Published by CGP.

Editors:
Ellen Bowness, Katie Braid, Joe Brazier, Charlotte Burrows, Polly Cotterill, Katherine Craig, Rosie Gillham, Paul Jordin, Hannah Nash, Rachael Powers, Dave Ryan, Jane Towle, Emma Warhurst.

Contributors:
Margaret Collinson, Kevin Cooper, Chris Critchlow, Michael F. Dean, Dr Tim Foulger, Paddy Gannon, Peter Goddard, Karen Holdich, Thomas Leverage (M. A.), Robert Morris, Helen Nurton, Sophie Watkins, Dennis Watts, Eileen Worthington BSc hons.

Proofreaders:
Roger Best, Sarah Hilton, Andy Park, Glenn Rogers.

With thanks to Laura Phillips for copyright research.

ISBN: 978 1 84762 135 1

Groovy website: www.cgpbooks.co.uk
Jolly bits of clipart from CorelDRAW®
Printed by Elanders Ltd, Newcastle upon Tyne.

Based on the classic CGP style created by Richard Parsons.

This book covers:

AQA
Edexcel

There ar[...] which b[...] It's also [...]

Photocopying — it's dull, grey and sometimes a bit naughty. Luckily, it's dead cheap, easy an[...] more copies of this book from CGP — just call us on 0870 750 1242. Phew!

The Hydrological Cycle

This section is mostly for AQA. There are some pages for Edexcel Unit 2 (Extreme Weather option) later on. These two pages are for AQA only. *What better way to start off a lovely new geography book than with some nice rivers...*

Drainage Basins are Local Open Systems

Water doesn't **come into** or **leave** planet Earth — it's continuously **cycled** between the **oceans** and the **atmosphere**, returning to the ocean when it falls as **rain** (or other forms of **precipitation**, e.g. snow). This is known as the **global hydrological cycle**.
The global hydrological cycle is a **closed system** — there are no **inputs** or **outputs**.
There are also **local** hydrological cycles, e.g. **drainage basin hydrological cycles**:

1) A river's **drainage basin** is the area **surrounding** the river where the rain falling on the land **flows** into that river. This area is also called the river's **catchment**.
2) The **boundary** of a drainage basin is the **watershed** — any precipitation falling **beyond** the watershed enters a **different drainage basin**.
3) Drainage basins are **open systems** with **inputs** and **outputs**.
4) Water comes **into** the system as **precipitation** and **leaves** via **evaporation**, **transpiration** and **river discharge**.

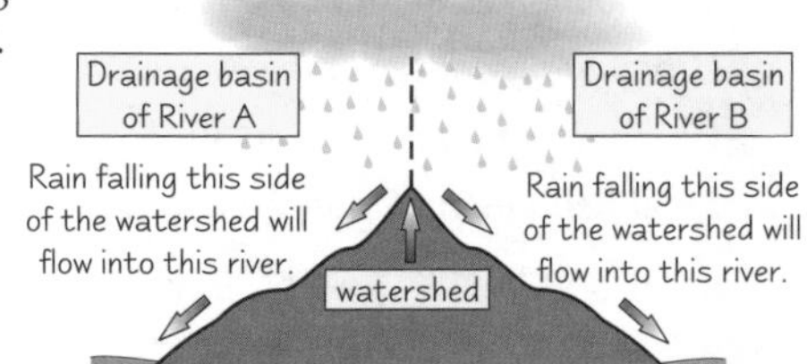

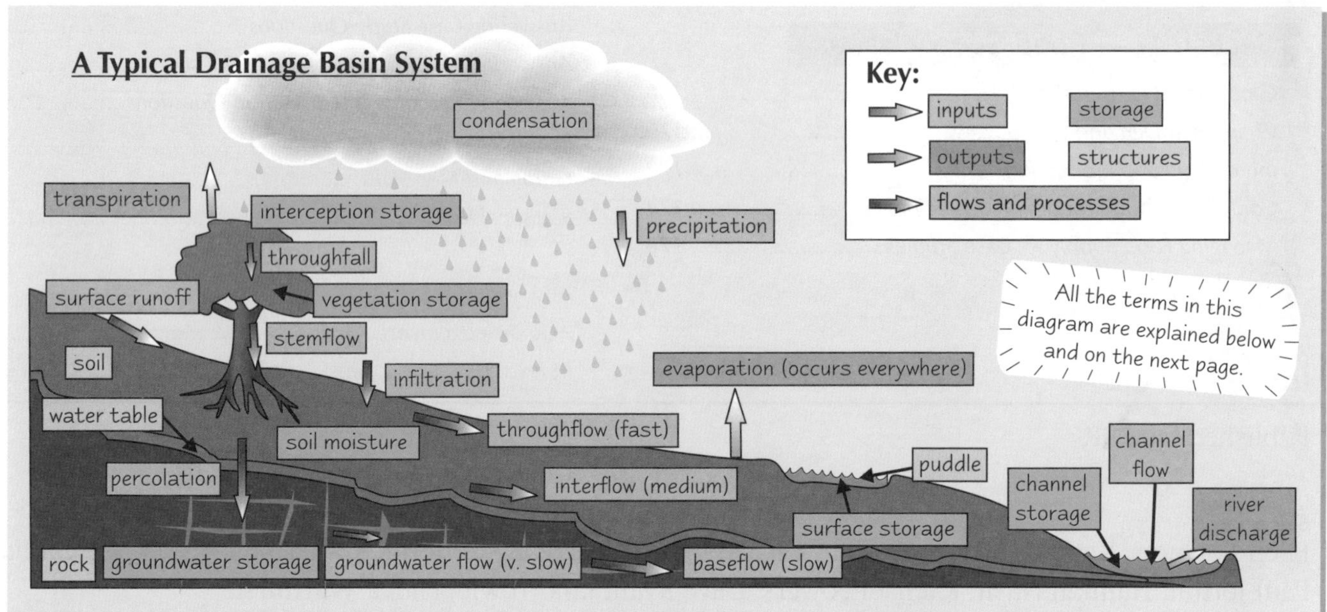

You Need to Learn All This Drainage Basin Terminology

Inputs — Water Coming into the System

Precipitation includes **all** the ways moisture **comes out** of the atmosphere.
Precipitation is mainly **rain**, but don't forget the other types like **snow**, **hail**, **dew** and **frost**.

Storage — Water Stored in the System

1) **Interception** is when some precipitation **lands on vegetation** or other structures, like **buildings** and **concrete** or **tarmac** surfaces, before it reaches the soil. Interception creates a **significant store** of water in **wooded areas**. **Interception storage** is only **temporary** because the collected water **evaporates** quickly.
2) **Vegetation storage** is water that's been **taken up** by **plants**. It's all the water **contained** in plants at any one time.
3) **Surface storage** includes water in **puddles** (**depression storage**), **ponds** and **lakes**.
4) **Groundwater storage** is water stored in the ground, either in the **soil** (**soil moisture**) or in **rocks**. The **water table** is the top surface of the **zone of saturation** — the zone of **soil** or **rock** where **all** the **pores** in the soil or rock are **full of water**. **Porous rocks** (rocks with lots of **holes** in them) that hold water are called **aquifers**.
5) **Channel storage** is so obvious that it's often overlooked — it's the **water** held in a **river** or **stream channel**.

The Hydrological Cycle

Flows and Processes — Water Moving from One Place to Another

1) **Surface runoff** (also called **overland flow**) is water **flowing over** the **land**. It can flow over the **whole surface** or in **little channels**. Surface runoff is common in **arid areas** where **torrential rain** falls on **hard baked** land.
2) **Throughfall** is water **dripping** from one **leaf** (or other plant part) to **another**.
3) **Stemflow** is water running down a plant **stem** or a **tree trunk**.
4) **Throughflow** is water moving slowly **downhill** through the **soil**. Throughflow is **faster** through **"pipes"** — things like **cracks** in the **soil**, or **animal burrows**.
5) **Infiltration** is water **soaking** into the soil. **Infiltration rates** are influenced by **soil type**, **soil structure** and how much water's **already in** the soil. In a heavy **storm**, water **can't** infiltrate fast enough, so it **flows** over the surface.
6) **Percolation** is water **seeping down** through soil **into the water table**.
7) **Groundwater flow** is water flowing **slowly below** the **water table** through **permeable rock**. Water flows **slowly** through most rocks, but rocks that are **highly permeable** with lots of **joints** (**gaps** that water can get through) can have **faster** groundwater flow, e.g. limestone.
8) **Baseflow** is groundwater flow that **feeds** into rivers through river **banks** and river **beds**.
9) **Interflow** is water flowing **downhill** through **permeable rock above** the water table.
10) **Channel flow** is the water flowing in the **river** or **stream** itself. This is also called the **river's discharge**.

Outputs — Water Leaving the System

1) **Evaporation** is water turning into **water vapour** — **turning** from a **liquid** to a **gas**.
2) **Transpiration** is **evaporation** from **plant leaves** — plants and trees **take up** water through their roots and **transport** it to their **leaves** where it evaporates into the atmosphere.
3) **Evapotranspiration** is the process of evaporation and transpiration **together**.
4) **River discharge**, or **river flow**, is another **output**.

Potential evapotranspiration (**PET**) is the amount of water that **could** be lost by evapotranspiration. **Actual evapotranspiration** is what **actually** happens. For example, in a **desert** potential evapotranspiration is **high** (because **heat increases** the amount of **evaporation**) but actual transpiration is **low** (because there **isn't** that much moisture in the first place).

*The **Water Balance** Shows the Balance Between **Inputs** and **Outputs***

Water balance is worked out from **inputs** (precipitation) and **outputs** (channel discharge and evapotranspiration).
The water balance affects how much water is **stored** in the basin.
The general water balance in the **UK** shows **seasonal patterns**:

1) In **wet seasons**, precipitation **exceeds** evapotranspiration. This creates a **water surplus**. The **ground stores fill** with water so there's **more surface runoff** and **higher discharge**, so **river levels rise**.
2) In **drier seasons**, precipitation is **lower than** evapotranspiration. **Ground stores** are **depleted** as some water is **used** (e.g. by plants and humans) and some flows into the **river channel**, but **isn't** replaced by precipitation.
3) So, at the **end** of a dry season, there's a **deficit** (**shortage**) of water in the ground. The ground stores are **recharged** in the next **wet season** (i.e. autumn).

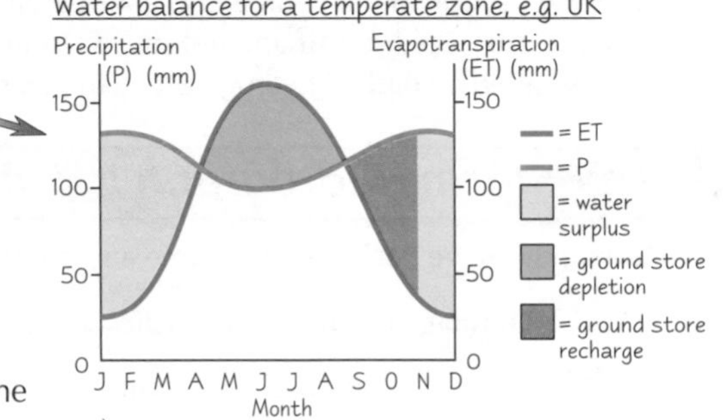

Practice Questions

Q1 List five ways in which water is stored in the hydrological cycle.

Q2 Water vapour evaporates from the leaves of plants. What is this process called?

Exam Question

Q1 Describe how the water balance of the UK changes with the seasons. [4 marks]

My grandad has issues with water flow...

There are loads of words that you need to remember on these pages. It might seem like a pain, but if you learn them all now it'll mean the rest of the section will make a lot more sense. And you thought geography was just about colouring in maps...

River Discharge

These pages are for AQA only. *Phew, I'm glad those last two pages are over — too many definitions for my liking. None on this page thankfully... OK, when I said none, I actually meant a few.*

River Discharge is the Volume of Water Flowing in a River

River discharge is simply the **volume** of water (in cubic metres, $\mathbf{m^3}$) that **flows** in a river **per second**. Unsurprisingly, it's measured in **cubic metres per second** ($\mathbf{m^3/s}$) — this is a bit of a mouthful, so geographers usually just shorten it to **cumecs**. River discharge is **affected** by:

1) **Precipitation** — the **more** precipitation, the **higher** the **discharge**.
2) **Hot weather** — the **higher** the temperature, the **lower** the **discharge** because the rate of **evaporation** is **higher**.
3) **Removal of water** from the river (**abstraction**) — also **reduces** the **discharge**.

Nelly was an abstraction master when she had a thirst on.

Hydrographs Show River Discharge Over a Period of Time

Hydrographs are graphs of river **discharge** over **time**. They show how the **volume of water** flowing at a certain point in a river **changes** over a **period of time**. **Storm hydrographs** show river discharge around the time of a **storm event**. They only cover a relatively **short time period** (hours or days, rather than weeks or months).

Bankfull discharge is the point when the water level reaches the top of the river channel.

1. **Peak discharge** — this is the **highest** point on the graph, when the **river discharge** is at its **greatest**.
2. **Lag time** — this is the delay between **peak rainfall** and **peak discharge**. This delay happens because it takes **time** for the rainwater to **flow** into the river. A **shorter** lag time can **increase peak discharge** because more water reaches the river during a **shorter period of time**.
3. **Rising limb** — this is the part of the graph **up to** peak discharge. The river discharge **increases** as rainwater flows into the river.
4. **Falling limb** — this is the part of the graph **after** peak discharge. **Discharge** is **decreasing** because **less water** is flowing into the river. A **shallow** falling limb shows water is flowing in from **stores** long after it's **stopped raining**.

A typical storm hydrograph

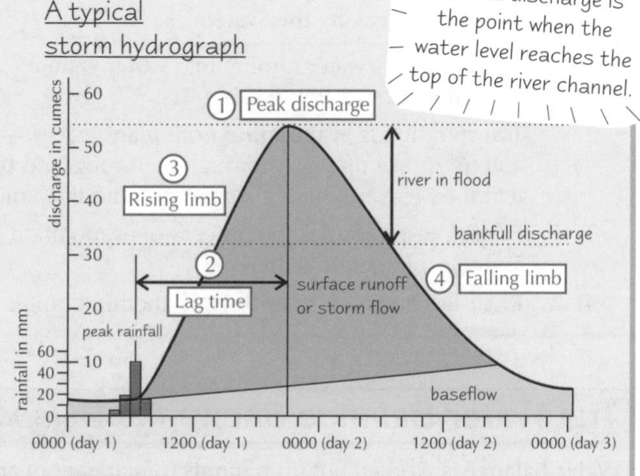

The **exact shape** of the hydrograph varies with each **river drainage basin** and each individual **storm event** (see below). A basin with **rapid runoff** and not much **storage** capacity gives a hydrograph with a **short lag time** and **high peak discharge**. This is called a "**flashy**" hydrograph — the graph has **steep**, roughly **symmetrical** rising and falling limbs.

The Storm Hydrograph is Affected by Physical Factors

Not all **drainage basins** are the **same** and the **weather** tends to vary too — these **physical factors** affect the storm hydrograph:

1) **Drainage basin characteristics** — the **physical features** of the drainage basin affect **lag time** and **peak discharge**.
   - **Larger drainage basins** can catch **more precipitation**, so they have a **higher peak discharge** compared to smaller basins. But **smaller basins** generally have **shorter lag times** because precipitation has **less distance** to travel, so reaches the main channel **quicker**.
   - **Steep-sided** drainage basins have **shorter lag times** than shallower basins — water flows **more quickly** downhill into the river on steep slopes. This can also **increase peak discharge**.
   - **Circular** basins are more likely to have a **flashy** hydrograph than **long**, **narrow** basins. This is because all points on the **watershed** are roughly the **same distance** from the point of discharge **measurement**. This means lots of water will reach the measuring point at the **same time**, **increasing peak discharge**.
   - Basins with **lots** of **streams** (high **drainage density**) drain **quickly**, so have **shorter lag times**.
2) The **amount** of water **already present** in the drainage basin ("**antecedent moisture**") — affects **lag time**.
   - If the ground's already **waterlogged** (the soil can't **absorb** any more water) then **infiltration** is **reduced** and **surface runoff increases**. Surface runoff is much **faster** than **throughflow** or **baseflow**, so rainwater reaches the river **more quickly**, **reducing lag time**.

River Discharge

3) **Rock type** — affects **lag time** and **peak discharge**.

- **Impermeable rocks** don't **store** water or let water **flow** through them. This **reduces infiltration** and **increases surface runoff**, **reducing lag time**. **Peak discharge** also **increases** as **more water** reaches the river in a shorter period.

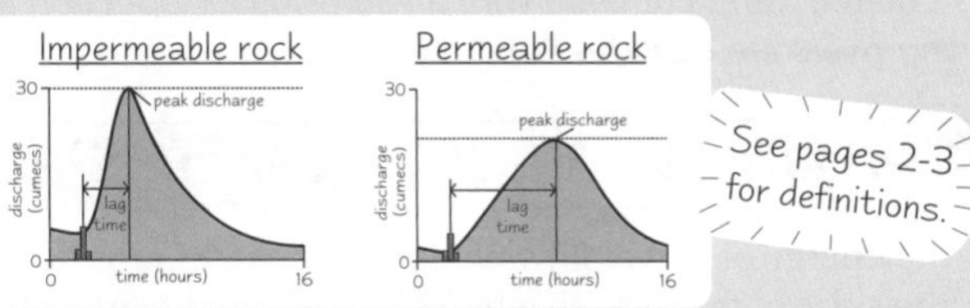

See pages 2-3 for definitions.

4) **Soil type** — affects **lag time** and **peak discharge**.

- **Sandy soils** allow a lot of **infiltration**, but **clay soils** have very **low infiltration rates**. Low infiltration rates **increase surface runoff**, **reducing lag time** and **increasing peak discharge**.

5) **Vegetation** — affects **lag time** and **peak discharge.**

- Vegetation **intercepts** precipitation and **slows its movement** to the river channel, **increasing lag time**. Interception is **highest** when there's **lots** of vegetation and **deciduous trees** have their **leaves**.
- The **more vegetation** there is in a basin, the **more water** is **lost** (through **transpiration** and **evaporation** directly from the vegetation) before it reaches the river channel, **reducing peak discharge**.

6) **Precipitation** — affects **peak discharge**.

- **Intense storms** will generate **more precipitation** and so **greater peak discharges** than **light rain showers**.
- The **type** of precipitation also affects **lag time** — e.g. snow that's fallen in a **winter storm** can **melt** (**meltwater**) and flow into the river in **spring**, giving a **very long lag time.**

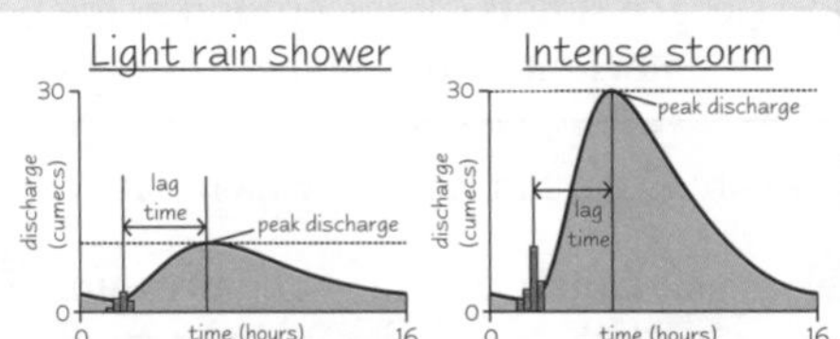

7) **Temperature** — affects **lag time** and **peak discharge**.

- **Hot**, **dry** conditions and **cold**, **freezing** conditions both result in **hard ground**. This **reduces infiltration** and **increases surface runoff** — **reducing lag time** and increasing **peak discharge**.
- **High temperatures** can **increase evapotranspiration**, so **less water** reaches the river channel, **reducing peak discharge**.

Human Activity Also Affects the Hydrograph

1) In **urban areas**, much of the **soil** is covered with man-made **impermeable** materials like **concrete**. Water **can't infiltrate** into the soil, which **increases surface runoff**, so water flows **more quickly** into the river. This makes the **lag time short** and **increases peak discharge**.
2) Man-made **drainage systems** affect the hydrograph in a similar way. Water flows down **drains** into the river before it can **evaporate** or **infiltrate** into the soil, causing a **shorter lag time** and **increased peak discharge**.

Practice Questions

Q1 What is river discharge?

Q2 What is the unit of measurement for river discharge?

Q3 How can human activity affect the storm hydrograph?

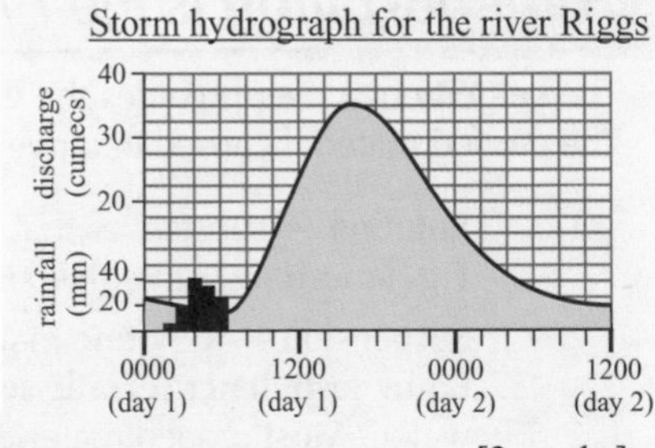

Exam Question

Q1 a) Give the lag time and peak discharge for the storm hydrograph shown above. [2 marks]

b) How might deforestation of the river Riggs drainage basin affect its storm hydrograph? Explain your answer. (Assume all other features, including precipitation, stay the same.) [4 marks]

I ain't saying she's a gold digger, but she loves her flashy hydrographs...

Storm hydrographs can look quite confusing, but they're not so bad once you've got your head round them. If you can explain how and why all the physical factors and human activities affect river discharge and lag time then you've nailed it, good and proper.

River Processes

These pages are for AQA only.
I could try and come up with an amusing introduction to erosion, but I'm only four pages into this section and rivers are really starting to wear me down.

Erosion Can Affect the *Length, Depth* and *Width* of a River

The **energy** of a river flowing **downhill** causes **erosion**. The **bed** (the **bottom** of the river channel) and **banks** (the **sides** of the river channel) of a river can be **eroded** — making the river **longer**, **deeper** and **wider**:

Headward erosion

Valley head
Banks
River
Key
Direction of water flow
Direction of erosion

Headward erosion makes the river **longer**. It happens near a river's **source** as **throughflow** and **surface runoff** causes **erosion** at the point the water **enters** the river channel (the **valley head**).

Vertical erosion

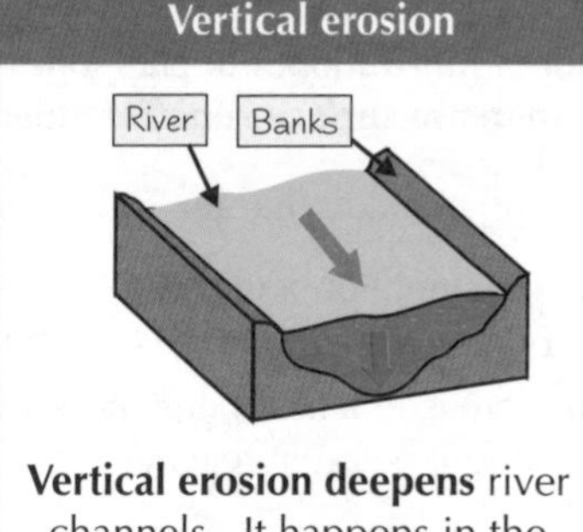

Vertical erosion deepens river channels. It happens in the **upper stages** of a river.

Lateral erosion

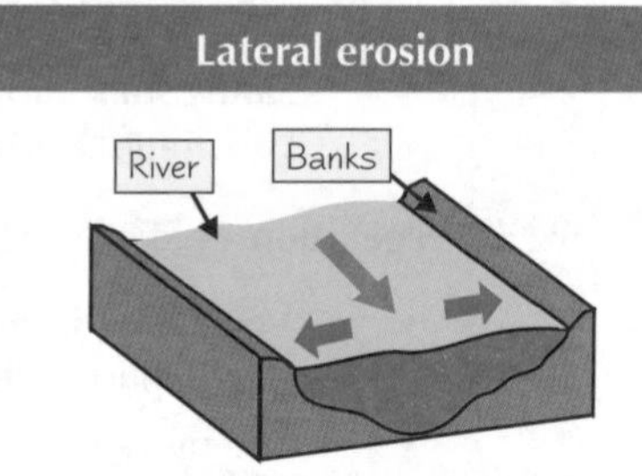

Lateral erosion makes the river **wider**. It happens in the **middle** and **lower** stages of a river.

There are **five** main ways in which river erosion happens:

1) **Hydraulic action** — the **pressure** of the **water** breaks **rock particles** away from the bed and banks. It's strongest in **rapids** and **waterfalls** (see p. 10), and during **floods**.

2) **Abrasion (corrasion)** — eroded pieces of rock in the water **scrape** and **rub** against the bed and banks, **removing material**. **Most erosion** of river beds and banks happens by abrasion.

3) **Attrition** — eroded rocks **smash** into each other and break into **smaller** fragments. Their edges also get **rounded off** as they rub together. Attrition **doesn't erode** the bed and banks — it just makes the particles of rock **in** the river **smaller** and **more rounded**.

4) **Cavitation** — **air bubbles** in turbulent stretches of water **implode** causing **shockwaves** that **break** pieces of rock off the banks and bed.

5) **Corrosion (solution)** — the dissolving of rock by **chemical processes**. **Carbon dioxide** dissolves in water to form a **weak acid**, which reacts with rocks like **limestone** and **chalk**, breaking them down.

The more eroded material a river carries, the more erosion it can cause by abrasion.

Transportation is the Process of *Eroded Material* Being Carried in a River

The **velocity** of a river provides the **energy** needed for it to **transport eroded material**.
The eroded material carried in a river is called its **load**, and it can be carried in **four** ways:

1) **Solution** — substances that can **dissolve** are carried along **in** the water. E.g. **limestone** is dissolved into river water that's slightly **acidic**.
2) **Suspension** — very **fine** material, like **silt** and **clay** particles, is whipped up by **turbulence** (**erratic swirling** of water) and carried along in the water. **Most** eroded material is transported this way.
3) **Saltation** — **larger particles**, like **pebbles** or **gravel**, are **too heavy** to be carried in suspension. Instead, the **force** of the water causes them to **bounce** along the river bed.
4) **Traction** — **very large** particles, e.g. **boulders**, are **pushed** along the river bed by the force of the water.

Material transported by **traction** or **saltation** is called the river's **bedload**.

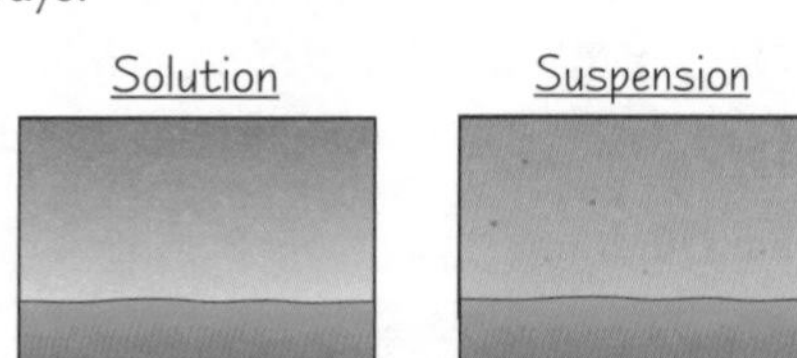

River Processes

Deposition is the Process of Dropping Eroded Material

Deposition happens when the river **loses energy**. When it **slows down**, it loses energy and **drops** some of its load. The speed and energy of a river can be reduced in many ways:

1) **Reduced rainfall** causes **lower discharge**, which means the river **slows down** and has **less energy**.
2) **Increased evaporation** or **abstraction** (taking water out of a river for human use) also causes **lower discharge**.
3) **Friction**, e.g. in **shallow** areas of the river and **close to the banks**, reduces the **speed** of the river, reducing its **energy**.
4) When the river is forced to **slow down**, e.g. before a **narrow section** of the channel, it **loses energy**.
5) A lot of energy is **lost** when the river meets the **sea** (the sea **absorbs** the energy).

The Capacity of a River is the Total Amount of Material It Can Carry

1) The **capacity** is the **total load** (measured in volume, weight or mass) that a river can **transport** at a given point.
2) The load of a river can be **divided** into **different categories** according to **particle size**. The particle sizes range from fine **silt** and **clay** (less than 0.1 mm in diameter) to **big boulders**.
3) The **competence** describes the **maximum particle size** that a river is capable of **transporting** at a given point.

The Hjulström Curve Shows the Link Between River Velocity and Competence

The **competence** of a river is affected by the amount of **energy** it has, which is related to its **velocity** — generally, the greater the velocity, the greater the energy. The **Hjulström curve** shows the **relationship** between river velocity and competence. It also shows how the **processes** of **erosion**, **deposition** and **transportation** vary with river velocity:

- The **critical erosion velocity curve** on the graph shows the **minimum velocity needed** for the river to **pick up (erode)** and **transport** particles of **different sizes** (in suspension or as bedload). It takes a **higher velocity** to **erode** material than it does to just **transport** material.
- The **mean settling velocity curve** shows the velocities at which particles of **different sizes** are **deposited**, i.e. it shows the **competence** of the river at different velocities.

The curves vary with river depth and characteristics.

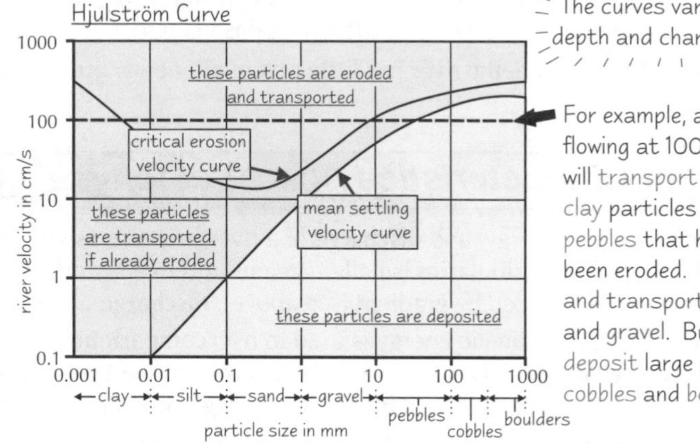

For example, a river flowing at 100 cm/s will transport small clay particles and small pebbles that have already been eroded. It will erode and transport silt, sand and gravel. But it will deposit large pebbles, cobbles and boulders.

The graph also shows that particles of **sand** (between 0.1 and 1 mm in diameter) can be **eroded** at **lower velocities** than **finer particles** such as **silt** and **clay**. This is because **silt** and **clay** particles **stick together more** than sand, which means they're **harder** to dislodge, so it requires **more energy** (greater velocity) to erode them.

Practice Questions

Q1 Name the four ways a river can transport its load.

Q2 Briefly describe two reasons why a river drops its load.

Q3 What is meant by the competence of a river?

Exam Questions

Q1 Describe the five main ways in which river erosion can happen. [5 marks]

Q2 Outline how the critical erosion velocity curve on a Hjulström graph varies with particle size. [6 marks]

Hjulström curve — sounds more like something you'd find in IKEA®...

OK, apart from that scary-looking diagram, this is all pretty simple. Bits of river beds and banks get knocked and scraped into the water (erosion). The river carries the material along while it's got enough speed and energy (transportation) and then drops it when it slows down (deposition). The faster the river is going, the more energy it has, so the more stuff it can carry. Not too bad...

The Long Profile and Channel Characteristics

These pages are for AQA only.
The long profile — well, it's long and, erm, a profile. And that's all I have to say about that. Well, not quite...

The **Long Profile** Shows the **River's Gradient** from Its **Source** to the **Sea**

1) A **long profile** shows you how the **gradient** of the river channel **changes** from the river's **source** to its mouth by showing the **height of the river bed** above the **base level** for the whole length of the river.
2) The **base level** is the **lowest point** that the river **can erode to** — usually **sea level** (or the level of a **lake** or **reservoir**).
3) The **total amount** of erosion and deposition along the **full course** of a river are **balanced**. But the **rates** of **erosion** and **deposition change** along the course of a river. This can result in the formation of **landforms** such as **waterfalls** (where the rate of **erosion** is **higher** than the rate of **deposition** — see p. 10), which make the profile **uneven**.
4) Because the **total** amount of erosion and deposition is **balanced**, the rate of erosion of landforms like waterfalls is **equal** to the rate of deposition elsewhere along the river. This means that **over time** the long profile will **change** from being uneven to a **smooth curve**. This is called a **graded profile** (but it hardly ever happens).

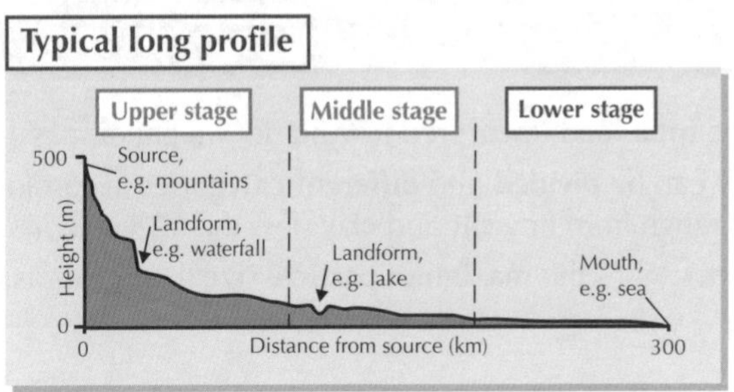

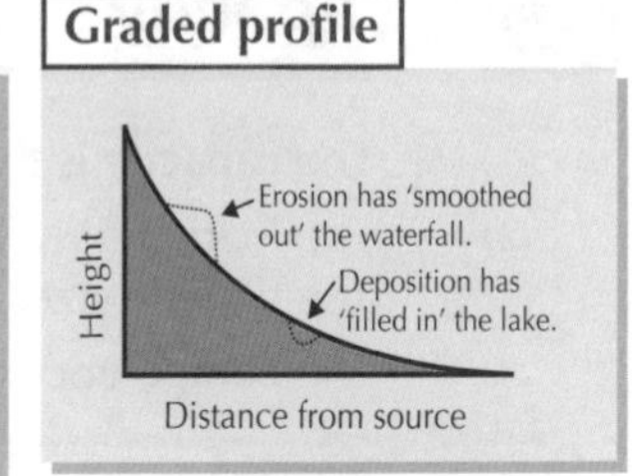

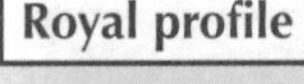

A river's course can be split into **three stages** — **upper** (near the source), **middle**, and **lower** (near the mouth). The **energy** of a river **varies** in each stage:

1) In the **upper stage**, the **gradient** is **steep** and the river is **high** above sea level, which gives it lots of **potential energy** (energy that can be **converted** into **other forms**, e.g. kinetic).
2) As the gradient **decreases** towards the **middle stage**, potential energy is converted to **kinetic energy** (movement) — the river **gains velocity**.
3) In the **lower stage**, the river has **little** potential energy, but **lots** of kinetic energy — it flows **faster**.

Channel Characteristics Affect **Velocity** and **Discharge**

The **velocity** (kinetic energy) and **discharge** of a river **increase** as you go **downstream** from source to mouth.
Discharge **increases** as **tributaries** (smaller streams and rivers) and **more surface runoff** join the main channel.
River velocity is influenced by **gradient** (see above), **discharge** and **channel characteristics** — the **shape** and **roughness**.

1) Most of a river's kinetic energy is used to **overcome friction** — the rest causes **erosion**.
   The **more energy** a river has available for **erosion** and **transportation**, the **more efficient** it is.
   An efficient river will have a **high velocity**, **high discharge** and **little friction**.
2) **Efficiency** is measured by **hydraulic radius**. The **larger** its hydraulic radius the **more efficient** a river is.
   - The **hydraulic radius** is the channel's **cross-section area divided** by the **length** of its **wetted perimeter** (the **total length** of the **banks** and river **bed** that are in contact with the water).
   - **Contact** between the water and the wetted perimeter creates **friction**, which **increases energy loss** and **slows the river down**.
   - A **larger hydraulic radius** means that a **smaller proportion** of water is in contact with the wetted perimeter. So **friction is lower**, which **reduces energy loss**, increasing **velocity** and **discharge**.
   - **Smooth**, **narrow**, **deep** channels (like channel **A**) have a **larger hydraulic radius** and so are **more efficient** than **shallow**, **broader** ones (like channel **B**).

A
Banks 5 m
Bed 5 m
Wetted perimeter = 15 m
Cross-section area = 25 m^2
Hydraulic radius = 1.7

B
Banks 2 m
Bed 7 m
Wetted perimeter = 11 m
Cross-section area = 14 m^2
Hydraulic radius = 1.3

3) **Channel roughness** also affects the efficiency. **Protruding banks** and **large**, **angular boulders** on the river bed **increase the wetted perimeter** and cause **more friction**. This **reduces** efficiency, velocity and discharge.
4) As channel roughness **increases**, so does **turbulence** (**erratic swirling** of the water in the main flow). Turbulent flow is **more effective** at **picking up** particles from the river bed than smooth flow — so turbulence causes **greater erosion**.
5) Channel roughness is **greatest** in the **upper stages** of the river. So although the **gradient** is steep, the river **loses** a lot of energy to **friction**, so discharge and velocity are **lowest** here during **normal conditions**.
6) In the **lower stages**, the banks and bed of the river are **smooth**, so there's much **less friction**. This means **less energy** is lost, so discharge and velocity are the **highest** in this stage.

The Long Profile and Channel Characteristics

River Processes Change *as the River Flows from* ***Source*** *to* ***Mouth***

Upper stage

EROSION
Mainly **vertical** and by **abrasion** (there's also some **hydraulic action**). **Erosion occurs** when there are **high-energy conditions** (i.e. when **velocity** and **discharge are high** after **heavy rain** or **ice melt**). The **rough channel** causes **turbulence** and the **large, angular bedload** is **dragged along** the **river bed**, causing **intense** downwards (**vertical**) **erosion**.

TRANSPORTATION
Mainly **large particles** such as **boulders** carried by **traction** or **saltation** during high-energy conditions.

DEPOSITION
Little deposition — mainly **largest particles** deposited in the **river bed** as **energy levels drop**.

Middle stage

EROSION
Mainly **lateral** and by **abrasion**. **Attrition** of **larger particles** in this stage means that sediment **particle size decreases** from source to mouth.

TRANSPORTATION
More material carried in **suspension** as particle size **decreases**. Some larger particles moved by **saltation**.

DEPOSITION
Sand and **gravel** are deposited across the **flood plain** as the river floods and **friction reduces** the river's **energy**.

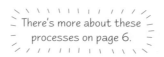

There's more about these processes on page 6.

Lower stage

EROSION
Although **velocity** and **discharge** are **highest** in this stage, there's **less erosion** because **turbulence is lower** and **sediment particle size** is **reduced** (**reducing abrasion**). Some **lateral erosion** occurs during the **formation of meanders**.

TRANSPORTATION
Mainly **smaller particles** such as **silt** and **clay** carried by **suspension**, or substances carried **in solution**.

DEPOSITION
Smaller particles such as **sand**, **silt** and **clay** are deposited on the **flood plain** when the river **floods** and in the **river mouth** as the **sea absorbs river energy**.

The ***Cross Profile*** *Shows the* ***Shape*** *of the* ***River Channel*** *and* ***Valley***

The **cross profile** of a river shows you what a **cross-section** of the **river channel** or the **river valley** looks like. The **valley** cross profile changes during the **different stages** of a river's **long profile**.

1) **Upper stage** valleys are **steep V shapes**. **Vertical** erosion creates **narrow** valley floors and **steeply sloped** sides.
2) **Middle stage** valleys are **wider**, caused by **lateral** erosion. **Deposition** creates a **flood plain** on the valley floor.
3) **Lower stage** valleys are **wide** with **gently sloping** sides. There's a much **wider flood plain** caused by **deposition**.

Upper stage

Narrow valley
Steep slope
Vertical erosion

Middle stage

Lower stage

Practice Questions

Q1 What does the long profile of a river show?

Q2 Describe the features of a lower stage river valley.

Exam Questions

Q1 What does the hydraulic radius tell you about a river, and how is it calculated? [3 marks]

Q2 Outline how the processes of erosion, transportation and deposition change along a river's long profile. [6 marks]

It's not the length of your wetted perimeter that counts, it's the hydraulic radius...

Phew, there's quite a lot of terms to learn on these pages: wetted perimeter, hydraulic radius, efficiency, roughness and turbulence. Learn what they all mean and how they affect velocity, discharge, erosion, transportation and deposition during the river's stages.

River Landforms

These pages are for AQA only.
Hurrah! After a few pretty dull pages, you get to learn about all kinds of brilliant river landforms.

Fluvial just means it's caused by rivers and streams.

Waterfalls**, **Rapids** and **Potholes** are Caused by **Fluvial Erosion

Waterfalls

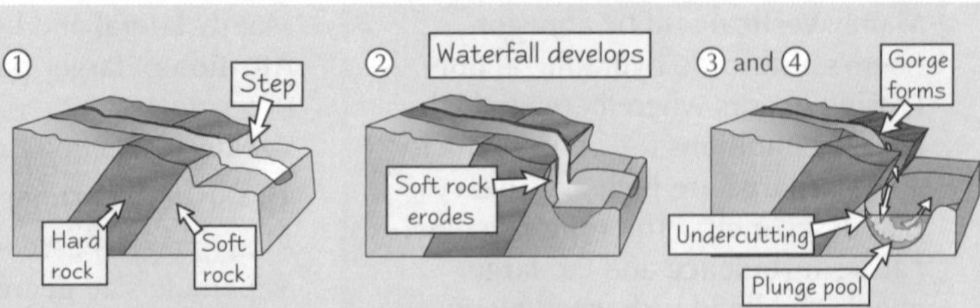

1) Waterfalls form where a band of **hard** rock meets **softer** rock. The soft rock is **eroded more** than the harder rock, causing a **'step'** in the river bed.
2) The water flowing over the step **speeds up** due to the **lack of friction** as it drops over the step. This increase in speed gives the water **greater erosive power**, causing further erosion of the soft rock and **undercutting** of the harder rock.
3) As the hard rock is **undercut**, it can **collapse**. A deep **plunge pool** is carved out by **abrasion** at the foot of the waterfall as the bits of **collapsed rock** are **swirled** round by **turbulence**.

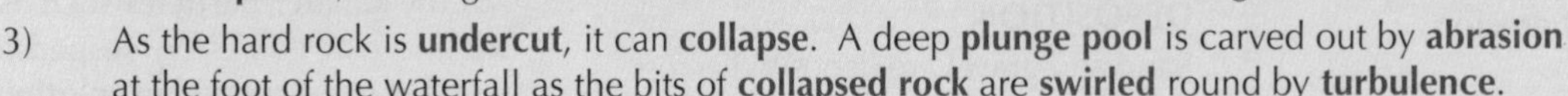

4) **Over time**, **more undercutting** causes **more collapse**. The waterfall will **retreat** (move **back up** the channel), leaving behind a **steep-sided gorge**.

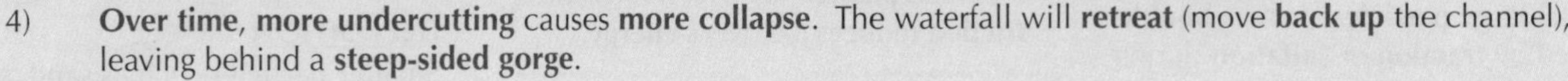

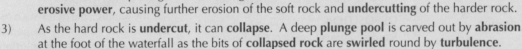

Potholes

Potholes are **small circular hollows** in the river bed.
They're formed by **abrasion** as **turbulence** swirls a river's **bedload** round in a **circular motion**, causing it to **rub** and **scrape** out holes.

Rapids

Rapids are relatively steep sections of river with **turbulent flow** where there are **several sections** of **hard rock**. They're a bit like **mini-waterfalls**.

Meanders** are Formed by **Combined Erosion** and **Deposition

Large, **sweeping curves** in a river's middle and lower stages are called **meanders**. They're formed by **erosion** and **deposition**.

1) **Meanders** form where **alternating pools** (areas of **deep** water) and **riffles** (**shallow** water) develop at **equally spaced intervals** along a stretch of river. The distance between pools is **5-6 times** the **width** of the river bed.
2) Because the river channel is **deeper** in pools it's more **efficient** (see p. 8), so it has **greater energy** and **more erosive power**. Energy is **lost** as the river flows over a riffle because of **friction**.
3) The **spacing** and **distance** between riffles and pools causes the river's flow to become **uneven** and **maximum flow** to be concentrated on **one side** of the river.
4) **Turbulence increases** in and around **pools** as the **water speeds up**, so the flow of water begins to **twist** and **coil**.
5) This causes **corkscrew-like** currents in the river called **helicoidal flow**, which **spiral** from bank to bank between pools.
6) The helicoidal flow causes more **erosion** and **deepening** of the pools. It also causes **eroded material** to be **deposited** on the **inside** of the **next bend**, where the river **loses energy**.

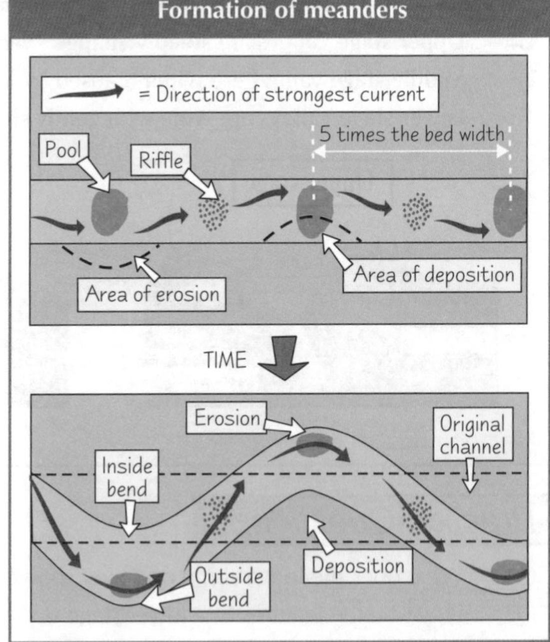

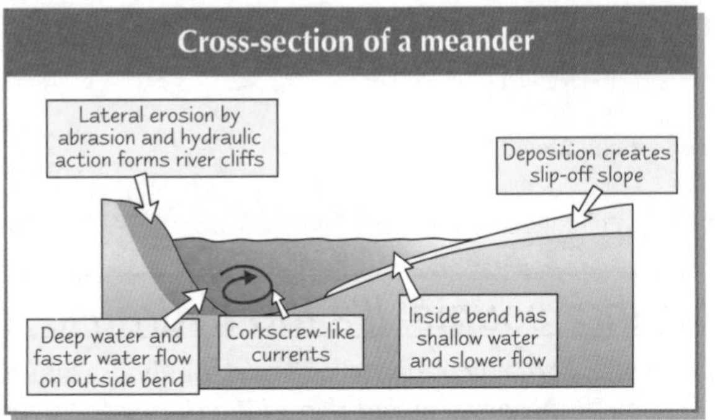

7) The **combination** of erosion and deposition **exaggerates** the bends until large **meanders** are formed. The combined processes also create the meanders' distinctive **asymmetric cross-section**.
8) **Oxbow lakes** are formed when the **neck** of the loop of a meander is **broken** through, often during **flooding**. **Deposition** dams off the loop, leaving an oxbow lake.

River Landforms

Braiding, Flood Plains, Levees and Deltas are Caused by Fluvial Deposition

Braiding

1) **Braiding** occurs when rivers are carrying a **vast** amount of **eroded sediment** (e.g. in meltwater).
2) If the river's **velocity drops**, or the sediment **load** becomes **too much** for the river to carry, sediment is **deposited** in the channel.
3) This causes the river to **divide** into many **small**, **winding** channels that eventually rejoin to form a single channel.

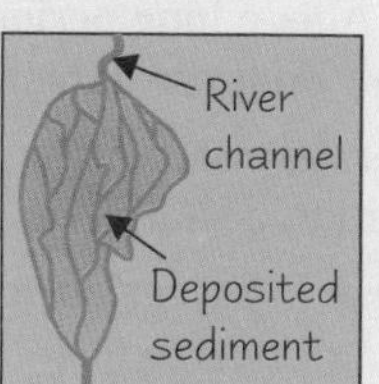

Flood plains

1) When a river **overflows** its banks and floods the flat land either side of the river (the **flood plain**), there's an **increase** in the **wetted perimeter** and **reduction** in **hydraulic radius**.
2) This **increases friction**, reducing the velocity of the river and causing fine **silt** and **sand** to be **deposited** across the flood plain.

Levees

1) **Levees** are natural, **raised embankments** formed as a river **overflows** its banks.
2) During a flood, material is deposited across the **whole flood plain** as the river **loses velocity** and **energy** due to **increased friction**.
3) The **heaviest** material (e.g. sand and gravel) is dropped first, **closest** to the river channel.
4) Over time, this material **builds up** on the river bank, creating a **levee**.

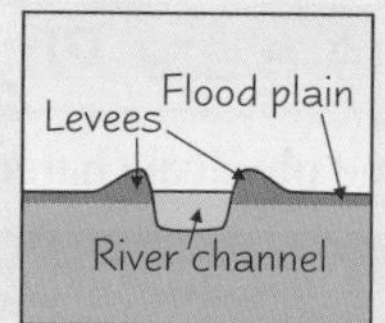

Deltas

1) When a river reaches the **sea** (or a **lake**), the **energy** of the **river** is **absorbed** by the **slower** moving water of the sea (or lake).
2) This causes the river to **deposit** its load. These deposits **build up** on the sea bed, until the **alluvium** (deposited sediment) **rises above** sea level, **partially blocking** the mouth of the river.
3) The river has to **braid** into several **distributaries** in order to reach the sea, forming a **delta**.

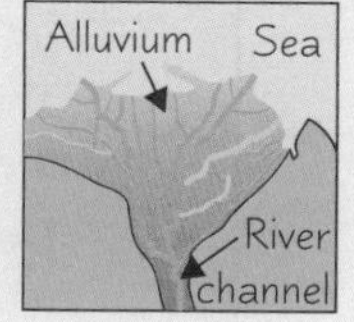

Rejuvenation Allows a River to Resume Vertical Erosion

See page 8 for the long profile.

1) A river is said to be **rejuvenated** if its base level is **lowered**. This can be caused by either the **ground level rising** (**crustal uplift**) or by a **drop in sea level**.
2) The drop in base level gives the river greater **potential energy**, increasing its **vertical erosion** potential.
3) The **long profile** of the river is **extended** and a **knickpoint** (a sharp change in gradient, often a **waterfall**) will form and mark the junction between the **original** long profile and the new one.

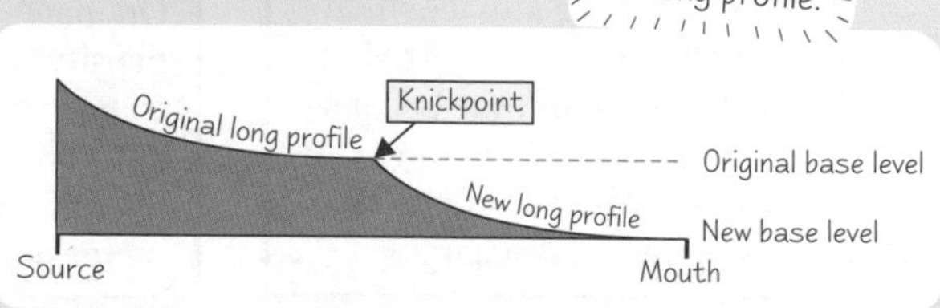

There are distinctive **landforms** associated with rejuvenation:

1) **River terraces** are former **flood plains** which have been left **above** the level of **present-day** flooding following increased **vertical erosion**.
2) **Incised meanders** are formed when a river keeps its meandering course as **vertical erosion** increases. The result is a **deep**, **winding valley** with **steep sides**. The river is left **far below** the level of the **former flood plain**.

Practice Questions

Q1 Briefly describe how waterfalls are formed.

Q2 Name two river landforms associated with rejuvenated rivers.

Exam Question

Q1 Describe the formation of levees. [4 marks]

Drove my Chevy to the levee — but the levee was just an old riverbank...

Don't be too rapid in going over the stuff on these pages — you'll only end up in deep water. But don't spend forever meandering around the facts. Slip off and take a break if you need to and come back rejuvenated. That's the best way to nick points in the exam.

Causes and Impacts of Flooding

These pages are for AQA and Edexcel Unit 2 (Extreme Weather option). *Right... time to learn what causes rivers to go wild (but not in a good way, unless you're a kayaker) and what happens when they do.*

Prolonged Rainfall and Heavy Rainfall are the Main Causes of Flooding

1) **Flooding** occurs when the **discharge** of a river is **so high** that the **river spills over** its **banks** onto the **flood plain**.
2) A **major cause** of **flooding** is **prolonged rainfall**. After a **long period** of **rain**, the **ground** becomes **saturated** (it **can't absorb** any more water). Any further rainfall **can't infiltrate**, which **increases surface runoff**, which **increases discharge**.
3) **Heavy rainfall** (e.g. the rain you get with **thunderstorms**) can lead to **rapid surface runoff** if the rainfall is **too intense** for **infiltration** to occur. This can lead to a **sharp rise** in **river discharge** called a **flash flood**.
4) **Melting snow** and **ice** also lead to a **huge increase** in a river's **discharge**. For example, **melting snow** in the **Himalayas** contributes to the **annual summer flooding** of the **River Ganges** in **Bangladesh**.

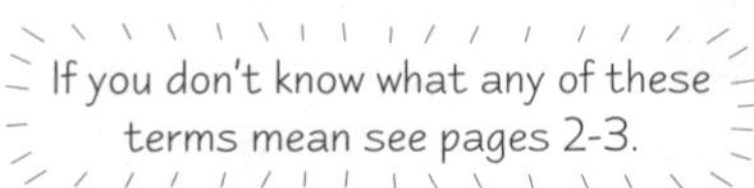

If you don't know what any of these terms mean see pages 2-3.

There are Physical Factors That Increase the Risk of Flooding...

Some **physical characteristics** of **drainage basins** can **increase** the **risk** of **flooding**:

Lag time is the time between peak rainfall and peak discharge.

Sparse vegetation or deciduous trees

- **Sparse vegetation** in the drainage basin means **little rainfall** is **intercepted**, so **more rain** reaches the **ground**. This **increases** the **volume of water** reaching the river, which **increases discharge**.
- **Deciduous trees** have **no leaves** in **winter**, which has the **same effect** as sparse vegetation — little rainfall is intercepted.

Impermeable ground

- **Clay soils** and some **rocks**, such as **granite** and **shale**, are **impermeable** — they **don't** allow **infiltration** of **surface water**. This **increases surface runoff**, which **increases discharge**.
- If the ground has been **baked hard** by the heat of the summer, or it's **frozen**, the **same thing happens** — water can't infiltrate, increasing surface runoff and discharge.

Circular drainage basins

Water draining into the main river channel will **all arrive** in a **short space of time** because all points in the basin are a similar distance from the river. This **increases discharge**.

High drainage density

Drainage basins with a **high drainage density** (lots of streams) drain **quickly**, so have **short lag times**. **Lots of water** flows from the streams into the main river in a **short space of time**, **increasing discharge**.

Steep slopes

If the **drainage basin** has **steep-sided valleys**, water will reach the **river channel** much **faster** because water flows **more quickly** on **steeper slopes**. This **increases discharge**.

...and Human Factors

A lot of these factors are the same as those that reduce lag time and increase the peak discharge on a flood hydrograph — see pages 4-5.

Humans often make flooding more **frequent** and more **severe** by **changing things** in the **drainage basin**:

Urbanisation

- **Urban areas** have **large areas** of **impermeable tarmac** and **concrete**, so when it rains **surface runoff** is **very rapid**.
- **Gutters** and **drains quickly** take **runoff** to **rivers**.
- Both of these things **reduce lag time** and so **increase discharge**.

Deforestation

- **Clearing trees** and plants **reduces interception** and **evapotranspiration**. This **increases** the **volume of water** that reaches the channel, which **increases discharge**.
- Deforestation leaves the soil **loose**. The soil is **eroded** by rainwater and **carried** to the **river**, which **raises** the **river bed**. This **reduces** the **channel capacity**, so it takes **less water** for the river to **flood**.

Flood management strategies

Flood management strategies (see pages 16-17) can actually end up making **flooding worse**. For example, if **dams fail** they release a **huge volume** of **water all at once** — giving a huge **increase** in **discharge**.

Agriculture

Overgrazing leaves areas with **less vegetation**, so has the same effect as deforestation (see above). **Overgrazing** and **ploughing** also **increase soil erosion**.

Climate change

Climate change could cause an **increase** in **rainfall** and **more storms** in some areas, which could **increase flooding**.

Causes and Impacts of Flooding

Flooding Affects **People**, the **Economy** and the **Environment**

Here are some of the **possible** impacts:

Social impacts

1) **People** and **animals** can be **killed**.
2) **Floodwater** is often **contaminated** with **sewage**, which can lead to a **lack** of **clean drinking water**.
3) **Contaminated water** can also put people at **risk** of **diseases** (e.g. **diarrhoea** and **dysentery**)
4) **Possessions** can be **damaged** by floodwater or **lost** (washed away).
5) People can be made **homeless** as their **properties** are **inundated** or **damaged**.

Economic impacts

1) **Businesses** often have to shut down as premises are **inundated** and **power supplies** are affected.
2) **Rescue work** and **repairs** are usually **costly**. **Insurance premiums** go **up** after floods.
3) **Unemployment levels** often **rise as businesses shut down** because they can't recover from the flooding.
4) **Public transport**, **roads** and **bridges** can be **destroyed**.
5) **Crops** can be **destroyed**. This can lead to a **rise** in the **price** of **food**.

Environmental impacts

1) Floodwater **contaminated** with sewage and rubbish can **pollute rivers**.
2) **River banks** are **eroded**.

Positive impacts include:

1) **River sediment** is **deposited** on the **flood plain**. This makes the land **more fertile**.
2) **Wetlands** can be created, e.g. **marshes** and **ponds**, which are **habitats** for many species.

The **social** impact is usually **higher** in **poorer countries** because flood defences are poorer, people are less able to evacuate, sanitation systems aren't as good and buildings are of a poorer quality. The **absolute economic** impact is usually **higher** in **richer countries** as they have more high value buildings and infrastructure. However, the **relative economic** impact is usually **higher** in **poorer countries** — the buildings and crops that are damaged are worth less money, but this affects the economy more because they have less money to recover from it (e.g. to rebuild homes).

Flood Frequency Can be **Calculated**

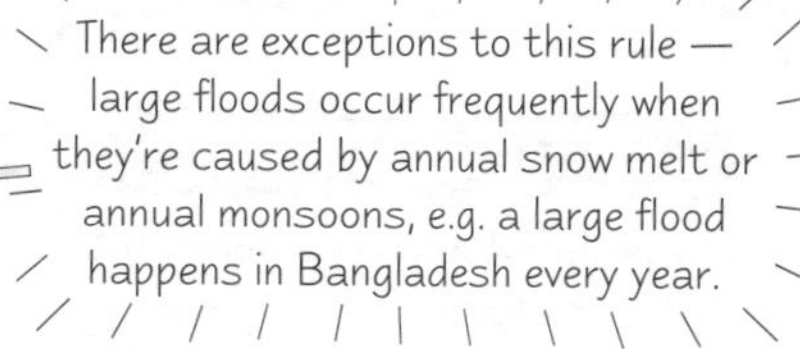

There are exceptions to this rule — large floods occur frequently when they're caused by annual snow melt or annual monsoons, e.g. a large flood happens in Bangladesh every year.

1) Floods of a **very large size** (**magnitude**) don't happen very often — they're **not very frequent**.
2) **Small floods** happen more often — they're **more frequent**.
3) Large floods usually occur due to **unusually** heavy or prolonged rainfall.
4) By keeping **records** over many **years**, people can **predict how often** a flood of a certain magnitude may **occur** — this is called the **flood return interval** (**RI**).

   For example, if a **2 m** high flood occurred along a river in **1701**, **1806** and **1899** — then the **return interval** of a 2 m high flood is about **100 years**.

5) A **small flood** may have an **RI** of **one** or **two years**, whereas a **huge flood** may have an **RI** of **100 years** or more.

Henry made sure he was definitely prepared for the flood this time.

Practice Questions

Q1 Why is prolonged rainfall a major cause of flooding?

Q2 Name two human activities that increase the risk of flooding.

Q3 Briefly describe the possible social impacts of flooding.

Q4 Briefly describe the possible economic impacts of flooding.

Q5 What is a flood return interval?

Exam Questions

Q1 Outline the physical characteristics of a drainage basin that would have a high risk of flooding. [6 marks]

Q2 Explain two ways in which urbanisation increases the risk of flooding. [5 marks]

If only the "getting wet" part of flooding were the worst part...

It's normal for rivers to flood occasionally, but us humans have made it more of a problem. You need to learn all the causes and impacts of flooding — use boring old list-making to help you. List the causes under two headings (natural and human) and the impacts under three headings (social, economic and environmental). Colour them nice and prettily. Oh yeah — then learn 'em.

Causes and Impacts of Flooding — Case Studies

These pages are for AQA and Edexcel Unit 2 (Extreme Weather option).
Just to make learning case studies more difficult, the causes and impacts of flooding are different in different places.
Flooding in poorer areas tends to have a much bigger impact on people's lives and health than flooding in wealthier areas...

Case Study 1 — Flooding of South Asia, 2007

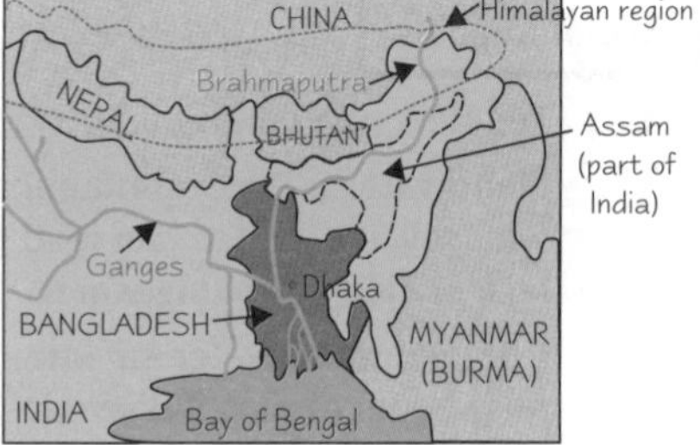

Parts of **South Asia** flood **most years**, usually in **late summer**. This is **because**:

1) **South Asia** has a **monsoon climate** — **80%** of **rain** falls in just **four months**.
2) Much of **South Asia** is **low-lying land**, particularly **Bangladesh** where **90%** of **land** is **less** than **10 m above sea level**.
3) **Melting snow** and **ice** from the **Himalayas** in the **late summer** months **increase** the **Brahmaputra River discharge**.

In **July** and **August 2007**, the **flooding** was **particularly severe** in **Bangladesh** and **India**.

Physical factors were the **main cause**...

1) The **monsoon** came **suddenly** after a **very dry, early summer**.
2) There was **heavy rainfall** — **Assam** had a **record 169.5 mm in 24 hours** on **22nd July**, and **900 mm** in **total** for **July**.
3) The **long duration** of **heavy rainfall** completely **saturated** the **soil**, **increasing surface runoff** and **increasing discharge**.
4) The **peak discharges** of the **River Ganges** and **Brahmaputra coincided**, which **increased** the river **discharge downstream**.

...but **human activities** made the **flooding worse**

1) **Deforestation** in **Nepal** and the **Himalayas** meant less rainfall was intercepted, which **increased discharge**.
2) The **growth** of **urban areas**, due to **migration**, also **increased surface runoff**.
3) **Collapse** of old **earth dams** in **Madhya Pradesh**, **India**, caused **further flooding**.

*The **Flooding** Had Major **Impacts**, Especially on **People***

SOCIAL IMPACTS

1) **Over 2000 people died.** The **death toll** was **high** for many reasons, e.g. many people were **reluctant** to **evacuate** (as they'd have to **leave** their **land** and **livestock unattended**) and many **children drowned** because they **couldn't swim. Poor transport links** meant **evacuation** was **slow**.
2) As **wells** became **polluted** with **sewage**, there was a **lack** of **clean drinking water**. **Over 100 000 people** caught **water-borne diseases** (e.g. dysentery and diarrhoea).
3) An estimated **25 million people** were made **homeless**.
4) **112 000 houses** were **destroyed** in **India**, as **porous mud bricks** became **saturated** by **floodwater**.
5) **Dhaka** (Bangladesh's capital) was **inundated**, especially the **poorer districts** and **shanty towns** near the river.
6) Children **lost** out on **education** as **4000 schools** were **affected** and **44 schools** were totally **destroyed**.

ECONOMIC IMPACTS

1) The **cost** of the **flood** was estimated at **US$ 1 billion**, including damage to **crops** and **property**.
2) **Factories** were **closed** around **Dhaka**, due to **flood damage** and **loss** of **raw materials** (e.g. **rice**). Many of the **poorest workers** became **unemployed**.
3) There was **widespread loss** of **livestock** (e.g. **cattle**). Since **80%** of **Bangladeshis rely on agriculture**, many **lost** their **livelihoods**.
4) **550 000 hectares** of **land couldn't** be **planted** with **rice** at **peak time**, because of **flooded fields.** A **lower rice crop** meant the **world price** of **basmati rice rose** by **10%**.
5) **10 000 km** of **roads** were **destroyed.** Landslides blocked roads in the **highlands** of **Nepal** and **Assam**.
6) **Debt increased**, both **individually** (e.g. farmers borrowed money for food and seeds) and **nationally** (e.g. governments imported food and medicine).

ENVIRONMENTAL IMPACTS

1) The flood deposited **fertile silt** on the **flood plain**.
2) **Rivers** were **polluted** with **sewage**.

Human Factors Made the Impacts Worse

1) **Bangladesh** is a **poor country** so there **aren't** many **flood defences** or **flood warning systems** in place.
2) **Low incomes**, **few savings** and **little insurance** limited people's **ability** to **recover** after the flood.
3) **Corrupt officials diverted aid money** away from the people most in need.

Causes and Impacts of Flooding — Case Studies

Case Study 2 — Flooding of Carlisle, Cumbria, 2005

The **River Eden** runs through **North Cumbria** and reaches the sea near **Carlisle**.

1) The **drainage basin** of the River Eden is **very large** so it **catches** a **large volume** of **rainfall**, leading to a **high river discharge**.
2) Some parts of the basin have **steep sides**, so **water** runs **quickly** down to the **river**.
3) There are **many streams** that **drain quickly** into the river, making the **lag time short**.

Carlisle River Eden

On **8th January 2005**, the **River Eden** flooded **Carlisle**.
The **flood return interval** (RI) of such a large flood is about **200 years**.

Physical factors were the **main cause**...

1) There was **heavy rainfall** on the **6th** January, for **36 hours**. **200 mm** of **rainfall** was recorded, which was the **equivalent of four months** rain.
2) Rain fell on **saturated ground** so the water **didn't soak** into the ground but **ran straight off** into the **river**.
3) This caused a **very high peak discharge** (**over 1520 cumecs**), compared to an **average discharge** of **52 cumecs**.

...but **human activities** made the **flooding worse**

1) Carlisle is a **large built-up area**, with **impermeable concrete** and **tarmac surfaces**, and **little soil** or **vegetation**. This meant there was **little infiltration** of rainfall and **high surface runoff**, which **increased discharge**.
2) **Drains** and **sewerage systems overflowed** in some areas — becoming a **source** of **flooding** themselves. **25%** of the **flooding problems** were associated with **overflowing drains**.

The Flooding Had Major Impacts, Particularly on Carlisle's Economy

SOCIAL IMPACTS

1) **Three people died** in the floods.
2) **Over 3000 people** were made **homeless** for up to a **year** and thousands of **personal possessions** were **damaged**. Living in **temporary accommodation disrupted lives** in many ways, e.g. **travel arrangements** were **disrupted**, people were **separated** from **community networks** and **friends**, and they had **problems receiving post**.
3) Children **lost** out on **education** as **four schools** were **severely flooded**. **Newman Catholic School** didn't re-open until **Easter**.
4) There was an **increase** in **stress-related illnesses** following the floods.

ENVIRONMENTAL IMPACTS

1) The flooding **increased river bank erosion** in some areas.
2) **Rivers** were **polluted** with rubbish and sewage.

ECONOMIC IMPACTS

1) It took about a **year** to **repair** the **damage** to homes and repairs **cost over £100 million**.
2) **350 businesses** had to **shut down** as there was **no electricity**, **telephone service** or **transport**. **Trade activities** from Carlisle **railway** station were **suspended**.
3) **United Biscuits**, the **largest employer** in Carlisle, was **flooded** with **3 m** of water that caused **over £5 million damage**. 33 out of 1100 employees **lost** their **jobs**.
4) **70 000 addresses** had **no power**. The **sewage works**, **police station**, **fire station** and **council offices** were **severely flooded**.
5) **80 buses** (most of the public transport fleet) were **destroyed**. Many **roads** and **bridges** were **damaged**, e.g. **Warwick Road**.

Practice Questions

Q1 Briefly describe the physical reasons why the 2007 floods in South Asia were particularly severe.

Q2 Briefly describe the economic impacts of the 2005 Carlisle flood.

Exam Question

Q1 Using two named examples, compare the impacts of flooding in poorer and wealthier countries. [10 marks]

Rain, rain, go away — come again another day but not all at once in one big downpour...

Flooding can cause havoc, and it takes a lot of time and money to get things back to normal again. And it's not just the sheer amount of water — don't forget the knock-on effects, like contaminated water supplies, landslides, job losses, food price rises...

Flood Management Strategies

These pages are for AQA and Edexcel Unit 2 (Extreme Weather option).
Flooding can cause major disasters, so unsurprisingly people try to stop it happening. There are various ways of doing this, but as usual there are various problems associated with each way.

There's Not Enough Money to Protect Everywhere from Flooding

1) The aim of flood management is to **protect homes**, **businesses** and the **environment** from **flooding**.
2) This is because flooding can have severe **social**, **economic** and **environmental impacts** (see p. 13).
3) It's **tricky** trying to **manage flooding** though — there **isn't enough money** available to **protect everywhere**.
4) Choosing **which** places are protected (and **how** they're protected) is done using **cost-benefit analysis**.
5) **Large settlements** and **important industrial sites** (e.g. power plants) are **more likely** to be protected than small settlements or farmland.

Flood Management Includes Hard Engineering and Soft Engineering

1 Hard Engineering Defences Involve Built Structures

Hard engineering defences are **man-made structures** that **reduce flooding**.
General disadvantages of hard engineering defences include:

1) They're **expensive** to **build** and **maintain**, and need **technical skill**. **Poorer countries** often **can't afford** these flood defences.
2) **Floods** happen **less often**, but they can be **more hazardous** if they do happen. E.g. if a **dam breaks** then a **huge** amount of water will **rapidly flood** the land.
3) **Natural processes** are **disrupted**, e.g. **crops** don't get **fertile silt** from river sediment during **low-level flooding**.
4) Some people think they're **ugly**.

Fortunately, flood defence strategies have progressed somewhat over the years.

Here are some of the **most common** types of **hard engineering defences**:

Scheme	How it works	Extra benefits	Disadvantages
Dams	Dams are huge walls built across rivers. A reservoir (artificial lake) is formed behind the dam. Flood water is caught by the dam, which prevents flooding downstream. The water is released as a steady flow throughout the year.	• Turbines are often built into the dams, which generate electricity. • Steady water release allows irrigation of land below the dam throughout the year. • People can use the reservoir for recreational activities, e.g. sailing.	• They're very expensive. • Land is flooded when a reservoir is created. This often destroys farmland and forces people to move elsewhere. • They affect wildlife, e.g. they can prevent salmon migrating upstream to breeding grounds. • They trap sediment normally carried in rivers. This can cause the dam to fail. It can also cause increased erosion downstream, as there's less protective sediment being deposited.
Channel straightening	Channel straightening is where meanders are removed by building artificial cut-throughs. This makes the water flow faster, which reduces flooding because water drains downstream more quickly and doesn't build up to a point where the river channel can't contain it any more.	It takes less time to navigate the river because it has been made shorter.	• Flooding may happen downstream instead, as flood water is carried there faster. • More erosion occurs downstream because the river flows faster. • Altering river channels disturbs wildlife habitats.
Levees	Levees are embankments built along rivers. The river can hold more water without overflowing and so it floods less often.	They allow the flood plain to be built upon.	• They're quite expensive. • There's a risk of severe flooding if the levees are breached.
Diversion spillways	Diversion spillways are channels that take water elsewhere if the water level in the river is too high. Water is normally diverted around an important area or to another river. They prevent flooding because river discharge is reduced. The spillways often have gates that can be opened, so the release of water can be controlled.		• An increase in discharge when the diverted water joins another river (or rejoins the same one) could cause flooding below that point. • If spillways are overwhelmed, water will flood areas not used to flooding, which could cause even bigger problems.

Flood Management Strategies

2) **Soft Engineering** Defences **Work With**, Not Against, the **Basin Processes**

Soft engineering defences use **knowledge** of the **whole river basin** and its **processes**, to try to **work with nature**. General **advantages** are:

1) They're **cheaper** to **maintain** than hard engineering defences — this is **especially important** for **poorer countries**.
2) **Flooding** is more **predictable**, **reducing** the **risk** of an **unexpected disaster**.
3) They can **improve opportunities** for **recreation**, such as **fishing**.
4) Some people think they're **more attractive** than hard engineering schemes.

Here are some of the **most common** types of **soft engineering defences** that **reduce flooding**:

Scheme	How it works	Extra benefits	Disadvantages
Land use management	Planning restrictions prevent buildings or roads being constructed on the flood plain. Use of the flood plain is restricted to things like playing fields, allotments or parks. More water can infiltrate so there's less surface runoff, which reduces discharge and flooding.	• There are no new buildings or roads on the flood plain to be damaged, so the impact of any flooding is reduced. • It provides recreational opportunities, e.g. football fields.	• It restricts development. This is especially a problem where there's a shortage of housing. • It can't be used in areas that are already urbanised.
Wetland and river bank conservation	Wetlands store flood water and also slow it down. This reduces flooding downstream. So conserving or re-establishing wetlands gives natural protection from flooding. Planting trees and shrubs along the river bank increases interception and lag time, and reduces discharge. This also decreases flooding.	• Vegetation protects the surface soil from erosion. • The vegetation provides habitats for wildlife.	Less land is available for farming.
River restoration	River restoration involves making the river more natural, e.g. by removing man-made levees. The flood plain can then flood naturally. As the water spreads out over the flood plain the river's discharge is reduced (because less water is in the channel), which reduces flooding downstream.	• Little maintenance is needed, as the river's left in its natural state. • The river provides a better habitat for wildlife.	Local flood risk can increase, especially if nothing's done to prevent major flooding.
Alteration of urban surfaces	Building porous pavements or soakaways increases infiltration, which reduces rapid surface runoff to the river channel. This increases lag time, which reduces discharge and flooding.	Any pollutants in the water are filtered out by the soil before the water reaches the channel.	It's expensive.

Areas of trees and shrubs along river banks are called riparian buffers.

Soakaways are hollows or trenches filled with gravel.

The **impact** of **flooding** can also be **reduced**:

Scheme	How it works	Disadvantages
Weather forecasts and flood warnings	The Environment Agency monitors weather forecasts, rainfall and river discharge. They warn people about possible floods through TV, radio, newspapers and the internet. This means people can evacuate before the flood happens, saving lives. People can also move possessions and use sandbags to help reduce damage if flooding occurs.	• Some people might not be able to access the communication network. • Flash floods may happen too fast for warnings. • People may ignore warnings if they were inaccurate in the past.

Soft Engineering is **More Sustainable** than **Hard Engineering**

Hard engineering is often **expensive** and **disrupts natural processes**. Soft engineering tends to be **cheaper** and requires **much less time** and **money** to **maintain** than hard engineering. Soft engineering is designed to **integrate** with the natural **environment** and it creates areas like **wetlands**, which are important **habitats** for **wildlife**. So soft engineering's a **more sustainable management strategy** than hard engineering because it has a **lower economic cost** and **environmental impact**.

Practice Questions

Q1 What is hard engineering? Give an example of a hard engineering flood defence.

Q2 What is soft engineering? Give two advantages of using soft engineering rather than hard engineering defences.

Exam Question

Q1 Explain how flooding can be reduced without the use of major man-made structures. [8 marks]

Flood management strategies — let the ideas come flooding in...

Flood management is a pretty difficult task — whatever scheme you decide on, there are drawbacks. Also, saving your own neck often causes a flood somewhere else — usually downstream of you (which isn't a very neighbourly thing to do, really)...

Flood Management Strategies — Case Studies

These pages are for AQA.
Here are two beautiful case studies for you — showing you how different places manage floods in different ways.

Hard Engineering is Used on the Yangtze to Control Flooding

1) The **Yangtze River** flows through **China**. At 6380 km long, it's the **third longest** river in the world.
2) **Seasonal flooding** is **common** around the Yangtze — China has a **rainy season** that lasts from about **June** until **August** and the huge **increase** in **river discharge** during this time often causes flooding. Flooding causes **huge problems** as there's lots of **farmland** and loads of **major cities** next to the river, e.g. **Wuhan** and **Nanjing**.
3) **Five major floods** have happened over the **last century** — in 1931, 1935, 1949, 1954 and 1998.
4) The flood of **1954** covered **193 000 km²** of land and **killed 33 169 people**. Over **18 million people** had to **move**. It covered the city of **Wuhan** for **over 3 months**.
5) The flood in **1998 killed** around **3000 people** and made **14 million** people **homeless**.
6) **Flood protection** is mostly done through **hard engineering** defences.

Defences Include Dams and Levees

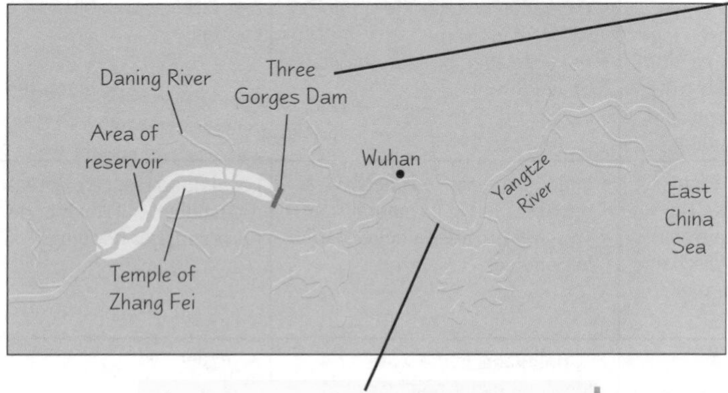

There are many **levees** along the river. E.g. there are **3600 km** of levees along the **middle** and **lower parts** of the river.

There are many **dams** on the Yangtze that reduce flooding (**46** are planned or under construction at the moment). The biggest of these is the **Three Gorges Dam**:

1) Work began on the **101 m high** Three Gorges Dam in **1994**.
2) A **reservoir** is building up behind the dam (it takes years to build up as the dam is huge). The reservoir **catches** any **flood water**, which can then be slowly released over time. The reservoir can store around **22 km³** of flood water.
3) It's also the largest **hydroelectric power station** in the world. The flow of water turns **26 turbines** built into the dam.
4) **Locks** have been built alongside the dam so **ships** can get past it.

Hard Engineering Has Reduced Flooding but Has Also Caused Problems

The construction of the **Three Gorges Dam** has had many **positive effects**, but also plenty of **negative effects**:

Positive effects

1) It's thought that the dam has **reduced major flooding** from **once every 10 years**, to once every **100 years**.
2) The turbines in the dam produce a lot of **electricity** — capacity is likely to reach **22.5 gigawatts** (enough to supply about **3%** of China's demand, which is loads).
3) The **reduction in flooding** has made it much **safer** to **navigate** up the Yangtze. **River shipping** has also **increased** as **bigger ships** can now travel up the river because the reservoir is deeper than the old river.

Levees have also caused problems:

1) In the **1998 floods** many levees **broke**, which contributed to **devastating flooding**.
2) After this, many levees were **reinforced**. They were **effective** at **reducing flooding** in the **2002 floods** (though the floods were **less severe** than the 1998 ones).

Negative effects

1) People have had to **relocate** as the water level in the reservoir has risen. It's thought that between **1.3** and **2 million people** in total will have to **relocate** by the time it's full — **13 cities** and **1352 villages** will be submerged.
2) The reservoir will also flood **farmland**, **657 factories**, and **1300** sites of **cultural** and **historic interest**. For example, as the water rises the **Temple of Zhang Fei** will be submerged.
3) A huge amount of **sediment** is normally carried down the Yangtze River. The dam will **trap** the sediment, which could lead to **failure** of the dam and cause **catastrophic flooding**.
4) The dam could **destroy habitats** and **endanger species**. E.g. the endangered **Siberian crane** spends the winter in wetlands below the dam, which are expected to be affected by less flooding. Fewer than 100 **baiji dolphins** are left in the Yangtze, and the dam could **reduce their food supply**.
5) The Three Gorges Dam **doesn't protect everyone** — rising water levels in the reservoir will **increase flooding** along the **tributaries** that lead into it, e.g. the **Daning River**. The increased water levels in the tributaries will also increase **erosion** of **riverbanks**, causing collapses and landslides.

Flood Management Strategies — Case Studies

Soft Engineering is Used in *Abingdon* to *Control Flooding*

1) **Abingdon**, a town in South-east England, was **built** on the **flood plains** of the **River Thames** and the **River Ock**.
2) **1500 properties** in Abingdon have a **1% chance** of **flooding** in a given year.
3) Abingdon has had **regular floods** over the years — in 1947, 1968, 1977, 1979, 1992, 2000 and 2007.
4) **Intense storms** in **July 2007** caused particularly bad **flash floods**. The **River Thames** and **Ock** burst their banks, flooding **660 properties** in **Abingdon**. **Increased surface runoff** in built-up areas made the flooding **even worse**.
5) **Hard engineering** defences have been considered but have been **rejected** for various reasons. E.g. a **diversion spillway** to transport Ock floodwater south of Abingdon was **too expensive**, and **flood barriers** to protect properties along the Ock would **increase flood risk downstream**. Flood protection is mostly done through **soft engineering** defences.

Defences Include *Land Use Management*, *Flood Warnings* and *Soakaways*

Gravel soakaways have been built along the **A34 road**.

Low-value land is allowed to flood, e.g. **Tilsley Park sports ground** is being considered as an additional **flood storage area**.

There are **planning restrictions** on **new housing developments** built on the **Ock flood plain**, stating they must have **improved drainage systems**.

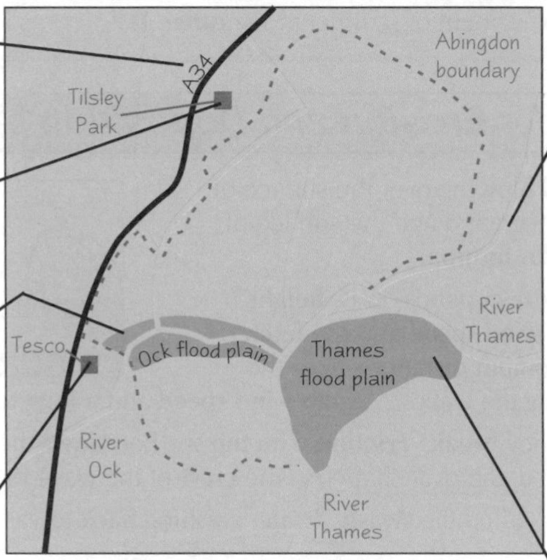

Tesco were forced to **revise** recent **extension plans** — they had to add **drainage improvements** such as **soakaways** and **permeable tarmac**.

The Environment Agency's **Local Flood Warning Plan** warns **specific areas** at risk and provides a **24 hour Floodline**.

Improvements have been made to **riparian buffers** along smaller rivers. Planting trees **reduces** the **volume** of **water** reaching the **Thames** and **Ock** rivers where the **flood problem** is **greater**.

Local voluntary **flood wardens** communicate **advice** and **warnings**.

There's **detailed advice** on the **internet** about **reducing flood damage**, e.g. by raising cupboards and using water-resistant plaster.

There are **restrictions** on **land use**, e.g. **planning permission** was **refused** for buildings on the **Thames flood plain**.

Soft Engineering Reduces Damage but *Floods Still Happen*

1) It's **difficult** to **measure** the **success** of flood defences because it's hard to figure out if any reduction in flooding was because of the **success** of new defences, or because the weather conditions were **less severe**.
2) Several **flood warnings** were issued by the **Environment Agency** in early **2008**.
3) The **Ock flood plain**, which has developments on, **didn't get flooded**. The **Thames flood plain did** get **flooded** but it's largely **clear of development**, due to **land use management** and **planning restrictions**.
4) The **2008 floods** did **less damage** than in previous years, with **minimal cost**, **little disruption** to community services, **no lives lost** and only a **few injuries**. However, **flooding** does still happen in **Abingdon**.

Practice Questions

Q1 List the types of hard engineering used on the Yangtze.

Q2 List the types of soft engineering used around Abingdon.

Exam Question

Q1 With reference to named examples, discuss the success of different engineering approaches to flood prevention. [10 marks]

Maybe if we all get together and ask the clouds to please not rain...

You can't ask for two case studies more different than these. You need to know who's built what, where, and why — and if it's successful.

Introduction to Coastal Environments

This section is for AQA (Coasts option) and Edexcel Unit 2 (Coasts option). These two pages are just for AQA.
Coastal environments are the areas where the land meets the sea. And they're almost as exciting as they sound...

Coasts are *Systems* — They Have *Inputs*, *Processes* and *Outputs*

1) **INPUTS** — **river sediment**, sediment from **cliffs** that have been **eroded** or suffered **landslides**, and sediment that has been **transported** by waves from **offshore** (out at sea).
2) **PROCESSES** — **wave action**, **tidal movement**, **erosion**, **weathering**, **transportation**, **deposition**.
3) **OUTPUTS** — sediment **washed out to sea**, or deposited **further along** the coast.

Coastal sediment cells (also called **littoral cells**) are lengths of coastline that are pretty much entirely **self-contained** for the movement of sediment. Each one is a **coastal system**. So **processes** going on in **one cell** don't affect the movement of sediment in **another** cell.

Sediment cells in England and Wales

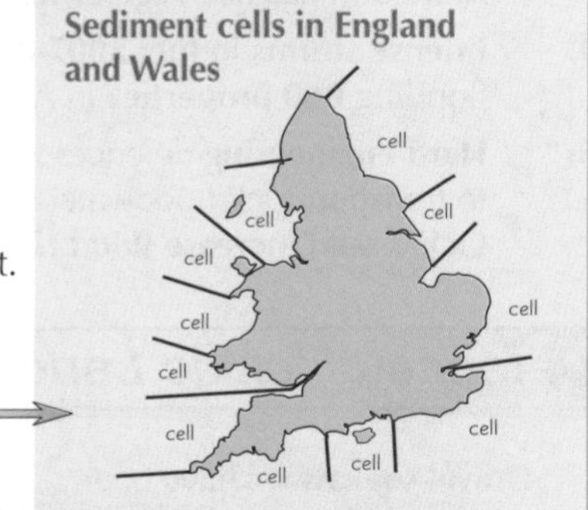

Waves are Responsible for *Erosion* and *Deposition* of *Beach Sediment*

1) **Waves** are created by the **wind** blowing over the surface of the sea. The **friction** between the wind and the surface of the sea gives the water a **circular motion**.
2) The **effect of a wave** on the **shore** depends on its **height**. Wave height is affected by the **wind speed** and the **fetch** of the wave. The fetch is the **maximum distance of sea** the wind has blown over in creating the waves. A **high wind speed** and a **long fetch** create **high** waves.

3) As waves approach the shore they **break**. **Friction** with the sea bed **slows** the bottom of the waves and makes their motion more elliptical (squashed and oval-shaped). The **crest** of the wave rises up and then **collapses**.
4) Water washing **up** the beach is called the **swash**. Water washing **back** towards the sea is called the **backwash**.
5) There are **two types** of wave:

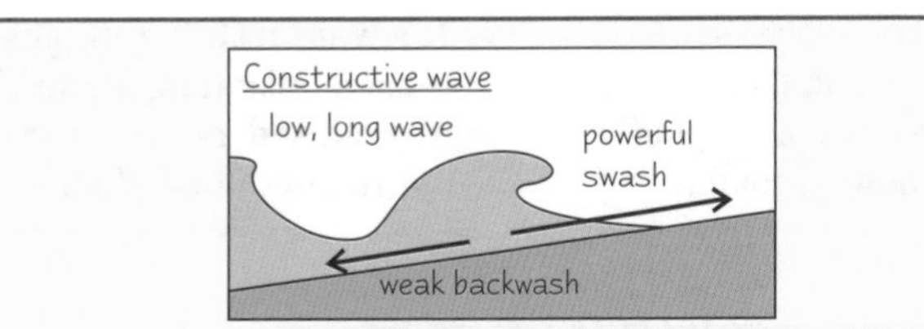

Constructive waves have a **low frequency** (only around **6-8** waves per minute). They're **low** and **long**, which gives them a more **elliptical** cross profile. The powerful swash carries material up the beach and **deposits** it.

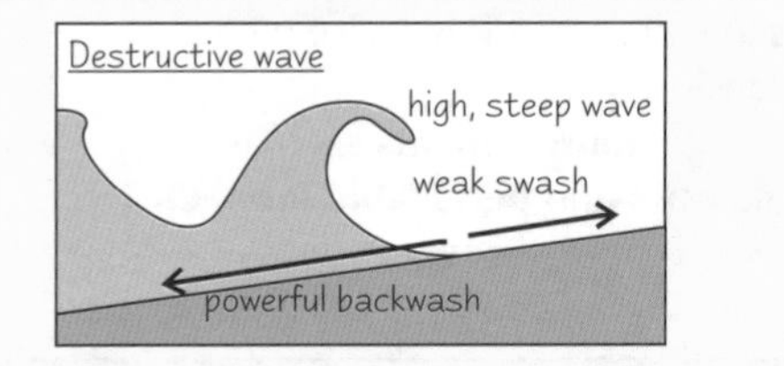

Destructive waves are **high** and **steep**, with a more **circular** cross profile. They have a **higher frequency** (**10-14** waves a minute). The strong backwash **removes** material from the beach.

6) The waves in an area are usually mainly constructive or mainly destructive.

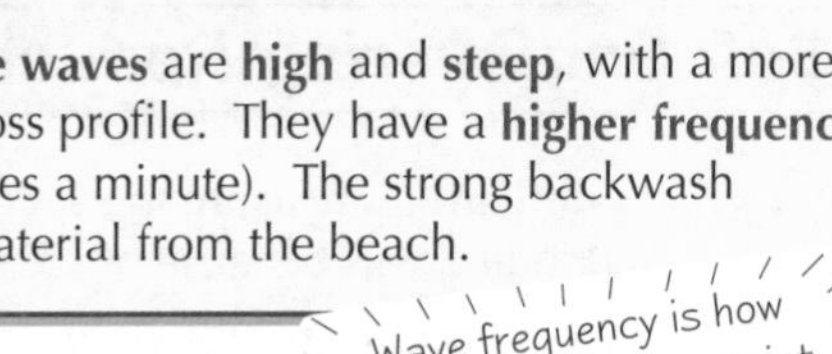

Wave frequency is how many waves pass a point in a particular time.

Tides Affect *Where Waves Break*

Tides are the periodic **rise** and **fall** of the **ocean surface**. They're caused by the gravitational pull of the **Moon** and the **Sun**. Tides affect the **position** at which **waves break** on the beach (at high tide they break higher up the shore). The area of land between **maximum high tide** and **minimum low tide** is where landforms are created and destroyed.

See page 58 for more on weathering.

Sub-aerial Weathering Occurs *Along* the *Coastline*

1) **Sub-aerial weathering** describes coastal processes that are **not linked** to the action of the sea. It includes **freeze-thaw weathering** and **salt weathering**. Weathering **weakens cliffs** and makes them **more vulnerable** to **erosion**.
2) **Throughflow** (the flow of water through the cliffs) and **runoff** (the flow of water over the land) caused by **heavy rain** can also make cliffs more **unstable** and increase the likelihood of **mass movement**.
3) Mass movement is the **movement** of material **downhill** due to gravity. It includes **landslides**, **slumping** (a type of landslide) and **rockfalls**.

Introduction to Coastal Environments

There are Five Main Ways Waves Erode the Coastline

Waves don't just erode beaches — they also erode **rocks** and **cliffs**. Here are the five main ways they do it:

1) **Abrasion/corrasion** — Bits of rock and sediment transported by the waves smash and grind against rocks and cliffs, breaking bits off and smoothing surfaces.
2) **Hydraulic action** — **Air** in cracks in cliffs is **compressed** when waves crash in. The pressure exerted by the compressed air breaks off rock pieces.
3) **Quarrying** — The energy of a wave as it breaks against a cliff is enough to detach bits of rock.
4) **Corrosion/solution** — **Soluble rocks** (e.g. limestone, chalk) get gradually **dissolved** by the seawater.
5) **Attrition** — Bits of rock in the water smash against **each other** and break into smaller bits.

The Rate at Which a Stretch of Coastline is Eroded Depends on Several Factors

1) **The width of beach** — i.e. the distance between high and low tide marks. Beaches slow down waves, reducing their erosive power. So a wide, flat beach will protect cliffs more than narrow, steeper beaches.
2) **The breaking point of the waves** — a wave that breaks directly at the foot of a cliff transfers the most energy to the cliff and causes the most erosion. Waves that hit the cliff before they break, or break further offshore will erode much less.
3) **The aspect** — if the coastline faces the dominant wind and wave direction, erosion will be faster.
4) **The fetch of the waves** — waves with a longer fetch are much higher and steeper, and have more energy, so will cause the most erosion.
5) **Rock type** — hard rocks like granite are much more resistant to erosion than softer rocks, e.g. clay.

See page 24 for a case study of coastal erosion.

Currents Transport Sediment

1) A **current** is the general flow of water in one direction.
2) Currents move material **along** the coast — this is called **longshore drift**.
3) **Swash** carries sediment (e.g. shingle, pebbles) **up** the beach, **parallel** to the prevailing wind. **Backwash** carries sediment back **down** the beach, at **right angles** to the shoreline.
4) When there's an **angle** between the prevailing wind and the shoreline, a few rounds of swash and backwash move the sediment **along** the shoreline.

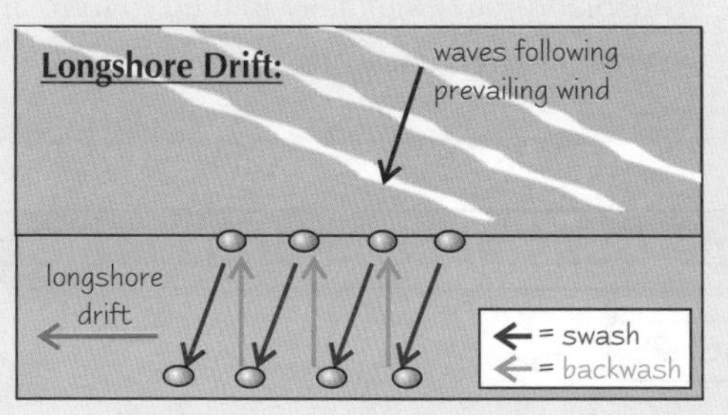

Practice Questions

Q1 Draw a table to show the main inputs, processes and outputs of a coastal system.

Q2 Sketch a diagram to show how longshore drift works.

Exam Questions

Q1 Describe the characteristics of constructive and destructive waves. [4 marks]

Q2 Outline how cliffs are eroded along the coastline. [6 marks]

What did the sea say to the beach — nothing, it just waved...

You really need to get your head around all the processes going on at the coast — cliffs are eroded and weathered, currents carry sediment about and constructive waves deposit it. Then there are destructive waves that annoyingly remove prime sunbathing spots.

Coastal Landforms

These pages are for AQA (Coasts option).
Get your bucket and spade ready — it's time to learn about coastal landforms. Wait a minute, where are the sandcastles...

Some **Coastal Landforms** are Caused by **Erosion**

CLIFFS AND WAVE-CUT PLATFORMS

1) **Cliffs** are a common coastal landform. Over time, cliffs **retreat** due to the action of **waves** and **weathering**.
2) Weathering and wave erosion cause a **notch** to form at the high water mark. This eventually develops into a **cave**.
3) Rock above the cave becomes **unstable** with nothing to support it, and it **collapses**.
4) **Wave-cut platforms** are **flat surfaces** left behind when a cliff is eroded.

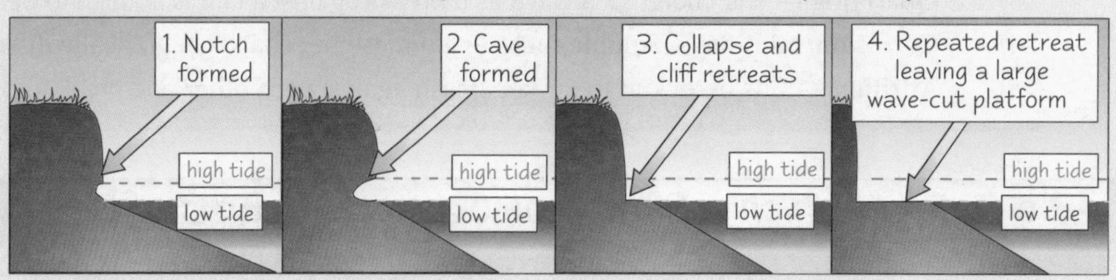

HEADLANDS AND BAYS

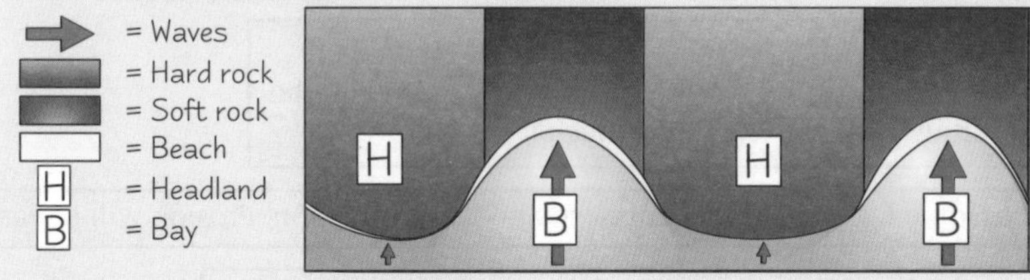

1) **Headlands** and **bays** form where there are **bands** of alternating **hard rock** and **soft rock** at **right angles** to the shoreline.
2) The **soft rock** is **eroded quickly**, forming a **bay**. The **harder rock** is **eroded less** and sticks out as a **headland**.

CAVES, BLOW HOLES, ARCHES AND STACKS

1) Weak areas in rock (e.g. joints) are **eroded** to form **caves**.
2) Occasionally, the roof of a cave is **weakened** along a major joint by **hydraulic pressure** and the roof **collapses** to form a **blow hole**.
3) Caves on the opposite sides of a narrow headland may eventually join up to form an **arch**.
4) When an **arch** collapses, it forms a **stack**.

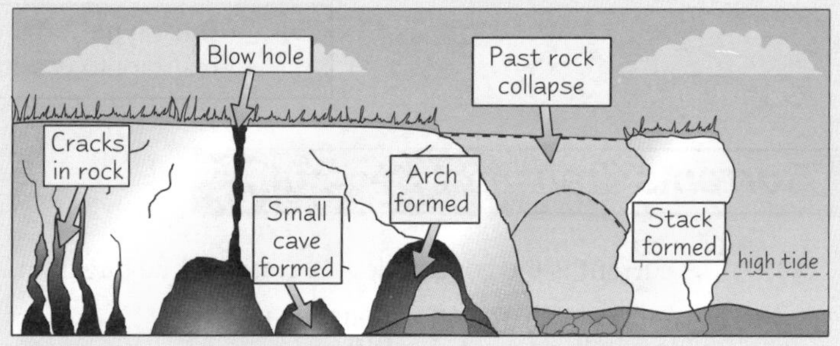

Some **Coastal Landforms** are Caused by **Deposition**

BEACHES

1) **Beaches** are formed when **constructive** waves **deposit sediment** on the shore.
2) **Shingle** beaches are **steep** and **narrow**. They're made up of **larger** particles, which pile up at steep angles. **Sand** beaches, formed from **smaller** particles, are **wide** and **flat**.

Beaches have their own **associated features**:

1) **Berms** are **ridges** of sand and pebbles (about 1-2 metres high) found at **high tide** marks. They're formed by deposition of coarse material at the limit of the **swash**.
2) **Runnels** are **grooves** in the sand running **parallel** to the shore. They're formed by **backwash** draining to the sea.
3) **Cusps** are **crescent-shaped indentations** that form on beaches of mixed sand and shingle. It's **not known** exactly how they form, but they develop in areas where waves break parallel to the beach and where there's a large **tidal range** (the difference in height between **high** and **low tides**).

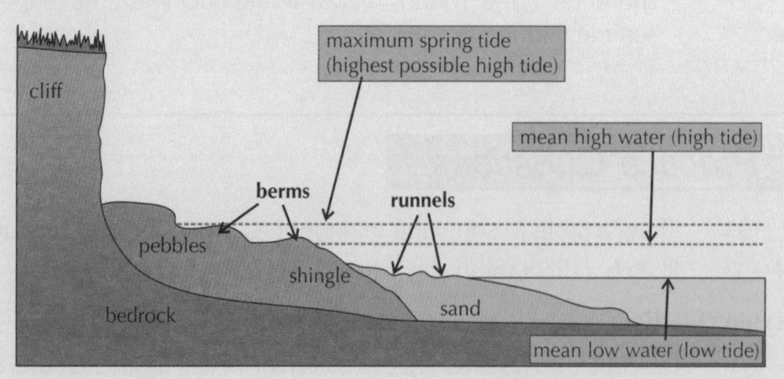

Coastal Landforms

SPITS

1) Spits tend to form where the coast suddenly **changes direction**, e.g. across river mouths. **Longshore drift** (see p. 21) continues to **deposit** material across the river mouth, leaving a bank of **sand** and **shingle** sticking out into the sea.
2) Occasional **changes** to the dominant wind and wave direction may lead to a spit having a **curved end** (the fancy name for this is a **recurved end**). Over time, several recurved ends may be abandoned as the waves return to their **original direction**.
3) The area **behind** the spit is **sheltered** from the waves and often develops into **mudflats** and **salt marshes** (see below).

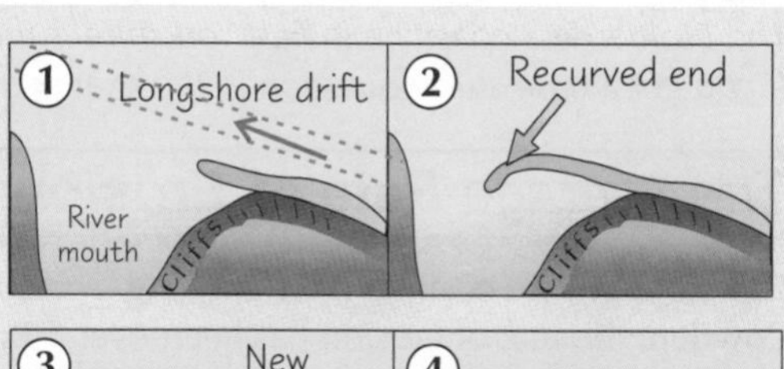

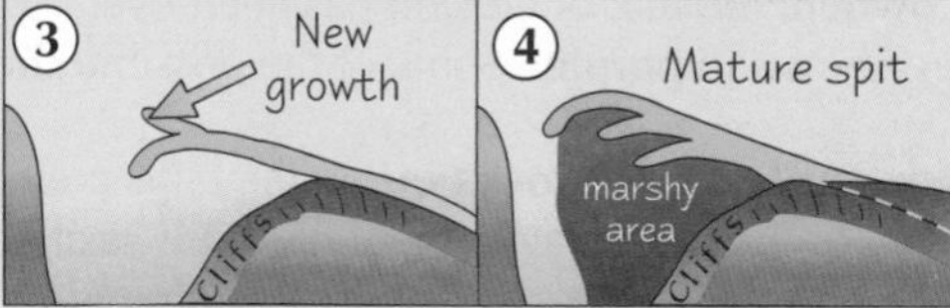

Chaz was a bit annoyed that the bar didn't go right across the river, but he was enjoying the lagoon...

BARS

1) Bars are formed when a **spit joins two headlands together**.
2) This can occur across a **bay** or across a **river mouth** (if the river isn't too strong).
3) A **lagoon** forms **behind** the bar.

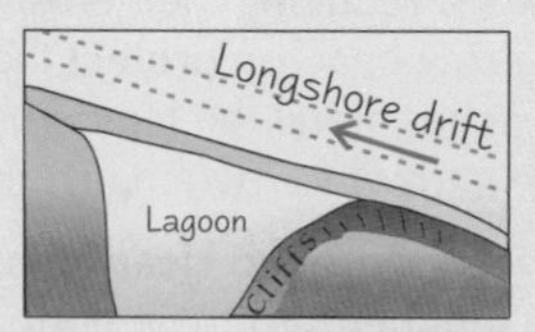

SAND DUNES

1) Sand dunes are formed when **sand deposited** by longshore drift is moved up the beach by the **wind**.
2) Sand trapped by driftwood or berms (see previous page) is colonised by **plants** and **grasses**, e.g. marram grass. The vegetation **stabilises** the sand and encourages **more sand** to accumulate there, forming **embryo dunes**.
3) Over time, the oldest dunes migrate inland as newer embryo dunes are formed. These **mature dunes** can reach heights of up to 10 m.

SALT MARSHES

1) Salt marshes form in areas of **sheltered water**, e.g. river estuaries or behind spits.
2) As **silt** and **mud** are **deposited** by the river or the tide, **mudflats** develop.
3) The mudflats are colonised by **vegetation** that can survive the **high salt levels** and long periods of **submergence** by the tide.
4) The plants **trap more mud** and **silt**, and gradually they create an area of marshland that remains **exposed** for longer and longer **between tides**.

Practice Questions

Q1 Name four landforms of coastal erosion and four landforms of coastal deposition.

Q2 What are berms, runnels and cusps?

Exam Questions

Q1 Describe how erosion can create a wave-cut platform. [5 marks]

Q2 Describe how spits are formed. [6 marks]

Man walks into a bar, gets his feet wet...

At AS level, the landforms you have to know are pretty much the same ones you have to know for GCSE (not much help if you didn't do GCSE, I know, but then they're not that hard to learn anyway). You just need to know more detail about the processes involved in their formation. And you thought it was going to be all excitement and glamour once you got to AS level. Sorry.

Coastal Erosion — Case Study

This page is for AQA (Coasts option) and Edexcel Unit 2 (Coasts option).
The Holderness coastline in East Yorkshire is the fastest eroding coastline in Europe (what a claim to fame).
If you get a case study question in the exam you need to have a bagful of juicy facts at the ready, so get learnin'.

The Average **Rate of Erosion** at Holderness is About **1.8 Metres per Year**

The Holderness coastline is **61 km long** — it stretches from Flamborough Head to Spurn Head. In some places, e.g. **Great Cowden**, the rate of erosion has been over **10 m/year** in recent years. The main **reasons** for this rapid erosion at Holderness are shown in **purple**. Some of the possible **social**, **economic** and **environmental impacts** of the erosion are also shown.

1) **Easily eroded rock type** — the cliffs are mostly made of **till** (or 'boulder clay'). Not only is till **easily eroded** through **corrasion**, but it's also prone to **slumping** when wet.

2) **Narrow beaches** — beaches slow the waves, **reducing** their **erosive power**. Narrow beaches **protect** the cliffs **less**. Beaches along the Holderness coast are narrow for two main reasons:
- **Flamborough Head stops sediment** from the north replenishing the beaches along Holderness. It's also made of **chalk**, which dissolves when eroded rather than making sand for the beaches.
- **Coastal defences**, e.g. at Mappleton (see p. 30 for why these lead to narrow beaches). This is a **human** cause of erosion.

3) **Powerful waves** — the waves are powerful because of:
- The **long fetch** (all the way from the **Arctic Ocean**).
- The coast faces the **dominant wind** and **wave direction** (from the **north-east**).

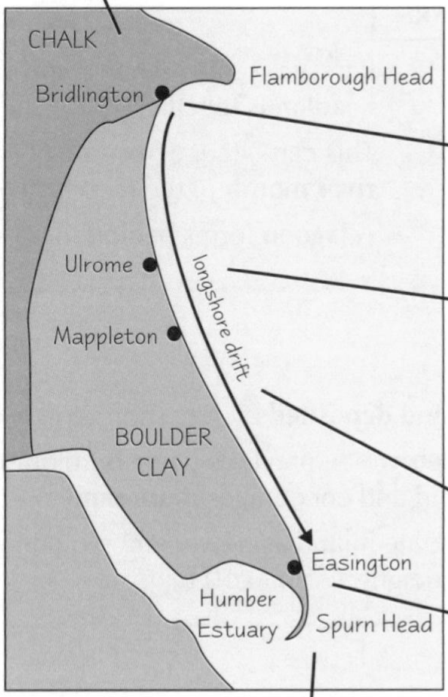

1) **Property prices** along the coast have **fallen** sharply for those houses at risk from erosion.

2) Around **30 villages** have been lost since **Roman times**.

3) **Visitor numbers** in **Bridlington dropped** by over **30%** between **1998** and **2006** (though this could have been due to other reasons).

4) Many **caravan parks** are at risk from erosion, e.g. **Seaside Caravan Park** at **Ulrome** is losing an average of **10 pitches a year**.

5) **£2 million** was spent at **Mappleton** in **1991** to **protect** the coast.

6) The **Gas Terminal** at **Easington** is at risk (it's only **25 m** from the cliff edge). This terminal accounts for **25%** of **Britain's gas supply**.

7) **80 000 m^2** of good quality **farmland** is lost each year. This has a huge effect on **farmers' livelihoods**.

8) Some **SSSIs** (Sites of Special Scientific Interest) are threatened — e.g. **The Lagoons** near **Easington** are part of an SSSI. It has a colony of over 1% of the British breeding population of **little terns**. The lagoons are separated from the sea by a narrow strip of sand and shingle. Erosion of this would connect the lakes to the sea and 'The Lagoons' would be destroyed.

You Need to Know How to **Research Erosion Rates** and **Causes**

This bit is for Edexcel only

CAUSES

1) Research what the **cliffs** are **made from** at **different locations**. E.g. in Holderness the cliffs are all made of till, but the different tills (e.g. Withernsea Till, Skipsea Till) will erode at different rates.

2) Research the effect of **coastal defences** on erosion rates. E.g. for Holderness you could compare erosion rates before and after the defences were built at Mappleton in 1991 — both at Mappleton and a little way to the south (down-drift), e.g. at Great Cowden.

EROSION RATES

1) A great way to calculate the erosion rate is to **compare** the **position** of the **coastline** on **maps** (or **satellite photos**) from **different years**. Don't forget that the maps and photos need to be at the **same scale** for easy comparison.

2) You could also simply research erosion rates on the **internet**. E.g. there's data available for sites all along the Holderness coast.

Coastal Erosion — Case Study

This page is for Edexcel Unit 2 (Coasts option) only — if you're doing AQA, skip straight to the questions.

You Also Need to Know **Fieldwork Methods** for **Erosion Rates** and **Causes**

CAUSES

1) You could **compare erosion rates** for locations just up-drift and down-drift of **sea defences** (e.g. at Mappleton) to tell you if sea defences are affecting erosion rates.
2) You could **measure** the **width** of **beaches** at different points to investigate whether width of beach affects the rate of erosion.

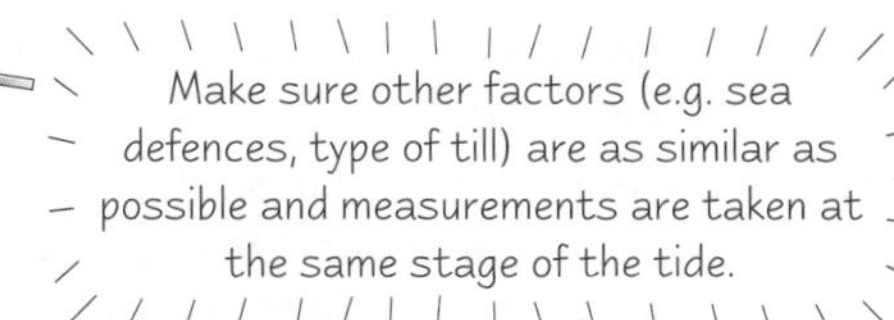
Make sure other factors (e.g. sea defences, type of till) are as similar as possible and measurements are taken at the same stage of the tide.

EROSION RATES

You could **compare** the **position** of the **present-day cliff-line** with recent **satellite photos** or **local maps** to estimate the rate of erosion.

You Need to be Able to **Research** the **Impacts** of **Erosion**...

SOCIAL

1) Use **old maps** and **historical records** to identify **villages** that have disappeared into the sea.
2) Research **census data** for the past 100 years to find changes in **population size** and **structure** for coastal areas.
3) Research **land** and **property values** to see if they've gone **down**.

Don't forget that you need to compare the trend to a similar area (so you can tell that the trend is due to erosion, not just general change in population in coastal areas).

ECONOMIC

1) Contact **insurance companies** to ask for data about **changes in premiums** for settlements along the coast.
2) Research **trends** in **tourist visitor numbers** to see if fewer tourists are visiting the area.
3) Research the impact on **industry** and **jobs** in the area.

For all these things, don't forget that you need to compare the trend to a **similar** coastal area.

ENVIRONMENTAL

Contact **Natural England** (the government body responsible for conservation) for information and data about how erosion is affecting the **environment** in the area.

The **local newspapers** will contain stories about all the different impacts. Watch out though — they can be unreliable.

You could also contact **local politicians** for their own and local residents' views on the impacts of erosion.

...And Do **Fieldwork** to Investigate Them

SOCIAL

1) Use a **questionnaire** to **survey local people**, asking how it's affected them. You could **analyse** the answers to find out **who's affected the most**, e.g. farmers, pub owners, retired people etc.
2) Use a **questionnaire** to **survey tourists** (e.g. in the main resorts of Bridlington or Hornsea), asking their opinions about whether coastal erosion has affected them or whether they will continue holidaying there.

ECONOMIC

Arrange to **visit** any **businesses** affected. E.g. go to a caravan park in Holderness and find out how it's affected their business.

Visiting businesses affected by coastal erosion was more pleasant than Raj originally thought...

Practice Questions

Q1 Describe how you could research the social impacts of coastal erosion.

Q2 Why do you need to compare the trends you find in your research to a similar area?

Exam Question

Q1 With reference to one named area describe and explain the causes of coastal erosion. [10 marks]

Like easily eroded till, I'll be gone when the morning comes...

You need to know a case study of coastal erosion as well as you know how to make beans on toast. Draw an annotated diagram to refresh your memory... toast, then butter, then beans, er... sorry, I mean label the physical causes, human causes and impacts.

Sea Level Changes

This page is for AQA (Coasts option) and Edexcel Unit 2 (Coasts option).
There's a fair bit to learn on these two pages. Just try and keep your head above the water...

Coastal Flooding is Now More Likely Because of Rising Sea Level

1) Sea level **varies** on a daily basis with the **tidal cycle. Onshore winds** and **low atmospheric pressure systems** also cause the sea surface to rise **temporarily**.
2) On a much longer time scale, global sea level is rising at almost **2 mm** each year, which is forecast to **increase** to **4 or 5 mm** a year by 2100.
3) This will increase both the **frequency** and **severity** of flooding in low-lying coastal areas.

Recorded and predicted sea level change

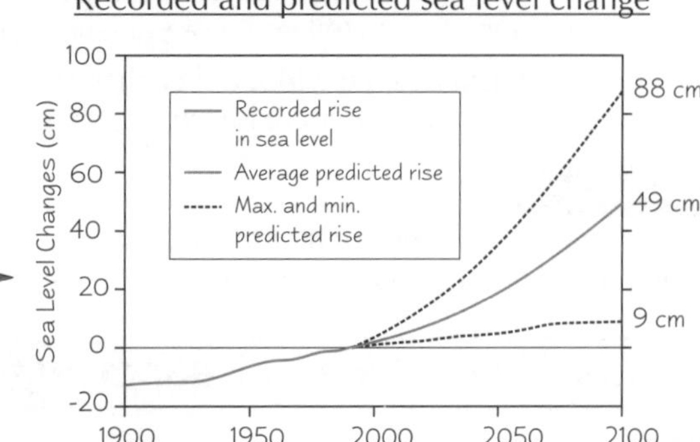

Sea Level Changes are Either Eustatic or Isostatic

EUSTATIC

Eustatic sea level change is caused by a change in the **volume of water** in the sea, or by a change in the **shape** of the **ocean basins**.

The effects are always **global** and the main **causes** are:

1) **Tectonic movements** of the Earth's crust that alter the shape (and so the volume) of ocean basins. E.g. sea floor spreading **increases** the **volume** of the basin and so **decreases** sea level.
2) **Changes in climate.** Different changes affect sea level in different ways:
   - An **increase** in **temperature** causes **melting** of **ice sheets**, which **increases** sea level. It also causes water to **expand**, which **increases** sea level further.
   - A **decrease** in **temperature** causes more precipitation to fall as **snow**. This increases the volume of water **stored** in **glaciers** and so reduces the volume of the sea, which **decreases** sea level.

ISOSTATIC

Isostatic sea level change is caused by **vertical movements** of the land **relative** to the sea.

Any **downward** movement of the land causes sea level to **rise** locally, while **uplift of land** causes sea level to **fall**.

The effects are always **local** and the main **causes** are:

1) **Tectonic** (crustal) uplift or depression, which occurs mostly at plate boundaries.
2) **Compression** or **decompression** of the Earth's crust due to accumulation or melting of **ice sheets**. Slow uplift of land can continue for thousands of years after the weight of a **retreating glacier** has gone. **Accumulation of sediment**, mostly at the mouths of major rivers, can also cause **compression**.
3) **Subsidence** of land due to shrinkage after **abstraction of groundwater**, e.g. drainage of marshland.

Sea Level Rise Can Have a Variety of Impacts

1) **More frequent** and **more severe coastal flooding**.
   Flooding of low-lying areas has increased with sea level rise and it will increase more with further rises. For example, at the beginning of the 20th century **St Mark's Square** in **Venice** flooded less than **10** times per year, and in **1996** it was flooded almost **100** times.
2) **Submergence of low-lying islands**.
   Lots of low-lying islands have **disappeared** as sea level has risen, and loads more are **at risk** of disappearing. For example, if the sea level rises by just **0.5 m** from the current level then most of the **Maldives** would be submerged.
3) **Changes in the coastline**.
   As sea levels rise the coastline changes — **islands** are **created** and the **area** of **land** is **decreased**.
   E.g. over the last 10 000 years sea level rise has separated Britain from mainland Europe.
   If the sea level rises **0.3 m** from the current level **8000 km²** of land in **Bangladesh** will be lost.

Barry and Ami wish they hadn't delayed their holiday to the Maldives.

Don't forget that all these impacts have **further impacts**, e.g. damage to coastal **infrastructure**, decrease in **tourism**, decrease in **agriculture**, loss of **homes** etc.

Sea Level Changes

This page is for AQA (Coasts option) only — if you're doing Edexcel, skip straight to the questions.

Sea Level Rise Results in Coastlines of Submergence

When sea level rises relative to the coast, the sea **submerges** (drowns) the existing coastline. This creates different **landforms**:

① **RIAS** are formed where **river valleys** are partially **submerged**, e.g. Milford Haven in South Wales is a ria. Rias have a **gentle** long- and cross-profile. They're **wide** and **deep** at their **mouth**, becoming **narrower** and **shallower** the further **inland** they reach.

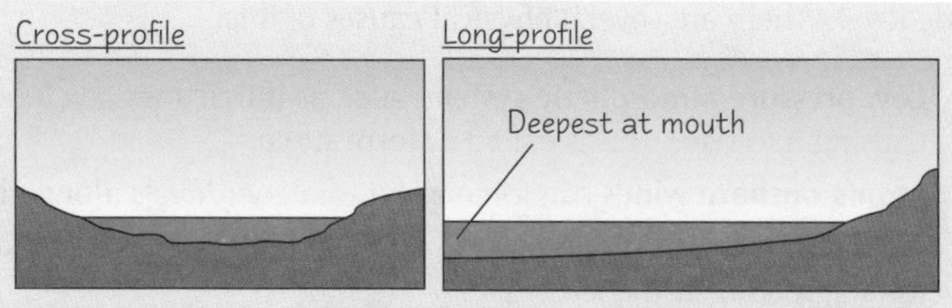

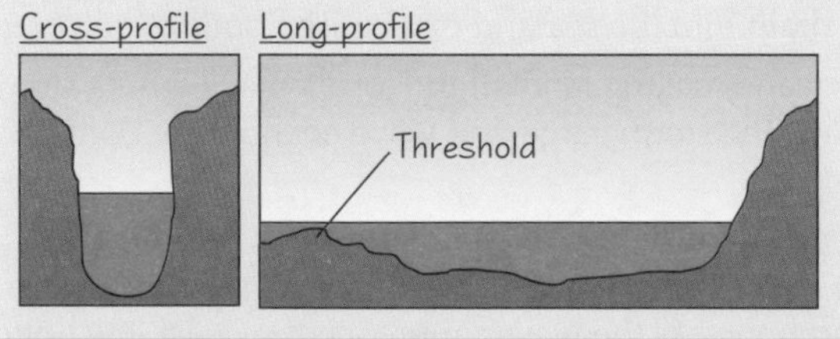

② **FJORDS** are a lot like rias, but they're **drowned glacial valleys** rather than drowned river valleys. They're relatively **straight** and narrow, with very **steep sides**. They have a **shallow mouth** caused by a raised bit of ground (called the **threshold**) formed by deposition of material by the glacier. They're very **deep** further **inland**, e.g. Sognefjorden in Norway is over 1000 m deep in places.

③ In areas where **valleys** lie **parallel** to the coast, an increase in sea level can form a **DALMATIAN COASTLINE**. Valleys are flooded, leaving **islands** parallel to the coastline. It's named after the Dalmatian coast in Croatia.

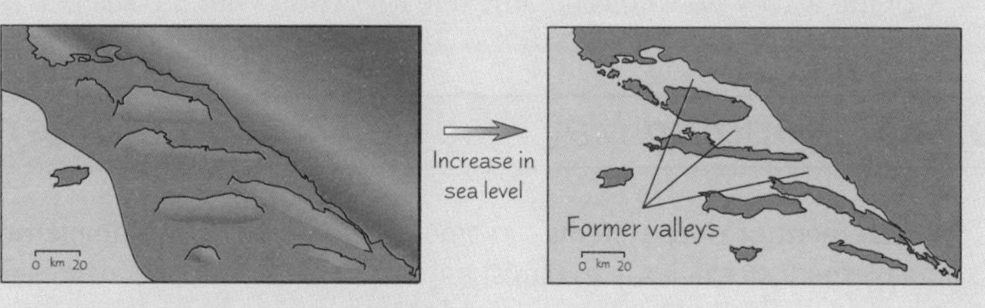

Sea Level Fall Results in Coastlines of Emergence

When sea level falls relative to the coast, new coastline **emerges** (appears) from the sea. This creates different **landforms**:

1) **Raised beaches** are formed when the fall in sea level **exposes wave-cut platforms** and their **beaches**. Over time, beach sediment becomes **vegetated** and develops into **soil**.
2) The **cliffs** above raised beaches are no longer eroded by the sea, and slowly get covered by **vegetation**. They're called **relict cliffs**. It's not uncommon to see **wave-cut notches**, **caves**, **arches** and **stacks** within relict cliffs. These **raised features** are gradually **degraded** (weathered) over time.

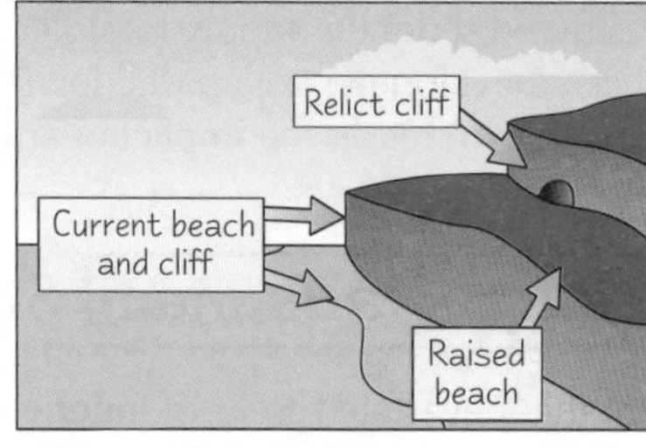

Practice Questions

Q1 State two causes of eustatic sea level change and two causes of isostatic sea level change.

Q2 Give two examples of landforms that show there must have been a drop in sea levels.

Q3 Sketch a diagram showing the cross-profile of a fjord.

Exam Questions

Q1 Describe the possible impacts of sea level rise. [8 marks]

Q2 Describe and explain how coastal submergence can result in a range of landforms. [8 marks]

I'd start moving up onto high ground now...

You need to know that sea levels are rising, and the impacts of sea level rise. Examiners love asking questions about current issues and rising sea levels are a hot topic in the news at the moment — so make sure you're hot on all the details too.

Coastal Flooding

These pages are for AQA (Coasts option) and Edexcel Unit 2 (Coasts option).
As well as a slow rise in sea level, coastal areas are at risk of flooding because of a number of physical and human causes...

Coastal Flooding Occurs Naturally Due to Physical Causes

Coastal lowlands (such as coastal plains, salt marshes and deltas) are liable to flooding when the sea rises above normal high-tide level. There are several **physical causes** of this:

1) **Low pressure atmospheric systems** such as **hurricanes** (cyclones) reduce atmospheric pressure on the sea surface, causing it to **rise**. This is called a **storm surge**.
2) **Strong onshore winds** can force water to higher levels along the coast, allowing waves further inland.
3) **Tidal currents** and **surges** may be funnelled into a coastal bottleneck such as the Bay of Bengal, or English Channel, forcing sea levels higher.
4) **High rainfall** may cause **high river discharge**. If sea level at the river mouth is high, e.g. due to high spring tides or storm surges, the large volume of river water may be **unable to drain** into the sea and can cause flooding.
5) When a **combination of the above factors** coincide. E.g. a hurricane making landfall in Florida may cause a storm surge and high rainfall (which may be unable to drain to the sea). The storm surge and wave energy may both be intensified by strong onshore winds.
6) **Tsunamis** are huge ocean waves caused when water is displaced by **landslides**, **volcanic eruptions** or **submarine earthquakes** that shift the ocean floor. When travelling in open water (i.e. out at sea) they have a very small wave height (less than a metre) and travel at hundreds of kilometres an hour. As the waves approach the coast, the bottom of the waves slow considerably due to friction with the sea bed, causing the wave height to increase enormously.

Coastal Flooding May Also be Caused or Intensified by Human Activity

1) **Management of river systems** — some management strategies (e.g. dams) trap sediment and so reduce the amount being deposited at the river's mouth. This causes deltas and salt marshes to shrink, providing less protection against high tides and storm surges.

2) **Management of coastal systems** — some management strategies alter sediment movement, reducing the amount of protective beach material further along the coast. E.g. coastal defences at Barton in Hampshire have reduced sediment transport to the east, allowing Hurst Spit to be breached more often, flooding lowlands behind.

3) **Building on coastal lowlands**, especially sand dunes, has restricted sediment supply to protective beaches and marshes. Development of coastal lowlands, such as Florida, also **increases** the **impact** of any coastal floods.

4) **Reclamation of coastal lowlands**, such as the Dutch polders, and reclaimed marshes along the east coast of England. Draining this land to reclaim it causes the land to shrink to become lower than sea level.

Case Study — a Tsunami Struck Southern Asia on 26th December 2004

The **tsunami** that devastated areas of **Indonesia**, **Sri Lanka**, **Thailand** and **India** in December 2004 was caused by a submarine **earthquake** in the Indian Ocean. The earthquake is estimated to have measured **9.0** on the Richter scale, making it one of the **strongest earthquakes** ever recorded. The map below shows some of the countries **most affected** by the tsunami.

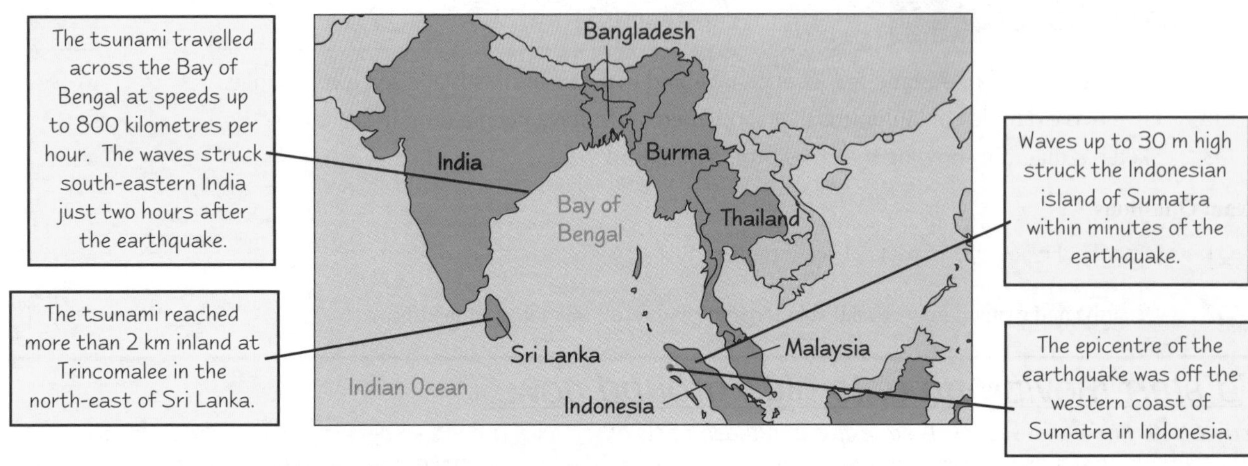
The tsunami travelled across the Bay of Bengal at speeds up to 800 kilometres per hour. The waves struck south-eastern India just two hours after the earthquake.
The tsunami reached more than 2 km inland at Trincomalee in the north-east of Sri Lanka.
Bangladesh
India
Burma
Bay of Bengal
Thailand
Sri Lanka
Malaysia
Indian Ocean
Indonesia
Waves up to 30 m high struck the Indonesian island of Sumatra within minutes of the earthquake.
The epicentre of the earthquake was off the western coast of Sumatra in Indonesia.

Coastal Flooding

The Tsunami Had Severe **Social**, **Economic** and **Environmental Impacts**

Social

1) It was the **deadliest** tsunami **ever recorded**, with an estimated **230 000** people **killed** or **missing**.
2) It's estimated that **1.7 million people** were made **homeless**.
3) Many sources of fresh **drinking water** were **polluted**, either by **sewage** or by **saltwater**.
4) An estimated **400 000 lost their jobs** in **Sri Lanka** alone.

The remains of a house in a destroyed village in Indonesia.

A destroyed fishing boat on a beach in Phuket, Thailand.

Economic

1) Estimates of the **cost** of the initial **damage** caused by the tsunami are between **$8 billion** and **$15 billion**.
2) **Fishing** is a large part of the economy for many of the areas hit by the tsunami. **Boats, nets** and other **equipment** were **destroyed** or **lost**, severely affecting the livelihood of fishermen.
3) **Salinisation** (increase in salt content) of land has severely **reduced soil fertility**. **Crop production** will be **lower** for several years to come.
4) **Tourism** is important to the economy of many of the countries affected. **25% of hotels** in southern **Thailand** were **closed** for at least **6 months** because of damage and the number of **foreign visitors** to the island of **Phuket dropped 80%** in **2005** as the area was perceived to be less safe.

Environmental

1) **8 million litres of oil** were released into the environment after **two oil plants** in Indonesia were **destroyed**. The oil caused widespread **pollution** at sea and **contamination** of the soil, posing **health risks** to humans in the area.
2) **Mangrove forests** as far away as the **East African coast** were **damaged** by the force of the waves, or **covered in layers of silt**.
3) The **high salt content** of the floodwater **destroyed** the natural balance of many **ecosystems**, e.g. the **Karagan Lagoon** in southern **Sri Lanka**.

Mangrove trees uprooted by the waves.

Human Activity Increased the Impact of the Flooding

1) **Mangrove forests** protected parts of the **Sri Lankan coast** by **absorbing wave energy**. Pressure for **tourist development** and the creation of intensive **prawn fisheries** has led to the **destruction** of mangrove forests in other areas around the Indian Ocean. It's estimated that **Thailand** has lost up to **half** of its mangrove forests since **1975**. The lack of protection meant that waves could reach **further inland** and the **flooding** was **much worse** than in areas protected by mangroves.
2) It's thought that healthy **coral reefs** surrounding the **Maldives** acted as a **breakwater** (reducing the power of the tsunami waves) and prevented the complete destruction of the low-lying islands. Illegal **coral mining** and the use of dynamite in explosive '**blast fishing**' has **destroyed** many offshore coral reefs in the Indian Ocean. This reduced the level of natural protection from the waves.

Practice Questions

Q1 What is a storm surge?

Q2 Describe how the characteristics of a tsunami change as it approaches the coast.

Q3 Describe three physical and three human causes of coastal flooding.

Exam Question

Q1 Describe and explain the causes and effects of coastal flooding in a named coastal area. [10 marks]

Coastal flooding — it really is no joke...

You can see from these pages the huge impact of coastal flooding on humans and the environment. Make sure you know a case study of the causes and effects of coastal flooding in a specific area — it's one the examiners love to ask you about.

Coastal Management

These pages are for AQA (Coasts option) and Edexcel Unit 2 (Coasts option). *Coastal management is a complex thing. Fixing up one coastal area can have the unintended effect of messing up another area nearby.*

See pages 24 and 29 for some examples of the impacts of coastal erosion and flooding.

Only **Some Parts** of the **Coast** are **Managed**

The aim of coastal management is to **protect homes, businesses** and the **environment** from **erosion** and **flooding.** This is because flooding and erosion of the coastline can have severe **social, economic** and **environmental impacts.** All coastal settlements want to be defended, but the amount of **money available** is **limited** so not everywhere can be defended. Choosing which places are defended (and how) is based on a **cost-benefit analysis.** The money available is usually used to protect **large settlements** and important **industrial sites**, rather than isolated or small settlements.

There are **Four Options** for **Coastal Management**

1) **Hold the line** — maintain the **existing** coastal defences.
2) **Advance the line** — build **new** coastal defences **further out to sea** than the existing line of defence.
3) **Do nothing** — build **no** coastal defences at all, and deal with erosion and flooding **as it happens**.
4) **Retreat the line** — build no coastal defences, but **move people away** from the coast.

Coastal Defences Include **Hard Engineering** and **Soft Engineering**

Hard Engineering Defences Involve **Built Structures**

Defence	How it works	Cost	Disadvantage
Sea wall	The wall reflects waves back out to sea, preventing erosion of the coast. It also acts as a barrier to prevent flooding.	Expensive to build and maintain	It creates a strong backwash, which erodes under the wall.
Revetment	Revetments are slanted structures built at the foot of cliffs. They can be made from concrete, wood or rocks. Waves break against the revetments, which absorb the wave energy and so prevent cliff erosion.	Expensive to build, but relatively cheap to maintain	They create a strong backwash, as above.
Gabions	Gabions are rock-filled cages. A wall of gabions is usually built at the foot of cliffs. The gabions absorb wave energy and so reduce erosion.	Cheap	Ugly
Riprap (boulders)	Boulders piled up along the coast are called riprap. The boulders absorb wave energy and so reduce erosion.	Fairly cheap	Can shift in storms.
Groynes (← longshore drift)	Groynes are fences built at right angles to the coast. They trap beach material transported by longshore drift. This creates wider beaches, which slow the waves (reducing their energy) and so gives greater protection from flooding and erosion.	Quite cheap	They starve down-drift beaches of sand. Thinner beaches don't protect the coast as well, leading to greater erosion and flooding.
Breakwaters (waves)	Breakwaters are usually concrete blocks or boulders deposited off the coast. They force waves to break offshore. The waves' energy and erosive power are reduced before they reach the shore.	Expensive	Can be damaged in storms.
Earth bank	Mounds of earth act as a barrier to prevent flooding.	Quite expensive	Can be eroded.
Tidal barrier	Tidal barriers are built across river estuaries. They contain retractable floodgates that can be raised to prevent flooding from storm surges.	VERY expensive	Really, VERY expensive.
Tidal barrage	Tidal barrages are dams built across river estuaries. Their main purpose is to generate electricity. Water is trapped behind the dam at high tide. Controlled release of water through turbines in the dam at low tide generates electricity. They also prevent flooding from storm surges.	VERY expensive	They disrupt sediment flow, which may cause increased erosion elsewhere in the estuary.

Coastal Management

Soft Engineering *Defences Involve Coaxing* ***Natural Processes Along***

1) **Beach nourishment** is where **sand** and **shingle** are added to beaches from elsewhere (e.g. **dredged** from offshore). This creates **wide** beaches, which **reduce erosion** of cliffs more than thin beaches.
2) **Beach stabilisation** can be done by **reducing the slope angle** and planting **vegetation**, or by sticking **stakes** and **old tree trunks** in the beach to stabilise the sand. It also creates **wide** beaches, which **reduce erosion** of cliffs.
3) **Dune regeneration** is where sand dunes are **created** or **restored** by either nourishment or stabilisation of the sand. Sand dunes provide a **barrier** between land and sea, **absorbing wave energy** and preventing flooding and erosion.
4) **Land use management** is important for dune regeneration. The vegetation needed to stabilise the dune can easily be **trampled** and destroyed, leaving the dune **vulnerable** to **erosion**. Wooden **walkways** across dunes, and **fenced-off areas** that prevent walkers, cyclists or 4×4 drivers from gaining access to the dunes, all **reduce vegetation loss**.
5) **Creating marshland** from mudflats can be encouraged by **planting** appropriate vegetation (e.g. glassworts). The vegetation **stabilises** the sediment, and the stems and leaves help **reduce the speed** of the waves. This **reduces** their **erosive power** and **how far** the waves reach **inland**, leading to **less flooding** of the area around the marsh.
6) **Coastal realignment** (also known as **managed retreat**) involves breaching an existing defence and allowing the sea to flood the land behind. Over time, vegetation will colonise the land and it'll become **marshland**.

Soft Engineering *is* ***More Sustainable*** *than* ***Hard Engineering***

Hard engineering is often **expensive**, and **disrupts natural processes**. Soft engineering schemes tend to be **cheaper** and require **much less time** and **money** to **maintain** than hard engineering schemes. Soft engineering is designed to **integrate** with the natural **environment** and it creates areas like **marshland** and **sand dunes**, which are important **habitats** for coastal plants and animals. So soft engineering is a **more sustainable management strategy** than hard engineering because it has a **lower environmental impact** and **economic cost**.

Management Strategies *for the Future Must be* ***Sustainable***

1) **Rising sea level** means **more** coastal management will be **needed** to protect coastal settlements and developments. **Storms** also seem to be getting **more frequent** and **more severe**, increasing the need further.
2) There's growing emphasis on the need for **more sustainable management strategies**, i.e. soft engineering.
3) Deciding how to manage a coastline is now done in a more **integrated** way to **improve sustainability**. For example, a **Shoreline Management Plan** (SMP) is a plan for how the coastline in one **sediment cell** (see p. 20) should be managed. SMPs are developed by **local authorities**. All the local authorities in one sediment cell **co-operate** when planning their coastal management strategy, so that defences in one area don't increase erosion in an adjacent area in the same cell.
4) The **process** of trying to come up with an integrated, sustainable management plan is called **Integrated Coastal Zone Management** (ICZM).

Practice Questions

Q1 What is the aim of coastal management?

Q2 What are: a) gabions,
b) groynes,
c) revetments?

Q3 What other options are there for coastal management, apart from hard and soft engineering?

Exam Question

Q1 Explain why soft engineering schemes are more sustainable than hard engineering schemes. [6 marks]

Do nothing? Retreat? Sounds like a lousy revision strategy to me...

Coastal management sounds like a difficult and unending job. Even after spending hundreds of thousands of pounds on a nice big concrete wall to keep the waves out, and some wooden groynes to hold the beach in place, it can still all go horrendously wrong. When it goes wrong, it costs even more money. These days they try to use sustainable methods instead, but it's still hard.

Coastal Management — Case Studies

These pages are for AQA (Coasts option) and Edexcel Unit 2 (Coasts option).
You need to know case studies of coastal management. Wait a minute, what's this I see...

Hard Engineering** Has Been Used Along **Holderness

The Holderness coast is the fastest eroding coastline in Europe. Page 24 outlines the main reasons for the rapid erosion and the social, economic and environmental impacts of the erosion. A total of **11.4 km** of the 61 km coastline is currently protected by **hard** engineering:

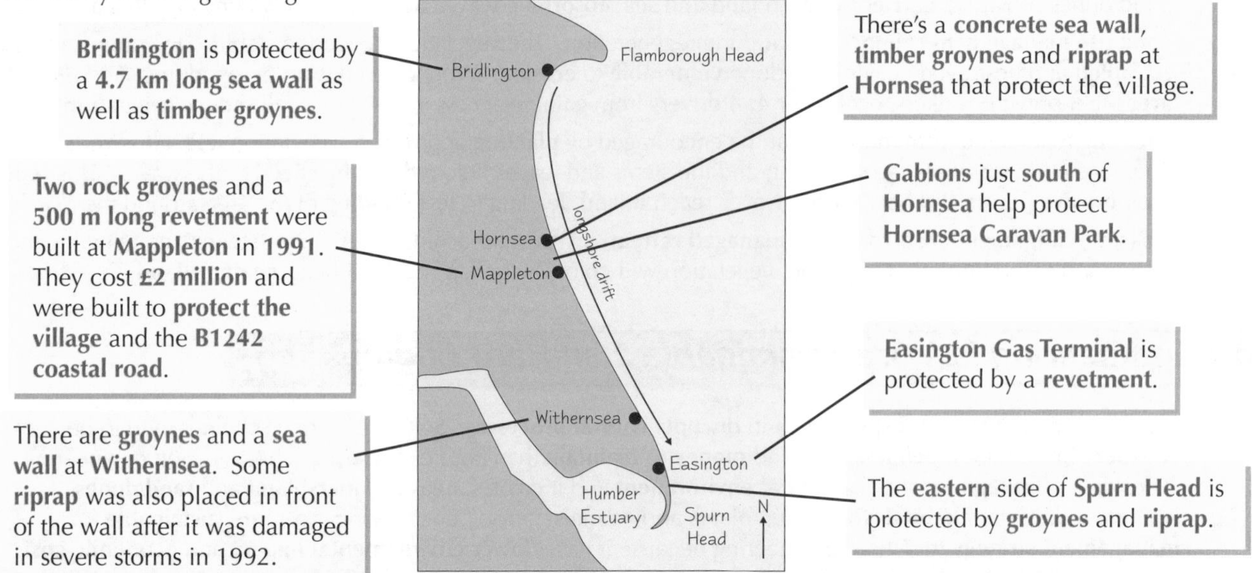

Bridlington is protected by a **4.7 km long sea wall** as well as **timber groynes**.
Two rock groynes and a **500 m long revetment** were built at **Mappleton** in **1991**. They cost **£2 million** and were built to **protect the village** and the **B1242 coastal road**.
There are **groynes** and a **sea wall** at **Withernsea**. Some **riprap** was also placed in front of the wall after it was damaged in severe storms in 1992.
Bridlington
Flamborough Head
Hornsea
Mappleton
longshore drift
Withernsea
Easington
Humber Estuary
Spurn Head
N
There's a **concrete sea wall**, **timber groynes** and **riprap** at **Hornsea** that protect the village.
Gabions just **south** of **Hornsea** help protect **Hornsea Caravan Park**.
Easington Gas Terminal is protected by a **revetment**.
The **eastern** side of **Spurn Head** is protected by **groynes** and **riprap**.

The **Schemes** are **Locally Successful** but **Cause Problems Down-drift*

1) The groynes **trap sediment**, increasing the **width** of the **beaches**. This **protects** the **local area** but **increases erosion** of the cliffs **down-drift** (as the material eroded from the beaches there isn't replenished). E.g. the Mappleton scheme has caused **increased erosion** of the cliffs **south** of Mappleton. **Cowden Farm**, just south of Mappleton, is now at risk of falling into the sea.
2) The **sediment** produced from the erosion of the Holderness coastline is normally washed into the **Humber Estuary** (where it helps to form **tidal mudflats**) and down the **Lincolnshire coast**. Reduction in this sediment **increases** the **risk of flooding** along the Humber Estuary, and **increases erosion** along the Lincolnshire coast.
3) The protection of local areas is leading to the **formation of bays** between the areas. As bays develop the wave pressure on headlands will increase and eventually the **cost** of maintaining the sea defences may become **too high**.
4) All these problems make the existing schemes **unsustainable**.

Possible Schemes** All Have **Problems

See p. 31 for more on SMPs.

1) The **SMP** for Holderness for the next 50 years recommends '**holding the line**' at **some settlements** (e.g. at Bridlington, Withernsea, Hornsea, Mappleton and Easington Gas Terminal) and '**doing nothing**' along more **unpopulated stretches**. However, this is **unpopular** with owners of land or property along the stretches where nothing is being done.
2) **Coastal realignment** of businesses has been suggested, e.g. relocating **caravan parks** further inland. This would be a **more sustainable** scheme as it would allow the coast to be eroded as normal without endangering businesses. However, there are issues surrounding how much businesses will be **compensated** by for relocating. Also, relocation isn't always possible, e.g. farmland can't be 'relocated', and there may be no land for sale to relocate buildings to.
3) A **sea wall** has been proposed to better protect **Easington Gas Terminal**. This would cost **£4.5 million**. The problem is that it would reduce sediment flow to the south, **increasing erosion** at the **village of Easington** (with a population of **700 people**). A **longer sea wall** could be built that would protect the village as well as the gas terminal, but that would cost **£7 million**.
4) **Offshore reefs** made from **concrete-filled tyres** have been proposed to protect the coastline. They act like **breakwaters**. Similar reefs have been built in the USA and have reduced erosion. Some people think that the reefs will **harm the environment** though (although there's currently no evidence of this).

Coastal Management — Case Studies

Soft Engineering Has Been Used Along *Blackwater Estuary*

Blackwater Estuary is part of the **Essex** coastline. Land in the estuary is being eroded at a rate of **0.3-1 m/year**. In some exposed areas (e.g. **Cobmarsh Island**) the erosion rate is **2 m/year**. The area is also **at risk from flooding** as sea level is rising and the **South** of England is **sinking** relative to the sea. There are some hard engineering schemes in the estuary, but these are becoming too expensive to maintain, so **soft** engineering approaches are now being implemented:

Coastal realignment was implemented at **Tollesbury Fleet** in **1995**. An existing **sea wall** was **breached** and **21 hectares** of farmland were flooded to encourage a **marshland** to form. A **new lower sea wall** was built **further back** on higher ground to protect from flooding.

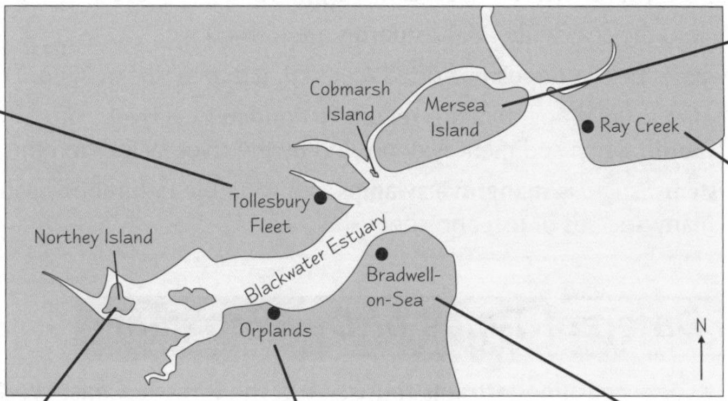

Beaches have been **nourished** along the estuary, e.g. at **Mersea Island**.

Marsh stabilisation has been carried out by planting **stakes** and **brushwood** on the water line to encourage sediment to build up, e.g. at **Ray Creek**.

In **1991** an **existing sea wall** was **lowered** and **breached** flooding **0.8 hectares** of land at **Northey Island**.

In **1995** a **sea wall** was **breached** and **40 hectares** of farmland at **Orplands** were flooded as part of **coastal realignment**.

Coastal realignment has been carried out at **Bradwell-on-Sea** by **breaching** an **old sea wall**.

The Schemes are *More Sustainable* than Hard Engineering Schemes

1) The schemes are **more sustainable** in the **long term**. E.g. to repair the sea wall at Orplands would have cost more than £600 000 (and it would only last for 20 years). The 40 hectares of farmland flooded was valued at around £600 000, but the marshland created would defend the coast for **longer** as it's **self-repairing**.
2) The schemes have created **more marshland**, which provides a larger **habitat** for **wildlife**.
3) However, some areas **haven't changed** to marshland (e.g. parts of the Orpland site are still bare mud, which is easily eroded). Also, **grazing land** has been **lost**.

The *Success* of *Coastal Management Schemes* Can be *Investigated*

This bit is for Edexcel only

RESEARCH

1) Research the **rates of erosion before** and **after** the scheme was implemented (both **at the site** of the scheme and **down-drift**). Data and maps could be obtained from **local agencies** (e.g. the **Council**) or from the **Environment Agency**.
2) Research the **flood risk before** and **after** the scheme was implemented — again using data and maps.
3) Search **local newspapers** to see whether local people have been positively or adversely affected by the scheme.

FIELDWORK

1) Visit the scheme and **record** the **structures** there, then **observe** the **effects** of the schemes **at the site** and **down-drift**.
2) Use a **questionnaire** to find out how the scheme has affected **local residents**, **business owners** and **tourists**.

Practice Questions

Q1 List the types of hard engineering used along the Holderness coast.

Q2 List the types of soft engineering used along the Blackwater Estuary in Essex.

Exam Question

Q1 Evaluate the success of a named coastal management scheme. [15 marks]

More case studies — what a pain in the groyne...

The best thing to do here is learn the annotated map for each case study. Draw them out over and over again until they're practically tattooed on the inside of your eyelids (it'll hurt a lot less than missing a load of easy marks in the exam, I promise).

Coastal Population Growth

The rest of this section is for Edexcel Unit 2 (Coasts option). If you're doing AQA, you've finished Section 2 now — hurrah!
Oh I do like to be beside the seaside, oh I do like to be beside the sea. And so does everybody else it seems...

Different Physical Factors Create Different Coastal Environments...

1) **Different rock types** and the process of **erosion** produce features like **cliffs**, **arches** and **stacks**.
2) Coastal **erosion** can also create **sheltered inlets** and deep **natural harbours**.
3) Where big **rivers** flow into the sea, wide tidal **estuaries** are formed.
4) **Beaches** are formed where the sea **deposits** eroded material, e.g. pebbles or sand.
5) **Flood plains** are wide, flat valley floors that are **regularly flooded** by a river.
   Deltas form at a river **mouth** when sediment is deposited by the river faster than the sea removes it.
6) Certain **coastal ecosystems**, such as **mangrove swamps**, are valuable natural environments, providing important **breeding grounds** for many species of fish and shellfish.

See pages 22-23 for how the features are formed.

...Which Encourage Different Types of Development

1) The **dramatic scenery** of some coastlines **attracts tourists**, e.g. the **Jurassic Coast World Heritage Site** in Dorset and East Devon attracts thousands of visitors each year.
2) Natural harbours allow **easy access** for the **import** and **export** of raw materials and manufactured goods by ship, which **attracts industry** to the area, e.g. companies such as **Shell** and **Esso** have located in **Rio de Janeiro**, Brazil.
3) **Estuaries** also allow **easy access** for ships, so encourage **port development** and **attract industry** to their **hinterlands** (the area surrounding the port), e.g. the **Port of Shanghai** on the **River Yangtze estuary** is the busiest port in the world.
4) Attractive **beaches** in areas with an **equable** (warm, temperate) climate will **attract tourists**, e.g. Costa Brava in Spain.
5) The nutrient-rich **alluvium** deposited by rivers on flood plains and deltas makes the **soil** very **fertile**.
   This **attracts agriculture**, e.g. the Nile Delta in Egypt has been farmed intensively for over 6000 years.
6) Some **coastal ecosystems** have a **high biodiversity**, which attracts **fishing** and **tourists**, e.g. the **Great Barrier Reef** in Australia attracts over a million tourists per year.

Increased Development Causes Coastal Population Growth

1) The physical factors of accessibility, fertile soil, equable climate, dramatic scenery and high biodiversity lead to an increase in fishing, tourism or industry.
2) An increase in **fishing**, **tourism** or **industrial/port development** in an area causes an **increase** in **population** because people are **attracted** to live there by the **opportunities for employment**.
3) Also, the **land** is often **flat** by the coast which means **homes** and **businesses** can be built much **more easily**. This **encourages** people to **live** and **locate businesses** in these areas, causing population growth.

Case Study 1: Brighton

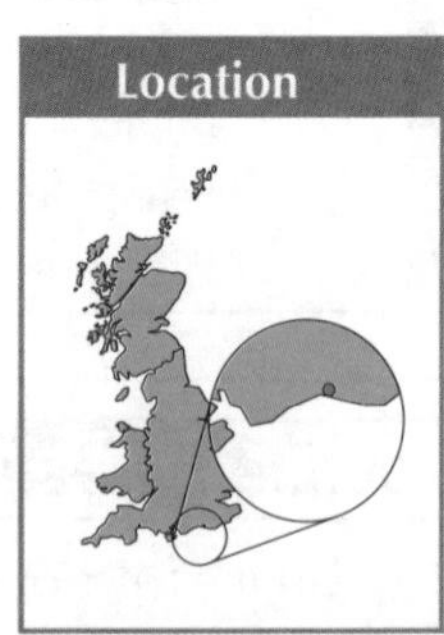

Brighton is a coastal city in **East Sussex** on the **English Channel coast**.
Brighton has seen population growth for many years due to different factors:

1) **Potential for fishing** — Brighton initially grew as a fishing village. People moved to the area because of the jobs available as fishermen.
2) **Tourism** — In the 18th century, it was believed that bathing in seawater was good for your health. Rich people, including the Prince of Wales, began to go to Brighton to be cured. This 'celebrity effect' saw Brighton attract wealthy tourists. People **migrated** to the area, attracted by the **jobs** that this new-found **tourism** provided.
3) **Accessibility** — In the Victorian period, a **railway** was built linking Brighton and London. Improved accessibility meant that working class people could travel to Brighton on day trips. This saw the growth of **mass tourism** and **exponential** population growth. Between 1841 and 1881, Brighton's population rose from **15 000** to over **135 000**.
4) **Industrial development** — Since the 1970s there has been a decline in tourists holidaying in British resorts. To fight this, Brighton has redeveloped itself as a centre for other **tertiary** and **quaternary** industries. It's now attracting large numbers of people who work in the **media** sector, particularly in "new media" such as the internet.

Coastal Population Growth

Case Study 2: **Dubai**

Dubai is in the **United Arab Emirates**, on the **Persian Gulf coast**.
It has experienced different periods of growth for different reasons:

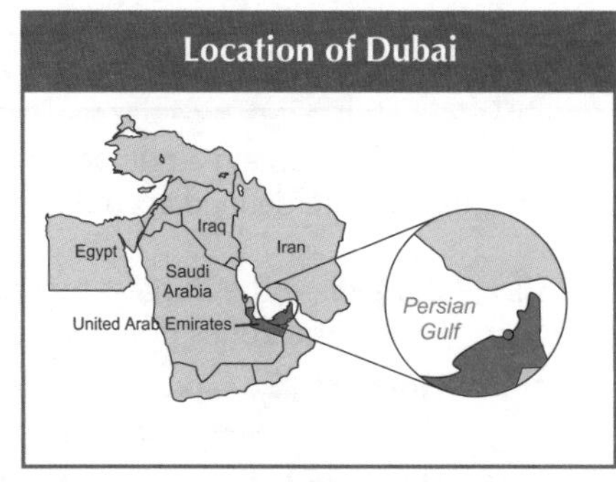

1) Dubai's **geographical proximity** to India made it an important **trading centre** between Asia and Europe and many traders eventually **settled** in the city. Until the 1930s it was known for its pearl exports.
2) In **1966 oil** was discovered. **Industrial** and **port development** followed as Dubai Creek was dredged to improve **accessibility**. This allowed large ships access to the city and a **new port** was built at **Jebel Ali**, the biggest in the Middle East. The population of Dubai City **quadrupled** from 1968 to 1975 as **foreign workers**, largely from India and Pakistan, flooded into the city to work in **construction** and **oil production**.
3) It was known that Dubai's oil reserves would not last, so money from oil exports was used to **diversify the economy** to promote continued growth. As well as the building of the port at Jebel Ali, a **Free Economic Zone** was set up adjacent to the port, offering tax incentives to international businesses. Global businesses such as Microsoft®, IBM®, CNN and Reuters located there, attracting both **domestic** and **international workers** to the area.
4) Over the last 10 years, **tourism** has become important to the growth of Dubai. In contrast to British resorts, which are having to diversify because of a drop in tourist numbers, the Dubai government is **investing heavily** in tourist **infrastructure** and hopes to attract 10 million tourists per year by 2010. Huge construction projects, which require a **skilled foreign labour** force, have contributed to a **doubling** in Dubai's population since 1993. **Less than 20%** of the 1.4 million people who now live in Dubai are **native**.

You Need to Know How to **Research** Factors Affecting **Population Growth**...

1) You could look at **historical documents** and **maps** to see how **land use** has changed over time. This may indicate a change in the factors influencing the growth of the population.
2) If you want to find out **population numbers** and how quickly populations have grown, look at **census data**.
3) You should check out **local newspapers** for the areas you're studying as they may have information on **development projects**, which could be tied to an increase in population. Foreign newspapers may have English language websites.
4) If the location being studied is a tourist destination, then you could look at **holiday brochures** to identify factors that attract people to the area.

...and Do **Fieldwork** to **Investigate** It

1) You could do **land use surveys** and look for **visible evidence** of economic development in a UK location, and then try to link the results to the factors on the previous page.
2) To find people's **reasons for moving** to an area, you could **survey** local people of a range of ages. Tourists can also be surveyed to find out what **attracted** them to the area.

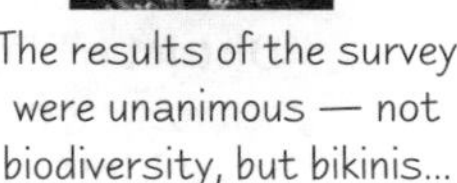

The results of the survey were unanimous — not biodiversity, but bikinis...

Practice Questions

Q1 Explain how soil fertility can influence coastal population growth.

Q2 List four factors, other than soil fertility, that can increase population growth at the coast.

Exam Question

Q1 For two contrasting coastal locations, explain why their population has grown rapidly. [10 marks]

You say Dubai, and I say hello...

Make sure you learn the physical and economic factors that influence population growth at the coast and can relate them to two contrasting case studies. You might also get asked a weirdy fieldwork and research question on all this stuff, so make sure you know what methods you used to investigate coastal population growth. All this talk of Dubai has made me fancy a holiday...

Coastal Development and Conflict

These pages are for** Edexcel Unit 2 (Coasts **option).
Ahhh land use models. Bet you thought you'd left all that behind at GCSE. Nope. Mwahahaha...

*A **Land Use Model** is a Diagram That Shows **How Land is Used** in Different Areas*

Land use models contain a number of different **zones**. They're **simplified** diagrams showing typical **patterns of land use** in an area (the zones are defined according to the **major** land use in that area). There are three popular urban land use models:

1) **Burgess** — The Burgess model shows a settlement growing out in concentric zones from the centre.
2) **Hoyt** — Hoyt's model also has concentric zones, but adds sectors that grow along linear features, like main roads or rivers.
3) **Harris and Ullman** — This land use model shows multiple nuclei of different land uses. It assumes that similar industries with common land use and financial requirements develop near to each other.

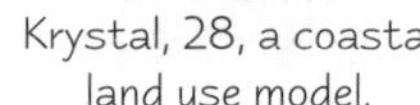
Krystal, 28, a coastal land use model.

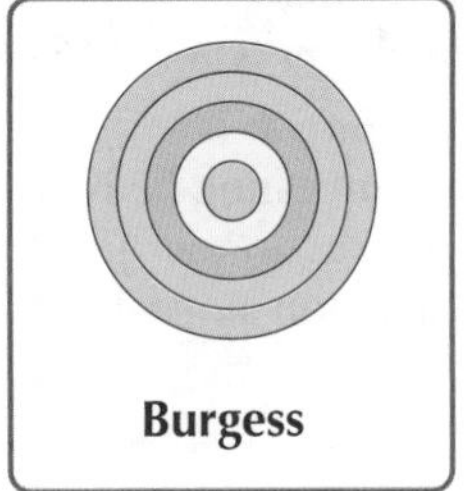
Burgess

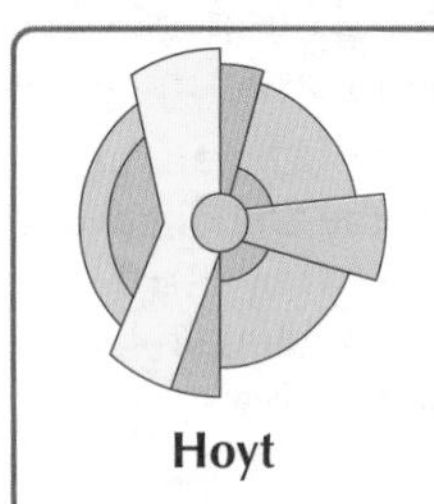
Hoyt

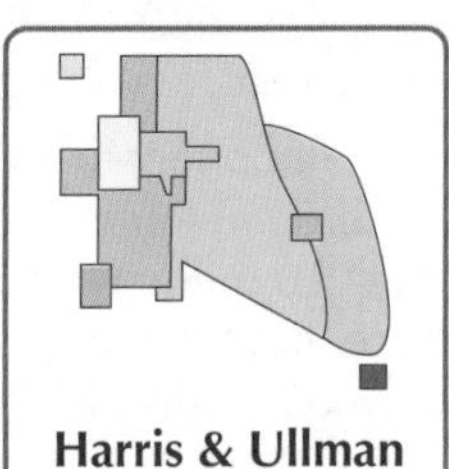
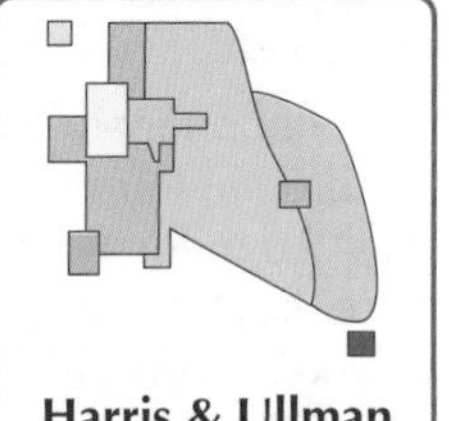
Harris & Ullman

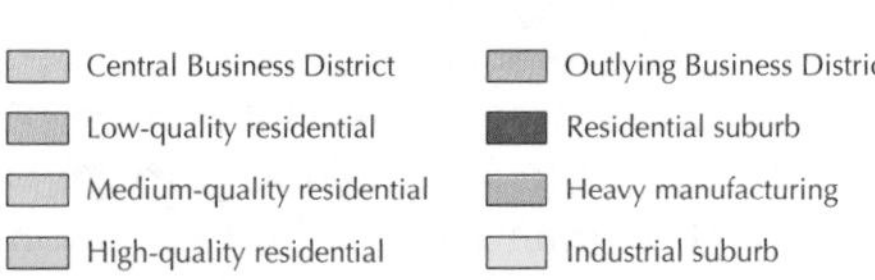

*Coastal Developments **Distort** Land Use Models*

Coastal development creates patterns of land use **zoning**. The diagram below shows a generalised land use model for a UK **seaside resort**. There are a number of characteristics to note:

1) **Shape** — The shape of land use zones is **distorted** in a coastal settlement, as the sea **limits growth** in that direction. **Linear zones** develop along the **sea front** and **main roads** away from the sea, similar to Hoyt's model. **Semicircular** zones may then grow **away from the coast**.

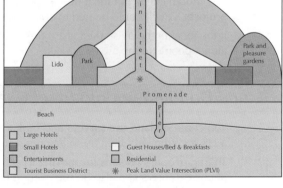

Main Street
Lido
Park
Park and pleasure gardens
Promenade
Beach
Pier
Large Hotels
Small Hotels
Entertainments
Tourist Business District
Guest Houses/Bed & Breakfasts
Residential
Peak Land Value Intersection (PLVI)

2) **Accommodation** — Hotels are attracted to sites with sea views or close to a promenade. The **larger hotels** will be based on the **sea front**, closest to the **Tourist Business District** (TBD). **Smaller hotels** will also try to locate on the sea front, but will be **further from the TBD**. This may lead to **multiple nuclei** of land use, like in Harris and Ullman's model. **Guesthouses** and bed and breakfasts, which can't charge as much for rooms, will be located **further** from the sea front, where land is **cheaper**. Residential housing will also be found further from the sea.

3) **Open spaces** — There may be **parks** or **pleasure gardens** on the sea front. Although land prices are now high, they will have been set aside at a time when prices were **lower**, e.g. during Victorian times. Strict **planning policies** prevent them from being developed.

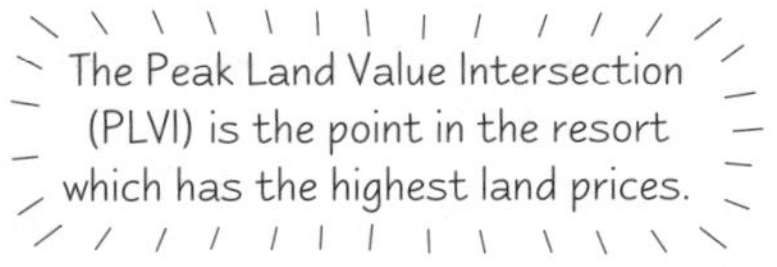
The Peak Land Value Intersection (PLVI) is the point in the resort which has the highest land prices.

4) **Entertainment** — Most tourist and recreational attractions are linked to key sites such as **piers**. They want to attract tourists, so they need to locate where tourists gather at the **sea front**. The **TBD** will usually be found along the **main street** running inland from the **Peak Land Value Intersection**. Sites that need a lot of **space**, such as golf courses, will be located near to the **edge** of the urban area.

Coastal Development and Conflict

Coastal Development Has Led to the Need for **Planning Control**

The rate of **development** at the coast is **increasing** as the coastal population continues to grow (see p. 34). However, the area of land available for development is decreasing and **fierce competition** is driving land prices up. To prevent unchecked growth of coastal areas and the possible destruction of important coastal ecosystems, strict **planning controls** are needed. The controls have to **balance** the **economic advantages** of development against the **environmental damage** caused.

Coastal Development Can Cause **Conflict** with **Coastal Conservation**

Different people have **different ideas** of how development should take place at the coast. These people are called **stakeholders** (and include tourists, small business owners, industrialists and conservationists). There's often **conflict** between stakeholders over **activity at the coast**. Some of the activities likely to cause conflict are:

1) Tourism

Tourism brings with it **job opportunities** and **increased spending** in local businesses (e.g. shops, cafés). However, there can be conflict between tourists and locals over **traffic congestion**, **parking** and **noise**. Tourism can also bring with it an **environmental impact**, as **demand for access** to tourist areas increases **road building** and **construction** of other **amenities**. These may be built on ecologically important land, leading to the **destruction** of valuable coastal **ecosystems**. Tourists can also contribute to **coastal erosion** by walking over **sand dunes** and destroying the plants that stabilise the dunes. This causes **conflict** between tourists and those responsible for protecting the ecology of the coast.

2) Overfishing

Fishing brings **jobs** and **money** to coastal areas but **overfishing** can lead to rapid decline and even **extinction** of fish populations. Efforts to conserve fish stocks cause conflict with the fishing industry. Treaties have been agreed by many countries to try to stop fish stocks from collapsing, e.g. the **EU Common Fisheries Policy**. But because these treaties **limit** the amount of fish that can be caught, they can lead to **job losses** and the **decline** of fishing communities.

3) Aquaculture

Demand for affordable fish and shellfish has led to the cultivation of aquatic animals in **'fish farms'**. This leads to **conflict** between the **producers** and **environmentalists**, due to the potential **negative effects** aquaculture can have on the surrounding ecosystem. High levels of fish waste can **decrease** dissolved **oxygen levels** in the water, which can lead to the **death** of **other fish** and plant life in the area. **Diseases** can spread **from farmed fish to wild fish**, which can then have a devastating effect on the natural population of certain species.

4) Industrialisation

As **ports** have **expanded** because of **industrial growth**, coastal **ecosystems** have come under threat. There's pressure to develop **salt marshes** at the coast as they provide flat land and sheltered water, ideal for ports and industry. There's a **conflict** between **industry** wanting to exploit the advantages of locating at the coast, and those trying to **protect** salt marshes and other **Sites of Special Scientific Interest** (SSSIs).

Pollution of both the sea and beaches from **industrial waste** has harmful effects for **swimmers** and **marine creatures**. This causes conflict between the **coastal industries** who are responsible for much of the pollution, and both **tourists** and **environmentalists**.

Practice Questions

Q1 Annotate a diagram to show the main land use zones of a seaside resort.

Q2 Describe the characteristics of the TBD.

Q3 Give a definition of the PLVI.

Exam Question

Q1 Examine the environmental impact of development at the coast and the conflict this causes. [10 marks]

Aquaculture — not an underwater opera...

There's quite a lot to learn on these pages, but it's all good nuts 'n' bolts geography stuff — land use models, development, conflict. Make sure you know the characteristics of the coastal land use model, and the issues surrounding rapid development of the coast.

Coastal Development and Conflict

These pages are for Edexcel Unit 2 (Coasts option).
Just when you thought you'd learnt everything for coasts, along come another two pages.
You're nearly there though — just a case study and some other bits and bobs to go...

Development in Dubai Has Caused Conflict

Dubai is in the **United Arab Emirates** (UAE), on the Persian Gulf coast. Page 35 outlines how and why Dubai developed.

The **rapid** coastal **development** since the 1970s has led to **conflict** in Dubai. This is because the **stakeholders** have **different opinions** and **ideas** about how development should proceed.

There are a number of **different activities** that cause **conflict** between stakeholders:

1. **OIL PRODUCTION** — Dubai produces over **150 000 barrels** of oil a day. Oil is very important to the **economy** of UAE as a whole, making up around a **third** of the country's **GDP**. Conflict between **oil companies** and **conservationists** occurs because **oil tankers** cause **pollution** in the Gulf. This can take 5-8 years to flush out because the Gulf is a semi-enclosed body of water. The pollution of the sea around Dubai also causes conflict with the **fishing industry** as it can affect **fish stocks**.

2. **FISHING** — **Overfishing** in Dubai is a problem as there are **no quotas** set to limit the numbers of fish that can be caught. Increasing **demand** from **tourists** for fresh local fish is putting further strain on fish stocks (certain species, such as the **hamour**, are in danger of being fished to **extinction**). Also, illegal **drift nets** are sometimes used, which affect **endangered species** such as the **hawksbill turtle**. This creates conflict between **conservation** agencies such as the **Environmental Research and Wildlife Development Agency (ERWDA)** and the **fishing industry**.

3. **TOURISM** — In **2007** the number of **hotel guests** staying in Dubai was about **7 million**. It's estimated to reach **14 million** by **2015**. This causes conflict between the **tourist industry** and **conservationists** because the increase in tourists will lead to **more sewage**, **litter**, and more **erosion** of the coastline. **Four-wheel-drive vehicles** used for tourist excursions have also **damaged turtle nesting beaches**.

4. **PROPERTY DEVELOPMENT** — Several 'mega projects' are being constructed in Dubai such as **The Palms** and **Waterfront** (artificial islands with houses, hotels and leisure facilities). They can **damage coastal habitats**, e.g. **Palm Jebel Ali** is being **built over coral reef**. Some of these developments are also being built on **land reclaimed** from the Persian Gulf using material **dredged** from the seabed. Dredging **destroys** the **seabed environment**. Many developments also **increase** the **number of tourists** and so increase the problems they cause. This creates conflict between **property developers** and **conservationists**.

A **conflict matrix** can be used to **record** the conflicts between **different stakeholders**.

For Dubai it would look something like this.

	Oil companies	Fishing industry	Conservationists	Property developers
Oil companies				
Fishing industry	-1			
Conservationists	-1	-1		
Property developers	0	0	-1	
Tourist industry	0	+1	-1	+1

+1 = interaction is positive
-1 = interaction is negative (conflict)
0 = no direct interaction

Tools Can be Used to Assess Conflict and Evaluate Developments

1) An **Environmental Impact Assessment** (EIA) is a process to determine the **environmental consequences** of a development project.

E.g. an EIA was undertaken for a proposed **combined power station** and **desalination plant** at **Hassyan** in **Dubai**. Data from **publications**, **internet research** and **satellite imagery** was studied. **Government officials**, **local interest groups** and **international experts** were consulted. An **ecological survey** to gather information on plants, animals, habitats and water quality was undertaken. A number of issues were identified, including:

1) **Seawater quality changes** — e.g. increased temperature and salinity.
2) **Modification** or **loss of coastal habitats** — e.g. **coral reefs** could be lost due to the seawater changes (corals are very sensitive to temperature changes).
3) **Loss** of the **Jebel Ali Wildlife Sanctuary**.

Coastal Development and Conflict

2) A **Cost-Benefit Analysis** (CBA) is a process that allows the **costs** and **benefits** of any development to be examined to see if it should go ahead. It can also be used to **compare different developments** to see which is best. All aspects of the development are given a **monetary value**, e.g. how much it costs to build, how much money it would bring to the area per year, etc. Then you can see if the total benefits **outweigh** the total costs. But, it's **difficult** to give a monetary value to **all** costs and benefits (e.g. the economic value of hamour fish is difficult to figure out), so it can be inaccurate.

3) **Values analysis** is another way of deciding if a development should go ahead. It's similar to a cost-benefit analysis, but involves examining the **viewpoints** of **different stakeholders** as well.

E.g. after analysing the costs and benefits of the **combined power station** and **desalination plant** at **Hassyan** in **Dubai**, it was **approved**. The viewpoints of different stakeholders were considered, but the decision was largely due to the **huge increase in the demand for water**. Dubai currently has the capacity to supply **260 m gallons/day**, but demand is expected to increase to **800 m gallons/day** by **2015**. The new desalination plant will be able to provide an extra **600 m gallons/day**.

You Need to be Able to *Investigate Coastal Development* and *Conflict*

FIELDWORK

1) To assess the **environmental value** of an area that may be affected by development you could **survey** the **biodiversity** of the area, e.g. by counting the number of **different species** present.
2) To assess the **recreational value** of an area that may be affected by development you could **survey** the **different recreational activities** on offer there.
3) To **assess** the **impact** of **tourists** attracted by a development, you could **survey** the amount of **litter**, **trampling of vegetation** and **erosion** in the area.

Don't forget that this would have to be done before and after the development, or you'd have to compare it to a similar area away from the development.

RESEARCH

1) To **identify** any **new developments** you could look at **planning applications**, or look in **newspapers** for articles about proposed developments. Looking at **land use maps** could also indicate new developments.
2) To **assess** the **environmental value** of an area that may be affected by development (e.g. fragile habitats like **dunes**, **salt marshes** and **SSSIs**) you could research if it **provides habitats** for **endangered species**.
3) To **assess** the **impact** of **fishing**, **aquaculture** and **tourism** you could look for **newspaper articles** or look on the internet for **reports** from the government or conservation groups.

SSSIs are Sites of Special Scientific Interest.

Development is *Threatened* by *Erosion and Flooding*

As if it wasn't enough that there's conflict surrounding coastal development, it's also **under threat** from two things:

1) Rapid **coastal erosion** (see pages 20-25 for more).
2) **Coastal flooding** caused by **rising sea level** and events such as **tsunamis** and **storm surges** (see pages 26-29 for more).

Practice Questions

Q1 List the four main activities that cause conflict between stakeholders in Dubai.

Q2 What is an Environmental Impact Assessment?

Exam Questions

Q1 Explain, with reference to one or more named areas, how economic development has threatened the coastal environment. [10 marks]

Q2 Describe and explain the fieldwork and research you could do to investigate development and conflict at the coast. [15 marks]

...hello, hello. I don't know why you say Dubai, I say hello...

See what I did there? Nice. Now here's a juicy case study related to all the stuff from the last few pages. Make sure you can remember your fieldwork and research on coastal development and conflict in case they ask you about it in the exam. And that's it — you've made it to the end of Section 2. I can't possibly tell you what's coming next — you'll just have to turn over...

Distribution of Cold Environments

This section is for AQA (Cold Environments option).
You're probably thinking that all cold environments are the same — they're all just, well, cold. Well it turns out that there are different types of cold environment, and it's not quite as simple as chilly, cold and blimmin' freezing.

There are **Three** Main **Reasons** Why Environments Might be **Cold**

1) They're at a **high latitude**. High latitudes are **colder** than lower latitudes because they receive **less solar radiation** (the Sun's energy hits the Earth at more of an **angle** at high latitudes so it's spread over a larger area).

Latitude lines go horizontally round the Earth, like the equator — the higher you go in latitude (either north or south) the further away you get from the equator.

2) They're at a **high altitude**. High altitudes are colder than lower altitudes because **air temperature decreases** with **increasing altitude**. **Less** of the Sun's energy **reflected** back from the Earth is **trapped** at higher altitudes, making it **colder**. Lower **air pressures** higher up also mean temperatures **drop**. It gets between 6 °C and 10 °C colder for every 1000 m you go up.
3) They're in the **middle** of **continents**. The middle of continents are cold because they're **far away** from the **sea**. In the summer, the **land heats** up **quickly** and the **sea** heats up **slowly**. In the winter, the **land cools quickly** and the **sea** cools **slowly**. So, in winter the sea **warms** the land **near the coast**, but **not** the **interior**. This effect is called **continentality**.

These factors control the **distribution** of the different **types** of cold environment — **glacial**, **periglacial**, **alpine** and **polar**.

Different Types of **Cold Environment** are **Found** in **Different Places**

1 **Glacial Environments** are Found at **High Altitudes** and **High Latitudes**

1) Glacial environments are areas of land permanently **covered by ice**. Land can be covered by **glaciers** or **ice sheets**:
   - Glaciers are masses of **ice** that flow **downhill**. There are two main types — **valley** glaciers and **corrie** glaciers. Valley glaciers **fill valleys** and can be **several kilometres long** (e.g. the Franz Josef Glacier in New Zealand is 12 kilometres long). Corrie glaciers are **smaller** glaciers that are found in bowl-shaped hollows high up in **mountains** (e.g. the Lower Curtis Glacier in Washington State, USA).
   - Ice sheets are **domes of ice** covering **huge areas** of land, e.g. the Antarctic Ice Sheet.
2) Glaciers and ice sheets only form where it's **really cold**, so glacial environments are found:
   - At **high latitudes**. E.g. the **Antarctic Ice Sheet** (in the southern hemisphere), and the **Greenland Ice Sheet** (in the northern hemisphere) are both entirely **above 60°** latitude.
   - At **high altitudes** (regardless of the latitude). E.g. glaciers are found in the **Himalayan mountains** even though they're at a **low latitude** (around **30°**). This is because it's the **highest** mountain range in the world. Glaciers even form at latitudes **close to** the **equator** (e.g. the Antizana glacier in Ecuador).

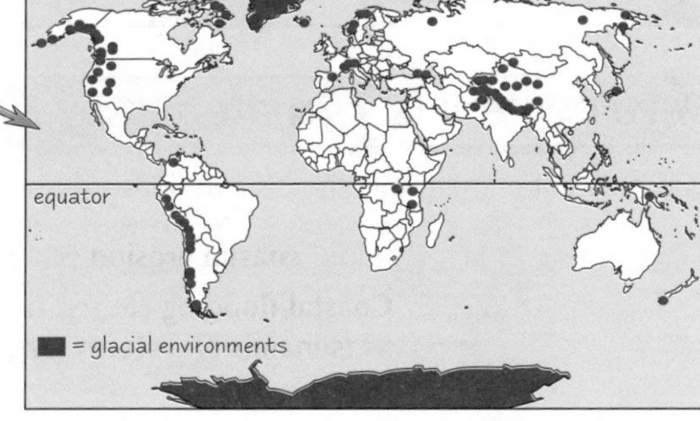

3) Even though it can be really cold on low altitude land in the middle of continents, glaciers don't form as there's not enough snow.

2 **Periglacial Environments** are Found at **High Altitudes** and **Latitudes** and in **Continental Interiors**

1) **Periglacial** environments are places where the temperature is frequently or constantly **below freezing**, but **not covered by ice**. They contain a layer of **permafrost** (permanently frozen ground) **on** or **below** the surface.
2) They form where it's persistently **below 0 °C**, so they're found:
   - At **high latitudes**. E.g. the northern parts of Asia, North America and Europe are all periglacial environments with large areas of permafrost.
   - At **high altitudes**. Periglacial conditions exist **around ice masses** in **mountain ranges**. They're also found on high altitude **plateau** areas, e.g. the Tibetan plateau in Asia, and the Bolivian plateau in South America.
   - In the **interior** of land masses. Periglacial conditions exist at lower latitudes and lower altitudes because of the effect of **continentality**, e.g. Siberia, central Asia.

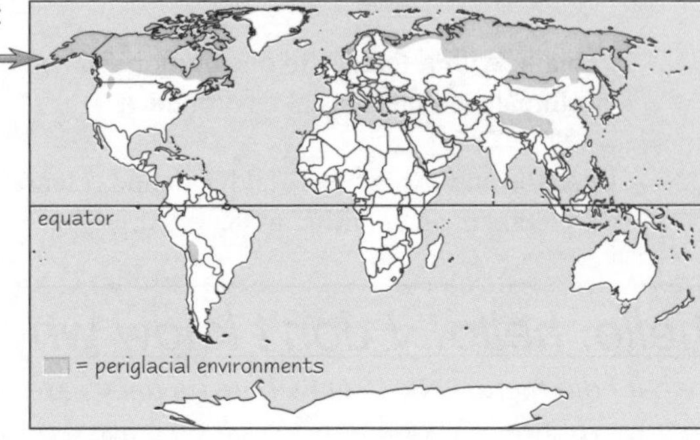

Distribution of Cold Environments

3 Alpine Environments are Found at High Altitudes

1) Alpine environments are cold areas of land at an altitude **above** the **treeline**. The treeline is the **limit** of the area that trees can grow in — above the treeline it's **too cold** for trees to grow.
2) Alpine environments are **always** found at **high altitudes**. Alpine conditions can be found above the treeline on **mountain ranges**, e.g. the Himalayas (Asia), the Andes (South America) and the Alps (Europe). They can exist at **any latitude**, e.g. alpine conditions exist along much of the Rocky mountains in North America, which run north to south from above 50° to around 30° latitude.

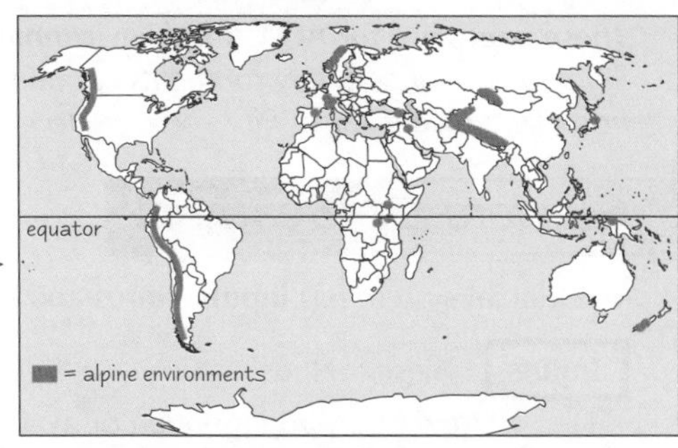

3) Alpine environments may **include periglacial** and **glacial** conditions. **Temperature decreases** as altitude increases — permafrost (periglacial conditions) may exist above (and below) the treeline, permanent snow and ice (glacial conditions) may exist even higher up.

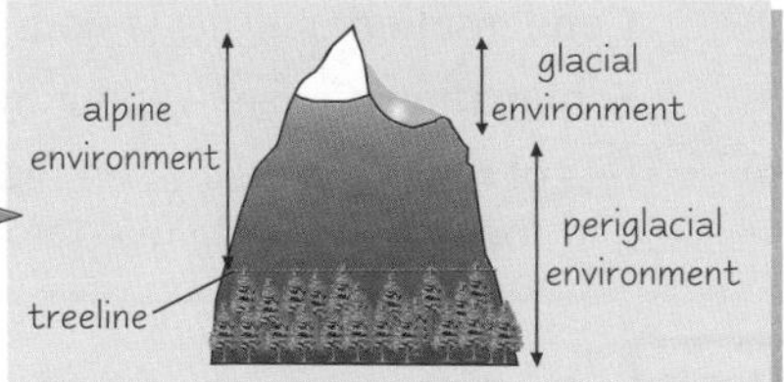

4 Polar Environments are Found around the Poles

There are **two** polar environments — one around the **North Pole** (the **Arctic**) and one around the **South Pole** (the **Antarctic**).

1) The **Arctic** polar environment is **cold** because it exists at a **high latitude**.
2) The Arctic polar environment can be defined either by the **Arctic circle** (**66° N**) or by the **10 °C July isotherm** (areas north of this line have an average temperature **below** 10 °C in **July**, the **hottest** month).
3) The area around the north pole is made up of **sea ice** (frozen sea water). The area of sea ice **shrinks** in the **summer**, leaving **open sea**, and **refreezes** in the **winter**.
4) Much of the Arctic polar environment is made up of the **northern land areas** of **Asia**, **North America** and **Europe**. The land-based polar environment can include **glacial** environments, e.g. the Greenland Ice Sheet, and **periglacial** environments, e.g. northern Russia.

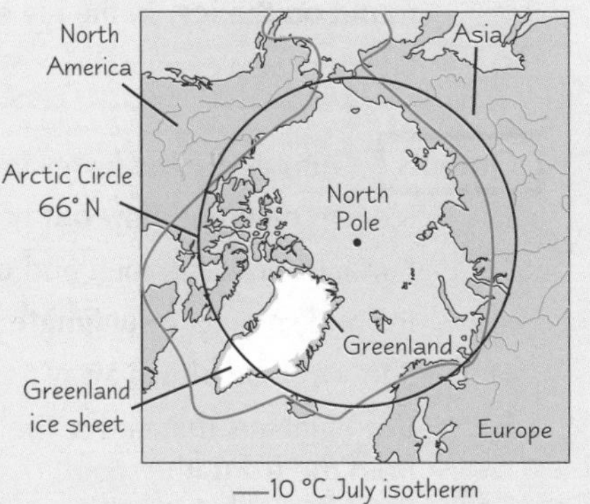

1) The **Antarctic** polar environment is **cold** because of its **high latitude** — the Antarctic circle (**66° S** latitude) doesn't go all the way round the land mass of Antarctica though, so the polar environment around the south pole can be defined by the **10 °C January isotherm** (the hottest month in the southern hemisphere).
2) Some of the Antarctic polar environment is also cold because it's at a **high altitude** — the ice in some places is so thick it reaches an altitude of over **4000 m**.
3) The **interior** of Antarctica is also **cold** because of the effect of **continentality** — the centre is hundreds of kilometres from the **warming** effect of the **oceans**.
4) A large area around the Antarctic land mass is made up of **sea ice**. The area of sea ice changes throughout the year, **shrinking** in summer and **refreezing** in winter.
5) Most of the Antarctic polar region is on the huge **land mass** of **Antarctica**. The land-based polar environment includes **glacial** environments, e.g. the Antarctic ice sheet.

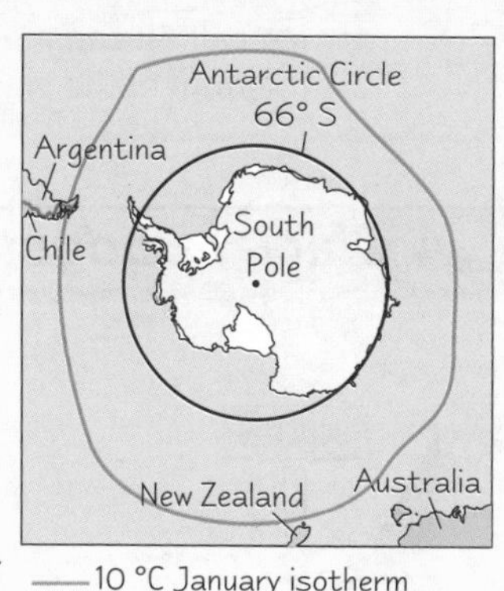

Practice Questions

Q1 Where are alpine environments found?

Q2 What's the latitude of the Arctic circle?

Q3 Give three reasons why Antarctica is cold.

Exam Question

Q1 Describe and explain the global distribution of glacial and periglacial environments. [15 marks]

So which is better — north or south? Let's take a poll...

It might not seem like it yet, but cold environments are actually pretty interesting. To really get yourself in the mood for these next few pages, try turning the heating off and opening all the windows, and read them with your scarf and gloves on.

Glaciers

These pages are for AQA (Cold Environments option).
Since plenty of cold environments contain glaciers, you need to know a fair bit about them.
I do like a nice glacier. Pity you have to go to the Alps or Norway to see the nearest ones.

Glaciers are **Systems**

The glacial system has **inputs**, **stores** and **outputs**.

Inputs These include:

1) **Snow** (from **precipitation** or **avalanches**).
2) **Condensation** of water vapour from the air (which then freezes).
3) **Sublimation** of water vapour from the air directly to ice crystals.
4) Bits of **rock** collected when the glacier carves away at the landscape, and rocks that have fallen onto the glacier from above.

Sublimation involves a direct change of state from a gas to a solid without passing through the liquid stage.

Stores

1) The main store is obviously **ice**.
2) **Meltwater** is a small part of the glacier. It can be found **on the ice**, **in the ice** or **below the ice**.
3) Glaciers also carry **debris** (rocks, gravel and sand).

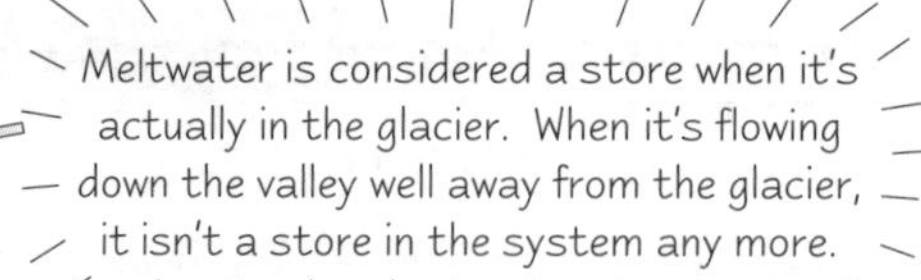

Meltwater is considered a store when it's actually in the glacier. When it's flowing down the valley well away from the glacier, it isn't a store in the system any more.

Outputs Outputs are the **losses** from a glacier.

1) Ice can **melt** and **flow out** of the glacier as **meltwater**.
2) Surface snow can **melt** and **evaporate**.
3) Ice and snow can **sublimate** to water vapour.
4) Snow can be **blown away** by strong winds.
5) With glaciers that end at the **sea**, blocks of ice fall from the **front** (the snout) of the ice mass into water to create **icebergs**. This is called "**calving**" — as if the glacier were a big old ice cow giving birth to a little ice calf. It can also happen where there's a **lake** at the front of the glacier.

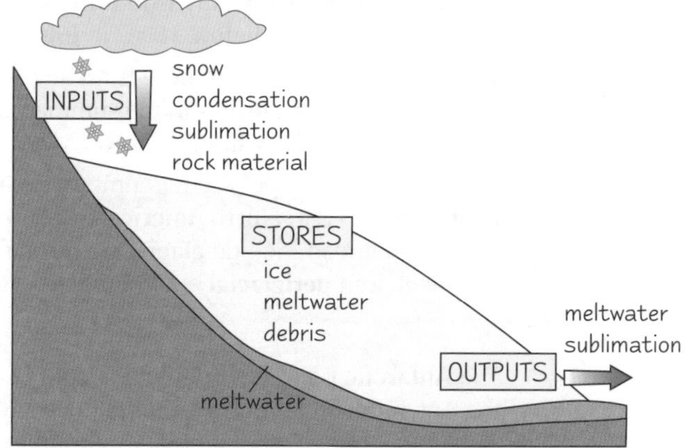

A **Glacial Budget** is the **Balance** between a Glacier's **Inputs** and **Outputs**

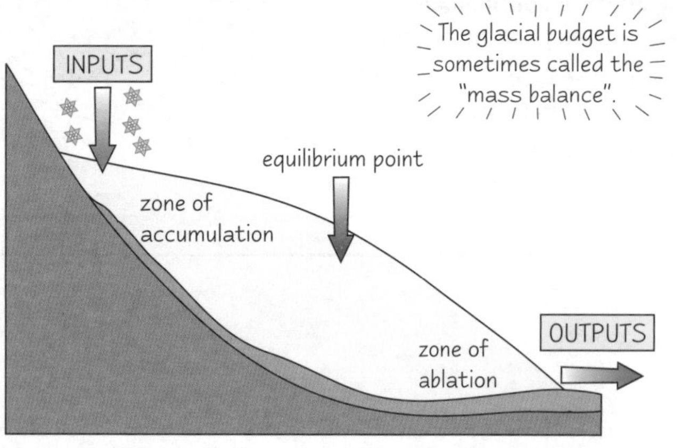

The glacial budget is sometimes called the "mass balance".

1) **Accumulation** is the **input** of snow and ice into the glacial system. Most accumulation is snow.
2) **Ablation** is the **output** of water from a glacier.
3) The **glacial budget** is the balance between accumulation and ablation over a year — it shows whether the volume of water in the glacial system has **increased** or **decreased**. This determines whether the **front** of the glacier **advances** forwards or **retreats** back.
4) You get **more accumulation** than ablation in the **upper** part of a glacier — so it's called the **zone of accumulation**.
5) You get **more ablation** than accumulation in the **lower** part of a glacier — so it's called the **zone of ablation**.
6) The place where accumulation and ablation are **equal** is called the glacier's **equilibrium point**.
7) If there's **more accumulation** than ablation over a year, the glacier has a **positive regime** (or a positive mass balance). The glacier grows and **advances** (moves forward).
8) If there's **less accumulation** than ablation over a year, this is a **negative regime** (or a negative mass balance). The glacier shrinks and **retreats** (moves back).
9) If there's the **same amount** of accumulation and ablation over a year, the glacier stays the same size and the position of the snout **doesn't change**.

Glaciers

The Glacial Budget Changes Throughout the Year...

1) You get **more ablation** during **warmer** times of the year — which makes sense, as more ice melts when it's warm.
2) During the **colder** months, there's **more accumulation** than ablation.
3) Over the year, this might **balance out** — the glacier **advances** in winter but **retreats** in summer, so overall the volume of water in the glacier **stays the same**.

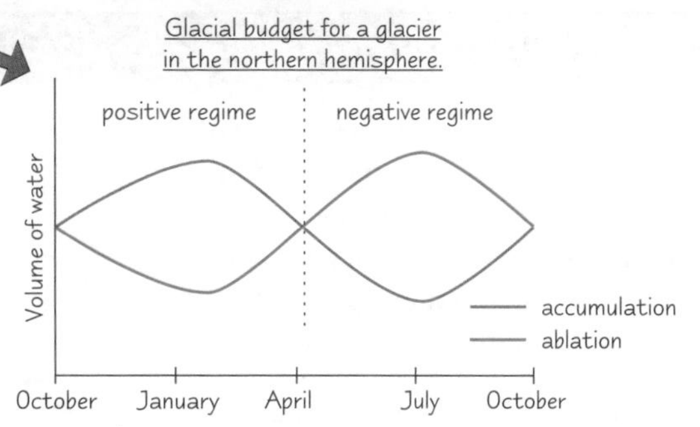

Hannah and Betty had a very positive regime.

...and Over Several Years

Changes in **global temperature** over long periods of time affect the glacial budget.

1) Temperatures in the **19th century** were **colder** than in the 18th century, so in general there was more accumulation than ablation. This meant that many glaciers **advanced** because they had a positive regime.
2) In the **20th century**, global temperature **increased** so glaciers tended to have a negative regime and **retreated**.

Glaciers Form when Snow Accumulates and Turns Into Ice

1) First, **snow settles**. It has a loose, fluffy, snowflakey consistency at this point.
2) The **weight** of **more snow** falling on top turns the snow into a denser, more granular kind of snow called **firn**.
3) **Air** is squeezed **out**, and particles of ice are **compressed together** by the continuing accumulation of snow and ice.
4) Water also **melts** and **refreezes** in the **air spaces**, making the ice **more dense**. Et voilà — a glacier is formed.

Glaciers can be Cold-Based or Warm-Based

Glaciers can be classified according to the **temperature** of their **base** (the bit where the ice touches the valley floor).

The melting temperature of ice at the base of a glacier is slightly lower than the normal melting point of ice (0 °C), because of the pressure of all the ice on top of it.

1) In **warm-based glaciers**, the base is **warmer** than the melting point of ice. It's warmer because of heat from **friction** caused by the glacier moving, or because of **geothermal heat** from the Earth. The ice at the bottom of the glacier melts, and the **meltwater** acts as a **lubricant**, making it easier for the glacier to move downhill. Ice at the **surface** also melts if the temperature reaches 0 °C, and meltwater moves down through the glacier, lubricating it even more. Lots of movement means **lots of erosion**.
2) In **cold-based glaciers**, the base is cold (the temperature is usually well **below** the ice's **melting point**) so there's very **little melting**. The ice is frozen to the base of the valley, so there's **very little movement**. There's hardly any melting at the surface either, even in summer. This means that cold-based glaciers **don't** cause very much **erosion** at all.

Practice Questions

Q1 What are the main inputs, stores and outputs in a glacial system?

Q2 What are accumulation and ablation?

Q3 How does the glacial budget change throughout the year in the northern hemisphere?

Exam Questions

Q1 What is a glacial budget? Explain how a glacial budget shows whether a glacier is advancing or retreating. [3 marks]

Q2 Describe the main differences between warm-based and cold-based glaciers. [5 marks]

Brrr. Might need an extra jumper on...

Nope, you're not reading an accountancy revision guide by mistake — glaciers have budgets too. Glacial budgets are all about the ins and outs of the glacier. Stuff comes in mainly in the form of snow, and goes out mainly as meltwater. If more comes in than goes out then the glacier advances, and if more goes out than in it retreats — not so hard after all.

Glacial Processes

These pages are for AQA (Cold Environments option).
Glaciers are moving all the time — they don't stop to think about the erosion they might be causing...

Glaciers Move Downhill under their Own Weight

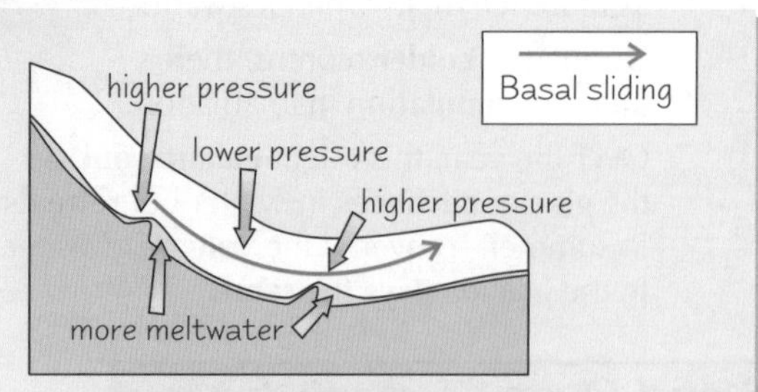

1) **Meltwater** underneath a glacier allows the glacier to **slide** over the ground. This is called **basal sliding**, and it's the main way that warm-based glaciers move.
2) There's **more melting** around bits of **rock protruding** from the valley floor, because there's **more pressure** on the ice (so the ice melts at temperatures lower than 0 °C). Meltwater can **refreeze** downstream of the obstruction where there's less pressure, so the flow tends to be faster around the obstruction, and slower downstream.

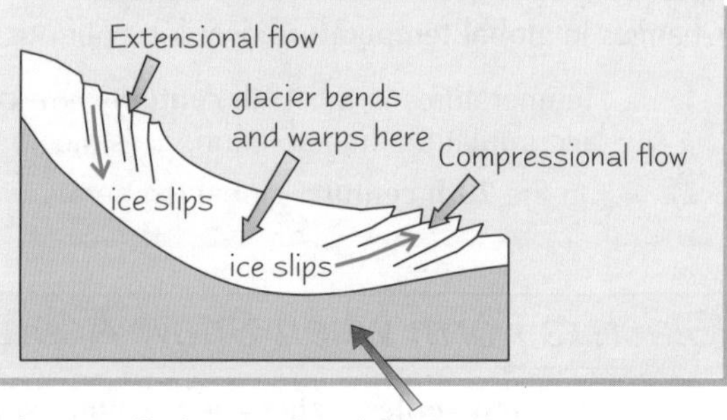

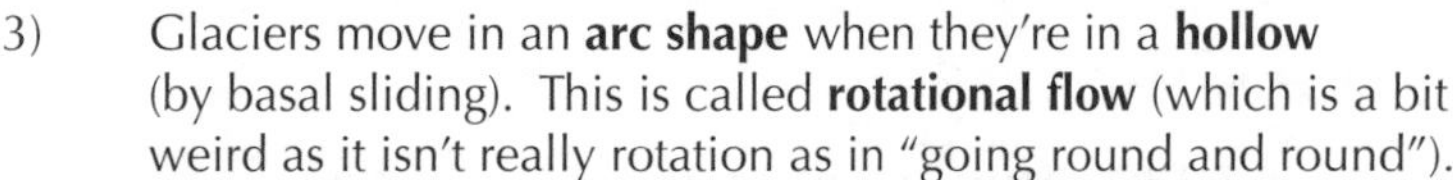

3) Glaciers move in an **arc shape** when they're in a **hollow** (by basal sliding). This is called **rotational flow** (which is a bit weird as it isn't really rotation as in "going round and round").

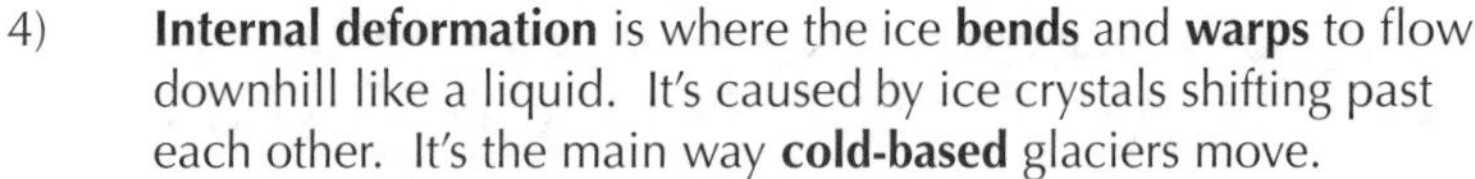

4) **Internal deformation** is where the ice **bends** and **warps** to flow downhill like a liquid. It's caused by ice crystals shifting past each other. It's the main way **cold-based** glaciers move.
5) At the **head** of a glacier the valley is steep, so there's a strong **gravitational force** pulling the ice downwards. This makes the ice **move quickly**. When ice moves quickly there's more **tension** (pulling apart forces), which causes the ice to **fracture** into thick layers. The **layers** then **slip downwards** — this is called **extensional flow**.
6) **Lower down** the glacier the ice is moving more **slowly** because the valley is less steep. The faster ice from the head of the glacier **pushes down** on the slower ice and **compresses it**. The **high pressure** causes the ice to **fracture** into layers, and the layers **slip forwards** — this is called **compressional flow**.

- The main things that determine the **speed** at which a glacier flows are the **gradient** of the valley floor, the **thickness** of the ice and the **temperature** at the base of the glacier.
- The **steeper** the valley, the **faster** the glacier will flow. The **thicker** the **ice** the **faster** it will flow — in a **warm-based** glacier thicker ice exerts **more pressure** on the valley floor, causing **more melting**, which makes it flow faster. In a **cold-based** glacier thicker ice means there's **more internal deformation**, which makes it flow faster. The **warmer** the **base** of the glacier the **faster** it will flow (see p. 43).
- Ice **moves faster** near the glacier's **surface** than at the **base** — **friction** at the base slows the glacier down.

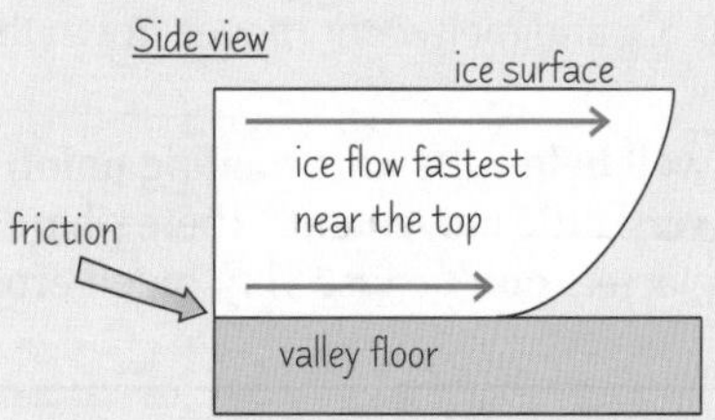

- Ice also moves faster near the **middle** than at the **edges**.

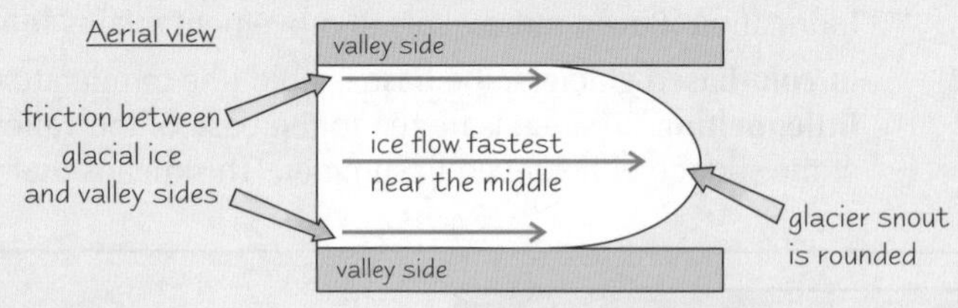

Glaciers Crack as they Move Down the Valley

1) Stresses and strains cause cracks called **crevasses** to form in the glacier.
2) Stress can be caused by **extensional** and **compressional flow**, **calving**, or **tension** between the ice attached to the **valley sides** and **back wall** and the rest of the glacier.
3) The tension caused by the glacier pulling away from the ice attached to the **back wall** produces a big **semicircular crevasse** at the back of the glacier called the **bergschrund**.

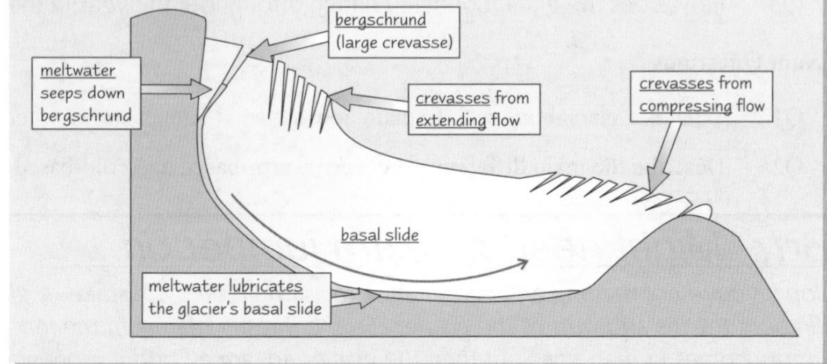

Glacial Processes

Glaciers Erode the Surrounding Rock

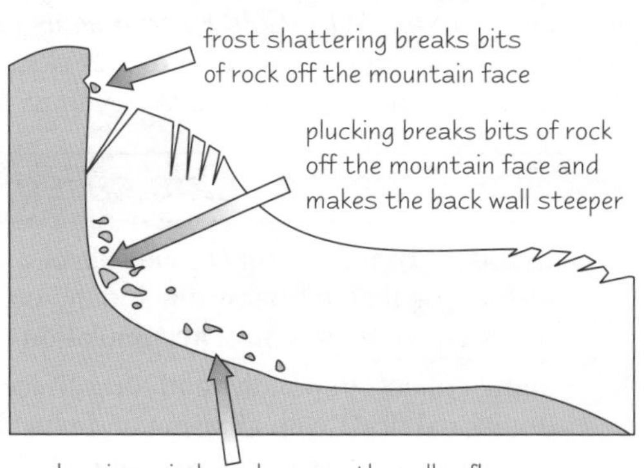
frost shattering breaks bits of rock off the mountain face
plucking breaks bits of rock off the mountain face and makes the back wall steeper
abrasion grinds and gouges the valley floor

Glaciers erode the valley floor and sides by plucking and abrasion

1) **Plucking** — ice in contact with rock surfaces can thaw slightly then **refreeze around rocks** protruding from the valley sides and floor. When the glacier **moves forward**, it **plucks** the rocks away from the valley sides and floor.
2) **Abrasion** — **debris** carried along by the glacier can **scrape** material off the valley walls and floor.

Meltwater erosion shapes the valley floor

Glaciers can produce huge quantities of **meltwater**, making streams that are powerful enough to erode the valley floor and sides by normal **fluvial (river) processes** (see p. 6).

The **amount** and **rate** of erosion is increased in areas of **less resistant rock**, and if the glacier is **thick** or if it's **moving quickly**. It's also increased if there's **lots** of **debris** or if the debris is made of **resistant rock**.

Weathering also contributes to the shaping of the glacial valley

Frost shattering breaks rocks off the **back** and **side walls** of the valley. **Meltwater** from snow gets into **cracks** in the valley walls and then **freezes** — when it freezes it **expands**, so it exerts **pressure** on the rock and bits of the rock get broken off. These bits of rock often **fall onto**, or **into**, the glacier (adding to the debris that **abrades** the valley).

Glaciers Transport Debris

1) Glaciers carry large loads of **debris** — this is material that the glacier has gathered by plucking, or bits of rock that have been broken off the back wall or valley sides and fallen onto (or into) the glacier. Debris ranges from **fine sediment** to **huge boulders**.
2) There are **three** main ways debris is transported. **Supraglacial** material is carried **on top** of the glacier's surface. **Englacial** material is carried **within** the body of the glacier. **Subglacial** material is moved along **at the base** of the glacier.

Glaciers Deposit their Load as they Move and as they Melt

1) The **unsorted** mixture of material **deposited** by the glacier is called **till** (it's sometimes called "boulder clay" too). It includes everything from massive boulders down to pebbles and clay. Glaciers drop any size of till anywhere.
2) **Lodgement till** is spread onto the valley floor beneath the ice by **moving** glaciers.
3) **Ablation till** is dropped by a glacier as it **melts**. The till is mainly deposited close to the glacier snout because this is where most ablation happens — the glacier drops debris as the ice around the debris melts.
4) Till **points** in the **direction** that the glacier is flowing.
5) Till is often **deposited** as landforms called **moraines** (see p. 47).

Practice Questions

Q1 What is rotational flow?

Q2 How is a bergschrund formed?

Q3 What are the main ways that debris is transported by a glacier?

Exam Questions

Q1 Explain what is meant by extensional flow. [4 marks]

Q2 Name and explain the two methods of glacial erosion. [4 marks]

Glaciers move r e a l l y s l o w l y — bit like you on a Sunday morning...

Alright, I'll admit that these two pages are slightly harder than the last two. It can be tricky at first to get your head around the different ways that glaciers move. Try reading over the first page a couple of times, then at least you'll know that rotational flow isn't a dance move. Don't forget that glaciers erode valleys in two different ways — by plucking and by abrasion.

Glacial Landforms

These pages are for AQA (Cold Environments option).
These pages are about the landscapes that glaciers leave behind them. Mountain climbers and geography teachers get very excited about the beauty of glacial landscapes. Whether or not they move you, you still need to learn about them.

Glaciers Create Basins called Corries (also called Cirques or Cwms)

1) Glaciers normally form on one side of a mountain peak — the side that gets **least sun** and the **coldest winds**. That's where there's **most accumulation** and **least ablation**.
2) Snow collects in hollows and turns to **ice**. **Basal sliding** (rotational flow) with **abrasion** and **plucking** deepen the hollow into a **corrie** (a bowl-shaped hollow).
3) When the ice in the hollow is thick enough, it **flows** over the lip and downhill as a glacier. Frost shattering and plucking **steepen** the back wall of the corrie.

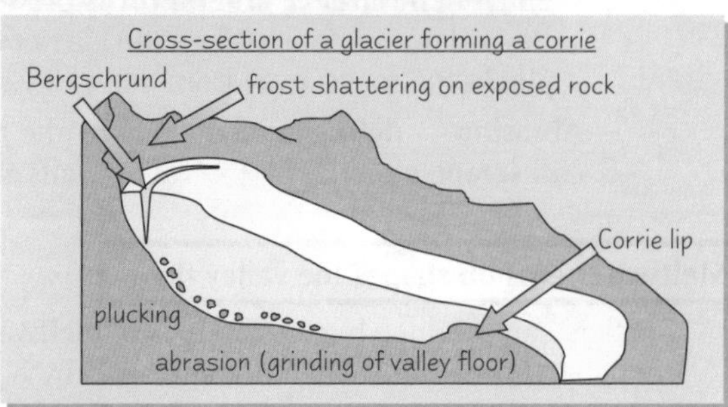

Glacial Erosion Changes the Landscape of Valleys

Glaciers moving through valleys produce **erosional landforms**, which change the way valleys **look** after the ice has **gone**.

1) An **arête** is a steep-sided **ridge** — it's formed when two glaciers flow in parallel valleys. The glaciers erode the sides of the valley, which **sharpens** the mountain ridge **in between** them.
2) A **pyramidal peak** is a pointed mountain peak with at least **three sides**. It forms where **three** or more **corries** form **back to back** (their back walls make the mountain peak).
3) **Glacial troughs** (also called **U-shaped valleys**) are **steep-sided valleys** with **flat bottoms**. They're formed by the erosion of **V-shaped river valleys** by glaciers. As the glacier erodes through the V-shaped valley it makes them **deeper** and **wider**.
4) **Hanging valleys** are valleys formed by **tributary glaciers** — they erode the valley floor much less **deeply** because they're **smaller** than the main glacier. So, when the glaciers melt, the valleys get left at a **higher level** than the glacial trough formed by the main glacier. You get **waterfalls** from hanging valleys into the main glacial trough.

A tributary glacier is a smaller glacier that flows into the main glacier.

5) **Truncated spurs** are formed when **ridges of land** (spurs) that **stick out** into the main valley are **chopped off** (truncated) as the main valley glacier moves past.
6) **Valley steps** are (funnily enough) steps in the glacial trough. They're formed when the glacier erodes the valley floor **more deeply**. This happens when **another glacier joins** it or where there's **less resistant** (softer) rock.
7) **Tarns** are **lakes** that form in **corries** after a glacier has retreated.
8) **Ribbon lakes** are long, thin lakes that form after a glacier retreats. They form in **dips** caused by erosion of bands of **less resistant** rocks, or **behind dams** of **debris** left by the glacier.
9) **Fjords** are long, deep inlets that form when a valley that's been eroded by a glacier is **flooded** by sea level rise after the ice has **melted**.
10) A **roche moutonnée** is a **resistant** (hard) mass of rock on the valley floor. The **upstream** (stoss) side is **smooth**, because it was smoothed by **abrasion** as the glacier went over it. The **downstream** (lee) side is steep and **rough** where the glacier **plucked** at it.

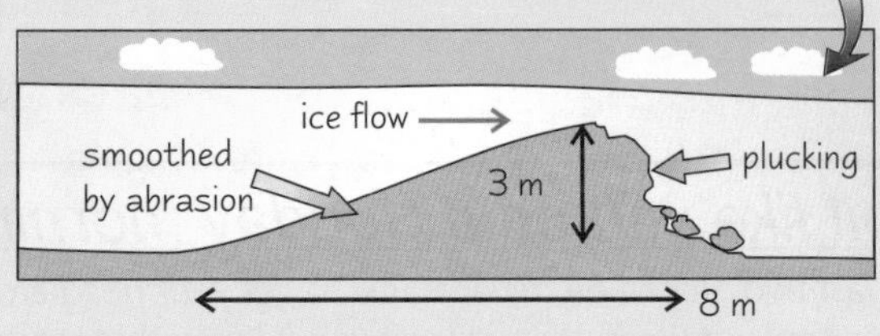

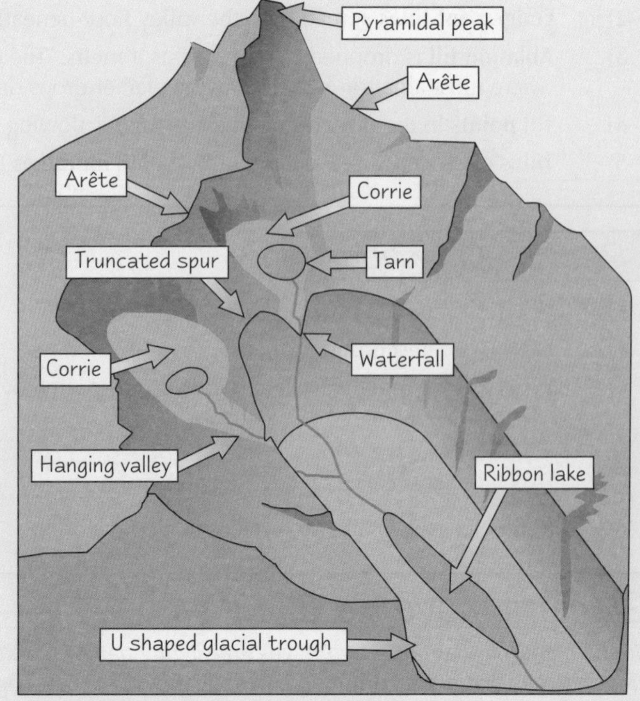

Glacial Landforms

Glaciers Form **Moraines** by **Depositing Till**

Moraine is the name for different formations of **till** deposited by a glacier as it melts. There are **three** different types of moraine:

1) **Lateral moraine** is deposited where the **sides** of the glacier were.
2) **Medial moraine** is deposited in the **centre** of the valley where two glaciers **converge** (the two lateral moraines join together).
3) **Terminal moraine** builds up at the **end** of the glacier, and is deposited as semicircular hillocks of till.

Till is all the stuff that a glacier leaves behind — unsorted boulders, stones and clay (see p. 45). Moraine is the name given to particular formations of till.

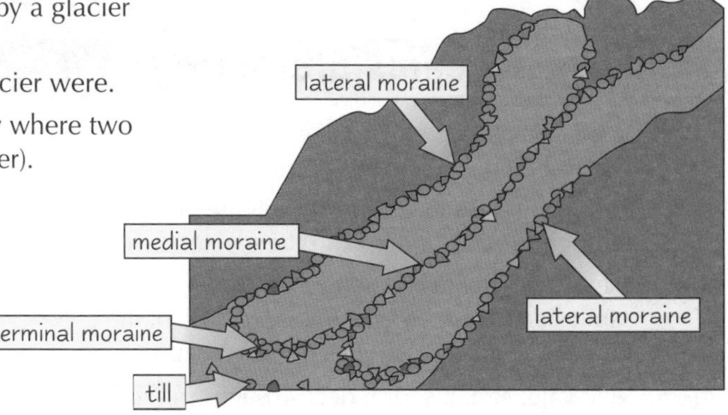

Till can also be Deposited as **Hills** called **Drumlins**

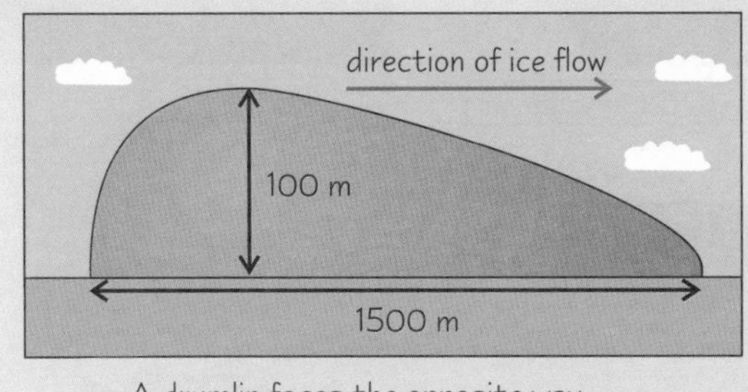

A drumlin faces the opposite way to a roche moutonnée.

1) **Drumlins** are **half-egg shaped hills** of till, up to 1500 m long and 100 m high. The **upstream** (stoss) end is **wide and tall**, and the **downstream** (lee) end is **narrow and low**.
2) Nobody's really sure **why** drumlins are egg-shaped — it may be that till got stuck around a rock or a little hill sticking out into the glacier. It may be that an original mound of dropped till got streamlined when the ice **readvanced** over it.
3) Drumlins often form in **groups**. There are drumlins in the **Ribble Valley** in Lancashire. There are also a whole bunch of drumlins under the water level in Clew Bay, Ireland.

Erratics are **Boulders** that have been **Carried** a **Long Way** by Glaciers

1) Erratics are rocks that have been **picked up** by a glacier or an ice sheet, **carried along** and **dropped** in an area of **completely different geology** (rock type).
2) For example, in the Yorkshire dales at Norber, loose black **Silurian** rocks sit on top of white **Carboniferous** limestone.
3) There are erratics in **Eastern England** that were originally picked up by an ice sheet in **Norway** and carried all the way to England during the Ice Ages.

Les was good at long-distance boulder carrying, but not quite as good as a glacier.

Practice Questions

Q1 What is the name of the ridge formed by two glaciers in parallel valleys?

Q2 Name three erosional features of glaciated valleys.

Q3 What is the name for rocks that are transported by a glacier or an ice sheet and dropped into an area with a different rock type?

Exam Questions

Q1 Describe and explain the landforms shown in the photo on the right. [8 marks]

Q2 Describe the three different types of moraine. [3 marks]

Corries? I'm more of an Emmerdale fan myself...

There are a fair few features to learn here, but don't let that get you down. You just need to learn the names of the features, what they look like and how they're formed. Even the names of the features are a bit tricky though — cirque, arête, roche moutonnée... anyone would think this was a French exam. At least you don't need to know how to pronounce them.

Fluvioglacial Processes and Landforms

These pages are for AQA (Cold Environments option).
The sad news for all you glacier fans is that glaciers don't always stay around forever. But don't worry, they don't go down without a fight — even when they're melting, they still manage to change the landscape.

Meltwater Streams Erode the Landscape

1) When glacial ice melts, water runs out and forms streams of **meltwater**. **Warm-based** glaciers and **retreating** glaciers produce **lots** of meltwater.
2) **Surface** meltwater **filters** through the glacier (e.g. through crevasses) and flows through **tunnels** underneath the glacier, before running out of the snout of the glacier.
3) Meltwater streams cause **erosion** in the same way as normal rivers — but they cause **more** erosion than rivers of the same size. This is because the pressure of the ice means that meltwater streams flow very **quickly** — so they can carry **lots** of material that **erodes** the landscape.
4) Meltwater streams form deep **troughs** in the landscape called **meltwater channels**. Because meltwater streams have a lot of **erosive power**, the meltwater channels they produce are very **wide** and **deep**. After the glacier has **retreated**, the deep meltwater channels are left with very **shallow streams** running through them.

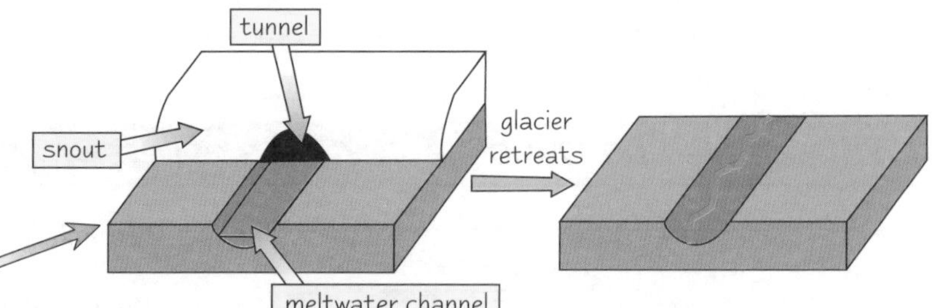

Fluvioglacial Deposits come from Glacial Meltwater

1) Glacial meltwater carries a **large load** of **sediment** of various sizes (from inside, on top of and underneath the glacier).

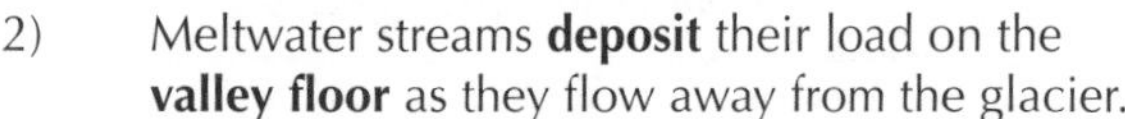

2) Meltwater streams **deposit** their load on the **valley floor** as they flow away from the glacier.
3) Meltwater streams are often **braided** — they split into lots of mini streams that cross over each other. This is because when the meltwater is flowing more **slowly** (e.g. in winter, when the amount of meltwater is lower) it can't carry its load — so it **deposits** the sediment on the ground, and **splits** into two streams to get round it.

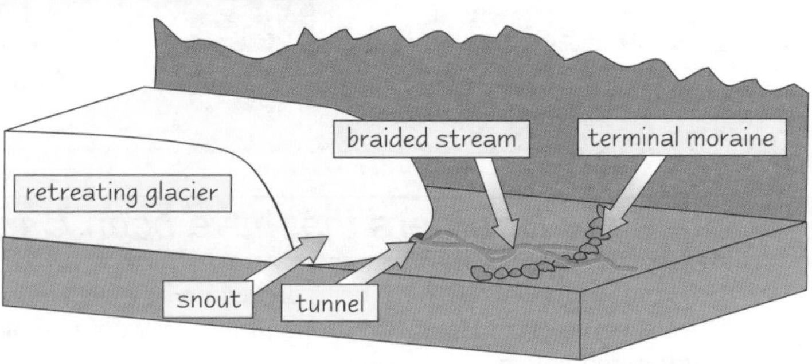

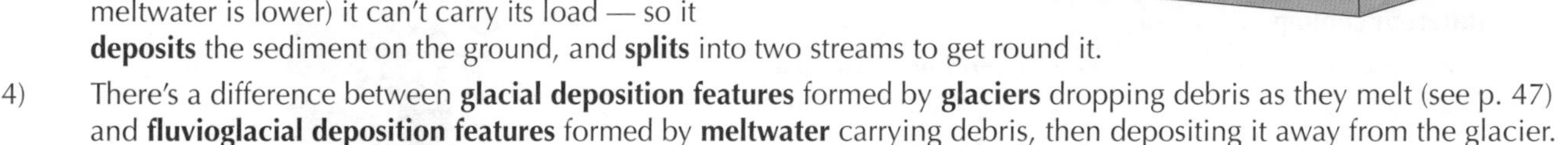

4) There's a difference between **glacial deposition features** formed by **glaciers** dropping debris as they melt (see p. 47) and **fluvioglacial deposition features** formed by **meltwater** carrying debris, then depositing it away from the glacier.
5) **Fluvioglacial** deposits are **sorted** — the fine sediment is **separated** from the larger sand, which is separated from the gravel, and so on. **Glacial** deposits are **unsorted**.

Melting Glaciers leave Outwash Plains and Kettle Holes

1) An **outwash plain** is a layer of gravel, sand and clay that forms in **front** of where the snout of the melting glacier used to be. Meltwater flows out of the glacier, and carries the sediment with it.

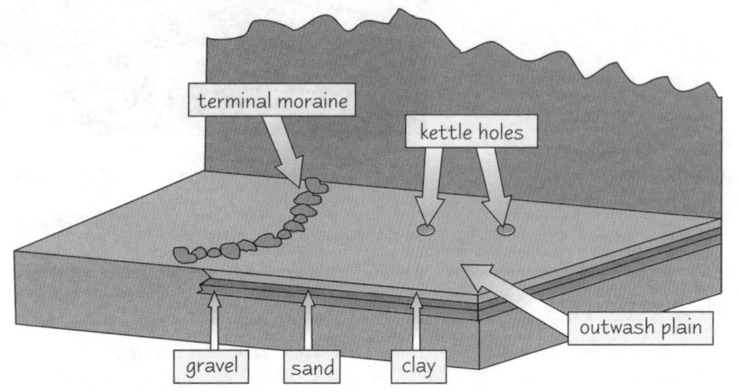

2) Sediments on outwash plains are **sorted** into layers. **Gravel** gets dropped **first** because it's **heavier** than sand and clay, so it forms the **bottom layer** of the outwash plain. **Clay** is dropped **last** and gets carried furthest away from the snout because it's the lightest sediment — it forms the **top layer** of the outwash plain.
3) **Blocks of ice** that have broken off from the front of the glacier can get surrounded and partly buried by the **fluvioglacial deposits**. When the blocks of ice **melt**, they leave **holes** in the outwash plain, called **kettle holes**.

Fluvioglacial Processes and Landforms

Meltwater Streams Deposit **Kames** and **Eskers**

1) **Eskers** are long, winding **ridges** of sand and gravel that run in the **same direction** as the glacier. They're deposited by meltwater streams flowing in **tunnels** underneath the glacier — when the glacier retreats and the stream dries up, the load remains as an esker. Eskers show you where the glacial tunnel used to be.
2) **Kames** are **mounds** of sand and gravel found on the valley floor. Meltwater streams **on top of** glaciers collect in depressions and **deposit** layers of debris. When the ice **melts** the debris is dumped onto the valley floor.
3) **Kame terraces** are piles of deposits left against the **valley wall** by meltwater streams that run between the glacier and the valley sides. They look like lateral moraine, but they're **sorted** into layers — meltwater streams deposit their **heaviest** loads first, so kame terraces have **gravel** at the **bottom** and **sand** on **top**.

This shows the kames and eskers that would be left after the glacier in the diagram in the middle of the previous page melts.

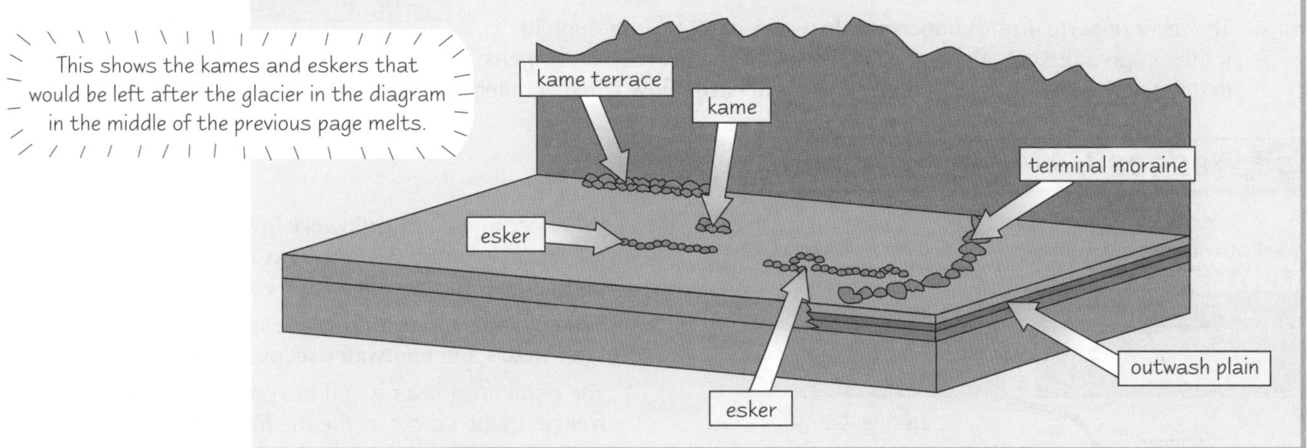

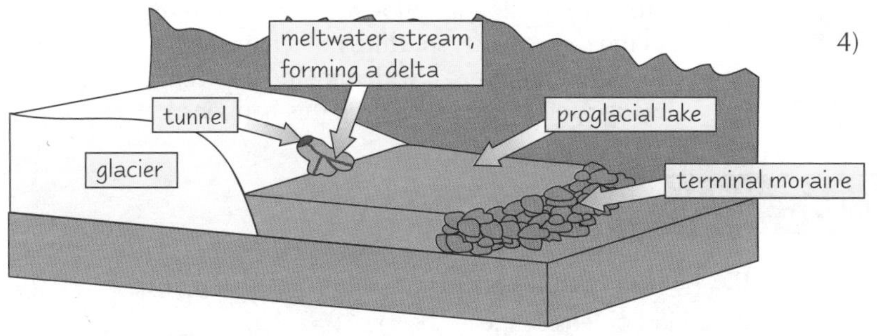

4) Lakes (called **proglacial lakes**) can form in front of glaciers, e.g. when the flow from meltwater streams gets dammed by the terminal moraine. As meltwater streams flow into a proglacial lake, they **slow down** and **deposit** their sediment on the ice — these deposits are known as **deltas**. When the ice melts, these deltas are dumped on the valley floor, forming **delta kames**.

Practice Questions

Q1 What are meltwater channels?

Q2 What's the main difference between glacial deposits and fluvioglacial deposits?

Q3 What is an outwash plain?

Q4 How are kettle holes formed?

Q5 What are eskers?

Exam Questions

Q1 Describe how kame terraces are formed. [2 marks]

Q2 Explain how delta kames are formed. [4 marks]

I'm melting! Meeeeeelting!

Well, this is just typical of glaciers if you ask me. Not content with ripping bits of rock out of mountains and scattering them all over landscapes, glaciers then have to go and melt, and wash all kinds of bits of rock all over the place. If only they didn't have to be so, well, messy about it — then you wouldn't need to know what a kame or an esker was. Oh well, tough luck, eh.

Periglacial Processes and Landforms

These pages are for AQA (Cold Environments option). *Periglacial areas are cold areas that aren't covered in ice. There's usually ice in the soil though — I knew it'd be there somewhere.*

Permafrost is Permanently Frozen Ground

1) **Periglacial** areas contain **permafrost** — **permanently frozen ground** with a top layer that can **melt** in the **summer** (called the **active layer**). **20-25%** of Earth's land surface is **permafrost**.
2) Areas of permafrost can be **continuous** (**all** the ground is frozen), or **discontinuous** (only **patches** of the ground are frozen).
3) For **discontinuous** permafrost to form the **mean annual temperature** needs to be **below 0 °C** for at least **2 years**. For **continuous** permafrost to form the mean annual temperature needs to be **below –5 °C**.
4) The layer of permafrost is **impermeable** (water **can't** flow through it). If the temperature gets **above 0 °C** in the summer, the active layer **melts**, but the water can't go anywhere. This means that the active layer gets **waterlogged** and will **easily flow** wherever there's a **gradient**. This flow is called **solifluction**.

Ice Wedges Develop in Permafrost Soil

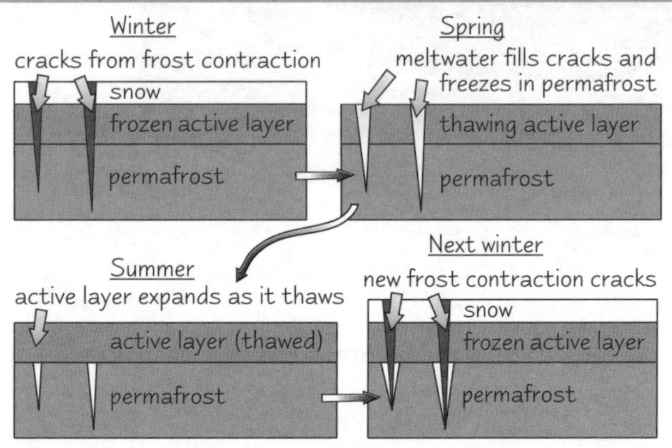

1) When temperatures **drop very low** in winter, the ground **contracts** and **cracks** form in the permafrost. This is called **frost contraction**.
2) When temperatures **increase** in spring, the active layer **thaws** and **meltwater seeps** into the **cracks**.
3) The permafrost layer is still frozen, so the water **freezes** in the cracks — the ice-filled cracks formed in this way are called **ice wedges**.
4) Frost contraction in following years can **re-open** cracks in the same place, **splitting** the ice wedge. More water seeps in and freezes, **widening** the ice wedge. The ice wedge gets **bigger** each time this happens.

Ground Water Freezes causing Frost Heave

1) Water **freezing** in the ground can make **humps** on the surface.
2) When the active layer **freezes** in winter, the ice forms a kind of **lens** shape.
3) In fine-grained soil (like silt or clay) the ice lifts (**heaves**) up the surface layers of soil. This is called **frost heave**.
4) Ice lenses also form underneath **stones** because stones lose heat **faster** than the soil around them, so when temperatures drop it's **colder** beneath the stones.
5) As the ice lenses **expand**, they push the stones **upwards** towards the surface of the ground. The **ice lenses** underneath the stones **stop** the stones from **slipping back down**. If the ice **thaws**, **fine material** fills in the space where the ice was, so the stones **don't fall down**. Eventually the stones **rise above** the **surface** of the ground.

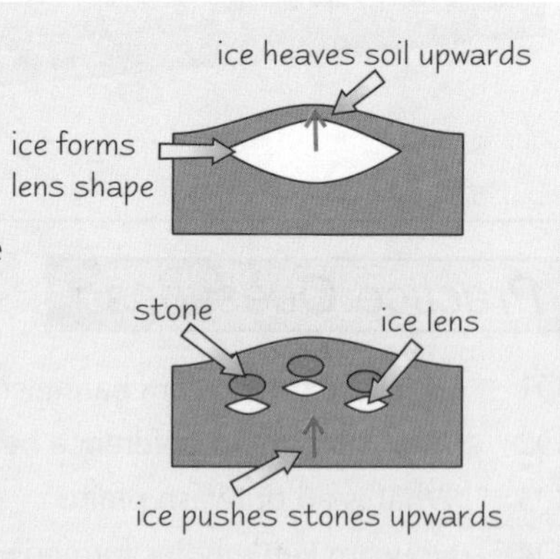

Patterned Ground is Formed by Frost Activity

Sometimes **stones** on the surface of the ground are arranged in **circles**, **polygons** or **stripes** — this is called **patterned ground**. Patterned ground can be formed in two ways — by **frost heave** and by **frost contraction**:

1) Stones can get pushed to the surface by **frost heave**. Once they reach the surface, they **roll down** to the **edges** of the **mounds** that have formed, so they form **circles** around them (**polygons** form when the mounds are **close together**). If the mounds are on a **slope**, the stones roll downhill and form **lines**.
2) **Frost contraction** causes the ground to **crack** in **polygon shapes**. The cracks get **filled in** with **stones**, forming polygon patterns on the surface.

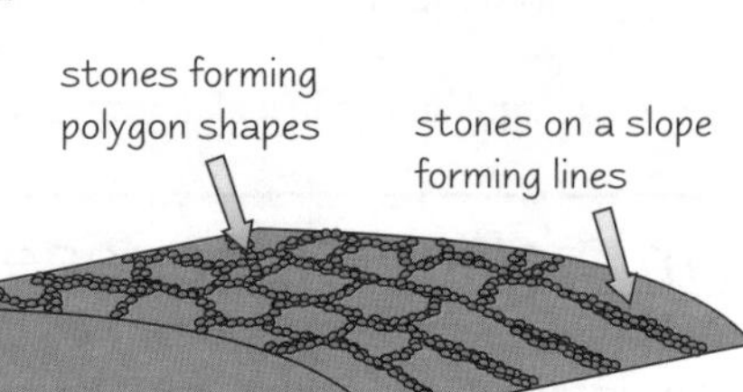

Periglacial Processes and Landforms

Nivation makes Hollows Deeper by Freezing and Thawing

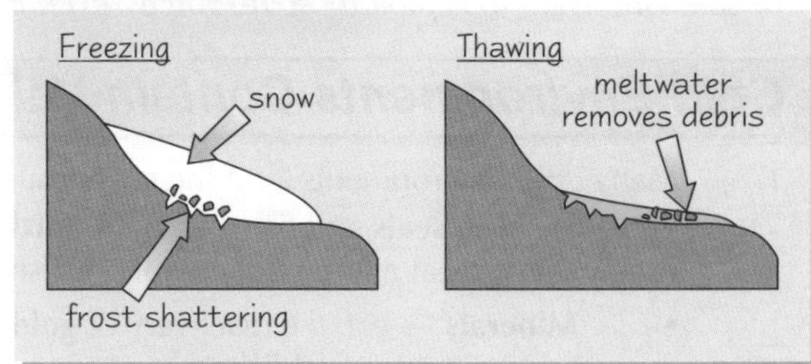

1) When snow gets into a **hollow** in the ground, it can **increase** the **size** of the hollow.
2) The temperature in periglacial environments often **fluctuates** around **0 °C**, so a lot of **freezing** and **thawing** happens — when the temperature's **above** 0 °C, the snow **melts**, and when it's **below** 0 °C, the water refreezes as **ice**.
3) Every time the ice **freezes**, it **expands**, so **frost shattering** eventually breaks bits off the rock at the base of the hollow. When the snow **melts**, the meltwater carries the broken bits of rock (debris) **away**.
4) Slopes **collapse** because they're **waterlogged** and they've been **eroded** — the material is **washed away** by meltwater.
5) Eventually the hollow becomes **deeper** and **wider**. The processes that cause this are collectively called **nivation**, and the hollows formed by nivation are called **nivation hollows**. Nivation hollows can be the beginning of a **corrie**.

Solifluction Produces Lobe Formations

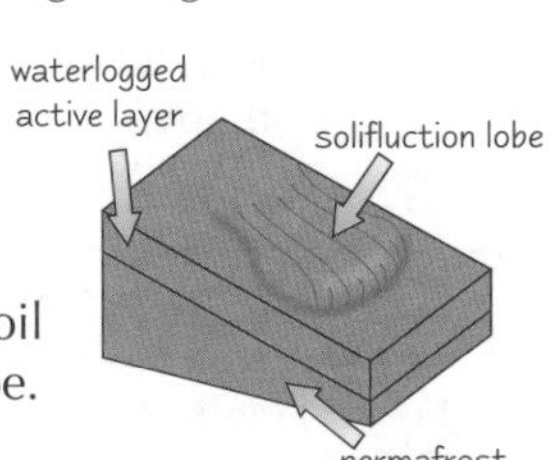

1) The **waterlogged active layer** of soil **flows** easily over the frozen impermeable layer beneath.
2) Solifluction produces **lobe** formations where one section of the soil is **moving faster** than the soil around it, e.g. because it's on **steeper** ground, so it flows down **further** to create a **tongue** shape.

Pingos are Ice-Filled Periglacial Hills

1) A pingo is a **conical hill** with a **core of ice**. Pingos can be as large as 80 m high and about 500 m wide.
2) There are **two types** of pingo — **open-system** and **closed-system**.
3) **Open-system pingos** form where there's **discontinuous** permafrost. **Groundwater** is forced **up** through the **gaps between** areas of permafrost (from unfrozen layers lower down). The water **collects** together and **freezes**, forming a **core** of ice that **pushes** the ground above it **upwards**.
4) **Closed-system pingos** form in areas of **continuous** permafrost where there's a **lake** at the surface. The lake **insulates** the ground, so the area beneath it remains **unfrozen**. When the lake **dries up**, the ground is no longer insulated and the permafrost **advances** around the area of unfrozen ground. This causes water to **collect** in the centre of the unfrozen ground. The water eventually **freezes** and creates a **core** of ice that **pushes** the ground above it **upwards**.
5) If the ice core **thaws**, the pingo **collapses**, leaving behind a **pond** of meltwater surrounded by **ramparts** (walls of soil).

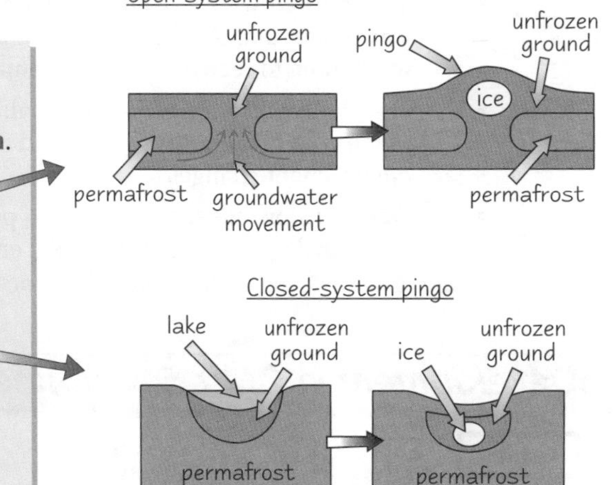

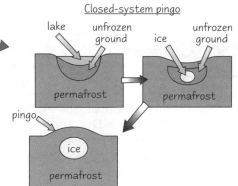

Practice Questions

Q1 What is permafrost?

Q2 How do ice wedges develop?

Q3 What's the difference between open-system pingos and closed-system pingos?

Exam Question

Q1 Describe the processes that lead to the formation of patterned ground in periglacial environments. [6 marks]

I always thought Pingo was one of the Beatles...

The trouble with this lot is that there are so many different processes going on, and all of them are to do with water freezing and then thawing. But at least you can sleep soundly now you know that patterned ground is caused by frost activity and not aliens.

Issues in Cold Environments

These pages are for AQA (Cold Environments option).
Cold environments might not be great for beach holidays, but they've still got some great resources. There'll always be people who want to exploit those resources, even if it means damaging the environment in the process.

Cold Environments Contain Valuable Resources, which Attract Development

1) Many cold environments (and the **seas** around them) **contain resources** that **attract development**. These include:
   - **Whales**, **seals** and **fish** — e.g. in **northern Russia** whales and seals are hunted for their skins, meat and blubber, while its **fishing industry** is one of the **largest** in the world.
   - **Minerals** — e.g. the discovery of **gold** in **Canada** and **Alaska** triggered gold rushes and led to the establishment of towns based around mining that still exist today.
   - **Oil** — e.g. **Alaska** has a lot of **oil**, and over the last few decades **oil companies** have moved into the area to **exploit** this resource.

Barry didn't like the sound of 'development'.

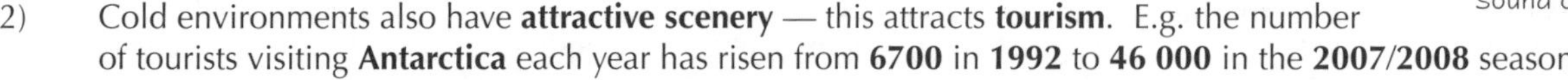

2) Cold environments also have **attractive scenery** — this attracts **tourism**. E.g. the number of tourists visiting **Antarctica** each year has risen from **6700** in **1992** to **46 000** in the **2007/2008** season.

3) Some cold environments have the potential for **hydroelectric power production** as they have natural lakes at high altitudes. **Norway** currently supplies **99%** of its domestic electricity through HEP plants.

Cold Environments have Fragile Ecosystems

1) Fragile ecosystems are ecosystems that struggle to **recover** from **damage**.
2) They're fragile because of the **harsh climate**:
   - The **short growing season** (when there's enough **light** and **warmth** for plants to grow) means that plants **don't have much time** to **recover** if they're **damaged**.
   - The **plants** and **animals** in cold environments are **adapted** to the cold conditions, so they find it hard to survive if their **environment changes**.
   - **Decay** is **slow** because it's cold, so **pollution** is **broken down** very **slowly** (and so remains in the environment for a long time).
3) **Tundra** is a fragile ecosystem found in some cold environments, e.g. in periglacial environments.

Tundra is found where it's **too cold** for **trees** to grow, either because of **high altitude** or **high latitude**. **Arctic tundra** is found in Greenland, northern Russia and Canada. **Antarctic tundra** is found in islands around Antarctica, e.g. South Georgia. **Alpine tundra** occurs in alpine environments. Vegetation includes **shrubs**, **grasses**, **mosses** and **lichen**. Animals found there include **seals**, **penguins**, **seabirds**, **hares**, **foxes**, **caribou** (reindeer) and **bears**.

Development in Cold Environments can Damage the Ecosystem

Fishing

1) Fishing can **disrupt food chains**, e.g. **krill** fishing in the **Southern Ocean** is depleting food supplies for **whales** and **penguins**.
2) **Overfishing** of a species can severely **deplete** its **population**, sometimes beyond recovery. Overfishing of the **Patagonian Toothfish** in the **Antarctic** is currently a concern.
3) **Bottom trawling** catches fish by dragging nets along the sea-bed. This **disrupts** the **ecosystem** (by **reducing light levels** through increasing turbidity) and **catches other species** as well as the target one. It's carried out in the **Gulf of Alaska**, the **Greenland Sea** and the **Barents Sea**.

Oil extraction

1) **Oil spills** can occur **during transport** of oil from the area. For example, in **1989** there was a huge **oil spill** off the coast of **Alaska** when the **Exxon Valdez oil tanker** crashed. Over **40 million** litres of oil spilled into the ocean, and over **250 000 birds** and **fish** were **killed**.
2) **Oil spills** can occur if **pipelines leak**. Between **1977** and **1994** there were, on average, **30 to 40** spills a year from the **Trans-Alaska pipeline**. Some of these were caused by **intentional attacks** and **forest fires**.

Hydroelectric power production

1) **Hydroelectric dams** can **block** the normal **migratory path** of fish. This can prevent them reaching **spawning grounds**, and so cause the fish **population** to **decrease**.
2) Hydroelectric dams also **heat up** the water, which can endanger **fish** that are used to **colder** temperatures.

Tourism

1) Large **cruise ships** increase **pollution** in the areas (from the ships and from the tourists).
2) Tourists and tourism developments (e.g. roads, hotels) disrupt **wildlife** and **damage habitats**, leading to **reduced biodiversity**.

Issues in Cold Environments

Mining

1) Mining can lead to **ground** and **surface water contamination**, either by **chemicals** used **during mining** or by the materials **being mined**. E.g. the lead-zinc mine in **Maarmorilik** (Greenland) was closed in 1990 but **lead** and **zinc** are still released, **polluting** nearby fjords.
2) Mining produces both **solid waste** and **wastewater** that has to be disposed of. In some cases, e.g. in the **Red Dog Mine** in **Alaska** and the **Kubaka** mine in **Russia**, the facilities are not built to deal with the quantities produced and the **waste** is **released** into the **environment**.

Development in Cold Environments has Affected the Locals

1) Even though the **climate** in **tundra** areas is very **harsh**, native **tribes** have lived there for **thousands** of years.
2) For example, the **Inuit** people are a group of tribes who live in the tundra in the northern parts of **Canada**, **Greenland** and **Russia**. Their traditional way of life involves **hunting** and **fishing** — they **eat** the **meat** and make **clothes** and **shoes** from the animal **fur** and **skin**.
3) **Newcomers** from Europe and the US started to take an **interest** in tundra areas during the **17th century** because of the opportunities for hunting **whales** and **seals**. **Seals** were hunted for their warm **fur** and their **oil** — the oil was used as **lamp fuel** and to make **leather**. **Whales** were mainly hunted for their **oil**, which was used to fuel **lamps**, make **candles** and also an ingredient in **margarine**.
4) The arrival of the **newcomers** had a very **negative** effect on the people living in the tundra, because they brought new **diseases** with them — many of the Inuit were infected and **died**. E.g. In the late 19th and early 20th century **90%** of the Inuvialuit (a Canadian Inuit tribe) were **killed** by diseases like tuberculosis, measles, smallpox and flu.
5) Also, an increase in **whaling**, **sealing** and **fishing** in the tundra areas **reduced** the **number** of whales, seals and fish available for the Inuit people to catch.
6) So development in tundra areas has had a big impact on the **lifestyles** of the indigenous people. E.g. in Canada:
   - There **aren't enough resources** for Inuit tribes to **support themselves** by hunting and fishing (and many young Inuits no longer learn the skills needed for this) so they have to find **paid employment**. This is difficult as the few job opportunities that exist are usually taken by the generally more educated white population.
   - With **unemployment** at nearly **50%** amongst some Inuit communities, they have to rely on government help.
   - The change of employment has also led to Inuits living in **permanent settlements** rather than being nomadic.

Development in Cold Environments can be Made More Sustainable

For development to be sustainable it has to **not deplete resources** and not cause **long-term environmental damage**.
It's pretty **difficult** for development to be totally sustainable, but there are things that make it **more sustainable**. For example:

1) **National parks** have been set up to allow **tourism** whilst **protecting** the environment — e.g. **Denali National Park** in Alaska was set up in 1917, and then expanded in 1980 to include a greater area of land. Cars and private vehicles are **banned** from the park, so visitors have to travel in park buses on approved routes. The most vulnerable parts of the park don't have any **roads** at all, so the ground is **protected** from the damaging effects of vehicles.
2) **Fishing quotas** have been introduced (e.g. in the **Barents Sea**), to **limit** the number of fish caught and **prevent overexploitation** of the resource.
3) **Oil pipes** have automatic **shut-off valves** in order to minimise **oil spills** if the pipelines are damaged.

Practice Questions

Q1 Name three resources that can be found in cold environments.

Q2 What kind of wildlife is found in tundra areas?

Exam Questions

Q1 Describe the impact of development on cold environments. [6 marks]

Q2 Explain how the traditional way of life of native tribes in tundra areas has been affected by development. [6 marks]

Personally, my main issue with cold environments is chilblains...

Exploitation of cold environments is kind of a sad story, but at least it's not too hard to get your head around. Just make sure you learn what kind of resources are found in cold environments, and how exploiting them can damage the environment and affect the lifestyles of the native people. And always check the label on margarine to make sure there's no whale oil in it — urgh.

Issues in Cold Environments — Case Study

These pages are for AQA (Cold Environments option).
You've probably noticed by now that geography teachers love a good case study. Well it turns out that the examiners are just the same — case studies are their absolute favourite thing in the world. So they'd probably love these pages...

The *Antarctic* is a *Unique Wilderness Area*

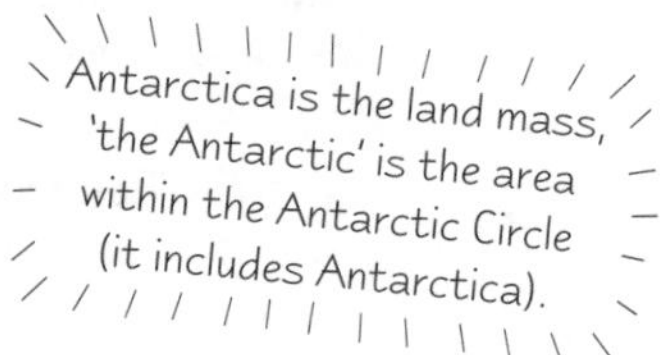

Antarctica is the land mass,
'the Antarctic' is the area
within the Antarctic Circle
(it includes Antarctica).

1) A wilderness area is an area that has been **unaffected** by large-scale **human activity**.
2) Antarctica is the **largest** wilderness area on Earth — it covers an area about **14 million km²**, so it's **larger** than **Europe**.
3) It contains **90%** of all the **ice** on Earth — around **70%** of all the Earth's **fresh water** supplies.
4) The **Antarctic ice sheet** covers most of the land mass of Antarctica all year round. The **ice sheet** extends into the **sea** — the ice masses that extend out over the sea are called **ice shelves**. The two largest ice shelves are the **Ross Shelf** and the **Ronne Shelf**. Chunks of ice can become detached from the ice shelves and fall into the sea as **icebergs**.
5) There are several **islands** off the coast of Antarctica, e.g. **Elephant Island**.

The *Antarctic* has a *Fragile Ecosystem*

1) There's **very little available water** in Antarctica for plants to grow. Inland areas receive **less than 166 mm** of precipitation per year (which is low enough to classify it as a **desert**) and most precipitation that falls is **frozen**.
2) It's **very cold** — the average temperature is **–49 °C**.
3) There's also **very little sunshine** in winter (the sun doesn't rise for several months because of the Earth's tilt).
4) This means that **very few** plants and animals **can survive** there, and the ones that do have to be specially **adapted**. Antarctica's plant life is mainly made up of **mosses** and **lichens**, and only **two** species of **flowering plants** grow. There's abundant **bird life**, e.g. **albatross** and **penguins**.
5) The lack of water, warmth and sunlight in Antarctica means that the land environment is very **fragile** — it takes a long time for it to **recover** from **damage**.
6) There's abundant **sea life**, e.g. **fish**, **seals** and **whales**.
7) The **sea ecosystem** is also **fragile** — if the population of one species **decreases** it affects other species in the **food chain**, e.g. if the population of krill decreases it would affect the whale population as some whales feed on them.

The *Antarctic* has Lots of *Valuable Resources*

1) Although the Antarctic appears to be **barren** it has a lot of **natural resources**:

There are around **300** species of **fish** and **eight** species of **whale** in the waters around Antartctica. The **Weddell** and **Ross Seas** are both rich in fish.

Antarctica has very **attractive scenery**.

There are large underground deposits of **coal** and **iron ore** in the **Transantarctic Mountains**.

There are large reserves of **oil** underneath the **Southern Ocean** around Antarctica.

2) These resources mean the Antarctic is an attractive area for **fishing**, **tourism**, **mining** and **oil extraction**.
3) The Antarctic is also very attractive to **scientific researchers** because it's unique.

The *Antarctic* is *Protected* by the *Antarctic Treaty*

1) Antarctica has **no native people**, so no one can claim the land as their own. This has caused **conflict** over the **ownership** of the region since it was discovered in the 18th century — lots of different countries have **tried** to **claim ownership** of bits of the continent and the right to **exploit** its **resources**.
2) Since the Antarctic has a **fragile** ecosystem the **impact** of any development on the **environment** could be **devastating**.
3) To try and **protect** the Antarctic from environmental damage, the **Antarctic Treaty** was set up **1961**. 12 countries agreed to set aside disputes over who owns Antarctica and came up with **laws** to **protect it**.
4) The treaty includes many **protocols** and **conventions** that **control** or **prohibit** certain activities (see next page for more).

Issues in Cold Environments — Case Study

Oil Extraction, Mining and Whaling are Currently Banned in the Antarctic

OIL EXTRACTION and MINING

1) Due to the **possible** huge **environmental impact** of oil extraction and mining in the area they're currently banned.
2) The **Madrid Protocol** (part of the Antarctic Treaty) came into force in **1998**, banning all mining activity and oil extraction. The ban is in force for **50 years** — it's due to be **reviewed** in **2048**.
3) Some people think the ban may be **lifted** in 2048 due to the **need for minerals** and **oil** (caused by depletion of reserves in the rest of the world).

WHALING

1) Whaling **was allowed** in the Antarctic, but caused a **decrease** in **whale populations**, e.g. it's estimated that there were **250 000 blue whales** in the Antarctic a century ago, now there are fewer than **1000**.
2) In **1994** the whole Antarctic area was declared a **whale sanctuary** and **commercial hunting** was **prohibited** (some whaling is still allowed for scientific research).

Efforts have been Made to Make Other Activities More Sustainable

1) Currently **tourism**, **scientific research** and **fishing** are allowed in and around Antarctica.
2) In the **2007-2008** season **46 000 tourists** visited the area.
3) There are around **5000 scientific researchers** in the Antarctic in **summer**, and about **1000** in **winter**.
4) **Fishing** is huge in the **Southern Ocean**, e.g. over **16 000 tonnes** of **Patagonian toothfish** were caught in **2000**.
5) These activities are controlled to **reduce** their **environmental impact** and to make them **more sustainable**:

Activity	Control
Tourism	• The Antarctic Treaty prohibits discharging of oil or plastics from cruise ships. • Tour operators have to stick to Antarctic Treaty rules, but they're mostly self-regulated by the IAATO (International Association of Antarctica Tour Operators). The IAATO imposes restrictions on tourist activity to reduce the environmental impact, for example no more than 100 passengers are allowed on shore in one place at a time and only one ship is allowed at a landing site at a time.
Scientific research	The Protocol on Environmental Protection came into force in 1998 as part of the Antarctic Treaty. It includes rules that protect Antarctica from damage caused by scientific research, e.g. scientists have to remove most of their waste from the Antarctic, and treat sewage before they dispose of it into the sea.
Fishing	The Convention for the Conservation of Antarctic Marine Living Resources came into force in 1982 as part of the Antarctic Treaty. It includes quotas (limits) on fish catches such as the Patagonian toothfish, krill and icefish.

6) **Not everyone** thinks that **tourism should be allowed**. The number of visitors is expected to increase to **80 000** per year by **2010**, which would **increase** the **environmental impact** of tourism.
7) It's very difficult to police the seas in the Antarctic so a lot of **illegal fishing** occurs despite the quotas, e.g. in the **2003-2004** season it was estimated that **2622 tonnes** of **Patagonian toothfish** were caught illegally.

Practice Questions

Q1 Name three of the resources that are found in Antarctica.

Q2 What is the Antarctic Treaty?

Exam Question

Q1 How is the Antarctic being protected from the impact of development? [15 marks]

Insert your own Aunt Arctica joke here...

Antarctica seems like quite a lively place considering nobody actually lives there. There's lots to learn on these pages, but at least it's all pretty interesting. Anyway, that's the end of cold environments — I hope you've enjoyed it as much as I have.

Desert and Desert Margin Characteristics

This section is for AQA (Hot Desert Environments option).
In my mind, deserts are full of towering sand dunes and camels, but in reality they're a bit different to that...

Rainfall is Low in Deserts and Desert Margins

1) **Deserts** are **arid** (dry) environments. Environments are classed as arid if they get **less than 250 mm** of **rainfall** a **year**.
2) **Desert margins** (land at the **edges** of a desert) are **semi-arid** environments. Environments are classed as semi-arid if they receive between **250** and **500 mm** of **rainfall** a **year**.
3) The **aridity** (dryness) of an environment depends on **rainfall** and the **rate of evapotranspiration**.
4) **Not all** deserts are **hot**, e.g. the **Gobi desert** in Asia is a **cold desert**. You **only** need to know about **hot** deserts for the **exam**.

Evapotranspiration is evaporation and transpiration (evaporation through plants).

Most Deserts and Desert Margins are Found...

1 Around 30° North and South of the Equator

1) Air moves in **circular patterns** between the **equator** and about **30° north** and **south** of it. These **circular air patterns** are called **Hadley cells**.
2) In a Hadley cell **air rises** at the **equator**. The air cools as it rises, moisture **condenses** and falls as **rain**, leaving the air **dry**.
3) The **dry air descends around 30° north** and **south** of the equator.
4) In areas where the **air descends** a zone of **high pressure** is created.
5) **Winds** blow **outwards** from high pressure areas — so **no moisture** can be **brought in** by the **wind**.
6) This means that the area has **very low precipitation**, which means desert margins and deserts are found there, e.g. the **Sahara**.

30° north
equator
30° south

2 In the Middle of Continents

1) The **central** parts of **continents** are usually **more arid** than coastal areas.
2) **Moist wind** from the sea **moves inland** and the **moisture** held is **dropped** as precipitation.
3) So when the **wind reaches** the **centre** of a large **continent** it's carrying **very little moisture**, so **very little rain** falls.
4) For example, the **Turkestan** desert exists because it's in the **central** part of **Asia**.

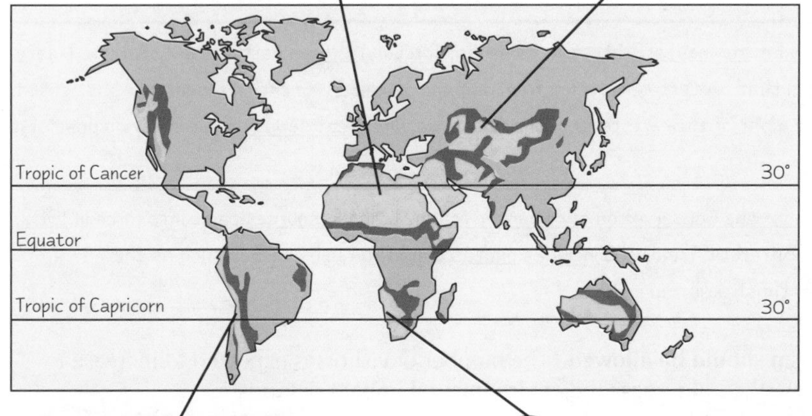

Desert (arid)
Desert margin (semi-arid)

3 Next to Mountain Ranges

1) Tall mountain ranges **force winds upwards**.
2) As the air rises it **cools** and its ability to **hold moisture** is **reduced**.
3) Any moisture held is dropped as **precipitation** over the mountains, so the wind that moves inland has **very little moisture**, which means that **very little rain falls** there.
4) This is called the **rain shadow effect**.
5) For example, the **Atacama** desert in South America exists because of the rain shadow effect of the **Andes** mountains.

4 Near Cold Ocean Currents

1) In some places **cold ocean currents** run along the coastline.
2) Wind is cooled as it travels over the cold water and its **ability to hold moisture** is **reduced**.
3) **Moisture** that's stored in the atmosphere is **released** as precipitation over the ocean **before** reaching **land**.
4) So when the wind **reaches** the **land** there's **very little moisture left**, so **very little rain falls**.
5) For example, the **Namib** desert in **Africa** exists because of the **Benguela Current** (a cold ocean current) that runs up the **west coast** of Africa.

Desert and Desert Margin Characteristics

Hot Deserts** are **Hot** and Have **Large Variations** in **Temperature

1) The **mean annual temperature** of most hot deserts is **high** — usually between **20 and 30 °C**.
2) There are large **seasonal variations** in **temperature** — up to **50 °C** in summer and **below 0 °C** in winter.
3) There are also large **daily variations** in **temperature** — up to **50 °C** in the day and **below 0 °C** at night. Large variations are due to the dry desert air, which can't **block sunlight** during the day or **trap heat** at night.

The temperature in **desert margins** is a bit lower:

1) The **mean annual temperature** of most **desert margins** is **lower** than in deserts — between **10 and 20 °C**.
2) The **temperature variations** in **desert margins** are usually **less extreme** (between **10** and **35 °C**).

*There's **Little Vegetation** in **Hot Deserts***

1) The **biomass** (total amount of living matter) in a desert is **low** because the **lack of water** makes it **difficult** for things **to grow**.
2) The amount of vegetation within a desert **varies** — there can be **none** where there are sand dunes, and a **variety** of small **shrubs**, **grasses** and **cacti species** in other areas.
3) Plants are **specialised** to **survive** in the hot and arid conditions, e.g. cacti have special ways to **collect**, **store** and **conserve** water.

Adaptations of Cacti

The enlarged stem stores water.
The thick waxy coating reduces transpiration and protects from strong winds.
Small spiny leaves reduce transpiration, and protect them from being eaten by herbivores.
Long, shallow roots absorb water from a large area, whilst longer taproots reach deeper water.

The vegetation in **desert margins** is a little different:

1) There's **more** vegetation in desert margins than in deserts.
2) Vegetation includes **shrubs**, **grasses** and **trees**.
3) The **amount** of vegetation generally **increases** the **further away** from the **desert** you go, because there's **more water**.

*The **Soil** in **Hot Deserts** is **Very Dry** and **Not Very Fertile***

1) You usually think of deserts as just being made from **sand**, but there are areas of **bare soil** and also **soil underneath** the sand.
2) Desert soils **aren't very fertile** because they don't contain very much organic matter. This is because **few plants grow** there.
3) The soils are often **sandy** (in areas with sand dunes) or **stony** (in rocky areas).
4) The soils are **very dry** due to the **low rainfall** and **high temperatures**.

The soil in **desert margins** is a bit better:

1) The soil in desert margins is **more fertile** than the soil in deserts, because there's more vegetation.
2) The soil contains **more water** than desert soil.
3) The soil is **less sandy** and **stony** than in deserts because there's **more weathering**.

Practice Questions

Q1 How much rainfall do desert margins receive per year?

Q2 Explain how the rain shadow effect causes aridity.

Q3 Why do deserts have large daily temperature variations?

Exam Question

Q1 The graph on the right shows the climate in Riyadh, Saudi Arabia.

a) Describe the climate in Riyadh. [6 marks]

b) Riyadh is 25° north of the equator. Explain how its location leads to low levels of precipitation. [5 marks]

c) Suggest what the vegetation in Riyadh is like, and explain your answer with reference to the climate in Riyadh. [4 marks]

WLTM hot desert — must have a dry sense of humour...

You need to know all about where deserts are, why they formed there and what they're like. So get learnin'. Now, with all this talk of deserts I can't stop thinking about chocolate chip cheesecake. Which reminds me — don't forget it's spelt with one 's'.

Processes in Hot Desert Environments

These pages are for AQA (Hot Desert Environments option).
It's a hard life being a rock in the desert — wind and water erode you and weathering makes bits fall off willy-nilly...

Rocks are Broken Down by Weathering

There are several **different types** of **mechanical weathering** that **break down rocks** in hot deserts. They include:

Thermal expansion and salt weathering cause the most weathering in hot deserts.

THERMAL EXPANSION

1) **Thermal expansion** is caused by **daily extreme temperature variations** in deserts.
2) During the **day** (when it's **hot**) rocks **expand**, and at **night** (when it's **cold**) they **contract**.
3) Sometimes **outer layers** of the rock **flake off** because they warm up and cool down at a **faster rate** than the inner layers. This is called **exfoliation.**
4) **Individual grains** may also fall off because **different minerals** within the rock expand and contract at **different rates**. This is called **granular disintegration**.

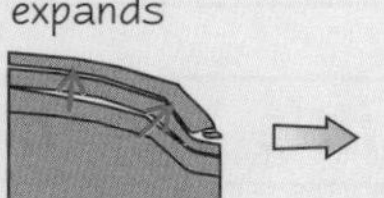

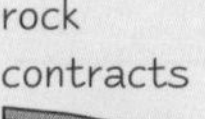

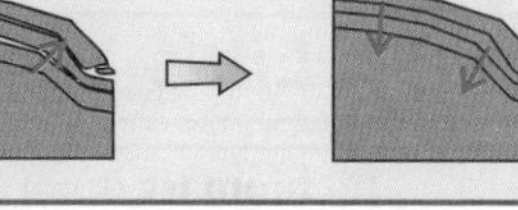

SALT WEATHERING

1) **Salt weathering** is caused by **saline** (**salty**) **water**, which comes from **rainfall** or from **groundwater** that's **drawn up** to the desert **surface** by **evaporation**.
2) This saline water **enters pores** or **cracks** in desert rocks.
3) The **high temperature** in hot deserts causes the **water** to **evaporate**, forming **salt crystals**. As the salt crystals **form** they **expand**, exerting **pressure** on the rocks.
4) As **more** evaporation occurs the salt crystals **expand** even **more**. This increases **pressure** in the rocks, causing **pieces** to **fall off**.

Rainwater can be slightly salty.

FROST SHATTERING

1) **Frost shattering** (**freeze-thaw** weathering) occurs in areas where there's **moisture** and **temperatures** that fluctuate **above** and **below freezing**.
2) Water from rainfall **enters** the **joints** and **crevices** in desert rocks.
3) At night, if the temperature **drops below 0 °C**, the water in the cracks **freezes** and **expands**.
4) Over time, **repeated** freeze-thaw action **weakens** the rocks and causes pieces to **fall off**.

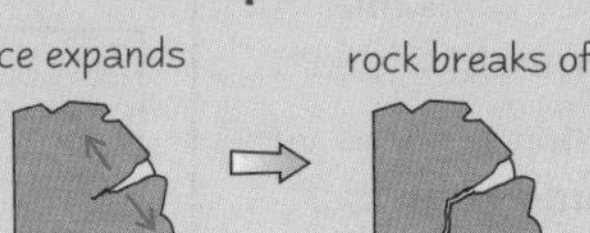

WETTING AND DRYING

1) Some desert rocks contain **clay**.
2) When clay gets **wet** (from rainfall), it **expands** and the **pressure** caused by this **breaks fragments off** the rock.

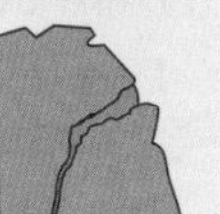

Wind Erodes Desert Rocks and Transports Particles

1) Wind can **erode** desert rocks in **two** ways:
   1. **Deflation** — the **removal** of **fine**, **loose particles** from the surface of rocks.
   2. **Abrasion** — **small particles** being **carried** by the wind **scrape off** particles from the rock surface.
2) It then **transports** the eroded material by **three** processes:

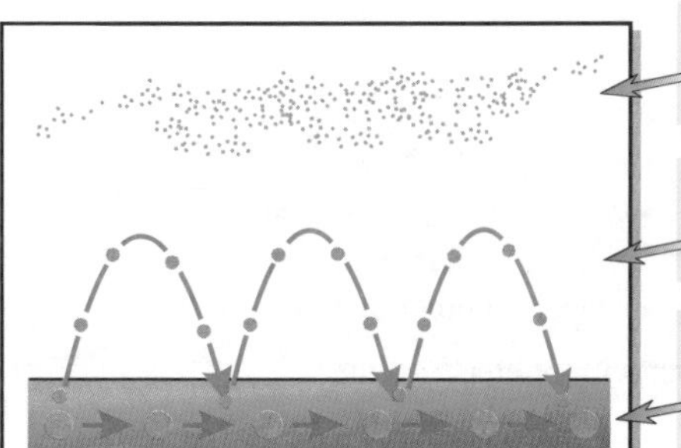

   1. **Suspension** is when **very small particles** (less than **0.15 mm**) are **picked up** and **carried** by the **wind**.
   2. **Saltation** is when **small particles** (**0.15-0.25 mm**) are **temporarily lifted** from the ground and **bounce** along.
   3. **Surface creep** is when **larger particles** (**over 0.25 mm**) are **hit** and **pushed along** the ground by particles being moved by **saltation**.
3) **More particles** are **transported** when the wind is **strong** and comes from a **constant direction**.
4) When there's a **reduction** in **wind speed**, the wind **drops** some of its **load** — this is **deposition**.

Processes in Hot Desert Environments

There are Three Types of River in Hot Deserts

1) **Exogenous** rivers have a **source outside** the **desert margin**. They flow **throughout the year** despite **evaporation** reducing their volume. For example, the source of the **Colorado river** in the **USA** is in the **Rocky Mountains**. It flows through the **Sonoran Desert** and the **Grand Canyon** to the sea.
2) **Endoreic** rivers **terminate inland** in the form of an **inland sea** or **delta**. For example, the **River Jordan** terminates in the **Dead Sea** — an inland sea in the **Middle East**.
3) **Ephemeral** rivers flow **intermittently** or **seasonally** after **rainstorms**. For example, the **Todd River** in the **Simpson Desert** (**Australia**) only flows a few days a year and remains a **dry river bed** for the rest of the year.

Derek promised them an ephemeral river was coming soon...

Flooding Erodes the Desert

Most **rainfall** in hot deserts is **light** and **infrequent**. However, **sometimes** there may be a **sudden**, **high intensity rainstorm** that lasts for a **short period** of time. This can cause **two types** of **flood** in a desert — **flash floods** and **sheet floods**.

Flash Floods

See page 6 for more on how water erodes and transports material.

1) A **flash flood** is a **sudden**, **strong** and **rapid** flow of water through a **channel**.
2) They occur because **heavy** rainfall **can't** be **absorbed** by the **dry**, **hard desert soil** — so the **runoff** collects in **channels** and **flows rapidly downhill**.
3) Flash floods have **enough energy** to transport **large pieces** of desert rock by **traction**. They also transport **pebbles**, **gravel** and **sand** by **suspension** and **saltation**. The rocks in the water are **eroded** into **smaller fragments** by **attrition** (rocks smashing into each other).
4) The material carried by flash floods **erodes** the channels by **abrasion**, making them **deeper**.
5) At the **mouth** of a channel, the flash flood waters **spread out**, **slow down** and **soak into** the **ground** (unless they meet another body of water).

Sheet Floods

1) A **sheet flood** is a **slow-moving**, **even flow** of water **over land** (i.e. it **isn't** confined to a **channel**).
2) Like flash floods, they occur **after** a period of **intense rainfall**, where water **collects** across the **dry**, **impermeable desert floor** and flows down **gentle slopes** as a **sheet** of water.
3) Sheet floods have **less energy** than flash floods, but can still **transport pebbles**, **gravel** and **sand** by **suspension** or **saltation**.
4) The **material** carried by sheet floods **erodes** the **desert surface** by **abrasion**.

Practice Questions

Q1 Name four types of mechanical weathering that occur in hot deserts.

Q2 Describe two ways in which wind can erode desert landscapes.

Q3 What is suspension?

Q4 What is surface creep?

Exam Questions

Q1 Describe the mechanical weathering processes that can occur in hot desert environments. [8 marks]

Q2 a) Describe the three types of river that can be found in hot desert environments. [3 marks]

b) Outline how flash floods and sheet floods can erode hot desert landscapes. [6 marks]

Surface Creep — Grandad's new disco dance move...

There are tons of technical terms to get to know on these two pages — saltation, exogenous, ephemeral... It's tricky enough to get the spelling right, let alone what they mean. But if you shut the book and test yourself a few times you'll soon have 'em sussed.

Landforms in Hot Desert Environments

***These pages are for** AQA (**Hot Desert Environments option**).*
Wind and water in the desert do really neat things, like sculpting crazy landforms. Ooooooh, aaaaaaaahh.

Wind Erosion Forms Yardangs and Zeugen

Yardangs

Yardangs are **narrow**, **streamlined ridges** that are usually **three to four** times **longer** than they are **wide**. **Strong winds** (blowing in **one direction**) carry sand in **suspension**, which **erodes rocks** by **abrasion**. **Softer** rock is **eroded faster** than **harder** rock, so **ridges** of hard rock are created (yardangs). The ridges **aren't** always **continuous**.

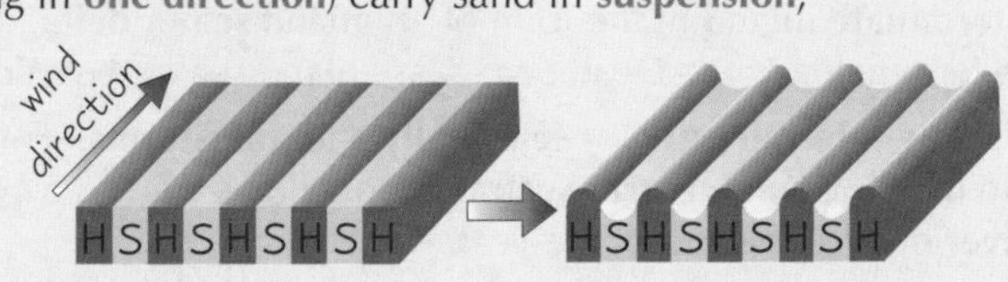

Zeugen! — That wind is capable of some nifty sculpting.

Zeugen

Zeugen are **long**, **block-shaped ridges** of rock (a **single** ridge is called a **zeuge**). They're formed in areas where a layer of hard rock sits **above** a layer of softer rock. If **cracks** form in the **hard rock** due to **weathering** processes such as **frost shattering** (see page 58), the **wind** can **erode** through the **cracks** and into the softer rock beneath by **abrasion**. Again, the **softer rock** is eroded **more** than the **hard rock**, and ridges (zeugen) are formed.

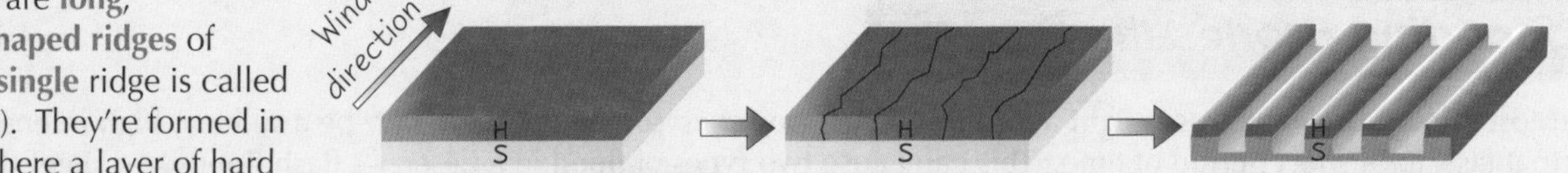

Sand Dunes Form When the Wind Deposits Sand

1) **Sand dunes** form when **sand grains** carried by **suspension** are **deposited** as the wind **slows down**.
2) **Vegetation**, **rocks** and **other dunes** slow wind down, causing it to **drop** its load.
3) The **shape** and **layout** of dunes is affected by several factors:
   - The **speed**, **direction** and **consistency** of the **wind**.
   - The **amount of sand** being transported — the **more** sand, the **larger** the dune.
   - The nature of the **ground surface** — e.g. **rocky outcrops** or **uneven ground** slow wind down.
   - The **amount** and **type of vegetation** — **deposition** occurs **downwind** from vegetation and **around its base**, **deforming** the shape of dunes. Also, **plant root networks** help to **stabilise sand** and **hold** dunes in place.
4) There are lots of **different types** of sand dune:

See page 58 for more on how wind transports sand.

Barchan dunes (crescent-shaped)

1) These are **isolated** dunes that develop from mounds of sand. They form in the **direction** of the **prevailing wind** as sand is **deposited**.
2) When the slope of the dune becomes **too steep**, **sand avalanches** occur, depositing sand at the **base** (downwind).
3) **Swirling wind currents** (**eddies**) help to keep the slope **steep**.
4) The dune **slowly moves forward** in the direction of the wind.
5) If there's a **lot of sand** being deposited, many barchan dunes **connect** with each other to form a **barchanoid ridge**.

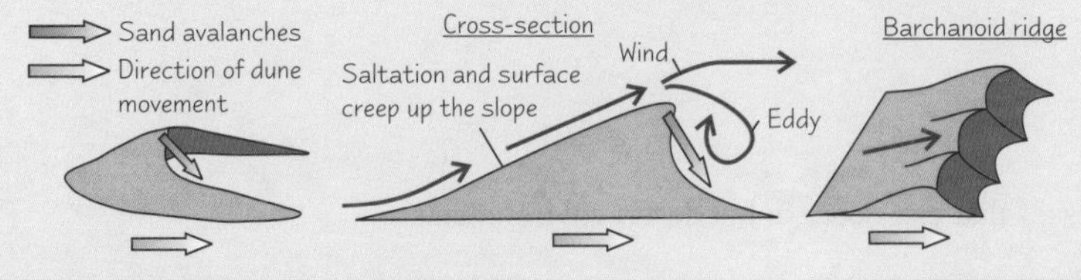

Seif dunes (long wiggly lines)

1) **Seif dunes** are **long**, **wiggly ridges** of sand.
2) They form **from barchan dunes** if a **change** of **wind direction** occurs.
3) When wind blows from **alternate sides** the 'arms' of barchan dunes are **elongated** and form a wiggly **line**.

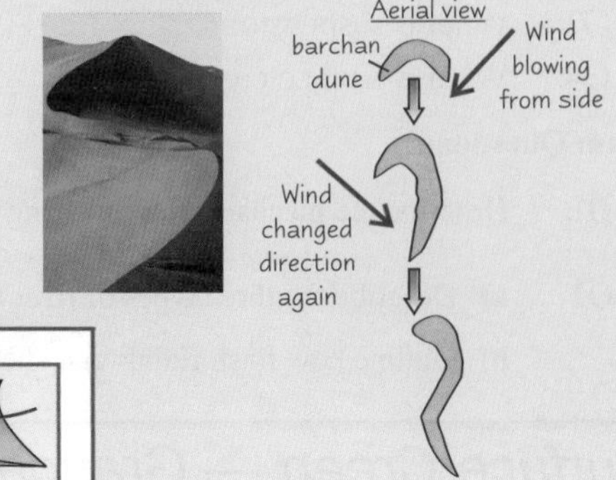

Star dunes (urm... star-shaped)

1) Star dunes have **multiple steep faces** caused by winds from **many directions**.
2) As more sand is added they grow in **height**.

Landforms in Hot Desert Environments

Water Erosion *Creates Many Different* ***Desert Landforms***

The **fast-moving water currents** that follow **torrential rainfall** in the **desert** can create many different **landforms**:

1) Pediments

Pediments are **desert plains** — **gently sloping** areas of **rock** (usually covered in a thin **layer of debris**). They're formed by the **erosion** of rock by **sediment** carried in **sheet floods** or **small streams**.

2) Inselbergs

Inselbergs (e.g. **Ayers Rock**) are **steep-sided hills** that rise up from pediments.
They're made of **hard rock** that's more **resistant** to **erosion** than the **surrounding rock**.
The surrounding rock is **eroded** by **water**, leaving the harder rock **standing out**. Inselbergs can also be formed by **wind erosion**.

Ayers Rock

3) Mesas and buttes

A **mesa** is an **isolated**, **flat-topped**, **steep-sided** landform found only in **arid** places. They're a **type** of **inselberg** composed of a **hard horizontal rock layer**. They form in the **same way** as inselbergs. **Buttes** are **smaller** and **narrower** versions of mesas.

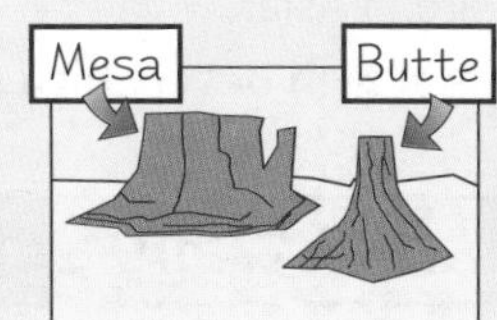

4) Salt lakes

Salt lakes form when **desert rivers**, which contain salt, are **endoreic** (**terminate** in an **inland sea**). The water can't **leave** the lake and **evaporation** is **high**, resulting in a lake with a **high salt content** (sometimes higher than **sea water**). Some salt lakes are **ephemeral** — evaporation is **so high** that they **dry up** at certain times of the year, leaving the salt behind to form **salt pans** (**ground** covered **with salt**).

5) Wadis and alluvial fans

A **wadi** is a **gully** or **ravine** that's been eroded by **seasonal rivers**. Depending on the **strength** of the river, a wadi can have **shallow** or very **steep** valley sides. If there's a flat desert plain at the **mouth** of a **wadis** the water **spreads out** on to the plain. This leads to **sediment** being **deposited** as **energy** is **dissipated**, forming an **alluvial fan**.

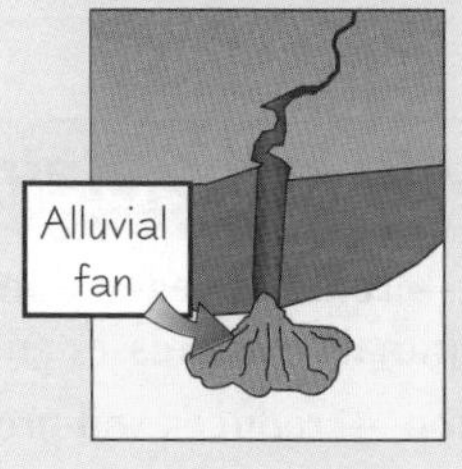

6) Badlands

Badlands are so called because they're **difficult** and **dangerous** to travel through. Badlands are **vast areas** of **uneven terrain** with **deep**, **interlocking canyons**, **steep ridges**, **loose sediment** and **deep sands**. **Wadis** and **buttes** can be found there. **Erosion** occurs from **flood waters** and **wind**. **Softer rock** layers and **clay soils erode** to form **canyons**, while **hard rock** layers are **eroded less** to form **ridges**.

Practice Questions

Q1 Give three factors that affect the shape and layout of sand dunes.

Q2 What are pediments?

Q3 Name two features of badlands.

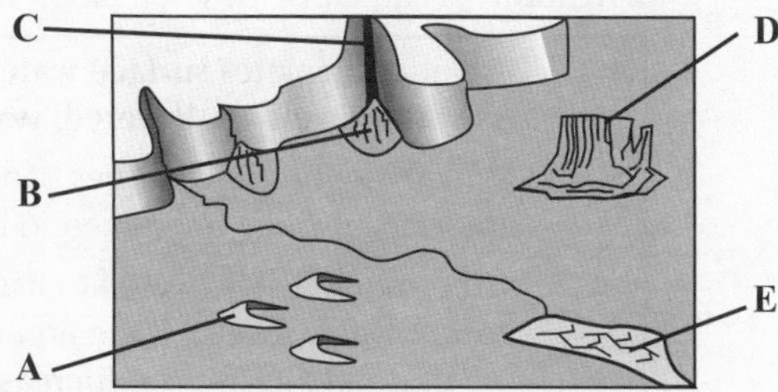

Exam Questions

Q1 Describe and explain the formation of yardangs and zeugen. [7 marks]

Q2 The diagram above shows a desert landscape.

a) Identify the landforms A, B and C. [3 marks]

b) Landform D is a mesa. Describe what it is and how it formed. [4 marks]

c) Suggest what E is and how it formed. [4 marks]

So, the yardangs fight the zeugen and the inselbergs save the world...

...what's that... we're not talking about Star Trek... Oh. Sounded like we were. Best make sure then that you really do know your yardangs from your zeugen, your pediments from your inselbergs — I suggest you get that butte into gear and sha-wadi-wadi.

Desertification

These pages are for AQA (Hot Desert Environments option).
Desertification isn't the cheeriest topic around but it's definitely important.

Desertification is a Form of Land Degradation

Desertification is the **degradation** of **semi-arid** land by **human activities** and **changes in climate**. It leaves land **unproductive**. **Africa** and **Asia** are the **worst affected areas** but desertification is a problem across the globe.

1) A **third** of land worldwide is **at risk** of **desertification**. ⟹
   110 countries have regions that are threatened, with those likely to be worst affected in **Africa**, **Asia** and **Latin America**.
2) **250 million people** across the globe are already affected by desertification, the **largest proportion** of which are in **Asia**.
3) **46%** of **Africa** is **at risk** of desertification (**25%** is at **high** or **very high risk**).

World map of desertification risk

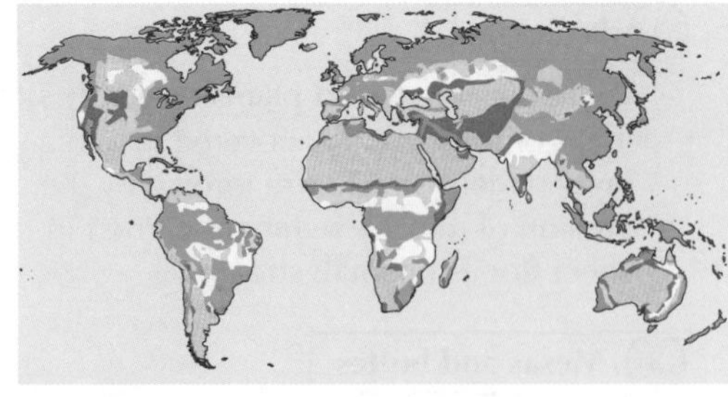

Climate Change is a Physical Cause of Desertification

Climate change is causing desertification by **reducing rainfall** and **increasing** the **temperature** in some areas:

Lower rainfall

1) Climate change will probably **reduce rainfall** in **sub-tropical regions** (where most semi-arid environments are).
2) If there's **less rain** then **surface water** and **groundwater** will be **reduced** (as it's used up or evaporates but isn't replenished).
3) This means that the volume of **water** available for **vegetation growth** is **reduced**, which leads to the **death** of vegetation.
4) The **roots** of **plants** and **trees bind** the **soil together**. **Fewer plants** and **trees** mean **fewer roots**, leading to **soil erosion**.

Higher temperatures

1) **Global surface temperature** has **risen** by **0.6 °C** over the last century and is predicted to **continue rising**.
2) As **temperatures increase** the **rate of evapotranspiration** also **increases**.
3) This **dries out soils** and **lowers surface water levels**, leading to soil erosion in the same way as lower rainfall does (vegetation dies).

Human Activity is the Main Cause of Desertification

1) **Overgrazing** — **reduces vegetation**, so leads to **soil erosion** (due to lack of **plant roots**). Trampling by large numbers of animals **compresses** and **breaks down** the **structure of soil**, which also makes **erosion more likely**.
2) **Overcultivation** — **reduces soil productivity** as the over-exploitation of the soil leaves it **without** enough **nutrients** to support plants. Without plants (and plant roots) the soil is **easily eroded**.
3) **Deforestation** — removing **trees** and therefore **tree roots** means that (once again) soil is more **vulnerable to erosion**. Forests are cleared to provide **land** for **farming** as well as **wood** for **fuel** and **building materials**.
4) **Irrigation** — can cause desertification in a number of ways:
   - Irrigation **depletes surface water** and may involve **unsustainable pumping** of **aquifers**. As **water levels** are **lowered**, **water availability** for plants **decreases**, leading to **soil erosion**.
   - Some **irrigation techniques** can **erode soil directly**, e.g. surface irrigation, where large amounts of water are added to the soil in a short amount of time, **washing topsoil away**.
   - If **too much water** is used to irrigate crops the excess can **sink** into the soil and **raise groundwater levels**. If the aquifer is **saline** this may bring **high concentrations** of **salt** too close to the surface, **increasing** the **salinity** of the **soil** too much for plants to survive.

   Aquifers are underground rocks containing water that can be extracted.
5) **Population growth** — **increases pressure** on the **land** as more and more **food** is needed to meet the **growing demand**. This leads to **further overgrazing**, **overcultivation**, **deforestation** and **irrigation**, therefore increasing desertification.

Desertification Impacts on Land, Ecosystems and Populations

As **fertile topsoil** is **eroded** the land becomes **less productive** (i.e. less can be grown). **Less plant life** means that **less animal life** can be supported and **biodiversity decreases**. If agricultural productivity decreases to the point where farmers **can't feed** their **families** or **earn a living** from the land then they have to **migrate** from the area. This **increases pressure** on the **land** in the **areas** that they **migrate to**. If people are **unable** to move then desertification can lead to **famine**, as families or whole communities are unable to produce the food they need from the degraded land.

Desertification

There are *Strategies* to *Manage Arid Environments*

Desertification can be **prevented** by using strategies that...

...make agriculture more sustainable by reducing overgrazing, overcultivation, and improving the fertility of the soil

1) Leaving areas of land **fallow** (not cultivated) — this allows the soil to **recover** from **grazing**.
2) Adopting **nomadic farming** — nomadic herders constantly move animals on, which **stops** areas being **overgrazed**.
3) **Rotating crops** — different crops need different nutrients, so rotating crops stops the same nutrients being **depleted** year after year. This **improves soil fertility**. Adding **compost** can also **improve soil fertility**.
4) **Planting legumes** (e.g. clover) — these **improve soil fertility** by **increasing** the amount of **nitrogen** present.

...make water use more sustainable by reducing use

1) **Growing crops** that need **little water** (e.g. millet, sorghum and olives) — this can **reduce water use**.
2) Using **drip irrigation** — this technique adds small volumes of water to the soil at a time. It **reduces wastage** of water and also **prevents** soil being **eroded** by large volumes of water being added in one go.

...increase or maintain the level of vegetation to reduce erosion

1) **Planting trees** — these act as **windbreaks**, **protecting** soil from wind **erosion**.
2) Using **alternative energy sources** — technology such as **solar cookers** can help **reduce deforestation** to provide wood for fuel. These cookers use the sun's energy to heat food and are cheap and easy to make.

External Aid May be *Needed* to *Implement* These *Strategies*

Implementing strategies to combat desertification **costs money**, either for **equipment** (e.g. drip irrigation systems) or for programmes to **educate** and **train** local people. In developing countries this money often comes from **external aid**. For example, in **1988** the International Fund for Agricultural Development funded a programme costing US **$1.5 million** to combat desertification in **Northern Sudan**.

Sustainable Strategies Address the *Causes* of *Desertification*

1) Most of the strategies above **are sustainable** because they **prevent desertification** and once implemented they can be **carried on** by the local community **without external help** or **money**. E.g. once people have been **trained** how to make a solar cooker, further external aid isn't needed as that **knowledge** is now within the community.
2) Some strategies just address the **problems caused** by **desertification** and so **aren't sustainable** (as they won't prevent desertification happening again in the future).
3) Examples of unsustainable strategies are **transporting water** to areas at risk of desertification, and using **external aid** to **provide relief** from **famine**.
4) To address the threat of desertification many countries are drawing up **National Action Plans**, which aim to prevent desertification using **sustainable solutions** and **involving local communities**.

Practice Questions

Q1 What is desertification?

Q2 Describe three strategies that reduce desertification.

Q3 What makes an anti-desertification strategy sustainable?

Exam Question

Q1 Outline the causes of desertification. [10 marks]

Dessertification — now that sounds like a topic I could get on board with...

If a third of land was at risk of being turned into sticky toffee pudding, the world would be a much better place. Sadly, that's not the case and desertification is causing problems across the globe. The good news is that if you take the time to learn these two pages really well it shouldn't cause you a smidge of a problem in your exam. Every cloud and all that...

Desertification Case Study — The Sahel

***These pages are for** AQA (**Hot Desert Environments** option).*
Down to specifics... The Sahel — it's a real place, with real problems.

Desertification is *Already Happening* in the *Sahel*

1) The **Sahel region** is a roughly **3900 km long belt** that runs east to west across **Africa**. It separates the hyper-arid Sahara from the wetter and more fertile savanna further south.
2) The Sahel runs through **10 countries** (see map), which are some of the poorest countries in the world.
3) It receives **200-600 mm** of rain per year, mostly between **May** and **September**, but **rainfall** can **vary** massively from year to year.
4) Some areas are **already suffering** from **desertification**, and others are at **very high risk**.

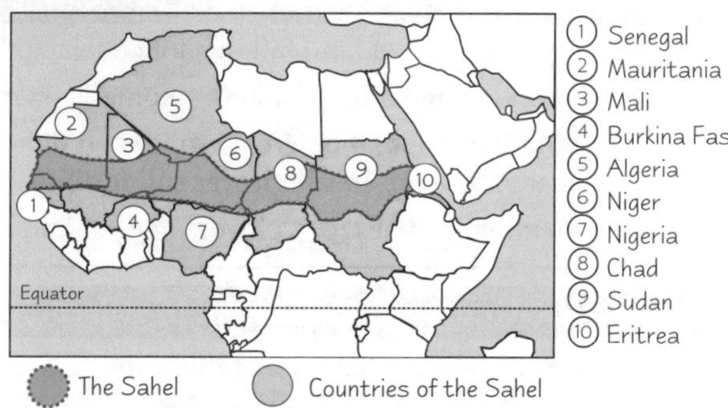

Desertification is *Caused* by *Climate Change*, *Agriculture* and *Deforestation*

Climate change

1) Between **1968** and **1997 rainfall** in the Sahel **decreased** between **29%** and **49%**.
2) Low rainfall led to a **five year drought** from **1968** to **1973** and **droughts** were **common** across the Sahel from then right through to the early 1990s. While drought alone **doesn't cause** desertification (well managed land will recover when the drought ends) it can **contribute** to desertification when the **land** is **badly managed**, as the land will become degraded to a degree that it **can't recover from**.
3) The **average temperature** of the region has **increased** over the last century. This **increases desertification** by **increasing evapotranspiration**, which **reduces ground** and **surface water supplies**.

Agriculture

1) Between **1968** and **1998** the **population** of the Sahel **increased** from **274 million** to **628 million**. As the population increases **more food** has to be produced from the land to feed everyone.
2) At the same time, the **area of good agricultural land** has **reduced**, as more and more land is used as **game parks** for **tourists**.
3) With **less land available** and **more people** to feed the **pressure** on remaining agricultural land has **increased**. This has led to **overcultivation** and **overgrazing**, which has **increased desertification**.
4) The **total** area of land that's used for agriculture has **increased** from **8 million hectares** in **1960** to over **16 million hectares** in **2000**, as land that's **less suitable** for agriculture is used.
5) **Restriction** of **nomadic farmers** (those who move their herds depending on the weather, season or state of pasture) by **border closures** has forced farmers to stay in **one area**, causing **overgrazing**. Some nomads have also adopted a more **settled lifestyle**, which has had the same effect as restricting movement.
6) **Political instability** and **war** has led to **migration** of people to refugee camps, putting huge pressure on the surrounding environment to provide **enough food** for the **enlarged population**. E.g. between **1998** and **1999**, **30 000** people migrated to **Sudan** to escape the war between **Ethiopia** and **Eritrea**.

Deforestation

1) To create **more space** for **agriculture** large areas of **forests** have been **cleared** in the Sahel (usually by burning), leaving the ground vulnerable to **erosion**.
2) **Deforestation** to provide **wood** for **fuel** is a major problem in the Sahel, where **82%** of **total energy** used in homes and for industry comes from **wood**.
3) The demand for fuel wood has led to some people switching **from agriculture to wood collection** to earn a living. As increasing amounts of wood are collected the area of land that's deforested also increases. Wood for use in **Zinder** (a city in **Niger**) is now collected up to **200 km** away from the town.

Desertification Case Study — The Sahel

Desertification Has Environmental, Social and Economic Impacts

1) Erosion of topsoil has **reduced** the **area** of **productive agricultural land** in the Sahel. In **Mauritania** all that's left is a **200 km wide** strip running across the country, whilst in **Niger 2500 km²** of land is lost **each year** to desertification.
2) As land area decreases, so does the **amount of food produced**. E.g. some areas of **Niger** now produce **less than a 20th** of the food they could **40 years ago**. This causes **loss** of **livelihoods** and, in the worst cases, **famine**.
3) Many people have had to **migrate** from areas where the **land can't support them** any longer. E.g. over **2 million** people have migrated from **Mali** and **Burkina Faso** as a result of desertification.
4) With **fertile soil** becoming increasingly **scarce**, **tensions** have grown between **settlement farmers** and **nomadic herders** over use of the land, sometimes leading to **violence**.
5) The **changing conditions** in the Sahel have led to **animal migrations**. E.g. **rodents** from the Sahara are travelling further south, **destroying crops** and bringing **new diseases**.

Strategies to Reduce Desertification are Being Implemented

Some strategies to reduce desertification are **traditional techniques** that have been used for many years. For example:

The plant ***Jatropha curcas*** is grown as hedges **around food crops** by farmers in **Mali**. It's able to grow in **poor quality soil** and **isn't eaten by animals**. Its roots help **bind soil together** and it **protects** the **soil** from wind and water **erosion**. **Oil** produced from the plant can be **sold**, providing a valuable source of **income**. This strategy has **reduced poverty** and **erosion** in the area. The plant can also be burnt as **fuel**, **reducing** the need for **deforestation**.

Contour bunding is a **low-cost** technique where stones are placed **around agricultural lands** to keep **rainfall** there long enough for it to **soak in**. It's used to **maximise water use** and **prevent soil erosion**. It's **increased** some **yields** by **40%** in **Burkina Faso**, but can only be used in areas with **sufficient stones**.

Other strategies are more **recent** developments and have relied on **external aid** for implementation. For example:

In **Niger**, **Non-Governmental Organisations** (NGOs) are helping farmers to **reduce soil erosion** by providing **free seeds** of plants that are **suitable** for growing in **arid conditions**. These plants grow an **extensive root system** that **holds** the **soil together**. Long roots also mean that the plant can **absorb water** from **deeper** in the ground, so they're **less vulnerable** to **drought**. This scheme has been successful in **reducing soil erosion** but some people are concerned that it **encourages poor farmers** to continue **agricultural production** that's **high-risk**.

Similar schemes are also run in Sudan and Senegal.

In **Eritrea**, a **more efficient** version of the **mogogo** (a traditional stove) has been introduced. It needs **50% less wood** than the older version and therefore **reduces** the need to **cut down trees** for fuel. **Funding** for the project has come from NGOs and **international aid agencies**. A similar project has been launched in **Chad**, where new stoves run on **manure** rather than wood, therefore **reducing deforestation** and the risk of desertification. The new stoves have **reduced pressure** on **wood supplies** and the number of **respiratory diseases** has **decreased** as they produce **less smoke** than the old ones.

In **Chad**, NGOs have launched schemes to **reduce soil erosion** by **educating villagers** about the importance of maintaining plenty of **vegetation** and by helping them grow and plant **seedlings**. The schemes also **promote cooperation** between **neighbouring villages** to try to avoid over-exploitation of resources and to **share techniques** for **good land management**.

External aid can have **negative impacts** if the projects they fund aren't managed properly. During the 1968 to 1973 drought thousands of **wells** were built using aid money. Many farmers used the wells to **increase** the **size** of their **herds**, but the land couldn't cope with the **overgrazing** that followed. **Large areas** of land became **desertified** as a result.

Practice Questions

Q1 How is agriculture causing desertification in the Sahel?

Q2 Describe the impact of desertification on the Sahel.

Exam Question

Q1 Evaluate the strategies used to reduce desertification in the Sahel. [15 marks]

I drought you'll have too much of a problem learning this...

Like with all case studies you need to make sure that you learn lots of details and examples. Having a general idea that there are some problems with desertification in the Sahel isn't going to cut it. You need to learn the causes, impacts and the strategies.

Desertification Case Study — Southern Spain

These pages are for AQA (Hot Desert Environments option). *It's not just developing countries at risk — desertification's causing problems all over the place. The Med may be fantastic for holidays, but all those tourists have an impact...*

Desertification is Already Happening in Southern Spain

1) **Spain** is in **Southern Europe**, close to North Africa and the Sahara desert.
2) Roughly **50%** of Spain is classified as **arid**, making it the **driest** country in Europe.
3) In 2008 it was estimated that **37%** of Spain is **at risk** of **desertification** (with **18%** of the land at **high** or **very high** risk).
4) The **most vulnerable areas** of the country are in the **south**, e.g. Andalusia and Murcia.

The map on the right shows the vulnerability of different areas to desertification.

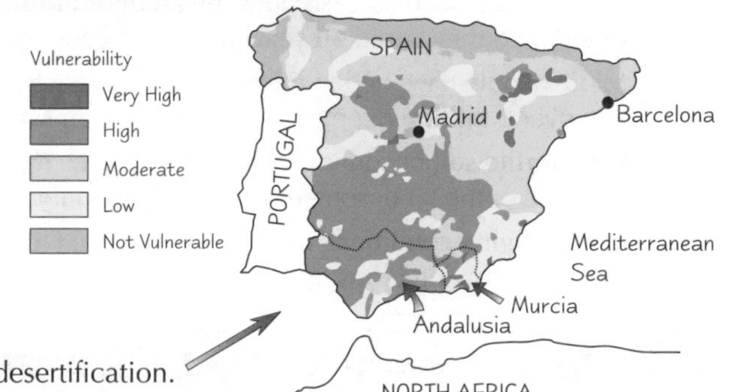

Desertification is Caused by Climate Change, Agriculture and Development

Climate Change

1) The **average temperature** in Spain has **risen** by **1.5 °C** in the last century, **increasing** the rate of **evapotranspiration**.
2) **Rainfall** has **decreased** throughout Spain. Between **1991** and **2000** rainfall in **Andalusia** fell by **9.5%**.
3) Higher temperatures and lower rainfall have **reduced surface water resources**. Less water is available to recharge groundwater supplies, leading to **falling groundwater levels**. As there's **less water fewer plants** can grow, meaning **fewer roots** to hold the soil together. This leads to **soil erosion** and desertification.
4) As the climate gets hotter and drier there's **increased risk** of **forest fires**, causing **deforestation** and desertification.

Agriculture

1) **Overcultivation** is causing desertification as the **nutrient content** of the soil is **reduced** to the point that it's no longer productive. **80 million tonnes** of **topsoil** is **lost** each year in **Andalusia** because of intensive cultivation of **olive trees**.
2) **Overgrazing** is **reducing vegetation cover**, causing desertification.
3) Groundwater resources are being pumped to **irrigate crops**. This is **lowering groundwater levels**. Increasingly more water is being used for irrigation because...
   - **Agriculture** is carried out in areas that **aren't** really **suitable** for it. E.g. the region of **Almeria** (in Andalusia) is an important agricultural area as produce grown there for export contributes **$1.5 billion** to the economy each year. Almeria is the driest area in Europe though, so this is only possible with **intensive irrigation**.
   - **Crops** that need **more water** than the area can **supply** are being grown for **export**. E.g. Spain is Europe's largest producer of **strawberries**, and **95%** of its exports are grown in **Andalusia**. As Andalusia is so arid **intensive irrigation** is needed to supply the strawberries with the **large amounts** of **water** they need to grow.

   Although there are restrictions in place to protect aquifers, many farmers are using **illegal boreholes** to secure water supplies for their crops.

Development

1) There's been a huge **increase** in **tourism** in Southern Spain in the last 50 years. In the last few years an estimated **180 000 holiday homes** have been built along the Spanish coast every year.
2) This is increasing strain on water supplies as there's more and **more demand** for **water** for **swimming pools**, **water parks** and **irrigation** of **golf courses**.
3) Although there are regulations in place to protect water supplies for agriculture, many developments get around them by **reclassifying** grass on golf courses as **"crops"** or holiday villas as **"farms"**. This ensures that, like farms, they get **allocated water**. This contributes to desertification by **depleting water levels**. It also **reduces water availability** for **farms**, **reducing** their **productivity**, which leads to desertification spreading.

Desertification Case Study — Southern Spain

Desertification Has Environmental, Social and Economic Impacts

1) The demand for water to fill swimming pools and irrigate crops and golf courses has led to **conflict** over water. A **black market** for water has developed, supplied by water from **illegal boreholes**. An estimated **40%** of land in some parts of the **Segura basin** (Murcia) is illegally irrigated and **10%** of wells in the **Guadalquivir river basin** (Andalusia) are illegal.
2) Exploitation of groundwaters has led to **loss of habitats**, such as wetlands, and **reduced biodiversity** in the region. E.g. nearly **150 000 ha** of **marshland** surrounding **Doñana National Park** has been **lost** since 1900 — most of which has been deliberately drained for farming.
3) As groundwater levels lower the water can become **salinised** (very salty). When this happens the water is no longer suitable for drinking or irrigation and the **resource** is **lost**. Many wells have had to be abandoned.
4) As **aquifers** become **salinised** so do the **soils** around them, which leads to **further desertification**.
5) Desertification leaves soil **unusable for farming** and deprives farmers of their **livelihood**.

Strategies to Reduce Desertification are Being Implemented

The government's **Programme of National Action Against Desertification** aims to tackle desertification in several ways:

The **National Hydrological Plan** was adopted in **2001** to ensure that water supply meets demand by:

1) **Transferring water** from areas with a **plentiful supply** to areas with **very little**.
2) Building **desalinisation plants** to produce fresh water from saline aquifers at a cost of **€1.2 billion**.
3) **Reducing** the amount of water **wasted** during irrigation by **improving irrigation infrastructure**, e.g. by investing in technology for sprinkling and drip irrigation. The aim is to **reduce** the amount of **water** used for irrigation by **10%** (from 2002 levels), whilst **increasing** the area of **land irrigated** by **7%**.
4) Reducing pressure on water supplies by **introducing management strategies** for **aquifers** and funding awareness-raising activities to **promote efficient use** of **resources**.

The National Hydrological Plan is **controversial** as it's very expensive and some elements **aren't sustainable**. **Raising awareness** and **improving infrastructure** can help **reduce desertification**, but transporting water from one area to another is only a **short-term** solution to the shortage of water (it doesn't tackle the overuse of water that's causing desertification). Irrigation will continue to **increase** and desertification will **spread**.

Areas at **high risk** of **forest fires** are being identified and **defence plans** drawn up for them so that fires can be dealt with quickly. Areas that are destroyed have to be **reforested** and many **new areas** are being planted with trees and bushes. Since the scheme was introduced **550 000 hectares** have been forested.

Reforestation and forest management **reduces soil erosion** and so desertification.

An official **water trading scheme** has been set up that allows farmers to buy water. It costs them three times the normal price but is **lower** than the **black market price** and therefore aims to **reduce illegal exploitation** of **aquifers**.

Water trading can help to reduce **illegal** exploitation of aquifers. If water resources are **sustainably managed** then the scheme could **reduce desertification**, but if resources continue to be **over-exploited** then water trading is unlikely to reduce desertification.

Practice Questions

Q1 Which areas of Spain are most vulnerable to desertification?

Q2 Why has the volume of water needed for irrigation increased?

Q3 Describe two impacts of desertification in Spain.

Exam Question

Q1 Compare the strategies used in Spain and the Sahel to tackle desertification. [15 marks]

Last year I went to sunny Spain — and helped spread desertification...

You know the drill by now — learn all the specifics, don't skimp on the examples, blah blah blah. The more information you know the more marks you can get. And once you've learnt these pages, you're done with deserts and arid environments. Finally.

Global Hazards

This section is for Edexcel Unit 1 (World at Risk).
A bit of mayhem and disaster always makes geography more interesting... Hazards are nasty things, as you might be able to guess. They come in all shapes and sizes and some of them are getting more frequent. I'm scared.

There are Different Types of Hazard

1) A **hazard** is something that's a **potential threat** to **human life** or **property**.
2) **Natural hazards** are caused by **natural processes**, e.g. a lava flow from a volcanic eruption.
3) Natural hazards can be divided into **two** types:

Hydro-meteorological hazards (caused by **climatic** processes) — these include **droughts**, **floods**, **tropical cyclones** and **storms**.

Geophysical hazards (caused by **land** processes) — these include **earthquakes**, **volcanic eruptions** and **landslides**.

You need to know these terms:

1) **Disaster** — when a hazard **actually seriously affects** humans.
2) **Risk** — the **likelihood** that humans will be seriously affected by a hazard.
3) **Vulnerability** — how **susceptible** a **population** is to the damage caused by a hazard.

A tropical cyclone is a hazard, but when it hits land and seriously affects people and property it's a disaster, e.g. Katrina (2005).

The Disaster Risk Equation Gives the Risk of a Disaster Occurring

The risk of a hazard **causing** a disaster can be shown using the **disaster risk equation**.
The risk of disaster **increases** as:

1) The **frequency** or **severity** of **hazards increase** (e.g. more and worse flooding).
2) People's **vulnerability increases** (e.g. higher population densities in areas vulnerable to flooding, like flood plains).
3) People's **capacity to cope** is **decreased** — capacity to cope is the ability to deal with the **consequences** of a hazard, e.g. people in remote areas are further from help than people in central areas, so have a lower capacity to cope.

$$\text{Risk (R)} = \frac{\text{Hazards (H)} \times \text{Vulnerability (V)}}{\text{Capacity to cope (C)}}$$

The disaster risk equation can be used to explain why **similar hazards** can cause disasters of **different degrees**.

Example

1) Similar sized earthquakes occurred in **Kashmir, Pakistan** (2005) and **Izmit, Turkey** (1999).
2) Although the hazard was **similar** (both were earthquakes), the disasters they caused were **different** — Kashmir suffered **more loss of life** with over 75 000 deaths compared to around 18 000 in Izmit.
3) The **disaster risk equation** can help to explain **why**:
   - The people of Kashmir had a **lower capacity to cope** — it's a remote, mountainous location, which makes **access difficult**. Access was made even worse by **landslides** that buried roads into the region.
   - The population of Kashmir is **vulnerable** — the people are **poor** and **buildings** are often **badly constructed**. When some of these buildings collapsed after the earthquake, people were buried.

Global Warming is Arguably the Greatest Current Global Hazard

1) **Global warming** describes the **recent increase in average global temperature**.
2) It's a type of **climate change** (a significant change in the weather of a region over a period of at least several decades).
3) It also **causes** other types of climate change (see page 80 for more).
4) There's a **scientific consensus** that global warming is due to **human activity** (see p. 79).
5) Global warming is a **context hazard** — it's **global** in scale (affects all parts of the environment) and has the potential to **trigger other hazards** or make them **worse**.
6) Global warming is also a **chronic** (long-term) hazard — it's a **constant threat** and can't be solved **quickly** or **easily**.
7) Hazards such as global warming highlight **issues of injustice** — it isn't necessarily the people **causing** the problem who are **most affected**, e.g. richer countries often contribute **most** of the pollutants that are thought to cause global warming, but poorer countries often **suffer more** from the effects.
8) Any **solution** to global warming will be **complex** because the **causes** and **effects** are complex and not fully understood. It's a global problem requiring **international cooperation** between **governments**, **businesses** and **individuals** (see p. 85).

There's loads more on climate change on pages 76-85.

Global Hazards

Hydro-meteorological Hazards are Becoming More Frequent

1) The number of **hydro-meteorological** hazards has been **increasing** in recent years.
2) But the number of **geophysical** hazards **hasn't changed** much.
3) It's thought that the **increase** in the number of hydro-meteorological hazards is due to the **increasing** effects of **global warming** — which is thought to be largely due to **human activity** (see page 79).
4) The number of **disasters** is **increasing**. → →
   This is because of a combination of **factors**:

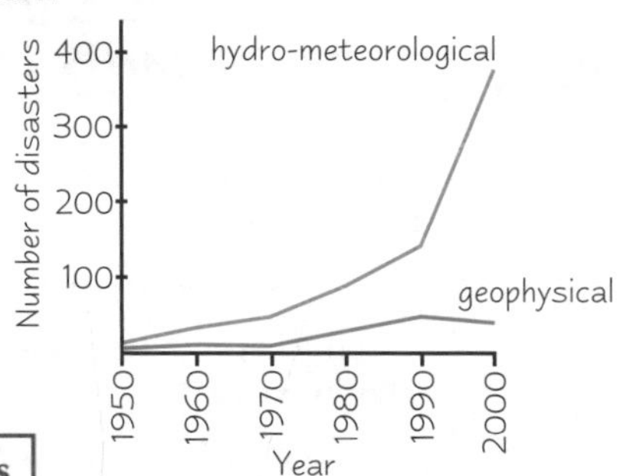

Human factors

- Rapid **population growth** and **urbanisation** — this increases the **number of people** who are **vulnerable** to hazards, especially in poor countries.
- **Increasing world poverty** — poor people are more **vulnerable** to hazards.
- **Exploitation** of **resources** — e.g. **deforestation** and **loss of wetlands** can lead to an **increased risk** of **flooding** and **landslides**.

Physical factors

- **Global warming** — it's thought to be increasing the number of **hazards**, e.g. floods and severe storms, which increases the number of **disasters**.
- **El Niño** events (oceanic current and temperature fluctuations) — these **change global weather** in an **unpredictable way**, which makes hydro-meteorological hazards more **unpredictable**.

5) Another reason why it may seem that the number of disasters has increased is because of **greater media coverage** — **more** disasters are **reported** than in the past, so it seems as if more are **actually happening**.

Deaths are Decreasing but Economic Losses are Increasing

1) The **number of deaths** caused by disasters has been **decreasing** because of improvements in **risk management strategies**:

- **Prediction** — improved technology means **some** hazards can be predicted, e.g. the **path** of **tropical cyclones** can be predicted to some extent. Advance warning means people can be **evacuated** and **property secured**.
- **Prevention** — natural hazards can't be stopped, but they can be **prevented from becoming disasters**, e.g. by using sandbags to **protect** against the effects of flooding.
- **Preparedness** — **educating people** on what to do in case of a disaster helps to **reduce** the number of deaths, e.g. **Japan** has a 'disaster preparedness day' each year when **practice earthquake evacuation drills** are carried out.

2) There's been a **levelling off** in the trend of decreasing deaths recently because the **increasing number** of **vulnerable people** in poorer countries means **more people** are being affected by disasters, leading to more deaths.
3) **Global economic losses** due to disasters are **increasing rapidly** though.

- **Actual financial cost** is the amount of money lost — this is **greatest** in **richer countries**.
- **Relative financial cost** is the amount of money lost relative to how much the people have to start with — this is greatest in **poorer countries**. **Less** actual money is lost, but the **effects** of the loss are **greater**.

Disasters can lead to further, indirect economic losses, e.g. if a country gets a lot of money from tourism, this could be affected by a disaster, which could affect the economy.

Practice Questions

Q1 Explain the difference between a hazard and a disaster.

Q2 Name one type of hazard that's increasing in frequency and give a possible explanation.

Exam Question

Q1 Describe and explain how the number of deaths and the amount of economic loss caused by disasters is changing. [15 marks]

Reality TV shows — a global hazard...

So, seeing your dad trying to be groovy on the dance floor is only a hazard as long as you keep clear of him. It causes a disaster when he tries to make you join in and waves at your friends — teenagers are particularly vulnerable to this.

Hazard Distribution

***These pages are for** Edexcel Unit 1 (World at Risk).*
Don't know about you, but I want to know where all these hazards are happening, so I can be somewhere else. Having said that, Britain's hardly a disaster hotspot, unless you attend a trainspotter's fashion show of course...

Geophysical Hazards Usually Occur Near Plate Boundaries

1) The Earth's **crust** is made up of huge plates called **tectonic plates** that sit on top of the **mantle**.
2) Plates are made of **two types** of crust:
   - The **thicker** (but **less dense**) crust is called **continental crust** — it's mostly **above** sea level.
   - The **thinner** (but **more dense**) crust is called **oceanic crust** — it's mostly **below** sea level.
3) The plates **move** because of **convection currents** in the **mantle** — the currents are caused by **temperature differences** within the mantle.
4) **Volcanoes** and **earthquakes** most commonly occur at the **boundaries** where the plates **meet**.
5) There are **three types** of plate boundary — **constructive**, **destructive** and **conservative**.

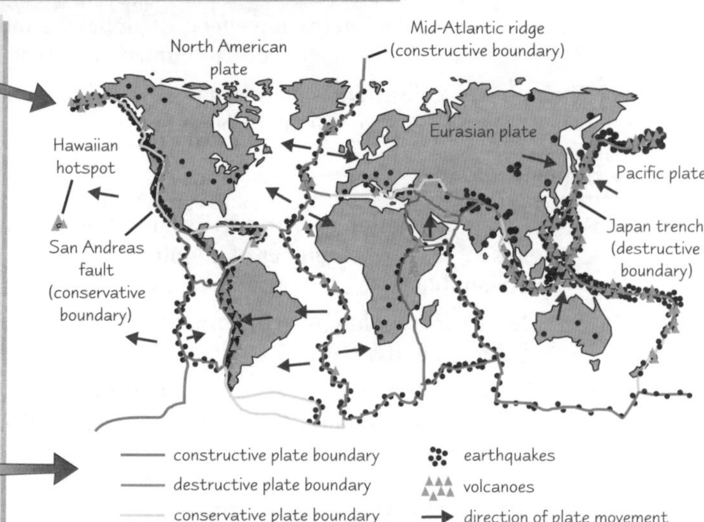

Volcanoes and Earthquakes Occur at Constructive Boundaries

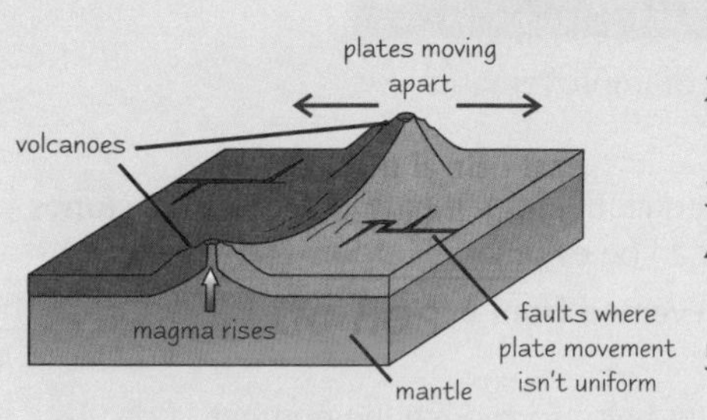

1) A **constructive boundary** occurs where two plates are moving **apart**.
2) The mantle is under **pressure** from the plates above. When they move apart, the pressure is **released** at the **boundary**.
3) The release of pressure causes the mantle to **melt**, producing **magma**.
4) The magma is **less dense** than the plate above, so it **rises** and can **erupt** to form a **volcano**.
5) For example, the **Eurasion plate** and **North American plate** are moving apart at the **mid-Atlantic ridge**. **Iceland** has been formed where magma has **risen** through the gap to form **volcanoes**.
6) The plates don't move apart in a **uniform way** — some parts move faster than others. This causes **pressure to build up**. When the pressure becomes **too much** the plate **cracks**, making a **fault line** and causing an **earthquake**. **Further earthquakes** may also occur along the fault line once it's been created.

A fault line is where a plate has cracked under pressure.

Volcanoes and Earthquakes Also Occur at Destructive Boundaries

A **destructive boundary** occurs where two plates are moving **towards each other**.

1) Where **continental crust** and **oceanic crust** are moving towards each other, the **more dense oceanic** crust is **forced under** the **less dense continental** crust (it's **subducted**).
2) The oceanic crust is **heated** by **friction** and **contact** with the upper mantle, which melts it into **magma**.

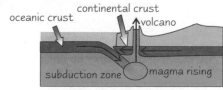

3) The magma is **less dense** than the continental crust above and will **rise** back to the surface to form **volcanoes**.
4) For example, the **Pacific plate** (oceanic crust) is subducting beneath the **Eurasian plate** (continental crust) at the **Japan trench**. The **Japanese island arc** has been formed where magma has **risen** through the crust to form **volcanoes**.
5) The same process occurs where **two plates** of **oceanic crust** are moving towards each other — the **denser** of the two will be subducted, e.g. this has formed the volcanic islands of **Indonesia**.
6) As one plate moves under the other they can **get stuck**. This causes **pressure to build up**. When the pressure becomes **too much** the plates **jerk** past each other, causing an **earthquake**.
7) Where two plates of **continental crust** are moving towards each other, **neither** is subducted so there aren't any volcanoes — but the pressure that builds up between them can cause **earthquakes**, e.g. the **Kashmir** earthquake (2005).

Hazard Distribution

Earthquakes Also Occur at Conservative Boundaries

A **conservative boundary** occurs where two plates are **moving past** each other.

1) The two plates get **locked together** in places and **pressure builds up**. As with destructive boundaries, this causes the plates to **jerk** past each other (or to **crack** forming **fault lines**) releasing the **energy** as an **earthquake**.
2) For example, the **Pacific plate** is moving past the **North American plate**. Many earthquakes occur along this boundary and at its fault lines, e.g. the **San Andreas fault** runs through **California**.

Conservative boundaries, laughed Winthorpe — they keep out the riff-raff, what!

Some Volcanoes Occur Away from Plate Boundaries

Volcanoes can occur **far away** from any **plate boundaries**, e.g. in **Hawaii**. These volcanoes are thought to be caused by **magma rising** from a **large chamber** beneath the crust. Areas like Hawaii are called **volcanic hotspots**.

Tropical Cyclones Occur over Warm Water

Tropical cyclones are huge **storms** with **strong winds** and **torrential rain**.

Global warming could lead to an increase in the strength of tropical cyclones because of increasing sea temperatures.

1) Tropical cyclones develop **above sea water** that's **26.5 °C or higher**. As warm, moist air **rises** and **condenses**, it releases energy which **increases wind speed**.
2) Tropical cyclones **lose strength** when they move **over land** because the **energy supply** from the warm water is **cut off**.
3) Most cyclones occur **between 5° and 30° north** and **south** of the **equator** — more than 30° away from the equator, the water **isn't warm enough** for cyclones to occur.
4) Cyclones spin because of the **Coriolis effect** (the force that deflects the path of winds due to the Earth's rotation).
5) Cyclones don't occur **0-5° either side** of the equator because the Coriolis effect there **isn't strong enough** to make them spin.
6) The Coriolis effect is also why they move **away from** the **equator**.
7) They move **westwards** due to the **east-west winds** in the **tropics**. For example, the **trade winds** move tropical cyclones westwards **across the Atlantic Ocean** towards the **Caribbean Sea**.
8) Tropical cyclones are also known as **hurricanes** (when they occur in the **Atlantic Ocean** or **Caribbean Sea**) and **typhoons** (when they occur in the **Pacific Ocean**).

Pacific ocean
Atlantic Ocean
Bay of Bengal
Tropic of Cancer (23° north)
Equator
Caribbean Sea
Indian Ocean
Tropic of Capricorn (23° south)
path of tropical cyclone
sea surface temperature 26.5 °C or higher

Practice Questions

Q1 Describe where tropical cyclones develop.

Q2 Explain why tropical cyclones don't develop within 5° of the equator.

Exam Questions

Q1 Explain why earthquakes occur at plate boundaries. [3 marks]

Q2 Describe and explain the global distribution of volcanoes. [10 marks]

Did you hear the one about the plate that went mad? It cracked...

So, the Earth's just like a big jigsaw puzzle, except with not many pieces. I love all this stuff about tectonics — I always found it really interesting, but then, I also have a lifesize cardboard cut-out of Han Solo in my room, so judge for yourself...

Disaster Hotspot Case Study — California

These pages are for Edexcel Unit 1 (World at Risk).
Maybe I was doing California a disservice when I said a trainspotter's fashion show was a disaster hotspot. California's the real deal — it's positively brimming with natural ways to be distinctly uncomfortable.

California is a Disaster Hotspot

Disaster hotspots are **vulnerable places** at risk from **two or more hazards**.

The state of **California** in the **USA** has many **highly populated** towns and cities at **risk** from a **variety of hazards**. The map below shows **examples** and **locations** of **past hazards** that have caused **disasters**.

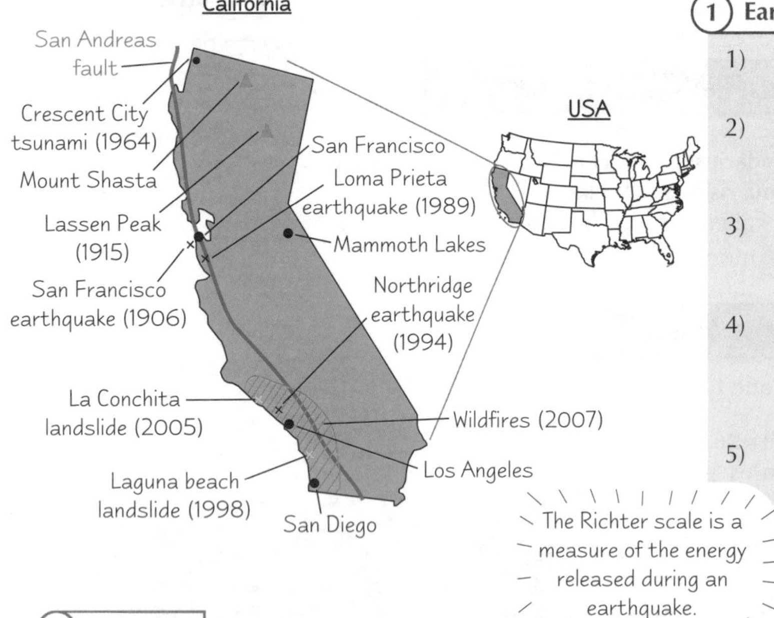

1) Earthquakes

1) The **San Andreas fault** runs the length of California — it's a **conservative** plate boundary (see p. 71).
2) **Earthquakes** occur when **pressure** between the plates **builds up** and then is **suddenly released** as they jerk past each other.
3) California has **two or three** earthquakes **each year** that are powerful enough to damage structures (5.5+ on the **Richter scale**).
4) Studies of the **frequency** and **magnitude** of **past earthquakes** show that there's a **good chance** of an earthquake of magnitude 7.0+ hitting the San Francisco Bay area **before 2025**.
5) Past disasters include the **San Francisco earthquake of 1906** (thought to have measured 7.8), which along with subsequent fires, **destroyed** much of the city.

The Richter scale is a measure of the energy released during an earthquake.

2) Droughts

Some hazards can increase the likelihood of other hazards occurring, e.g. droughts make wildfires more likely.

1) Drought in California can be caused by **anticyclones** (**long-lasting** periods of **high air pressure** with **sinking, dry air**). Dry, sinking air means **no rain**.
2) Drought can also be caused by **La Niña** events (periods when the **surface water** in the **eastern Pacific Ocean** is **cooler**). This means **less evaporation**, so there's **less precipitation**.
3) Another cause of drought is **increased wind** blowing westward from the **desert areas** that are east of California, e.g. from Arizona. The dry air has **no moisture** to cause **precipitation**.
4) The most devastating effect of drought in California is **wildfires** — dry vegetation is extremely flammable, so fires **spread quickly** over **wide areas**.
5) The wildfires in **southern California** in October 2007 **killed 22 people** and destroyed **1300 homes**.

3) Tsunamis

1) A **tsunami** is a series of **large waves** that can **flood coastal areas**.
2) They can be **caused by earthquakes** on the sea bed, or **landslides** into the sea.
3) Earthquakes under the **Pacific Ocean** could cause a tsunami along the California coastline.
4) An earthquake off the coast of **Alaska** in 1964 caused a tsunami to strike the coast of northern California, **killing 12 people** in **Crescent City**.

Volcanoes in California — they'll be back.

4) Landslides

1) **Landslides** occur on **unstable steep land**. Land can be made unstable by **coastal erosion** or **extreme weather** (rainstorms). Landslides can also be **triggered** by **earthquakes**.
2) The risk of landslide disasters in California is high because of **building on and around steep slopes**, as well as building on **coastal land** overlooking the ocean, e.g. **La Conchita**.

5) Volcanoes

1) There hasn't been a **volcanic eruption** in California since **1915** (**Lassen Peak**).
2) But there are volcanoes **being monitored** for **potential eruptions**, e.g. **Lassen Peak**, **Mount Shasta** and the volcanoes around **Mammoth Lakes**.

Disaster Hotspot Case Study — California

*California is **Wealthy** but **Parts** of the **Population** are **Vulnerable***

Even **wealthy parts** of **wealthy nations** have populations that are **vulnerable** to the risks from hazards:

1) More than **70%** of California's population live **within 50 km** of a **fault line** (see p. 70).
2) There's a lot of building on **unstable land** — this can lead to **soil liquefaction** during earthquakes (where the ground can become more like a **liquid**), which damages buildings and **increases** the **risk of landslides**. This was a major problem during the **Loma Prieta** earthquake in 1989.
3) There are many buildings along the **coast** that are vulnerable to **tsunamis**.
4) California is a **wealthy state**, but there are very **poor areas within it** — around **20%** of the residents in **Los Angeles** live **below** the official **poverty line**. These people have the **lowest capacity to cope** when affected by a hazard (see p. 68).
5) California has a **massive economy**, so there are likely to be **huge economic losses** when a disaster occurs.

*You Need to **Research Hazard Risk** in **Your Local Area***

Looking at **disaster hotspots** shows that some places are at **more risk** than others. California's obviously a bit of a nasty spot for hazards, but you need to think about places **closer to home** — in the exam they might ask you about **real** (where hazards do occur) or **potential** (where they could occur) **hazard risk** in your **local area**. You need to be able to talk about:

1) Any **past events** that might have happened in the area you live, e.g. rivers that have **flooded**.
2) Any **likely future events** that could happen, e.g. landslides caused by **coastal erosion**.
3) The **impact** of these events on **people**, **property** and the **environment**.

It's important to think about how the risk of hazards in your area may be **changing** because of things like **global warming**. If global warming causes more **extreme weather**, or **rising sea levels**, it'll affect the **potential risk** in your area.

You can research **hazard patterns** and **risk potential** in different ways:

1) Use **Ordnance Survey® (OS®) maps** to find **where** potential hazards could happen, e.g. to find the location of **rivers** and the **populations at risk** if they flood.
2) Use OS maps to look for **vulnerable populations** near to **potential hazards** — where it's more likely a **hazard** could cause a **disaster**, e.g. housing estates on a river flood plain.
3) Use **Geographical Information Systems (GIS)** — **computer programs** that are used by geographers to look at hazard patterns and risk potential on a **local** scale. They usually look at different bits of **locational information** together (like different maps overlaid on top of each other). For example, a map of the **tectonic plate boundaries** could be overlaid with a map showing **river flood plains** — this would show where the two hazards **coincide**.

Practice Questions

Q1 Define the term disaster hotspot.

Q2 Describe one way you could research hazard risk potential in your local area.

Exam Question

Q1 Using specific examples, explain why California is considered to be a disaster hotspot. [15 marks]

Landslides — not as much fun as they sound...

California's a great place and everything, but crikey, I can think of more sensible places to build a load of massive cities — it's got the lot — volcanoes, earthquakes, massive waves (in a bad way surfers), landslides, droughts, dragons, alien invasions... Maybe I got carried away a little, but my point stands. There have already been some disasters and it's likely there'll be more.

Disaster Hotspot Case Study — The Philippines

***These pages are for** Edexcel Unit 1 (World at Risk).*
If you thought California was a bad spot for people who like their surroundings to not try to kill them, then wait till you get a load of the Philippines...

The Philippines is a Disaster Hotspot

The Philippines is a group of islands in **south-east Asia** with a **vulnerable population** at **risk** from a **variety of hazards**. The map below shows **examples** and **locations** of **past hazards** that have caused **disasters**.

1) Volcanoes

1) The Philippines is near to a **destructive plate boundary** (see p. 70), where the **Philippine plate** is being **subducted** beneath the **Eurasian plate**.
2) The islands were formed by a combination of **folding** at the boundary and **volcanoes** formed from magma that has **risen** to the surface from the mantle below.
3) **Mount Pinatubo** is a volcano that erupted in 1991. Many people were **evacuated**, **buildings collapsed**, **crops** were **destroyed** and **agricultural land** was **ruined** by falling ash.

The Philippines
plate boundary
Angeles
Luzon earthquake (1990)
Mount Pinatubo (1991)
Manila
Philippine plate
Asia
path of typhoon Xangsane (2006)
Mount Mayon
Eurasian plate
southern Leyte landslide (2006)
fault lines
area affected by the Moro Gulf tsunami (1976)

2) Earthquakes

1) The **Philippine plate** and the **Eurasian plate** can become **locked together** as one moves under the other. This causes **pressure** to **build up**. When the pressure is too much the plates **jerk** past each other, causing an **earthquake**.
2) Earthquakes also occur at **fault lines** in the area, where the plate has **cracked** under pressure.
3) Earthquakes occur **daily**, but most **can't be felt** (they're low on the **Richter scale**).
4) An earthquake of **magnitude 7.8** occurred on **Luzon island** in 1990, killing over **1500 people**.

Multiple hazards in one area can increase the likelihood of other hazards occurring, e.g. falling ash from a volcanic eruption can combine with typhoons to cause mudflows (lahars).

3) Landslides

1) The Philippines get a **lot of rain**. If a lot of rain falls in a **short space of time** in areas with **steep slopes**, **landslides** can occur.
2) Landslides can also be **triggered** by **earthquakes**.
3) A landslide occurred on **Leyte island** in 2006 after it had been raining heavily for **10 days**. A whole village was **buried** (including a school), **killing hundreds**.

Some people love a good lahar at the end of a hard day.

4) Typhoons

1) The Philippines have around **10 typhoons** (tropical cyclones, see p. 71) **every year**.
2) They **develop** in the Pacific Ocean and move **westwards** over the islands.
3) **Typhoon Xangsane** swept across **Manila** and the surrounding **densely populated area** in the North in 2006. High winds and torrential rain **destroyed homes** and caused **flooding**, **landslides** and the **loss** of power and water.

5) Tsunamis

1) **Earthquakes** in any of the oceans surrounding the Philippines could cause a **tsunami** (see p. 72).
2) In 1976 an earthquake of **magnitude 7.9** caused a tsunami that hit the coastline around the **Moro Gulf** on the southern island of Mindanao. **Thousands were killed** and several cities were **devastated**.

Disaster Hotspot Case Study — The Philippines

6 Droughts

1) Some parts of the Philippines have a distinct **wet** and **dry** season, e.g. **Manila** (and the surrounding densely populated area) is **dry** between **November** and **April**, and wet between **May** and **October**.
2) **Drought** can occur when the wet season hasn't brought **enough rain** to last the dry season, or the dry season is particularly **harsh**.
3) There was a **drought** on **Luzon island** in **2005**. The reduction in rainfall decreased water flow in rivers, which affected **power production** from **hydroelectric** power plants. This affected the **power supply** to the **entire region**. Without power for an **extended period**, **economic** and **social** activity were severely **reduced**.

7 Flooding

1) During the wet season, **floods** can be caused by **typhoons** and **heavy rain**.
2) Flooding affects many areas, even some that are also affected by **drought**.
3) **Major floods** occurred in the **lowland areas** around **Manila** in the 1970s and in recent years. **Crops** were **devastated** in this major rice growing region.

*The **Population** of the Philippines is **Vulnerable***

The Philippines isn't a really poor country (some bits of it are very wealthy), but much of its population remains **vulnerable** to the effects of a hazard, or has a **low capacity to cope**.

1) When a hazard strikes a **densely populated area**, there's a **greater risk** it will become a **disaster**, e.g. the island of **Luzon** and the area around **Manila** are more at risk because they have a **high population density**.
2) **Population pressures** have led to **deforestation** of upland areas for agriculture. This **increases** the risk of **landslides** in populated areas.
3) The Philippines has a **fast growing economy**, but there are still many people **below the poverty line** who will be most severely affected by a disaster.
4) Some **fast growing settlements** have been built near to **hazardous areas**, e.g. **Angeles** was built near to **Mount Pinatubo**. It wasn't thought of as a threat because it hadn't erupted for a **long time** (since 1380).
5) Many people live in **unstable locations**, e.g. the **Aeta tribe** were living on the slopes of **Mount Pinatubo** when it erupted in 1991.

Practice Questions

Q1 Name four hazards from which the Philippines are at risk.

Q2 Give two reasons why the people of the Philippines are vulnerable to disasters.

Exam Question

Q1 a) Mark on the map of the Philippines (right) the location of any plate boundaries and fault lines, as well as one example of an earthquake disaster and one example of a volcanic disaster. [4 marks]

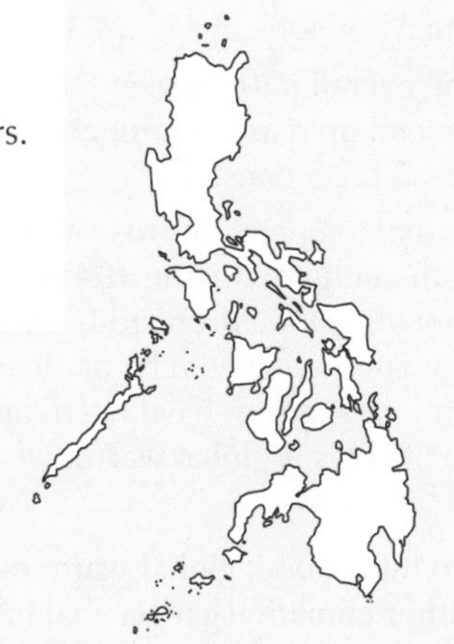

b) Using specific examples, compare and contrast the Philippines with California as a disaster hotspot. [15 marks]

I like my cup of typh-oooooon milky with three sugars...

As my geography teacher used to say, case studies are here to 'put the meat on the bones'. Hmm, regardless of how odd that may sound, the point is that it's all very well learning the theory, but with geography it's really important that you know details of real-world examples (case studies) — that's how you'll get top marks in your exam.

Evidence for Climate Change

***These pages are for** Edexcel Unit 1 (World at Risk).*
Climate change is the big cheese, the head honcho and the top dog when it comes to hazards at the moment. Global warming's a big part of how the climate's changing right now, but it's not the first time the climate's changed...

Climate is Constantly Changing

Climate change is any **significant** change in the **weather** of a region over a period of at least **several decades**, e.g. increasing average **temperature** or **rainfall**, or a change in the usual **wind direction**.

The climate **constantly changes** over **long**, **medium** and **short** time scales, it **always has**, and it **always will**.

Long-term climate change

1) Taking **temperature** as an indicator of climate, there have been **huge changes** over Earth's history — temperatures have been much **higher** at some points in the **past** than they are **today**.
2) Looking at more detailed data for the **last 400 000** years, you can see a more detailed **fluctuation.**
3) Climate shifted between **cold glacial periods** that lasted around 100 000 years and **warmer interglacial periods** that lasted around 10 000 years. We're in an **interglacial period now**.

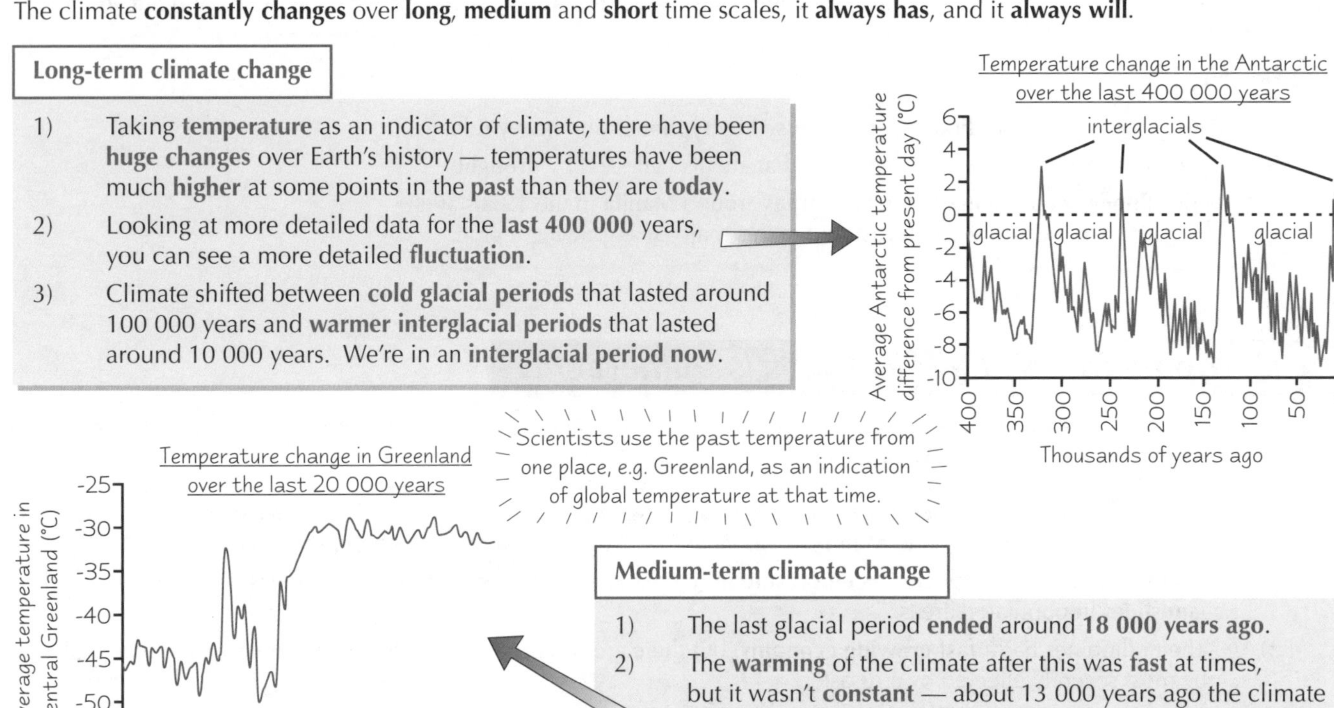

Medium-term climate change

1) The last glacial period **ended** around **18 000 years ago.**
2) The **warming** of the climate after this was **fast** at times, but it wasn't **constant** — about 13 000 years ago the climate **switched back** to cooler conditions for about 1000 years.
3) Around 5000 years ago, temperatures were **1-2 °C higher** than today.

Short-term climate change

1) **Global warming** is the term used for the **rapidly increasing global temperature** over the **last century** — there's been a **sharp rise** in temperature when you look at the last **1000 years**.
2) The **overall pattern** over the last century shows a general **increase** in **temperature**, but the pattern hasn't been **constant**.
3) Global temperatures **rose steadily** from the **early 20th century** until the **1940s** (although they fluctuated annually), then **dropped** back down. Scientists thought there would be another **glacial period**, but temperatures have **risen rapidly** again **since** the 1970s (this is **global warming**).

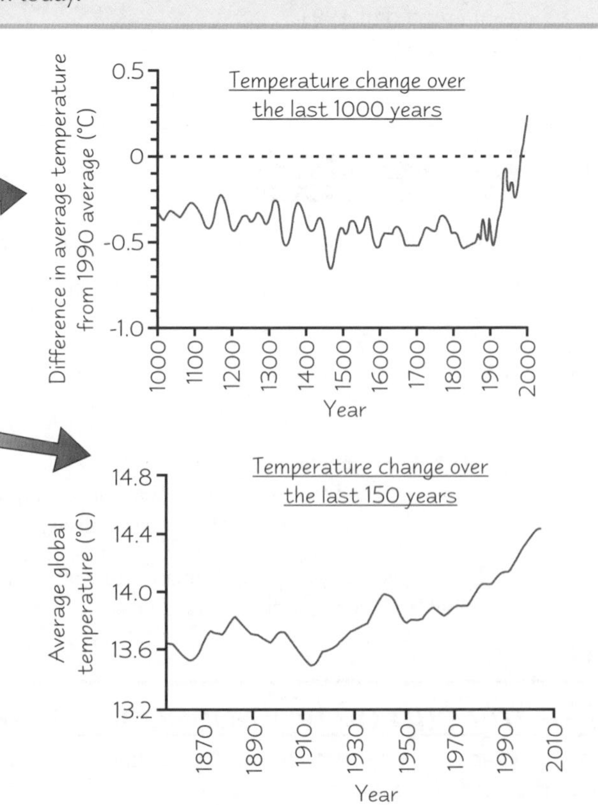

You need to think about **global warming changes** in the context of all the **other climatic changes** that have occurred.

It's important to remember that climate change **isn't fully understood** — but the **changes in temperature** (and the **speed** at which they're occurring) over the last century are **worrying** because they're **thought to be unprecedented** (never seen before).

Evidence for Climate Change

There's Evidence for Long, Medium and Short-Term Climate Change

Long-term change

① Ice cores

1) Scientists drill deep into **ice sheets** (**huge masses of ice**) to extract **cores of ice**. Ice sheets are made up of **layers** of ice — **one** layer is formed **every year**. So the ice at the bottom of the core is really, really old.
2) They can analyse the **gases** trapped when the ice formed to tell what the **temperature** was each year. Then they can figure out how temperature has **changed over time**.
3) E.g. a core has been extracted from the **Antarctic ice sheet** to a depth of **3000 m** and has been used to show temperature for the last **400 000 years** (see long-term climate change graph on previous page).

② Pollen analysis

1) **Pollen** from plants is often **preserved** in **sediment**.
2) The preserved pollen can be **identified** and **dated** to show when it was **released**.
3) Scientists know the **conditions** that plants live in now. When they find preserved pollen from similar plants, it indicates that **conditions** were **similar** when that pollen was **produced**.

③ Sea level change

1) **Sea level** is affected by things like the volume of water **stored as ice**.
2) Past sea levels are shown by **raised beaches** (formed when sea levels were **higher**). Raised beaches can be **dated**. They can indicate that **less water** was stored as **ice** (i.e. it was **warmer**).

Medium-term change

① Historical records

Historical records can **indirectly** indicate **different conditions** in the past. E.g. **agricultural reports** (such as harvest times) show changing conditions throughout **human history**.

② Tree rings

1) A new **tree ring** is formed each year as a tree grows. If conditions that year were good, the tree ring produced will be **thick**.
2) Scientists can take **cores** and count the rings to find the **age** of a tree. They then look at the **thickness** of each ring to see what the climate was like **each year**.
3) Tree rings can reliably **show** and **date** climate conditions up to **10 000 years ago**.

③ Retreating glaciers

1) Scientists can tell **how big** a glacier was and how far it **extended** by looking at the position of **rocks deposited** by it. These rocks can be **dated** to show when they were deposited.
2) The **distance** of the rocks from the current glacier **indicates climate change**. E.g. if the front of the glacier is now miles away from the rocks it indicates that **temperatures** have **increased** over that period of time.

Short-term change

① Weather records

1) Details of **weather conditions** have been consistently **collected since 1861**.
2) These can be used to show detailed **climate changes** over the short time period they've been collected.

② Polar ice melt

1) Current research into the behaviour of **polar ice** shows a **reduction** in the amount of ice at both poles.
2) Changes in the **extent of polar ice** shows changes in the climatic factors affecting them, e.g. **increased melting** shows **increased temperatures**.

③ Ecosystem changes

Changes in temperature affect the availability of **food** and **shelter**. This affects what **species** live in an area. So scientists can use **changes** in how species are **distributed** to indicate changes in the **climate**.

Practice Questions

Q1 Suggest two ways of investigating medium-term climate change.

Q2 Suggest two ways of investigating short-term climate change.

Exam Question

Q1 Outline the sources of evidence for long-term climate change. [10 marks]

Ice cores tells us that ice was mostly mint flavoured 100 000 years ago...

Another thing my geography teacher used to say was 'Does that make some sort of sense?' I'd say 'Yes, it makes perfect nonsense.' Hopefully, this is all OK — the climate's always been changing, but global warming's an unusually large and rapid change.

Causes of Climate Change

***These pages are for** Edexcel Unit 1 (World at Risk).*
So here's the answer to what's causing all this climate change — aliens. I wish. Actually, it's a little more complicated...

The **Causes** of **Climate Change** May be **Natural** and **Human**

Some changes in climate are caused by changes in how the **Sun's energy** is **received**, **trapped** and **distributed** around the Earth, e.g. when **more energy** is received, the Earth will get **hotter**. When **less energy** is received, the Earth will get **cooler**.

However, some changes in climate are caused by **human activity** (see next page).

Earth's Climate Changes **Naturally** Without **Human Influence**

1) Variations in the Earth's orbit

The way the Earth **moves around** the Sun **affects** the way the Earth **receives energy** from the Sun. Earth's movement around the Sun **gradually changes** in **three ways**, which in turn affect **global climate**.

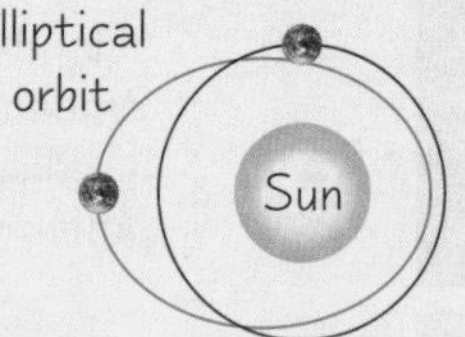

1) Stretch
   - The path of the Earth's orbit around the Sun **changes** from an almost perfect **circle** to an **ellipse** and back again about every **96 000** years.
   - This changes the **distance** from the Sun to the Earth, and so the **amount of energy** the Earth receives from the Sun (at different times of the year).
   - Earth's orbit is **elliptical** right now — it's **closest** to the Sun in **January** and furthest away in **July**.

Earth's axis
23.5°
24.4°
21.8°

2) Tilt
   - The Earth is **tilted** at an angle as it orbits the Sun, called its **axis** (currently 23.5°).
   - This changes between about 21.8° and 24.4° over a cycle of about **41 000** years.
   - The change in **tilt** changes the **amount of energy** that different **latitudes** receive, **changing global climate**.
   - When the tilt is **greater** (24.4°) areas that receive **lots of energy**, such as **the tropics**, will be **larger**. Other climate regions, such as the **temperate zones** beyond the tropics, will be **smaller**.

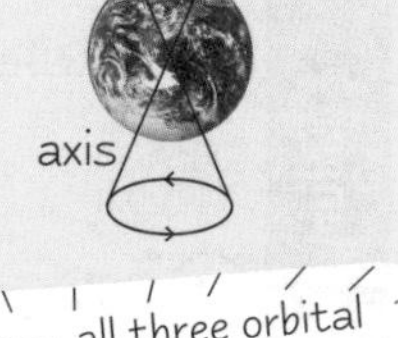

3) Wobble
   - The axis of the Earth also **wobbles** like a spinning top on a cycle of about **22 000** years.
   - Because Earth is closest to the Sun in January, winter in the northern hemisphere is **mild** and summer is **cool**.
   - The wobble of the axis means this **gradually changes** — the **seasons** will eventually **swap over**.
   - When this happens, the Earth will still be closest to the Sun in **January**, but this will now be **summer** in the **northern hemisphere**. The Earth will still be furthest away from the Sun in **July**, but this will now be **winter** in the **northern hemisphere**.
   - So in the northern hemisphere, winter would then be **colder** because it would be at the time when the Earth is **further** from the Sun, and summer would be **hotter**, because it's at the time when the Earth is **closer** to the Sun.

Remember — all three orbital changes are going on at the same time, affecting each other.

2) Variations in solar output

1) The Sun's output of **energy** isn't **constant**.
2) **Sunspots** are darker areas on the Sun that **increase** solar energy output.
3) They're thought to **increase** and **decrease** in number in an **11 year cycle** — though there's variation within this cycle.
4) E.g. a period of **cooling** in the late 17th century called the **little ice age** is thought to have coincided with a period when sunspot activity was very **low**.

3) Meteor impacts

1) The impact of a **meteor** (up to 10 m across) or an **asteroid** (larger than 10 m across) forms a large crater and can throw up huge amounts of **material** into the **atmosphere**.
2) This can result in a lot of **sunlight** (energy) being **blocked** out for **months** or even **years**, changing the climate.
3) E.g. the mass extinction of the **dinosaurs** is widely thought to have been caused by the **climate change** brought about by a massive **asteroid impact**.

Causes of Climate Change

4 Volcanic eruptions

1) Major **volcanic eruptions** also eject large quantities of **material** into the **atmosphere**.
2) This can also block out **sunlight (energy)**, which changes the climate.
3) E.g. the eruption of **Mount Tambora** in **Indonesia** in **1815** is thought to have **lowered global temperature** by about **0.5 °C**.

Human Activity is Causing the *Recent Change in Climate*

The recent **rise** in **global temperature** (**global warming**) and the **rate** of this increase is **unheard of** in **historical terms**. There's a **scientific consensus** that this temperature rise is **caused** by human activity (it can't be **explained** by **natural causes**, which usually happen **more slowly**).

Climate is affected **most** by **two human activities**:

Ozone is a greenhouse gas in the lower atmosphere. Don't get it confused with the ozone layer higher in the atmosphere (which filters out harmful UV). Human activity has caused a reduction in the ozone layer in some places, e.g. above the Antarctic.

1. Enhanced greenhouse gas emissions

- **Greenhouse gases** include CO_2, **methane**, **ozone** and **water vapour**.
- The **greenhouse effect** is where greenhouse gases absorb **outgoing energy**, so less is **lost** to space. It's **essential** for keeping the planet **warm**.
- But **too much** greenhouse gas in the atmosphere means **too much** energy is trapped and the planet **warms up**.
- CO_2 is **released** into the atmosphere when **fossil fuels** like coal, oil, natural gas and petrol are **burnt**, e.g. in power stations or in cars.
- Since the industrial revolution in the mid-19th century levels of **atmospheric** CO_2 have **increased** from **280 ppm** (parts per million) to **380 ppm**. The level had been **broadly stable** for the previous 10 000 years.
- The **increase** in CO_2 has caused the **increase** in **temperature** (**global warming**) over the same period because of the **enhanced greenhouse effect**.

2. Destruction of natural CO_2 sinks

- CO_2 **sinks store** CO_2, keeping it out of the atmosphere — so it's **not contributing** to the greenhouse effect.
- The biggest sinks are the **oceans** — CO_2 **dissolves** in sea water and gets moved to the deep ocean by natural currents.
- Another big sink is **plants** — plants **take in** CO_2 and convert it into **organic matter** using photosynthesis. It's also stored in the soil as **dead organic matter**.
- CO_2 is **released** into the atmosphere when trees are **burnt** by forest fires or to make way for agriculture.
- It was thought that a lot of **greenhouse gas emissions** from humans could be **stored** in CO_2 sinks. It's now thought they **won't** be able to **keep pace** with **increasing** emissions, so more CO_2 will go directly into the **atmosphere**.

Practice Questions

Q1 Name two natural events that can affect climate change.

Q2 Explain how one variation in the Earth's orbit can affect climate.

Exam Question

Q1 Describe and explain how human activity is affecting climate change. [15 marks]

Destruction of sinks — no more washing up for me then...

So, the unusually large and rapid change I was talking about has rather a lot to do with us. It isn't just that the planet's as fickle as a fridge that thinks it's an oven — I'm hot, no, I'm cold, hang on, I'm roasting, no, I'm freezing, I'm burning, I'm melting...

Impacts of Climate Change

***These pages are for** Edexcel Unit 1 (World at Risk).*
Oooo, now we're getting into the juicy bits — what's going to happen to us and the planet and how we can predict it. Come on, I'll give you a pound if you can guess how accurate our predictions are.

Global Warming is Causing **Ice** to **Melt**...

Don't forget — global warming is a type of climate change.

1) The melting of **ice on land** (e.g. the Greenland and Antarctic ice sheets) means that water **stored** as ice returns to the oceans.
2) This **increases** the **volume of water** in the oceans and causes the **SEA LEVEL** to **RISE**. This kind of sea level change (caused by an increase in water volume) is called **eustatic** sea level change.
3) If **all the remaining ice sheets** melted it would cause global sea level to rise by between **60 and 80 metres**.
4) Increased global temperatures also means that the oceans get **warmer** and **expand**. This **thermal expansion** also **increases** the **volume** of the water, causing sea level to rise **further**.
5) This could raise sea levels by between **8** and **80 cm** for each increase in global temperature of **1 °C**.

Only melting ice on land affects eustatic rising. If sea ice, such as Arctic ice, melts it just replaces its own volume in the water.

Predictions of how much sea level will rise in the future are **uncertain** and **differ a lot** (see next page). An international group of scientists, called the **Intergovernmental Panel on Climate Change** (**IPCC**), look at the **risks** of climate change — they think sea levels could rise by between **18 and 59 cm** by the end of the century.

Any rise in sea levels will have a **global impact**, but it will be **greater** in some places than others. For example:

Larry the lamppost looked fondly on his last sunset before the sea swallowed him forever.

Bangladesh

1) **80%** of the land area in Bangladesh is **low-lying**. Any rise in sea level will **submerge large areas**.
2) This would affect lots of people as Bangladesh has a **very high population density** (around 1000 people per km^2).
3) The situation would be made worse as it's a **poor country** — the population are **vulnerable**, with a low **capacity to cope**.

The Maldives

1) The Maldives are an extremely **low-lying** set of islands in the **Indian Ocean**. A rise in sea level of 0.5 m would submerge most of the **country**.
2) Although the population isn't poor, the economy is **dependent** on **tourism**, which would be threatened by a rise in sea level.

...And **Permafrost** to **Thaw**

1) Permafrost is **ground** that has been **permanently frozen** for two years or more. It covers around 20% of the Earth's land surface.
2) Areas of permafrost are **natural sinks** of CO_2 (see p. 79). It's stored as organic material in the soil. Thawing of permafrost **releases** some of this, contributing further to global warming.
3) Thawing of permafrost causes the **collapse** of **buildings** and **pipelines** built on it. It may also bring **economic benefits** to **humans** though, e.g. it's easier to look for and extract **natural resources** (like fossil fuels) in areas of **unfrozen ground**.

Global Warming is Also **Causing** Other **Changes in Climate**

Changes in global temperature affect **global weather patterns**. For example, global warming is thought to be causing:

1) An **increase** in the **frequency** of **extreme weather events**, e.g. increasing ocean temperatures may mean an increased risk of **tropical cyclones** over a wider area.
2) A **change** in the **distribution of climatic regions**, e.g. **colder polar** regions may **shrink** and **warmer tropical regions** may **advance** to higher latitudes.
   - This affects **ecology** (the distribution and abundance of organisms). Species will have to **migrate** to remain in a suitable climate and, if they can't migrate, they may become **extinct**.
   - It also affects **agriculture** — e.g. some areas become unsuitable for **cultivation** as **climatic factors** such as **temperature** and the **timing of the seasons** alter.
   - Regional climate changes may bring **benefits** to some **human activities**, e.g. **economic benefits** of **tourism** where the climate has become warmer.

Impacts of Climate Change

Emissions Scenarios are Used to Predict Impacts of Global Warming

There's a scientific consensus that human factors, such as **CO_2 emissions**, are **causing** global warming. Scientists try to **predict** how **emissions** will **change** in the future, so they can try to predict the **change in climate** and its **impacts**:

1) The **IPCC** has produced a number of **emissions scenarios**, which are **predictions** of how human CO_2 emissions will **change** up until 2100.
2) Scenarios include:
   - Emissions **not increasing** much more (scenario 5, minimum emissions).
   - Emissions continuing to **grow** as they are now (**'business as usual'**).
   - Emissions **increasing** by a lot (scenario 1, maximum emissions).
   - Emissions being controlled by **sustainable management** strategies.
3) They can put all these different scenarios into **global climate models** (computer models of how the climate works), to see how the climate could **change** with each scenario, e.g. how much global temperature will **rise**.
4) Then these can be used to show how the **different climate changes** can cause **different impacts**, e.g. different levels of **sea level change**.

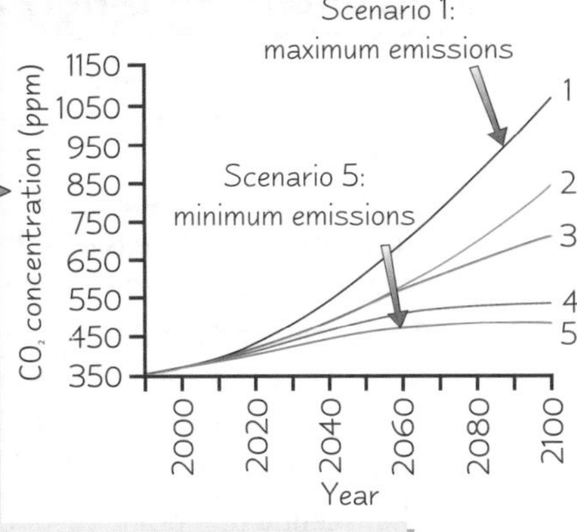

Scenario	Sea level rise between 2000 and 2100
2	0.23 - 0.51 m
3	0.21 - 0.48 m
4	0.18 - 0.38 m

It's **difficult to predict** the impacts of changes in the climate because there's so much **uncertainty**:

1) We don't actually know how emissions will **change**, i.e. which emission scenario is most **accurate**.
2) We don't know how much of the emissions will be **absorbed** by things like **natural CO_2 sinks** (see p. 79).
3) We don't know what exact **climate changes** each emission scenario will **cause**.
4) The extent of climate change due to **natural causes** (without human influence) **isn't known**.
5) We don't know what attempts there will be to **manage the impacts** of climate change, or how **successful** they'll be.

Combined Impacts May Lead to a Tipping Point

Climate change could reach a **tipping point** — where a slight rise in temperature would cause **catastrophic** and **irreversible** changes to the environment, creating a much **more hazardous** world.

This may happen because of **positive feedback loops** — where a **change** in the climate is **speeded up** by the impacts it's **already caused**. For example:

> Global warming causes **melting** of Arctic **sea ice**. As sea ice melts it leaves **darker sea water** in its place. Sea water has a **lower albedo** (the amount a surface **reflects** the sun's radiation) than ice, so **more radiation** is **absorbed** by the water. This **warms** the **water**, which **causes more ice to melt**, and so on...

The boys on board the good ship Titanic II knew all about tipping points.

The **combined effect** of positive feedback on several of the impacts of global warming, e.g. ice melt and the destruction of CO_2 sinks, may lead to a **tipping point**.

Practice Questions

Q1 Explain how global warming causes eustatic rise in sea level.

Q2 Other than eustatic sea level rise, name two other potential impacts of global warming.

Exam Question

Q1 With reference to IPCC emissions scenarios, explain why the impacts of global warming are difficult to predict. [15 marks]

I.P. in the C. — and the sea level rises...

Did I say a pound? I meant a pound of potatoes. Predicting climate change and its impacts isn't an exact science — maybe nothing will change and the future's just rosy, or maybe the whole world's going to blow up/melt down/sink. Take your pick.

Climate Change — Case Studies

These pages are for Edexcel Unit 1 (World at Risk).
Aaaah we're back in case study land — a chance for you to make some real-life sense of my theoretical jibber-jabber. Global warming's affecting the whole planet, but some places are really getting it in the neck.

*The **Arctic** is a **Vulnerable Environment***

The **Arctic** is the area around the **North Pole**. It includes the northern parts of Asia, North America and Europe. **Global warming** is affecting the Arctic **directly**:

1) The **area** of **Arctic sea ice** (frozen sea water) has been **shrinking** at an increasing rate — some scientists think there won't be any sea ice in the summer by **2030**.
2) The **Greenland ice sheet** is **melting** — most scientists think the rate of melting has **increased** in recent years.
3) The **permafrost** (see p. 80) **boundary** is moving **north** and the area covered by permafrost is **shrinking**.
4) The **treeline** (the point beyond which trees can't grow) is moving **north** and the area where trees can't grow is **shrinking**.

These effects are having **indirect impacts** on the **environment** and **ecology** (the **distribution** and **abundance** of organisms) of the Arctic.

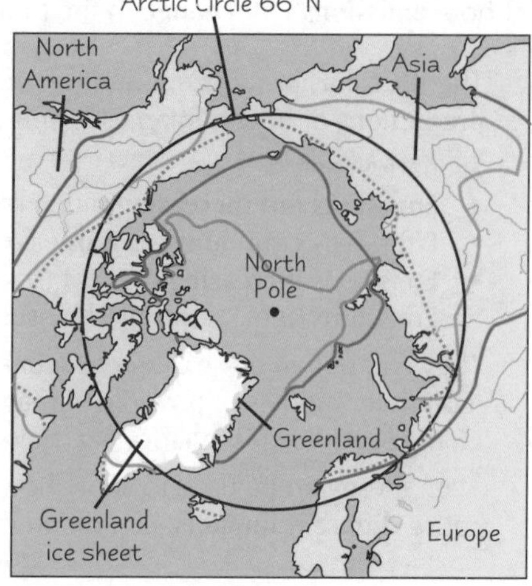

Global Warming Will Have a Variety of Impacts on the Arctic

Environmental impacts

1) Melting of ice sheets like the **Greenland ice sheet** will mean an injection of **fresh water** into the sea. This will cause changes in the **density** of the water and could **disrupt ocean currents** like the **north Atlantic drift**.
2) Thawing of permafrost **releases** more CO_2 and methane — permafrost's a **natural sink** (see p. 79).

Ecological impacts

1) Changing **climatic regions** (see p. 80) means the **habitats** (where species live) of some species are being **reduced** or **lost**. E.g. polar bears use areas of **sea ice** to hunt for food. As this is lost polar bears may become **endangered** in the wild.
2) Some parts of the Arctic have very **sensitive ecosystems** — there are **few species**, so the loss of one may have **devastating** impacts on other species that rely on them.
3) In other parts of the Arctic, like the ocean, the **number** and **diversity** of **species** (e.g. fish) may **increase** as **sea ice coverage** is **reduced** and **temperatures increase**.

Socio-economic impacts

1) Shrinking sea ice could open up **new shipping routes** in the summer.
2) **New natural resources** may be exploited, e.g. less sea ice increases the area available for **fishing**.
3) It's also thought there are **undiscovered oil** and **gas** reserves in the Arctic — unfrozen ground would make them easier to **find** and **extract**.
4) Access to new resources may lead to **conflict** over which countries **own them** though.
5) **Warmer** soils and climate may **increase** the **opportunity** for **agriculture** or **forestry**.
6) **Thawing of permafrost** can result in **collapsed buildings** and **broken pipelines** where ground has become **less stable**.

It's an **unfair world** — it isn't necessarily the people **causing** climate change who are **most affected**. As with the Arctic, the greatest **environmental and ecological** damage often happens **away** from those causing the problems.

Arctic Warming Has Consequences for the Rest of the World

The **impacts** of global warming on the Arctic will affect the rest of the **planet** too.

Interlinked systems — if you change one system, all the others change too.

1) **Melting ice sheets** will add to **rising** global **sea levels**.
2) **Ocean currents** in the Arctic are affected by **salinity changes** (freshwater from melting ice sheets changes the **density** of sea water), which affects **global ocean currents** because they operate as an **interlinked system**.
3) Changing **temperatures**, **sea ice** and **landscapes** affect **air currents** in the Arctic. This also affects **global weather patterns** because the atmosphere also operates as an **interlinked system**.

Climate Change — Case Studies

Africa's Population is Vulnerable to the Impacts of Global Warming

Africa has a range of **different climates** from dry deserts to tropical rainforests.
Global warming is having **different** impacts in **different** areas.

1) Areas that are **already dry** (arid and semi-arid environments) are getting **drier**.
2) **Wetter areas** (tropical and sub-tropical environments) are getting **wetter**.
3) The whole continent is getting **warmer** — around **0.5 °C warmer** in the last century.

Because Africa's population is **vulnerable** (poor countries and people) the **economic impacts** of global warming in Africa are **complex** and the **relative financial costs** are massive:

1) Poor people have a **reduced capacity to cope**, e.g. **subsistence farmers**, who only grow enough to meet the needs of their family and have **no income**, will be at risk of starvation if **climate change** affects their crops.
2) Poorer countries are less able to **prepare for** and **respond to** the impacts of climate changes.
3) **Political turmoil** can mean the appropriate responses **aren't made**, making the impacts of climate change worse.

Here are some **examples** of impacts:

Global warming is causing **desertification** — the process by which **fertile** land becomes **unusable** for agriculture. It's a major problem in the **Sahel region** (the belt between the Sahara desert and the fertile area to the south). This causes a **decrease** in **agricultural production**, which leads to more **poverty, unemployment, malnourishment** and **starvation.**

Global warming has caused a **reduced growing period** over much of the continent. This **decreases agricultural production.** In the Sahel region agriculture forms around 70% of the **employment**, so any reduction leads to increased **unemployment, poverty, malnourishment** and **starvation.**

Global warming means **tropical areas** are experiencing **longer growing periods**, and may **financially benefit** from better agricultural conditions.

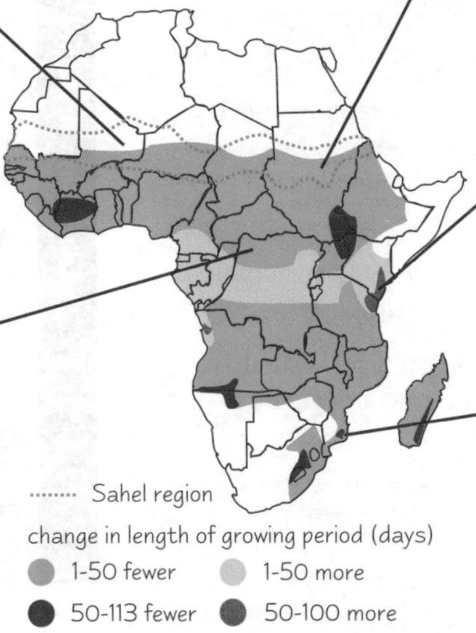

Global warming may have improved **conditions** in some areas of Africa for **mosquitoes** that spread **malaria** — a disease which kills over a million people each year. The **costs** of health care and the **reduction in productivity** (combined with reduced interest in **tourism and investment**) mean the economies are put under **strain** and prevented from **growing.**

Global warming is causing a more **erratic climate.** E.g. **Mozambique** suffered **drought** and **widespread crop failure** in **1995**, then **flooding** in **2000**, which displaced lots of people. Homes and infrastructure are **destroyed** in areas where people are unable to **rebuild** and **recover.**

It's an **unfair world** — the poorest people of Africa have contributed **little** to the causes of global warming and yet suffer the **most**. The **economic losses** that would be **minor** in well developed countries can have more **disastrous consequences** in poorer countries, resulting in **loss of life**.

Practice Questions

Q1 Describe one environmental, one ecological and one socio-economic impact of global warming on the Arctic.

Q2 Describe one environmental change caused by global warming in Africa.

Q3 Describe one way in which global warming changes in Africa could affect the economy.

Exam Question

Q1 Explain the environmental and ecological impacts of global warming in a named area of the world. [10 marks]

What's white, furry and has a hole in the middle — a polo bear...

Hmm, I'm thinking the world's a little bit unfair, and it's a little bit more than 'ref that was never a penalty' unfair. It's always the most vulnerable people and places that suffer the most, and more often than not, they didn't cause the hoo-ha in the first place. Try to learn as much as you can, and even, shock horror, do some extra research on these case studies — it'll help in the exam.

Coping With Climate Change

These pages are for Edexcel Unit 1 (World at Risk).
So, what to do about global warming and all its impacts? It's a toughie for sure — there are loads of great ideas, but the problem is trying to get all those world leaders to agree on what's best. And they normally get on so well...

There are Different Strategies for Coping with Climate Change

Approaches to coping with the climate changes caused by **global warming** can be divided into **two categories:**

1) **Mitigation strategies** involve taking action to **reduce how much** climate change **occurs**, e.g. **reducing emissions** may help to **slow** the temperature increase, so **less ice** may melt and the sea level would **rise less.**
2) **Adaptation strategies** involve taking action to **reduce** the **impacts** that the changes are having, e.g. sea levels are rising so **defences** could be built to **protect** vulnerable settlements.

Here are some examples:

Mitigation strategies

- **Carbon tax** — taxing companies or people who produce CO_2. Increasing costs discourages overconsumption of energy.
- **Changing the energy mix** — changing the mix of sources of energy, i.e. lowering the proportion of energy made from fossil fuels and increasing energy from sources that produce less greenhouse emissions, e.g. nuclear power.
- **Modified agricultural practices** — cut methane generation from farm animals, e.g. by developing new types of feed.
- **Emission-cutting technologies** — carbon capture and storage involves storing the CO_2 produced (e.g. by power plants) using methods like injecting it into geological formations, e.g. coal seams.
- **Energy conservation** — using less energy, e.g. switching off home appliances when they're not being used.
- **Waste strategies** — increasing the amount of waste that's recycled, which should directly cut methane emissions from landfill sites.
- **Tree planting** — planting new trees creates new carbon sinks so more CO_2 will be stored as organic matter.
- **Carbon offsetting** — individuals and companies can calculate the amount of CO_2 their activities are producing, then offset them by paying for activities that take up an equal amount of CO_2 (like tree planting).

Adaptation strategies

- **Lifestyle adaptations** — people adapt the way they live to suit the new conditions, e.g. planting new crops that will flourish in the new climatic conditions.
- **Improved risk assessment** — looking at the likelihood that people or property will be damaged by climate change impacts, and evaluating the need for insurance policies.
- **Flood adaptations** — building physical defences such as flood barriers to reduce the impacts of flooding, and having better flood warning systems.
- **Water resource management** — using freshwater resources more efficiently to cope with drought conditions, e.g. installing water meters in homes to discourage people from using a lot of water.
- **Community awareness** — educating local communities on the potential impacts of climate change. Emergency action plans can be tailored for specific communities.

1) Some of these strategies need to be applied on a **global scale** (e.g. changing the energy mix, introducing emission-cutting technologies) while others can be done at a **local scale** (e.g. community awareness, waste strategies).
2) **International agreements** (see next page) are another example of **global** strategies to tackle climate change.
3) Many of the strategies have only a **small impact** on their **own**, e.g. energy conservation in homes, but when all the strategies are **combined** the impacts can make **long-term** differences.

Strategies Have Limitations and Side Effects

Some strategies have **limitations** which reduce their effectiveness, while others have **side effects** that impact on other things:

1) **Limitation** — e.g. building physical flood defences works whilst flooding remains **below** a certain point. If sea levels continue to **rise** defences like the **Thames barrier** won't be **high enough** to cope with the higher flood waters.
2) **Side effect** — e.g. changing the energy mix would **reduce emissions**, but using more **nuclear power** would produce more **nuclear waste**. It's a long time before the waste becomes **safe**, so it's **expensive** and **dangerous** to dispose of.

Coping With Climate Change

Agreeing on How to Cope with Climate Change is Complex

Strategies to cope with climate change need to be **developed**, **managed** and **carried out**. This is done at **different levels** by **various groups**. There are **key players**, each with a **different role** that can sometimes be conflicting:

1) **Governments** — develop strategies on an **international**, **national** and **local** scale.
2) **Businesses** — can be responsible for **contributing** to climate change, or can help to **slow it down**. They may **lobby** governments to **reduce restrictions** and allow them to continue producing greenhouse gases, or they may help by investing in **new technologies** to **combat** climate change.
3) **Non-governmental organisations (NGOs)** — can have many roles and views depending on what they're set up to do and who their members are, e.g. **Greenpeace** is an environmental pressure group that tries to **persuade governments** to recognise and take action **against** climate change.
4) **Communities** and **individuals** — strategies developed on a larger scale are carried out at a **local level**, e.g. a government may decide to encourage recycling, but the recycling is actually done by **individuals**.

There are different **views** and **levels** of **influence** between and within the key players, e.g. not all governments **agree** on the right thing to do, and some key players may have **more power** than others to influence decisions.

Developing agreements on the nature of climate change and how to respond is very **complex**. Here's an example:

The Kyoto Protocol

1) The Kyoto Protocol is an **international agreement** between more than **180 countries** to **monitor** and **cut** greenhouse gas emissions by **2012**.
2) The agreement divides the countries into two groups — **developed** and **developing**.
3) **Developed countries** have agreed to **cut emissions** (overall by 5%).
4) **Developing countries** don't have to cut emissions, but need to **monitor** and **report** their emissions.
5) The agreement has set up a **market** to trade in **carbon 'credits'** — all countries and businesses are given a **limit** on the **emissions** they can produce. If they produce less, they can **sell** the **extra carbon credits** — if they produce more, they need to buy more credits. They can also gain credits by helping to **reduce emissions** in developing countries — so developed countries **invest** in developing countries to help them develop in a **sustainable way**.
6) **Four countries** with the **highest emissions** (the **USA**, **Australia**, **China** and **India**) **didn't sign up** for the original agreement in 1997. The **USA** and **Australia** felt signing would affect their **economies** and that the developing countries should have targets **as well**. **China** and **India** thought it would slow their **rate of growth**.
7) Most have now joined the agreement but there's still lots of **criticism** — some people feel the targets aren't **high enough** and others think there's no point if the highest polluters **aren't included** (the **USA** still hasn't **fully** joined).

Individuals Can 'Act Local, Think Global'

A carbon footprint is the amount of greenhouse gases a person produces, i.e. how much they might be contributing to global warming.

International agreements help at the largest scale, but changes need to be coordinated at **all levels**. Most people think the approach should be to **'act local**, **think global'** — **individuals** can make **small changes** that will help the global problem, e.g. reduce their **carbon footprint**.

Some people think that if everyone took steps to **decrease** their carbon footprint, it would make a **big difference**. Others believe that individual impacts **aren't significant**.

It's likely that changes to emissions will be **incremental** rather than gradual (change occurring in **steps**, rather than **constantly**), as large-scale initiatives and changes to attitudes cause **sudden changes**.

Practice Questions

Q1 Explain the difference between mitigation and adaptation strategies.

Q2 Name three adaptation strategies for coping with climate change.

Exam Question

Q1 Using a named example, explain why global agreements on coping with climate change are complex. [15 marks]

The Kyoto photocall — these politicians are so vain...

After lots of talking, plenty of arguing and several lost dummies, international agreement on coping with climate change still isn't there. Hmm, maybe if you learn all the strategies I've written out then you can come up with a better solution than they can.

Global Hazards — The Future

These pages are for Edexcel Unit 1 (World at Risk).
And finally, let's end the section on an upbeat, optimistic note. Oh, hang on a minute, turns out the world is getting more hazardous and the impacts of the hazards are getting in the way of our efforts to manage them. Sorry, I tried.

The *World* is Becoming *Increasingly Hazardous*

Global **risk** and **uncertainty** are **increasing** as many hazards increase in magnitude and frequency (see p. 69). This threatens **major disruption** to **people** and the **environment**.

One problem associated with increasing risk and uncertainty is **water shortages**, which lead to reduced **food security** (the **availability** and **access** to food).

Here's an example of how increasing **global warming** is causing **water shortages** and **reduced food security**:

1) Global warming causes changes in **precipitation** and **temperature patterns**.
2) In some areas, this results in **drier** conditions, which leads to **water shortages** and a **decreased ability** to grow food.
3) Many **poorer** parts of the world are affected in this way, e.g. **sub-Saharan Africa**.
4) **Poorer areas** have less money to find **technological solutions** such as dams, or to **import** sufficient food supplies.
5) **Dehydration** and **famine** (widespread shortage of food) can occur in areas where global warming has affected a **vulnerable environment** with a **vulnerable population**.

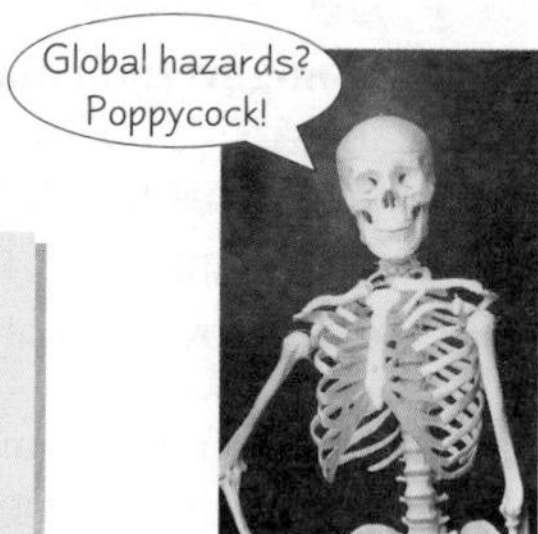

I didn't believe the world was a hazardous place — look what happened to me.

Global warming affects the **supply** of **water** and **food**, and many developing countries have **rapidly increasing** populations — so the **vulnerability** of the population is increased and the **risk** of a **disaster** is much higher (see p. 68).

The Impacts of *Climate Change* May Lead to *Conflict*

The problems of water shortages and food security have caused **political disputes** between countries and can even lead to **armed conflict**. Conflicts can **escalate** as risk and uncertainty **increase** because of hazards like global warming:

1) **Egypt** relies heavily on the river **Nile** for its **water supply**.
2) The two main **tributaries** that feed the Nile flow through **Ethiopia** and **Sudan**.
3) Egypt built a dam called the **Aswan High Dam**, which created a large lake to **store water** (Lake Nasser).
4) Droughts in the 1980s led to **famine** in **Ethiopia** and **Sudan**, but **Egypt wasn't affected** because enough water was **stored** in Lake Nasser.
5) If global warming continues to cause **shortages** of water and Ethiopia or Sudan **increase** their water use, Egypt's supply might be **reduced**.
6) Egypt has stated that it's ready to **use force** to protect its **access** to the waters of the **Nile**.

Conflict can occur **within** countries and **between** countries where any type of resource **isn't enough** to support the population — and this will only **get worse** as climate change affects the **supply of resources**.

Other *Global Problems* Make *Managing Hazards More Difficult*

Conflict, **famine**, **poverty** and **climate change** make managing global hazards more **difficult**.

1) These problems **increase** the **vulnerability** of the population — they may become **poorer** and **less healthy**, and the **infrastructure** to provide help may become **inadequate**.
2) **Risk** is **increased** where the population is vulnerable — a **hazard** may become a **disaster** (see p. 68).
3) A country suffering **other problems** like famine won't have the **resources to manage** the impacts of any other global hazards such as global warming. The **priority** will be to feed the nation, rather than **reduce** greenhouse gas emissions or stop deforestation.
4) A **downward cycle** can occur where the hazards cause problems that eventually increase the risk of more hazards (**positive feedback**, see p. 81).

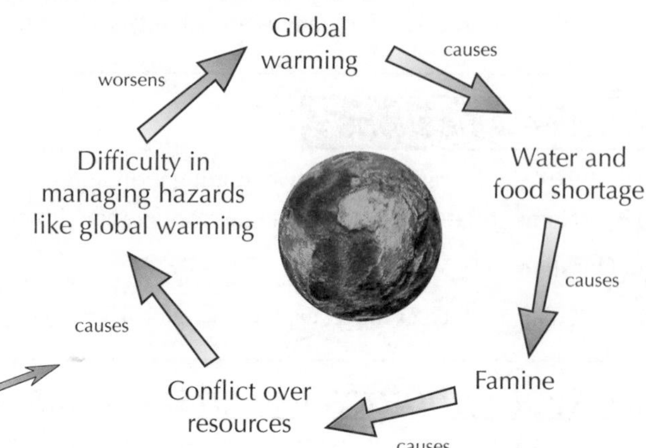

Global Hazards — The Future

Global Warming may be the Greatest Hazard to Life and Property

Global warming is considered to be one of the **biggest challenges** the world has faced:

1) Global problems like **famine**, **poverty** and **conflict** cause massive **loss of life**, but global warming has the potential to cause **much more loss of life** and **damage to property**.
2) It can be the **cause** of many other global problems and hazards (e.g. **famine**, **poverty** and **conflict**), and can **worsen** their effects — it's a **context hazard** (see p. 68).
3) It's a long-term hazard and the impacts may be **permanent** and **irreversible**.
4) Global warming affects the **entire planet** whereas other problems tend to occur in more **localised regions**.

There are lots of **strategies** that have been **proposed** and are **currently being used** to **cope** with the impacts of global warming:

1) **Increasing energy efficiency** — making the energy we produce **do more**.
2) **Energy conservation** — using **less** energy.
3) **Decreasing carbon emissions** — directly **slowing** the rate of global warming.
4) **Increasing alternative energy use** — using energy sources that produce less **greenhouse gases**.
5) **Reafforestation** — replanting trees to **increase** CO_2 uptake from the atmosphere.

See p. 84 for more on strategies to cope with climate change.

It's thought that global warming will be the **most difficult** and **costly** to manage of all global problems.

1) The **Stern Review** (2006) looked at the **economics** of climate change.
2) It concluded that an investment of **1%** of the world's **GDP** (Gross Domestic Product, the **total value** of production over a given period) would be needed to prevent the **worst effects** of global warming.
3) If this investment isn't made, GDP could be reduced by up to **20%** in the future.

You need to understand all these strategies and assess which are the most **cost-effective** for the **benefits** they'll bring — **cost-benefit analysis**. Achieving a balance requires **innovative solutions** (ideas that haven't been tried before) so governments perform this kind of analysis when deciding what approaches to take.

It's likely the most cost-effective and beneficial solutions in the long-term will be those that are **sustainable** (can be used **indefinitely** without **harming** the environment or **depleting resources**), e.g. **renewable energy sources** like solar power. But strategies are **most effective** when they're carried out by **everyone**, so the problem needs to be **recognised by everyone**.

Solutions to Hazards Should Focus on Risk and Vulnerability

The solutions to a hazardous world, whether they're on a **local** or **global** scale, need to focus on **assessing** and **altering** the **risk** the hazard poses (the **likelihood** the hazard will impact on humans) and the **vulnerability** of the population (how **susceptible** the population is to the impacts of a hazard).

The **United Nations** (**UN**) set up a programme in 1992 called **Agenda 21** which outlines action to be taken at **global** and **local** levels to help **sustainable development**. The first section looks at **vulnerability** and is about combating **poverty**, **changing consumption** and promoting **better health**. The second section looks at **reducing risk** by changing **emissions**, working against **deforestation** and protecting **environments**. Together they should help reduce **risk** and **vulnerability**.

Practice Questions

Q1 How does global warming lead to water shortages?

Q2 Outline two strategies used to cope with global warming.

Exam Question

Q1 Explain how global warming could increase water shortages, famine and conflict. [10 marks]

Stern Review — nothing to do with parents' evening...

I wish politicians talking about risk meant they were playing world domination board games. Alas, the board is in fact the real world, and the risk is the likelihood that something nasty's going to happen to us. Global warming's a big part of it all, and if there's going to be a solution it needs to focus on what and where the risk is and how vulnerable people are.

Extreme Weather Events

This section is for Edexcel Unit 2 (Extreme Weather option). *Some extreme things are fun, like extreme sports and, um, extreme ironing (yes, it exists, honest). Other extreme things, like extreme weather events, really aren't. Read on...*

Extreme Weather is Severe or Unexpected

1) **Extreme weather** is weather that's **unusually severe** (e.g. when hot weather turns into a heatwave) or that occurs in an area **where** it **isn't expected** (e.g. drought in a usually wet area).
2) There are many different **types** of extreme weather — **temperate storms**, **tornadoes**, **tropical cyclones**, **heatwaves**, **droughts**, **blizzards** and **ice storms**.

Temperate Storms are Caused by Depressions

1) **Temperate storms** are **weather systems** with **strong winds** and **heavy rainfall**.
2) They're **caused** by **extreme low pressure systems** called **depressions**. Here's how a depression forms:

1) **Warm air** constantly moves **out** of **tropical areas**, **towards** the **poles**. A **warm front** is the **leading edge** of a **warm air mass**.
2) **Cold air** moves **out** of **polar regions**, **towards** the **tropics**. A **cold front** is the **leading edge** of a **cold air mass**.
3) Where the air masses **meet** (in the **temperate zone**) the **warm air** heading towards the pole **rises** above the cold air heading towards the tropics (because **warm air** is **less dense** than cold air).

4) The rising **warm air** means there's **less air** at **ground level**, so atmospheric **pressure** is **reduced**.
5) **Strong winds** blow into this area of low pressure in a **spiral fashion**.
6) The direction of these winds combined with the fact that **cold fronts move more quickly** than warm fronts leads to the cold front **catching up** the **warm front**.
7) When this happens the **warm air** behind the warm front is **undercut** by the incoming cold front and is **lifted** away from the ground entirely. It now sits **above** the **cold air** — this is an **occluded front**. The warm air rises into the **upper atmosphere** and the depression **dissipates**.

3) **Depressions** are **common**, but some **cause strong winds** (due to extremely low pressure) and **heavy rainfall** (due to cooling and condensation when warm air rises).
4) When the winds get **stronger** and rainfall **heavier** they are classed as **temperate storms**, e.g. the Great Storm of October 1987 in the UK. The diagram on the right shows the weather conditions of a temperate storm.
5) Temperate storms occur in **temperate areas** (**25-65° latitude**) where the **winds** come mainly **from** the **west**. This means they're **common** in **north-west Europe** and **North America**.

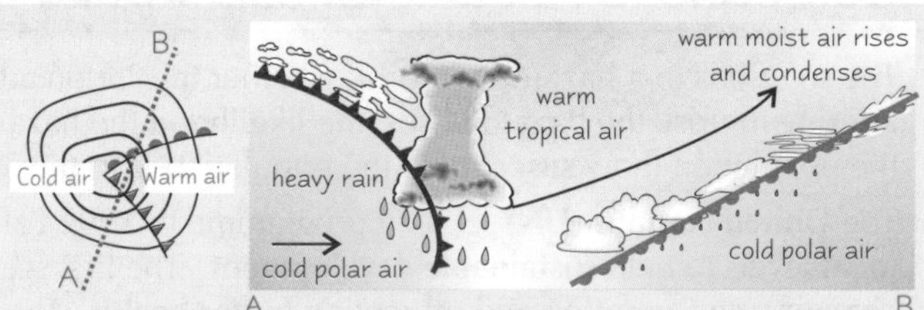

1) As the **warm front** passes there is **light rain**.
2) Rain **stops briefly** as the warm air mass passes.
3) The **cold front** brings **heavy rain**.

Tornadoes Form Inside Massive Storms

1) A tornado is a **rotating column of air** that is **in contact** with the **ground surface** and the **clouds** above.
2) Tornadoes have **wind speeds** of **up to 480 kph** and can **travel over land** for **many kilometres**.
3) They **form** when **rotating air** high in the **atmosphere** gets **turned on** its **side** into a **vertical column** and is **dragged down** to the **surface** by **descending air**. This happens in **large storms** (e.g. temperate storms or tropical cyclones).
4) This means tornadoes occur anywhere there are **temperate storms** — they're most common in the **USA** (there were over 1000 tornadoes there in 2007) but also occur in **north-west Europe**.
5) Tornadoes can also be found where **tropical cyclones hit land** — **south-east Asia**, **Australasia** and **southern Africa**.

They're visible because a funnel of condensation forms along with strong winds.

Extreme Weather Events

Tropical Cyclones Form Over Warm Water

Tropical cyclones are also called hurricanes or typhoons.

1) Tropical cyclones are **huge spinning storms** with **strong winds** and **torrential rain** that **develop over water**.
2) Scientists don't know exactly **how** cyclones are formed but they do know the **conditions** needed. These include:
   - A **disturbance** near the sea-surface that triggers the cyclone (e.g. an area of low pressure).
   - **Sea water** that's **warm** (above **26.5 °C** at the **surface**), so that it will **evaporate**.
   - The **Coriolis effect** (see page 71) — to make the **winds spin**.
3) Tropical cyclones form around the **tropics** because the water there is **warm** (as it receives a lot of **solar radiation**).
4) They **don't form below 5° latitude**, because the **Coriolis effect isn't strong enough** to make the winds **spin**.
5) The **energy** that keeps the cyclone going comes from the **condensation** of **water vapour**, so tropical cyclones maintain **strong winds** over **warm water** (due to high levels of evaporation from the sea).
6) Tropical cyclones **dissipate** over **land** (because the **supply** of **warm, moist air** is **cut off**).

Tropical cyclone **Katrina** developed in the **south-eastern Bahamas** in **August 2005** and **moved** over **land** in **Florida**, where it **weakened**. It then **strengthened** as it moved over the **warm waters** of the **Gulf of Mexico** and **struck land** again in **Louisiana**, southern USA.

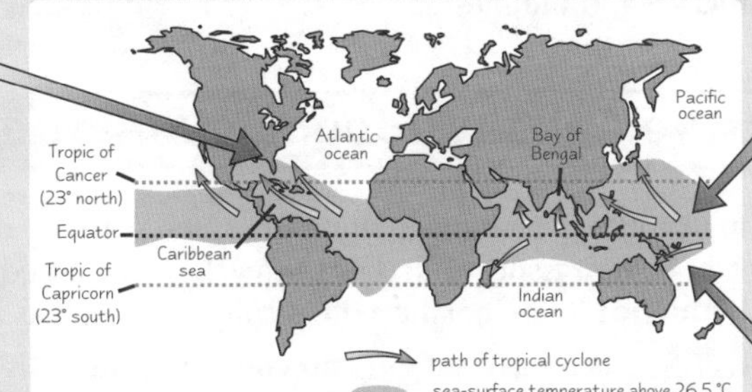

Tropical cyclones **move westwards** due to the **east-west winds** in the **tropics**, e.g. the trade winds move cyclones west across the Atlantic ocean.

They **move away** from the **equator** because of the **Coriolis effect**.

Extreme Weather Events can Cause Flooding

Flooding isn't a type of extreme weather, but it's often caused by storms and cyclones.

Flooding is when an area of **land** that **isn't** usually covered in **water** becomes **submerged**. **Different types** of flooding occur in **different places** including:

River Flooding — **Rivers flood** when the **water level** becomes **so high** that the river **spills** over its banks onto the **flood plain**. This can be caused by **constant rainfall** over a **long period** of time or a **massive input of water** over a **short period** of time (e.g. heavy rainfall in a **temperate storm** or **cyclone**). Any **low-lying area near** to a **river channel** is **at risk** from **river flooding**, e.g. large areas of China are flooded by the river Yangtze.

Coastal Flooding — **Coastal areas** can **flood** when the **sea surges** onto the **land**. This can happen when **temperate storms** or **cyclones** cause a **storm surge** — they reduce the atmospheric pressure on the sea surface, causing it to **rise**. Strong **onshore winds** associated with storms can also force water to higher levels along the coast. Any **low-lying area** near the **coast** is potentially **at risk** from coastal flooding, e.g. a storm surge in 2004 off the west coast of Indonesia caused widespread flooding in south-east Asia

Flooding can be particularly **severe** when **several factors** are **combined**, e.g. **melting ice** and **snow** in the **Himalayas**, **high rainfall** from the **monsoon** and **tropical cyclone Yemyin** together caused **widespread flooding** in **southern Asia** in **2007**.

Practice Questions

Q1 What is the definition of 'extreme weather'?

Q2 Briefly explain how a depression forms.

Exam Question

Q1 Describe the conditions needed for tropical cyclones to form and explain their distribution. [10 marks]

Toto, I've a feeling we're not in Kansas anymore. We must be over the rainbow...

Well, there may have been a tornado in the Wizard of Oz, but there certainly wasn't any depression — bit annoyingly optimistic that Dorothy, don't you think? You need to know what different types of extreme weather there are and where they occur. Easy.

Extreme Weather Events

These pages are for Edexcel Unit 2 (Extreme Weather option).
Oh joy, there's more. We've done too windy and too wet, now we're on to too dry and too cold.

Drought is When Conditions are Drier than Normal

1) A drought is a **long period** (weeks, months or years) during which **precipitation** is **consistently below average**.
2) The **conditions** of a drought are **different** in **different places**, e.g. the worst drought in Britain since records began lasted 16 months (from May 1975 to August 1976), whilst droughts in some African countries can last for more than a decade.
3) The **map** on the right shows the **areas** of the world that were **affected** by **drought** in **November 2008**.
4) Areas **most at risk** from drought are **north-eastern Africa**, the **Sahel**, **southern Africa**, the **Middle East**, **Australia** and parts of **eastern South America** and **Indonesia**.

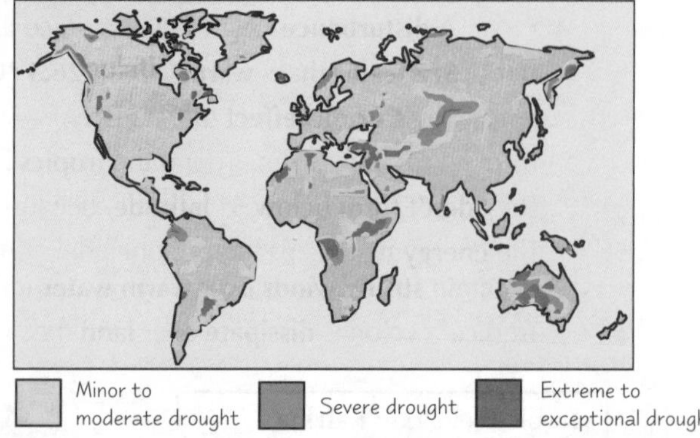

Areas of High Pressure Cause Drought in Subtropical and Temperate Zones...

1) **Air circulates** around the Earth as weather systems — in some places it **rises** and in others it **sinks**. Where air **sinks** an area of **high pressure** called an **anticyclone** is formed. Anticyclones commonly occur over **Europe** and **North America** in the **northern hemisphere**, as well as across **most** of the **southern hemisphere**.
2) Anticyclones **stop air rising**, which means there's **no condensation**. This leads to **clear skies** and **no precipitation**.
3) The **position** of an anticyclone is **affected** by **jet streams** — **narrow currents** of **fast moving air** high up in the **atmosphere**. When an **anticyclone** is **cut off** from a **jet stream** it can remain **stationary** for **long periods** (days or weeks). These anticyclones **block incoming depressions** (they're diverted around them) — so they're called **blocking anticyclones**. This results in **no precipitation**, and possible **drought** conditions (e.g. drought in the UK in 1979).

...and also in Tropical Regions

1) Some **tropical regions** (e.g. the Sahel in northern Africa and Malawi in southern Africa) are already **very dry** because **rain only falls** during the **wet season**. Seasonal rainfall is caused by the **Intertropical Convergence Zone** (ITCZ) — a zone of **low pressure** created by air circulation patterns, **moving north** in July and **south** in January.
2) The **rest** of the **year** the **climate** is **dry**. This is due to **bands of high pressure** present at around **30° north** and **south** of the equator. Here, **sinking dry air** causes continually **dry conditions** in tropical regions.
3) **Changes** in **atmospheric circulation** can cause the **ITCZ** to **stay closer** to the equator than normal for the time of year, or cause the band of high pressure to move. This can cause some regions to receive a lot **less rain** during the wet season, leading to **drought**.
4) These atmospheric conditions may last for **several years** causing a **long-lasting** and **severe drought**, e.g. the ITCZ shift contributed to the **drought conditions** in the **Sahel** that lasted from the **1960s** to the **1980s**.

A Heat Wave is when Conditions are Hotter than Normal

1) A **heat wave** is a **long period** (days or weeks) during which the **temperature** is much **higher** than **normal**.
2) The **conditions** of a **heat wave** are **different** in **different places**, e.g. the conditions considered a heat wave in the **UK** would be much **cooler** than in a country like **Spain**, where higher temperatures are **expected**.
3) Heat waves are also caused by areas of **high pressure**.
4) In **temperate areas**, **blocking anticyclones** (see above) in summer can result in **reduced cloud cover**. This means **less** solar radiation is **reflected back** into space and **more** is **absorbed** by the land, causing an **increase** in **temperature**. Blocking anticyclones can last for a long period of time, leading to a **heatwave**.
5) Another way a heatwave can occur in temperate zones is due to **shifts** in **bands of high pressure**. Changes in **atmospheric circulation** can cause the bands to **move polewards**, bringing **hot**, **dry conditons** with them. For example, in 2003 the northern band moved further north and brought conditions commonly found in **north Africa** to **southern Europe**. These conditions were **abnormal** in Europe and led to the **2003 European heatwave**.

Extreme Weather Events

Drought and Heat Waves can Cause Wildfires

1) Wildfires are **uncontrolled fires** that usually **start** in the **natural environment** (e.g. **forests, grassland**) and can **spread** into **human environments** (buildings and land).
2) Wildfires are a **natural phenomenon**. However, these fires can spread rapidly and cause **widespread destruction**.
3) Fires often **start** during **droughts** and **heat waves** (see previous page) because **low precipitation** and **high temperatures dry out vegetation**. Vegetation can then **easily** be **ignited** by many things, e.g. **lightning strikes**.
4) Wildfires **spread quickly** where there are **warm, dry winds**.
5) They're common in **environments** where there's **lots of vegetation** and **dry weather**, e.g. parts of **Australia, South Africa** and **North America**.

Winter Weather Happens Where Temperatures Fall Below Freezing

1) Winter weather includes **low temperatures**, **ice** and **snowfall**.
2) In areas at **high altitude** and **high latitude** winter weather is **expected**.
3) Winter weather occurs at **high latitudes** (**above 40°**) because **less solar radiation** is received than at lower latitudes. **Temperatures** fall **below freezing**, resulting in **ice** and **snow formation**. E.g. **northern** parts of **Asia**, **Europe** and **North America** and **southern** parts of **South America** and **New Zealand** experience winter weather every year.
4) Winter weather occurs at **high altitudes** because **temperature decreases** by about **6-10 °C** for every **1000 m** gained.

The extreme winter weather called for extreme winter clothing.

5) Winter weather can become **extreme** when conditions are **more severe** than usual (e.g. **blizzards** and **ice storms**) or when they're very **prolonged**, or they occur in **places** that **don't** usually **experience them** (e.g. **lower latitudes**).
6) More **severe conditions** can happen when **temperate storms** (see p. 88) occur during **winter**, resulting in a **blizzard** or an **ice storm**:

Blizzard

- A blizzard is a **winter storm** with **high winds** and **snowfall**.
- They happen when an **intense low pressure system** forms during **winter**.
- Blizzards occur in the **higher latitudes** of the **temperate zone** (**40°** to **60° latitude**) where there are **freezing temperatures** and **low pressure systems**, e.g. **Canada**, **northern Europe** and **southern New Zealand**.
- For example, in the **'storm of the century'** (USA, March **1993**) a **huge low pressure system** formed over the **east coast** of the **USA**. It caused **massive snowfall**, **low temperatures** and **high winds**, from **Canada** down to **Cuba**.

Ice Storm

- An ice storm is a **storm** in which the **ground** and **surfaces** (e.g. of buildings) get **covered** in a layer of **ice**.
- This happens when **rainfall** (from a **storm**) **passes through** a **layer** of **cold air** at (or near to) the **ground**. So the **rain freezes** as it **hits** the **surface** covering everything in **ice**.
- For example, in the **'Great Ice Storm'** of **1998** in **North America**, **warm**, **moist air** from the **Gulf of Mexico rose** above **cold air** trapped at **ground level**. This caused an **ice storm** for **several days** over a **wide area**.

Practice Questions

Q1 Explain how drought can lead to wildfires.

Q2 Explain why winter weather commonly occurs at high latitudes.

Exam Question

Q1 Describe how an anticyclone can lead to extreme weather events. [10 marks]

I don't like extreme weather — I'm anti-cyclone...

This stuff isn't too bad really — high pressure leads to anticyclones, which cause bad things like droughts and heatwaves to happen. Simple. OK, there's a bit more to it, but that's the general idea. All you have to do now is go back and learn the details.

Extreme Weather — Fieldwork and Research

These pages are for** Edexcel Unit 2 **(Extreme Weather option).
Weather diaries aren't exactly fascinating. I can't see 'The Secret Weather Diary of Joe Bloggs Aged 17¾' becoming a bestseller. Synoptic maps are a tad better — they're the funny-looking ones that weathermen use. Ooh, the excitement...

A Weather Diary is a Primary Source of Data on Weather Patterns

A **weather diary** is a **record** of the **weather conditions** (e.g. temperature, precipitation, air pressure, wind speed) over a **period of time** in a **specific area**.

Making your **own weather diary** is one way of collecting **primary data** (first-hand information).
You can use this data to help you **understand** the **weather patterns** you've studied, like **depressions** and **anticyclones**.

Here's how to make a weather diary...

1) **Choose** the **elements** of the **weather** you're going to **observe**, e.g. pressure and wind direction. The **more elements** you record the **more detailed** your **data** will be, which is **helpful** when you're looking for **patterns** in the weather.
2) You need to **take** and **write down** readings for **each element** you're observing.
3) Take your readings at the **same time** each day, or at **set time intervals** over the course of the day.
4) Take your readings in the **same place** each day — **avoid** anything that would **affect** the readings. E.g. do it in an **open space** away from buildings that could affect the wind, and **surfaces** that **reflect** lots of **heat** (like tarmac).
5) It's best to take **readings** for a **few days** or even **weeks** because it's more likely you'll record **different weather conditions** and be able to see **distinct patterns**.

A Weather Diary Should Look Something Like This...

By carrying out **fieldwork** like making a weather diary, you can see when a **front** is **passing**, what kind of **pressure system** (high or low) is present and what kind of **air mass** the area's in (warm or cold).

Here's an **example** of a **weather diary** that shows the **weather conditions** as a **depression** (see p. 88) passes over:

Your weather diary can be used alongside secondary sources (e.g. news reports and synoptic maps — see next page) to help you understand what your observations show.

Time	Temp (°C)	Rainfall (mm)	Pressure (millibars)	Windspeed & direction (Beaufort scale)
6.00	9.8	0.0	990	South-easterly 4
8.00	10.2	2.8	986	South-easterly 4
10.00	11.6	4.6	979	Southerly 5
12.00	12.2	7.3	974	South west 6
14.00	12.3	0.9	975	South west 4
16.00	11.9	1.1	975	South west 5
18.00	8.2	9.5	984	North-westerly 9
20.00	8.6	1.5	990	North-westerly 9
22.00	9.7	0.8	994	North-westerly 7
0.00	10.1	0.0	998	North-westerly 4

1 Ahead of the warm front:
- Temperatures **begin to rise**.
- **Drizzly rain**.
- Pressure **falls**.
- Wind speed **increases** and direction **begins to turn**.

2 As **warm front** passes:
- **Temperatures rise**.
- Rain becomes **heavier**.
- Pressure **falls**.
- Wind is strong and **blustery**. Wind **turns** direction.

3 **Warm air** overhead:
- Temperatures remain **steady**.
- Rain is **light** and **may stop**.
- Pressure remains **steady**.
- Wind speed **decreases**, **turns** direction **slightly**.

4 As **cold front** passes:
- Temperatures **drop** suddenly.
- **Heavy rain**, **storm** conditions.
- Pressure **rises** suddenly.
- Wind speed **increases** to **gale force**, **turns** direction **sharply**.

5 **Cold air overhead**:
- Remains **cold**.
- **Rain showers**.
- Pressure continues to **rise**.
- Wind speed **falls gradually**.

Extreme Weather — Fieldwork and Research

Synoptic Maps Display Weather Data from Different Primary Sources

1) **Synoptic maps** are a type of **secondary data** (second-hand information) about the weather.
2) They **display** weather data from a **range** of **primary sources** (e.g. weather stations).
3) You can **use** them to **find** the **positions** of **fronts**, **air masses** and **pressure systems** (see p. 88).

Synoptic maps have **lines** called **isobars**. These **link** together **points** of **equal atmospheric pressure**, which is measured in **millibars** (mb).
Here are **two synoptic charts**, one showing a **depression** and the other an **anticyclone**.

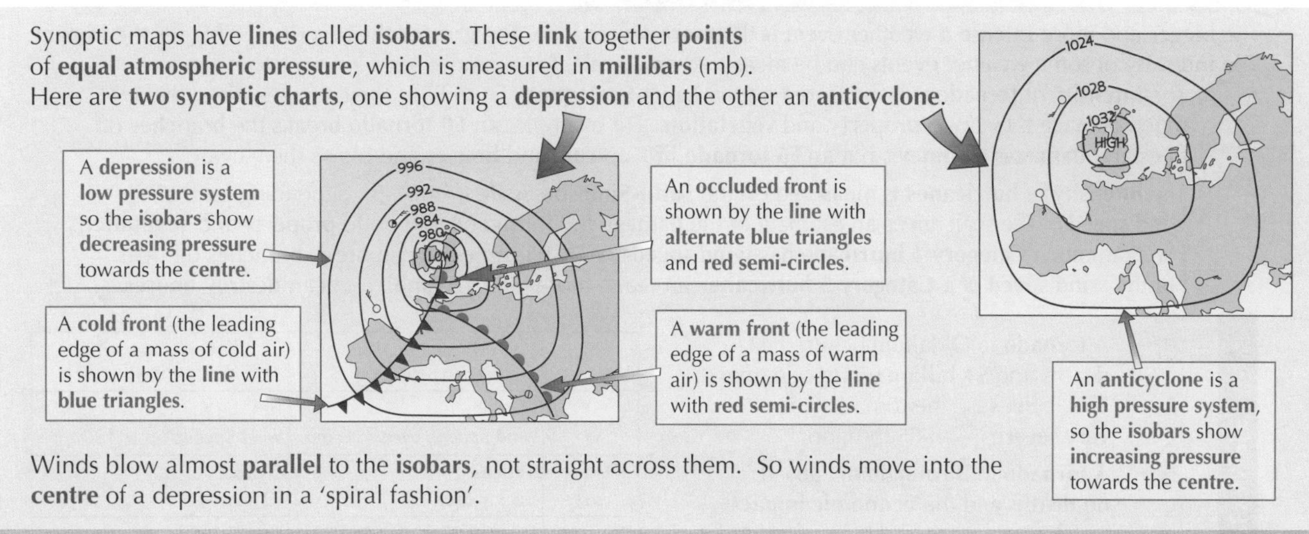

A depression is a low pressure system so the isobars show decreasing pressure towards the centre.
A cold front (the leading edge of a mass of cold air) is shown by the line with blue triangles.
996
992
988
984
980
LOW
An occluded front is shown by the line with alternate blue triangles and red semi-circles.
A warm front (the leading edge of a mass of warm air) is shown by the line with red semi-circles.
1024
1028
1032
HIGH
An anticyclone is a high pressure system, so the isobars show increasing pressure towards the centre.

Winds blow almost **parallel** to the **isobars**, not straight across them. So winds move into the **centre** of a depression in a 'spiral fashion'.

Synoptic maps use a variety of symbols:

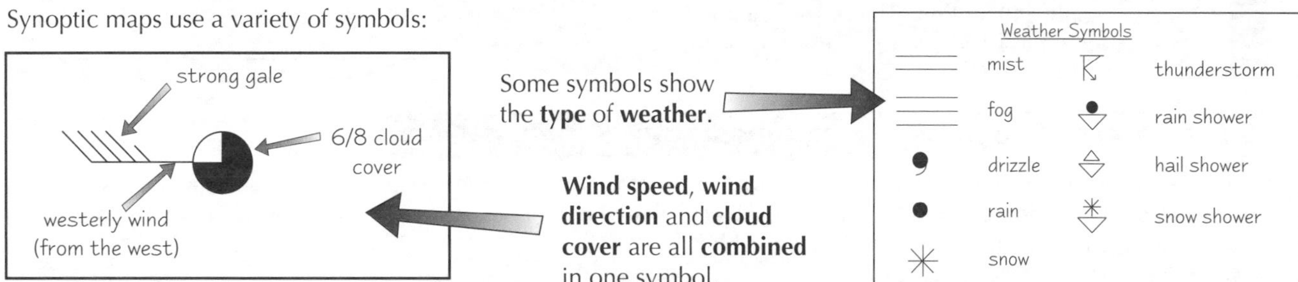

strong gale
6/8 cloud cover
westerly wind (from the west)
Some symbols show the type of weather.
Wind speed, wind direction and cloud cover are all combined in one symbol.
Weather Symbols
mist
fog
drizzle
rain
snow
thunderstorm
rain shower
hail shower
snow shower

You can Use Other Secondary Sources to Research Weather Patterns

You can **use secondary sources** of weather data to **find out** about **extreme weather events** in the **past**:

Example

To research a **storm** (e.g. the Great Storm of October 1987) find **synoptic maps** (from the Met Office), **satellite images**, and **newspaper** and **online articles** about the storm. The **synoptic maps** will show the **position** of the **warm** and **cold fronts** (and air masses). If you look at synoptic maps for different times you can see the **development** of the **low pressure system**. **Articles** and **satellite images** will tell you about the associated **weather patterns** (heavy precipitation, strong wind). Using these together you can show the **progressive nature** (i.e. the stages) of the **depression** as it passes across the country.

Practice Questions

Q1 Why is it important to take measurements for a weather diary in an open space?

Q2 What do isobars show?

Exam Question

Q1 Describe and explain a programme of fieldwork and research you would use to investigate the links between weather conditions and a depression. [15 marks]

What do people drink at the iso-bar? Strong gale...

The examiners think 'examining a developing depression, cold snap or heatwave' is an 'ideal scenario'. It doesn't seem like an ideal scenario for a Sunday afternoon, or a hot date, so I guess it means fieldwork.

The Impact of Extreme Weather

These pages are for Edexcel Unit 2 (Extreme Weather option).
Now you know why extreme weather events occur, it's time to take a look at their impact. And it's not pretty.

Three Key Factors Influence the Impact of Extreme Weather Events

1 The Severity of the Extreme Weather Event

The **bigger** and **more intense** a weather event is the **more severe** it is. The **greater the severity** the **bigger the impact**. The **intensity** of some weather events can be measured on a **scale**, for example:

- The **intensity** of **tornadoes** is measured on the **Fujita Scale** (from F0 to F5). They're categorised by how much **damage** they do to **property** and **vegetation**. For example, an **F0 tornado breaks** the **branches** off trees and **damages chimneys**, but an **F5 tornado lifts** up **cars** and **houses** and blows them away.
- The **intensity** of **hurricanes** is measured on the **Saffir-Simpson Scale** (from 1-5), depending on their **wind speeds**. The scale gives an estimate of the **damage** the hurricane will do to **property** and **vegetation**. For example, a **Category 1 hurricane** has **wind speeds** of **74-95 mph** and can **break branches** off trees, but the **wind speed** of a **Category 5 hurricane** can reach more than **155 mph** and can **destroy houses**.

EXAMPLE

1) A **tornado** in **Oklahoma** caused **41 deaths** and **$1 billion** worth of damage. This is because the tornado was **very severe** — an **F5** tornado.
2) A **tornado** in **Birmingham** caused **no deaths** and the **economic impact** was **lower** than the Oklahoma tornado — only **£40 million**. This is because the tornado was **less severe** — an **F2** tornado.

	Oklahoma, USA (1999)	Birmingham, UK (2005)
Severity	F5 Wind speeds over 300 mph	F2 Wind speeds up to 130 mph
Death toll	41 dead 583 injured	0 dead 19 injured
Economic impact	$1 billion (£620 million) 4300 houses damaged or destroyed	£40 million 4449 houses damaged

2 The Level of Economic Development in the Affected Area

Generally, the **economic impact** of an extreme weather event is **greater** in **more economically developed areas**. But, the **social impact** is **greater** in **less economically developed areas** because people have a **lower capacity to cope** with extreme weather events (they're **more vulnerable**).

EXAMPLE

1) **Hurricane Mitch** hit **less economically developed** areas, e.g. Honduras. The **death toll** was **high** for a number of reasons. **Inadequate roads** and **bridges** were **quickly destroyed** so people **couldn't evacuate** easily and there were **shortages** of **food** and **water** immediately after the hurricane. **Poor sanitation systems**, e.g. broken sewers, meant flood water became contaminated, which **spread disease**. The **poor infrastructure**, **poor sanitation** and **poor emergency responses** (common in less economically developed areas due to lack of money), meant that the **impact** of the hurricane was **high**.
2) **Hurricane Wilma** hit **more economically developed** areas, e.g. Florida. The **death toll** was **lower** because these areas are better **able to cope** with the **disaster**, e.g. by providing **warnings**, **shelters** and quick **evacuation**. But the **financial cost** of the hurricane was much **higher** because the property and infrastructure destroyed was **more valuable**.

	Hurricane Mitch (1998)	Hurricane Wilma (2005)
Areas hit worst	Honduras and Nicaragua	Mexico, Cuba, Florida
Severity	Category 5	Category 5
Death toll	Over 11 000	63
Economic impact	US$6 billion	US$29 billion

3 The Vulnerability of People in the Affected Area

The **poorer** the country is, the **more vulnerable** the population, but some **groups** of people **within** a population also have a **lower capacity to cope**, so are **more vulnerable**. The **impact** is **greater** on vulnerable people. They have a lower capacity to cope with extreme weather because of...

- Their **age**, e.g. the elderly are more susceptible to the effects of a heatwave.
- Their **health**, e.g. disruption of health care affects people who need regular medication more than those who don't.
- Their **wealth**, e.g. hurricane evacuation is more difficult for those who don't own a car because they're poor.
- Where they **live**, e.g. tornadoes affect people who live in mobile homes more than people in permanent homes.

EXAMPLE

The **heatwave** in **England** and **Wales** in **2003** lasted for 10 days and may have caused over **2000 deaths**. In southern England **excess mortality** (the percentage extra deaths during that time, compared to previous years) was **33%** for people **aged 75 and over**, compared to **13.5%** for those **under 75**, during the heatwave. Therefore the **elderly** were **more vulnerable** during the heatwave, possibly because dehydration has more serious effects on the elderly.

The Impact of Extreme Weather

*Case Study — **Hurricane Katrina** hit South-eastern **USA** in **August 2005***

In **August 2005**, the USA was hit by **Hurricane Katrina** — a **Category 5** hurricane. **Louisiana** was the worst hit — over 85% of deaths occurred there. The hurricane had many **social**, **environmental** and **economic** impacts:

1) The **death toll** was **1836**, with about **700** people still **missing**. Many people **lost family members**, **homes** and **jobs**. Over **1 million** people **moved** to other parts of the USA following the hurricane.

2) Around **300 000** homes were **destroyed** and many **more** were **damaged**.

3) People were **injured** directly by the hurricane. At one hospital emergency department the **number** of **patients treated rose** by **83.6%** in the week following the hurricane.

4) **Storm surges** caused substantial **beach erosion**. Many **coastal habitats**, which were **breeding grounds** for sea turtles, marine mammals and migrating birds and fish were **lost**.

5) Many major **highways** and **bridges** were **damaged**, e.g. the **Rigolets Bridge** in New Orleans. Some were completely **destroyed**, e.g. the **Biloxi Bay Bridge** on the US Route 90 highway.

6) Agricultural **crops** (e.g. cotton, sugar cane) and **forests** were **destroyed**. The **oil** and **gas industry** was **disrupted** (**30 oil platforms** were destroyed and **9 refineries** closed).

7) In **Louisiana**, over **70 000 businesses** were affected. Around **230 000 jobs** were **lost**.

8) The hurricane caused around **$300 billion of damage**.

*There are **Three Reasons** why **Katrina's Impact** was so **High***

Severity	Hurricane Katrina was a **Category 5** storm, but weakened to **Category 3** before it hit land. This is still fairly severe, which meant that its **social**, **environmental** and **economic impacts** were **high**.
Level of economic development	Hurricane Katrina affected **more economically developed** areas, so the **economic impact** was **high**.
Vulnerability of those affected	Hurricane Katrina hit **poorer areas** of New Orleans. People from these regions **weren't able** to **evacuate** as easily and the **buildings** and **infrastructure** were of a **lower quality** and therefore more easily damaged. The **ill** were also **badly affected**, with **hospitals flooding** and **equipment failing**.

*The **Impact** was **Made Worse** by **Inadequate Levees***

1) Most of **New Orleans** lies **below sea level**. It relies on **levees** (see p. 16) to **protect** the city from **floods**.
2) During Hurricane Katrina, **storm surges** generated **waves** about **8 m** high. The **levees** catastrophically **failed**, causing **80%** of **New Orleans** to be **flooded** — this was blamed for much of the damage and loss of life.
3) **Reports** found that **faulty design**, **incomplete sections** and **poor construction** all contributed to **levee failure**.
4) It's been estimated that if the **levees** had **not failed**, up to **two-thirds** of the **deaths** could have been **avoided**.

Practice Questions

Q1 Describe a scale used to measure the intensity of an extreme weather event.

Q2 Give an example of a vulnerable group of people.

Q3 Describe the social impacts of Hurricane Katrina.

Exam Question

Q1 Explain the factors that influence the impact of extreme weather events. [10 marks]

The Fajita Scale — used for measuring the spiciness of Mexican food...

I always thought the severity of tornadoes was measured by how many cows they could pick up. As in, "Did you see that tornado? Must have been a 3 cow-er, at least." Guess not. The important thing to remember from these pages is that the effect of an extreme weather event is always dependent on three key factors — severity, economic development and vulnerability. Sorted.

The Impact of Extreme Weather

These pages are for Edexcel Unit 2 (Extreme Weather option).
They say lightning never strikes twice — but these two pages are just one extreme weather event after another. Literally.

Case Study — Major Drought in South-Eastern Australia Since 2002

Australia is suffering from **severe**, **long-term drought**. The **worst hit** area is the **Murray-Darling Basin** in south-east Australia, which is Australia's most **important agricultural region**. This drought has many **social**, **environmental** and **economic** impacts:

1) The drought has led to **water use restrictions**. The **3 million people** who rely on the **River Murray** for their water supplies have had their **allocation reduced.**

2) Over **10 000 farming families** have been **forced** to **leave** the Murray-Darling Basin in the **last five years** because they can **no longer make a living** from **agriculture**.

3) The drought is **increasing groundwater salinity** in **over 35 towns** in the river basin. This causes **structural damage** to homes. Many **properties** are **losing value**.

4) **Financial hardship** caused by the drought is affecting the **mental health** of many people. The **Government** has spent over **$10 million** on strategies, such as **mental health workshops**, to help communities cope with mental health issues.

5) The drought has caused **vegetation loss** and **soil erosion**, as well as increased **wildfires** and **dust storms**. **Depleted rivers** and **lakes** are suffering from **outbreaks** of **toxic algae**. This damage is **threatening** the **habitats** of many species, some of which are **endangered** (e.g. the **Purple-spotted gudgeon**).

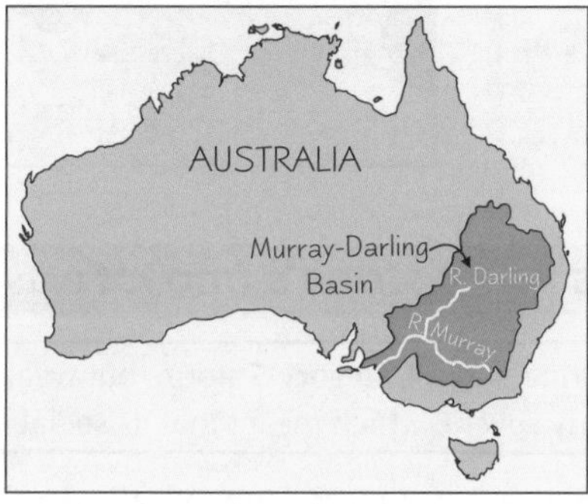

All these impacts are <u>ongoing</u> because Australia is still suffering from drought.

6) Agricultural production of **cereals**, **fruit**, **vegetables**, **dairy** and **livestock** has **decreased** due to lack of water. Crops that rely on **irrigation** (watering) have been particularly badly affected, e.g. **rice production** has fallen to just **2%** of pre-drought totals. All of this has **increased food prices.**

7) Many **farms** and **small businesses** have **closed. Production levels** and **incomes** of many other businesses have **decreased**. This has caused **unemployment** levels to rise to **7% above** the **national average**.

8) More than **23 000** rural families and **1500 small businesses** receive **income support** to help them survive.

Three Factors Influence the Impact of the Drought

1) Severity of the event

1) It's Australia's **worst drought** on **record** — **rainfall** in **June 2008** was the **lowest** recorded in **117 years**. This has increased the **severity** of the impacts shown above.
2) Parts of the Murray-Darling Basin have been in **drought** since **2001** and water levels are now **so low** that it'll take **years of high rainfall** for the basin to **recover**. Therefore even after the drought some of the impacts will be ongoing.

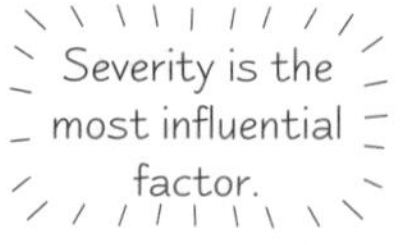

2) Level of economic development

1) Australia is a **more economically developed** country, so it's **more able** to **cope** with some of the **impacts** of drought (e.g. the Government can afford to spend money on **tackling mental health problems**).
2) However, the Murray-Darling Basin is a **rich agricultural area** (responsible for **34%** of Australia's gross value of **agricultural production in 2000/2001**) — so drought in this region is having a huge impact on Australian agriculture as a whole and is causing **large financial losses**.

3) Vulnerability of the affected populations

1) **Poorer people** are badly affected by the drought because they **can't afford** the **high prices** of **food**.
2) The large numbers of **farmers** in the area are also badly affected as they depend on water for their **livelihood**.

The Impact of Extreme Weather

Case Study — Flooding in Carlisle in January 2005

You need to know the **social**, **economic** and **environmental impacts** of **flooding**. Look at the **Carlisle flood** case study on p. 15.

Three Factors Influenced the Impact of the Flood

Severity influenced the impact of the flood the most.

1 Severity of the event

1) The **River Eden** flowed at its highest recorded level of **1520 cumecs** — this would be expected **about once every 200 years**. At **Eden Bridge**, flood waters rose **over a metre higher** than the **previous highest waterline**.
2) The **severity** of the flood meant that its **impact** was **high**.

2 Level of economic development

1) Carlisle is an urban area in a **more economically developed** country so **money** was spent on **flood defences**. These performed well, protecting over **6000 properties**. **Emergency services responded well** after the flood, **decreasing** its **impacts**.
2) Most people's **financial needs** (e.g. to repair houses) were met by **insurance** companies, **decreasing** the **economic impact** on **individuals**.
3) However, the economic impact was **high** because Carlisle has a lot of **high value property** and **infrastructure**. Some businesses were **badly hit**, e.g. **United Biscuits**, Carlisle's largest employer, had **over £5 million** pounds worth of **damage**.

3 Vulnerability of the affected populations

1) The **failure** of **landlines** and **mobile phone networks** meant that people were unable to call for **assistance**. This particularly affected the **elderly** and **ill** as they had the **most difficulty evacuating**.
2) People on **lower incomes** were **less likely** to have had **insurance** and so they suffered the most from **property damage**.
3) The increased **costs** of living in **temporary accommodation** also particularly affected **people** on **lower incomes**.

Use Fieldwork and Research to Investigate the Impact of Extreme Weather

It's most likely that any **fieldwork** you'll do in this country will be on **flooding**:

Fieldwork

- **Visit** an **area** that's **prone** to **flooding**. Use a **land-use map** of the **flood plain** to **count** how many **houses** and **businesses** could be flooded.
- Design a **questionnaire** asking **local** people and businesses about the impact of previous flooding. You'll need to ask **closed** questions like *'How much did it cost to repair the damage?'* to get specific, detailed responses.

However, you can carry out research on lots of extreme weather events:

Research

- Study (online) **newspaper articles** to find out about the **intensity** and **amount of damage** of a past **hurricane**.
- Look at the **flood reports** and **maps** on the **Environment Agency website**, to find out about the **physical extent** of past UK floods.
- Visit the **Met Office Library** in Exeter, or look at its **website** to find **meteorological data** (e.g. rainfall data) on previous UK extreme weather events (e.g. storms, droughts).
- Look at the USA's **National Oceanic & Atmospheric Administration** (NOAA) **website** for **official reports** and **interactive maps** on past and current extreme weather events.
- Look at recent reports and the current drought monitor map on the **website** of the **UCL Department of Space and Climate Physics**.

Practice Questions

Q1 Describe the severity of the 2005 Carlisle flood.

Q2 Give an example of how you could research the impact of hurricanes.

Exam Question

Q1 With reference to one or more named examples, describe and explain the impact of an extreme weather event. [10 marks]

Best way to learn about flooding? Give it some welly(s)...

It's a bit grim this stuff. Seems unfair that some people get way too much rain and others don't get enough... There's quite a bit to learn here, but it's not actually too bad once you get going. Start by jotting down the social, economic and environmental effects of these extreme weather events — then see if you can remember how the three factors affect the impact.

Increasing Risk from Extreme Weather

These pages are for Edexcel Unit 2 (Extreme Weather option).
It's not good news, I'm afraid — extreme weather events across the world are becoming more common.

Extreme Weather is Getting More Frequent and More Severe

International weather records show that **extreme weather events** have **increased** in **number** and **severity** during the **last 50 years**. For example:

1) The graph below shows the **global frequency** of **hurricanes** (an extreme weather event) and **floods** (an event that can be caused by extreme weather), compared to the frequency of **earthquakes**, which are **not** weather related. It shows that the **frequency** of **hurricanes** and **floods** has **increased** since **1980**, while the **frequency** of **earthquakes** has stayed more **constant**.

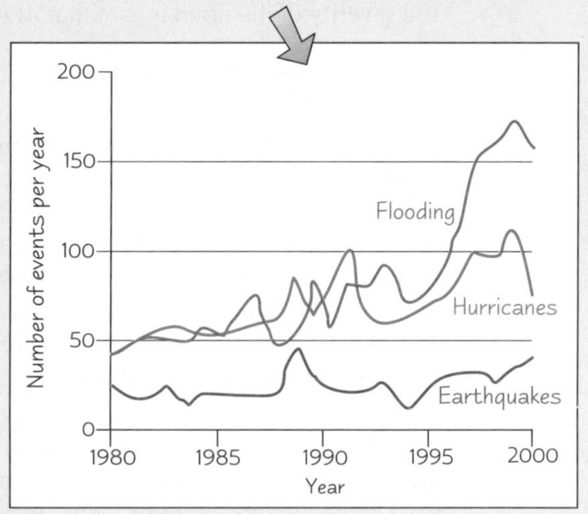

2) Globally, the **proportion** of **Category 4** and **5 hurricanes** has **risen** from **20%** in the **1970s** to **35%** in the **1990s**.
3) The **frequency** of **heavy rainfall** and **severe floods** has **increased** over **most land areas** in recent years. In the **UK**, the **frequency** of **intense winter rainfall** events and the **risk of flooding** have **increased** over the **last 40 years**. British **insurance companies** paid out **£6 billion** on **weather damage claims** between **1999** and **2004** — over **twice** the amount paid during the **previous 5-year period**.
4) Worldwide, the **percentage** of **land** area affected by **serious drought** more than **doubled** between the **1970s** and the early **2000s** — going from **10-15%** to **30%**.

The more **frequent** and more **severe** the events, the **greater** the **risk** of them **affecting humans**.

Global Warming is Increasing the Risk of Some Extreme Weather

Global warming (see p. 76) is a type of **climate change**. Many scientists think that global warming is **contributing** to the **increasing frequency** and **severity** of **extreme weather events**. Here are some of the most **common arguments** for a **link** between the two:

DROUGHTS

Higher temperatures due to **global warming** cause **changes** in **global air circulation** and **ocean currents**. This means some areas will experience **less rainfall** than usual, and some areas will experience **more rainfall**. Areas experiencing **less rainfall** may have **more frequent** and **more severe droughts** (e.g. the long-lasting drought in the Australian Murray-Darling River Basin — see p. 96).

HURRICANES

1) **Hurricanes** can **only form** when the sea surface **temperature** is **warmer than 26.5 °C**. Global warming **increases ocean temperatures**, making the **conditions** hurricanes need to form **more frequent**.
2) **Increased temperatures** also **increases** the **energy supply** for **hurricanes**, making them **more severe**. One study found that for **every 1 °C rise in sea surface temperature, hurricane rainfall increased** by **6-18%** and **wind speed increased** by up to **8%**.

They didn't care that it increased the risk of hurricanes, it was soooo warm...

STORMS

Higher temperatures due to **global warming** cause **changes** in **global air circulation** and **ocean currents** (see above). This means **some places** will have a **higher frequency** of storms and get **more severe storms**.

An **increase** in the **frequency** and **severity** of **storms** and **hurricanes** can lead to an **increase** in **flooding**.

Climate change can increase the risk of flooding in other ways that aren't related to weather, e.g. causing ice caps to melt, leading to a rise in sea level.

Increasing Risk from Extreme Weather

Poor Land Management Increases the Risk of Flooding Occurring

1) An increase in **storm frequency** or **severity increases** the **risk** of **flooding**.
2) But **poor land management** increases the risk of an extreme weather event **resulting in flooding**:

   1) **Urbanisation** on flood plains **increases** the area of **impermeable surfaces** (e.g. concrete), which **increases surface runoff**, leading to **higher river levels.**
   2) **Agricultural practices** can **affect** the **volume** and **rate** of water reaching a river, e.g. **drainage systems** allow water to flow more quickly into a river channel. Other farming practices (e.g. **removal of vegetation, overgrazing**, use of **heavy machinery**) increase **soil erosion**, which leads to more soil being **deposited** in a river. This **lifts up** the **river bed, decreasing** the **capacity** of the **channel** and increasing the risk of flooding.
   3) **Deforestation reduces interception** and **evapotranspiration**. This **increases** the **volume of water** that reaches the river channel, which **increases discharge** and the risk of flooding.

Page 3 explains interception and evapotranspiration.

Population Growth Along Rivers and Coasts Increases the Number at Risk

1) As the **world's population increases, more people** will be **at risk** from **extreme weather** events and **flooding.**
2) One reason for this is that a **large proportion** of the **world's population** lives near **rivers** or **coasts**, which are **prone** to **flooding**. Some **coastal areas** are also at **risk** from **hurricanes**. As the population **grows, more people** live in these areas, which **increases** the **number** of people experiencing **flooding** and **hurricanes.**
3) In **2006/07**, local **planning authorities** in **England** gave **permission** for **13 major developments** to go ahead **against Environment Agency advice** on flood risk. Around **two million properties** in England and Wales are on the **flood plains** of rivers or on low-lying land **close to the coast**, so are **at risk** from **flooding**. For example, the UK city of **York** is built on the **flood plain** of the **River Ouse** and despite severe floods, several **new housing developments** have been built on the **flood plain** in recent years.
4) Some people believe there's **no alternative** to using **flood plain land** for **development** because sometimes it's the **only land** available to support a **growing population**.

Various Factors may Contribute to Increased Risk from Extreme Weather

EXAMPLE — Flooding along the River Ouse, UK

1) **Various factors** have been **blamed** for the **increase** in the **frequency** and **severity** of **flooding** along the **River Ouse** in **Yorkshire**. These include **global warming, housing developments** on the **flood plain, overgrazing** in the **drainage basin** and **poor flood defences.**
2) The **relative importance** of each of these **factors** is **disputed** by **different groups** including the **Environment Agency, farmers, developers** and **local councils** — partly because all these groups have **different self-interests.**
3) There's **evidence** to suggest **all these factors** may play a part — but **proving** that **one factor** is the **most important** is **very difficult**. Most people now recognise that a **range of factors** all have **some impact** — so **each factor** is addressed in **flood management strategies.**

There's more information about factors that increase the risk of flooding on page 12.

Practice Question

Q1 Give two ways in which global warming is thought to lead to an increased risk of hurricanes.

Exam Question

Q1 Explain the factors that may have led to an increased risk of flooding in the UK. [10 marks]

Extreme weather is getting more violent — now it's sandbags at dawn...

Bad news, it's getting worse... Extreme weather that is, not this book. You need to learn what makes it worse, what's making it more likely to cause flooding, and why it's not always great to live by water. So, what are you waiting for — cover the page and get scribbling.

Increasing Flood Risk — Fieldwork and Research

***These pages are for** Edexcel Unit 2 (Extreme Weather **option**).*
Those examiners just won't be happy until you're standing knee deep in a freezing cold stream with a tape measure...

You Need to be Able to **Investigate Why** a **River Floods**

There's loads more about these factors on p. 12.

To investigate why a river floods you need to know the **factors** that **increase flood risk** — they include:

- **Meteorological factors**, e.g. heavy precipitation, prolonged precipitation, warm conditions causing snow melt.
- **Other physical factors** (characteristics of the drainage basin), e.g. impermeable ground, steep slopes, sparse vegetation.
- **Human factors** (land use), e.g. urbanisation, increased agriculture, deforestation.

1 You can do **Fieldwork** to Show the Link Between **Precipitation** and **Flooding**

Heavy and **prolonged precipitation** are major causes of river **flooding**. A good way to investigate the **link** between **precipitation** and **flooding** is to **measure precipitation** and **estimate river discharge** (the volume of water that flows in a river per second). It's best to do this at **one or more locations** along a river, over a **period of time** (hours or days).

1) You can **measure** the amount of **precipitation** (in mm) using a **rain gauge**.
2) You can **measure water velocity** (in m/s) by **timing** how long something that floats takes to **pass between two points**.
3) You can **estimate** the **cross-sectional area** (in m^2) by taking **depth measurements** at **several points** across a river. You can use these to draw the river's **cross section** on **graph paper**, and **count** the **squares** to work out the area.
4) To **calculate river discharge** (in m^3/s), multiply the **water velocity** by the **cross-sectional area** of the channel.
5) Once you've recorded precipitation and river discharge **over a period of time**, you can plot them both on one graph called a **hydrograph**. A hydrograph allows you to see the **link** between **precipitation** and **river discharge**, and from your hydrograph you can work out the river's **lag time** (the delay between peak rainfall and peak discharge).
6) If you carry out your fieldwork when a river floods you'll be able to **estimate** the **discharge** needed for the river to **flood**. This is called the **bankfull discharge** — the discharge at which the water level reaches the top of the river channel. If the **discharge** of the river **rises above** the **bankfull discharge**, the river will **flood**.

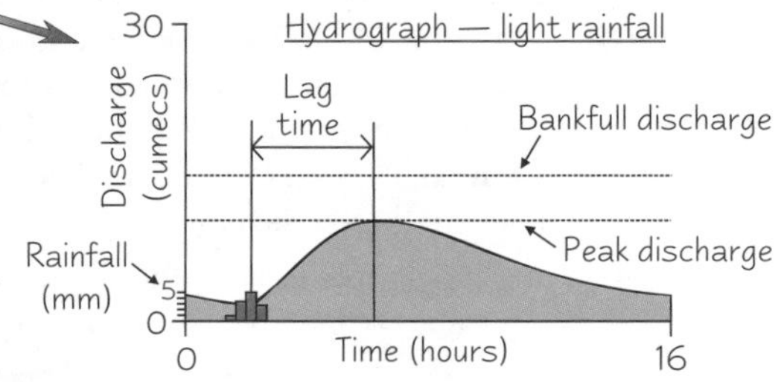

2 You can **Measure Physical Factors** that Affect **Flooding**

There are a few **physical factors** (other than precipitation) that affect flooding:

1) **Surface runoff** (water running over the ground) — the **amount** and **speed** of **surface runoff** affects the risk of flooding because the **sooner** precipitation reaches the river channel, the more chance there is of the river level rising above **bankfull discharge**. Surface runoff can be **measured directly** by digging a ditch of a known area and using a container to **collect runoff**. You need to **divide** the **amount of runoff** collected **by the rainfall** at each location so you can **compare** locations **fairly**.
2) **Infiltration** (water soaking into the soil) — a **high infiltration** rate **reduces surface runoff** and vice versa. **Infiltration rates** can be measured using an '**infiltration ring**' that you push into the soil — you pour a **known volume** of water into the ring and then **record the time** it takes to **soak away**.
3) **Vegetation cover** — the **more vegetation** cover there is, the **more rainfall** will be **intercepted**, and so **less water** will **reach** the **channel** (and vice versa). You can **map** the **vegetation cover** of an area of land.

There are **other physical characteristics** of the drainage basin that affect flooding (see p. 12), which you can **measure**, e.g. the **gradient** of the **drainage basin slopes**, **soil type**.

3 You can **Monitor** how **Changes** in **Land Use** are **Increasing Risk**

Changing land use can **increase** the **risk** of **flooding**. E.g. more **urbanisation** creates large areas of **impermeable ground**, increasing surface runoff and river discharge, which can cause flooding. **Agriculture** and **deforestation** also have an effect on the risk of flooding — these are all **human factors** and they're explained in more detail on page 12.

Land use can be **mapped** to record the **amount of urbanisation** (e.g. developments on flood plains, areas of impermeable surfaces like concrete), **agricultural land** and **deforestation**. This can then be **combined** with **research** (see next page) to investigate the **link** between **flooding** and **changing land use**.

Increasing Flood Risk — Fieldwork and Research

Research can be Used to Gather **Reliable Long-Term Data**

Fieldwork provides you with **primary data** about factors that affect flooding, but you'll also need to do some **research** to gather reliable **long-term**, **secondary data** to support your **conclusions**.

1 You can **Research** the Link Between **Precipitation** and **Flooding**

1) You can get **rainfall data** from **local weather stations** or the **Met Office** — **meteorological data** and **weather reports** go back to the **1860s**. You can also look at **weather diaries** from the **18th century**. You can use this data to investigate the **long-term links** between **precipitation** and **flooding**, e.g. you could see whether **historical flood events** occurred in periods of **high rainfall**.
2) You can get **river discharge data** (including **hydrograph records**) from the UK **National River Flow Archive** (NRFA) or **local gauging stations**. These records often go back **many years**. You can use this data to **investigate** the **long-term links** between **river discharge** and **flooding**, e.g. you could find out **how high** the **river discharge** was when **past floods** occurred.
3) Information about the **size** and **impact** of **previous floods** can be found in **newspaper archives**, **council reports** and **National Water Archive sources**. This information can be useful in calculating **flood return intervals** (how often a flood of a **certain magnitude** is likely to **occur** — see p. 13).

2 You can **Research** How **Physical Factors** Affect **Flooding**

1) You can use **Ordnance Survey® maps** to work out the **size** and **gradient** of river **drainage basins** you're studying. Rainfall in drainage basins with **steep slopes** will reach the river more quickly, **increasing discharge**.
2) Look at **maps** on the **British Geological Survey** website to find out the **rock type** in different areas. Rocks like **granite** are **impermeable** (don't allow infiltration), which **increases surface runoff**.
3) You can use maps to investigate the **link** between **vegetation cover** and **flooding**. **Woodland** areas **reduce river discharge** because the vegetation **intercepts** precipitation before it hits the ground.

3 You can **Research** How **Changing Land Use** Affects **Flooding**

1) You can look for **historical maps**, **land use surveys**, **old photographs** and **historical diaries** (e.g. Samuel Pepys' diary) in **libraries** and **online**. These sources can show how land use has changed over the years, so you can **investigate the links** between **land use changes** (e.g. urbanisation) and **flooding**.
2) There are **flood risk maps** on the **Environment Agency** website. The maps show **areas at risk** from **flooding**, areas benefiting from **flood defences** and **flood management plans** for the future. You can use this data to see if flood defences have reduced the risk of flooding in some areas.
3) The **Environment Agency** also produces **reports** giving details about **previous floods**. You can use these reports to look at the **human factors** associated with **previous floods**, e.g. floods that have been made worse by **blocked drains** and **concrete driveways**.

Practice Questions

Q1 What instrument could you use to measure precipitation?

Q2 What data do you need to plot a hydrograph?

Q3 What is infiltration and how could you measure it?

Q4 Where can you obtain long-term rainfall data from?

Exam Question

Q1 Describe and explain a programme of fieldwork and research you have carried out to investigate the physical factors that affect flooding. [15 marks]

I'm a meteorological dater — I just love Siân Lloyd...

Yup, you guessed it — it's another one of those exciting fieldwork and research topics. And I bet you've been lucky enough to go out and play pooh sticks in a river somewhere. So make sure you put that information to good use — if you get a question about fieldwork and research, dazzle the examiners with your detailed methods... they'll just love it.

Managing Extreme Weather

These pages are for Edexcel Unit 2 (Extreme Weather option). *Weather's getting worse — please tell me we can manage this...*

There are Strategies that Reduce the Impact of Extreme Weather

It's **not possible** to **prevent** extreme weather events from occurring. The only way to **manage** them is to implement **strategies** that **reduce** their **impacts**. Here are some **examples** of strategies:

There's loads more about flood management strategies on pages 16-17.

Flooding

Flooding can be an **impact of extreme weather**, but there are ways to **prevent** it. Strategies include:

1) **Hard engineering** strategies — **built structures** that prevent flooding, e.g. dams, levees.
2) **Soft engineering** strategies — encouraging **natural protection** from flooding, e.g. conserving wetlands.

If flooding does occur, there are ways to **reduce** the **impact** (to **minimise loss of life** and **property damage**). Strategies include:

1) **Forecasting** and **warning systems** — **weather forecasts** are used by **government organisations** to **predict flooding events**, so **warnings** can be given for people to **protect** their **property** or **evacuate**. E.g. before Carlisle flooded in 2005, the **Environment Agency** issued **flood warnings** via the **media** and direct **door knocking**, and sent **automatic voice messages** to over **5000 properties at risk**.
2) **Emergency plans** — **rescue plans**, **evacuation routes** and **emergency supplies** are put in place in areas **vulnerable** to **flooding**, to **minimise loss of life**. E.g. the **RAF** are **trained** in how to **rescue** people from floods using helicopters.
3) **Community education** — **information** about **what to do** in the event of a flood and how to **protect** your **home** is provided by organisations like the **Environment Agency** and **local councils**.

You can do **fieldwork** on flood strategies, e.g. **mapping where** they are and **recording** the **types**.
You can **research** flood strategies **online**, e.g. on the **Environment Agency** and **local UK councils' websites**.

Drought

1) **Conservation** of **surface water** and **groundwater** — e.g. **water use restrictions**.
2) **Changing agricultural practices** — e.g. planting crops **less dependent** on **water**, encouraging practices that **improve infiltration** and **retention** of **soil moisture**, **avoiding overgrazing** and **minimising erosion**.
3) Building **canals** or **redirecting rivers** to **irrigate** areas suffering from **drought**.

You can **research** drought strategies **online**, e.g. at the **Food & Agriculture Organisation website**.

Hurricanes

1) **Forecasting** and **warning systems** — national weather forecasting bodies (such as the **National Hurricane Center** (**NHC**) in the USA) issue **hurricane warnings** via **radio** and **television** so people can get **supplies**, **secure** their **homes** and prepare to **evacuate**. E.g. the **NHC** issued **warnings** two days **before Hurricane Katrina** hit New Orleans, so a lot of people were able to **evacuate**, which **saved** many **lives**.
2) **Emergency plans** — **rescue plans**, **evacuation routes** and **emergency supplies** are put in place in areas **vulnerable** to **hurricanes**, to **minimise loss of life**. E.g. **refuges** with **emergency supplies** were set up for people who couldn't leave **New Orleans**.
3) **Community Education** — **governments** provide **information** about **what to do** and how to **protect** your **home**.

You can **research** hurricane forecasting systems **online**, e.g. at the **National Hurricane Center** website.

Some Strategies are More Successful than Others

You can use **fieldwork** and **research** to **evaluate** the **success** of existing **disaster management strategies**, for example:

1) You could visit somewhere that suffers from **frequent extreme weather events**, e.g. York suffers from flooding.
2) You'll need to **compare** the **impact** of **similar extreme weather events** — **before** and **after** the **management strategies** were put in place. E.g. **compare** the **impact** of the **1982 flood** in York (before river embankments were raised and sluice gates constructed) with the impact of the **2000 flood** (which happened after their construction).
3) Find **data** to help your **comparisons**. E.g. look at the **Environment Agency website** and **newspaper articles** to find the **size** of the area flooded, the **cost** of the damage and the **number** of **houses flooded** in the 1982 and 2000 floods.
4) Using the **data**, decide whether or not the **impact** was **lower** when the management strategies were in place (**not** all strategies are **successful**). Also look for any **unwanted side effects**, e.g. damage to natural habitats.

Managing Extreme Weather

New Technology *and* **More Powerful Technology** *has* **Led** *to...*

1 More Accurate Weather Forecasts

As **computers** and **radars** get **more powerful**, **forecasts** of **extreme weather** become **more accurate** and **more detailed**. This means **earlier warnings** can be given, so people have **more time** to **protect** their **property** or **evacuate**, which **reduces damage** and **loss of life**. Here are some **examples** of how technology is improving the accuracy of forecasts:

1) The **Met Office** is responsible for UK weather forecasting. It uses **supercomputers**, which are **more powerful** and have **faster processing speeds** than previous models. This means scientists can run **more complex weather models**, making the forecasts **more accurate**. Forecasting **accuracy** (e.g. correctly predicting the next day's rainfall in a particular place) rose from **79%** in **1980**, to **86%** in **1996**, because of **computer upgrades**.

2) The **National Oceanic and Atmospheric Administration** (**NOAA**) in the **USA** warns of **dangerous weather events** such as **storms** and **hurricanes**. In the **1980s** and **1990s**, NOAA **replaced** its **conventional weather radars** with **doppler radars**, which can **measure** the **speed** of **precipitation particles** as well as their **position** and **intensity**. Scientists can now **identify wind patterns** that could cause **tornadoes**. By **2011**, NOAA will have a network of **radars** that will help scientists identify **rain**, **hail** and **snow**, allowing **more accurate predictions** of extreme weather.

2 Better Coordinated Disaster Response

A **Geographic Information System** (**GIS**) is **software** that's used to **compare** and **analyse** different **sets** of **geographical data** — different maps are **overlaid** on top of each other. GIS can be used to **highlight densely populated areas** that are most **at risk** from an extreme weather event, so **search and rescue teams** can be **sent** to these areas and the **right areas** can be **evacuated**. For example, the **Federal Emergency Management Agency** (**FEMA**) can use GIS to **map** where **populations** are at **most risk** from **river flooding**. It does this by mapping the **flood plains**, then mapping the **densely populated areas** near to them and putting both maps **together** — the **overlap** shows the areas where most people are at risk.

3 Better Communications

New **communication technologies** include **portable cellphone towers** and **communications support trucks** with **satellite uplink**. These all help provide **better communication** during extreme weather events, **reducing loss of life** and **minimising damage**. For example, communications support trucks help **emergency services** stay in **contact** with **each other** and **weather forecasters**. This helps them perform **rescue operations efficiently** and keeps them **updated** on the **progress** of the **weather event**.

4 Drought-resistant crops

Advances in **genetic engineering technology** have led to the development of **drought-resistant crops**, which can **withstand long periods of drought**. They can help to **reduce loss of life** (from starvation) in drought-prone areas by providing **food**. However, many of these crops are still in the **experimental stage**, e.g. some don't grow well when it does rain.

5 Hurricane-Proof and Flood-Proof Buildings

Hurricane-proof and **flood-proof buildings** are buildings that have been **designed** to **withstand** floods or hurricanes. This means that when a flood or hurricane occurs there's **less structural damage**, leading to **reduced financial cost** and **loss of life**. At the moment the **technologies** involved are **expensive**, but in the **long-term** they may work out **cheaper** than the cost of **rebuilding** after disasters.

Practice Questions

Q1 Briefly describe two strategies that reduce the impact of drought.

Q2 Briefly describe two strategies that reduce the impact of hurricanes.

Exam Question

Q1 Outline the ways in which new technology and more powerful technology have improved the management of extreme weather events. [10 marks]

NOAA uses powerful computers to ensure the animals come in two by two...

Crikey, there seems to be an awful lot of text on these two pages... Don't worry, just make sure you know the strategies used to reduce the impact of extreme weather, how you can investigate if they're successful and how new technology is helping us. Phew.

Drought and Water Management

*These pages are for **Edexcel Unit 2 (Extreme Weather option).** Droughts tend to last for longer than other extreme weather events, like tornadoes — in fact droughts can last for years. So their impact needs to be managed using sustainable strategies.*

Managing Drought Involves Physical, Social, Economic & Political Responses

Governments, **water authorities**, **agricultural organisations**, **businesses**, **communities** and **individuals** all have **different strategies** for **reducing** the **impacts** of **drought** by **managing water supply** and **use**. Strategies include:

- **Physical responses** — e.g. **diverting** rivers and canals from wetter areas to **drier areas**.
- **Social responses** — e.g. **recycling water** from treated waste to use for flushing toilets.
- **Political responses** — e.g. **policies** to **regulate** water **supply** and **use**.
- **Economic responses** — e.g. **grants** to help **farmers** introduce **water-saving technologies**.

A drought management strategy is **sustainable** if it **permanently reduces water use** and **doesn't deplete resources** (e.g. money).

Case Study 1 — Drought And Water Management In Australia

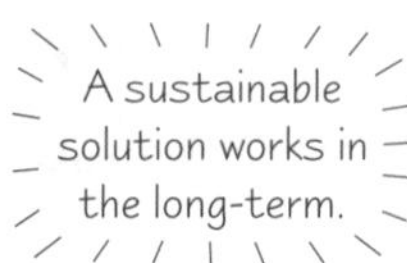
A sustainable
solution works in
the long-term.

Parts of **Australia** have been suffering from **severe drought** for **several years** (see p. 96).
Various **strategies** have been used to try to **reduce its impact**:

1) **Perth** has a **desalination plant** that supplies the city with **17%** of its **water**. The plant continuously **filters**, **treats** and **desalinates** (removes the salt from) **seawater** and **mixes** it with the **public water supply**. It's **powered** by **renewable energy** from **wind farms** and seawater is a **renewable resource** — so it's a **sustainable** strategy. **More** desalination plants are **planned** in Australia.

2) Many Australian regions have **temporary** or **permanent water use restrictions**, e.g. the **Murray-Darling Basin** region. **Water restrictions** include **banning** people from **watering lawns**, **washing vehicles**, **cleaning windows** and **refilling swimming pools**. Permanent water restrictions will **permanently reduce water use**, so they're a **sustainable** strategy.

3) Over **500 sewage treatment plants** in Australia now **recycle** some of their **treated wastewater** and **sewage**. **Households** have both a **drinking water supply** and a **recycled water supply**, which is used for **watering gardens**, **washing cars** and **flushing toilets**. Water recycling schemes **permanently reduce water use** and so are a **sustainable** strategy.

Mmm, tasty recycled water.

4) The Australian **Government** has introduced **rules**, **guidelines** and **educational programmes**, e.g. **labelling schemes** — products like washing machines must have a label showing their **water efficiency**. These schemes aim to **permanently reduce water use**, so they're a **sustainable strategy**.

5) The **Government** provides **direct economic assistance** (e.g. income support, interest rate subsidies) to **farmers**, **rural communities** and **small businesses** that are **dependent** on **agriculture**. Over **$1000 million** was provided in **drought assistance** in **2007**. These assistance schemes have a **high financial cost**, which **can't** necessarily be **maintained** in the long-term, so they're **not sustainable**.

6) Many people believe that **farming certain crops** (e.g. cotton) in **some areas** of Australia **can't** be **maintained**. So, the Government offers **'exit grants'** of up to **$170 000** to **help farmers leave** their **land**, **relocate** and **retrain**. Exit grants can **permanently reduce water use** so they aim to be **sustainable**, but they have a **huge financial cost** so will only work as long as the Government can **afford** them.

7) The **Government** also **funds research** into **strategies** such as **cloud seeding** (dispersing substances such as sliver iodide into clouds, to induce rainfall), **water-conserving agricultural techniques** and growing **drought-resistant crops**. These strategies may be **sustainable** if they **permanently reduce water use** but it depends on how **expensive** they are to introduce.

These strategies have some **disadvantages**:

1) The **cost** of **building** the **desalination plant** in Perth was **very high**.
2) Many people **dislike** the **idea** of using **recycled water** as **drinking water**. E.g. **people** in **Toowoomba**, in the Murray-Darling Basin, **rejected** a proposal (**62%** against) to use **recycled water** for **25%** of the town's **drinking water** supply.
3) **Not many farmers accept exit grants**, e.g. because they may feel **forced** into **abandoning** a **family history** of **farming**.
4) **Cloud seeding doesn't work** in **cloudless skies**, which **limits** its use.

Drought and Water Management

Case Study 2 — Drought in South-East England

South-east England is prone to **dry weather** and **water shortages** — a recent **drought** lasted from **2004** to **2006**. Various **strategies** are being used to **reduce its impact**:

1) **Water companies** are trying to **fix leaking pipes**, which **waste** huge amounts of **water** — over **900 million litres** of water are lost **every day** in **London** through **leaking pipes**. This is a **sustainable** strategy because it **permanently reduces water wastage**.

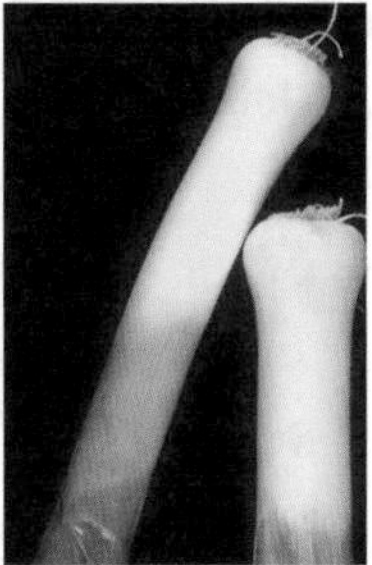

The real culprit of drought...

2) The UK's first **desalination plant** has been approved for **east London** and is expected to be completed in **2009**. It will only operate in **periods** of **drought** or **low rainfall** and will treat **Thames estuary water** to provide almost a **million people a day** with **drinking water**. Even though it's **costing a lot** (an estimated **£250 m**) to build the plant, **Thames Water** are committed to running the plant on **100% renewable energy** (initially **biodiesel**, with wind power a possibility in the future). They also plan to use **waste energy** to **provide heating** for nearby homes. The desalination plant **won't deplete resources** so will be **sustainable**.

3) When **water levels** are **low**, **water companies restrict public water use** (e.g. hosepipe bans, sprinkler bans, car-wash bans) and the **Environment Agency restricts water** being used for **agriculture**. If these water restrictions are only **temporary**, they won't permanently reduce water use so **won't be sustainable**.

4) The **Government**, **Environment Agency** and **water companies** encourage **water conservation** through **campaigns** to **educate** people and **promote water efficiency** in homes, businesses and industry. For example, companies offer **free devices** to place in **toilet cisterns**, so **less water** is used when **flushing**. These **schemes** aim to **permanently reduce water use** so are **sustainable**.

5) The **Government** plans to **review water tariffs** and install **water meters** in areas **worst affected** by drought. Water metering means that people are **charged** for the **exact amount** of water they **use** — so they create a **financial incentive** to **use less** water. It's hoped the plan will **permanently reduce** water **use** and be a **sustainable** strategy.

These strategies have some **disadvantages**:

1) It's **not** always **easy** for water companies to **repair leaks**, e.g. because they might need **council permission** to **close roads** while the leaks are fixed. Fixing leaks can also be **expensive** and can take a **long time**.
2) Desalination plants are **very expensive** and some people think there's **no need** to spend such a huge amount of money building one in London — they think **fixing** the **leaking pipes** will **solve** the **water shortage**.
3) Some people argue that **compulsory water meters** are **unfair** to families living on a **low income** because they **won't** be able to **afford** the amount of water they **need**.

Practice Questions

Q1 What's meant by a 'sustainable' drought management strategy?

Q2 List five strategies used in Australia to manage the impacts of drought.

Q3 Give two disadvantages of Australia's drought management strategies.

Q4 List four strategies used in south-east England to manage drought.

Q5 Why do some people object to London's new desalination plant?

Exam Question

Q1 With reference to at least two named examples, discuss the sustainability of a range of drought management strategies. [10 marks]

Exit Grant — not just a stage direction from Eastenders...

I think I might be behind the times with that gag — he's not been in it for years, has he? Anyway, exam questions on drought are likely to ask you to compare the sustainability of drought management strategies, so make sure you know if they permanently reduce water use or if they deplete resources. Desalination plant or recycled water — it's a tough call...

Introduction to Globalisation

This section is for Edexcel Unit 1 (Going Global).
Globalisation — the process that's bringing the world closer together. I know that sounds like an advert for some sickeningly soppy film, but the world really is coming together and it's happening faster than it used to. Read on...

Globalisation is How Countries Become More Closely Integrated

Globalisation's important because it's a big part of **how** and **why** the world's **changing** to become one **big global community**:

1) Every country has its own **political** and **economic systems** as well as its own **culture**.
2) **Globalisation** is the process of all the world's systems and cultures becoming more **integrated** — it's the **whole world** coming together like a **single community** with **similar**, **shared** systems and cultures.
3) Globalisation changes how people think of **distance** and **time**. People can **interact easily** with other people anywhere in the world, no matter how **far apart** they are — it feels like the world's **shrinking**.
4) For example, in a **globalised world** Great Britain could **potentially** have as much **political**, **economic** and **cultural interaction** with countries on the **other side** of the world, like **New Zealand**, as it can with its immediate neighbours, like **France**.

Bless my soul! She's in Peru but I can hear her through this box.

If everyone stayed in their own country and **didn't interact** in any way with other countries there would be **no globalisation**. If everyone **interacted freely** and countries were **fully integrated** so the global community acted like a **single society**, there would be **total globalisation**. The real world is somewhere **in between**. But as countries and people **interact more**, globalisation is **increasing**.

You can look at globalisation as a process that changes the **connections** between **people** and **environments** across the globe:

1) The connections between places are **lengthening** — **new links** are being formed between places that are **far apart**, e.g. you can fly to pretty much **any country** and companies operate in **multiple countries**.
2) The connections between places are becoming **deeper** — **more** people's lives are increasingly involved with far-away places, **not** just the richest people. E.g. **anyone** can buy products imported from **all over the world** in their **local supermarket**, and you can **easily reach** anyone in the world by **phone** or the **internet**.

Globalisation's a really important concept, but people have **different ideas** about what it means. Some people only think about **economic globalisation** (e.g. **trading goods** with people all over the world). Other people are only concerned with **cultural globalisation** (e.g. the adoption of **Western lifestyles** by many countries).
Remember, globalisation is about **all** these things — global **political**, **economic** and **cultural** integration.

Globalisation has Been Happening for Thousands of Years

Although globalisation might seem like a **recent concept**, in one form or another it's been going on for a **long time**:

1) **Exploration** and **war** have led to **interactions** between different populations for **thousands of years**. This has resulted in the **trading** and **sharing** of different **cultures**, **politics** and **beliefs**. For example, the **Roman Empire** spread across (and controlled) large areas of the world around **2000** years ago. They brought a new political system, **new technology** and a different culture, some of which **remained** long after they left.
2) **Goods** have been traded around the globe for a **long time**, though the **global economic system** we know today is a fairly **recent development**. The recent system started when **large companies** began to operate in **several countries**, e.g. in the 17th century the **East India Company** traded a lot with British colonies throughout **east Asia**.
3) Globalisation **accelerated** in the **19th century** because of **increasing trade** between **European empires**. Acceleration continued in the **20th century** because of increasing trade with the **USA**. Global trade was **slowed** by the First and Second **World Wars** because they **severely damaged** European economies, slowing globalisation.
4) Globalisation has really **accelerated** since the 1980s. Huge **global brands** and **corporations** have **easy access** to most countries and are known **all over the world**, helping to create a sense of **global community**.

We've come to conquer... Ahem, I mean share our culture.

Introduction to Globalisation

Globalisation is Accelerating

Globalisation is occurring at an **increasing rate** due to four **key factors**:

GDP (Gross Domestic Product) is a measure of a country's income.

1 Trans-National Corporations (TNCs)

1) TNCs are companies that **produce**, **sell** or are **located** in **two or more** countries, e.g. **Sony** manufacture **electronic products** in **China** and **Japan**, and **sell** many of them in **Europe** and the **USA**.
2) Some TNCs generate **more money** than the GDP of some nations, e.g. oil companies like **Shell**.
3) TNCs bring lots of **investment** into countries, spread **new technologies** and can promote particular **cultures**, e.g. **McDonald's** bring **Western-style** fast food to other countries.
4) **Potential investment**, the **creation of jobs** and access to **new technology** means TNCs can have **political influence**.
5) TNCs have **grown in size** and **number** in the last 50 years, and are **continuing** to move into **more countries**.
6) They're thought to be one of the **main driving forces** behind globalisation because of the economic, political and cultural **interactions** that occur **between** the countries where they operate.

TNCs are covered in more detail on pages 110-111.

2 New markets

1) The **increasing prosperity** of developing countries opens up **new markets** for companies, e.g. Western companies can sell more to countries like China and India, which have **large populations** and **increasing wealth**.
2) Global share trading involves buying and selling **shares** at **stock exchanges**. Exchanges in **less developed** countries are getting **bigger** and attracting **more investment**, e.g. **Mumbai** (India) and **Shanghai** (China).
3) The availability of **new markets** and **stock exchanges encourages** more **global trade**, which **accelerates** globalisation.

3 Improved communications

1) Communications can mean **transport mechanisms**, e.g. aeroplanes and high-speed rail, or **information exchanges**, e.g. the internet and e-mail.
2) Transport mechanisms have been **improving** since the mid-20th century. More people have **easier access** to **new products** and to places that are **further away**, making people **better connected**.
3) Electronic information exchanges allow **instant communication** for **individuals** and **businesses** to any part of the world.
4) Better communications make the world seem **smaller** — distance becomes much **less important**, allowing **businesses** and **individuals** to interact with **anyone**, **anywhere** (the world is **shrinking**).

4 International organisations

1) International organisations bring **people**, **money** and **information together** — helping to accelerate globalisation.
2) The **World Bank** offers **money** to poorer nations to help them **develop**. It provides **loans** to fund **development projects**, e.g. building schools and better roads. **Improved infrastructure** means poorer countries are more likely to attract **international investment**, helping to create **connections** between **rich** and **poor** countries.
3) The **International Monetary Fund** (**IMF**) is an organisation that **regulates** the global financial system and lends money to make countries more **financially stable**. Countries with **failing economies** find it hard to **trade** or **attract investment**. IMF loans **increase** economic stability, helping these countries to participate in **global trade**.
4) The **World Trade Organisation** (**WTO**) regulates the **rules of trade** between countries. It's designed to **reduce barriers** to trade between countries, e.g. setting up agreements where **tariffs** (**taxes**) on trade are **reduced** or **removed**. This increases **trade** between countries, which increases **interaction** and **globalisation**.

Practice Questions

Q1 Describe globalisation.

Q2 Name one international organisation involved in accelerating globalisation.

Exam Question

Q1 Describe and explain why globalisation has been accelerating. [15 marks]

Lengthening connections — I just use an extension cable...

Aaaaw, globalisation's making the world into one big happy family, and the fatherly forces of TNCs, big new markets, improved communications and international organisations are making sure the global family gets more quality time together.

Global Groupings

***These pages are for** Edexcel Unit 1 (Going Global).*
As globalisation increases and the world becomes more connected, it's useful to group countries together in certain ways. Global groupings are important because they show how money and power are shared out (and who's best buds with who).

Countries can be put into **Economic** and **Political Groupings**

Countries can be put into **broad economic** and **political groups** because **wealth** and **power** aren't shared out **equally** around the world. These groups **change** over time as the **wealth** and **power** of countries **change**. For example, most countries used to be classified as either **More** or **Less Economically Developed** (**MEDCs** and **LEDCs**). It's now thought that this system is too **simplistic** — there are too many **stages** of **economic development** to put all countries into only **two categories**.
You need to learn these **three** groupings:

LDCs

1) **Least Developed Countries** (**LDCs**) are a group of around **50** countries that are defined by **very low incomes**, **poor health**, **low education**, **economic instability** and their **heavy debt** to richer countries, e.g. **Mozambique**.
2) Their economies are usually based on **agriculture**, so crop failures can lead to economic **disaster**.
3) Countries are **moved out** of the LDC group when conditions **improve**, e.g. **Botswana**.

NICs

1) **Newly Industrialised Countries** (**NICs**) aren't yet classified as **developed** countries (like the **UK**), but aren't thought of as **LDCs** (like **Bangladesh**) either.
2) Their economies are usually **growing** very fast, and there has often been a **recent move** from a mostly **agricultural** economy to one involving **manufacturing** and **exporting**.
3) The term was originally used for the **Asian 'Tiger'** economies of **Singapore**, **Hong Kong**, **South Korea** and **Taiwan**, although some people now argue they're **fully developed** and so shouldn't be referred to as NICs any more.
4) There's **no official** list of NICs, though **China** and **India** are **currently** thought of as NICs.

Ex-Soviet states — Middle-income countries

1) **Russia** and some of the surrounding countries in **central Asia** and **eastern Europe** used to make up **one large state** called the **Soviet Union**. A lot of **independent countries** have been created since the Soviet Union **collapsed** in 1991 — these are mostly now classed as **middle-income countries**, e.g. **Estonia**.
2) **Middle-income countries** have **growing economies**, but the growth isn't as **rapid** as the **NICs** and their development hasn't reached the **same level**, e.g. **Ukraine**.
3) Recent **growth** in some ex-Soviet states is due to the exploitation of **natural resources**, e.g. oil and gas in **Kazakhstan**.
4) The **privatisation of industries** (**state controlled** in Soviet times to **privately controlled** now) has led to economic **recovery** and **growth** in many ex-Soviet states, e.g. **Belarus**.

Countries can be **Members** of **Voluntary Groups**

The G8 is one of the world's most powerful and wealthy groups — it's made up of Canada, France, Germany, Italy, Japan, Russia, USA and the UK.

Some countries form voluntary groups to gain **mutual economic benefits**:

OPEC

1) The **Organisation of Petroleum Exporting Countries** (**OPEC**) is a group of **13** major **oil-producing** countries, e.g. **Venezuela**, **Iran**, **Angola** and **Indonesia**. OPEC countries control around **two-thirds** of global oil reserves.
2) Because they're a **large group** in control of a large amount of oil, they can make sure they get a **fair price** from oil-consuming countries (e.g. the **UK**).
3) Some members have **left** since OPEC was founded because they wanted to produce **more oil** than the agreed **OPEC quotas** allowed, e.g. **Gabon**. Other countries have also been invited to **join**, e.g. **Bolivia** and **Sudan**.

OECD

1) The **Organisation for Economic Cooperation and Development** (**OECD**) is a group of around **30** of the **richest** and **most powerful** countries. The top eight are called the **G8**.
2) They meet to **discuss** and provide possible **solutions** to **economic**, **environmental** and **social issues**.
3) Members of the OECD are always **changing** too, e.g. potential **new members** include **Brazil**, **China** and **India**.

Global Groupings

Countries can Group Together for Mutual Advantage

Trade blocs

Trade blocs are groups of countries that make **agreements** to **reduce barriers** to trade, e.g. by removing **tariffs** (**taxes** on imported goods). Blocs **increase** trade between members, and members can work together as a **larger organisation** to trade with non-members. **Benefits** of membership of a trade bloc are linked to **two** important concepts:

1) **Economies of scale** — the **advantages** companies gain because of **increased sales**. There's a **larger market** for all companies within the trade bloc because it's **easier to trade** with all the other member countries. This **increases sales**. More sales means **more products** need to be made, so companies can buy the **raw materials** for their products in **greater numbers, saving money**. Buying raw materials in **bulk** means each product **costs less** to make, so companies can make **more profit**.
2) **Comparative advantage** — countries can **concentrate** on developing **specific industries**. Being in a trade bloc means it's **easier to trade** for all the **different** goods and services a country needs, because trade is **less restricted**. So countries can **specialise** in producing the things they're **good** at making and trade for the things they're **not good** at making. Production will **increase** in each member country because they're concentrating on **what they do best**, so production will **increase** in the trade bloc **overall**.

Trade bloc example — NAFTA

1) The **North American Free Trade Agreement** is an example of a trade bloc. It's called NAFTA because it's an agreement between the countries of North America — **USA**, **Canada** and **Mexico**.
2) It's made **trade** between the members **easier** by removing things like **import taxes** on some goods.
3) Trade between all three countries has **increased** but there are **other impacts**, e.g. **job losses** in the **USA** because the manufacture of some goods has been moved to **Mexico**, where labour is **cheaper**.

There are Inequalities in Wealth and Power Between Countries

These groupings of countries highlight the **inequalities** in **wealth** and **power** around the world. **Most** of the wealth and power is in the hands of a **few countries**, e.g. the **G8** have over **60%** of the **gross world product** (the **total income** of the world), and control most of the **military power**, even though they're **only eight** countries.

These groupings also show how wealth and power can **change**. For example, **Russia** didn't officially join the **G7** (to form the **G8**) until 1997 because of the power issues of the **cold war** (a period of **political struggle** between the **USA** and the **Soviet Union**) and **economic problems** in Russia after the **collapse** of the Soviet Union.

Because **wealthy countries** often form groups **together**, they become more **closely integrated**. This means they're more likely to get **even wealthier** and **develop solutions** to their own economic, environmental and social **problems** at a **faster rate**. This can lead to a **widening of the gap** between **poorer** and **wealthier** countries.

The annual meeting of the Jovial Organisation of Kipper Eaters (JOKE) was unexpectedly busy.

Practice Questions

Q1 Suggest one reason why some middle-income countries are growing in wealth.

Q2 Name the voluntary group that includes about 30 of the richest and most powerful countries in the world.

Q3 Name one example of a trade bloc and list the countries it involves.

Exam Questions

Q1 Compare and contrast LDCs with NICs. [4 marks]

Q2 Describe comparative advantage and state how countries in a trade bloc can benefit from it. [2 marks]

NICs — I thought they were a basketball team...

So there are global groupings that countries belong to because of how rich and powerful they are. Then there are global groupings countries agree to be in because it'll help them out, like OPEC and the OECD. It all sounds like the playground to me — there are the geeks and the jocks... I've gone all American — well that's globalisation for you.

Trans-National Corporations

***These pages are for** Edexcel Unit 1 (Going Global).*
Trans-National Corporations (TNCs) are worldwide companies that are bringing countries together by spreading themselves, and their cash, all over the world. Unfortunately, they don't seem to have spread any cash into my bank account.

TNCs are the Agents of Global Change

Remember — TNCs are companies that produce, sell or are located in two or more countries (see p. 107).

TNCs **accelerate globalisation** by **linking together** groups of countries through the **production and sale of goods**. In large **assembly industries**, the parts are often **made** in one country, **assembled** in a second country, then **sold** in a third. For example, **BAE Systems** make defence vehicles like **submarines**. They use components from **all over the world**, assemble the vehicles in large factories like the ones in **Barrow** (UK), then sell the vehicles to **other countries** such as the **USA**. TNCs **create links** between different countries in several ways:

1) **Mergers** — a merger is where **two companies** (usually of **similar size**) agree to become one **bigger** company, e.g. the two oil and gas companies **BP** and **Amoco** merged in 1998. This helps **links** form **between** the countries where the two companies operate.
2) **Acquisitions** — an acquisition is where one company **buys** another (usually **smaller**) company, e.g. the **US** car company **Ford** bought the **Swedish** company **Volvo Cars** in 1999.
3) **Using Sub-contractors** — TNCs can use **foreign** companies to **manufacture products** without actually **owning** the businesses, e.g. **NIKE** products aren't always made in factories NIKE **own**. This **links** the countries of the TNC and the sub-contracted company **together**.
4) **Foreign Direct Investment (FDI)** — this is any **investment** that gives a TNC a **long-term interest** in a country **outside** the one they're from. It can involve mergers, acquisitions and using sub-contractors, e.g. if **HSBC acquire** a bank in **Indonesia**, they're investing money in Indonesia (that's FDI).

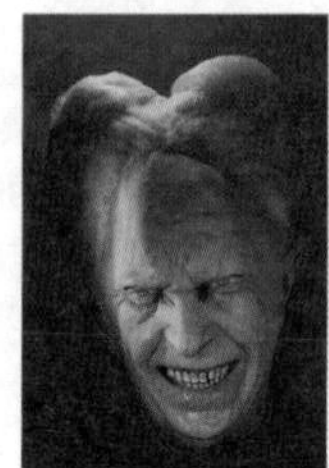

Hi, I'm into murders and executions... I mean mergers and acquisitions... ahem.

A major **criticism** of TNCs is that much of the profit they make from foreign operations doesn't **remain** in the foreign countries — some of it **goes back** to the country of origin. E.g. some of the money made by **Volvo Cars** will be invested back in the **USA**, not **Sweden**.

TNCs can accelerate globalisation by bringing the **culture** from their **country of origin** to many **different countries**. The countries become **linked** by **common patterns of consumption**, e.g. companies like **McDonald's** sell **similar products** in **every country** they operate in. People in different countries are **linked together** because they can **buy** similar products.

Trade Blocs can Help or Hinder TNCs

Trade blocs can reduce or remove **import taxes** between countries in the bloc (see previous page). TNCs operating **within** a trade bloc benefit from these **reduced taxes**, but TNCs that operate across countries that are **in and out** of the trade bloc will have to pay **normal** import taxes. This affects where TNCs **locate** their operations, for example:

1) **Nissan** manufacture cars in **Sunderland** (UK) rather than in their country of **origin** (**Japan**) because it means they don't have to pay **tariffs** to import the cars into the **EU** (**European Union**, a trade bloc in Europe).
2) TNCs from the **USA** gain benefits from the **NAFTA** trade bloc (see p. 109). They can produce goods in **Mexico**, but still sell them in the USA and pay less or no **import tax**. This means they can **cut costs** and **increase profit** because labour is **cheaper** in Mexico and they can still sell at the same prices in the **USA**.

Wal-Mart® is a Retail TNC from a Wealthy Country

Wal-Mart is a chain of discount **department stores** (**ASDA** is part of Wal-Mart). It's one of the **largest** TNCs in the world and the largest **retail** TNC (many of the top TNCs are **oil companies**). It's a case study, so here's your background information:

1) Wal-Mart began when **Sam Walton** opened the first discount store in **Arkansas, USA**.
2) More **stores** opened across Arkansas, then across the USA, and more recently across the **globe** via the **acquisition** of other retail companies. E.g. **Seiyu** in Japan, **ASDA** in the UK and **Bompreço** in Brazil.
3) Some Wal-Mart stores continue to trade under their **own name**, e.g. ASDA.
Others have been **re-branded** as Wal-Mart, e.g. some stores in **Canada**.
4) Some acquisitions **weren't successful**, e.g. Wal-Mart was forced to sell its stores in **Germany** after **struggling** to **compete** with existing discount retailers there (like Lidl).
5) Wal-Mart is starting to **expand** into **NICs** like India, which have huge **new markets**.
For example, Wal-Mart and an **Indian** company called **Bharti Enterprises** are opening new retail outlets **together** in the **style** of Wal-Mart stores.

Trans-National Corporations

Wal-Mart® Helps to Accelerate Globalisation

Like other TNCs, Wal-Mart helps to **accelerate globalisation** — it **links** countries together through the flow of **money**, **people**, **trade** and **information**. It also brings the **culture** of its country of origin (**USA**) to other countries.

In the USA, Wal-Mart gives customers all they need in **one building** at **low cost**. They've **successfully** introduced this in other countries, e.g. ASDA now stocks more non-food items. This hasn't been **successful** in all countries. They're trying a **different approach** in **India** where people like to shop in **traditional markets** rather than supermarkets.

Although Wal-Mart is a global brand it's retained a **local approach** by buying **local companies**. Its stores **aren't** all exactly the **same**, though many of the **products** are, e.g. **George** clothing supplies ASDA in the UK and Wal-Mart in the USA. Selling the **same products** globally helps to create **common patterns of consumption** between different countries.

Wal-Mart Divides Labour Across Different Countries

The **spatial division of labour** is basically splitting up the work of a company so that **each part** is carried out in a **different** location. Companies do this so each part is carried out in the most **cost-effective** place. For example, goods are manufactured where there's **cheap labour** (e.g. developing countries), but **research and development** is carried out where there's a **highly educated**, **skilled** workforce (e.g. more developed countries).

Wal-Mart's workforce is divided because it **sources** products from **all over** the globe and sells them in **many countries**.

1) Some **electronic goods** are made in factories in **China** and **Malaysia**. **Cheaper labour** and **bulk buying** mean Wal-Mart can sell these products at **lower prices** than if they bought goods made in the **USA**.
2) **Clothing** for Wal-Mart (and ASDA) is made by companies like **George**, a **British** company. Criticism of supermarkets for exploiting **cheap labour** in countries like **China** and **India** has led companies like George to **switch** some of their production to the **UK**.

There are Inequalities in Wal-Mart's Global Operation

When TNCs like Wal-Mart **divide** labour across the globe, people from different countries are **linked together** because they **work** for the **same** company. But this doesn't mean **working conditions** or **wages** are **equal**:

1) **Factories** in **China** — workers earn **less than $1** an hour.
2) **Factories** in the **USA** — workers earn the minimum wage of **around $6** an hour.
3) **Headquarters** in the **USA** — executives earn **hundreds of thousands of dollars** a year.

This may seem unfair, but it's the **relative amount** that matters — the **cost of living** in China is **lower** than the USA, so $1 goes **further**. Also, TNCs can offer **more reliable** wages than income from jobs like **subsistence farming**, even if the money isn't great.

I don't think you guys really understood when I said 'people are linked together'.

Practice Questions

Q1 Describe how TNCs link countries together through the production of goods.

Q2 How do trade blocs help TNCs?

Q3 Describe one inequality in Wal-Mart's global operation.

Exam Questions

Q1 Name four ways in which TNCs can create links between different countries. [4 marks]

Q2 Describe the growth and spatial division of labour of one named TNC. [10 marks]

I'm Agent Global Change from the FDI, I'd like to ask you a few questions...

If globalisation's a big juggernaut heading towards a unified world, then TNCs are in the driving seat and they're hitting the gas. They're changing the world by growing and investing their cash in loads of countries. It links together all the countries they're in, all the people that buy their stuff, and all the people that work for them. For Wal-Mart, that's basically the whole world.

Global Winners and Losers

***These pages are for** Edexcel Unit 1 (Going Global).*
Revising with CGP products makes you a winner. Using other, inferior brands will make you a loser.
Right, now you've got that covered let's do some geography — globalisation helps to create global winners and losers.

Some Places are **Switched-on**, Others are **Switched-off**

Air travel, **tourism**, **global businesses** (TNCs) and **communication systems** create global networks — they **connect** different places together, accelerating **globalisation**. Global networks allow **trade**, **money**, **people** and **information** to **flow** around the **world**, e.g. air travel and tourism allow **more people** to travel to different countries, bringing **money** and **information** with them.

Global networks have helped to create places that are **switched-on** (**well connected** to global networks, usually rich and powerful) and places that are **switched-off** (**poorly connected**, usually not wealthy or powerful).

Switched-on places

1) These are the most **highly-connected countries**, as well as the **important cities** in poorer countries, e.g. **Singapore** is an important **port**, **financial centre** and **tourist destination**.
2) Because they're **well connected**, trade, money, people and information **flow easily** between them and elsewhere — they're **global hubs** because global networks flow **through them**.
3) People in switched-on places are significant **consumers** and **producers** of goods and services because they're well connected.
4) **Energy usage** and the **ecological footprint** (how much a place **impacts** on natural resources) are **large** because of the **high levels** of production and consumption.

Switched-off places

1) These are the **worst-connected countries**, as well as some **remote places** in more wealthy countries, e.g. **Bhutan** is a **landlocked** country in the Himalayan mountains, where **tourism** and access to the **internet** are **restricted**. The **economy** is based on **agriculture**, with little foreign influence.
2) Some **money** does flow into switched-off places, often in the form of **aid**. Also, they may grow some crops to make money (**cash crops**, e.g. coffee), but they **trade little** and receive **very little** for the crops.
3) People in switched-off places aren't significant **producers** or **consumers** because they're not well connected to global networks and aren't a **potential market** for **TNCs**.
4) **Energy usage** and the **ecological footprint** are **low**.

You need to know the difference between places that are **interconnected** and places that are **dependent**.

1) **Interconnected** places have a roughly **equal exchange** in the flow of trade, money, people or information, e.g. the number of tourists **visiting** a country is **equal** to the number of citizens from that country that **travel**.
2) One place is **dependent** on another if there is an **unequal exchange** in the flow of trade, money, people or information — more is **coming in** than **going out**, e.g. **lots** of tourists **visit** a country, but **few** citizens of that country **travel** abroad.

The **multiplier effect** also helps connected places to **grow** in **wealth** — money **spent** in one place **causes** more money to be **made** in that place, e.g. **more tourists** visiting a town means **more hotels** and **restaurants** are needed, so more money is **invested** in the city and more local people are **employed**. They'll spend their **increased earnings** in the city, and so on...

New Technologies Make the **World More Interconnected**

1) **Technologies** like telecommunications, the internet and air travel create **global networks**, for example:
   - **Long-distance telecommunications** began when copper **telegraph cables** were laid across the Atlantic in 1866. Now there's a **global phone network** linking all countries.
   - **The internet** allows people in offices that are far apart to work together at the same time.
   - Low-cost **air travel** means it's **cheap** and **easy** to travel long distances for **work** and **holidays**.
2) Global networks lead to a **shrinking world** — **distances** don't seem as far because places are very **well connected**.
3) Here's an example of how global networks can create global patterns of **connectivity**:

EasyJet is a low-cost airline that helps to connect many places by making it easier for **more** people (not just the **wealthy**) to get to **more** places (not just **popular places**). It makes a **pattern** of connectivity, made up of all the places it flies to. The connections it forms can help make places **switched-on**.

For example, **Tallinn** is the capital of **Estonia**, an ex-Soviet state. EasyJet has made Tallinn **more connected** by setting up **flights** to and from there to other European countries (e.g. the UK). This has **increased** the flow of **people**, **information** and **money** between Tallinn and other countries, helping to make Tallinn **switched-on**.

Either the world's shrinking, or this woman's enormous.

Global Winners and Losers

Physical and *Human Resources* Create *Global Winners*

The **winners** in a globalised world are countries that have **useful resources** that are in demand — this helps them **connect** to **global networks**, so they become **switched-on**.

Winners can use their **comparative advantages** (see p. 109) — they're **well connected** so they can easily **trade** for the things they **need**. This means they don't have to produce **everything**, but can concentrate on using their physical and human resources where they'd be **most useful**. The **multiplier effect** (see previous page) can also help them to become **more** wealthy.

Here are a couple of examples of how **physical** or **human resources** have helped create global winners:

<u>Physical — Saudi Arabia</u>

1) **Saudi Arabia** is an **oil-rich** country in the **Middle East** that gets most of its wealth (about half its GDP) from the **trade** of oil — this is called **petrodollar** wealth.
2) Saudi Arabia has **coasts** on two sides so oil can be easily **shipped** out to other countries.
3) Saudi Arabia uses the money it makes from its **comparative oil advantage** to **develop** other parts of its economy. This helps to **increase** its **global connections** and keep it **switched-on**.

<u>Human — China</u>

1) **China** is a **NIC** (see p. 108) with a **huge population** (more than 1.3 billion).
2) China can provide lots of **cheap** but relatively **skilled** labour, e.g. the manufacturing industry in China has **grown rapidly** because of **investment** from Chinese and foreign companies. Cheap, skilled labour means costs are **reduced** and profit can be **increased**.
3) China's **comparative advantage** in **human resources** has allowed other parts of its economy to grow because of the **multiplier effect**. This has helped to increase its **connectivity** and make it **switched-on**.

Physical Difficulties or *Poor Leadership* Create *Global Losers*

Global losers are countries that remain **switched-off** from **global networks**. This can be because of **difficult physical conditions** (e.g. landlocked countries) or **poor leadership** leading to **political isolation** (e.g. a corrupt government). For example:

Zimbabwe is a **landlocked** country in south-east **Africa** that is cut off from global networks. It has been **politically isolated** because of the **undemocratic** way the country has been **governed**. This has led to **economic sanctions** from the EU and USA, reducing the flow of **trade**. Also, many airlines **refuse** to fly to Zimbabwe, **reducing** its connectivity further.

The **consequences** of being switched-off from global networks mean global losers may be **left further behind**:

1) **Valuable resources** may be **wasted** or left **unused** because there's no investment to help **trade** in them.
2) **Conflict**, **starvation** and **disease** may make it less likely that global connectivity will **improve**.
3) Switched-on countries are more likely to work **together**, helping them to **progress** faster. This means the **gap** between switched-on and switched-off places will only **get wider**.

There are Some *Odd Winners and Losers*

Odd winners — some areas are in **difficult** physical locations, but are still **switched-on**. E.g. **Las Vegas** is a city in the Nevada desert (**USA**), but is a **global hub** for **tourism** (and **money**) because **gambling** is **legal** there.

Odd losers — some places are **rich** in a **natural resource** but remain **switched-off**. E.g. **Sierra Leone** (West Africa) is rich in **diamonds** but hasn't been able to generate much wealth from them due to **civil war** and **government corruption**.

Practice Questions

Q1 What factors create global winners?

Q2 What factors create global losers?

Exam Question

Q1 Describe and explain what a 'switched-on' country is. [4 marks]

Switched-on, switched-off — wax on, wax off...

Switched-on, switched-off, winners, losers... to make some sense of all this just remember that we're still talking about globalisation here. Countries that are well connected to other countries are switched-on and will benefit from globalisation.

Consequences of Globalisation

***These pages are for** Edexcel Unit 1 (Going Global).*
Globalisation's brought countries together and made plenty of people rich, but as always, someone or something's gotta pay for it. There are negative consequences of globalisation for people and the environment.

There are Economic Consequences of Globalisation

For more on NICs and the OECD see p. 108.

Globalisation has caused an **increase** in **global trade** (because of the spread of global business by **TNCs**, see p. 107). Trade has increased in **most countries**, but especially in **Newly Industrialised Countries** (**NICs**) and countries in the **Organisation for Economic Cooperation and Development** (**OECD**). Increased trade has **different effects** on their **economies**:

Richer nations (e.g. OECD members)

Globalisation has caused the **deindustrialisation** of many **richer countries** — **manufacturing** industries have **moved** from richer countries to poorer countries mainly because **wage costs** are **lower**. For the **growth** of their economies to continue, rich countries have had to change to a **post-industrial economy** — one that's based mainly on the **service sector**.

- **Positive consequence** — this has led to **increased wealth** for many people. One reason why many rich countries, like the UK, **educate** their population to a **high level** is that this attracts **investment** from TNCs because more people can work in the **highly paid service sector**.
- **Negative consequence** — many manual workers **lost their jobs** and struggled to find new work because of **deindustrialisation**. The **economies** of some cities (e.g. **Sheffield** in the UK, famous for **steel manufacturing**) were **ruined** by deindustrialisation. Recovery has been slow because the economies were based almost **entirely** on **one industry**.

NICs

Globalisation has caused the **industrialisation** of many countries — manufacturing industries have been moved to **NICs**, changing their economy from **agriculture-based** to **manufacturing-based**.

- **Positive consequence** — **increased wealth** in poorer countries. NICs, like China, **attract investment** from TNCs because of **large workforces** with **lower wage demands** than richer countries. This has brought **wealth** to **some people** in NICs.
- **Negative consequence** — the **income gap** between rich and poor people has become **wider**. The wealth isn't **spread evenly** in NICs (e.g. Indonesia) — a **few people** become wealthy, while **many remain poor**.

There are Moral and Social Consequences of Globalisation

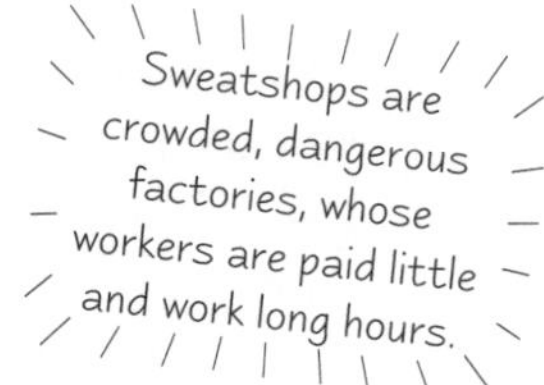

Sweatshops are crowded, dangerous factories, whose workers are paid little and work long hours.

Globalisation has meant many countries have become **more industrialised**. TNCs **move** factories from richer countries to NICs, and **sweatshops** are also set up for **sub-contract** work. Agricultural workers from **rural areas** move to **urban areas** to work in the factories and sweatshops — **rural-urban migration** (see p. 132). This can lead to the **exploitation of workers**:

1) Workers are **paid very low wages**.
2) Many workers are **killed** or **injured** in accidents because there are fewer **health and safety** regulations, e.g. **Yongkang** is an industrial city in **China** famous for the number of amputees from **factory accidents**.
3) Workers have **fewer rights**. If they **strike** because of poor conditions they may **lose their job**, or the factory may be **moved** to another place (where the workers **won't strike**).

Some people think the effects of globalisation are **morally wrong**:

1) **Dangerous, poorly-paid work** has just been **moved** from richer countries to poorer countries, instead of being **stopped altogether**.
2) Some sweatshops employ **children**, which is **illegal** in richer countries.
3) Products made in NICs are **cheap** because conditions are **poor** and wages are **low** — **exploitation**. Many think people in richer countries should take more **responsibility** and pay **higher prices** for products produced in NICs, so the workers get a **fairer wage**.

Other people think the effects of globalisation are **helpful** in some countries:

1) Urban **working conditions** and **standards of living** might be **better** than those in rural areas.
2) Sweatshops are the **first steps** towards a **wealthier economy**. They existed in the UK and the USA in the 19th century and helped the **economy** to **grow**.
3) Poorer countries have to focus on what they can **do best** — use their **comparative advantage** (see p. 109). They can't supply the **high levels of education** (needed for **service sector jobs**), but they can supply **cheap labour**. This means their economies will **grow** and in time conditions will **improve**.

Consequences of Globalisation

There are Environmental Consequences of Globalisation

Increase in **global trade** also creates **environmental problems**:

1) **Oil pollution** — increased global trade means **more shipping**. **Ecosystems** (the wildlife and the physical environment) are **damaged** by oil pollution from **shipping**, e.g. in the major shipping lanes near **Alaska**.
2) **Deforestation** — increased global trade has meant countries in tropical areas can **make money** by growing **crops** to sell for **profit** (cash crops), e.g. oilseed plantations for alternative fuel. They **clear forests** to make **space** for crops. **Tropical forests** are a massive **sink** of the greenhouse gas CO_2 (see p. 79). When trees are cleared by **burning**, CO_2 is released into the **atmosphere**, adding to global warming.
3) **Carbon emissions** — globalisation has meant products can be sold a **long way** from where they're made. So, they're transported a **long distance** before they're **bought**. Transporting products creates **pollution** because planes and ships release pollutants like **carbon dioxide**, which contributes to global warming (see p. 79).
4) **Waste** — increased global trade means people have access to **more products** at **low prices**, so they can afford to be more **wasteful**, e.g. people **throw away** damaged clothes instead of **repairing** them because it's cheaper to just **buy more**. Lots of waste ends up as **landfill** if it's not **recycled**.
5) **Recycling issues** — **increased waste** created by global trade means there's **more recycling**. Waste can be moved a **long way** to be recycled though, e.g. a lot of paper and plastic from the **UK** is shipped to **China** for recycling. This can lead to more **greenhouse gases** being produced, adding to **global warming**.

The distance food products are transported is called 'food miles'.

Solutions to the Consequences of Globalisation can be Local or Global

The problems caused by globalisation can be handled at a **local** or **global** scale, by **governments**, **businesses** and **individuals**:

Governments

Trading carbon credits — international agreements like the **Kyoto Protocol** (see p. 85) set countries **carbon emission limits** (measured in **credits**). If they emit **less** they can **sell** the extra credits, but if they emit **more** they have to **buy** credits. This **encourages** reductions in **carbon emissions** caused by transportation, and reduces the amount of **shipping** and **oil pollution**. It **discourages deforestation** as countries can **gain** carbon credits by **planting trees** instead of **cutting them down**. It takes a **long time** for governments to create these agreements, so it may not reduce emissions **quickly**.

Businesses

Stating distance transported — businesses can **label** products to show where they've come from. This could **encourage** consumers to buy products that haven't **travelled** as far, helping to **reduce carbon emissions**.

Using recycled materials — businesses can use recycled materials, e.g. recycling old **drinks cans** to make new ones. This **reduces** the amount of **waste** that goes to **landfill**, but could **increase carbon emissions** and **oil pollution** if the recycled material is shipped **long distances** (though it's often **still better** than making new products from raw materials).

Individuals

Fair trade — individuals can buy products that are **fair trade**. The producers are **guaranteed** a **fair price** for their goods (e.g. bananas). This can **increase wages** and the **security** of income for some of the poorest workers. Some argue that fair trade **prevents economic growth** — the guaranteed prices of the products are **higher** than their **market value** (what the product is **worth**). So people are encouraged to produce **too much**. This results in an **excess**, which causes the market value of the products to **fall**. Anyone who **isn't** part of the fair trade agreement will **lose out**.

Buying local — individuals can buy **local products** that haven't been transported a long way, helping to reduce **carbon emissions**. But many workers (especially in poorer countries) **rely on exporting** their goods to make money. If people **only** buy locally (especially in richer countries), millions of **workers** in **poorer countries** could **lose out**.

Recycling — individuals can **recycle more** waste, **re-use** products and **refuse** to buy products that aren't made from recycled materials. This has the **same effect** as businesses using more recycled materials (see above).

Practice Questions

Q1 How has globalisation changed the economies of richer nations?

Q2 Name one social consequence of globalisation.

Exam Question

Q1 Evaluate the strategies used to solve the problems caused by globalisation. [15 marks]

Globalisation has econo-socio-enviro-moral consequences. Gotcha.

There's plenty of debate about whether globalisation's doing more good than bad, and how effective all the solutions to the problems really are. You need to make sure you talk about both sides of the debate to get top marks in your exam.

Population Change Basics and the DTM

This section is for AQA and Edexcel Unit 1 (Going Global). These pages are for both exam boards.
Populations are dynamic — they're always changing. These pages will help you understand how and why — it's all to do with birth and death rates and population migrations. And don't forget the famous DTM.

There are Loads of Terms and Definitions to Learn

1) **Birth rate** — the **number** of live **births** per 1000 people, per year.
2) **Death rate** — the **number** of **deaths** per 1000 people, per year.
3) **Fertility rate** — the **average number of children** a woman will have between the ages of **15** and **44** (**reproductive** age).
4) **Infant mortality rate** — the **number** of **children** (out of every 1000 born **alive**) who **die before their first birthday**.
5) **Life expectancy** (**longevity**) — the **average age** (in years) a person can **expect to live**.
6) **Migration rate** — the **difference** between the **number** of people who **migrate in** (**immigrants**), and the number of people who **migrate out** (**emigrants**) per **100 000** (or 1000) of the population, per year.
7) **Population density** — the **number** of people per **square kilometre** (km^2). It's the **total population** of an area **divided** by the **size of the area** (in km^2).
8) **Changes in the population over time**:
   - **Natural change** — the change in population (**increase** or **decrease**) because of the **difference** between **birth rate** and **death rate** (not including changes due to **migration**). For example, when **birth rate > death rate**, the population will **grow naturally** (if migration rate is **zero**). When **death rate > birth rate**, the population will **fall** (unless enough people **migrate in**).
   - **Zero growth rate** — the population is **neither increasing** nor **decreasing** (e.g. **birth rate = death rate**).

Migration is the movement of people between or within countries.

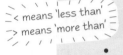

< means 'less than'
> means 'more than'

The Demographic Transition Model (DTM) Shows Population Change

The **demographic transition model** (**DTM**) shows how the **population** of a country **changes** over time through **five stages**. The model shows changes in **birth rate**, **death rate** and **total population**.

'Demographic' means it's to do with human populations.

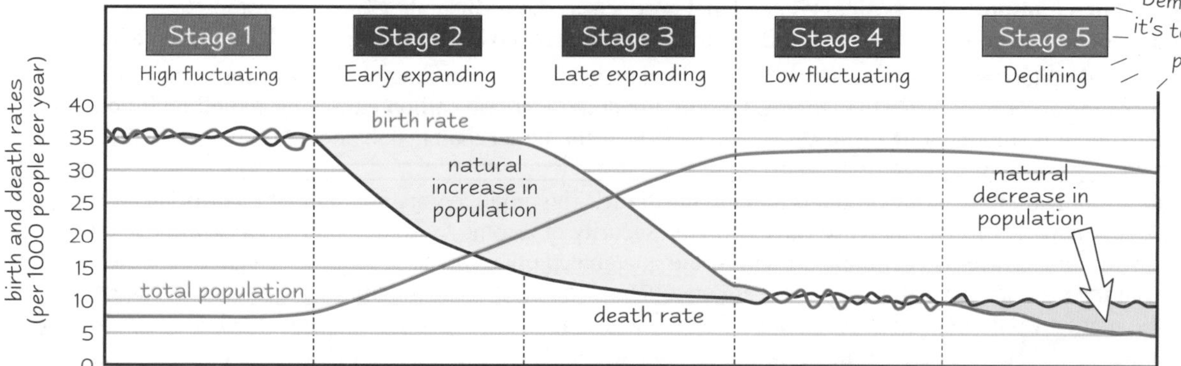

As Countries Develop They Move Through the Stages of the DTM

As countries become **more developed** their birth rate and death rate **change**, which causes the **total population to change**.

Stage 1 — high birth rate and high death rate

Birth rate and death rate **fluctuate** at a **high level** — the population remains **stable** but **low**. There **aren't any countries** in **Stage 1**, but some **tribes** in the rainforests of **Brazil** are in this stage.

1) **Birth rate** is **high** because there's **no birth control** or **family planning**, and **education is poor**.
2) It's also high because there's **high infant mortality**, so people have **more children** to replace those who've **died**.
3) **Death rate** is **high** and **life expectancy** is **low** because there's **poor health care**, **sanitation** and **diet** — leading to **disease** and **starvation**.

Birth rate — around **35/1000**

Death rate — around **35/1000**

The values for the birth rate, death rate and population for each stage are just rough estimates, not exact figures.

Population Change Basics and the DTM

Stage 2 — high birth rate, death rate falls

Death rate **falls**, but birth rate remains **high** — the population **increases rapidly**.
Countries like **Nepal** and **Afghanistan** are in **Stage 2**.

1) **Birth rate** is still **high** as there's still **little birth control** or **family planning** and **education is poor**.
2) Birth rate also stays **high** for **labour reasons** — family members (including **children**) **all** have to **work**, e.g. on **farms**. A **larger** family can tend to a **larger** farm, helping to bring in **more food** and **money**.
3) **Death rate falls** and **life expectancy increases** due to improved **health care**, **sanitation** and **diet**.

Birth rate — around **35/1000**

Death rate — falls to around **15/1000**

Stage 3 — birth rate falls a lot and death rate falls slightly

Birth rate **declines rapidly**, while death rate **falls slowly** — the population **increases** at a **slower rate**.
Countries like **Egypt** are in **Stage 3**.

1) **Birth rate decreases** due to the **increased** use of **birth control** and **family planning**, and **improvements** in **education**.
2) The **birth rate** also **drops** as the **economy** moves towards **manufacturing** — **fewer children** are needed to **work** on farms, so having a **larger family** isn't as **advantageous** as it once was.
3) **Birth rate falls** further still as **more women work** rather than stay at home to have children.
4) Some countries introduce **government population policies** to try to **reduce the birth rate**.

Birth rate — falls to around **13/1000**

Death rate — falls to around **10/1000**

Stage 4 — low birth rate and low death rate

Birth rate and death rate **fluctuate** at a **low level** — the population remains **stable** but **high**. Most **developed countries**, e.g. most of **Europe** and the **USA**, are in **Stage 4**. **Birth rate stays low** because **increased access** and **demand** for **luxuries** like **holidays** and **material possessions** means there's **less** money available for having children (they're **expensive** to raise). Also, there are **fewer advantages** to having children, e.g. they're **not needed** to work for the family.

Birth rate — falls to around **10/1000**

Death rate — around **10/1000**

Stage 5 — birth rate drops below death rate

Birth rate begins to **decline** further while death rate remains **stable** — the population begins to **decrease**. Some **highly developed** countries, e.g. **Japan**, are in **Stage 5**.

1) The **birth rate decreases** because children are **expensive** to raise and many people have **dependent** elderly relatives, so lots of people choose **not** to have children.
2) **Death rate** remains **steady** as there are **more elderly people** so more people die (of **old age**) despite **advances** in health care.

Birth rate < **Death rate**

Hmm, have children or buy myself a shiny new car...

Practice Questions

Q1 Define fertility rate.

Q2 Define population density.

Exam Question

Date	Birth rate (per 1000 per year)	Death rate (per 1000 per year)	Population (millions)
1600	38	37	2
1700	35	34	3
1800	35	18	7
1850	26	15	15
1900	18	12	21
1950	12	10	26
2000	8	10	28

Q1 The table shows some population data for a country since 1600.
With reference to the DTM, describe and explain the changes in the population shown by the data. [10 marks]

Rabbits never seem to get much past Stage 2...

You're expected to know your way around the DTM. Make sure you understand the diagram and how all the different rates change over time. You need to be able to explain why the rates change too. Then you can apply it to any country or set of stats.

Applying the DTM

These pages are for AQA only.
So you're now a dab hand at the ol' DTM and how the stages differ from one another. It's a nice model but it doesn't work for every country, and you get to learn why. Joy.

Most MEDCs are in Stages 4-5 of the DTM

1) **Most countries** that are classed as **MEDCs** (**More Economically Developed Countries**) have **passed through** Stages 1, 2 and 3. They have **low birth and death rates**, **long life expectancies** and **slow population growth**.
2) During Stages 2 and 3 their **rapid population growth** was accompanied by **industrial growth**, **farming improvements** and **increasing wealth**. This is where they **changed** from being **LEDCs** (**Less Economically Developed Countries**) to **MEDCs**.
3) Some MEDCs are in **Stage 5**, e.g. **Italy**, **Japan** and **Germany**. Birth rate is **lower** than death rate, causing the population to **shrink**. The population is also **ageing**, as **more people** live for **longer** — a **greying population**.
4) Being in Stage 5 can cause **problems** for a country:
   - There are too **few children** to **replace** the current, ageing **workforce** — the workforce may not be large enough to carry out the work, which could cause the **economy** to **slow down** or **stop growing**.
   - A **smaller population** means a **reduction** in **spending**, which could also cause the **economy** to **slow** or **stall**.
   - There are **fewer taxpayers**, so there's **less money** for **services**. This is made worse by the **increasing cost** of **services** for the **elderly** — **more old people** means **more money** is needed for **pensions** and **health services** (**carers** etc.).

Most LEDCs are in Stages 2-3 of the DTM

1) Most countries classed as **LEDCs** are in **Stage 2** (e.g. **Afghanistan**) or **Stage 3** (e.g. **India**).
2) Lots of countries entered **Stage 2** in the **1950s**, e.g. **Kenya** and **Bangladesh**. **Improved health care** and **sanitation** led to a **reduced death rate**, while birth rate **stayed high**. Many of these countries have become **overpopulated** — they don't have the **resources** (e.g. **money** or **services**) to **cope** with the expanding population.
3) Some **former LEDCs** have moved into **Stage 3** in the last few decades, e.g. **Newly Industrialised Countries** (**NICs**) like **Malaysia** and **Taiwan**. The **death rate** is still **falling**, leading to **increasing populations**. Some **governments** have introduced **policies** to reduce **birth rate** and **prevent** overpopulation, e.g. **one-child** policies.

You need to be aware that although most countries used to be classified as either MEDCs or LEDCs, it's now thought that this system is too simplistic — there are too many stages of development to divide countries into only two categories.

The UK's Demographic History Matches the DTM Model

Stage 1 (prehistoric times to about 1760)

Total population was **small** — e.g. **6 million** in **1700**. **Poor diet** and **hygiene**, as well as **wars** and **diseases** such as the **Black Death** and **cholera**, caused a **high death rate**, which **cancelled** out the **high birth rate**.

Stage 2 (1760-1880)

The population **grew quickly** — it was **5 times** bigger by the **1880s** (6 million in 1700 to **30 million** by **1881**). Improvements in **farming** and **medicine** reduced **starvation** and **disease**, so **death rate fell**. **Birth rate** remained **high** and the **economy grew** quickly. **Urban populations** grew particularly **rapidly**.

Stage 3 (1880-1940)

The population was still **growing**, but at a **slower rate** — **47 million** by **1941**. **Birth control** improved and was used **more** frequently, so the **birth rate fell**. **Death rate continued to fall** (except during **World War 1**) as **food supply**, **medicine** and **hygiene** continued to **improve**.

Stage 4 (1940-today)

Population growth has **slowed down** — **56 million** by **1981**. **Death rate** was **low**, except during **World War 2**, and **birth rate** was also **low**, except for **baby booms** (**large increases** in **birth rate**) **after** World War 2 and in the **1960s**.

Stage 5 (today+)

Death rate today is **almost** exactly the same as birth rate and the population is **ageing** — pensioners **outnumber** children and it's been estimated that by **2030**, **a quarter** of the UK's population could be **over 65**. The population could begin to **decline** if birth rate **drops below** death rate because there are too few young people, or death rate becomes larger than birth rate because the large population of elderly people **die**.

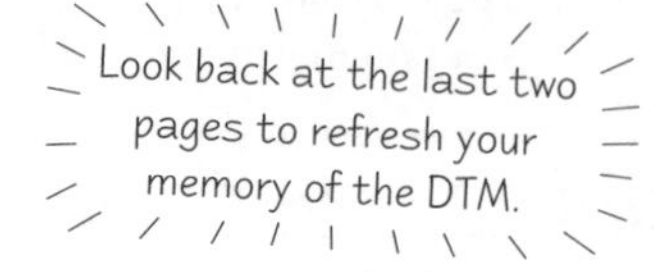

Look back at the last two pages to refresh your memory of the DTM.

Applying the DTM

The **DTM** is **Useful**...

1) The **DTM** gives a good **generalised** picture of how a **population** can **change** over time.
2) It's easy to **compare** a **country** with the DTM — if you know a bit about how the **population** and **birth** and **death rates** of a country have changed, you can analyse what **stage** of the DTM it's in.
3) You can then **forecast** how its population may change — which can help governments decide on **policies** such as **one-child limits** and **immigration laws**.

Winning major sporting events is often linked to mini peaks in birth rate — I blame it on the short shorts.

...But It Has **Limitations**

1) The **original data** used to **create** the DTM was from **more developed**, richer countries (e.g. **European** countries, **Japan** and the **USA**). This means it might **not** be a **valid model worldwide** — what happened in these countries might not be the **same** as what's happening in others, e.g. countries in **Asia** or **Africa**.
2) The original DTM **didn't** have **Stage 5** — it's been **added** since some countries have moved **out of Stage 4**.
3) The DTM doesn't take things like **education** and the role of **women** into account separately and these affect **birth rate** quite a lot, e.g. **increased higher education** means more people **delay** having a family.
4) The **population** in countries with **different customs** may change in different ways, e.g. the **Catholic** church **condemns contraception**.
5) **Extreme poverty** and **low levels of development** may cause a **lack of population growth** and **prevent** many **LEDCs** from passing through **all** the stages.
6) The DTM **can't predict** exactly **when** countries will **reach** each stage, or **how long** each stage will **last**.
7) It doesn't consider **migration** — **international migration** can have a large effect on **population change**.
8) **Other factors** can also affect the population so a country **no longer fits** the DTM:

Population control policies (e.g. France and China)
High levels of **population growth or decline** have forced some governments to introduce **population policies** — **discouraging** or **encouraging** larger families. For example, population growth in **France** is very **low**, so the government has introduced things like **subsidised childcare** to encourage **larger families**. In **China**, the **opposite** is occurring. The government has tried to **reduce** birth rate using a **one-child per family policy**.

Infectious disease (e.g. HIV/AIDS, Malaria)
Some countries may have particularly **high levels** of **infectious disease**, which keeps the **death rate high**, **reducing** the population or stalling population **growth**. For example, some **African countries** like **Nigeria** and **Botswana** have very **high HIV/AIDS** rates, leading to **high death rates**.

Civil War (e.g. Rwanda, Sierra Leone, ongoing in Sudan)
War leads to an **increased death rate** and **decreased birth rate**, especially if **large numbers** of men and women of **reproductive age** are **killed** or **involved** in the conflict. Also, **civil war** often leads to **emigration**, decreasing the population, as people **flee** the fighting. For example, thousands of people **died** during the civil war in **Sierra Leone** (**1991-2002**) and thousands more **fled** to **neighbouring countries**.

Practice Questions

Q1 Describe two problems faced by countries in Stage 5 of the DTM.
Q2 In 1800, what stage of the DTM was the UK in?
Q3 Describe one factor that can affect the population size so that a country no longer fits the DTM.

Exam Question

Q1 Discuss the uses and limitations of the DTM. [15 marks]

Baby boom — the noise babies make as they break the sound barrier...

OK, so not the greatest CGP pun ever, but at least I'm trying. You better be trying to learn all these DTM facts — my blood, sweat and tears have gone into this page. Well tears anyway — that joke really isn't great, it's a 'must try harder' for sure.

Population Structure and Migration

These pages are for AQA and Edexcel Unit 1 (Going Global).
Population structure pyramids are very exciting — not as exciting as cheerleader pyramids, but still better than nowt.

Population Structure is How the Population is Made Up

Population structure is the **number** or **%** of **males** and **females** in different **age groups** within a population.
Population pyramids (**age-sex pyramids**) **show** population structure. You can **learn** a lot about the **demographics** of a place from its population pyramid. For example, the pyramid below shows the **population structure of France**:

Ⓐ Some people are living to be **100**, which shows a **high life expectancy**.
Ⓑ **Women** are living **longer** than **men**.
Ⓒ There are **fewer** people aged **75-85**, because there was a **low birth rate** when they were **born** (around **World War 1** – WW1) and they've suffered from a **high death rate** (lots killed in **WW2**).
Ⓓ There are also **fewer** people aged **50-60**, also because of a **low birth rate** when they were born (around **WW2**).
Ⓔ There are **lots** of people aged **25-50** because of a **baby boom** after WW2.
Ⓕ There are **fewer** people aged **0-10** because of a **low birth rate** for the last 10 years.

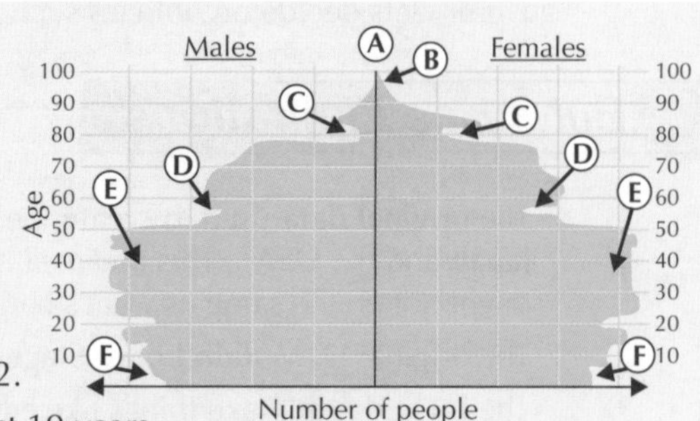

Population Structure Varies from Place to Place and Over Time

1) Population pyramids for **different countries** vary because of different **demographic factors** — **birth** and **death rates**, **fertility rates**, **wars**, **migration** etc.
2) A country's population structure **changes** through **time** as it moves through the **stages** of the **DTM** (see page 116).
3) This means a **population pyramid shape** can show **which** stage of the DTM a country is in:

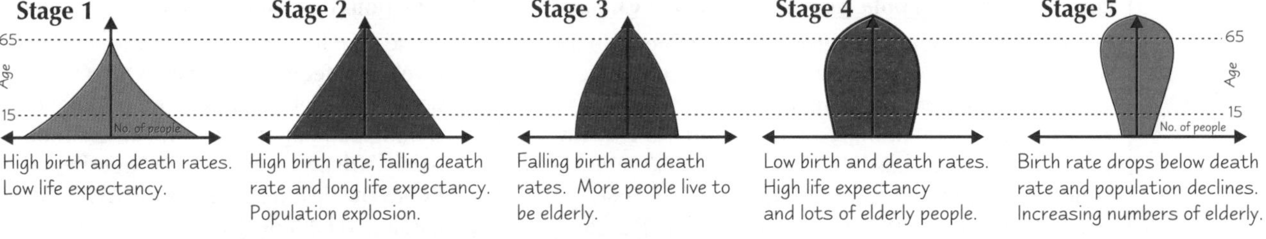

Migration Can Change Population Structure

Migration is the (often permanent) movement of people **between** or **within** countries. **Immigration** is the movement of people **into a country** (or area) and **emigration** is the movement of people **out of a country** (or area). Migration can **alter population structure**, which can be seen in the **population pyramids** for the areas affected. Migration can affect **any part** of the population pyramid — it depends **how old** the migrants are.
Here are some examples:

1) **Internal migration (migration within a country)**
Internal migration from **rural** areas to **urban** areas often affects the number of **young adults** (people of **working** and **reproductive age**). They **move away** from the countryside **into** the cities to find **jobs**. This is called **rural-urban migration**. This can **affect birth rate** too as the migrants are of reproductive age.

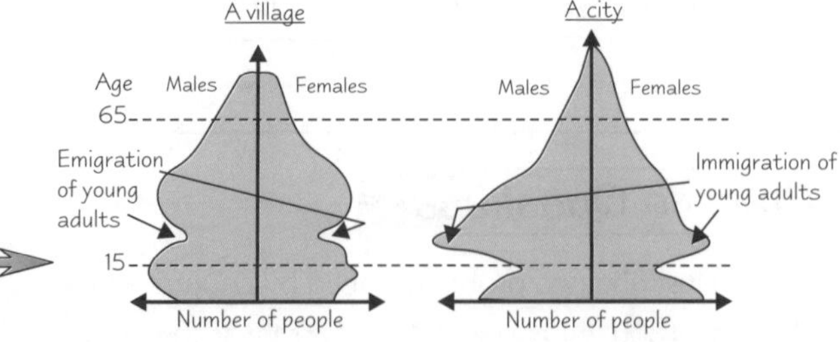

2) **Emigration away from countries at later DTM stages**
Emigration **away** from countries at **later** DTM stages **into** other countries **decreases the population** of the country they've left. E.g. **elderly people** in the **UK retiring and emigrating** to other countries. This **reduces** the number of elderly in the UK, but **increases** the number in the countries they **move to**.

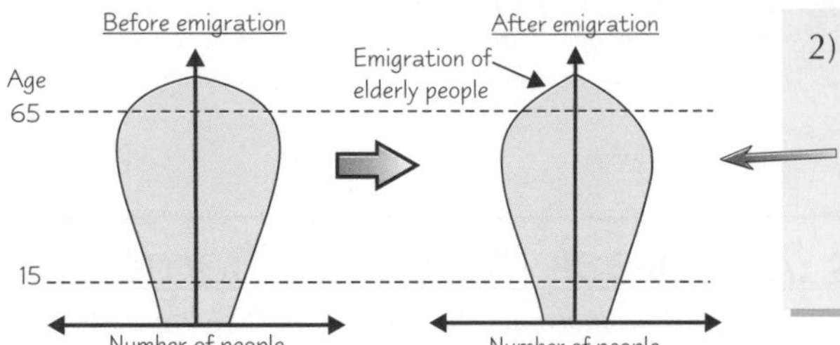

Population Structure and Migration

3) **Immigration into countries at later DTM stages**

Immigration **into** countries at **later** DTM stages (e.g. MEDCs) from those at **earlier** DTM stages (e.g. LEDCs) **increases the population** of people of **working** and **reproductive age**. This **increases** the population of young people and **increases birth rate**. For example, immigration **into** the **UK** (Stage 4).

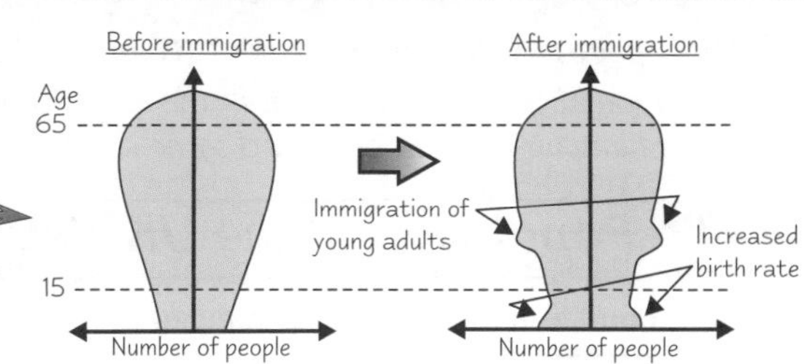

Migration Occurs Because of Push and Pull Factors

The **reasons** for migration can be divided into **push** (**negative**) and **pull** (**positive**) factors:

Push factors — these are things that **make** people want to **move out** of the place they're in. They're **negative factors** about the place they're **leaving**, e.g. **lack of jobs** or **poor living conditions** and **services**, fear of **political persecution**.

Pull factors — these **attract** people to a **new place**. They're **positive factors** about the place they're **moving to**, e.g. **better jobs** and **more job opportunities**, **better** living conditions and **services**.

Migration is also affected by **obstacles** and **opportunities**:

Obstacles — these are things that make migration **more difficult**, e.g. the **cost** of moving.

Opportunities — these are opportunities individuals **encounter** that mean they **stop** before they reach their **intended destination**, e.g. **Polish** migrants heading for **Ireland** for **work** might stop in **London** because there are plenty of **jobs** there.

Globalisation Affects Migration

This bit is for Edexcel only.

Globalisation (see Section 7) has many **different effects** but generally it **brings countries** and the **people** in them **closer together**. Globalisation can **affect migration** too — it can **encourage** it or **discourage** it:

Effects that encourage migration

1) **Open-door** policies between **EU members** — **anyone** from a country **within** the EU can **live** and **work** in **any other** EU country. (But **not all** EU countries **allow unlimited immigration** from **new** EU members, e.g. from **Poland**.)
2) **Ease of movement** of an international **elite** — **highly skilled** or **important** individuals are in **demand** around the world. **Globalisation** means they can go where they're **most needed** with **fewer restrictions** than other people, e.g. **footballers** move between **clubs** in **different countries** with relative **ease**.
3) **Increased urban investment** — investment from **Trans-National Corporations** (**TNCs**) is often **focused** on **urban areas**, which can cause an **increase** in **rural-urban migration** as people move for **new** or **better jobs**. E.g. **44%** of **Chinese** people live in urban areas **today** — it was **26%** in **1990**.

Effects that discourage migration

1) There are **restrictions** on migration **into** an **EU country** if you're **not** from one originally — **closer connections** between European countries makes migration **between** them **easier**, but makes it **more difficult** for people **outside** the EU. This is why Europe is sometimes called '**fortress Europe**' — it's **hard** to **enter**.
2) **Mexico** and the **USA** are **closely connected** by the **NAFTA trade bloc** (see p. 109), but this doesn't extend to the movement of **people** — migration **into** the USA is **strictly controlled** with a **heavily guarded border**.

Practice Questions

Q1 What is population structure?

Q2 What do population pyramids show?

Exam Question

Q1 Describe what is meant by push and pull factors. [4 marks]

Large, shiny tractors — rural pull factors...

The diagrams on these pages might look horribly complicated, but they're a good visual way of showing how populations change (plus the colours look nice). I'd bet they make great revision aids and pretty handy additions to exam answers. Hint hint...

Changes in the UK Population Since 1900

***These pages are for** Edexcel Unit 1 (Going Global).*
The population's changed loads in the last 100-odd years. Some of it's to do with stuff that's gone on in the UK (e.g. changing governments) and some of it's caused by global issues (e.g. war). Let's get factualising...

The **Population** of the **UK** Has **Changed** During the **20th Century**

The **population** of the UK has **changed** in lots of ways **since** the **1900s**:

Family size

1) **Family size fell** during the **early 20th century**, then **increased** towards the **mid-20th century**. In **1900** women had an average of **3.5 children** during their **reproductive years** (15-44), but women born in the **1920s** had only **2.07** (probably due to WW2). It rose after this to **2.46** for women born in **1934** (due to a **baby boom** after WW2).
2) Family size **fell** again **later** in the 20th century — for women born in **1955** it was **2.03** children.
3) It's expected to **fall even further** — women born in the **1980s** are **projected** to have an average of **1.74** children.
4) So women are having **fewer children** and **more women** are remaining **childless**:
   - **40%** of women born in **1934** had **three or more** children, but since then it has **fallen** to around **30%**.
   - **9%** of women born in **1945** had **no children**, but this might **rise** to **20%** for women born in the **1980s**.

Population structure

1) The **population pyramid** (see p. 120) of the UK **today** shows how the population structure has **changed**:
   - The **bulges** at **60 years old** and at **35-45** show that there was a **high birth rate** in the **40s** and **60s**.
   - The **dips** in population around **30 years** and at **5-15** show a **drop in birth rate** in the late **70s** and **90s**.

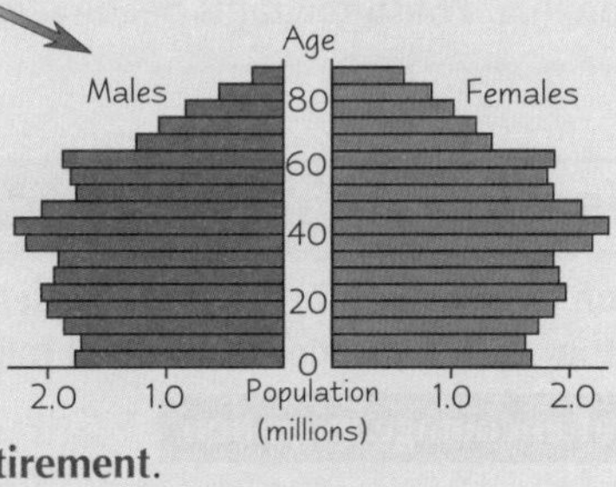

2) Today, about a **fifth** of the population is made up of the **under 16s** and about a **fifth** the over **60s**. This has changed from a **higher proportion** of **under 16s** when the larger generations were young, e.g. in the 1940s and 50s. In the future, it'll change to a **higher proportion** of **over 60s**, as the larger generations **reach retirement**.
3) **Life expectancy** has also **increased** from around **50** in **1900** to **77** for **men** and **81** for **women today**.

Migration and Ethnicity

See pages 128 and 130 for more on migration to the UK.

1) **Before WW2** many **Germans** (particularly **Jews**) and **Irish people** migrated to the **UK**. **After the war**, **immigrants** came from the countries of the then **Soviet Union**, e.g. **Ukraine**.
2) In the **50s-70s** large numbers of immigrants came from countries that were once part of the **British Empire** (**Commonwealth countries**). Most came from **India**, **Pakistan** and the **Caribbean**.
3) Lots of people have come from **central** and **eastern European** countries like **Poland** since they joined the EU in 2004.
4) All this migration has **changed** the **ethnic mix** of the UK — we're now a **multicultural country**. About **15%** of the population are **immigrants** themselves or are **descended** from immigrants. For example, there are now **over 1 million** UK **citizens** who class themselves as **Indian**.

Employment

1) **Employment** in the **primary sector** (e.g. **agriculture**) and **secondary sector** (e.g. **manufacturing**) has **declined** in the last 100 years. E.g. in **1901**, about **51%** of jobs were in the secondary sector, but this had fallen to **20%** by **2001**.
2) **Mechanisation** has meant fewer jobs in agriculture, whilst manufacturing **industries** have **moved abroad** where there's **cheaper labour**.
3) **Improvements** in **education** have led to a **rise** in **tertiary sector** jobs (e.g. **banking** and **insurance**), up from about **40%** in **1901**, to **78%** by **2001**.

Social status

Social class can be defined by things like **education** and **occupation**. The **main traditional** social classes in the UK are:

1) **Upper class** — the **nobility**, often people who hold **titles** or have **inherited wealth**.
2) **Middle class** — usually **highly educated** people with **professional** jobs and **above average** earnings, e.g. **doctors**.
3) **Working class** — **less well educated** people with **semi-skilled** or **unskilled jobs** with **below average** earnings, e.g. workers in **car assembly plants**.

It's thought that the social classes have been **changing**, e.g. the middle class is **growing** as the number of people in **higher education increases**, causing an **increase** in the **average wage** and **higher-class** activities like **skiing holidays**.

Changes in the UK Population Since 1900

Changes in *Population* are *Caused* by *Internal* and *External Factors*

Changes to the population of the UK have been caused by **internal factors** (things happening **within** the UK) and **external factors** (things happening on a **global scale** that affect the UK).

Internal factors

1) Family size (e.g. fertility rate)
   - The **suffragette movement** (early 20th century) — the **equal rights** movement for women led to changes in **attitude**, giving women more **freedom**. This caused a **reduction** in **birth rate** as women felt free to pursue their **own careers** and **delay** having children, or have **fewer children**.
   - **Legalisation of abortion** (1967) — more women could choose **not to have a child**.
2) Population structure (e.g. life expectancy)
   Establishment of the NHS (1948) — **free health care** for everyone led to **increased** life expectancy.
3) Employment and social status
   Increasing A-level and university take-up — greater levels of education have caused changes in **employment**, e.g. more **jobs** in the **tertiary sector**, and changes to **social status**, e.g. **increasing** numbers of **middle class**.
4) Migration
   More jobs created in the tertiary sector — this has been focused around the **south-east** of the UK. But the **loss of jobs** caused by the **decline** of the **secondary sector** has mostly affected the **north**. This has led to the **internal economic migration** of people to the south-east (the **south-east drift**).

External factors

1) Family size (e.g. fertility rate)
   - **Periods of global recession** — during global recessions (e.g. the great depression of 1929) people have **less money**, which means they **can't afford** to have lots of children. So birth rate **decreases**.
   - **Global conflict** — birth rates **fell** during the two World Wars because of the **economic stresses** of war and because men were **away from home**. After World War 2 there was a **baby boom** — birth rate **increased**.
2) Population structure (e.g. life expectancy)
   Decrease in dangerous jobs — the number of jobs that cause **poor health** and **loss of life**, e.g. in **mining**, has declined. Workers in the UK now carry out **less dangerous** work, so **life expectancy** has **increased**.
3) Employment
   Loss of manufacturing to overseas — factories have been **moved** to other countries where there's **cheaper labour**, e.g. **NICs** (see p. 108). This has caused a **decline** in the **secondary sector** in the UK, so many people have **lost** their job or have had to **change** jobs.
4) Migration
   Open-door policies — EU membership means people from other member countries can **live and work** in the UK. This has **increased immigration** into the UK.

You Can Research the *Changes* in *Population* in *Your Local Area*

The changes in population are **different** in different **parts** of the country, e.g. immigrants aren't **spread out evenly** — they tend to settle in particular areas. You can **research** how the population has changed over the last century in your **local area**:

1) Look at **census data** — a census is carried out every **10 years** in the UK. It's a survey where **data** is collected about the **whole population**, including things like **employment**, **family size** and **ethnic background**. The data goes as far back as **1841** and it's available on the internet. You can look at how the data has changed for your local area over the last 100 years.
2) Research your own **family history** (**genealogy**) — look at changes in things like **employment**, **family size** and if any members of your family **migrated** to the UK. You can research it by talking to **older members** of your family, or carry out research in a **local library** or on **genealogy websites**.

Practice Questions

Q1 Describe how family size has changed in the UK throughout the 20th century.

Q2 Outline one external factor that's caused changes to employment in the UK.

Exam Question

Q1 Describe and explain how internal factors have caused changes in the UK population in the 20th century. [10 marks]

I say, this census makes no sense-us...

You need to learn all about the changes in population that have occurred in the UK since the 1900s, e.g. changes in family size, population structure, etc. You also need to carry out your own research into how it's been changing in your local area. What fun...

Impacts and Management of Population Change

These pages are for AQA and Edexcel Unit 1 (Going Global).
Some countries are full of old people, some are full of young people, and some are full of little green men...

The Dependency Ratio Shows How Much of the Population is Dependent

The **dependency ratio** gives the **proportion** of the population that has to be **supported** by the **working population** (aged **15-64**). **Young people** (aged **0-14**) and **older people** (**over 65**) are generally **dependent** on the working population — they need to be **looked after** or **supported financially**. The **equation** for the dependency ratio is given below:

A **high dependency ratio** means there's a **greater proportion** of dependent people, e.g. **Uganda** has a **high dependency** ratio of **1.1** — there's **more than one** dependent person for **each** working person.

$$\text{Dependency ratio} = \frac{\text{Young people (0-14) + Old people (over 65)}}{\text{Working age population (15-64)}}$$

There are Social and Economic Impacts of an Ageing Population

An **ageing** (or **greying**) **population** means the **proportion** of older people is **increasing**, which causes an **increase** in the **dependency** ratio. This has **social** and **economic effects**:

Social

1) **Increased pressure on public services** — there's **greater demand** for services like **hospitals** and **hospices**. **More** people are needed to **care** for the elderly, so **more carers** and **nurses** will need **training**. Also, more people will act as **unpaid carers** to their **own** elderly family members, putting pressure on them **socially** and **financially**.
2) **Unequal distribution of older people** — e.g. **Eastbourne** in the UK is a **resort** with a high proportion of **retired**, older people. Areas like this may have **inadequate facilities** for **young people**, e.g. **bars** or **youth clubs**.
3) **Reduced population growth or population decline** — the working population may have **fewer children** because they already have older dependants, leading to a **reduction** in **birth rate**.
4) **Longer working life** — the **state pension** is **low** because there are **so many** retired people. It's often **not enough** to support people in their retirement so some may have to **work beyond** normal **retirement age** — to build up **personal pensions** or **savings**, or to **add to their income** from the state pension.

Economic

1) **Reduced work force** — a **smaller proportion** of the population is working, which may **slow economic growth**.
2) **Increased taxes** — **pensions** and **services** are paid for by **taxes**. A greater proportion of older people **claiming** pensions and support could mean **higher taxes** for the working population.
3) **Spending** — the elderly have **savings** and **pensions** to spend (the **grey pound**).

There are Social and Economic Impacts of a Youthful Population

This bit is for AQA only.

A **youthful population** means there's a **large** proportion of **young people** in the population.
This has **social** and **economic effects**:

Social

1) **Increased pressure on public services** — greater demand for services like **schools** and **childcare**.
2) **Rapid population growth** — the large numbers of children grow up and have **families** too, **increasing** the population. This may lead to **overpopulation** if there **aren't enough resources** to cope with the number of people.

Economic

1) **Too few jobs** — there **aren't enough jobs** for young people when they grow up. **More unemployed** means more people are dependent on **government support**.
2) **Increased poverty** — **more** young people are born into families that are **already poor**, so there are **more people in poverty**. Some children may have to **work** to help **support** their large family, so they **can't go to school**, which means they can't **break out of poverty**.

There are Political Impacts of Ageing and Youthful Populations

This bit is for AQA only.

Whether a population is getting **older** or **younger**, the impact on **politics** is the same — it changes what's important in **elections** and how people **vote**, and it affects **policies** such as **immigration laws** and **taxes** and **pensions**.

1) **Ageing population** — elderly issues will be important to **voters**, e.g. changes to **national pensions** or **heating allowances**. **Immigration laws** may be **relaxed** to encourage people of **working age** to **enter** the country.
2) **Youthful population** — youth issues will be important, e.g. **student loans** and **childcare provision**. The government may need to **increase teacher salaries** to **encourage** more people into the **profession**.

Impacts and Management of Population Change

This page is for AQA only. If you're doing Edexcel, you can skip straight to the questions.

There are ***Strategies*** *to* ***Manage Ageing Populations***

1) **Encouraging larger families** — e.g. the **Swedish government** makes having children more **manageable** by giving **both** parents **18 months' paid leave** when they have a child. Encouraging larger families should result in a **larger working population** when the children grow up, which can provide **more taxes** for **better pensions** and **services**.
2) **Raising retirement age** — the **working population** is made **larger**, so **more people contribute** to the **state pension fund** and to personal pensions for **longer**. People will also **claim** the state pension for **less time**.
3) **Encouraging the immigration of working-age people** — e.g. in recent years **Japan** has **increased** its number of **foreign workers** because there **aren't enough** working-age Japanese people to fill the jobs **available**. This **increases** the **working-age population**, which helps to support the ageing population by **paying taxes**.
4) **Increasing health care provision** — large numbers of older people puts pressure on **health care systems**. This **doesn't** manage the **population change** but it could help ease the problem of **poor health** in the **elderly**.

There are ***Strategies*** *to* ***Manage Youthful Populations*** *Too*

1) **Controlling birth rate** — some countries that are **overpopulated** try to **slow** further growth by introducing policies that **limit** the number of children couples can have. For example, **China** introduced a **one-child policy** for some couples in **1979**. It's thought this has **prevented** more than **300 million births** since it was introduced.
2) **Limiting the immigration of younger people** — **limiting** the number of immigrants of **reproductive age** (15-44) would mean birth rates aren't **made any higher** by immigrants having children.
3) **Encouraging family planning and the use of contraception** — governments can offer **sex education** and **free** contraception, allowing couples to **plan** and **limit** the number of children they have.
4) **Increasing childcare provision** — countries can **invest** in **more** and **better childcare** so parents can **work** instead of caring for children. This **doesn't** manage the population change, but helps to address some of the **problems caused** by a younger population.

Management Strategies *Should Aim Towards* ***Sustainable Development***

Sustainable development is all about developing and **growing** to meet the **needs** of people **today**, without **hindering** the ability of people in the **future** to meet their **own** needs. It involves **getting** what we need now without **damaging** or **altering** the **environment** in an **irreversible** way.
Generally, the **strategies** to manage growing elderly or youthful **populations** don't help sustainable development **on their own** — achieving sustainable development requires **lots** of **strategies** in lots of **different** areas.

1) **Encouraging larger families** — this creates an **even larger population** that'll need **housing**, **transport**, **food** etc. This **isn't** sustainable unless the population's **needs** are met in a **sustainable way**, e.g. **carbon-neutral homes**, **low** or **no** emission transport, food that's produced in an **environmentally friendly** way with **few food miles**.
2) **Encouraging the immigration of working-age people** — on its **own** this doesn't help towards sustainable development. E.g. **more** working people require **more jobs**, which could be in **heavily polluting industries**, or in **offices** that use **electricity** etc. Unless **these needs** are met in a **sustainable way**, this strategy on its own isn't sustainable.
3) **Controlling birth rate** — this **helps towards** sustainable development as the population **won't** get much **bigger**. But if the needs of the population still **aren't** met in a sustainable way, then it **just** stops the problem getting any **worse**.

Practice Questions

Q1 What does the dependency ratio tell you about a country or area?

Q2 Describe one strategy used to manage the effects of a youthful population.

Exam Question

Q1 Describe and explain the social and economic impacts of an ageing population. [15 marks]

This book'll have a social impact on you — you'll have to stay in and revise...

I'm sorry about this geography stuff taking up your valuable time, but think of it as an early warning. The population's ageing, so there'll be a lot of people for us to look after, and believe it or not, we'll all be old one day too so these strategies better work.

Managing Populations — Case Studies

These pages are for AQA and Edexcel Unit 1 (Going Global).

And you thought I'd forgotten about the case studies. Case studies are good for you — you should have some for your tea.

The UK Has an Ageing Population

If you're doing Edexcel see pages 122-123 for more on how the UK population has changed.

Like most **wealthy** and **developed countries**, the population of the UK is **ageing** (it's a **greying population**) — people **over 65** make up a **large part** of the population and it's **increasing**. In **2005**, **16%** of the population of the UK were **over 65**. This is expected to rise to **25%** by **2041** — here are a few reasons **why**:

1) **Increasing life expectancy** — between **1980** and **2006** life expectancy **rose 2.8** years for **women** and **4** years for **men**. It's currently **81.3** for **women** and **76.9** for **men**. As people live **longer**, the number of older people **increases**.
2) **Baby booms** — **lots of babies** were born in the **1940s** and **60s**. These large generations are starting to **retire**, **increasing** the number of elderly people.
3) **Falling birth rate** — there are **fewer** young people, so the **proportion** of older people is **greater**.

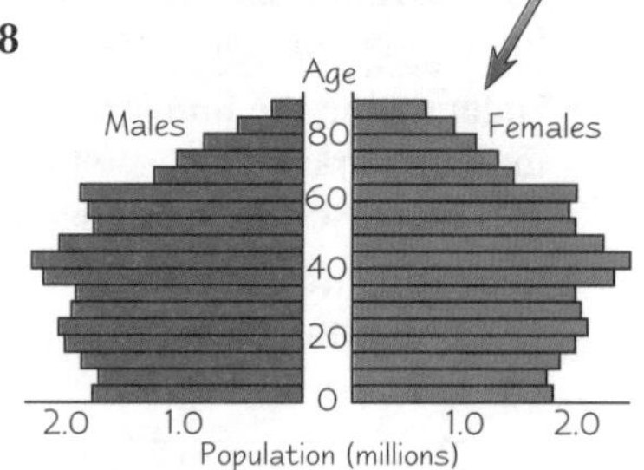

The Ageing UK Population Causes Problems

1) **Pressure on the pension system** — there aren't enough people of **working-age** to pay for an **adequate pension** for the **retired** population. **State pensions** are paid for by the **working population** through **taxes**.
   - Today, **60%** of the population (the people of **working-age**) are paying taxes that go towards the pensions of **19%** of the population (the people of **retirement age**).
   - By **2030**, only **56%** of the population will be of **working-age** but the taxes they pay will have to pay for the pensions of the **27%** of the population of **retirement age**.
2) **More elderly people living in poverty** — the state pension **isn't very large**, and many people don't have **other savings**. The working population **isn't large enough** to provide a **better pension** (see above).
3) **Pressure on the health service** — older people often need **more medical care** than younger people, e.g. the average stay in hospital in **2005** for people **over 75** was **13** nights, but only **8** nights for the UK population **as a whole**.

Different Strategies Aim to Manage Ageing Populations

1) **The age of retirement has been increased** — retirement age in the UK is currently **65** for men and **60** for women, but it will be raised to **68** for everyone by **2050**. Increasing the retirement age means people have to work for **longer**, **increasing** the size of the **working population**.
2) **Encouraging immigration of working-age people** — the UK has allowed **unlimited immigration** of people from countries who joined the **EU** in **2004**, e.g. **Poland**. In 2004, around **80%** of immigrants that came to the UK from the **new EU** countries were **34 or under**. This also **increases** the size of the **working population**.
3) **Encouraging more women to have children** — new UK **pension** proposals mean **women** won't lose out on **state pensions** if they take **career breaks** to have children. This could encourage women to have children. **Working family tax credits** support women (and men) who go back to **work** once their children are born, which might also encourage **more couples** to have children.

Strategies Need to Work Towards Sustainable Development

This bit is for AQA only.

As mentioned on the **previous page**, strategies to **manage** ageing populations should support **sustainable development**. But usually they can't do this on their **own** — other actions need to be taken to help **achieve** sustainable development.

1) **Increasing retirement age** — this **helps towards** sustainable development because it **doesn't increase** the **population**. But it might mean **more jobs** are needed, as people work for longer. This could **hinder** sustainable development if the **new jobs** aren't provided in a way that works towards **sustainability**, e.g. **building** and **working** in new **coal-powered** power plants versus **wind-turbine** power plants.
2) **Allowing immigration** — this is only **sustainable** if the **needs** of the new people are met in a sustainable way. E.g. meeting the **increased energy demand** by increasing energy production from **renewable sources**, building new **energy-efficient** homes with **good insulation** and **natural heating systems**.
3) **Encouraging more children** — this could **increase** the **population** of a country, and so is similar to immigration.

Managing Populations — Case Studies

This page is for AQA only, if you're doing Edexcel skip straight to the questions.

Uganda Has a Youthful Population

Like many **poorer** and **less developed** countries, **Uganda** has a **youthful population**. In **2007**, **50%** of the population were **under 15** and only **3%** were **over 65**. The population is becoming **more youthful** — here are a couple of reasons **why**:

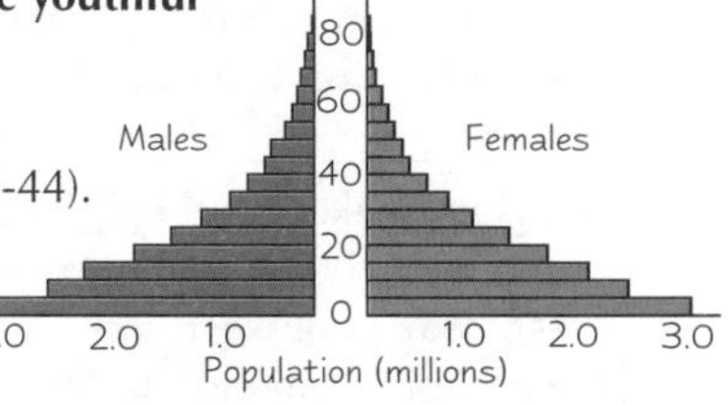

1) **High birth and fertility rates** — every year there are **48** babies born for every 1000 people, and women have an average of **7 children** during their reproductive years (15-44).
2) **Low life expectancy** of around **52** years — there are **very few** older people, which means the **proportion** of the population made up of young people is **very high**.

The Youthful Population Causes Problems for Uganda

The main problem caused by a **youthful population** is **overpopulation**, which is caused by a **high birth rate**. The population of Uganda is currently around **30 million**, but by **2025** it's thought it will grow to about **56 million**. When there are **too many people** for the **resources** the country has, things like the **health service** and levels of **employment** suffer:

1) **Pressure on the health service** — around **6000** women already **die** each year in **childbirth**. When the youthful population reaches **reproductive age** the pressure on the health service will be **even greater**, potentially leading to **more deaths**. The health service is also **stretched** because of **HIV/AIDS** (a deadly disease). It's passed on from **mother to child** and through **unprotected sex**, so HIV/AIDS may **spread** further when the youthful population start to have children, putting **even more strain** on the health system.
2) **Unemployment could get much worse** — in **2003** unemployment in **Uganda** was **3.2%**. However, 50% of the population are under 15 and so weren't **counted** in these figures. When the **large youth population** reaches working age there **won't be enough jobs** for them all, so unemployment will **rise further**, causing **poverty** to **increase**.

Some Strategies Have Been Introduced to Address These Problems

1) **Encouraging the use of contraceptives and family planning** — the use of contraceptives among married women is **less than 25%**. New policies **encouraging** the use of **contraceptives** allow women to plan **how many** children they have and **when they have them**, e.g. the government has brought in **free contraceptives like condoms**. However, family planning clinics **aren't widespread**, so many people don't have **easy access** to birth control. Since 1991, **birth rate** has **increased**, suggesting this population management method **isn't working**.
2) **Policies to combat the spread of HIV/AIDS** — in the late 1980s a programme of **education** called the **ABC approach** was used (**A**bstain from sex until marriage, **B**e faithful to one partner and use **C**ondoms). This strategy **worked** — HIV **infection** rates **fell** from **15%** of all adults in **1991** to **5%** in **2001**.

These Strategies Should Help to Achieve Sustainable Development Too

1) **Encouraging contraception** — this should **reduce birth rate** and help prevent **overpopulation** from getting any worse. This means the country can **focus** on sustainable development for the current population, without the population **increasing dramatically** and putting **pressure** on sustainable development strategies.
2) **Reducing the spread of disease** — this **relieves** pressure on the **health care system**, which **frees up** money to be used elsewhere, e.g. in **developing sustainable** irrigation techniques for **rural farming** communities.

Practice Questions

Q1 Describe one problem caused by the ageing population in the UK.

Q2 Describe one problem caused by the youthful population in Uganda.

Exam Question

Q1 With reference to a named example, evaluate the strategies used to manage population change. [10 marks]

Youthful populations — not exactly like Neverland...

You're all too old, you're all too young — hang on, nobody's the right age here. Population structures are constantly changing, causing lots of different problems. Just think, one day the youthful populations will be old, then they'll be ageing populations.

Migration into Europe

***These pages are for** Edexcel Unit 1 (Going Global).*
Europe's totally the place to move to — it's soooooo in vogue these days, darling.

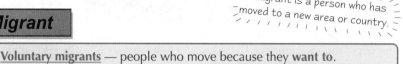

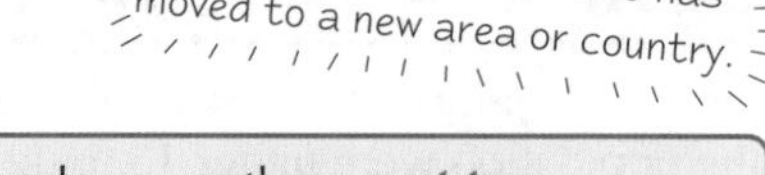
A migrant is a person who has moved to a new area or country.

There are Different Types of Migrant

Economic migrants — people who **move abroad** to find **work** or a **better paid job**.

Voluntary migrants — people who move because they **want to**.
Involuntary migrants — people who are **forced to move** against their will.

Asylum seekers and refugees — people who move because they're at **risk**, e.g. from **war** or **persecution**. Asylum seekers apply for **permission to live** in a country (**asylum**), but if it's **denied** they're **refused entry**, or may be **sent back** (**deported**).

Illegal immigrants — people who **enter** or **stay** in a country **without permission**. Illegal immigration may be for **economic reasons**, or it may be to **escape war** or **persecution**. Illegal immigrants may be people who've applied for asylum, been **rejected** and have **stayed on**, or they may be people who've **crossed the border** without the country **knowing** about it.

Lots of People Migrated into Europe from Former Colonies...

Before the **mid-20th century**, some **European countries** had been **colonising** other places around the world, building **empires**, e.g. the **British Empire** included **India**, **Australia** and some **Caribbean** islands.
After **World War 2**, these empires **broke up** and there was a flow of people **into Europe**. This is called **post-colonial flow**.

1) Immigrants from the **former British Empire** — the **British Government invited** people from the **former colonies** to migrate to the **UK** where there was a **shortage of labour** and **lots of work** available to rebuild the **damaged economy**:
   - More than **60 000 Indians** had **migrated** to the **UK** by the **mid-1950s**. A shortage of trained UK doctors meant the NHS **recruited** many doctors from India, as well as Pakistan, Bangladesh and Sri Lanka. There are currently more than **1 million** people in the UK who describe themselves as **Indian**.
   - People from the **Caribbean islands** began emigrating to the **UK** in large numbers in **1948**. Today there are around **550 000** people in the UK who describe themselves as **Caribbean**.
2) Immigrants from the **former French empire** — from the 1950s to the 1970s loads of **people** migrated into **France** from **former French colonies** in **North Africa** (e.g. **Algeria**, **Tunisia** and **Morocco**). Many were **economic migrants** attracted by **jobs** created by **labour shortages** (lack of workers). Others were **fleeing persecution** occurring as colonies gained independence, e.g. around **1 million** people fled Algeria between 1962 and 1964 after it **became independent** in 1962.

...and from Other Countries

People have also migrated **into Europe** from countries that **aren't former colonies**:

1) West **Germany** made up for its **shortage of labour** in the **1960s** by **inviting** workers over from **Turkey** (**economic migrants**). **Today** there are more than **1.7 million Turks living** in Germany.
2) A lot of **asylum seekers** were created by the invasion of **Iraq** in **2003** (around **2 million** people). **Sweden** has accepted over **40 000** of these.
3) Huge numbers of **illegal immigrants** enter Europe every year, e.g. many **Africans** try to cross the **strait of Gibraltar** (the narrow gap between **Morocco** and **Spain**). It's **not known** how many people **try** to get across, but in **2001**, **45 000** people were caught and **refused entry** to **Spain** alone. Many people **die** in the attempt to cross.

Links Between Europe and the Wider World Explain Migration Patterns

1) **Former colonies** have **political links** (e.g. systems of **government**), **economic links** (e.g. flows of **trade**) and **cultural links** (e.g. a **shared religion**) with the country that used to **rule them**. People like to migrate to countries that they have some **familiarity** with.
2) Countries are **linked** by ties between **family** and **friends**, because migrants usually leave **people they know behind**. Migrants are often later **joined** by family and friends, who move to a country because they **already know someone** there.
3) Countries are **linked** by a **shared language**. For example, migrants whose **first language** is English (e.g. from **Australia** and **South Africa**) have come to Britain to **work** and **study**. Others might speak English as their **second language**, e.g. migrants from **India**. Sharing a language makes it easier to **find work** and become **integrated** into a new **society**.

Migration into Europe

Migration into Europe Has Many Consequences

A destination country is where migrants are heading to. A source country is where they've come from.

Demographic

Migration changes the **population structure** (see p. 120) of the **destination** and **source** countries.

- **Source** countries will have a **reduced proportion** of people of **working** and **reproductive age**. **Destination** countries will have an **increased proportion** of people of **working** and **reproductive age**.
- An **increase** in the number of people of **reproductive age** may **increase birth rate** in **destination** countries, e.g. around 25% of children born in the UK in 2006 had at least one parent who had migrated from another country. A **decrease** in the number of people of **reproductive age** may **decrease birth rate** in **source** countries.

Economic

Many migrant workers **send money back** to families in their **country of origin**. E.g. in **2006** over **$25 billion** was sent back to **India** from other countries. This money can form a large part of the **national income** (GDP, see p. 130) in poorer **source** countries. **Destination** countries **lose out** because the migrant workers **earn** the money in that country, but it gets **spent** in another country.

Social

Illegal immigrants (see previous page) don't have access to legal **employment**, **healthcare** or **benefits**. They live in the destination country **illegally**, so if they try to access these things they risk being **deported**. They may carry out **dangerous work** for **little pay**, e.g. in **2004 more than 20** illegal immigrants from **China drowned** when picking cockles in **Morecambe Bay** in the **UK**.

Cultural

1) Migrants bring their own **culture** (e.g. their **religion**) to the countries they move to. This has caused problems of **racial tension** in some countries, e.g. there was widespread **rioting** across **France** in **2005** because **immigrant communities** didn't think they were being treated **fairly**.
2) Where immigrant groups from several **different countries** have settled, you get a **mixture** of **different cultures**. This leads to new **hybrid cultures** of **music**, **fashion** and **food**, e.g. **Indian** food has become so popular in the UK that some **new dishes** have been created **specifically** for the **UK** population.

Political

1) Large numbers of immigrants can lead to **changes** in **government policies**, e.g. the UK government is changing its policy on **immigration** to a **points-based system**. Points are awarded based on an immigrant's **age**, **skills** and **experience**. They get **more points** if their age, skills and experience **match** what the **UK needs**. Migrants are allowed to **stay** and **work** if they have enough points.
2) **Racial tensions** have led to some **nationalist political parties** becoming **more popular**, e.g. the **British National Party** (**BNP**) is a political party that thinks there **shouldn't be any more immigration** to the UK. They've **become more popular** — in the 2006 local elections they **more than doubled** the number of **political seats** they held.

Environmental

Travel by planes and ships causes **pollution** and migration means a **lot of people** travel **long distances**. This leads to increased **CO_2 emissions**, which increases **global warming** (see p. 79).

Practice Questions

Q1 Describe one major migration of people into Europe from a former colony.

Q2 Explain one link between Europe and the wider world that might encourage migration to Europe.

Exam Question

Q1 Discuss the consequences of migration into Europe. [10 marks]

No Terry, this page is about Euro-revision, not Eurovision...

I'm assuming all the people that want to migrate to Europe haven't seen the Eurovision Song Contest. Most people migrate to Europe to make a better life (not for the music). This has consequences for Europe and the countries they've come from.

Intra-EU Migration

These pages are for Edexcel Unit 1 (Going Global).
As if all this global movement wasn't complicated enough, people are dashing about within Europe too. Crikey.

Many People Have **Migrated** from **Poland to the UK**

People who come from a country **within the EU** can live and work in **any other EU country**. When **new countries** join the EU the **current members** can **choose not to allow immigration** from the new countries for a **few years**. In **2004**, **10** countries in **central** and **eastern Europe** became new members of the EU, including **Poland**. Between **2004** and **2007**, more than **half a million** people from **Poland** migrated to the **UK** — most were **economic migrants**.

Here are a few reasons why they decided to **leave Poland** (**push factors**, see p. 121):

1) **High unemployment** — around **19%** in **2004**. People of working-age **left** Poland to **find work** in the UK — they were **economic migrants** (see p. 128).
2) **Low average wages.** People of working-age **left** Poland to find **higher wages**, e.g. the **average income** in the EU in 2004 was nearly **three times greater** than it was in Poland.
3) **Low availability of housing.** People left Poland because there **weren't enough houses** for them to move into, e.g. in **2004** there were just over **300 dwellings** for every **1000 people**.

When people move from newly joined countries it's called post-accession flow.

Here are a few reasons why they decided to **come to the UK** (**pull factors**, see p. 121):

1) **Ease of migration.** Only the **UK**, **Ireland** and **Sweden** decided to **allow unlimited migration** from the new member countries in **2004**. Other countries **restricted entry**, but they will have to allow it by 2011.
2) **Good exchange rate.** **A few pounds** earnt in the UK were worth **lots of zloty** (Polish currency, **one pound** was worth **seven zloty in 2004**), so migrants could **send a few pounds** back to Poland and it would make a **big difference.**
3) **Plenty of jobs** and **better paid jobs.** There was a **labour shortage** for certain occupations in the UK, e.g. a shortage of **tradesmen** such as **plumbers** (who are also **paid more** in the UK than in Poland).

Migration Has **Consequences** for Both **Poland** and the **UK**

Demographic

Poland's population has **shrunk** because so many people have **migrated** to other countries, e.g. it **fell 0.3%** between **2003** and **2007**. The **birth rate** also **decreased** between **2003** and **2005**, partly because a lot of the people that have left are of **reproductive age**. The population of the UK has **increased** as a result (especially those of **reproductive** age).

Economic

The UK economy **loses out** because money **earnt** in the **UK** by **Polish** workers **isn't all spent** in the UK. The Polish economy **grows** because money is **sent back** to Poland by migrants, e.g. in 2006, around **€3.45 billion** was sent to Poland from abroad. Migration has also had a **bad effect** on the Polish economy — there's a **shortage of labourers** (most migrants were of **working-age**) so **less work** can be done, which means the economy **doesn't grow as much**.

Social

Migration of working-age people has **helped** the problems caused by the UK's **ageing-population** (see p. 126). Young migrant workers **pay taxes** and these are used to **support** the older retired people, e.g. they pay for **pensions**.

Cultural

Shops selling **Polish products** have **opened** in areas where lots of Polish people have **settled**, e.g. the **West Midlands**. The number of people attending **Catholic church services** in the **UK** has **increased** because most of the Polish migrants are **Catholic**.

Political

The **immigration policy** of the UK has been **changed** because of the **influx** of **Polish migrants**. When **Romania** and **Bulgaria** joined the EU in **2007**, the UK **didn't allow unlimited migration** like it had for Poland.

Environmental

Increased immigration from Poland has meant **more air traffic** between **Poland** and the **UK**, e.g. there were just over **500 000** passengers to and from the UK in **2003** and **3.3 million** in **2006**. Increased air traffic means more **greenhouse gases** are released, making **global warming** worse (see p. 79).

Migration to the **UK** Might Not be **Permanent**

In **2008** lots of migrants **moved back** to **Poland**. Here are a few reasons **why**:

1) **Less work** is available in the **UK** — the economy of the UK is thought to be **shrinking**, so **less money** is being spent on things like **house renovation**, which means there's **less work** for tradesmen.
2) **More work** is available in **Poland** — the economy is **growing**, providing more work. Poland's **GDP** (the total value of goods produced and services provided) **grew by 6.5%** in 2007.
3) **Less favourable exchange rate** — **one pound** was worth about **4.5 zloty** in **November 2008**. This means the money immigrants send back **isn't worth as much** as it was in **2004**.

Intra-EU Migration

Many People *Have* ***Migrated*** *from the* ***UK to Spain***

Lots of people **migrate** to **Spain** from the **UK** when they **retire**. The largest numbers migrated in the **1980s** and **90s**, and more are **still going**. It's difficult to know **exact numbers** because lots of people move **temporarily** — they live in **Spain** for **part** of the year, and in the **UK** for **part** of the year. It's thought that around **1 million** British people own a **property** in Spain.

There are **push factors** (see p. 121):

1) The **cost of living** is **rising** in the UK. Shopping, fuel, electricity and mortgage payments are getting **more expensive**, but people's earnings **aren't increasing** at the **same rate**, so they have **less to spend** on **other things**.
2) The **UK** has a **cool, wet** and **changeable** climate.

There are **pull factors** (see p. 121):

1) The **cost of living** is **lower** in **Spain**, so people have **more money** to spend on **other things**.
2) **Spain** has a **hot, dry** and **less changeable** climate than the **UK**. Retired people move because they **prefer** the **Spanish climate**.

Spain and the **UK** have become more **interlinked**, making it **easier** for people to **migrate**.

1) The increase in **budget air travel** from companies like **EasyJet** has meant that people can **afford** to visit **family** and **friends** they've **left** in the **UK several times** a year.
2) **Improved communications** such as **cheap telephone calls** and use of the **internet** means people can keep in **close contact** even when they're living **far away**, e.g. **Skype™** allows people to make **free calls** over the **internet**.

There are ***Consequences*** *for the* ***UK*** *and* ***Spain***

Demographic

The **population structure** of the UK and Spain is **altered**. The people that **retire to Spain** are mostly older (**over 65**) so the population structure of **Spain** will have a **greater proportion** of older people, while the **UK** will have a **reduced proportion** of older people.

Environmental

Many UK migrants don't live in Spain **all year** (e.g. there were about **230 000** part-time residents in **2008**) — they regularly **return** to the UK. This leads to **increasing air traffic**, which causes **more pollution**.

Social

A lot of migrants were in their **50s** or **60s** when they migrated in the **1980s** and **90s**. They're now reaching an age where they'll need more **long-term medical care**. It's **not known** whether the Spanish **health system** will be able to **cope**. Also, **UK-born Spanish residents** don't have the **same right** to **health care** in the **UK** as UK residents do, e.g. they don't qualify for things like **nursing home places**.

Cultural

UK migrants have set up **communities** with **British-run shops** and **restaurants**. Some **don't speak Spanish** so they don't **interact** with the **local community**. This can lead to **tensions** between UK migrants and local people.

Economic

Jobs are created in Spain to provide for the **needs** of UK migrants, e.g. more **home help** and **construction workers** to build houses. UK migrants **spend** their **savings** in **Spain** instead of the **UK**, **helping** the Spanish economy to **grow**, whilst the UK economy **loses out**.

Political

Local elections in Spain are affected by UK immigrants — they have the **right to vote**, and many are standing as **candidates** in local elections. E.g. more than **100 UK immigrants** stood as candidates in local elections in **2007**. Also, some Spanish people think the **health care** that UK migrants receive should be **paid for** by the **UK NHS**.

Practice Questions

Q1 Describe one push factor and one pull factor that help to explain why people in Poland migrate to the UK.

Q2 Describe one push factor and one pull factor that help to explain why retired people in the UK migrate to Spain.

Exam Question

Q1 Using a named example, discuss the reasons for intra-EU migration and the consequences it has for the countries involved. [10 marks]

Entrance to the UK — if your name's not down, you're not comin' in...

People migrate when they've got good reasons to — they don't want to stay where they are (push factors), and they're drawn towards another place (pull factors). Unlike my herd of Pushmi-pullyus — they don't know whether they're coming or going.

Rural-Urban Migration

These pages are for Edexcel Unit 1 (Going Global).
Lots of people are heading for the cities to seek their fortune where the streets are paved with gold. It's mostly happening in countries that are developing quickly, like China. Maybe I'll book a holiday to one of these cities of gold...

Most Population Movement is Rural-Urban Migration

Rural-urban migration is the **movement of people** from **rural areas** (areas with a **low population density**, e.g. the **countryside**) to **urban areas** (areas with a **high population density**, e.g. **towns** and **cities**). It causes **urbanisation**, which is the **growth** in the **proportion** of people living in **urban areas**.

More than **50%** of the world's population live in **urban areas** (**3.4 billion** people) and this is **increasing**. **Urbanisation differs** between **developed** and **developing** countries:

- **Most** of the population in **developed** countries **already live** in **urban areas**, e.g. more than **80%** of the **UK's** population live in urban areas.
- This is because most **rural-urban migration** in **developed countries** has **already happened**, e.g. in the **late 18th** and **early 19th century** in the **UK** (during the **Industrial Revolution**).
- **Less** of the population in developing countries **currently** live in urban areas, e.g. around **25%** of the population of **Bangladesh** live in urban areas.
- Most **rural-urban migration** that's happening in the **world today** is going on in **developing countries** — it's causing **rapid urbanisation** (see p. 134).

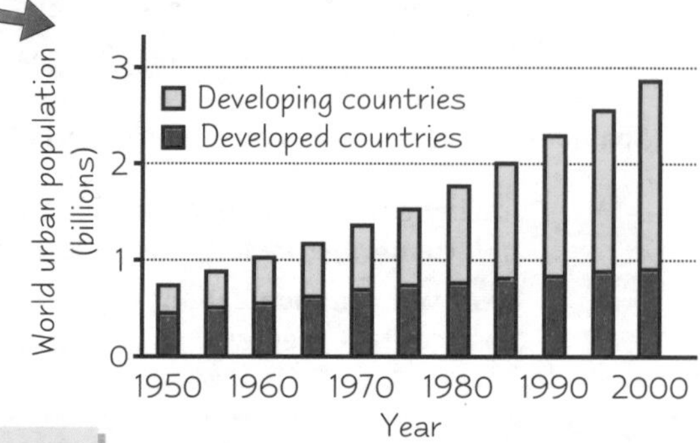

There are Many Factors Causing Rural-Urban Migration

Migration to **urban areas** in **developing** countries is **triggered** by **two** main factors:

1) **Foreign investment** from **TNCs** (see p. 110) is **concentrated** in **urban** areas because the **population density** is **high**, so there's access to a **large workforce**. This means **new job opportunities** are created in urban areas.
2) **Increased access** to **technologies** (like **television** and **radio**) as well as **transport links** (like **road networks**) mean people in **rural** areas **learn more** about the **opportunities** available in **urban areas**.

Here are a few reasons why people **leave rural areas** in **developing** countries (**push factors**, see p. 121):

1) **Inconsistent income** and **food supply** — in rural areas many people are **subsistence farmers**. They grow **food** to meet the needs of their **family** and sell any **extra** to make a **small income**. Crop failures can mean they make **no income** and even risk **starvation**.
2) **Overpopulation** in rural areas — there are **too many** people for the **resources** in many rural areas, e.g. not enough land for everyone to **farm**.
3) **Low standard of living** — there's often little access to adequate **health care** and **education**, and the **demand** is **high** because **birth rates** are **high**. Not everyone has access to **electricity** or a **clean water supply**.

Here are a few reasons why people **migrate to urban areas** in **developing** countries (**pull factors**, see p. 121):

1) **Job opportunities** — **more** jobs are available in **urban** areas.
2) **Higher wages** — jobs in urban areas usually offer a **higher** and **more stable income**.
3) **Higher standard of living** — better access to **health care** and **education**. Also, **greater access** to things like a **clean water supply** and **electricity**.

Yee-haw! We're a-heading for the city.

Rural-Urban Migration Creates Million Cities and Megacities

Increasing rural-urban migration means **metropolitan areas** (**cities** and the surrounding areas from which people commute to that city) are **growing**, helping to create more **million cities** and **megacities** around the world:

- **Million cities** are cities with a population of **1 million people or more** — there are more than **400** of them.
- **Megacities** are metropolitan areas with a population of **over 10 million people** — there are more than **22** megacities.

Most **new** million cities and megacities are being created in **developing countries** in **Africa** and **Asia** where the **greatest rates** of **rural-urban migration** are taking place.

Rural-Urban Migration

China's Experiencing **Massive Rural-Urban Migration**

There are a **huge number** of people migrating from rural to urban areas in **China**.

1) **300 million** rural **Chinese** people are now thought to live in **cities**, e.g. in **1990** around **74%** of the population lived in **rural areas**, but in **2006** it had decreased to around **56%**.
2) There's a movement of people **towards** the **east coast** because most of the **cities** in China are **concentrated** there, e.g. **Beijing** and **Shanghai**.
3) Rural-urban migration in China has helped to create lots of **million cities**, e.g. there are **more than 90** cities with a population of more than 1 million people in China **today**.

Ready, set, migrate!

Rural-Urban Migration in *China* is *Caused* by *Different Factors*

Rural-urban migration in China has been **triggered** by a couple of factors:

1) **Foreign investment** from **TNCs** (see p. 110) — lots of companies have opened **factories** in **urban areas** in China. This has created **jobs**, **attracting** people from rural areas, e.g. **Ford** has a large factory in **Nanjing**, north-west of **Shanghai**.
2) **Technologies** and **transport links spread knowledge** to **rural** areas about **opportunities** in **urban** areas. **China National Highway 312** is a **4800-km** road from the major urban areas in the **east** (e.g. **Shanghai** and **Nanjing**), through the **rural central areas** to the major city in the far **west** (**Urumqi**). People in **rural** areas **find out about** the **opportunities** available in the **urban** areas to the **east** and **west** because of the **highway**.

Here's why people are **leaving rural areas** in China (**push factors**, see p. 121):

1) **High unemployment** — the use of more **machinery** has made agriculture more **efficient**, which has meant **fewer workers** are needed in **rural areas**. This has created **high unemployment**, e.g. **150 million** rural people were unemployed in **2004**. So people have been **leaving** rural areas to **find work**.
2) **Poverty** — in 2004 there were **26.1 million** people in **rural areas** in **absolute poverty** (too poor to afford enough **food** and **clothing**). People have been **leaving** rural areas to **escape poverty**.
3) **Lower standard of living** — **services** like **education** and **health care** are funded by taxes collected within the **local area**. This means poor rural areas don't have the **money** to improve their **services**, so people **leave** to **improve** their standard of living.

Here's why people are **migrating to urban areas** in China (**pull factors**, see p. 121):

1) **Higher employment** — large-scale **industrialisation** since the 1970s has focused on **urban** areas. Large numbers of **manufacturing jobs** have been **created** by **foreign** companies (**TNCs**, see above) and by **Chinese** companies.
2) **Higher wages** — average income is **three times higher** in **urban** areas than **rural** areas (and the **difference** is getting **bigger**). People migrate to urban areas to **increase their income** and **escape poverty**.
3) **Higher standard of living** — the **quality** and **availability** of services like **education** and **health care** is better in urban areas because there's more **money** available to pay for **them**, e.g. in **1998** there were **7 doctors per 1000** people in **urban** areas and **1 doctor per 1000 people** in **rural** areas. People migrate to urban areas to have **better access** to **adequate** services.

Practice Questions

Q1 Define rural-urban migration.

Q2 Describe one factor that triggers rural-urban migration in developing countries.

Q3 What's the definition of a megacity?

Exam Question

Q1 Describe the push and pull factors for rural-urban migration in a named country. [10 marks]

Megacity — wasn't he a massive, seriously evil robot...

Basically, rural-urban migration is the mother of all migrations and it means loads of enormous cities are popping up in a lot of places. It happens because people are pushed out of rural areas and pulled towards urban areas. All sounds a bit rough to me.

Megacities

***These pages are for** Edexcel Unit 1 (Going Global).*
Remember, megacities are urban areas with a population of 10 million people or more.

The cycle of urbanisation isn't really a cycle — cities don't start back at the beginning once they've been through all four stages.

Cities Undergo a Cycle of Urbanisation

The **different patterns** of population **movement** that happen in cities make up the **cycle of urbanisation**. Cities **don't** just go through the stages **one by one** though — **different population movements** can be happening in a city at the **same time**.

1) Urbanisation

- The **growth** in the **proportion** of people living in **urban areas**.
- It occurs because of **migration** — especially **rural-urban migration** (see pages 132-133).
- Urbanisation is happening **quickly** in **developing countries** (where most megacities have recently developed) because of the massive **rural-urban migration**. One of the ways the cities have **grown** is by poor migrants setting up **shanty towns** — **unplanned** and often **illegal** settlements where people build their own homes out of whatever they can find, usually on the **outskirts** of the city.

2) Suburbanisation

- The movement of people from the **city centre** to **lower density housing** on the **outskirts** of a city.
- As **urbanisation increases** city centres become **overcrowded** and people want **more space**. Improvements to **public transport** mean people can **live further away** but still reach the **city centre** easily.
- As megacities grow, **more suburbs** are **added** so older suburbs **aren't** on the **outskirts** any more.
- A **complex pattern** of **wealthy** and **poorer** areas develops. **Wealthy people** live in suburbs on the outskirts of the city because they can **afford** larger houses with **more space**. **Wealthy people** also **move into poorer suburbs** closer to the centre and **renovate** the houses — this process is called **gentrification**.

3) Counter-urbanisation

- The movement of people **out of the city** into surrounding **villages** and **rural areas**.
- Improvements in **transport** and **communications** mean people can **commute** to work or **work from home** over the internet.
- This happens because of **high property prices** and **overcrowding** in cities. People may also **prefer** more **quiet rural areas**.

4) Re-urbanisation

- The movement of people **back** into **redeveloped city centre** residential areas.
- In **developed countries** lots of city centres have been **redeveloped**. This attracts **young, affluent people** who want to be near to the **cultural activity** of the city centre, e.g. redeveloped canal areas such as **Brindleyplace** in **Birmingham**.

London is a Megacity in a Developed Country

London is a **megacity** in the south-east of the **UK**. The London metropolitan area (**Greater London** and much of the **surrounding counties**, including towns like Slough, Luton and Potters Bar) has a population of around **13 million** people. Greater London is on the **flat land** around the mouth of the river **Thames** and has a population density of about **4800** people per km^2. It's very **different** to megacities in other countries, e.g. **Mumbai** (see next page). Here's what's been going on in London:

Urban cycle

The population of London is **growing**, but not **rapidly**, e.g. the population of Greater London has grown by **less than 1 million** people since 1981. People are moving **into, out of** and **around** the city:

1) **Urbanisation** is still occurring — people are **migrating** to Greater London from **abroad**, e.g. in 2006 there was a **net gain** of almost **70 000** international migrants. **Almost all** parts of Greater London gained, but the **biggest** gains were in **central** areas, e.g. **Westminster** and **Camden**.
2) **Counter-urbanisation** is also happening — people are moving **out** of Greater London to the **rest of the UK**, e.g. in **2006** there was a **net loss** of around **80 000** people to other parts of the UK.
3) **Re-urbanisation** has happened around **London Docklands** — the area **east** of **central London** that used to be a **major port**. The port **moved upriver** between 1965 and 1980 and the area was left **derelict**. It's been **redeveloped** since the 1980s and the population has more than **doubled**.

Economy

London has a **post-industrial economy** — the economy used to be based on **industry** and **manufacturing**, but now it's mostly based on **services**, e.g. **85%** of the people employed in London work in the **service** industry.

- It's a major **financial** centre. London has one of the largest **stock exchanges** in the world. Many **global banks** have their headquarters in the centre of London, e.g. **HSBC**.
- **Tourism** is a major part of the **economy**. London is one of the **most popular** cities to visit in the world, e.g. it attracted more than **15 million foreign tourists** in **2006**.

Megacities

Housing patterns

London has a **complex residential pattern** that includes contrasting **rich** and **poor** areas.

1) **Parts** of poorer areas in the east of inner London, e.g. **Hackney**, have been **changed** because of **gentrification**. **Richer** people have moved in, making a **mixed pattern** of **rich** and **poor** people living **near** to each other.
2) **Suburban growth** has meant **villages** around London have **become suburbs** of London, e.g. **Streatham** was a **village** that became a **wealthy suburb** as London grew in the **19th century**. Other suburbs have **grown around it**. Wealthy people still live there, but it's also a **destination** for **poorer immigrants**.

Mumbai is a Megacity in a NIC

Mumbai is a **megacity** on the west coast of **India**. The **Mumbai metropolitan area** (**Mumbai city** and neighbouring areas such as **Navi Mumbai** and **Thane**) has a population of more than **20 million** people. **Greater Mumbai** is on an **island** separated from the mainland by the river **Ulhas**. It has a **high population density** — there are more than **20 000** people per km^2. Although Mumbai's also a **megacity**, it's very **different** to **London**.

Urban cycle

The population of Mumbai is **growing rapidly**, e.g. the population of Greater Mumbai has grown by more than **6 million** people since **1971** and people are **still moving into** the city:

- Massive **urbanisation** is occurring — people are migrating to Mumbai from **all over India**, e.g. from **1991-2001** more than **1.1 million** people migrated to Greater Mumbai from **outside Maharashtra** (the **state** Mumbai's in).
- **Suburbanisation** is occurring — some people are moving **north**, **away from** the **inner city** on the **southern tip** of the island. **Suburbs** are being built **along** the main **rail** and **road routes out** of the city.

Economy

Mumbai has a **fast growing** economy based on **manufacturing**, but the **service industry** is becoming more important:

- Until the 1980s, the economy was based mainly on **textiles manufacturing** and **shipping** (it's still a **major port**).
- There's been an increase in **IT** and **financial services** recently.
- Mumbai's a major centre for **out-sourced work** — companies in Mumbai work for **foreign companies**, e.g. the **UK-based financial services** company **Prudential** has its **call centre** in Greater Mumbai.
- Mumbai's a **major media centre** for **India**, e.g. the **Bollywood** film industry is based in Mumbai. It's one of the **largest** film industries in the world, e.g. in **2002** Bollywood films sold **3.6 billion** tickets **worldwide**.

Housing patterns

The **residential pattern** of Greater Mumbai is **complex**:

- The **wealthiest** area (**Malabar Hill**) is **near** to the **Central Business District** (**CBD**).
- Around **half the population** of Greater Mumbai live in **shanty towns**. They're **squeezed in** wherever there's **space**, e.g. **Dharavi** is the **biggest** shanty town (more than **600 000** people live there) — it's **next** to the **CBD**.
- **Wealthier suburbs** have been built along the **road** and **rail routes** that run north out of the CBD, but **shanty towns** are also squeezed in as near to the **transport links** as possible.

London and Mumbai are Interlinked

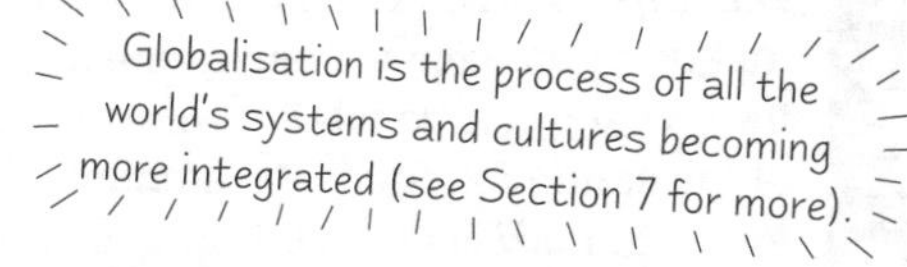

Globalisation is the process of all the world's systems and cultures becoming more integrated (see Section 7 for more).

Flows of **trade**, **money**, **people**, **information** and **culture link** London and Mumbai **together**, accelerating **globalisation**. For example:

1) **Cadbury** has its global headquarters in **London**, and its subsidiary company, **Cadbury India**, has its main office in Greater Mumbai. There are flows of **trade**, **money**, **information** and **people** between the two parts of the same company.
2) There are **close links** between the **film industries** in **London** and **Mumbai**, e.g. in **2006** more than **40 Bollywood films** were made in **London**. This means there's a flow of **trade** and **money** as well as **culture** between the two cities.

Practice Questions

Q1 Define urbanisation.

Q2 Define suburbanisation.

Exam Question

Q1 Compare two megacities that you have studied. [10 marks]

Urban cycle — I'm more of a mountain biker actually...

Jeez, people just can't make up their minds. They move into the city, then they move to the outer suburbs, then they move to the countryside, then they move back to the centre of the city. Why don't they just sit down and have a nice cup of tea, eh?

Urban Sustainability

These pages are for Edexcel Unit 1 (Going Global).
Urban areas keep growing and it causes a hatful of problems. These'll only get worse unless the areas can start developing in a sustainable way. That means making sure what we're doing now isn't going to adversely affect people in the future.

There are Consequences of Urban Growth

Urban populations are predicted to carry on **growing**, e.g. the population of **Shanghai** in **China** is currently around **18 million** and it's predicted to grow to up to **25 million** by **2020**. The continued **growth** of **urban** areas will have **consequences**:

1) **Housing shortages** — there won't be **enough houses** for everyone. This will have different effects in different places though, e.g. in **developed** countries it may mean children have to live with their parents for **longer**. In **developing** countries more people could end up living in **overcrowded shanty towns** — these cause other problems such as **poor health** because of **insufficient and unclean water supplies** and a lack of **sewage removal**.
2) **Increased ecological footprints** (how much a place **impacts** on **natural resources**), e.g. **more power** will be needed as the population **grows**. This could mean that more fossil fuels are **burnt** to produce the power. This **reduces** the amount of fossil fuels **available** in the **future**.
3) **Transport problems** — lots of people use **bikes** and **scooters** to get around in **megacities** in **less developed** countries. But as **more people** move in and become more **affluent**, car ownership will **increase**. This will cause an **increase** in **pollution** and the number of **accidents**. The **transport system** (e.g. road networks) may not be able to **cope** so it will become **more difficult** to get around the city.
4) Increased effect on **climate change** (see p. 79) — more **greenhouse gases** will be emitted because **more power** is used as the **urban** area **grows**. This could mean that **climate change** is **accelerated**. Some natural hazards are **increasing** because of climate change, e.g. **hydro-meteorological** hazards (see p. 69), which means people may be at **greater risk**.

Innovative solutions are needed to combat growing transport problems.

Urban Areas Need to Become More Sustainable

Sustainable development means **growth** in a way that lets the people living **now** have the things they **need**, but without reducing the ability of people in the **future** to get what **they need**. Basically, it means developing in a way that **doesn't irreversibly damage** the **environment** or **use up resources faster** than they can be **replaced**. For example, an urban area that's growing by generating **all** its **power** from **fossil fuels** will **exhaust** its supply and **accelerate climate change**, so the people in the future **won't have any** fossil fuels and the **environment** will be **damaged** — it's **unsustainable**.

Megacities require so many **resources** that it's **unlikely** any megacity could ever develop in a **truly sustainable** way, i.e. develop **without depleting any non-renewable resources**. But things can be done to make them develop in a way that's **more sustainable**:

1. Build more **carbon-neutral homes** — buildings that **generate** as much **energy** as they **use** (from sources that **don't damage** the **environment**). They have things like **solar panels** to produce **energy**, and lots of **insulation** to reduce the amount of energy that's **lost**, e.g. **BedZED** is a carbon-neutral housing development in London with these features. Building more carbon-neutral homes provides **more housing** without **increasing** the **ecological footprint** of the city. However, carbon-neutral homes can be **expensive** to build so they **can't always** be used to **solve housing shortages**.

2. Generate more power from **renewable energy sources** — burning **fossil fuels** to generate power isn't sustainable because they'll **run out**. They also **increase** the rate of **climate change** because burning them produces **greenhouse gases**. Megacities could use **more power** from sources that **don't run out**, e.g. Los Angeles uses **hydroelectric power** from the **Hoover Dam**. Greater **energy needs** can be **met** without **increasing** the **ecological footprint** of the city. This means people's **ability** to generate power in the **future** is **less affected**. However, at the moment renewable energy sources can't generate **enough power** on their **own** to **support** large cities.

3. **Recycling** more **waste** — **increased** recycling means **less resources** are **used**, e.g. tin cans can be melted down and used to make **more tin cans**. **Less waste** is produced, which **reduces** the amount of waste that goes to **landfill**. Landfill is **unsustainable** because it **uses up resources** — **finite resources** (e.g. metal) that are thrown away and the resource of **suitable landfill sites**. **Decomposition** of landfill also releases **greenhouse gases**.

4. **Water conservation** schemes — only as much water should be **taken from the environment** as can be **naturally replaced**. If natural stores, e.g. **lakes** or **groundwater**, are reduced **too much** there **won't be enough** for future generations. Water conservation schemes reduce the amount of water **used**, but don't affect how the **needs** of people using the water are met, e.g. collecting **rainwater** for use on **gardens** or **installing toilets** that use **less water** to flush.

Urban Sustainability

5 **Improving public transport** — using **buses, trains** and **trams** that generate **little or no harmful emissions**, e.g. some buses in London are powered by **hydrogen** and only emit **water vapour**. The **ecological footprint** of the city is **reduced** (provided the **electricity** used to produce the hydrogen fuel comes from **renewable sources**) because the buses and trains are **producing less harmful emissions**. The number of **buses** and **trains** can also be **increased**, as well as the **area they cover**. **Improved** public transport **networks** will mean **fewer cars** on the road, so **emissions** will be further **decreased**.

They're **Attempting** to **Build** a **Sustainable City** in **China**

There are **attempts** going on in the world to make **urban** areas that are more **sustainable** — in **China** they're **planning** to build an **'eco-city'** — a **city** that's **as sustainable as possible**, called **Dongtan**. It's planned for the island of **Chongming** near to **Shanghai**. It's a **new city** (the island is currently a **wetland** used for **farming**) — the idea is to help solve the **problems** of **urban growth** in **Shanghai**, but in a way that will help to achieve more **sustainable development**.

Here are some of the **plans** to make it a **sustainable city**:

1) **Carbon-neutral homes** — the **housing** in the city has been designed to **generate** as much **energy** as it **uses**.
   - All the homes will produce **their own power**, e.g. using **solar panels**. They'll be **well insulated** to prevent **energy loss**, e.g. **green roofs** (with **soil** and **grass** on top) provide **good insulation**.
   - Dongtan will be more **sustainable** because it will provide **housing** to help Shanghai's **housing shortages**, but the housing won't **increase energy use** or **deplete the resources** available to the city.
2) **Renewable energy production** — the city's **designed** to **generate** all **its own** energy.
   - Power will be provided by **wind turbines** outside the city as well as **smaller wind turbines** on the **buildings**.
   - **Biofuels** will also be used — generating power by burning **waste biological material**, e.g. **rice husks**.
   - Dongtan will be more **sustainable** because **less resources** will be used, e.g. fossil fuels, but **enough power** will be produced to provide for the **needs** of the population. Using **waste biomass** to **generate energy** also means less waste goes to **landfill** so less landfill space is **used up**.
3) **Green transport strategies** — the city's designed to have **very low emissions**.
   - Vehicles that run on **petrol** or **diesel won't be allowed** in the city.
   - The city will have a **network** of **cycleways, walkways** and **canals**.
   - The **public transport system** will use **low-emission vehicles**, e.g. **solar-powered water taxis** along the canals.
   - Dongtan will be more **sustainable** because **few emissions** will be **produced** by the city's **transport systems**, but it **shouldn't affect** people's **ability to get around** the city.

There are **reasons** why China's plans for **sustainable urban living** might **not be achievable**:

1) There's **not enough governmental support** for **sustainable development** — **political leaders** need to **make** and **enforce laws** to **change** the way urban areas are **developed**. E.g. the government **hasn't renewed** the **planning permission** for Dongtan, so some people **don't think** it'll **ever happen** as it's been planned.
2) It **costs a lot** and takes **a long time** to build **more sustainable** urban areas. Shanghai's **urban growth problems** may need **cheaper** and **quicker solutions**, so **plans** for Dongtan may be **compromised** to get it finished **sooner**.
3) Even if all the plans were carried out **in full**, Dongtan still wouldn't be **truly sustainable** — **huge resources** would be used to **construct** the city, and **some emissions** would be caused by **housing** and **transport**.
4) It's **difficult** to make **existing urban areas** sustainable. Even if **new** urban areas are made to be **more sustainable**, old urban areas are still **unsustainable** — they're **using up resources** and **damaging the environment**.

Practice Questions

Q1 Describe one problem caused by urban growth.

Q2 Define sustainable development.

Exam Question

Q1 Describe and explain how an urban area could become more sustainable. [10 marks]

If I can sustain this revision it'll be a miracle...

Sustainability's a tough cookie, but the overlords of geography just love it to bits. In a more sustainable city, people can get what they need without reducing the ability of people in the future to get what they need, so it's about preserving the environment.

Urban and Rural Characteristics

These pages are for AQA only.
For anyone who thinks that urban characteristics is a dance beat with a groovy bass line — read on...

Urban** and **Rural Areas** Have **Different Characteristics...

Urban areas can be divided into **zones** based on the **major land use** in each area. In **developed** countries, as you **move away** from the **town** or **city centre**, the **major urban zones** are: the **inner city**, the **suburbs** and the **rural/urban fringe**. Each of these urban zones, and the **rural area** beyond them, have their own characteristics. The table below shows the **typical characteristics** of a large urban area in the UK:

Characteristic	Inner city	Suburbs	Rural/urban fringe	Rural area
Housing	High-density terraced housing built in the 19th century and high-rise blocks of flats built in the 1960s. Some old warehouses may have been redeveloped into luxury apartments.	A mix of 20th century detached and semi-detached houses with gardens. Closer to the inner city, a high proportion of properties will be council-owned. Further out, properties will be privately owned and larger, with garages and driveways.	Low-density, high-quality private housing. May also be higher density outer-city council estates.	Larger, privately owned housing and new estates with privately owned houses.
Ethnicity	High proportion of ethnic minorities.	Proportion of ethnic minorities tends to decrease as you move out of the city. →		Majority white.
Age structure	High proportion of younger people (students and young professionals).	Mostly families with children.	Mostly families with children. More elderly people.	Higher proportion of elderly people.
Wealth	The poorest sections of the urban population tend to live here. You also get more wealthy people living in redeveloped areas.	Wealth tends to increase as you move out of the city. →		Wealthiest residents who've moved out of the city. Also, some less wealthy original rural residents.
Employment	High proportion of students, unemployed and unskilled or semi-skilled workers. Some young professionals living in redeveloped areas.	More employment in tertiary sector (e.g. services, clerical and professional) and skilled manual workers.	Proportion employed in tertiary sector tends to increase. →	High proportion of workers in professional and managerial sectors (e.g. doctors, lawyers and bankers). Also agricultural workers.
Provision of services	Today, often an area of urban decay with derelict warehouses and industrial sites. But it's close to the city centre, which has lots of shops and services.	Some local shopping parades. Good transport routes to city centre and good availability of public transport.	The location for out-of-town shopping complexes, airports and recreational facilities such as golf courses.	Village shops may have closed as more residents shop in urban areas on their commute to work. Lack of public transport facilities.

...Which Affect the Welfare of the People Living in Each Zone

As you **move out** of the urban area **towards rural areas**, there tend to be **fewer environmental**, **social** and **economic problems**. These problems are **factors** affecting the **social welfare of people** living in each zone.
In **general**, these problems and social welfare **improve** as you **move away** from the inner city:

Environmental

1) Old, **poor quality housing**, often in a state of **disrepair**, creates a **poor living environment** in the **inner city**.
2) **Graffiti** and **vandalism** levels are **highest** in the **inner city** where there may be many **empty** and **derelict buildings**. Vandalism can also be high in the **suburbs** where there's a larger population of **children** and **teenagers**.
3) **Air pollution** is highest in the **inner city** due to remaining **industrial sites** and the **high volume of traffic**.

Social

1) There can be **tension** between people of **different ethnicities** in the **inner city** because of the **higher proportion** of **ethnic minorities**. This can occur in **rural areas** too if **large numbers** of immigrants move there.
2) The **crime rate** is **high** in the inner city — possibly due to the high levels of **unemployment** and **poverty** in this area. There are often **poor relationships** between the **police** and the **community**. Crime rates tend to **fall** as you **move away** from the inner city.
3) **Rural areas** can also experience social problems, e.g. a **lack of public transport** services can **isolate** people, particularly the **elderly**, and out-migration can lead to the closure of services like **shops** and **post offices**.

Economic

1) **Industrial decline** and **lack of investment** can lead to **high levels** of **unemployment** in the inner city. Although **employment levels** are generally **higher** as you **move away** from the inner city, there is **increasing unemployment** in **rural areas** because of **agricultural decline**.
2) **Poverty** is highest in the **inner city**. This can lead to **higher death rates** and **poorer general health** due to **poor nutrition**, **poor education** and a **lack of access to services**.

Remember, environmental, social and economic problems all affect social welfare.

Urban and Rural Characteristics

Population Change and Migration Have Affected Urban and Rural Areas

The **character** of **urban** and **rural areas** can be affected by **population change** and **migration** (including both **rural-urban migration** and **immigration**).

Housing

1) In **developed countries**, most migrants occupy the **cheaper**, **run-down** areas of housing in **urban areas** such as those found in the **inner city**.
2) In **developing countries**, **rural-urban migration** has resulted in the growth of **shanty towns** — **unplanned** and often **illegal** settlements, usually on the **outskirts** of the urban area, where people build their **own homes** out of whatever they can **find**. Theses areas have **limited services** such as clean **water** and **power**.

Ethnicity

1) High numbers of **immigrants** can change the character of areas by bringing their **existing culture** and **customs** with them. If they **fail to integrate** into the existing community, then '**ghettos**' may form — areas of cities where members of an **ethnic minority** group live, **segregated** from the rest of the city.
2) Although most immigrants move to **urban areas**, some move to **rural** areas seeking **work** in **agriculture**. This can have a **greater impact** on the **character** of small rural **villages** than it does on a large city, especially if all the migrants are from one country. E.g. Polish workers moving to the UK countryside might open Polish **shops** and **cafes** in small **villages**, which may have **few shops** for the **original residents** already.

Age Structure

1) In **developed countries**, rural areas have increasingly ageing populations due to the **out-migration** of **younger people** and the **inward migration** of **retired people**.
2) The **provision of services** will be affected by this **changing age structure**, e.g. in **rural** areas **schools may close** due to reduced demand, whilst there may be **increased** demand for **services for the elderly**, e.g. nursing homes.

There's more about the effects of changing age structure on p. 124

Wealth

1) In **developed countries**, increasing numbers of **second-home owners** and **commuters increases** the **wealth** of **rural areas**. This leads to **rising house prices**, which can force **younger residents** to leave as they **can't afford housing**.
2) As **young**, **wealthy professionals** move to **redeveloped urban areas**, they **increase** the **wealth** there. This can **improve inner city areas**, but can also mean **younger original** residents **can't afford** to buy houses there.

Employment

1) **Unemployment** will **increase** if **many people** move to urban areas without there being **enough jobs** available.
2) This is a big problem in **developing countries** as there's often a very **high rate** of **rural-urban migration** for work.
3) In rural areas, the large number of people **moving away** for work could eventually lead to a **lack of available workers**.

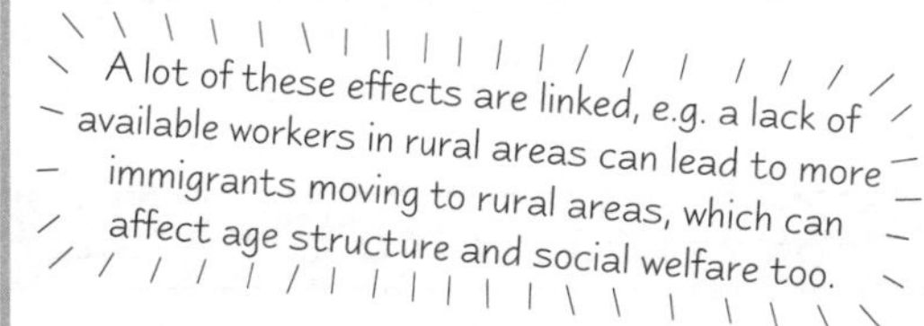

A lot of these effects are linked, e.g. a lack of available workers in rural areas can lead to more immigrants moving to rural areas, which can affect age structure and social welfare too.

Services

1) **Shops and services** in rural areas suffer because **residents who commute** may use shops **closer** to their **work**. Services like **bus routes** can also close as the **newer residents** tend to use **cars** instead. This could be a problem for the **original residents** of the rural areas if they rely on **public transport** to get about.
2) As people of **reproductive age** move to an area, there'll be increased need for **childcare services** and **schools**. When **elderly residents** move to an area, it **increases** the need for **carers**, **home help** and **health care**.

Practice Questions

Q1 How does the proportion of ethnic minorities in each zone change with distance from the city centre?

Q2 In which zone would you expect to find 19th century terraced housing?

Exam Question

Q1 Explain how population change and migration can affect the character of urban areas. [6 marks]

My barber gave me a rural/urban fringe — that affected MY social welfare...

Wow, there's quite a lot on these two pages — make sure you know the different characteristics of urban and rural areas and how they affect the welfare of the people who live there. As if all that wasn't enough, you also need to know how these characteristics can be affected by population change and migration. Look on the bright side though — it could be worse... probably...

Urban and Rural Characteristics — Case study

These pages are for AQA only.
Now it's time to take all that lovely theory and apply it to the real world — that's what geography's all about.

Different Areas in Preston Have Different Characteristics

The map below shows **four areas** in and around **Preston**, a city in the **North-west** of **England**. The areas correspond to **wards** (areas of roughly **equal-sized population** defined by the **city council**). There's **one area** from **each of the zones** discussed in the table on page 138. The characteristics of **housing** and the **provision of services** are **different** in **each of the areas**:

LEA — an area on the **rural/urban fringe**. It has large **semi-detached** and **detached** houses with **gardens** and **driveways**. Many of the houses are built on **modern estates**. There are **no** out-of-town **shopping centres**, but there are small shopping **parades** and a **supermarket**. There's a regular **bus service** to the city centre and there's also a **golf course** in this ward.

FISHWICK — an **inner city** area. Here there's mainly **high-density**, 19th century **terraced housing** built during the **industrial revolution** when Preston's **cotton industry** was at its peak. It has a few **corner shops** that sell convenience goods (e.g. **bread** and **milk**), but it **doesn't have** any **parades of shops** or **shopping centres**. Residents travel to the **city centre** for these services.

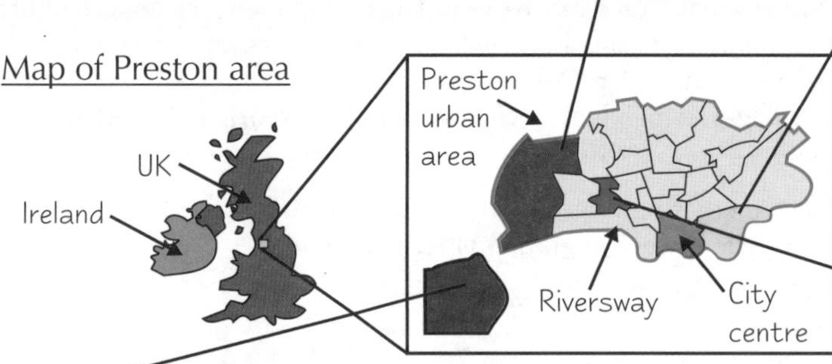

ASHTON — a **suburban** area. It has **terraced housing** to the east of the ward. To the west, there are **larger detached** and **semi-detached** houses with **gardens** that border **Ashton park**. The **Lane Ends** shopping area has over 40 shops and there are many **bus stops** with **frequent services** to the city centre.

LONGTON — a **rural area**. Many new **housing estates** have been built here since the **1960s**. Housing consists of **large detached** and **semi-detached** properties with **gardens** and **garages**. The **A59 Longton By-Pass** provides easy **access** to Preston city centre for **commuters**. Longton village has a **supermarket** and many **shops** and **services**.

*These Areas **Fit the Expected Pattern** for **Urban** and **Rural Zones**...*

The table below shows **data** from the **2001 census** about the **characteristics** of the **population** in each ward.
The **four areas** of Preston fit the **generalised** characteristics for **different zones** (as described on p. 138) quite well:

Characteristic	Statistic	Fishwick	Ashton	Lea	Longton
Housing	% of houses privately owned	60.5	81.5	81.7	92.7
	% of houses without central heating	17.5	17.5	5.6	3.7
	% of houses with 1+ occupant per room	4.8	0.5	0.6	0.3
Ethnicity	% of population in ethnic group 'white'	66.5	93.2	95.7	99.2
Age structure	Average age (years)	32.9	38.4	35.6	43.4
	% of population aged 60 years or over	15.0	20.4	15.8	28.4
Wealth	% of households owning at least 1 car	57.4	75.7	86.2	88.5
Employment	% of 16-74 year olds unemployed	5.9	2.1	2.0	1.1
	% of working population employed in management or professional sector	15.7	28.3	30.8	30.7

The % of privately owned houses **increases** as you **move away** from Fishwick (inner city).

The proportion of **ethnic minorities decreases** as you **move away** from Fishwick.

The % of **elderly** residents roughly **increases** as you **move towards** Longton (rural area).

The proportion of people **employed generally increases** as you move **away from** Fishwick. Also, more people are employed in **tertiary sector jobs** as you move away from Fishwick.

There's **no direct** data on **wealth**, but **car ownership** can be used as a rough **indicator** of the wealth of an area — the **greater the %** of car ownership, the **greater the wealth**. The number of people owning cars **increases** as you move **towards Longton**.

Urban and Rural Characteristics — Case study

... **But** There are **Some Exceptions**

There are a **couple** of ways in which these areas **don't** fit the generalised characteristics:

1) There are **no** out-of-town **shopping** centres in **Lea** (**rural/urban fringe**). This could be because of the **huge redevelopment** of **Preston Docks** in the neighbouring ward of **Riversway**. This has provided shopping and **leisure** facilities (such as a **cinema**, **bars** and **restaurants**). The residents of Lea can **travel** here easily, resulting in **less demand** for these services **within** Lea itself.
2) There are **more services** in **Longton** than might be expected for a **rural area**. Many commuters use the regular **bus service** from Longton to **Preston**, rather than **driving** into the city centre. This could be because of the **difficulty** of parking in the **centre**. Because the bus services are used **more frequently**, they're less likely to get **cancelled**. It also means that commuters are more likely to do their **shopping** in **Longton**, rather than **carry** it home on the bus. This might explain why there are **lots of shops** and a **supermarket** in Longton.

The **Different Characteristics** Have **Implications** for **Social Welfare**

The **social welfare** of people living in and around Preston is **affected** by the **characteristics** of the different areas. **Social welfare** tends to be **worse** in the **inner city**, and improve as you move **further towards** rural areas:

1) **74%** of people in **Lea** described their **general health** in the 12 months leading up to the 2001 census as **'good'**. In **Fishwick**, only **65%** described their general health as **'good'**. This may be because a **higher percentage** of people in Fishwick live in houses that are likely to be **cold and damp** due to the **lack** of **central heating** (see table). Also, the **higher occupancy rate** in Fishwick means that **germs** spread more easily from person to person, **aiding** the spread of **disease**.
2) The **Preston Crime Audit** found that there were **161 crimes** per 1000 people in **Fishwick** between 2003 and 2004, compared to **52** in **Lea**. The high levels of **unemployment** and **low levels of wealth** in inner city areas like Fishwick can lead to **higher crime rates**. **Theft of vehicles** and theft **from** vehicles are also **higher** in Fishwick. This could be because most of the houses **don't** have **driveways** or **garages**, so vehicles are **less secure**.
3) The level of **education** is **lower** in **Fishwick** than it is in other areas — in **Ashton**, **21.4%** of the population have **no qualifications**, but in Fishwick it's **44.7%**. **Fewer** people are in **higher education** in Fishwick too — **10.3%** of the **18-74** year old population in **Ashton** are classed as **students** in **full-time education**, but this is only **6.2%** in Fishwick. Lower levels of education mean residents can't apply for **more highly skilled** or **professional work** (see data table).
4) **Less skilled workers** are usually paid **lower wages** than highly skilled professionals — this affects the **wealth** of the area. In the table, **car ownership** (i.e. wealth) **increases** towards Longton, **as the proportion** of **managers** and **professional** sector workers **increases**. A **lack of wealth** in an area can lead to other social welfare **problems** such as **increased debt**, and less money for **entertainment** and **sporting activities**, which can add to **health issues** such as **depression** and **obesity**.

Practice Questions

Q1 Name four wards found in the Preston area.

Q2 Which ward in Preston consists of mainly 19th century terraced housing?

Q3 Describe the general pattern of ethnicity for wards in the Preston area.

Exam Question

Q1 For a named region, choose **two** of the following areas:
- inner city
- suburb
- rural/urban fringe
- rural area

For these two areas, compare their characteristics and explain how they affect the social welfare of the resident population. [15 marks]

It's been a long-ton coming but you prest-on and got to the end...

Hurrah — that's the end of Population. Well, not the end of population as in the end of the world — that wouldn't be anything to cheer about. But that's the Section finished. It might have been tough at times, but you 'pressed on' and got there in the end.

Introduction to Inequalities

This section is for Edexcel Unit 2 (Unequal Spaces option).
Calling all human geographers... Here's a nice section for you — lots of rural and urban differences, some causes and effects, and a little bit of economics thrown in. Dosage: take two pages at a time with a large cup of tea.

Unequal Spaces are Areas That are Unbalanced

Unequal spaces are **areas** with **uneven levels** of **wealth**, **social opportunity** and **environmental quality**. They're caused by **movements** of **people** and **money**, and **changing opportunities** between different areas. The **differences** between unequal spaces need to be **recognised** in order for the **balance** to be **restored** and people's lives to be **improved**.

Differences Between Areas are Called Inequalities

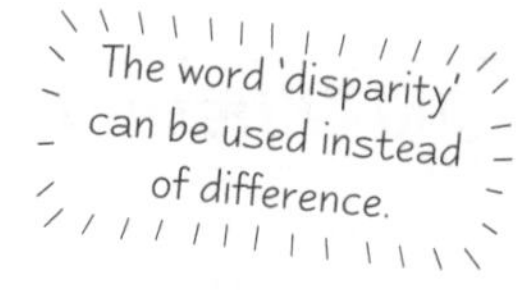

The word 'disparity' can be used instead of difference.

1) The **differences** in levels of **wealth**, **social opportunity** or **environmental quality** between different areas are called **inequalities**. For example, the south of England is **more wealthy** than the north, which means there's **economic inequality** between these two areas.
2) All inequalities can **contribute** to a person's **quality of life** (degree of **wellbeing**).
3) The table below shows examples of how different inequalities can be **measured**.

Inequality	Includes differences in...	Examples of measures
Economic (wealth)	Income, economic assets (e.g. house, pension, inheritance)	Average income, average house price, proportion of people on benefits, car ownership
Social	Type of employment, education, amenities, access to services, health, incidence of crime, community life	Unemployment level, proportion of GCSE passes, number of people per doctor, burglary rate
Environmental	Pollution, green spaces/gardens, housing quality	Air quality, area of green space/number of parks, proportion of buildings with graffiti

4) A single **measure** can show **more than one** type of **inequality**, e.g. **vandalism** is a **crime** (creating **social inequality**) but it also **damages** the environment people live in (creating **environmental inequality**).
5) Some **measures** are **more useful** than others depending on the **areas** you're studying. E.g. the **number of people per doctor** is a useful measure of social inequality **between countries**, but it **isn't** very useful when comparing **different regions** of the **UK** because the figures are fairly **similar**.
6) **Indexes of inequality** have been developed to take into account **several different measures**. E.g. the **Human Development Index** (**HDI**) includes measures of life expectancy, literacy, education, standard of living and GDP (Gross Domestic Product — the total value of goods and services produced in a country in a year).
7) '**Spatial inequalities**' are **inequalities** between **different geographical areas** (it's a fancy geography term). E.g. the inequalities that exist between the **north** and **south** of **Cardiff** (see page 148).

Inequalities Exist on Global, Regional and Local Scales

The following table gives examples of **different inequalities** and their **measures** at **different scales**:

INEQUALITY	GLOBAL SCALE	REGIONAL SCALE	LOCAL SCALE
Economic (wealth)	Japan has greater wealth than Central Africa. E.g. in 2005, the GDP per person was $32 000 in Japan, compared to $1000 in Central Africa.	The north of England is more wealthy than the south. E.g. in 2004, average gross disposable household income (per person) was £15 300 in London and £10 900 in the north-east of England.	Differences in wealth exist between different areas of a city. E.g. the estimated average weekly household income in 2001/02 for Bristol was £640 in Redland and £470 in Southville.
Social	Japan has greater social opportunity than Central Africa. E.g. in 2002, enrolment in primary education in Japan was 99%, compared to 44.4% in Central Africa.	The incidence of disease varies across the UK. E.g. in 2005 the incidence of tuberculosis was 14.8 per 100 000 in England, compared to 6.3 in Scotland, 5.4 in Wales and 3.9 in Northern Ireland.	Urban areas have more services and amenities than rural areas. E.g. in January 2004 the road distance to a supermarket was 20 km for the village of Cartmel and only 0.6 km for the town of Ulverston.
Environmental	There's greater access to clean drinking water in Japan than in Central Africa. E.g. in 2000/02, 50% of people in Central Africa had no access to clean water, compared to 0% of people in Japan.	River quality varies across the UK. E.g. in 2006, the percentage of rivers that had 'good chemical quality' was 95% in Wales, compared to 66% in England.	Inner city areas often have less green space than suburban and rural areas. E.g. the City of London has 5% green space, compared to South Lakeland (Cumbria) that has 86% green space.

Introduction to Inequalities

There are Many Causes of Inequality

1) There are **many different causes** of inequality, but most can be **linked** to the **economy**. For example, **economic decline** in an urban area causes a **decrease** in **employment** in particular industries (**social inequality**), which **leads to** lower average family incomes (**economic inequality**) and **dereliction** as industries and people move away (**environmental inequality**).
2) Inequalities are usually **interlinked** — the **effect** of one inequality can **cause** another inequality. E.g. **economic inequality** in an urban area means that people have **less money** to spend in shops in that area, so businesses may **collapse** or **move away**, causing **social inequality** (because of a lack of amenities).
3) All this interlinking can lead to a **cycle of decline** — one inequality causes **deprivation**, which leads to **more inequalities**, which cause **more** deprivation, leading to more inequalities, and so on. A cycle of decline can also be called a **vicious cycle**, **negative feedback** or a **cycle of inequality**.

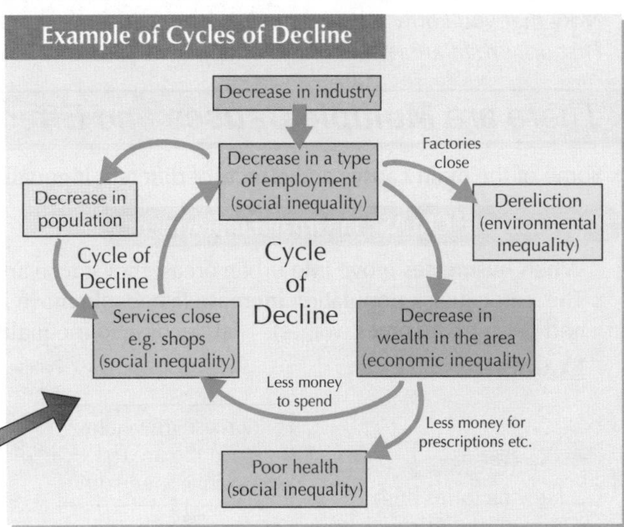

Deprivation is where there are social, economic and environmental problems in an area, e.g. poor housing, lack of services.

Inequalities Lead to Reduced Opportunities

One **effect** of inequalities is **reduced opportunities**. For example, people living in an area that has **economic inequality** caused by **low incomes**, are **less likely** to go on to **further education** (e.g. university, which is expensive) — so economic inequality leads to **reduced education opportunities**. Reduced opportunities include:

- Reduced **employment** opportunities — caused by many different social inequalities, e.g. lack of jobs in a particular field, lack of access to the internet to look for jobs, lack of transport to get to jobs.
- Reduced **housing** opportunities — caused by economic and social inequalities, e.g. low incomes, lack of affordable housing.
- Reduced **education** opportunities — caused by economic and social inequalities, e.g. low incomes, lack of good teachers, lack of local funding.

Fashion inequality has always existed between Essex and the rest of the UK.

Practice Questions

Q1 What are unequal spaces?
Q2 What are the three main types of inequality?
Q3 Give one measure of social inequality.
Q4 What are spatial inequalities?
Q5 Give one example of global economic inequality.
Q6 Give one example of regional social inequality.

Measure	Bradford	Harrogate
Total population (2001)	467 665	151 336
Average detached property selling price (Aug 2001)	£112 723	£191 024
% unemployed (2001)	4.4	1.8
% people of working age claiming a key benefit (Aug 2001)	17	8
% people with 'not good' general health (2001)	10.2	7.21
Police recorded offences of theft from a motor vehicle (Apr 01 - Mar 02)	9961	698
% 15 year old pupils achieving 5 or more A* - C GCSE grades from schools within the area	37.3	68.6
Total number of students aged 16-17 (2001)	10 256	3041
Area of green space (km^2) (Jan 2005)	0.27	1.25

Exam Question

Q1 Outline how well the information in the table shows the inequalities between Bradford and Harrogate. [10 marks]

Unequal spaces — so that's why I can't parallel park...

I reckon if you tell anyone that you're studying 'Unequal Spaces' they won't have a clue what you're going on about — it might make you sound intellectual though. When they find out what it really is, they may just fall asleep. Unfortunately you need to learn this basic stuff really well 'cause it'll make the rest of this section much easier to understand.

Causes and Effects of Urban Inequalities

These pages are for** Edexcel Unit 2 (Unequal Spaces **option).
Now that you know what inequalities are, you can apply the ideas of inequality to different areas. First up, urban areas — a round of applause please...

*There are **Multiple Causes** and **Effects** of **Urban Inequalities***

Some of the **main causes** and **effects** of different **inequalities** are shown below:

1 Cause: INCREASE in Urban Employment

When **businesses** move **into** urban areas, they cause an **increase** in employment in one or more industries. This can cause a population **increase** (as people **move into** the area for **work**), affecting **services, housing** and people's **incomes** (wages) — all leading to **inequalities.**

EXAMPLE

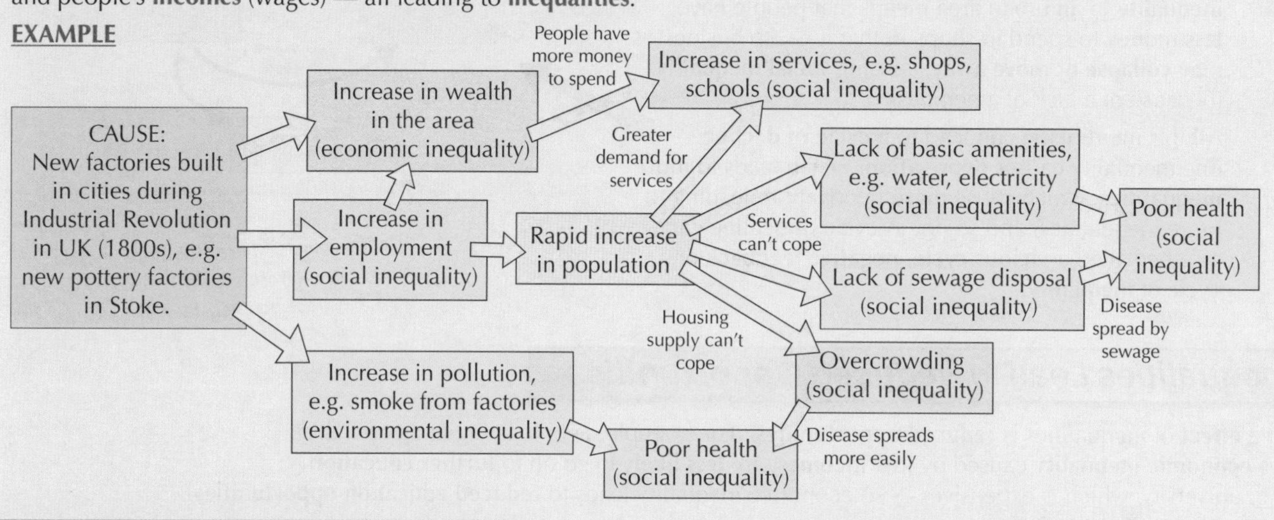

2 Cause: DECREASE in Urban Employment

When **businesses shut down** in urban areas, they cause a **decrease** in employment in one or more industries, which can cause a population **decrease**, affecting **services, housing** and people's **incomes** (wages) — all leading to **inequalities.**

EXAMPLE

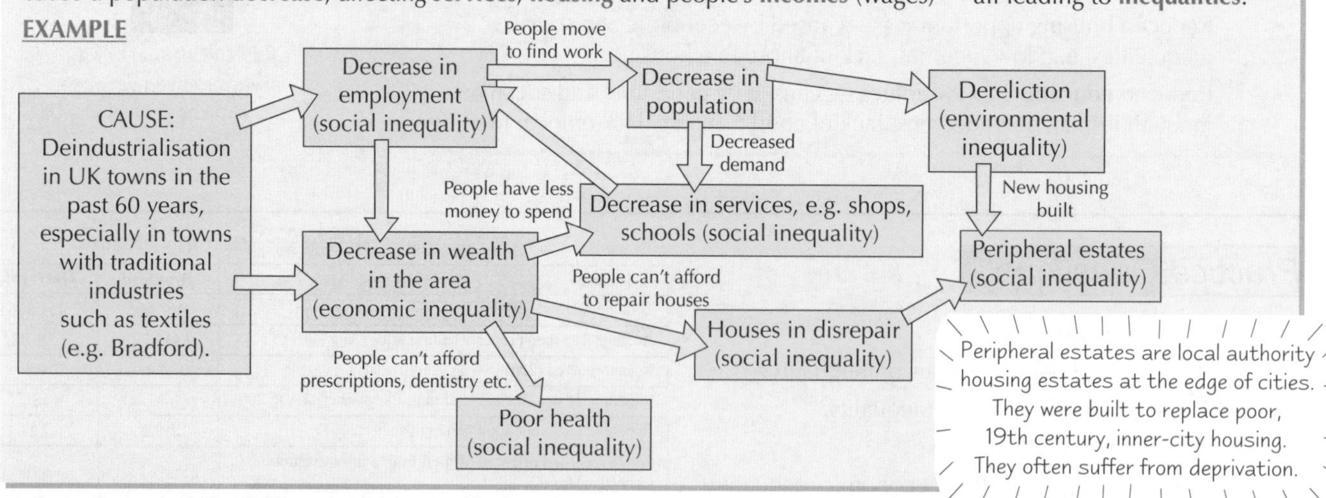

Peripheral estates are local authority housing estates at the edge of cities. They were built to replace poor, 19th century, inner-city housing. They often suffer from deprivation.

3 Cause: Rural-urban Migration

In many countries there's **mass migration from** rural areas **into** urban areas, due to **push factors** (reasons people leave, e.g. lack of employment in rural areas) and **pull factors** (things that attract people, e.g. perceived better quality of life in urban areas). This can cause many **urban inequalities.**

EXAMPLE

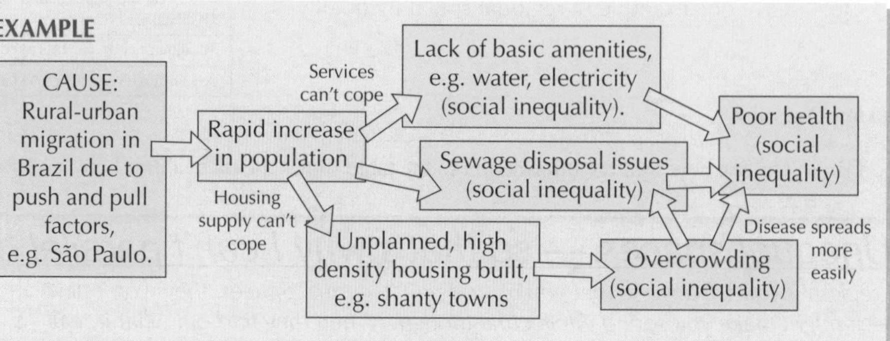

Causes and Effects of Urban Inequalities

4 Cause: INCREASE in House Prices

House prices vary for lots of reasons — e.g. an **influx** of people into an area **for work** can cause an **increase** in house prices, which results in **inequalities** and **polarisation** (see below).

EXAMPLE

CAUSE: Rapid increase in house prices in southern areas of the UK from the late 1990s until recently.
→ Only wealthy can afford houses (economic inequality) → Increase in buy-to-let → Wealthier get richer as house prices rise (economic inequality) → Rich get richer → Increased polarisation between the rich and the poor
→ Lack of affordable housing (social inequality) → Increase in buy-to-let; → Decrease in population → Decrease in services (social inequality) → Increased polarisation between the rich and the poor; → Increase in debt, e.g. loans to buy houses (economic inequality) → Poor get poorer → Increased polarisation between the rich and the poor

Inequalities Can Cause Polarisation

Polarisation is when there are **extreme inequalities** between **geographical areas**.

For example, an **increase** in **house prices** can cause **other inequalities** between the **rich** and the **poor** in an **urban area**. The rich can **afford** high priced housing, which is often in areas with **better services** and **better schools**. This leads to **better education**, and **better jobs** and **incomes**, **adding to** economic inequality — **polarisation** between the rich and poor.

Polar-isation was becoming a problem in some urban areas.

People Can be Excluded from Society Due to Inequalities

Social exclusion is the **exclusion** of **individuals** or **groups** of people from society on the basis of **gender**, **age**, **race**, **religion**, **education**, **health** or **disability**. **Economic exclusion** is the exclusion of individuals or groups on the basis of their **wealth**. Social or economic exclusion can be **caused by inequalities**.

For example, in urban areas of the **UK** there's been an **increase** in **jobs** in the **service industries**, e.g. financial services. Many of these jobs require certain **qualifications** or **skills** (e.g. IT skills), which can **exclude** some people from applying. This effect leads to **more** economic inequality in urban areas, as those **with** the desired skills gain **more wealth**.

Exclusion Can Result in Marginalised Groups

Marginalised groups may occupy or use a particular area of a city — called a ghetto.

Marginalised groups are groups of people that are **relegated** to the **edge** of **society**, usually **due to** social or economic **exclusion**. Marginalised groups may find it **hard** to **integrate** into the rest of the community. This might make it harder for them to **find jobs** etc., **increasing** the inequalities within the area.

For example, **unemployment** among **males** from **ethnic minorities** in Leicester was **16.11%** in 1991 — **double** that of the **white male population**, which was **8.04%**. This **economic inequality** may contribute to the **marginalisation** of **ethnic minority groups** in Leicester, as they **can't afford** the **services** and **lifestyle** enjoyed by white males.

Practice Questions

Q1 Describe polarisation.

Q2 Explain what social exclusion means.

Q3 What is a marginalised group?

Exam Question

Q1 The table provides information about lone-parent families and two-parent families in the UK. Discuss the possible causes and effects of the inequalities shown. [10 marks]

Measure	Lone-parent families	Two-parent families
% employed (2006)	56	81
% of total number of part-time students (2004 - 05)	8	31
% receiving income related benefits (2004 - 05)	89	62
% living in a detached house (2005)	8	28

Star Trek fans are definitely a marginalised group...

When you're learning these two pages (in between watching the telly) remember that I haven't been able to cover ALL the causes and effects of inequalities on these pages — that would take about a gazillion years, especially if I explained how they're all interlinked too. So make sure you understand the causes and effects on these pages and how they're all interlinked.

Strategies to Reduce Urban Inequalities

***These pages are for** Edexcel Unit 2 (**Unequal Spaces option**).*
You should be a bit more comfortable with inequalities now, which, let's face it, aren't great. So, next you need to know what's being done about them — it's called 'delivering solutions' in exam-board speak. I know, it sounds thrilling.

Different Organisations Help to Reduce Urban Inequalities

Different groups work at **different scales** (e.g. local, regional, national and international) to **reduce** urban inequalities. The **key players** are shown in the diagram below — they're in **order** of **increasing scale** of **operation**, **impact** and **cost**.

Increasing scale of **operation**, **impact** and **cost**

Individuals	— An individual who **picks up litter** in their neighbourhood helps to **reduce local environmental inequality**.
Small groups	— A small group of people **cleaning graffiti** off buildings helps to **reduce local environmental inequality**.
Community action groups	— A community group **collecting and distributing food** for the elderly helps to **reduce local social inequality**.
Local charities	— North London Action for the Homeless helps to **reduce social inequality** by providing **literacy classes** for the homeless in North London.
Local authorities	— The South Lakeland District Council sets up designated **parking areas** (so people don't park on grass verges) to **reduce environmental inequality** between local areas.
Regional charities	— Alzheimer Scotland runs **drop-in centres** so people with dementia and their carers can socialise, **reducing social inequality** in Scotland.
Regional authorities	— Cumbria County Council runs **recycling schemes** to **reduce environmental inequality** between regions.
National governments	— The **UK** government sets the **minimum wage** (the lowest hourly wage employers can legally pay workers in the UK) to help **reduce economic inequality** across the country.
International organisations	— The **World Health Organisation** (WHO) carries out immunisation programmes to **reduce social** (health) **inequalities** between **countries**.

There are Many Strategies to Reduce Urban Inequalities

1) Self-help Schemes — to help people reduce inequalities in their local urban environment

1) **Shanty builds** — schemes created by **people living in shanty towns** to **build** their **own homes, services** and **amenities**. They aim to **improve** their own living conditions and **reduce social inequalities** by building **better housing**, and getting **clean water supplies** and **electricity**. Some **governments** support these schemes by providing **building materials** and **basic services** (e.g. clean water, sewage disposal).
2) **Residents' associations** — associations formed by **groups** of people **living** in a **particular area**. Members meet to discuss **local issues** (e.g. **planning** applications, levels of **crime**, management of **green space**) in order to work out how they can **reduce social** and **environmental** inequalities in their own neighbourhood.
3) **Neighbourhood watch** — **local organisations** that aim to **reduce crime** in **neighbourhoods** where they're set up. Members agree to **look out** for signs of **crime** and **report** it to the local authorities. This helps to **reduce social** and **environmental** inequalities (e.g. antisocial behaviour, vandalism, graffiti). The **success** of a neighbourhood watch group can be **monitored** by looking at **crime statistics** in the area **before** and **after** the group was set up.

2) Traffic and Public Transport Strategies — to reduce social and environmental inequalities caused by urban road traffic

1) **Park-and-ride schemes** — schemes that let people **park** their cars **near to** city centres, then use **public transport** to **reach** the centre. They help people **avoid** the **high cost** of **city centre parking** and aim to **reduce** problems caused by **city centre traffic** (e.g. **air pollution, noise, accidents**). The **success** of park-and-ride schemes can be **measured** by looking at **air quality** in the city centre **before** and **after** the scheme was introduced.
2) **Congestion charging** — a scheme where **motorists** are charged to take their vehicles **into** city centres. Many cities have these schemes (e.g. **Singapore, London, Stockholm**) to **reduce** city centre traffic and the problems described above.
3) **Oyster cards** — a system of **electronic tickets** that makes it **easier, faster** and **cheaper** to pay for **London public transport**. This aims to **encourage** people to use public transport in London to **reduce** city centre traffic.

3) Business Initiatives — local and government schemes to reduce economic inequalities in urban areas

1) **The minimum wage** — the **lowest** hourly **wage** employers can **legally** pay workers in the UK. It's set by the **UK government** and aims to **reduce** economic inequality by providing workers with a **decent wage**. The **success** of this policy can be **measured** by looking at **how many people** were living in **poverty before** and **after** its introduction.
2) **Furniture schemes** — unwanted furniture is collected for **free** and sold at **affordable prices** to people on **low incomes**, helping to reduce social inequalities (lack of furniture) **caused by** economic inequalities (low income).

Strategies to Reduce Urban Inequalities

4) Town Planning Initiatives — government-led programmes to help improve the urban environments of a country

1) **Sustainable urban communities** — communities that aim to **meet human needs** while **preserving** the natural and urban **environment**, by promoting efficient land use, less pollution etc. For example, the **Masdar Initiative** in **Abu Dhabi** aims to make **Masdar City** a **'zero-carbon, zero-waste, car-free city'**. This will **reduce environmental inequalities** (e.g. reduced air pollution) and **economic inequalities** (e.g. fewer people affected by rising fuel prices).
2) **The WHO Healthy Urban Planning Initiative** — this scheme encourages **local governments** to **improve urban health** through projects that address **social inequalities** (health) and **urban poverty**. Over **1200 cities** are involved in it.

Successful Strategies Must *Address Causes* of Inequality and be *Sustainable*

Strategies to reduce urban inequalities have a **greater chance** of being **successful** if they:

1) **Address** the **root causes** of urban inequalities — they need to promote **long-lasting solutions**.
For example, strategies to help **homeless people** are more likely to be successful if they **enable** homeless people to find **secure employment** so they can **support themselves**, rather than just giving them a **bed** for the night. Schemes to help **starving communities** are more likely to be successful if they enable the community to produce their **own** reliable **sources of food**, rather than just giving them **free food**.
If strategies **don't** address the root causes of inequalities, they will only provide **short-term** solutions.
2) **Are sustainable** — they need to be **maintained** in the **long-term**.
For example, schemes that require **high levels** of **financial support** are **less likely** to be successful because they'll only continue for as long as financial support is **available**. **Cheaper** or **self-financing** schemes are likely to run **long-term**.

EXAMPLE — Urban-rural migration in Asia, Africa and South America

- In Asia, Africa and South America **urban inequalities** are often **caused** by **mass rural-urban migration**. This is because mass migration into cities causes **rapid population growth**, so there isn't enough affordable housing, resulting in **shanty towns**. Shanty towns have **many** social, economic and environmental **inequalities**.
- In order to **reduce** and **prevent further** urban inequalities the **root causes** (**push factors**), as well as the **existing urban inequalities**, need to be addressed.
- Push factors are the **reasons** why people **leave** the rural areas. They can include **famine**, **drought**, **natural disasters**, **poor living conditions**, **lack of education**, **lack of health care**, **agricultural change** (leading to job shortages) and **conflict**.
- Some of the push factors can be **reduced** by **improving rural areas** (e.g. building water sources, building health care facilities, developing industry in the area) and encouraging their **sustainable economic development**.
- **Schemes** can be **introduced** in urban areas to **reduce inequalities**, e.g. **shanty builds** (see previous page).

Melanie had a lack of push factors...

Practice Questions

Q1 Give an example of an organisation that works to reduce urban inequalities at a local scale.

Q2 What are sustainable urban communities?

Q3 What are push factors?

Measure	1995	2005
Average number of visitors to city centre per month (thousands)	1224	1315
Average number of vehicles passing through city centre per month	753 124	215 376
Number of bus services to/from city centre	15	25
Average nitrous oxide concentration in the air ($\mu g/m^3$)	18.2	10.1

Exam Question

Q1 In the UK in 1998, City X introduced some schemes to reduce inequalities caused by city centre traffic. The table above shows data about City X before and after the schemes were introduced.
Using data from the table, describe two schemes that City X may have introduced and evaluate how successful the schemes have been. [10 marks]

Revision — an exam self-help scheme...

Okay, I think I've got it... There are many different schemes to help reduce each type of urban inequality and they're carried out by people at different scales — from individuals up to international organisations. To be a success these schemes must address the causes of inequalities and be sustainable. And the success of a scheme can be measured in different ways. By Jove, I've got it!

Urban Inequalities — Case Study

These pages are for Edexcel Unit 2 (Unequal Spaces option).
You were bound to get a case study sooner or later. It's what geography's all about. (PS — try not to fall asleep.)

There are **Inequalities** Between **North** and **South Cardiff**

Cardiff is the **capital** of **Wales**. The **north** of the city is relatively **wealthy**, but the **south** of the city shows signs of **deprivation**.

EXAMPLE — Cathays and Butetown

The map on the right shows two different areas of Cardiff — **Cathays** and **Butetown**. Cathays is in the **north** and includes part of the **city centre**. Butetown is in the **south** and includes some of the **docklands**. **Data** on these areas (from the **2001 Census** and **Cardiff Community Profile 2002**) is summarised in the table below.

North Cardiff
South Cardiff
Cathays
Butetown

This data shows economic inequality.

Over twice as many people in Butetown have 'not good' health.

Measures	Butetown	Cathays
% 16 - 74 year olds unemployed	5.2	1.8
% owner occupied households that own house outright	12.5	20.9
% 16 - 74 year olds with no qualifications	33.6	9.73
% people with 'not good' general health	14.1	6.23
Reported incidents of crime per 1000 population (in 2000)	1121.4	1189.7

There are over 3 times as many 16 - 74 year olds with no qualifications in Butetown than Cathays (that's quite high).

Both areas have similar, high levels of crime (there's only a 6% difference).

The table shows that the **incidence of crime** per 1000 population is **high** for **both** areas. This may be because the areas include the **city centre** and **bay**, which both attract **large numbers** of **visitors**. However, the crime figures are worked out by **reported** incidents of crimes per 1000 of the **resident** population — it doesn't include visitors. This means the data is **distorted** — the crimes **could** involve **visitors**, but they're **only** divided by the **number of residents**, so it seems **high** for the number of people who live there.

The table shows that **Butetown** has a **higher percentage** of **unemployed** residents, which means the **average income** is likely to be **lower** in Butetown. **Housing** can be the **greatest expense** for a household, so it's not surprising that in the poorer area of Butetown **only 12.5% own** their own **home**, compared to **20.9%** in Cathays. **Over three times** as many **16 – 74 year olds** in **Butetown** have **no qualifications**, compared to Cathays. This all means that families in Butetown **live** in an area of **higher unemployment** and have **fewer qualifications**, which leads to **lower income jobs** and **poorer health** (e.g. **less money** for **food**, **prescriptions**). This causes a **cycle of decline** (see p. 143).

There are **Multiple Causes** of **Inequalities** in **Cardiff**

1) The **decline** of the **coal** and **steel industries** in the **late 20th century** (e.g. **coal exports** from Cardiff port **stopped** in **1964**, the **steelworks closed** in **1978**) caused **high unemployment** in Cardiff, especially in the south where workers from the docklands lived. This led to **dereliction** in the **docklands** and in residential areas as people **moved away** to **find work**. The **decrease** in **employment** caused **further inequalities**, leading to a **cycle of decline**.
2) The **south** of Cardiff has some of the **most densely populated** and **poor quality housing** estates. People on lower incomes are likely to **buy** poor quality housing because it's **cheaper**. This causes **polarisation** (see p. 145) between the north and the south of Cardiff because the poorer people are all **concentrated** in the south.
3) The **population** of Cardiff has **rapidly increased** during the last decade (by more than 1% a year). This population growth **hasn't** been even across the city and has caused **overcrowding** in the **south**, leading to **further** inequalities.

Inequalities Reduce Opportunities and **Cause Social Exclusion**

The **effects** of the **inequalities** between the north and south of Cardiff include:

1) **Reduced employment** in the **south** of the city — due to the **decline** of **industries** (see above) and an **increase** in the **population** (so there are **fewer jobs** to go round). This has led to **lower average wages** and **more** inequalities.
2) **Poorer education** in the south — e.g. because there are **larger** class sizes (due to **more children**) and good teachers are **less likely** to be attracted to the area (because of the inequalities).
3) **Poorer health** in the south — e.g. due to **less money** for **food, poor housing** that could be **damp** etc.
4) **Environmental issues** in the south — e.g. **poor quality housing** and **high crime rates** (e.g. **vandalism**).
5) **Social exclusion** (see p. 145) of some groups (e.g. **lone-parent families, ethnic minorities**) in the **south** — e.g. **lone parents** may find it **harder** to get work because they don't have **child-care facilities**.

The redevelopment of Cardiff Bay (see next page) has created more jobs in the south of the city, but unemployment there is still high.

Urban Inequalities — Case Study

Strategies *Have Been Used to* ***Address Inequalities*** *in* ***Cardiff***

The success of a scheme depends on addressing the root causes (see p. 147).

1990s Redevelopment of South Cardiff

Scheme: In the **1990s**, **£2.4 billion** was spent on regenerating Cardiff **docks** and **waterfront** (south Cardiff), including new **residential**, **business**, **retail** and **leisure** developments.

Success: **High unemployment rates** were addressed by the **17 000 new jobs** created. These new jobs have **decreased** unemployment in some areas, e.g. unemployment in **Butetown** fell from **8.6% 1991** to **5.2% in 2001**. **Inadequate housing** has been addressed by **6000 new homes**. However, **wealthy** people have moved **into** the new homes and the **older housing estates** have just become **'boxed in'**, which has led to **increased** feelings of **exclusion** in those areas. The scheme is **long-term** — there are plans for **further redevelopments** of the **south** of Cardiff (e.g. there's a new health centre, shopping parade and affordable housing planned in Butetown).

Butetown Community Centre

The **Butetown Community Centre** aims to **improve** the **quality of life** for **local** people by providing **educational**, **recreational**, **health** and **leisure opportunities** (e.g. the community food co-op provides **cheap**, **good quality**, **fresh** fruit and vegetables to local people). The **success** of this scheme could be **measured** by looking at the **number of people using** the centre or the **perceived increases in local opportunities** (via **questionnaires**).

Ethnic Minority Communities Programme

The **Ethnic Minority Communities** programme aims to **support** ethnic minority groups across Cardiff and **reduce deprivation** within these communities. The success of this programme could be **measured** by examining **census data**, such as the **level** of **unemployment** in ethnic minority groups **before** and **after** it was set up.

You Can ***Investigate*** *the* ***Causes*** *and* ***Effects*** *of* ***Inequalities*** *in an* ***Urban Area***

You can use a **range** of **fieldwork** and **research techniques** to **study** the causes and effects of **inequalities**. For example:

1) You could examine **census data** to look for **inequalities** in **house prices**, **education** or **health** and to **analyse changing patterns** in **employment** or **population**. Census data can be obtained from the **Office for National Statistics**, the **local authority** or **websites**.
2) You could examine **CVA scores** (**Contextual Value Added scores**) to find out **how well** schools are **performing** and enable you to **identify social** (educational) **inequalities** between areas.
3) You could use **questionnaires** to determine **mobility patterns** (how easy it is for people to **get around** in an area), perceived **quality of life** and **environmental quality**. These factors can **indicate** other inequalities, e.g. a person's mobility is affected by **personal transport** (e.g. car ownership). If a questionnaire shows that an urban area has **low car ownership**, it may indicate **economic inequality** (as people on low incomes **can't afford** a car). However, questionnaires are based on people's **opinions**, which can be **biased**, so they need to be backed up with **other forms** of **data**.
4) You could carry out **surveys** to **collect data**. For example, you could **count** the number of **bus services** in **two areas**. A **lack** of bus services could show **social inequality**, because people will have to rely on their **own cars** to get around. If they **can't afford** their own cars they will find it **harder** to **access other services** and **employment**.
5) You could also assess the **environmental quality** of two areas by visiting them and recording factors like how many houses have **chipped paint**, how many **gardens** are **unkempt** and how many buildings have **graffiti**. These are useful factors when trying to find **correlations** between **economic** and **environmental inequalities**.

The success of a strategy to reduce inequalities can be measured by looking at these things before and after the strategy was introduced.

Practice Questions

Q1 Describe one strategy used to tackle the inequalities between north and south Cardiff.

Q2 How could you measure the success of the Ethnic Minority Communities programme?

Q3 Suggest three ways to investigate inequalities in your area.

Exam Question

Q1 With reference to one named example, discuss the causes and effects of urban inequalities. [10 marks]

2001 Census data shows that 98% of students are bored with revision...

Did you know that 'census' comes from the Latin word meaning 'assess'? I guess it makes sense, because every 10 years a UK census is taken, which assesses the levels of health, education etc. across the country. One of the ways this data can be used is to find out how successful strategies to reduce urban inequalities have been. So the census is still useful today.

Causes and Effects of Rural Inequalities

These pages are for Edexcel Unit 2 (Unequal Spaces option).
I hope you saved some of your enthusiasm for these pages. After all, we're nearly at the end of the section — just need to learn the causes, effects, strategies and a case study for rural inequalities and we're done. Easy peasy, lemon squeezy. (Oh dear...)

There are Multiple Causes and Effects of Rural Inequalities

Just like urban inequalities, **rural inequalities** have **many causes** and **effects**. They include:

1 Cause: DECREASE in Rural Employment

Industry may be **lost** from a rural area due to **changes** in **technology**, or **cheaper** labour **elsewhere**, or because companies go **out of business**. This has **huge effects** on the local community and can lead to **inequality**.

EXAMPLE

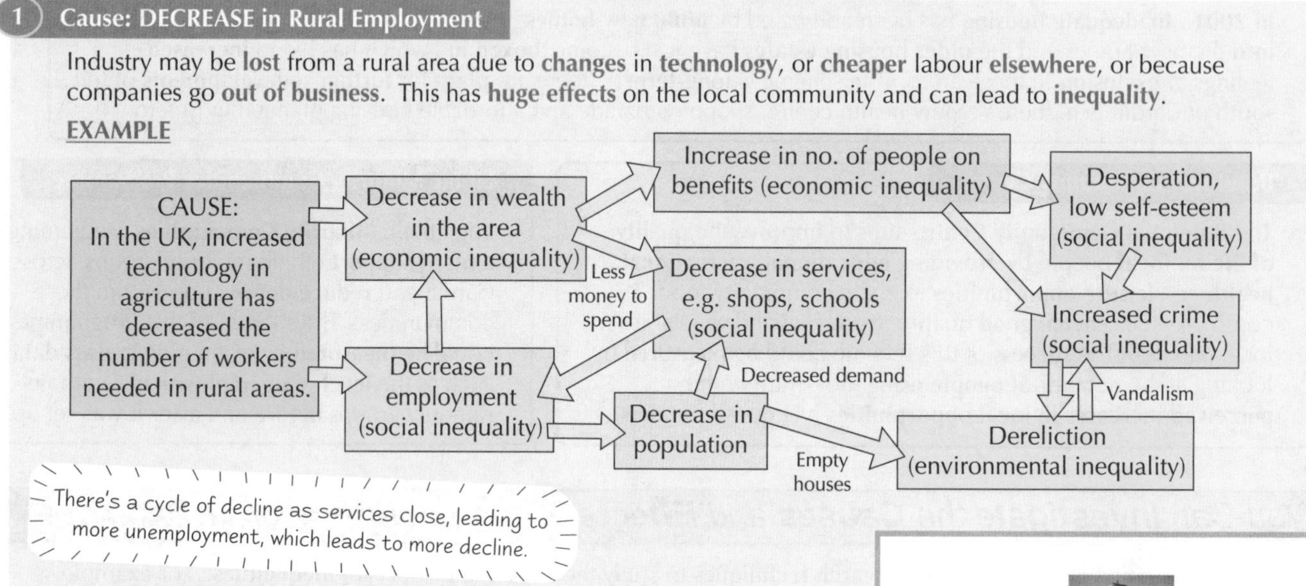

Be careful when making **generalisations** about inequalities — in the example above you could say that **reduced employment** in rural areas may lead to **poor health** because people have **less money** for food, prescriptions etc. However, **health is affected** by **many factors**. People in rural areas tend to suffer from **fewer** mental health problems and often have access to **fresher**, local **food**, which can have a **positive effect** on health.

Betsy couldn't understand why people thought living in rural areas was boring...

2 Cause: INCREASE in House Prices

House prices in rural areas are **higher** than those in **urban areas** — in 2007 house prices in rural areas were **14% higher** than in urban areas. However the **average income** in rural areas is **lower** than in urban areas. This **economic inequality** can lead to many **more** social and economic inequalities, as shown below.

EXAMPLE

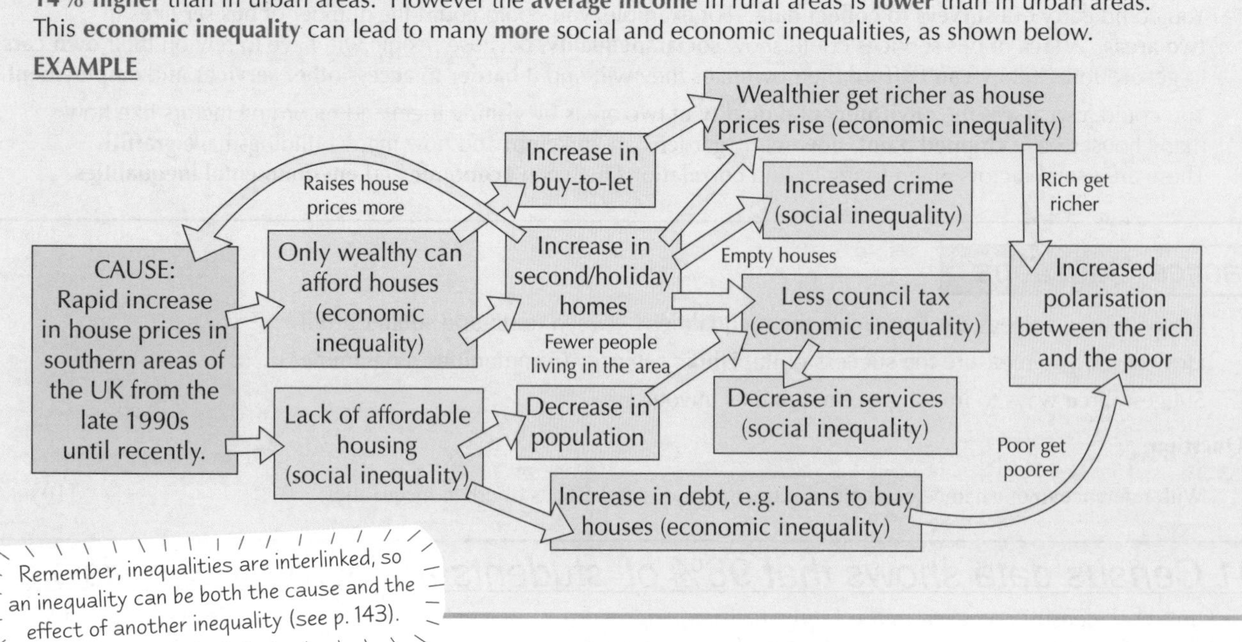

Causes and Effects of Rural Inequalities

3 Cause: Environmental Changes

Environmental changes, such as droughts, floods and land degradation, have **massive effects on rural communities**, especially those that **rely** on **agriculture** to survive. They usually **worsen inequalities** already present in rural areas.

EXAMPLE

You can find out more about cyclones on p. 71.

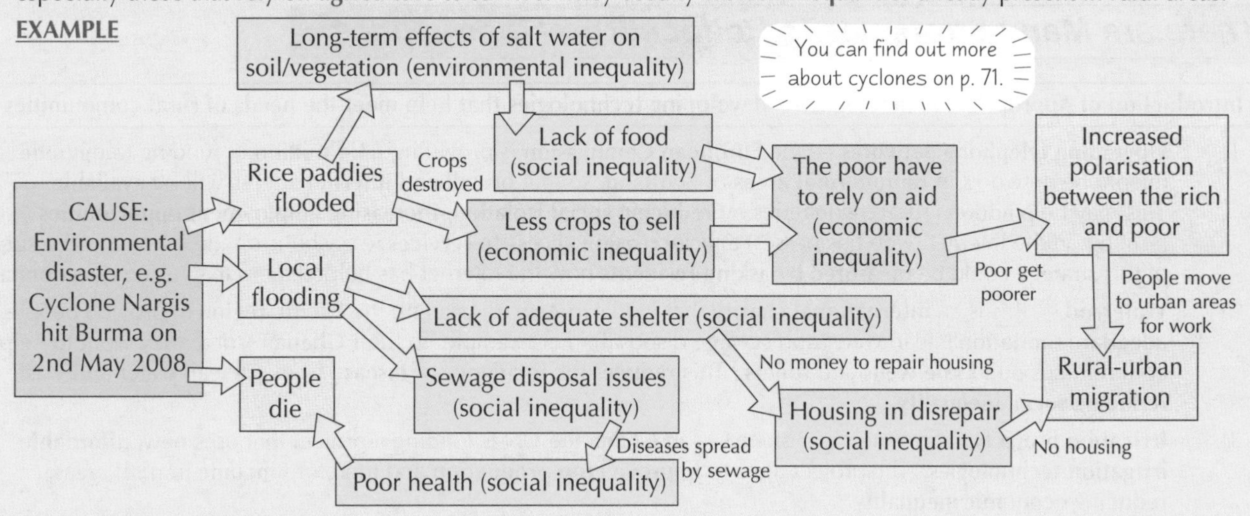

Inequalities are Barriers to Equality

Inequalities, opportunities and barriers are all interlinked — inequalities reduce opportunities, creating barriers.

Inequalities can **reduce opportunities** because they're **barriers** to equality. Barriers that occur in **rural areas** include:

1) Lack of **affordable housing** (economic inequality) — this **reduces** housing opportunities for people on **lower incomes** in rural areas and so is a barrier to **housing equality**.
2) Lack of **local employment** (social and economic inequality) — this reduces **employment opportunities**, so people have limited **job choice**, often associated with **low incomes**. It's a barrier to **economic** and **employment equality**.
3) Lack of **services** (social inequality) — e.g. a lack of **public transport** means people find it hard to travel to **work**, limiting the **jobs** they can do. This reduces **employment opportunity** and so is a **barrier** to **economic equality**.

Polarisation and Exclusion Occur in Rural Areas

Polarisation occurs when **inequalities** between two groups become **extreme** (see p. 145). Rural inequalities often lead to polarisation **between** the **rich** and the **poor**. E.g. an **increase** in **house prices** means **only** the **wealthy** can **afford** to buy homes. Wealthy people may visit **scenic** rural areas and buy **second homes** there to use as **holiday homes**. This **increases** the house prices **even more**. Less wealthy, local people are **priced out** of the **market** and wealthy homeowners become **more wealthy** as their properties **increase** in **value**.

Different groups of people can experience **exclusion** in **rural areas**. E.g. people who are **unemployed** in rural areas (e.g. due to a decrease in agricultural jobs) will have **lower family incomes** and may be on **benefits**. This means they are **less likely** to be able to **afford** a **home**, **car**, **good clothes**, **social activities** etc. Therefore they're **excluded** from some areas of **society** on the **basis** of **income** (economic exclusion).

Practice Questions

Q1 Describe how a decrease in employment can lead to one rural inequality.

Q2 Describe how environmental changes can lead to one rural inequality.

Exam Question

Q1 Explain how the causes and effects of inequalities in a rural area can lead to polarisation. [10 marks]

Cow poo — the worst inequality between rural and urban areas...

Yep, you're right, there are lots of similarities between the causes and effects of inequalities in rural and urban areas. E.g. a root cause of inequality in both areas is an increase in houses prices. One of the effects of this is a boom in the rental market in both areas. However, rural areas are also affected by people buying second homes. Gosh, it's all made my head go funny...

Strategies to Reduce Rural Inequalities

These pages are for** Edexcel Unit 2 (Unequal Spaces **option).
You've learnt about strategies that can help to decrease inequalities in urban areas and now you need to learn about them for rural areas too. So go grab some biccies and prepare yourself for some quality revision time...

*There are **Many Strategies** to **Reduce Rural Inequalities***

1 Introduction of Appropriate Technologies — developing technologies that help meet the needs of rural communities

1) **Upgrading telephone networks** — the **European Commission** is providing **£3.4 million** of funding to **upgrade** telephone networks in **remote rural areas** of **Scotland**, so that **broadband internet** access will be **available**. This may help **address** rural inequalities by **reducing social isolation, increasing employment opportunities** (e.g. job hunting on the internet, web businesses) and **increasing access to services** (e.g. shops on the internet). The **success** of this strategy could be **measured** by **asking residents** how the internet has helped them (e.g. using **questionnaires**).
2) **WaterAid** — this is an **international charity** that works in **Africa**, **Asia** and the **Pacific region** to provide people with **adequate sanitation** (clean water and sewage disposal). For example, in rural **Ghana** (Africa) they work to help communities build **safe wells** and **toilets**. This **reduces** the **incidence** of **disease** from unclean water and waste, **reducing social inequality**.
3) **Irrigation projects** (crop watering systems) — in **Ghana** the **UN** is funding a project that uses **new**, **affordable irrigation technologies**. The project aims to **improve crop production** and therefore **income** in rural areas, **reducing economic inequality**.

2 Community Schemes — to help rural communities reduce inequalities in their own areas

1) **Village Action Plans** — these are being developed by many **rural communities** in the **UK** as part of the **'Vital Villages' scheme** run by the **Countryside Agency**. They help local communities **identify** rural inequalities and they work together to **organise** more specific **schemes** to **address** these inequalities.
2) **The Devon Social Inclusion Programme** — this programme works with **small rural communities** to tackle **social exclusion**. The programme **supports** many **community groups** (e.g. youth clubs) and **community events** (such as festivals and family fun days).
3) **The Village Enterprise Fund** — this is a scheme in **rural East Africa** that aims to address **economic inequalities** in the region by helping rural communities **create their own businesses**. The scheme provides **business training**, **financial grants** and **mentoring** to **give** people the **skills** and **means** to create and operate small businesses, e.g. small farms, carpenters', tailors', bicycle repair workshops and cafes. The **success** of such a scheme could be monitored by **counting** the **number** of **small businesses** in a part of rural East Africa **before** it's introduction and **six months after**.

3 Transport and Services Schemes — to help increase access to transport and services in rural areas

1) **Rural Wheels scheme** — a **UK** scheme, based in **Cumbria**, that provides **door-to-door transport** on **demand** and at a **reasonable cost**. The scheme involves **different transport providers** (e.g. taxis and patient transport services). People book a journey **48 hours in advance**, so that the **best use** of transport can be made. The scheme **reduces social inequality** as it helps tackle **social isolation, dependence on car ownership** and **lack of access to services.**
2) **Vital Villages scheme** — a **UK** scheme to help **villages** in **Warwickshire** and **Worcestershire** gain **access** to the **services** they need, reducing **social inequality**. The scheme provided **grants** to **improve village shops** and **support** for **new developments** (e.g. new community-run shops, internet cafes and delivery services). The **success** of such a scheme could be measured by asking residents how they **perceive** improvements in local village shops etc., via questionnaires.
3) **Peru Decentralised Rural Transport Project** — this project aims to **address rural poverty** (economic inequality) in **Peru** by **improving access** to **goods**, **social services** and **income-generating opportunities**. The project involves **improving transport infrastructure** and **reducing transport costs** in rural areas, to **help** people become **more mobile**.

4 Local Employment Schemes — to help create new jobs in rural areas

1) **Changes to EU agricultural policies** — these aim to **encourage farmers** to **move away** from **intensive farming techniques** and use more **environmentally friendly methods** (e.g. organic farming). This **increases** the **labour** needed, **creating** more **employment opportunities** in **farming** and decreasing social inequality. The **success** of these policies could be **measured** by **counting** the **number** of **workers** on farms **before** and **after** their introduction.
2) **Business Development Scheme** — this is run by **Lancaster Council** and **promotes job creation** in rural areas by providing **grants** to **existing** businesses and to businesses **relocating** into rural areas.
3) **National Rural Employment Guarantee Programme** — this is run by the **Indian** Government and provides the **legal right** of **100 days of employment per year** at a **minimum wage** to rural households. This means **job opportunities** are **provided** by the **government**, e.g. building irrigation systems, digging wells.

Strategies to Reduce Rural Inequalities

Local Development Frameworks (LDFs) Target Local Areas

Local Development Frameworks (**LDFs**) are **plans** for the **development** of **local areas** (e.g. for new roads, schools, housing etc.) in England and Wales. Before LDFs, development was **planned** at the **county** and **district level** — taking into account the **needs** of a county as a whole, **not** the specific needs of smaller areas within the county. In contrast, LDFs **aim** to meet the needs of **small**, **local** areas, which means they're more **flexible**. E.g. they may use **different planning strategies** for **adjacent**, local areas because they recognise that **even** adjacent rural locations can have **different issues** that require **different solutions**.

For example, inequalities across rural **Cumbria** have **different causes** and require **different solutions**. In the heart of the **Lake District National Park** traffic **congestion** (environmental inequality), **second homes** and a **lack of affordable housing** (social inequality) are **key issues**. However, in more **remote west Cumbria**, **employment** and **inaccessibility** (social inequalities) are key issues. LDFs mean that any plans for development in these areas will aim to **solve** the **specific key issues** for the area, instead of **general**, **county-wide** issues.

Successful Strategies Address Root Causes and are Sustainable

Strategies to reduce rural inequalities have a **greater chance** of being **successful** if they:

Address the root causes of rural inequalities

If strategies **don't** address root causes, they will only provide **short-term** solutions. For example, the **UK government** has announced plans to provide **young people** in poor, isolated, rural areas with **free computers**. It hopes that **computer access** will **reduce** social and economic inequalities in rural areas by **increasing** young people's **employment opportunities** (e.g. people can gain **computer skills** or **look for jobs** advertised on the internet). However, this scheme doesn't address the **root cause** of the inequalities, which is a **lack** of **local employment** — it doesn't help having a computer to **search** for jobs if there **aren't** any in the first place. A more successful scheme would have been one that **created jobs** in rural areas **too**.

Are sustainable

Successful strategies need to be able to be **maintained** in the **long-term**. For example, **Africa Now** (an international development organisation) runs a **commercial bee-keeping project**. The project introduces **small-scale farmers** to commercial bee-keeping by providing **training** and access to **equipment**. To ensure the project is **sustainable**, a **private company** has agreed to buy the honey produced at a **fair price**, enabling the **reinvestment** of any money earned.

Rural Inequalities and Urban Inequalities are Linked

1) **Rural-urban migration** leads to **inequalities** in **both** the **rural** and **urban** areas.
2) In **poorer countries** (e.g. Brazil) rural-urban migration leads to a **decrease** in the **young**, **able population** in rural areas. The older, less able people left behind have **less help** with **daily activities** (**social inequality**) and there's **less chance** of **services** being **created** for a **smaller population** (**social inequality**).
3) In **richer countries** rural-urban migration also leads to a **decrease** in the **population** in rural areas, which can cause a **decrease** in **services** (**social inequality**) and **dereliction** (**environmental inequality**).
4) **Strategies** that **address rural inequalities** will **reduce push factors** (see p. 147), which will **decrease** rural-urban **migration** and also **reduce urban inequalities**.

Practice Questions

Q1 Describe one example of how appropriate technologies can help reduce rural inequalities.

Q2 What are LDFs?

Q3 Why do schemes to solve rural inequality need to be sustainable?

Exam Question

Q1 With reference to one or more named examples, describe strategies that are used to reduce rural inequalities. [10 marks]

'STRATEGY' — I'm sure that was a song by Steps...

There are loads of strategies (carried out in loads of different communities) to reduce all types of rural inequalities — so make sure you know a good range of them for the exam. Also, it's important to think about how you'd monitor the success of these strategies — this could include using questionnaires, surveys and census data. Right, on to the next page we go. Whoop whoop.

Rural Inequalities — Case Study

These pages are for** Edexcel Unit 2 (Unequal Spaces **option).
If you've found the last few pages on rural inequalities a bit unexciting then never fear here's another case study...

There are **Inequalities** Between **Areas** in the **Brecon Beacons National Park**

The **Brecon Beacons National Park** is situated in **south-east Wales**. It's a large, **rural** area dominated by **agricultural land**. Many areas in **central** parts of the park have a thriving **tourist industry** and are relatively **wealthy**. However, there are some **deprived areas** situated on the **outskirts** of the park.

EXAMPLE — Llanelly Hill and Llangynidr

Llangynidr is a small area situated near the **centre** of Brecon Beacons National Park. **Llanelly Hill** is an area situated on the **outskirts** of the park.

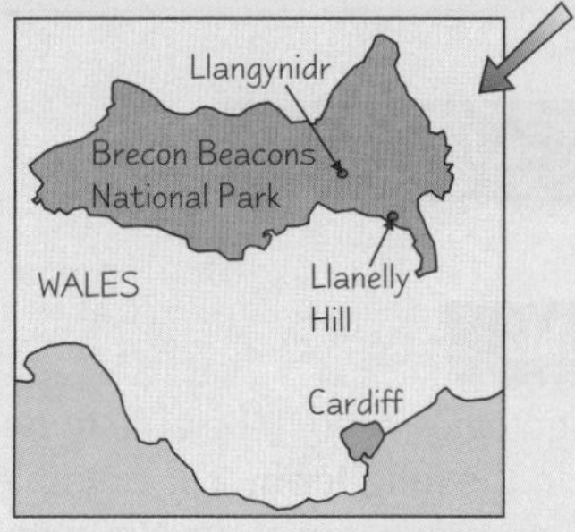

This table shows some **statistics** for the two areas from the 2001 census:

Measures	Llangynidr	Llanelly Hill
Population	1005	3810
% houses that are second or holiday homes	4	0.6
% aged 16-74 unemployed	1.7	3.0
% 'not good' health	8.9	13.3
% 16-74 year olds with no qualifications	19.7	28.1
% households with no vehicle	6.6	15.9

More people own second homes or holiday homes in Llangynidr.

Llanelly Hill has a larger population

More than twice as many households in Llanelly Hill have no vehicle.

- Llanelly Hill has a **higher unemployment rate** of **3.0%**, compared to only **1.7%** in **Llangynidr**. This is probably because Llanelly Hill is situated on the **outskirts** of the Brecon Beacons National Park and so **doesn't** have as many **jobs** created by the **tourist industry** as areas in the centre of the park, like Llangynidr.
- **More houses** are used as **second homes** or **holiday homes** in **Llangynidr** — probably because it's situated **further into** the National Park. This can **drive house prices up**, causing **economic inequality**.
- A **higher percentage** of people in Llanelly Hill have **'not good' health**, possibly because they **don't** have **enough money** for **prescriptions** and **health care**.
- A higher **percentage of 16-74 year olds** in Llanelly Hill have **no qualifications** (**28.1%** compared to **19.7%** in Llangynidr). This can lead to **further unemployment** as people **don't** have the right **qualifications** to get jobs, leading to **further decline** in the area. This creates a **cycle of decline** (see p. 143).
- **Fewer people** have no vehicle in Llangynidr (**6.6%**) compared to Llanelly Hill (**15.9%**). This can also lead to **further unemployment** as people might have trouble **travelling** to work. Also, this can cause **social inequality** as people are **less mobile** and have to rely on public transport to get around.

There are **Multiple Causes** of **Inequalities** in the **National Park**

1) The **decline** of the **coal** and **iron industries** to the **south** and **south-east** of the National Park caused **high unemployment** in the **south** of the park, e.g. **Llanelly Hill** was badly affected when the nearby **Blaenavon coal mine closed** in **1980**. Llangynidr, with its long-established **tourist industry**, **wasn't** so badly affected.
2) There's a **lack of affordable housing** in the **National Park**. This is because the houses are in a **desirable** area, which **pushes prices up**. Also people from outside the area are likely to buy **second homes** there, **increasing prices further**.
3) There's a **lack of access to transport services** in the National Park, due to a **low population**. This affects the people in Llanelly Hill more because **fewer** of them **own vehicles**.

Inequalities Reduce Opportunities and **Cause Social Isolation**

The **effects** of the **inequalities between areas** in the Brecon Beacons National Park include:

1) **Lack of affordable housing** (e.g. in both areas above) — first-time buyers **can't** get on the 'housing ladder'.
2) **Reduced employment** opportunities on the **outskirts** of the park (e.g. Llanelly Hill) — this leads to **lower family incomes** and a **reduced population** as people **move away** to **find work**.
3) **Social isolation** in the **poorer**, **southern** areas of the park — because of a **lack of car ownership** and **public transport**. This also leads to **reduced employment opportunities** as it's **difficult** to **commute** to work.

Rural Inequalities — Case Study

Strategies *are Being Used to* ***Address Inequalities*** *in the* ***National Park***

1. A new **Unitary Development Plan** for the **Brecon Beacons National Park** was approved by the **National Park Authority** in March 2007. It includes **policies** and **proposals** that will **control development** in the National Park up to **2016** and beyond, so the park is **protected** and the **needs** of **local communities** are met. It includes **quarry planning permission** for an area to the north-east area of **Llanelly Hill**, which could **provide jobs** in the area. Also a **housing allocation** for an area to the south of **Llandgynidr** is included, which could provide more **affordable housing**.

2. The **Beacons Project** was started in **2000** and involves several organisations including the **Brecon Beacons National Park Authority**, the **Brecons Trust**, the **National Park Authority**, **Powys County Council**, **local tourism operators** and **local agricultural businesses**. It aims to **improve employment** and **training opportunities** for **young people**, **support** the **local economy**, **conserve** the **landscape** and help **keep local services open**. The project has run many schemes, including a **marketing campaign** to boost **tourism** across the **whole park**. This may help **provide more jobs** in **tourism** in **less wealthy areas**, such as Llanelly Hill, and generate **more trade** for **local businesses** there too. The success of a scheme like this could be measured by **examining data** on the **number of tourists** to the National Park **before** and **after** the marketing campaign was introduced.

3. The **National Park Authority** is developing its **agricultural policies** to encourage more **environmentally friendly farming methods** and **farm diversification**. This may **increase employment opportunities** in agriculture. The **success** of these policies could be measured by looking at **data** on **unemployment** in areas of the park **before** and **after** new policies are introduced.

4. **Blaenavon** (the **coal mine** — see previous page) has been designated a **World Heritage Site** and is investing in its **tourist industry**, which could **provide jobs** for people in **Llanelly Hill**.

5. The **Brecon and District Disabled Club** run a **'dial-a-ride service'**. **Disabled** people can **ring up** and **book transport**, which **increases transport services** for the **disabled** across the park. It's been running for over 30 years and is funded by several organisations, e.g. the **National Lottery**. The **success** of this **scheme** can be measured by **monitoring** the **number of users** and **surveying** the users to see how it **affects** their lives.

6. A **community action group** in **Llanelly Hill** obtained **EU** and **council funding** to **renovate** the **village hall**. It's now used as a **venue** for **computer classes**, a **youth club**, **bingo**, a **food co-operative** and a **playschool**. The success of the village hall could be measured by **distributing** a **questionnaire** to **local people**, asking **how many** of them **use** the village hall and how they **perceive** its success.

You Can ***Investigate*** *the* ***Causes*** *and* ***Effects*** *of* ***Inequalities*** *in a* ***Rural Area***

The **fieldwork** and **research techniques** that you can use to **study** the **causes** and **effects** of **rural inequalities** include the **same** ones that are used to **investigate urban inequalities** (see p. 149), such as **census data**, **CVA scores**, **questionnaires** and **surveys**. You could also map **zones of exclusion** — areas with **no bus service**, **shops** or **secondary schools** for **2 miles**. These maps can **indicate** the areas that are the **most deprived** and are most in **need** of **schemes** like the ones above.

Michael found a perfect example for his fieldwork on deprivation in rural areas.

Practice Questions

Q1 Describe two inequalities between Llanelly Hill and Llangynidr.

Q2 Give one cause of the inequalities between Llanelly Hill and Llangynidr.

Q3 Describe a strategy that has been used to address the inequalities in the Brecon Beacons National Park.

Exam Question

Q1 With reference to one named example, discuss the causes and effects of rural inequalities. [10 marks]

I didn't know that whales have inequalities — boom, boom...

Oh dear, it's the end of the section. I hope you've enjoyed all this juicy information. Remember that inequalities in rural and urban areas are pretty similar. And that all inequalities are interlinked. Also, make sure you learn the case studies because you'll probably have to answer a question that needs references to a 'named example'. Right, that's all from me now... ter-rah.

Introduction to Rebranding Places

This section is for Edexcel Unit 2 (Rebranding option).
Rebranding is all about improving a place's image so that people will want to go there, and take their wallets...

Rebranding** Aims to **Improve** a **Place** and Its **Image

1) **Rebranding** a place usually involves **regeneration** — making actual **improvements** to an area, e.g. new buildings and services.
2) It also involves **re-imaging** — using **marketing** to improve the **image** and **reputation** of a place.
3) Rebranding is aimed at **internal** users (e.g. residents and employees) and **external** 'customers' (e.g. visitors and potential investors).
4) It occurs at all **scales**, from rebranding individual **villages** to changing the image of an entire **country**, like **China**.
5) Its aims can include improving the **quality of life** for **residents** and **attracting new residents**, **tourists** and **businesses**.
6) Ideally a '**virtuous cycle**' will be created.

Regeneration is often followed by re-imaging — to make people aware of the improvements that have been made.

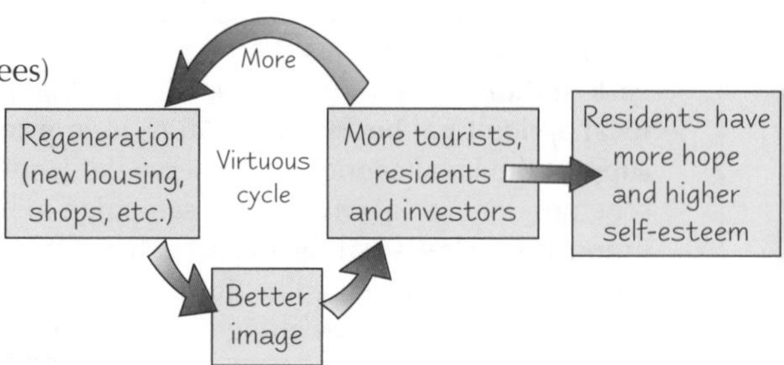

Rebranding** is **Needed** When a Place is in **Decline

A place can be in **decline** due to **social**, **economic** and **environmental** problems. Each of these problems causes **more problems**, creating a **spiral of decline**. In the UK, places that need rebranding fall into **three** groups:

Urban areas

1) Many **industrial** towns have lost their **factories** and so have seen a massive **decrease** in manufacturing **jobs**.
2) The **loss of industry** results in **high unemployment**, creating **economic problems** as people have to live on **low income** or **income support** (welfare).
3) The economic problems lead to a **spiral of decline** as people **move out** of the area to look for **work**, which leads to **services closing** (e.g. shops), leading to **fewer** job opportunities, resulting in further **economic** and **social decline**.
4) Rebranding is **needed** to **encourage new investment** that should bring **jobs** and **money** to the area. **Improvements** in **housing** and the **local environment** will **attract** people **back** to the area.

Rural areas

1) The **decline** of **agriculture** has led to **reduced employment** and **economic problems** in **rural** areas.
2) The lack of **job opportunities** leads to the **out-migration** of **young** people, resulting in an **ageing population**.
3) Services such as **shops**, **schools** and **post offices** close as people **move away** for **work**, leading to a **spiral of decline** as **economic problems** and **social isolation** become worse.
4) Attracting new **business** and **tourists** to the area through **rebranding** will increase **employment** and **services**. This will then encourage **young people** to **stay** in the area, and **new people** to **move** to the area.

Coastal Resorts

1) **Cheap flights** abroad mean **fewer British tourists** are visiting **UK** coastal resorts, so resorts are **losing money** and **businesses** are **closing**.
2) The **decline** of the **fishing industry** has also led to **fewer jobs** and further **economic problems**.
3) This leads to the **out-migration** of **young people** and a **spiral of decline** as **problems** get worse.
4) As with urban and rural areas, **rebranding** encourages new **investment**, bringing **jobs** and **money** to the area.

*You Need to be Able to **Investigate** the **Need** for **Rebranding***

Here are some ideas for **fieldwork** and **research** you could carry out into the **need** for **rebranding**:

Fieldwork

- Design a **simple questionnaire**, asking **local** people whether they think there's a **need** for rebranding and **why**.
- Conduct an **environmental quality survey**, scoring areas for **greenery**, **litter**, **graffiti**, **vandalism**, **dereliction**, **pavement quality**, **pollution**, **noise levels** and **state of repair of housing**. This could show whether an area is in **decline** and so in **need** of **rebranding**.

Research

- Conduct an **internet image search** to find out what sort of pictures are **typical** for a specific place. If they're all **negative**, rebranding may be required.
- Look at **census** data for information on **unemployment**. If an area has **high** unemployment, it may be in **need** of a rebranding scheme that will **create** more **jobs**.
- Use **GIS** to overlay **census** data on **deprivation** with **environmental quality data**. You could use this data to identify the locations most in **need** of **rebranding**.

Introduction to Rebranding Places

Rebranding Can Use Many Different Strategies

1) There are lots of different ways to **rebrand** an area. Projects can **focus** on:
   - **Attracting tourists** — with **leisure** and **sports facilities**, **culture** and the **arts**.
   - **Improving conditions for residents** — with **better housing** and more **amenities**.
   - **Attracting investment** — with new **shops**, **commercial buildings** and **waterfront developments**.
2) Rebranding can be **achieved** through projects that help to **regenerate** or **re-image** a place:

Regeneration

Developing new...
- Housing
- Shops
- Commercial buildings
- Art and cultural centres
- Technology
- Leisure and sports facilities

Re-imaging

Promoting...
- National parks
- Rural and historical heritage
- Festivals
- Food towns (see below)
- Links with the media
- Leisure and sports
- Art and culture

3) There's a lot of **overlap** between **regeneration** and **re-imaging**, and **most** projects involve a bit of **both**.
4) Focusing on **one strategy** can **speed up** the rebranding process by acting as a **catalyst** for **further change**.
5) For example, **culture** has been used as a **catalyst** for rebranding **Liverpool**. Since being named **European Capital of Culture** for 2008, it's begun a major **redevelopment process**. This includes new **housing**, a **cruise-liner terminal**, and the £900 million **Paradise Street shopping** complex. It shows how **re-imaging** can lead to **regeneration**.
6) In **successful** rebranding projects the **strategies** will be **linked**. The aim is to create a **virtuous cycle**, where the **first** change leads to **further** improvements, and so on. For example, building a shopping centre creates **more jobs**, bringing **more money** and **visitors** to an area. This helps to improve a place's **image**, attracting **more visitors**, etc.

Rebranding Can Involve Flagship Projects...

Flagship projects are **large-scale**, **expensive** projects designed to make a **radical change** to a place's **image** and generate **media interest**. They're '**top-down**' initiatives, which means the **idea** and **funding** come from local or national **government** and **big business** (the 'top'). The **Guggenheim Museum** in **Bilbao**, **Spain** is an example of a flagship project:

1) The **decline of industry** in **Bilbao** (an **industrial port**) in the 1970s and 1980s led to **high unemployment** and many **social problems** in the area.
2) The **Guggenheim Museum** was opened in 1997 as a **flagship project** designed to act as a **catalyst** for **regeneration** of the Bilbao area.
3) The **art museum** is housed in an **eye-catching building** that attracts around **1 million visitors** and an estimated extra **150-200 million euros** each year.
4) **Further regeneration** of the area has included new **tram** and **bus lines**, further **cultural centres** and **concert venues**, and **improved buildings** and **services**.

CARLOS DOMINGUEZ / SCIENCE PHOTO LIBRARY

...or Community Projects

Community projects tend to be **smaller** than flagship projects. They're '**bottom-up**' initiatives, which means they're started by **local** people (the 'bottom'). The rebranding of **Ludlow** is an example of a community project:

Ludlow is a **market town** in Shropshire (**UK**). It started to be rebranded as the '**slow food town**' in 1995 when a few **local people** came up with the idea of holding a **food festival** there. The festival now more than **doubles** the town's population for **one weekend** each September. It attracts visitors with top-class **restaurants** and **independent shops** selling **local produce**.

Practice Questions

Q1 What is the difference between regeneration and re-imaging?

Q2 What is the difference between a flagship project and a community project?

Exam Question

Q1 Describe why urban, rural and coastal areas in the UK might require rebranding. [10 marks]

Re-e-brand, when the crowd say bo' selecta...

This stuff isn't too tricky really, but remember that rebranding doesn't have to be limited to towns and cities. Something as small as a school or as big as a country can benefit from a new image. Heck, you could even rebrand yourself. All it takes is some PVA glue, a couple of pillows, a pair of scissors and a bit of determination and hey presto! You've rebranded yourself as a chicken...

Urban Rebranding Strategies

***These pages are for** Edexcel Unit 2 **(Rebranding option)**.*
Urban rebranding can be a bit of a complicated business — it takes a lot of people and a lot of money to get it right.

Urban Rebranding** Involves **Many** Different **Players

Rebranding an **urban** area **can't** be done by one **organisation** on its **own**. It needs many different **players** (people who have an **interest** in the rebranding). Each of these players will have **different roles** and **different reasons** for getting involved:

Player	Likely Role	Possible Reasons
Local government (e.g. district or city council)	Funding and planning permission.	To improve urban areas for social and economic benefit, to increase income from taxes, and to gain votes.
National government	Funding.	
Urban Regeneration Companies (URCs)	Coordinating government and private investment and deciding priorities for rebranding.	It's the job of these companies to support regeneration and rebranding.
Private companies	Project funding.	Publicity, association with vibrant modern projects.
	Moving into the rebranded area.	Profit — taking advantage of the likely increase in business as a result of rebranding.
Private investors (e.g. venture capitalists)	Funding local projects and companies.	Profit — taking advantage of the likely increase in business as a result of rebranding.
Not-for-profit organisations (e.g. Arts Council England)	Funding, support and advice.	Regeneration is often the aim of the organisation or it supports the aim (e.g. improving social problems).
Local tourist board	Marketing and promotion.	Leads to increased tourist numbers and improved visitor experience.
The local community	Backing the rebranding process and helping to decide priorities for rebranding.	Desire to live and work in a place with improved facilities, environment and reputation.

Urban** Rebranding Can Involve **Regeneration

One of the most obvious ways to regenerate an urban area is to **improve** its **buildings**. This can involve **smartening up existing** buildings or building eye-catching **new** ones. Building **improvements** tend to focus on **four** main areas:

1 Residential

Improving **existing** housing or building **new** estates, e.g. the 1700 new homes in **New Islington, Manchester** (see p. 160).

2 Shopping

Building **new shopping centres** or improving **existing** ones to attract **consumers** and **investors** to the area.

3 Commercial

New **business** buildings — e.g. the **Burj Al Arab hotel** in **Dubai**. This **flagship** building shows that Dubai wants to **promote** itself as a **tourist destination** for the **jet-set** — it's not just an oil industry city or a business location.

4 Waterfront developments

Regenerating former **industrial** areas like **docks**. This can be done with new **housing**, **shops** and **commercial buildings**. Waterfront projects also often focus on **culture** — e.g. the **Baltic Mill** in **Gateshead** (UK) has been turned into a **modern art gallery**, helping to **increase tourism**.

***Urban** Rebranding Can Involve **Promoting** an **Existing Image**...*

1) Cities often **promote** themselves by **reinforcing** a **positive aspect** of their **identity** that people already know about, rather than actually **changing** anything about the place.
2) For example, **historic centres** can promote their existing links with history to combine **heritage** and **tourism**, e.g. **York** is marketed as '**England's first city of history**'.
3) Promoting an existing image can create a **virtuous cycle** — people are persuaded to **visit**, which encourages more **investment** (e.g. by encouraging businesses to relocate there), which encourages more **visitors** and so on.
4) For example, **Hay-on-Wye** (UK) set up a **literary festival** in 1988 on the back of its **reputation** for second-hand bookshops. The originally small festival **developed** into a big attraction, bringing over **80 000** visitors and an **extra £3 million** to the town **each year**.
5) However, promoting an image can sometimes be **risky**, as developers can be **accused** of '**spin**' if they just **remarket** the place **without** actually making any **improvements**.

Urban Rebranding Strategies

...or Marketing a New Image

Sometimes promoting a city's identity involves **changing existing** perceptions of the place. For example, **Amsterdam** has tried to **alter** its **reputation** for **prostitution** and **drugs** by promoting itself as a **historic** place filled with **art** and **culture**. **Declining coastal towns** can also benefit from a **new image**, e.g. **Eastbourne**:

1) **Eastbourne** is known for being a popular **tourist** and **retirement destination** for **older people**. When the **number** of elderly visitors started to **decline**, **Eastbourne Borough Council** launched the **'Change Your View'** poster **campaign** in **2004**. It aimed to diversify the tourist economy by attracting **younger visitors** and **families** with children.
2) The campaign **promoted** Eastbourne as a place to enjoy **extreme sports**, **live bands** and **theme parks**.
3) The rebranding seems to have been **successful** — **visitor numbers** are **increasing** (they increased 66% from 2007 to 2008) and over **half** of the **4 million** people who **visited** Eastbourne in **2008** had **never** been **before**. This suggests that the campaign had **reached out** to a **different 'types'** of tourist.

Urban Rebranding Can Use Sport as a Catalyst for Change

1) **Sport** can act as a **catalyst** for **rebranding** — it **speeds up** urban rebranding by generating **publicity**, attracting **visitors** and **investors**, and creating **jobs** for residents.
2) **Hosting** a **major sporting event** can have a **huge** impact on an area. For example, the **Chinese government** was willing to spend over **$40 billion** on hosting the **Beijing 2008 Olympic Games** because the massive **global publicity** would raise China's **profile** around the world. The aim is that this will **increase tourism** and **international investment** in China.
3) On a smaller scale, building **new sports facilities** can help **rebrand** an area too:

The development of **Arsenal Football Club's** £430 million **Emirates Stadium** in Ashburton Grove, **North London** has provided **2600 new jobs** for the area and **2500 new homes**. The project has also replaced the old **recycling facilities** and provided a **nursery** and a **health club** for the local community.

Urban Rebranding Can Have Disadvantages

Sometimes urban rebranding can have a **negative** impact. A particular problem is that **unrebranded** areas can become **isolated** as a result of rebranding **elsewhere**. For example:

1) Over the last 20 years, **Manchester** has been rebranded as a **'happening place'**. The **regeneration** included **improving** former **run-down suburbs** like **Hulme** and **derelict industrial areas** like **Eastlands** (where the **City of Manchester Stadium** was built for the **Commonwealth Games** in 2002).
2) But **research** by the **William Temple Foundation** has revealed that as a result, **crime** and **poverty** have become **more concentrated** in places that **haven't** been **regenerated** yet, like parts of **Moss Side**.
3) This **gap** between **regenerated areas** and **unregenerated areas** has led to:

- A **decline** in **local shops** in the **unregenerated** areas because there are **large-scale retail outlets** nearby.
- **Fear of crime**, particularly among **older people**, in the areas that **haven't** been **regenerated**.
- A **reduction** in **volunteer work**, **social interaction** and **local clubs** and **societies**. This has happened particularly in the **regenerated areas** as **young professionals** have moved **in** and **families** have moved **out**.

Practice Questions

Q1 Name two players that might be involved in urban rebranding.

Q2 Outline the four main areas that building improvement regeneration strategies can focus on.

Q3 Briefly describe how sport can act as a catalyst for rebranding.

Exam Question

Q1 With reference to named examples, explain how rebranding strategies might regenerate urban areas. [10 marks]

If you're using football as a catalyst — you'll need at least 11 players...

Once a town or city gets a bit grotty then you've got to make a choice about what to do to improve it. You could knock down all the buildings and redo all the houses and shops from scratch, smarten up the docks, build a new sports centre, or spend billions of pounds hosting the Olympics. Or you could just give it a lick of paint and get a new sign. Genius...

Urban Rebranding — Case Study

***These pages are for** Edexcel Unit 2 (Rebranding **option**).*
You might have to write about an urban rebranding case study in detail in your exam. Well, look what I have here...

The **Cardroom Estate** in **Ancoats** Needed **Rebranding**

1) The **Cardroom estate** was built in the **1970s** in the **Ancoats** area of **Manchester**, just **east** of the **city centre**.
2) The estate was built to **replace** the **old**, **cramped** Victorian housing in the area.
3) By the **mid 1990s** the estate had become **run-down** and had a **bad reputation**. **50%** of the **houses** were **empty** or being used as **squats**.
4) The area suffered from a **spiral of decline** caused by **economic** and **social problems** like **high unemployment**, **burglary**, **joyriding**, **drug problems**, **graffiti** and **vandalism**.

The **Cardroom Estate** Has been **Replaced** by the **New Islington** Development

1) **New Islington** is a **flagship housing development** that has **replaced** the **Cardroom estate.**
2) The estate was chosen as the location for the rebranding because it's a **brownfield** site that was an area of **deprivation** and **dereliction**. It's a good location because it's within **walking distance** of the **shops**, **offices** and **entertainment facilities** in the city centre.
3) **New Islington** has **colourful**, **eye-catching buildings** and lots of **new facilities**:

A brownfield site is one that has been built on before. It's the opposite of a greenfield site — one that has never been built on before.

Facilities in New Islington

1700 new homes	**Restaurants and cafes**	**Angling club**
Primary school	**Orchard**	**Tram links**
Health centre with 8 GPs	**31 acre ecopark**	**50 moorings on the Ashton and Rochdale Canals**
Village hall	**Community football pitch**	

4) The **total cost** of the redevelopment has been estimated at **£250 million**.
5) It's being managed by property developers **Urban Splash** and the urban regeneration company **New East Manchester** (NEM) Ltd — a partnership between **Manchester City Council, English Partnerships** (the government's regeneration agency) and the **Northwest Regional Development Agency** (NWDA).
6) It's hoped that the **regeneration** will **improve** the area's **image** and **encourage** more people to **move** there. It will also **attract** more **businesses** to the area, which in turn will **create jobs** and **increase wages** (a **virtuous cycle**).

The **Rebrand** Has **Involved** the **Local Community**

Despite being a multi-million pound **flagship development**, the **local community** has been **involved** in the **decision-making**. Everything that's happened at New Islington has followed **consultation** with **residents** of the **Cardroom estate**.

1) There have been regular **meetings** between the **developers** and the **locals** in the **Cob o'Coal pub**. The choice of design for the **new council houses** was a **result** of these **consultations**.
2) Each **Cardroom estate resident** was offered a **new house** in New Islington, or a **transfer** to **another Manchester estate**.
3) In one area of New Islington people can **design their own homes**. The idea is that **each house** on the terraced street will be **different** and the **residents** will take real **pride** in their home. This is called the **Tutti Frutti development**.

New Islington Will be More **Environmentally Sustainable**

The development includes a number of **environmentally friendly initiatives**:

- A '**Combined Heat and Power**' (**CHP**) **station** to supply **heat** and **electricity**.
- **Extensive** new **recycling facilities**.
- **Energy-efficient buildings** and lots of **green space**.
- The **water supply** will come from the development's own **borehole** (which used to supply the **Boddington's** brewery).

The new borehole was an instant hit with the locals.

Urban Rebranding — Case Study

The **Rebrand** Has Involved **Modern Marketing Methods**

The **internet** has played a vital role in **marketing** New Islington.

1) Internet searches for **New Islington** bring up some feel-good **video clips** set to **upbeat music**. They show happy **young professionals** living in **designer flats**.
2) The development has its own **website**, with colourful **photos** and artists' impressions of the project. The website helps to **communicate** the **brand message** that New Islington is **quirky**, **vibrant**, **community-focused** and **eco-friendly**.

The **New Islington** Development Has **Good Points**...

There's been a lot of **focus** in the **planning** on New Islington's **long-term impact**.

1) **Locals** have been **involved** in the **planning** and they've been **consulted** at **all stages** throughout the development. This means they're more likely to **support** the development and **stay** in the area, which in turn gives it a **better image**.
2) The regeneration has created **new businesses**, such as a **newsagents**, a **greengrocers** and a **gastro pub**. This creates lots of **new jobs**, helping to **decrease** the **high unemployment** in the area and leading to a **virtuous cycle**.
3) There's a focus on **improving infrastructure**. New Islington has a new **tram stop**, which gives the area better **public transport links**. This makes the area more **attractive** to **new residents**, and should stop it from becoming **isolated**.
4) **Conservation** is important in New Islington. It's built on a **brownfield site**, which is **better** for the **environment** than building on a **greenfield site**. The **buildings** have been designed to be as **energy-efficient** as possible, and the **CHP station** and new **recycling facilities** mean there should be much **less waste** than there was previously.

...and **Bad Points**

New Islington has been **criticised** by **different groups** for **various reasons**:

Residents

- Some **residents** of the old **Cardroom estate** have **complained** that they're considered to be **less important** than the **new residents**. This is because the **social housing** area of the development, where they've been **rehoused**, is at the **opposite end** of the site from the **public spaces** and **amenities**.
- All the houses have **locked gates** over the **doors**, which has led some residents to voice **concerns** about the emphasis on **personal security** in the development. They're worried that it might **damage** the **community spirit** that the developers are keen to **promote**, because it suggests that people can't **trust** their neighbours.

The media

New Islington is named after a **street** on the old **Cardroom estate**, and was **chosen** by **local residents**. However, some **newspapers** have **criticised** it because it suggests the area is trying to be like the trendy suburb of **Islington** in **London**.

Experts

Some **experts** on rebranding have **criticised** New Islington for **not** providing enough **council houses** for residents of the old Cardroom estate. The development has been described as "**a bit light on social housing**".

Practice Questions

Q1 Why was the Cardroom estate chosen as the location for a major rebranding project?

Q2 Name five new facilities in New Islington.

Q3 Name two environmentally friendly initiatives in New Islington.

Exam Question

Q1 With reference to a named example, outline and evaluate an urban rebranding scheme. [10 marks]

I want to be a part of it — New Islington, New Islington...

Who'd be an urban developer eh? You do the best you can but you'll never be able to please everyone. I had to get out of the rebranding game in the end, it was too much stress — endless meetings and rows and the hours were awful. Plus, I look terrible in a hard hat. So now I just spend my days doing sudoku and listening to country and western, and I've never been happier...

Rural Rebranding Strategies

***These pages are for** Edexcel Unit 2 **(Rebranding option)**.*
It's not just towns and cities that need to be rebranded — rural areas can benefit from a bit of restyling too.

Rural Rebranding Involves Many *Different Players*

1) As with **urban areas**, **rebranding** a **rural** area **can't** be done by **one organisation** on its **own**.
2) Creating a **virtuous cycle** (see p. 156) needs the **involvement** of **many** different **players**.
3) These players are basically the **same** as those for **urban** areas (see the **table** on p. 158). The main **differences** are:

Less money is available

- **Rural** locations in need of **rebranding** are **unlikely** to generate as much **money** as **urban** areas, because not as many people live there.
- This means there's **less interest** from **'big business'**.
- **Exceptions** to this include **energy developments** like **nuclear power stations** and **wind farms**.

Planning permission can be hard to get

- It's **harder** to get **planning permission** in **rural** areas than it is in **run-down urban** areas.
- It can be **especially difficult** to get planning permission in **National Parks**. National Parks Authorities might **not approve** new buildings because they want to **preserve** the **landscape**, even if the buildings would be **good** for **rebranding**.

Technology and the *Media* Can Help with *Rural Regeneration*

The internet

- With the advent of the **internet**, there's been an **increase** in the number of people able to **move** to **rural** areas and **work from home**.
- But there have been **problems** with this because **high-speed broadband connections** have been focused on more **densely populated** areas where there are **more customers**.
- To **tackle** this in the most **remote** parts of **Scotland**, the **Scottish Executive** (the government) and the **Highlands and Islands Enterprise** (**HIE**) have funded a **£70 million project** to **connect** every **community** to **high-speed broadband**.
- This has been used by the **HIE** to **market** the **Highlands and Islands** as a good place to **base small businesses** for people who want a **slower pace** of life.

Jo and Nancy couldn't wait to work from home — their boss wore horrific aftershave.

Community radio

- Community radio **reaches out** to **rural communities** by catering to their **specific needs**. For example, since 1994 a lot of community radio stations have been set up in **South Africa**. They **discuss** local **issues** in the local **dialect**, and play local **music**. They also often have an **educational** function, e.g. they broadcast plays on topics like **HIV/AIDS**.
- Many people in rural parts of South Africa **can't read or write**, so they can feel **isolated**. Community radio can help them to feel **part** of their community, e.g. people can **drop in** to the station and **get involved** in the **broadcasts**.
- This can help **rebrand** an area by making **residents** feel more **positive** about it. This gives it a **better image** and **encourages visitors** and **investors**. Stations can also **advertise** an area's **good points** and **support local businesses**.

Films

- **Rural areas** can be **rebranded** as good **locations** for **filming**. The **National Trust** promotes rural locations and **hires out** properties like **stately homes** to film-makers. This is particularly **popular** for **period dramas** like **Pride and Prejudice**.
- This brings **business** to the area and **generates interest** while the filming is taking place. The area can also be **promoted** as the **film location after** the film is **released**, attracting more **fans** and **tourists** (see below).

Rural Rebranding Can Involve *Re-imaging*

1 *Promoting* Links with the *Media*

If a successful **film** or **TV series** is set in a particular rural area then it can attract more **visitors** to the area.
If the film or TV series portrays a particular **image** of the area, then this image can be used to help **rebrand** it. For example:

1) The children's TV programme **Balamory** is filmed in the village of **Tobermory** on the **Isle of Mull**, **Scotland**.
2) Since Balamory launched in **2003**, the island has attracted up to **160 000 extra visitors** each year.
3) Many of these visitors are families with **toddlers**, so the island has developed attractions specifically for them, e.g. **Tobermory Open Farm** and a business selling Balamory **souvenirs**.
4) The series has contributed an estimated **£5 million a year** to the **tourist economy** of Mull.

Rural Rebranding Strategies

2 *Promoting Heritage and the Arts*

Rural rebranding can involve promoting the **art** and **heritage** that's **unique** to an area. Here are some examples:

Art

The **Angel of the North** is a huge steel **sculpture** on a hill by the side of a road near **Gateshead** (UK). It's **regenerated** the site of a **disused mine** and helped attract **visitors** and **investors** to the area.

Rural Heritage

The production of **whisky** in **Scotland** has become a way of **attracting tourists** to the region. People can go on **tours** of **distilleries** to see how whisky is produced. This brings **visitors** who also **spend money** on **accommodation** and **leisure activities**.

Cultural Heritage

The **Lake District** is often called **'Wordsworth Country'** because the poet **William Wordsworth** lived there and wrote many of his poems **about** the area.

Historical Heritage

The **World Heritage Site** (and surrounding area) between **Newcastle** and **Carlisle** on the **border** of **England** and **Scotland** has been branded **'Hadrian's Wall Country'**, because of the **Roman wall** built by the **Emperor Hadrian**.

3 *Giving an Area National Park Status*

Large areas of **natural beauty** can be **re-imaged** as **National Parks**.

1) For example, the **New Forest** (an area of heathland and forest in **Southern England**) became the country's **newest National Park** in **2005**.
2) The **aim** is to attract **more visitors** and **protect** the area from **overdevelopment**.
3) This will hopefully create a **virtuous cycle**, where the **extra visitors** will bring more **money** to the area, which means **more** can be **spent** on **conservation**, which will then attract **more visitors** because they know the area is **unspoilt**, etc.

Integrated Projects are Good for Rural Rebranding

Integrated projects involve **more than one** rebranding **strategy**. They're more likely to be **successful** than other projects because they're **more sustainable** — if one strategy **fails** then there are **others** to **fall back** on. Integrated projects include:

1) Joining up **social**, **economic** and **environmental** strategies — to try to tackle **all** of these issues together.
2) Involving both **public sector activity** (EU, national or local government) and **private sector business development** in the rebranding project — e.g. linking government-funded **tourist boards** with new **tourist businesses**.
3) Having different **business sectors** working **together** — e.g. the rebranding of **Ludlow** as a **specialist food town** brings together **farming**, **food processing**, **restaurants** and **tourism** (see p. 157).

Integrating Projects Leads to Diversification

- The **decline** of **agriculture** in many places means that rural areas have to find **other ways** to generate income from the **post-production countryside**. This means lots of rural rebranding projects involve **diversification**.
- Many farms have **diversified** in order to make money in different ways, e.g. attracting visitors with **maize mazes**, **nature trails** and **farm shops**. **Diversification** can also create **new jobs**, which **encourages young people** to **stay** in the area.
- For example, **Lobbs Farm**, a small **farm** in **Cornwall**, has **branched out** and now has a **farm**, a **shop** and an **educational visitors' centre**. After only **three years** of opening it made over **£600 000** in additional sales.
- It's an **integrated project** that involves **farming**, **leisure** and **tourism**, with a focus on **sustainability** and **rural heritage**. It makes use of **farm buildings** that might otherwise become **derelict**. This **improves** the **image** of the area, which attracts even more **visitors**.

Practice Questions

Q1 Why can it be harder to get planning permission in rural areas compared to urban areas?

Q2 Outline three different strategies that can be used to re-image rural areas.

Exam Question

Q1 Using named examples, describe the rebranding strategies often used in rural areas. [10 marks]

Links with the media — Trainspotting didn't work so well for Edinburgh...

There's not too much to worry about with these pages because the examiners have done you a bit of a favour. Rural rebranding is really quite similar to urban rebranding — it's still about attracting visitors and investors and whatnot, just with more cows and mud.

Rural Rebranding — Case Studies

***These pages are for** Edexcel Unit 2 (Rebranding **option**).*
These pages cover some examples of rural rebranding in a bit more detail. Joy of untold joys...

The **Eden Project** is Helping to **Regenerate Cornwall**

Cornwall's economy used to **rely** on **farming**, **fishing**, **mining** and **quarrying**. These industries have been in **decline** since the **1970s**, which has **damaged** the **local economy** and the **landscape**, forcing people to **leave** the area to **find work**.

- The local economy relies on **tourism**, but most **jobs** in the **tourist industry** are **seasonal** and **low-paid** — Cornwall has the **lowest weekly wages** in Britain. This has led to the **out-migration** of **young people**.
- **Low wages** also leads to **young people leaving** because they **can't afford** to **buy property**. **House prices** have **risen** as people have bought **holiday homes** in the area. This means **rural areas** are **under-populated** for much of the year, so **small businesses** have to **close** because of a **lack** of **trade**. The **lack of services** makes the areas more **isolated**, which encourages more people to **leave**. All this leads to a **spiral of decline**.

Developers have aimed to regenerate the area with **flagship projects**:

The **Eden Project** near St Austell in **Cornwall** opened in **2001**. It's an example of **rural diversification** and **rebranding**. It's **changed** the **rural landscape** and aims to **regenerate** the local area through **ecotourism** (tourism that focuses on the **appreciation** of **nature** and has **minimal negative impact** on the local **ecosystem**). It's a sort of **'eco theme park'** in a former **china-clay quarry**, made up of huge, futuristic **plastic domes**. There's a **tropical zone**, a **Mediterranean zone** and an **outdoor temperate zone**. They contain **plants** from each location and focus on **sustainable farming**.

The project has:

1) **Changed** the **image** of this part of Cornwall from a **summer-only**, **beach holiday** destination into a **year-round** destination for **ecotourists**.
2) Attracted over **1 million extra visitors** a year to the area, and attracted **visitors inland**, to the previously **run-down** former **mining** area.
3) Developed **scientific research** and **education resources**.
4) **Boosted** the **local farming** and **food processing industries** by using **local suppliers** wherever possible by working with **county** and **local councils** as part of an **Integrated Area Plan** (**IAP**).

The **Eden Project** is helping to create a **virtuous cycle** — the **extra business** creates **more jobs** and **higher salaries**, which encourages young people to stay in the area. It also means that **more money** is being **spent**, so **extra business** is **created** and rural services **stay open**, encouraging more people to **visit** and making **locals** more likely to **stay**.

The **Eden Project** Has **Attracted Tourists** But Created **Other Problems** Too

The **Eden Project** has been **very successful** in **rebranding St Austell** as a centre for **ecotourism**, but it's **not** all **good news**.

Positive effects

1) A **visitor survey** in **South Cornwall** showed that **36%** of people visited the area mainly **because** of the **Eden Project**.
2) The Eden Project buys over **£7 million** of **local food produce** every year.
3) It's generated an estimated **£150 million** each year in **extra revenue** to **local businesses**.
4) The Eden Project itself has **created over 500 jobs**, and an estimated **2500 jobs** have been created because of the effects of the **virtuous cycle**.
5) It's led to a **£75 million facelift** project for **St Austell town centre**.
6) In a **local business survey**, **22%** of responses specifically mentioned the **positive impact** of the area's **improved image** as a **result** of the **Eden Project**.

Negative effects

1) All the **extra visitors** have created serious **traffic problems** in the area, particularly in the **summer**. This **lowers** the **quality** of the **visitor experience** and **reduces** the chance that people will **visit again**.
2) The **extra cars** produce extra **greenhouse gas emissions** — a big **drawback** given the project's **focus** on **environmental sustainability**. The **Eden Project** and **Cornwall County Council** have addressed this with **reduced entry price** for **walkers** and **cyclists**, **cycle routes** from **local towns**, and the **Eden Branch Line** bus-rail link.
3) Another **criticism** of the project is that it keeps needing **more public money**. Despite a **£15 entry fee** and **high food prices**, the project has needed **£150 million** in donations from the **Millennium Lottery fund**, the **South West England Regional Development Agency** (**RDA**), the **EU** and **Cornwall County Council**.

Rural Rebranding — Case Studies

The **Dorset** and **East Devon Coast** Has Become the **Jurassic Coast**

1) The **coast** of **Dorset** and **East Devon** was awarded **World Heritage Site** status by **UNESCO** in **2001**, because of the **prehistoric rocks**, **fossils** and **dinosaur remains** that are found there. It's since been **rebranded** as the **Jurassic Coast**.
2) The area was in **need** of **rebranding** because the local **economy** mostly relied on **tourists** visiting the beaches in the **summer**. This meant that it **couldn't** generate much **income** for the **rest** of the **year**.
3) The rebranding is mainly focused on **increasing visitors** to the area, especially at times **other than** the peak **summer season**. It aims to attract visitors to the area with **facilities** to **educate** them about the **coastal features**, **rocks** and **fossils**.
4) The rebranding was **also** designed to inspire **local communities** to **enjoy** the area, and **businesses** to **invest** in it.

The **Jurassic Coast Rebranding** Has Had **Positive** and **Negative** Effects

Positive effects

1) The number of **visitors** to the area has **increased**, especially **out-of-season**. Events like the **Lyme Regis Fossil Festival** attract **5000 extra visitors** to the town **one weekend** each April. The **best** time to **collect fossils** is after a **winter storm**, so this **attracts visitors** who might **not** otherwise visit until the **summer**.
2) **West Bay's** new **£16 million Jurassic Pier** has helped to **double** visitor numbers there since it was built in **2004**.
3) **New** or **renovated visitor centres** at **Beer**, **Exmouth**, **Swanage** and **Charmouth** have **increased** visitor numbers.
4) The **Bournemouth** to **Exeter X53 Jurassic Bus** service saw a **130%** rise in **passenger numbers** between **2002** and **2005**. This means that not all the extra visitors are coming by **car**, which **benefits locals** (as there's not as much traffic congestion) and it's **more environmentally friendly**.
5) Because the area is spread along **150 kilometres** of **coastline**, it's **avoided** a lot of the **traffic problems** faced by attractions like the **Eden Project**, which is in **one location**.
6) The **cliffs** of **Charmouth** and **Lyme Regis** are **well managed** in terms of **safety**, **litter** and **erosion**. In **2006 UNESCO** reported that the coast is in as **good** a **condition** as it was when it gained **World Heritage Site** status in **2001**.
7) Changing the coast's **image** and building **visitor attractions** has **increased** the number of **visitors** to the area. This has generated more **income** for the **tourist economy**, and attracted more **investors**. This in turn will bring even more **visitors** and **create more jobs** for local people (another **virtuous cycle** — they get everywhere).

Negative effects

1) There's **concern** that the **rebranding** is **focused solely** on **tourism**, rather than **wider business** and **community benefits**. This is **risky** because it means that a **decline** in **tourism** could have a huge **negative impact** on the **local economy**.
2) Some **locals** feel that the rebranding has been **top-down** (the **decisions** have been made by local or national **government** and **big business** — the 'top'). Locals have complained that they **haven't** been **consulted** about the **changes**.

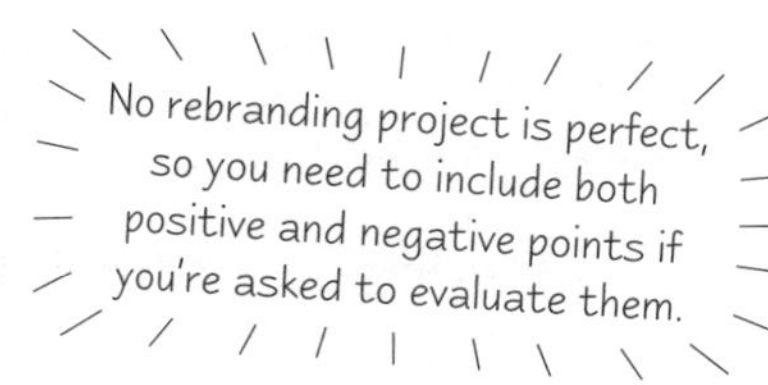

No rebranding project is perfect,
so you need to include both
positive and negative points if
you're asked to evaluate them.

Practice Questions

Q1 How has the Eden Project tried to boost local farming?

Q2 Why is traffic a problem for the Eden Project?

Q3 What has been done to attract tourists to the coast of Dorset and East Devon?

Exam Question

Q1 Using named examples, compare the success of different rural rebranding schemes. [10 marks]

Jurassic Coast — I think I saw that at the cinema...

It's a scary place — I can't believe it's still open really. It's like a theme park — you go round in a jeep and look at dinosaurs they've cloned from a mosquito or something. I thought it must have been shut down after the T-Rex went on the rampage and someone got eaten on the toilet. Still, I reckon you can't argue with loads of extra visitors. I guess that's the beauty of rebranding...

Evaluating Rebranding Strategies

These pages are for Edexcel Unit 2 (Rebranding option).
It's been written that only a lucky few will ever be told the secret of evaluating rebranding strategies. Read on, chosen ones...

The *Impact Rebranding* Will Have in the *Future* Has to be *Considered*

1) For a rebranding project to be **successful**, it needs to be **sustainable** — it needs to lead to **long-term benefits** and be possible to **maintain** in the **future**.
2) To achieve this, the project should involve **more than one strategy**. If it only focuses on one thing, like attracting tourists, a decline in that industry could be devastating.
3) It's also important for a rebranding project to be **self-sufficient**, which means creating a **virtuous cycle** (see p. 156). For example, in a **tourist destination** the rebranding needs to attract **more tourists**, which will bring in **more money**, which will lead to **more improvements**, which will lead to **more tourists**, and so on...

Sustainable Rebranding Can be *Achieved in Different Ways*

You need to look at whether a strategy is sustainable when you're **evaluating** how **successful** it's been.
There are **four key ways** to make sure that a rebranding project will be **sustainable**, so make sure you look out for them:

1) Involve local people in the planning

- Strategies are more likely to be **successful** if **local people** are **behind** it. They're more likely to **support** the scheme if they're able to make **suggestions** and **decisions.**
- Developers can involve local people by conducting **surveys** to find out what **residents** want.

2) Improve infrastructure

- **Infrastructure** is the structures that **support a society**, e.g. **roads, public transport** and **power grids.**
- Improving things like the **public transport network** can attract more **residents** and **visitors** to an area. This can **improve** the area's **image** and bring in more **investment** — it helps create a **virtuous cycle.**

3) Build legacy facilities

- **Legacy facilities** are those that can **keep** being used once the **first stages** of rebranding are **over** — e.g. a **stadium** that the **public** can use **after** a sports event has finished.
- It's important for a rebranding strategy to leave a **legacy** if it's going to have a **long-term impact.**
- Legacy facilities often focus on **social improvement**, like **education** and **reducing crime.**

4) Include conservation measures

- It's important to consider the **environmental impact** of a strategy — if there's too much **waste**, it won't be **sustainable.**
- Showing concern about things like **energy efficiency** will also make the scheme more **popular**, so it's more likely to get **public support.**

An example of a rebranding strategy that has **planned** for the **future** is the **London 2012 Olympic Games.**
The **site** chosen for the Olympic Park is **Stratford** in **East London** — an area in **need** of **rebranding.**
The **strategies** involved in creating the Games and rebranding the area focus on **sustainability**:

1) **Planning** — the **Olympic Delivery Authority** has **written** to local residents to **inform** them of major planning decisions, and they've carried out **public consultations** to get **feedback** from local residents.
2) **Infrastructure** — £17 billion is being invested in **public transport.** By 2012 there will be **ten** railway lines into **Stratford.**
3) **Legacy** — sports facilities being built for the **athletes** will be available for **locals** to use **after** the Games.
4) **Conservation** — improved public transport should help **reduce traffic** in the area in the long term.

Evaluation Involves Looking at an Area *Before* and *After Rebranding*

1) To find out whether rebranding an area has been **successful**, you need to **compare** what the area's like **now** to what it was like **before** the rebranding.
2) This means that the **rebranding processes** should begin with a detailed **assessment**, measuring the **economic**, **environmental** and **social** state of the place before rebranding **starts.**
3) **Later evaluations** can then measure any **changes** by **comparing** the **data** — e.g. whether more **residents** are happy with the **facilities** after rebranding. They should also take into account the **impact** on **different groups** — e.g. **local businesses** and **visitors.**
4) **Comparing** the **data** can be a good way of measuring whether the rebranding has been **successful**, but it can **never** be completely **reliable** — e.g. residents might be **happier**, but that could be because the residents who **weren't** happy with the rebranding have **moved away.**

The rebranding of Whifftown sewer as a beach was a huge success.

Evaluating Rebranding Strategies

You Need to be Able to Do **Fieldwork** into the **Success** of **Rebranding**...

Your fieldwork should focus on the **economic**, **social** and **environmental** impact of rebranding:

Economic

- **Interview shoppers** and ask how far they've **travelled**, and if they would have come **before** the rebranding.
- You could then use this information to draw a rough **map** of the **spheres of influence** (the area the shoppers have come from) for **before** and **after** the **rebranding**.
- If **more** people **travel** from **far away** to shop there now, rebranding has been **successful**.

Social

- **Interview locals** to find out if there are people who have **moved away** or felt **marginalised** (left out) as a **result** of the rebranding. You can then see if the rebranding has had any **negative impact**.
- Where a city has had a rebranding campaign focusing on its **identity**, you could conduct a **survey** asking **local people** and **visitors** whether their **opinions** on the place's **image** have **changed**.
- If locals feel that the image has **improved**, they're more likely to want to **stay** in the area. This will lead to a **virtuous cycle**, attracting **more** people and investors to the area.

Environmental

- **Interview local people** and ask them if they think the **environment** has got **better** or **worse** since the rebranding.
- Ask **specific questions** about people's views on **litter**, **graffiti** and **access** to **green spaces since** the **rebranding**.
- If locals think the environment has **improved**, the scheme has been **successful**. **Residents** are more likely to **stay** in the area and other people are more likely to want to **visit**.

...and **Research** to **Support** Your Fieldwork

Economic

- Ask the **shop owners** for **data** about **shopper numbers**.
- **Compare** your findings with data from **similar nearby places** that **haven't** been **rebranded**.
- If the **rebranded** place gets **more** shoppers, then the scheme has been **successful**.
- Research **local trends** in **unemployment figures** for **before** and **after** rebranding.
- If the scheme has been **successful**, unemployment will have **decreased**.

Social

- Research **crime statistics** for **before** and **after** the **rebranding**. Be aware that a **drop** in **crime figures** in **one area** of a city could just mean that crime has **shifted** to a **different location**.
- Look on the **local newspaper's website** to find out **local opinion** of the scheme. **Public support** can help to **improve** a place's **image**, which can lead to more **benefits** like **more investment**.

Environmental

- Use the **internet** to research whether the scheme has **won** any **environmental awards**.
- Ask the **local council** for any **Environmental Impact Assessment** (**EIA**) they've done in the area. Compare the data from **before** and **after** the **rebranding** to find out the **environmental impact**.
- If a rebranding strategy includes providing more **recycling facilities**, you could look up **recycling rates** on the **local council website** and **compare** the **amount** of **recycling** done **before** and **after** the **rebranding**. This should tell you whether residents are using **new recycling facilities**.

Practice Questions

Q1 What are legacy facilities?

Q2 Suggest one piece of fieldwork you could do to analyse the economic success of a rebranding scheme.

Exam Question

Q1 Describe the results of your fieldwork and research into the success of a rural rebranding scheme. [15 marks]

Reinforced concrete toilets — just one example of legacy facilities...

To evaluate a rebranding strategy you need to look at whether it's improved the area, what problems it's caused, and whether it's sustainable. That's it really. Once you've got to grips with that then you can go and treat yourself to a nice cup of tea...

Global Food Distribution

This section is for AQA (Food option). *And it's all about one of my favourite topics of conversation — grub. So tuck in.*

Global **Food Production** is **Unevenly Distributed**

Some countries produce **large amounts** of food and some countries produce **very little**. The map below shows the production of barley by country from 2000 to 2002. The production of other food follows a similar pattern.

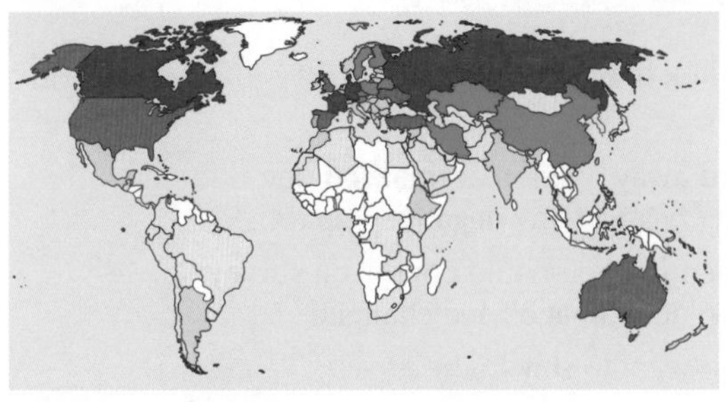

Metric tonnes (1000s)
9001 — 17200
4001 — 9000
1501 — 4000
501 — 1500
0 — 500
No data

East Asia, **North America** and **Europe** produce a lot of food due to:

1) **Climates** that are **good** for farming.
2) Lots of **investment** in farming.

South America and **Africa** only produce small amounts of food due to:

1) A **lack of resources** and **funding** for farming equipment.
2) Large areas of **land** that are **unsuitable** for farming as they are either **mountainous**, have **poor quality** or **little soil**, e.g. the Sahara desert.
3) **Unsuitable climates** — **low rainfall**, **too hot** or **too cold**.

There are **Several** Different **Food Production Systems**

1) **Commercial** farming — the production of crops or livestock to make a **profit**.
2) **Subsistence** farming — when just enough food is grown to **feed the family**. It's common in Africa and Asia.
3) **Intensive** farming — **produces as much as possible** from the land. There are **two types** of intensive farming:
   - **Capital-intensive** farming has a high input of capital (money), and a low input of labour for the area of land. It often involves using fertilisers, pesticides and labour-saving machinery.
   - **Labour-intensive** farming doesn't involve much capital but uses a lot of labour.
4) **Extensive** farming — the **opposite** to intensive farming. It has a **low capital** and **labour input** for the area of land so produces **less food** than intensive farming. Small numbers of livestock grazing large areas of land is an example. Extensive farming has **less impact on the environment** and provides **better animal welfare** than intensive farming.
5) **Arable** farming — **plants** are grown for food, fuel, animal feed or materials (e.g. wood).
6) **Livestock** farming — **animals** like sheep, pigs or cows are raised for food or for materials (e.g. leather).
7) **Mixed** farming — farming of **plants and livestock**.

Global **Food Consumption** is Also **Unevenly Distributed**

Food consumption, like production, **varies** between countries. The map on the right shows the **daily calorie intake** of people in different countries.

1) **More developed** areas like **North America** and **Europe** **consume a lot**. They can afford to import a large variety of foods, have a **culture** of **consumerism**, and many people have **high disposable incomes** so can **afford more food**.
2) **Less developed** areas like **Africa**, **South America** and parts of **Asia consume less food** per person as they **can't afford** as much.
3) **China** and other **newly industrialised countries** are **consuming more** as their **wealth increases**.

Large populations consume more than small populations but this map shows consumption per person.

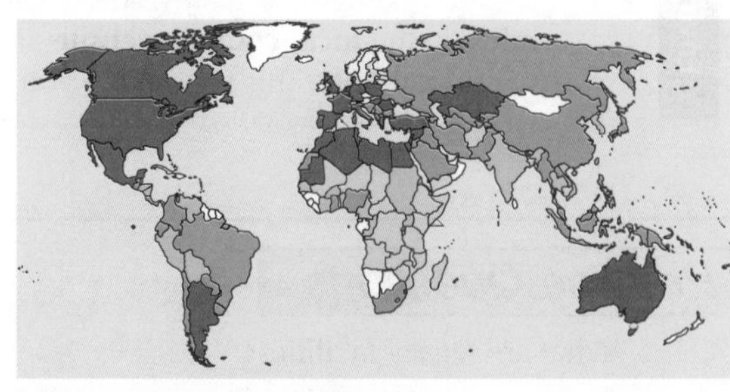

Daily calorie intake per person (1995)
Over 3400
2900 to 3400
2500 to 2900
2100 to 2500
1579 to 2100
Not estimated

Food is **Traded Between Countries**

1) Countries that are able to **produce lots** of food often **export** it to those that can't.
2) North America, Europe, Australia, Argentina and Brazil all **export large amounts** of food.
3) Africa, Japan and Middle Eastern countries such as Saudi Arabia all have to **import large amounts** of food.

Global Food Distribution

Trans-National Corporations *Play an* ***Important Role*** *in the* ***Food Industry***

Trans-National corporations (**TNCs**) are companies that operate in **more than one country**.
Many TNCs play a **major role** in the **production**, **processing** and **distribution** of food.

E.g. **Cargill™** is a TNC based in the USA. It's the largest privately owned company in the world and operates in **66 countries**.

1) **Production**: Cargill™ **sells products** like fertilisers, equipment and seeds to farmers to help them grow crops. It then **buys** the crops from them. It also **produces its own** food, e.g. palm oil in Papua New Guinea.
2) **Processing**: It **owns processing plants** across the globe, e.g. soya bean processing plants in Paraguay, corn processing plants in China and cocoa processing plants in Ivory Coast.
3) **Distribution**: The worldwide distribution of many Cargill™ products is run from an office in Switzerland. It has its **own distribution network** in some countries, e.g. Venezuela, and **employs local people** to trade products in others, e.g. Pakistan.

ADVANTAGES OF TNCs

1) **Lots** of foods can be produced **cheaply**.
2) The **range** of foods available is **increased**.
3) TNCs **provide jobs** and **improve economic security** in countries where they operate.
4) They **invest** in **research** and **development** of new products and technologies that can increase farming yields.

DISADVANTAGES OF TNCs

1) They **control** the **price** of products such as seeds, fertilisers and machinery, the cost of processing and distribution, and the price of foods produced. If these prices are too high **some countries can't afford them.**
2) **Smaller companies can't compete** and **go bankrupt**. This causes supplies of food to become **delocalised** (countries have to buy from TNCs instead of local companies), leading to **less self-sufficiency**.
3) The **intensive farming methods** of TNCs can cause **environmental problems** (see page 172).
4) It can take a long time to process and transport the food — **reducing** its **nutritional value.**

The ***Geopolitics*** *of Food Involves* ***Different Issues***

1) Food production and trade are **very important** to all governments for many reasons.
2) All countries want '**food security**' — they want to make sure that **their supply** of food (either from their own country or from another) **isn't disrupted** by things like poor yields, wars, or other political issues.
3) If their food supply **is** disrupted it can result in **food shortages**. These can cause serious **health issues** as well as **social** and **political instability** in that country. Not good.
4) Also, food production can account for a **huge proportion** of a country's **economy**.
5) So, countries make **agricultural policies** that **protect** their **home production** and **control** the **import** of food (see pages 174-175 for more).

Practice Questions

Q1 Why is food production in Africa low?

Q2 What is subsistence farming?

Q3 Describe the global pattern of food consumption.

Exam Questions

Q1 Compare the main characteristics of intensive farming and extensive farming. [5 marks]

Q2 Discuss the advantages and disadvantages of the involvement of TNCs in the global food industry. [8 marks]

Food fights — a serious threat to the even distribution of food...

OK, I'm fully aware that your main interest in food is probably the part where you shovel it into your mouth — but you do need to learn all the bits that lead up to that. So take the time to learn these pages properly — you could get asked about any of it.

Changes in Demand

These pages are for AQA (Food option). *Back in yesteryear, olden times and days of yore people had to eat whatever they could grow, which I imagine made mealtimes a trifle dull. Luckily for you and me, all that has changed...*

In the Last 50 Years the Food Industry Has Become Globalised...

Before the 1960s the food we ate was usually grown in our **own country**, and was often from the local area.
Since then there has been an **increase** in the **global trade** of food to satisfy **rising levels of consumption** and the increasing demand for a **wide range** of foods **all year round**. This increase in global trade is called **globalisation**.

...Which Has Had a Negative Impact on the Environment

Countries can make a lot of **money** by **exporting food** so it's in their interests to **produce large amounts**. Unfortunately, producing and transporting all this extra food can be damaging to the environment:

See page 172 for the damaging effects of intensive farming methods.

1) Countries that **export food** want to **produce as much as possible**. This means that they want **more land** for **farming**, which often leads to **deforestation** to provide the land.
2) The **greater** the **area** of land that's farmed, the **bigger** the **environmental impact** of farming. Growing food for export can also mean a change to more environmentally damaging **intensive farming methods**.
3) As **food exports increase**, so does the amount of **transportation** needed and the amount of **carbon dioxide** released by vehicles. Carbon dioxide is a greenhouse gas, so the more that's released the bigger the contribution to the **greenhouse effect** and **climate change**. '**Food miles**' is the distance food travels from **producer** to **consumer** and gives an indication of **how much** carbon dioxide is **released** as the food is transported.

The Type of Food That's in Demand Has Changed

1 Demand for SEASONAL PRODUCTS ALL YEAR ROUND has INCREASED...

1) In the 1960s most of the fruit and vegetables on sale in the UK were **locally produced** and **seasonal**. Seasonal food isn't available all year round — you can only buy it during the months that it grows.
2) Today, you can buy seasonal products at **any time** of year.
3) This is because fruit and vegetables are **imported** from **abroad**. E.g. peaches grow in the UK from August to September, but are imported all year round from Spain, Italy, France and Greece.

2 ...and so has demand for HIGH VALUE FOOD EXPORTS from POORER COUNTRIES.

1) **High value foods** are, unsurprisingly, foods that have a **high value**. They include things like exotic fruits and vegetables, coffee and chocolate.
2) Between 1980/1 and 2003/4 **high value food** exported from **poorer** countries to **richer** countries **quadrupled** — from $26 billion to $106 billion.

Crops that are grown for export are called cash crops.

Both these changes in demand were caused by...

1) A rising culture of **high consumption**.
2) **Rising incomes** in developed countries, which means more people can afford to buy the imports.
3) The **increasing popularity** of **exotic** products.

Dave was thrilled to discover his favourite vegetables were now available all year long.

There are **negative** effects of importing seasonal and high value food:

1) There are **food safety** and **agricultural health concerns** because standards vary between countries.
2) Importing food **increases food miles**, which increases the **negative impact** of transporting food on the **environment**.
3) There's **less food produced** in developed countries because it becomes cheaper to import food than produce it. This leads to **lower food security** as countries rely more and more on imported foods.
4) Many people are concerned about the fairness of **workers' pay** in developing countries, and that these countries are selling their best produce abroad at cheap prices.
5) The **best land** is often used to grow **high value foods** for exportation. This may leave **little** or **poor quality land** to grow **food** to feed the local population, which can lead to **food shortages**.

Changes in Demand

Demand for **ORGANIC** food has **INCREASED**...

Between 1993/4 and 2003/4 **organic food sales** in the UK **increased** over **10 times** — from £105 million to £1119 million.

This trend is caused by people's concern that...

1) **Intensive farming damages** the **environment**.
2) Eating food that may contain **pesticide residues** is **harmful**.

There are negative effects of organic produce:

1) It's more vulnerable to **pests** and **disease**.
2) It's more **expensive** to produce and buy.
3) There's **not enough** organic produce grown in the UK to **meet demand** so some has to be **imported**, which **increases food miles**.

...and so has demand for **LOCAL PRODUCE**.

From 2005 to 2006 the number of UK shoppers buying **local produce increased** by 6%.

Reasons for this change in demand include more awareness of...

1) **Environmental issues**, i.e. food miles.
2) **Social issues** — the possible exploitation of workers in the developing world.

The negative effects are:

1) Local foods can be **more expensive** to produce and buy.
2) If we **import less** from the **developing world**, the **producers** there may **suffer**.

Foods Can be Produced in a More Sustainable Way...

For food production to be **sustainable** it has to **not damage** the **environment** and **not deplete resources**. Hardly any food production systems are totally sustainable, but there are ways to make them **more sustainable**:

1) **Relocalising food supplies** (buying food produced locally). This would **reduce food miles**.
2) Replacing intensive farming with **organic farming**. This would reduce the impact on the environment.
3) Using **less food packaging**. This would **reduce energy use** and **waste**.
4) Using **fairtrade systems**. This would give growers in developing countries **fair pay** and improved **social** and **environmental** standards.

... But There are Challenges to Doing This

1) Food **can't** always be **grown locally** — the land might not be suitable for farming.
2) **Organic** farming methods are usually **less productive** than intensive farming methods — so **more land** is required to produce the same amount of food.
3) **Climate change**, **soil degradation** and demand for **biofuels** is **reducing** the area of **land** available for farming.
4) Also, in many areas where the **land** available for **farming** is **reducing**, the **population** is **increasing** and therefore **more food** is needed.
5) So, with **less land** available and **more people** to feed, it would be very **difficult** to **produce enough food** using **only organic farming methods** as they're **less productive** than **intensive farming methods**.

Practice Questions

Q1 What are high value food exports?

Q2 List the negative effects of the growth of high value food exports from developing countries.

Q3 List some of the ways that food could be produced in a more sustainable way.

Exam Questions

Q1 Describe and explain the changes in demand that have driven globalisation of the food industry. [4 marks]

Q2 Describe the environmental impacts of the globalisation of the food industry. [8 marks]

'Newsflash: Jet-setting vegetables to destroy planet.' Just as I suspected...

The key thing here is to be able to explain yourself. It's all very well knowing how our food supply has changed but if you can't explain why, you're going to come unstuck, which is never good. So read these pages through, scribble the details down, and you'll be able to explain to all and sundry why you can buy peaches in December. Whether they want to know is a different issue.

Increasing Food Production

These pages are for AQA (Food option).
So, there's no shortage of demand for good food, which leads us seamlessly on to the fact that...

Global **Food Production** Needs to **Increase**

Food production needs to increase to cope with **population growth** and **increasing consumption** in countries with increasing wealth, e.g. China, India and Brazil.

There are a Range of **Strategies** That **Increase Food Production**

1 The **Green Revolution** Increased the Use of **Technology** in Agriculture

The **green revolution** began in the 1940s and **spread** the use of **technology** and **intensive farming methods** across the world.

Food production increased through the use of:

1) **Higher yielding crops** and **animals** (developed by selective breeding).
2) **Monocultures** — growing just one crop over a large area.
3) **Irrigation technologies**, e.g. groundwater pumping, electric sprinklers.
4) **Agrochemicals**, e.g. fertilisers, pesticides and herbicides.
5) **Mechanisation**, e.g. use of machines for sowing, harvesting, weeding and spraying.

Example

India began a green revolution programme in **1961**. It **financed agrochemicals**, **developed irrigation systems** and **imported high yielding** varieties of **wheat** and **rice**. Productivity increased rapidly as a result, e.g. **rice yields tripled** by the **1990s**.

The **negative impacts** of the green revolution are:

1) Bankruptcy of **small farms** that **can't afford** the **technology**, leading to **rural unemployment** and **food shortages**.
2) **Lower food security** — monoculture crops can be wiped out by a single pest, drought or disease, and there's no alternative crop to rely on.
3) The **intensive farming methods** of the green revolution can **damage** the **environment**:
    - Monoculture **reduces biodiversity**.
    - Over-irrigation can lead to **lower ground water levels**, **waterlogging** and **salinisation** (increase in saltiness) of soil and water.
    - Agrochemicals can cause **pollution**.
    - Mechanisation and over exploiting the land leads to **reduced soil fertility** and **increased soil erosion**.
    - Using pesticides could lead to the evolution of "**superpests**" that are resistant to pesticides, which could result in **more damaging pesticides** being used.

2 **Genetic Modification** is a **High Technology** Approach

Genetically modified (**GM**) **crops** are crops that have been altered by the addition of genes that give them **beneficial characteristics**.
They were introduced in the 1990s.

Crops can be modified to make them:

1) **Produce pesticides** — making them **resistant** to some **pests**.
2) **Herbicide** and **pesticide tolerant** — this means farmers can use these chemicals without harming the plant.
3) **Resistant** to **disease**.
4) **Higher yielding** — either by increasing their size, or their rate of growth.
5) **Longer lasting**, i.e. with an increased shelf-life.
6) **Resistant** to **harsh** environmental **conditions**, e.g. drought or frost.

All of these modifications **increase food production**.

A small number of **GM animals** are also being developed, e.g. quick to mature salmon, cows that produce enriched milk, and pigs that produce lower fat bacon.

Example

'**Bt maize**' and '**Bt cotton**' contain a **gene** from bacteria that enables them to produce a **toxin** poisonous to insect pests (called Bt toxin). **20% less insecticide** is needed on these crops.

Because GM is a new technology it's still unclear what all of its **disadvantages** are.
Some concerns include:

1) If crops are grown that are resistant to agrochemicals farmers might be tempted to use **more agrochemicals**, which can **damage** the **environment**.
2) Some GM crops are able to **cross-pollinate** and **transfer** their **genes** to other plants. This could lead to a gene for herbicide tolerance being transferred to a weed, which would then be difficult to kill.
3) The pesticides produced by some GM crops could **harm non-pest species**, e.g. butterflies.

Increasing Food Production

3 Land Colonisation and Land Reform Provide Agricultural Land

Land colonisation and **reform** can **increase food production** by giving people **access to land** to grow food.

Land colonisation is when humans **move** to an area of land that **hasn't been used before**, e.g. rainforests.

Example

2 million hectares of the **Amazon rainforest** are **cleared** each year to make way for subsistence and commercial **farms**.

The disadvantages include **environmental damage** (such as **deforestation**) and possible **conflicts** with indigenous populations.

Land reform is when land is **redistributed**, e.g. land owned by the government is given to local people.

Example

In **Albania** in the 1990s **216 large state farms** were **redistributed** to create **380 000 small farms** owned by former state **farm workers**.

Disadvantages include **conflicts** over who is entitled to the land (or over compensation for previous landowners). **Human rights violations** are also a concern if the previous landowners were forcibly removed.

4 Commercialisation is the Change from Subsistence Farming to Commercial Farming

Commercialisation **increases production** through the use of capital-intensive **green revolution technologies.** Commercial farms produce **high value food** for export and produce **cash crops.**

Example

Commercialisation of small farms in **Kenya** since the 1960s has led to it becoming the world's **4th largest exporter** of **tea.** Tea is now Kenya's **main source** of foreign **income.**

There are disadvantages to **commercialisation**:

1) The **best land** is usually used to produce food. This can lead to **food shortages** as there's less high quality land left to produce food for the **local population**.
2) Also, the move from subsistence to commercial farming involves the use of **green revolution technologies** and the **problems** that they cause (see previous page).

5 Appropriate Technology Solutions are Low Cost

Appropriate technologies are **simple, low cost** technologies that **increase food production.** They're **made** and **maintained** using **local knowledge** and **resources** only, so aren't dependent on any outside support, expensive equipment or fuel.

Appropriate technology is also known as intermediate technology.

Example

The **treadle pump** is a **human powered** pump **developed in Bangladesh** in the 1980s. It **pumps water** from below the ground to **irrigate small areas** of **land.** This is important in Bangladesh as the main crop (**rice**) needs **lots of water** to grow. It costs US $7 to buy. It has **increased** Bangladeshi farmers' average annual **incomes** by roughly **$100**, through increased irrigation and therefore increased crop yield.
Local workshops, village dealers, well drillers and pump installers have all benefited from the business that the local production and distribution of the pump has brought.

The main **disadvantage** of appropriate technology solutions is that they tend to be **labour intensive**.

Practice Questions

Q1 How have green revolution technologies increased agricultural production?

Q2 What is the difference between land colonisation and land reform?

Q3 What is commercialisation of agriculture?

Exam Question

Q1 Explain the disadvantages of using green revolution technologies to increase food supplies. [6 marks]

Food glorious food — turns out everybody wants some more...

So there you have it — five ways to increase food production. It isn't edge-of-your-seat stuff, but you could be asked to explain or compare any of these strategies, so you need to know each strategy and its disadvantages really well. Sorry about that.

Controlling Food Production and Supply

These pages are for AQA (Food option).
Just when you thought you had food production sussed, it turns out there's a lot more to it...

Food Production and Supply Needs to be Controlled

Production and supply of food have to be controlled in order to:

1) Ensure **food availability** and **security**, but **prevent overproduction**.
2) Ensure **fair living standards** for farmers and the **survival** of **rural communities**.
3) Encourage farmers to act as '**stewards of the landscape**' and **preserve** the natural **environment**.

In **Europe** food production and supply is controlled by the **Common Agricultural Policy** (**CAP**). CAP is a set of policies laid out by the European Commission — it controls production and supply through a range of **market** and **non-market policies**.

Market Policies Control How Profitable Products Are

Market policies control food production by controlling **how profitable** it is to farm certain produce.
There are several different **types** of **market policies**:

1 Subsidies — Paying Farmers to Produce Certain Products

Subsidies are **payments** made to **farmers** to **grow certain products**. This maintains home grown supplies and **food security**. It also ensures **fair living standards** for farmers.

Example: The EU is the second largest **dairy** exporter in the world due to the **subsidies** that support the industry. **€1 billion** was paid out in dairy subsidies in **2006**.

Negative effects of subsidies:

1) The **cost** of paying farmers.
2) It can cause **overproduction**. This can lead to **export dumping** (when food is sold abroad for less than the cost of production).
3) Export dumping causes **disruption** of **international markets** and **problems** in **developing countries** (because farmers are unable to compete with the artificially low price of the dumped food).

2 Quotas Limit Production and How Much is Imported

Quotas limit the production of some food to **prevent overproduction**.
Import quotas protect the market by **limiting** the amount of **imported produce**.

Example: **Milk quotas** were introduced in the **1980s** following overproduction that created **'milk lakes'** and **'butter mountains'** (huge amounts of produce that couldn't be consumed or exported). Milk quotas have gradually been **increased** as **demand** has **increased**.

Negative effects of import quotas:

1) They **prevent consumers** obtaining **cheap imports**.
2) They can **influence** international **production** and **trade**.

3 Intervention Ensures Farmers Can Sell Their Produce

1) **Intervention** is when the EU **buys produce** from farmers. It improves food security by ensuring farmers can **sell** their **produce** even when demand is low. Intervention stock is either **stored** for later **resale**, **exported** or **disposed** of.

Example: Currently, the EU will buy up excess stocks of **grain**, **butter** and **sugar**. The EU had over **1.5 million tonnes** of sugar **stored** in warehouses in January 2006.

Negative effects of intervention:

1) The **cost** of **transport**, **storage** and **disposal**.
2) It can cause **overproduction**.
3) The risk of **export dumping** and **disruption** of **markets**.

2) **Intervention** involves **guaranteeing** a **minimum price** for certain products (pricing). It **controls production** by encouraging farmers to **produce** or **stop producing** particular products.

Example: The EU aims to **cut sugar production** by 6 million tonnes by 2010 to allow developing countries to export lower cost sugar. In 2006 the **guaranteed price** for sugar was **cut** by 36% to encourage farmers to **stop producing** sugar.

Negative effects of pricing:

1) **Cost** of paying farmers.
2) **Increased cost** to **consumers**.

Controlling Food Production and Supply

4 *Tariffs* Protect the Market for Domestic Farmers

Tariffs are **taxes** applied to **imported goods** — they stop imports from **undercutting** domestic produce.

Example: The EU can produce **94%** of the beef that it needs, but if it was **cheaper** for consumers to buy **imported beef** then it would **not be profitable** for EU farmers to produce it and **production** (and so **food security**) would **decrease**. To prevent this, a **tariff** of 18 to 28% is applied to **imported** beef products, making them **more expensive** than locally produced products.

Negative side effects of tariffs:

1) They **prevent consumers** buying **cheap imported products**.
2) They can **affect international production** (by reducing trade of products with high tariffs and increasing trade of products with low tariffs).

Non-market Policies Control Production *Without Affecting Markets*

Non-market policies also **control food production**, but **don't affect** how **profitable** certain products are to farmers. There are different **types** of **non-market policies**:

1 *Diversification Schemes Promote Enterprise*

Diversification schemes encourage farmers to develop **new enterprises**, reducing dependence on subsidies for agricultural products.

Example: **Rainton Farm** in Scotland has **diversified** by producing and selling **ice cream**, and providing **tourist facilities** such as a farm shop, tea room, adventure playground, 3D maze and nature trails.

2 *Environmental Stewardship* Protects *Nature*

Environmental stewardship involves paying **subsidies** to farmers to use **conservation methods** when farming.

Payments are made for schemes that:

1) Protect **wildlife**.
2) Maintain or enhance **landscape quality**.
3) Protect the **environment** and **natural resources**.
4) Promote **public access** to the **countryside**.

Example: In the **Lake District** farmers receive subsidies to **restrict cultivation** and **grazing**, **reduce fertiliser** and **pesticide** use, **manage hedges**, **maintain ditches** and **repair** stone walls.

Benefits of **non-market policies**:

1) They prevent **overproduction**.
2) They prevent **land degradation**.
3) They promote **sustainable farming**.
4) They promote a **sustainable rural economy**.

Negative effects of **non-market policies**:

1) **Cost** of paying farmers.
2) **Reduced productivity** (this can be a benefit if overproduction is an issue though).

Practice Questions

Q1 What are agricultural subsidies?

Q2 Describe the negative effects of intervention.

Q3 What are the benefits of environmental stewardship schemes?

Exam Question

Q1 Describe how EU market policies control the level and nature of agricultural production. [15 marks]

More food, less food, environmentally friendly food, grrrr — enough already

Managing food supplies for a whole continent is tricky stuff — the balance needs to be just right. Luckily for you, you only need to be able to explain these policies — pity the people who actually have to come up with them. Or laugh at them. Whichever.

Managing Food Supply — Case Studies

These pages are for AQA (Food option). *Two highly interesting, hugely important and crucially contrasting case studies for you.*

Case Study 1: Bangladesh — Production Doesn't Meet Demand

1) Bangladesh is a **developing country** with a high poverty rate.
2) Rates of **malnutrition** are **high**.
3) **Food production doesn't meet demand** due to **fast population growth** and **climatic events** that **damage production**. E.g. the annual monsoon and cyclones cause flooding as the country is situated on low-lying river deltas.

Food Supplies are Managed Through a Range of Strategies

Various organisations are working to increase productivity and ensure food supplies are sufficient. These include the government, foreign aid agencies, international research institutions and non-governmental organisations (NGOs). These groups have put a range of strategies in place to increase food supplies:

1 Investment in Technology

The government provides **subsidies** and **loans** for farmers to invest in **green revolution technologies**. The use of **high yielding rice seeds**, **agrochemicals** and **increased irrigation** increased rice production from 11.7 to 23.1 million tonnes between 1974 and 2000. There has also recently been more investment into **appropriate technology solutions**, due to the negative effects of green revolution technologies (see page 172).

2 Free Market Policies Encourage Food Imports

The government has **removed** many **subsidies**, **eliminated quotas**, and **reduced import tariffs** to **encourage imports**, which are essential to feed the population. **Disadvantages** of this strategy include **susceptibility to rising food prices** — in 2008 the rising price of grain pushed 4 million people below the poverty line.

3 Diversification is Encouraged

Bangladesh relies heavily on **rice**, which needs four times more water than most crops to grow — a problem in a country with falling water levels. **Food security**, **nutrition** and **health** would all improve if a **greater range** of **foods** was produced.

Diversification is encouraged in several ways:

1) **Small and medium businesses** are **supported** by projects that provide expertise and training.
2) **Financial incentives** are given to livestock farmers, e.g. tax holidays and duty exemptions.
3) **EU trade preferences** allow goods to be exported to Europe **without duties** or **quotas**.

4 Investment in Infrastructure

There's been **investment** into **infrastructure** that **supports food production**:

1) **Maintaining** and **building roads** to improve the transport of produce. Between 1995 and 2000 the US funded the construction of 15 000 km of farm-to-market roads.
2) **Increasing electricity supplies** — between 1977 and 2000 over 80 000 irrigation pumps were electrified.
3) **Building flood defences** and **improving water flow** to allow damaging flood water to recede quickly.

5 Food Aid is Provided Where it's Needed Most

The government and other organisations operate **schemes** to **provide food**. For example:

1) The **'Food for Work'** programme gives people the opportunity to **work for food** on projects that **improve rural infrastructure** or the **environment**.
2) The **'Food for Education'** programme gives food to families who send their children to school instead of work — **increasing education** and **decreasing child labour**.

These Strategies Have Advantages and Disadvantages

Advantages:

1) Diversification and investment in infrastructure are long-term **sustainable** solutions.
2) Strategies such as "Food for Education" provide **health** and **social benefits**.
3) Diversification would **benefit** the **economy**, providing a wider range of export goods.

Disadvantages:

1) All these strategies cost **money** to initiate.
2) Food imports and food aid are **not sustainable** solutions.
3) Some technologies **damage** the **environment**.

Managing Food Supply — Case Studies

Case Study 2: China — Priority is Self-sufficiency

With 1.3 billion citizens China is the world's **most populated country**. It has had a **history** of **food shortages** so its **goal** is to be **self-sufficient**. It aims to achieve this through focusing agricultural policy on **grain production**. China currently produces 90% of its own grain, despite having only 7% of the planet's arable land and 20% of its population.

Food Supplies are Managed Through a Range of Strategies

1 State Control of Grain Production

Grain production and **distribution** are **controlled** by the **central government**. Farmers are required to produce at least 50 million tonnes of grain that are sold at **government controlled prices** and 40 million tonnes that are sold to the government at **negotiated prices**. This grain is distributed to **urban areas** and sold at **low prices**.

2 Incentives to Grow Grains

Provincial governments are responsible for making sure **enough grain** is **produced**. Provinces that **don't produce enough** have to **buy produce** from those that have a **surplus**. **Incentives** put in place by the provinces to encourage grain production vary but include **subsidies**, **guaranteed minimum prices**, **tax exemptions** and **free education**.

3 Modernisation of Agriculture

There's been **investment** into **modernising agriculture**:

1) **Transportation infrastructure** has been **improved**, speeding up transport of produce (slow distribution has caused famine in the past).
2) **Losses** during **processing** and **distribution** have been **reduced** using Western technology in packing, refrigerating and canning.
3) **Agricultural research** and **development** have become a **priority**. Research into rice breeding, biological pest control and genetic engineering have been funded with the aim of **improving crop yields**.

4 Domestic Supplies are Protected

China is cautious, **protecting** its **supplies** by:

1) **Stockpiling surplus grain**. In 2008 China held a reserve supply equivalent to 30 to 40% of its annual consumption (the UN regards 17% as a safe minimum).
2) **Limiting grain imports**. This protects the domestic market for home-grown produce.
3) **Reducing grain exports**. In 2007 a global shortage of grain resulted in soaring prices worldwide. Exports to many countries were stopped to protect domestic supplies.

These Strategies Have Advantages and Disadvantages

Advantages:

1) Modernisation of agriculture is a **long-term investment**.
2) Prioritising self-sufficiency leaves **less chance** of **disruption to food supplies** by external events.

Disadvantages:

1) **Urbanisation** is **reducing** the area of **arable land** so food **self-sufficiency** may **not** be **sustainable** as a policy.
2) The focus on grain **prevents farmers** from **growing high value foods** for export, **increasing rural poverty**.
3) **Reducing grain exports** can **adversely affect food supply** in **countries** that **depend** on **imports**.

Practice Questions

Q1 Why doesn't agricultural production meet demand in Bangladesh?

Q2 What strategies are used in Bangladesh to increase food production?

Q3 How has agriculture been modernised in China?

Exam Questions

Q1 Discuss the sustainability of strategies to manage food supplies in Bangladesh. [10 marks]

Q2 Compare the management of food supply in Bangladesh and China. [15 marks]

Chinese agriculture — just like the good life, but on a slightly larger scale...

These case studies are mega important. Loads of questions ask you to give examples to back up your points and there's tons of specifics here. So pick out some quotable statistics and learn them — then go over them again. And again. And again.

Energy Resources

***This section is for AQA (Energy option)**. What with the palaver over climate change and petrol prices energy is a hot topic these days. So here's a whole section devoted to it, just for you, to help you do stunningly well in your exams.*

There are Different Types of Energy

Energy comes in many different types (e.g. heat, electrical, light, chemical, potential), and although it can't be created or destroyed, it can be **converted** from **one type** to **another**. Energy can be classified as either **primary** or **secondary energy**:

1) **Primary energy** is released from a **direct source**, e.g. heat energy is released from burning coal.
2) When primary energy is **converted into a different form** it becomes **secondary energy**, e.g. when heat energy from burning coal is used to generate electricity.

Primary Energy Resources can be Renewable or Non-renewable

Renewable Resources

1) A **resource** is **renewable** if it can be **replenished** at a **similar rate** to which it's **used**.
2) Renewable resources are also known as **flow resources**. There's a constant energy transfer occurring, which if balanced will be sustainable.
3) **Tidal energy**, **wind energy** and **solar power** are all renewable resources because you can't use them up.

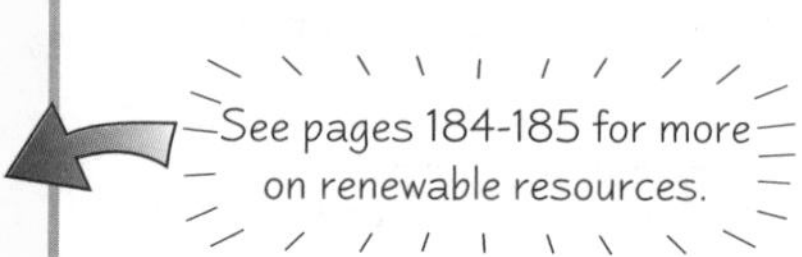
See pages 184-185 for more on renewable resources.

Non-renewable Resources

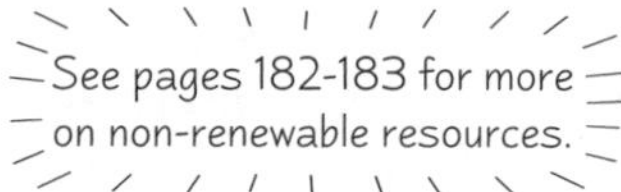
See pages 182-183 for more on non-renewable resources.

1) **Non-renewable resources** can **run out** and **can't be replaced** in the **foreseeable future**.
2) They're also known as **stock resources** as the planet has a limited 'stock', which when used up won't be replaced.
3) **Fossil fuels** (**coal**, **oil** and **natural gas**) and **nuclear energy** are non-renewable resources.

Some Resources are only Renewable if Carefully Managed

Whether a resource is renewable or not depends on **how fast** the resource is being **used compared** to **how fast** it's **replenished**. If the rates are **roughly equal** then it's a **renewable resource**.

1) Some resources are **clearly** renewable and will be available **no matter how much we use**, e.g. solar power.
2) Other resources have to be **carefully managed** if they're to be considered **renewable**. For example:
   - **Wood** — if **too much wood** is used in a **short space of time** the **natural cycle of replenishment** is **disrupted** and the resource is **used up**. If wood is **managed carefully** (using techniques like coppicing and replanting) to ensure that it's **replaced** at roughly the **same rate** that it's **used**, then it can be considered **renewable**.
   - **Geothermal reservoirs** — tectonic heat is used to turn water into steam at geothermal power stations, but if the **power station** is **too large for the site** then continually pumping water into the ground will end up **cooling the ground**. This means the resource is lost, so it's **not renewable**.
3) Some **non-renewable** resources **can be replaced** but **aren't** considered **renewable** because of the **timescale** involved, e.g. fossil fuels. **Fossil fuels** are **hydrocarbons** that have formed under high temperatures and pressures beneath the Earth's crust. This process hasn't stopped (fossil fuels are still being made), it's just that they take many **millions of years to form** and we're **using them** much **faster** than they are being **replaced**. So because they can't be replaced in the **foreseeable future** they're **not** a **renewable** energy source.

Energy Resources

The Primary Energy Mix Describes the Sources of Energy a Country Uses

1) Countries need energy for industry and transport, as well as for use in homes.
2) Many countries **aren't able to supply** all of their **energy needs** from **one source**, or they might not want to for energy security reasons. They use a **variety** of sources instead.
3) The **amount** of **each resource used** is called the **energy mix** and it's usually shown as **percentages**.

Solar and wave energy were the ideal mix to satisfy Sam's energy needs.

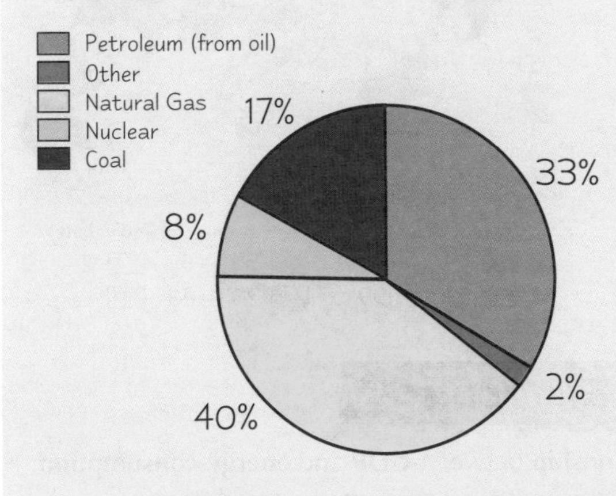

The pie graph on the left shows the **UK's energy mix** in **2008**.

1) **Over 70%** of the UK's energy supply is provided by **oil** and **gas**, which makes sense as the UK has **reserves** of both.
2) Since the early 1970s the UK's **consumption of oil increased** due to the discovery of North Sea oil in 1969 and the growing demand for transport fuel.
3) Use of **natural gas** has **increased** by **85%** since 1990.
4) Despite having **large reserves**, use of **coal** has **fallen** by **40%** since 1990, due to closure of mines and the move to using less polluting oil and gas.
5) Use of **renewable resources** has **increased**, as the government aims to move towards a more sustainable energy supply. It's still below the EU average of 6% though.

The pie graph on the right shows **France's energy mix** in **2004**.

1) France has **limited coal and oil reserves** and most of their supplies have to be **imported**. Coal mining stopped completely in France in 2004 so energy production from coal is low. Energy production from oil remains high though, due to the demand for transport fuel.
2) The proportion of **natural gas** that France uses has **increased** by over 50% since 1990, but is still below the EU average of 24%.
3) As it has limited fossil fuel resources France began investing in **nuclear power** in the 1970s in order to **secure energy supplies**. **41%** of France's energy supply now comes from **nuclear power**. It's the biggest producer of nuclear power in the EU, and the second biggest in the world.
4) Most of France's renewable energy comes from **hydropower** and **biomass**.

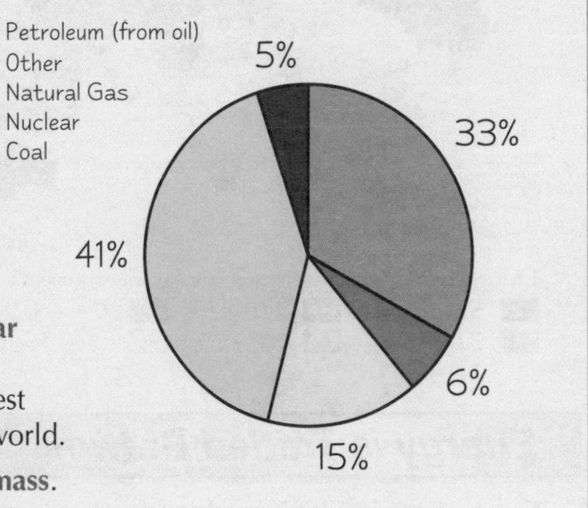

Practice Questions

Q1 What is the difference between primary and secondary energy?

Q2 What is a fossil fuel?

Q3 What is meant by 'primary energy mix'?

Exam Questions

Q1 Explain the difference between renewable and non-renewable resources. [6 marks]

Q2 Describe the energy mix of one named country and explain how it has changed recently. [6 marks]

50% pizza, 30% cake, 20% chocolate — the perfect energy mix...

The important thing to learn here is what the words renewable and non-renewable mean and why the boundary between them is a bit blurry. A good way of testing how well you understand this is to try explaining it to someone else. So once you think you know it well, pick a victim and explain away. This also doubles up as a handy way of getting rid of people you don't like.

Global Energy Distribution

***These pages are for** AQA **(Energy option)**. With 6.6 billion people in the world, supplying everyone with energy isn't simple.*

Global **Energy Production** *is* **Unevenly Distributed**

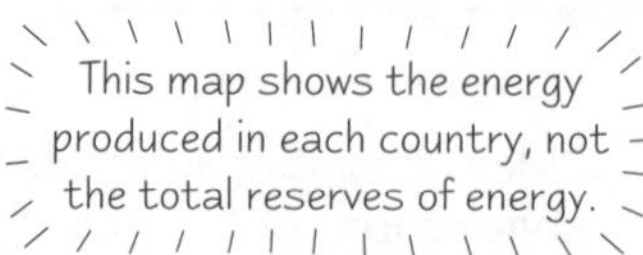

This map shows the energy produced in each country, not the total reserves of energy.

The map on the right shows energy produced from fossil fuels, per country, in 2004.

1) Some countries produce **lots of energy** because they have **large energy reserves** and the **money** to **exploit** them. For example:
   - Iran, Saudi Arabia — large oil reserves.
   - China, Australia — large coal reserves.
   - UK, Russia, Canada — large oil and gas reserves.
   - USA, Indonesia — large coal, oil and gas reserves.
2) Some countries produce **little energy** because they have **few resources** or are **unable** to **exploit** their resources due to lack of **money** or **political instability**.
   - Sudan — politically unstable and lack of money.
   - Ireland — few recoverable resources (resources that can be extracted using current technology).

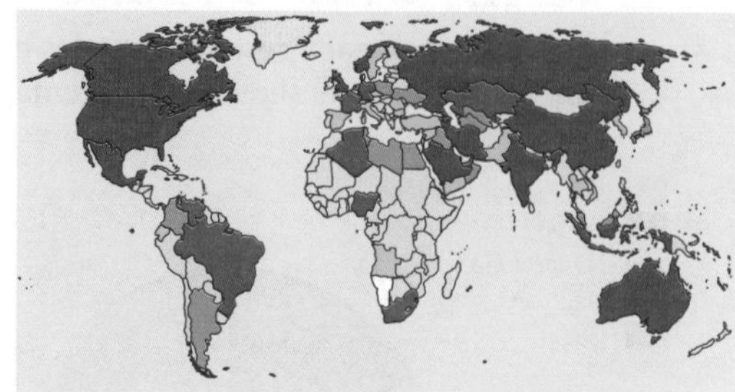

Global **Energy Consumption** *is also* **Unevenly Distributed**

The map below shows the energy consumption per person across the world in 2004.

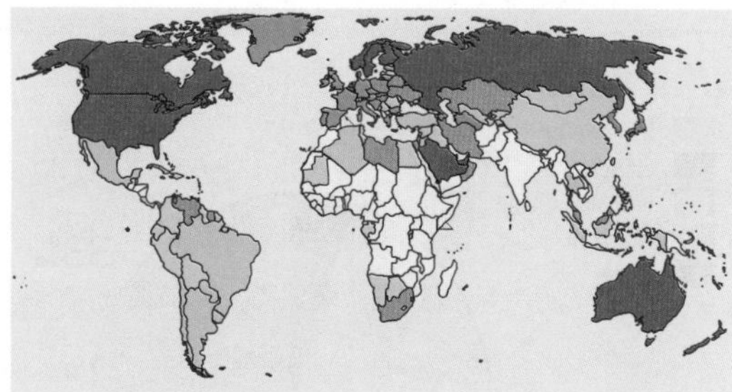

There's a **strong relationship** between **GDP** and **energy consumption**:

1) **Wealthy countries** tend to **consume lots of energy** per person because they're wealthy and **can afford to**. **Most people** in these countries have **access** to **electricity** and **heating**, and use **energy-intensive devices** like cars. E.g. **Australia**, **Sweden**, **USA**.
2) **Poorer countries consume less energy** per person as they are **less able to afford it**. **Less energy** is **available** and lifestyles are less dependent on high energy consumption than in wealthier countries. E.g. **Burkina Faso**, **Pakistan**.

Some countries don't consume much energy per person, but consume a lot overall because they have large populations. E.g. Brazil consumes less energy per person than Ireland, but has a higher total energy consumption.

Energy *is* **Traded Between Countries**

Some countries don't produce much energy but still **consume a lot**, and vice versa. This is possible because **energy** is **traded between countries**.

1) Countries that are able to produce a lot of energy **export** it to those that can't.
2) Canada, Saudi Arabia, United Arab Emirates, Denmark and Venezuela all **export large amounts** of **energy**.
3) Ireland, Italy, Spain and Japan all **import large amounts** of **energy**.

Electricity is traded between neighbouring countries, while coal, oil and natural gas can be transported around the world.

Trans-National Corporations *Play an* **Important Role** *in the* **Energy Industry**

Trans-National corporations (**TNCs**) are **companies** that **operate** in **more than one country**.
Many TNCs play a **major role** in world **energy production** and **distribution**.

E.g. **ExxonMobil** is an **oil** and **gas TNC** based in the USA. It's the largest company in the world (based on revenue) and **operates** in **over 200 countries** worldwide, **producing 3%** of the **world's oil** and **2%** of its **energy**.

1) **Production:** ExxonMobil **explores** for oil and gas on every continent except Antarctica. When found the oil is **extracted** and sent to ExxonMobil **refineries** (e.g. in the USA, Norway, Thailand or the UK) for **processing**.
2) **Distribution: After processing** ExxonMobil uses its **own transportation system** to **transport products** to **distribution centres**, either its own or independent ones, e.g. Acculube, TrAchem Ltd. These then **sell** to **customers** such as CATERPILLAR® and Singapore Airlines, as well as to individuals for transport fuel.

Global Energy Distribution

The Geopolitics of Energy is a Big Issue

Energy security is an **important** issue for **all governments**, for several reasons:

1) **All countries** are **dependent** on **energy supplies**, e.g. for transport, heating, electricity and manufacturing.
2) Global **energy use** is **increasing** and **fossil fuel reserves** are **decreasing**. Many people believe we're coming to an "**energy crisis**", so governments are more concerned than ever about how to **secure future supplies** of energy.
3) To make the situation trickier, the **largest reserves** of **oil** and **gas** are often in areas that are either **politically** or **economically unstable**, e.g. Russia, which means that **energy supplies** are often at risk of being **disrupted**.
4) So in order to **secure supplies**, **agreements** are often reached between **exporting** and **importing regions**. For example, the EU will become increasingly dependent on imports as North Sea oil runs out, so it opened talks with Russia in 2000 to try to guarantee access to Russian gas supplies. In return Russia wanted investment into production of fuel and improved access to EU markets.
5) At times agreements can't be reached and **concerns over energy security** can **lead to conflict** or the **threat of conflict**. E.g. the 1980 Carter Doctrine stated that the USA would use military force if necessary to protect its interests in the Middle East and secure the free movement of oil.
6) As energy consumption increases, so does the **impact** of energy use on the **environment** (see page 182). **International agreements**, e.g. the Kyoto Protocol, are drawn up to try to **address these problems**, but these too can lead to political **conflict** if environmental protection clashes with other national interests, e.g. economic growth.

Patterns of Energy Production, Consumption and Trade Can Change

Changes in Production

1) **Energy production** has **increased** in countries where **new reserves** have been **discovered**, e.g. in **Nigeria** and **Algeria**.
2) There have also been **increases** in places that have become **more politically stable**, e.g. **Angola** (after the end of the civil war).
3) The production of energy has **decreased** in other countries as **resources** are **used up**, e.g. **North Sea oil** production has declined since 1999, reducing production in the **UK**, **Norway**, **Denmark**, **Germany** and the **Netherlands**.
4) **Production** often **decreases** in areas that become **more unstable**, e.g. **Sudan** oil production decreased due to civil war between 1983 and 2005.

Changes in Consumption

1) **China** has the largest population and one of the fastest growing economies in the world. As **standards of living** and **industrial output increase** China **consumes** more and **more energy**.
2) Other **newly industrialised countries**, e.g. **India**, **Malaysia** and **Mexico**, are also **using more energy** as they **develop**.

Changes in Trade

As **production** and **consumption** of energy **changes**, so does the **trade of energy**.

1) **Exports** from ex-Soviet central Asian countries like **Kazakhstan** are **increasing**. These countries are attractive as suppliers to the **EU**, **USA** and **China** because the region is **more stable** than the **Middle East** and **isn't controlled by Russia**, **reducing dependence** on these two areas.
2) **Brazil** and **Denmark** were once **heavily dependent** on **imports** but are now both **energy self-sufficient**, due to **development** of **renewable energy** and **discoveries** of **domestic oil reserves**.

Practice Questions

Q1 Why do wealthy countries consume more energy per person than poorer countries?

Q2 What role do TNCs play in the energy industry?

Exam Question

Q1 Explain why global patterns of energy production, consumption and trade change. [15 marks]

Revision — a serious threat to the energy reserves of sixth formers...

So there you have it — the energy supply of an entire planet on one double page. Doesn't seem too bad to me — some places have loads of energy and some don't have enough, so politicians pal up and shunt it about a bit. Don't see what the fuss is about.

Impacts of Energy Production

***These pages are for AQA (Energy option)**. Imagine you're running a country — you've got yourself a nice secure supply of energy, you're feeling pretty smug. Only thing to worry about now is the impact of the energy on your shiny new country.*

Fuel Wood Gathering can Damage the Environment...

Although **fossil fuels** supply **87%** of the **world's energy**, a significant proportion of the world's population use **wood** as an **energy source**, usually to provide energy within the home. Wood that's burnt for fuel is called **fuel wood**.
The **gathering** of **fuel wood** can **damage the environment** in several ways:

1) **Deforestation** — most fuel wood gathering isn't regulated and can seriously deplete local woodland.
2) **Habitat loss** — deforestation can damage or destroy the habitats of a wide range of wildlife.
3) **Soil erosion** — tree roots bind soil together. If the trees are removed the soil isn't held together as well and can be washed away by rain or blown away by winds.

Example

The **Copperbelt** in **Zambia** is a densely populated industrial area that relies heavily on fuel wood. Between **1972** and **2000** an average of **3125 hectares** of woodland were **cleared** each year for **fuel wood**. Heavy **tropical rains** from November to April resulted in dramatic **erosion of topsoil** as there were fewer trees to hold the soil together. This left much of the land **barren** and **unsuitable for agriculture**, as well as **preventing** the **re-growth** of **woodlands**.

...and so can Using Fossil Fuels

The **extraction** of fossil fuels, e.g. by mining, can damage the environment.
Transportation can also cause environmental damage, e.g. through **oil spills**.
The **use** of fossil fuels has **negative impacts** on the **environment** as well, such as **acid rain** and **global warming**.

1 Acid Rain

Burning fossil fuels releases various **gases**. Some of these **dissolve** in **water vapour** in the atmosphere, which then falls as **acid rain**. Acid rain can:

1) **Kill fish** and other **aquatic life**, which can lead to **reduced biodiversity**.
2) **Kill trees** and other **plant life**, which also **reduces biodiversity**.
3) **Reduce** the **nutrient content** of **soil** so that some species of plants can't grow, or grow more slowly.
4) **Corrode rocks**, e.g. limestone, sandstone.

2 Global Warming

The largest environmental problem created by the use of fossil fuels is **global warming**. **Burning fossil fuels releases** the greenhouse gas **carbon dioxide** into the air. This **enhances** the planet's natural greenhouse effect, **increasing world temperatures** and causing **climate change**. This could lead to:

1) **Rising sea levels** and **increased flooding**.
2) **More frequent** and **severe extreme weather events**, e.g. hurricanes, droughts.
3) **Habitat loss** (which leads to **loss of biodiversity** and the **extinction** of species).

3 Problems Associated with Mining

Coal mining involves disturbing or removing large areas of land, which can lead to:

1) **Wildlife** being **displaced**.
2) **Habitat Loss**.
3) **Reduced air quality** as dust and other particulates are released.
4) **Contamination** of **surface water** with acidic or toxic substances.

The impact of each of these varies depending on the location of the area affected and the severity of the problem.

4 Oil Spills

Oil spills happen when **pipes**, **oil wells** or **tankers** transporting oil **leak**, dumping oil onto land or into seas or oceans. The effects of oil spills last for a long time and lead to the **death of wildlife**. There are many reasons for this:

1) **Oil reduces** the **ability** of animals to **move freely**, which makes it more difficult for them to swim, fly or forage.
2) **Hypothermia**. When **feathers** and **fur** become **coated in oil** it reduces the animal's ability to control its body temperature.
3) **Consumption of oil**.

Impacts of Energy Production

Fossil Fuel Resources Won't Last For Ever

It's **hard to know how long fossil fuel reserves will last**. This is because **new reserves** might be found, or we might find **more efficient ways to use them**. This would **increase** the length of **time** we can **depend on them**.

A 2006 estimation of **proven** reserves suggested that, worldwide, there were:

- 1000 billion barrels of oil left (enough to last 40 years).
- 150 trillion cubic metres of natural gas left (enough to last 60 years).
- 1000 billion tonnes of coal left (enough to last 250 years).

They might label him a pessimist now, but Rob knew he'd have the last laugh.

Eventually **fossil fuels will run out** (or become too difficult to extract) so an **alternative energy source** needs to be found.

Nuclear Power could be an Alternative to Fossil Fuels

In **nuclear power stations heat energy** released from **uranium** or **plutonium** is used to **generate electricity**.
The first commercial nuclear reactor opened in 1956 and there are now 439 reactors in 31 countries around the world.
They supply 15% of the world's electricity, which is 6.3% of the total energy consumption.
There are **advantages** and **disadvantages** of using nuclear power:

Advantages of nuclear power

1) It has **low carbon dioxide emissions**, so contributes little to global warming.
2) **Less toxic waste** is released into the environment than from fossil fuel plants. (Fossil fuel plants release ash containing heavy metals such as mercury, cadmium and lead).
3) **Large amounts of energy** are generated from **small amounts** of **fuel**.
4) **Electricity** produced by nuclear power is **cheap**.

Example

In **France 78%** of **electricity** is produced from **nuclear power**. France has the **cleanest air** of any industrialised country and the **cheapest electricity** in Europe.

Disadvantages of nuclear power

1) **Nuclear waste** is **highly radioactive** and has to be **stored carefully** for **thousands of years**. This is very **expensive**. Some people argue that as technology improves this problem will be solved, but there's no guarantee of this.
2) **Accidents** causing **radioactive waste** to **leak** into the **environment** can have devastating consequences, e.g. **human**, **animal** and **plant deaths** and **illnesses**, **destruction** of the local **environment** and **contamination** of **large areas of land**. The damage lasts for a **long time**. The **explosion** of nuclear power **plants** causes similar problems.
3) There's only **limited amounts** of **uranium** and **plutonium** so it's a **non-renewable** resource.
4) **Decommissioning** power stations at the end of their life is **very expensive**.

Example

The 1986 explosion at the **Chernobyl** nuclear power plant in the Ukraine directly caused **56 deaths** and radiation released caused **thousands of deaths** and **illnesses**. **Radioactive material** from the disaster was detected as far away as **Ireland**, a **4 km² area of forest** around Chernobyl **died**, **food supplies** (particularly of fish) were affected in **Scandinavia** for several years after the accident and the Chernobyl area is **still heavily contaminated** today.

Practice Questions

Q1 What is meant by the term fuel wood?

Q2 What environmental problems are associated with coal mining?

Q3 Why is nuclear power a non-renewable source of energy?

Exam Question

Q1 Discuss the advantages and disadvantages of using nuclear power as a replacement for fossil fuels. [10 marks]

Fossil fuels are dwindling — they'll be going, going and then gone

So it's either fossil fuels that damage the environment and will run out soon, or nuclear power, which can also damage the environment and will run out. Guess we'll just have to go back to no electricity and wood fires... No, wait, that damages the environment too. But don't despair. It may seem doomy and gloomy on this page, but there could be a solution. Read on...

Sustainable Energy

These pages are for AQA (Energy option). *Sustainable energy is so important there are four whole pages of it coming your way...*

Sustainable Energy Sources are Always Renewable

For **energy production** to be **sustainable** it **musn't deplete resources** or cause any **long term environmental damage**. Energy production using **non-renewable resources isn't sustainable** as it's environmentally damaging and the resource will one day run out. Energy produced from **renewable resources** is **sustainable** as it doesn't usually cause long term environmental damage and the resource won't run out. There are many different types of renewable energy resources:

1. *Wind Energy is Harnessed by Wind Turbines*

Wind energy is responsible for **1%** of the world's electricity production. **Carbon dioxide** is released during the **production** and **installation** of wind turbines but once that's done **no greenhouse gases** are released and **no fuel** is needed.

1) **Wind turbines** are built in **open exposed areas** where there's a high chance of **strong** and **regular winds**.
2) The energy of the wind turns the blades of the turbine, **converting wind energy** to **mechanical energy**, which is then converted to **electrical energy** by a **generator**.
3) **Large-scale wind power** involves **wind farms** that may have thousands of turbines. The electricity generated is fed into an **electrical grid** that **transports electricity** to consumers. Wind farms can be **offshore** (out at sea) or **onshore** (on land).
4) **Small-scale wind power** involves small turbines that might be connected to a grid but often just **supply one building**.

EXAMPLE

Denmark has been investing in wind power since the 1970s, establishing **wind farms** onshore and offshore. Families are offered **tax exemptions** for generating their **own electricity**, either by investing in community turbines or by buying their own. By 2004 over 150 000 households had joined this scheme. Denmark now produces **19.7%** of its **electricity from wind power**, the highest proportion in the world.

Disadvantages of wind energy:

1) Wind energy is **unpredictable**. The amount of electricity generated varies with wind strength.
2) **Large numbers of turbines** are needed to produce significant amounts of electricity, which takes up **lots of space**.
3) The **most appropriate places for turbines** are often **protected areas** of natural beauty.
4) Wind farms produce a constant humming **noise**, which some people living nearby don't like.
5) Turbines can **kill** or **injure birds** and **bats**.

2. *Biomass is Material That's Burnt for Power or Used to Produce Biofuel*

1) **Biomass** is material that **is** or was **recently living**.
2) It includes **wood**, **plants** and **animal waste**.
3) These materials can be **burnt** to release energy.
4) Biomass can also be **processed** to produce **biofuels**, which are then **burnt** to release energy.
5) A common way of producing biofuel is to **ferment sugar cane** to produce **alcohol**, which can then be burnt. **Methane** and **biogas** are also types of **biofuel** produced using fermentation.
6) Using biomass as an energy source can involve a lot of technology (if biofuels are being made), or very little (if biomass is being burnt directly). This means that biomass is a **suitable energy source** for a **wide range of countries**.
7) Biomass energy is released by **burning**, which produces **carbon dioxide**. Biomass **doesn't contribute to global warming** though, as the amount of **carbon released equals** the amount of **carbon taken in** when the material was growing. This means there's **no overall increase** in the amount of **carbon dioxide** in the **atmosphere** from the burning of biomass.

EXAMPLE

Brazil has been running an **ethanol fuel programme** since the 1970s. The ethanol is made by fermenting sugar cane, and any leftover cane is burnt for heating and power. Ethanol supplies **18%** of **transport fuel** and cars either run on **ethanol** or a **petrol and ethanol mix**. This has **decreased** Brazil's **dependence on imported oil**.

Disadvantages of biomass:

1) **Large areas of land** are needed to produce sufficient amounts of biofuels. This **reduces** the **area of land** available to grow **food crops**, which could lead to **food shortages**.
2) Biomass is only a renewable energy resource if it's **carefully managed** (see page 178).
3) **Fossil fuels** are often used to **process** and **transport** biomass.

Sustainable Energy

3. Solar Power Depends on Energy from the Sun

1) **Solar power** comes from the **sun** and can be used in lots of different ways.
2) **Solar water heaters** use **solar energy** to **heat water**, which is then pumped to a storage tank ready for use.
3) **Solar cookers** work by **concentrating sunlight**, converting it to **heat energy** and then trapping it for use in cooking.
4) **Photovoltaic (PV) cells** convert **light energy** into **electrical energy**, which is used in the home or exported to a grid.
5) **Materials** that **absorb** the **sun's heat** during the day and release it at night can be used to **keep houses warm**.

EXAMPLE

In the Chinese city **Rizhao**, **99%** of buildings have **solar water heaters** (it's now compulsory for new builds), over **6000 households** use **solar cookers** and most **traffic** and **street lights** are powered by **PV cells**.

Disadvantages of solar power:

1) **Carbon dioxide** is released in equipment production.
2) PV cells are **expensive**.
3) **Large areas** of solar panels and **sunny climates** are needed to produce **large amounts** of **electricity**.

4. Tidal Energy is a Reliable Source of Energy

1) **Tidal energy** comes from the movement of tides. It's **less variable** than wind or solar energy as tides are regular, unchangeable events. Tidal energy can be harnessed using **tidal barrages** or **tidal stream systems**.
2) **Tidal barrages** (dams) are built across **estuaries**. As the tide flows in and out water passes through gates in the barrage, turning **turbines** that **generate electricity**. Some turbines are only turned by outgoing tides, some by incoming as well.
3) **Tidal streams** are fast-flowing currents caused by the tide. They turn **turbines** placed in their pathway to **generate electricity**.

EXAMPLE

The **Rance estuary** tidal barrage in Northern **France** began operating in **1967**. It's the **largest** tidal power station in the world, producing enough **electricity** for over **19 000 homes**.

Disadvantages of tidal energy:

1) The equipment is **expensive** and making it releases **carbon dioxide**.
2) Barrages **disrupt ecosystems**, and **turbines** can **kill aquatic animals**.

5. Wave Energy is Created by Wind Blowing over Water

1) **Wave energy** is harnessed by using a **wave generator** — a chamber with a hole at the top that contains a **turbine**.
2) When a wave flows into the bottom of the chamber, the increased mass of water forces **air** in the chamber upwards and through the hole, which **turns the turbine**.
3) The turbine is connected to a **generator** that **produces electricity**.

EXAMPLE

In 2000 **LIMPET** in Scotland became the world's first device that used **wave energy** on a **commercial scale**. It **generates electricity** for the **national grid**.

Disadvantages of wave energy:

1) Wave energy is **unreliable**, as there aren't always waves.
2) The generators are **expensive** and making them releases **carbon dioxide** into the atmosphere.

6. Hydroelectric Power Uses the Energy of Falling Water

Hydroelectric power (**HEP**) supplies about **20%** of the world's electricity and is responsible for over 60% of all electricity from renewable sources. Once plants are built they **release no greenhouse gases**.

1) At HEP plants **dams** are built to **trap** large volumes of **water**. Tunnels containing **turbines** are built into the dams.
2) The **pressure of the water** above drives water through the tunnels, **turning the turbines**.
3) **Generators** then convert this energy into **electricity**.

EXAMPLE

The **Nurek Dam** in **Tajikistan** is the tallest dam in the world and has **nine hydroelectric turbines** in it. In 1994 it supplied **98%** of the country's **electricity**.

Disadvantages of HEP:

1) Creating reservoirs can mean **destruction** of **communities** and **habitats**.
2) If the **dam fails** then large areas of land are likely to be **flooded** rapidly.
3) **Ecosystems** and **fish migratory paths** are **disrupted**.
4) The plants are **expensive** and making them releases **carbon dioxide**.

Sustainable Energy

Keep going...

Appropriate Technology is Technology That's Suitable for the Area

1) **Appropriate technologies** are **simple**, **low-cost** technologies.
2) They're **made** and **maintained** using **local knowledge** and **resources** only, so aren't dependent on any outside support, expensive equipment or fuel.

Appropriate Technology can Contribute to Sustainable Development

1) Using appropriate technologies to produce energy **isn't always sustainable**, e.g. they could be dependent on local sources of non-renewable energy.
2) Some **appropriate technologies** do produce energy from **renewable sources** though, so it's **sustainable**. Producing energy in a sustainable way contributes to **sustainable development** — growth in a way that doesn't stop future generations getting what they need (i.e. by not depleting resources or permanently damaging the environment).

Example

In mountainous regions of developing countries **clay stoves** have been introduced as an **appropriate technology** that makes **energy use** for **cooking and heating more sustainable**.

1) In **high altitude** areas of **developing countries** many indigenous people rely on **burning biomass** on **open fires** as their main **energy source**.
2) Fuel is usually **straw**, **crop roots** and **pasture grass**. One family can burn up to 6000 kg a year.
3) At high altitudes the temperature is lower and **plants grow more slowly**, which often means **crops** are **removed faster than they can be replenished**.
4) As energy supplies are depleted there are fewer plant roots in the soil to support it. This causes **soil erosion** and a **decrease** in soil **productivity**.
5) **Burning biomass in this way** is therefore **unsustainable**.

Clay stoves are **more efficient** than open fires and can lead to a **75% reduction in fuel consumption**. This means fuel is **harvested more slowly**, allowing the **crops** to **replenish** themselves. This leads to decreased soil erosion and increased soil productivity. Using a stove rather than an open fire also has **health benefits**, as the smoke from open fires can cause eye and lung diseases.

Clay stoves are an **appropriate technology** as they can be made by **local** craftsmen from metal and clay, providing a source of income for local people. They **reduce** the quantity of **biomass burnt** and therefore help to maintain the **natural cycle of replenishment**. This makes the resource **renewable** (see page 178) and therefore **sustainable**. So, they contribute to sustainable development.

Energy Conservation is Important for Sustainable Supply

Energy supply can be made **more sustainable** by **conserving** as much **energy** as possible. By **reducing overall use of energy** fewer resources are used up and the **environmental effects** of energy use are **limited**, e.g. emission of greenhouse gases. **Homes**, **workplaces** and **transport** can all be **designed** to **conserve energy**:

Buildings can be made more sustainable...

Energy can be **conserved** in **homes** and **workplaces** in several ways:

1) **Reducing** the amount of energy needed for **heating** by installing **double glazing**, **draught-proofing**, **loft insulation** and **cavity wall insulation** to **reduce heat loss**.
2) **Installing energy-efficient boilers**. They're more efficient because a greater proportion of the heat energy they generate is used to heat the water in the boiler and **less energy** is **lost** to the surroundings.
3) Using computers, printers and faxes that **turn themselves off** after a period of time instead of staying on (stand-by mode can consume nearly as much energy as being turned on permanently).
4) Building in **features** that help **absorb** and **retain** the **sun's energy** (e.g. **large south-facing windows**) to provide **heat** as well as **light**.

Iain understood the importance of insulation but this was a step too far. He looked like a fool and he knew it.

Sustainable Energy

5) Using **energy-saving appliances** wherever possible, e.g. **energy-saving light bulbs**.

Example

The **City of Calgary Water Centre** in Canada was designed to conserve energy. Lots of **south-facing windows** let natural light reach all areas, which **reduces the need** for **electric lighting**. The electric lights only come on when they're needed as they're controlled by **light** and **motion sensors**. The **windows** and the **shape** of the building help to **warm the building** in winter, **reducing the need** for **heating**. An **overhanging roof** keeps the heat out in summer so **less energy** is **needed** for **air-conditioning**. A **radiant ceiling slab cooling system** has been built in to **reduce the need for air-conditioning** further. This system draws cold night air through pipes set into concrete, cooling it down. The cooled concrete helps to keep the building cold throughout the next day. These methods have **reduced** annual **energy consumption** by **58%**.

...and so can *Transport*

Energy can be conserved in **transport** by:

1) Changing to **vehicles that don't need any fuel**, e.g. **bicycles**. Employers receive tax exemptions for loaning or selling bicycles to employees as part of the **Cycle to Work** scheme. This encourages people to switch cars for more sustainable bicycles.
2) Establishing out-of-town **park-and-ride schemes** and **investing in public transport**. This **reduces fuel consumption** by reducing the number of vehicles on the road.
3) Introducing **congestion charges**. This **encourages public transport use** and is used in London, Singapore, Rome and Stockholm.

Example

The **London congestion charge** was **introduced in 2003**. It charges drivers for entering a central zone of the city during normal working hours. It aims to reduce congestion and raise money for public transport improvements. Since the scheme started the **number of vehicles** within the zone has **decreased** by **21%** (70 000 fewer cars each day) and **carbon dioxide emissions** have **decreased** by **20%**. In 2007/2008 **£137 million** was raised, which was **invested in public transport**. **Bicycle use** has **increased** by **12%** since 2003, and use of **public buses** has **increased** by **6%**. There's been an **increase in congestion** in the area **surrounding the central zone** though and some small businesses within the zone (e.g. shops and restaurants) claim that the charge has **reduced trade**.

Transport can also be made more sustainable by using **technologies** that run off **sustainable energy sources**:

- **Hydrogen fuel cell buses** run on electricity produced from **hydrogen**. The hydrogen that fuels the bus is **made from water**. The process **uses electricity**. So, for hydrogen fuel cells to be sustainable this initial electricity must be produced from **renewable resources**.
- **Electric buses**, e.g. the **Islay Wave Bus** runs off **wave power generated electricity** from LIMPET (see page 185).
- Using **hybrid fuel vehicles** (vehicles that run off a mixture of two fuels). If one fuel is from a **renewable** source then the vehicle is **more sustainable**, e.g. use of **ethanol-petrol hybrid fuel cars** in Brazil (see page 184).

Practice Questions

Q1 How is wind energy harnessed?

Q2 Give three examples of biomass.

Q3 What are the disadvantages of solar power?

Q4 What does HEP stand for?

Q5 What are appropriate technologies?

Exam Questions

Q1 Explain what biomass is and how it's used as an energy source. [4 marks]

Q2 Compare wave energy and tidal energy. [6 marks]

Q3 Explain how energy use in the home can be made more sustainable. [8 marks]

Q4 Describe and explain how transport can be made more sustainable. [10 marks]

Brain chargers and memory plugs — now they're appropriate technologies...

Well done — you made it. I know there's loads to learn here and I'm guessing you're not too happy about it, but I've not put it in for the good of my health (you do need to know all about sustainable energy for the exam). Don't forget to learn the examples as well — the examiners will expect you to be able to spew some up for any questions they ask on this topic. They're evil like that.

Managing Energy — Case Studies

These pages are for AQA (Energy option). *So, you know the different sources and impacts of energy, you're crammed full of interesting facts and impressive knowledge. You just need to make a tiny bit of space in that grey blob for these case studies...*

Chad has **Very Low Energy Consumption** per Person

Chad is a **developing country** in **North Africa**. It's very **unstable politically** and is one of the **poorest** and **most corrupt countries** in the world. Despite having **large reserves of oil**, annual **energy consumption** is very **low** at only **0.005 tonnes of oil equivalent** per person (average consumption in the EU is 3.8 tonnes). **80%** of the **population** live **below** the **poverty line**.

Chad's Main **Energy Resources** are **Oil** and **Biomass**

Chad is an **oil exporter**...

1) Chad has **large reserves of oil**.
2) **TNCs** like ExxonMobil, Chevron and Petronas began **exploiting the oil** in **2003**.
3) It's **exported** via a **pipeline through Cameroon** to the Atlantic coast. The pipeline was **part funded** by the **World Bank** on the condition that **80% of the revenue** from the oil was **spent on projects to reduce poverty**.
4) The Chadian government **didn't keep to this agreement**.
5) So although oil is an **important source of income** for Chad and **could** help **improve economic** and **social conditions** for Chadians, the **corruption** and **political instability** in the country at the moment mean that **it doesn't**.

...and also an **oil importer**

1) Chad **can't use its own oil** because it doesn't have any way of **refining** it.
2) Instead, it has to **rely on imports** of refined oil from **Cameroon** and **Nigeria** to supply its only major power station.
3) The cost of doing this means that the **electricity** generated is **very expensive**, and most Chadians **can't afford it** (only 2% of the population have access to electricity).
4) Also, **delivery problems** caused by the **poor transport system** can lead to **shortages**.
5) So importing oil is **expensive**, **unreliable** and **doesn't support** the **energy needs** of most of the population.

Most Energy is supplied by **Biomass**

90% of Chad's **total energy** and **98%** of **household energy** is supplied by **wood**. There's no control over wood production or use, so it's **overexploited**. In 1998 the **World Bank** and the **Chadian government jointly funded** the **Household Energy Project** to address this problem by:

1) Using **non-governmental organisations** (NGOs) to **educate** local people about the **need for conservation**.
2) Setting up **village resource management schemes** that **limit** the amount of **wood cut down**. This can involve **charging** people for **collecting wood**.
3) **Giving villages ownership** of the local **resources**. This allows them to **make money** from wood, so makes it a **more valuable resource** to them and **worth conserving**.
4) **Improving energy use in homes** by introducing **more efficient cooking stoves** that use less fuel than open fires (see page 186).

The Household Energy Project **only operates on a small scale** at the moment though (about 100 villages near the capital city).

1) At the moment Chad's **energy supply isn't sustainable**.
2) Chad's oil policy doesn't help it meet its energy needs, and as oil is **non-renewable** it's **unsustainable** anyway.
3) Most energy is provided by **biomass**, which has the **potential to be sustainable** if it's **managed properly**.
4) The **Household Energy Project** could help to make the supply of biomass sustainable but **needs to be implemented more widely**, which takes time and money.
5) There is the potential to do this using money from exporting oil, but political corruption and instability could be a barrier to this.

Practice Questions

Q1 What are Chad's main energy resources?

Q2 Why does Chad have to import oil?

Exam Question

Q1 Discuss the potential for Chad's energy supply to become sustainable. [15 marks]

Managing Energy — Case Studies

Norway has **High Energy Consumption** per Person

Norway is a **wealthy**, **developed country** in **Northern Europe**. **Energy consumption** is **high** in Norway, at **6.2 tonnes of oil equivalent** per person, and **electricity consumption** per person is the **highest in the world**. It has **large reserves of oil** and **gas** (located under the North Sea) and utilises its **high potential for hydroelectricity**, with **99%** of **electricity** being generated from hydroelectric plants. Overall, **39%** of its **energy** comes from **fossil fuels** and **61%** from **renewables**.

Norway's Main **Energy Resources** are **Oil**, **Gas** and **Hydroelectricity**

Norway is an **oil** and **gas exporter**

1) Norway is the **5th largest exporter of oil** and the **3rd largest exporter of gas** in the world.
2) These **fossil fuels** are an **important source of income** for the country, with oil alone providing about **25%** of **GDP**.
3) Despite being oil-rich, Norwegian **fuel prices** are among the **highest in Europe** due to **high taxation**. This fits in with Norway's energy policy of increasing the proportion of their energy supply that comes from renewable sources by **discouraging** the **use of oil**.
4) Almost **all** of Norway's **gas** supplies are **exported** as it's not used much domestically.
5) So, like Chad, Norway **exports most of its fossil fuel** resources, but for different reasons. Chad needs the income from exports and can't exploit the resources itself, whereas Norway **chooses to use other sources of energy** and actively discourages the use of oil.

Most electricity is supplied by **hydropower**

1) With **natural lakes** at **high altitudes** and **lots of rain** Norway is able to generate **99%** of its **electricity** and **50%** of its **total energy** from **HEP**.
2) This makes it the **6th largest producer** of hydropower in the world and the **largest in Europe**.
3) As many lakes are natural the plants have **less impact on the environment** than **artificially created** reservoirs.
4) Whilst Chad's main source of energy (biomass) has the potential to be renewable if it's managed carefully, **Norway's main source** (hydropower) **is renewable** by nature, and is therefore **sustainable**.

Norway is **investing** in **renewable energy**

1) One of Norway's energy aims is to **reduce** its **dependency** on **hydroelectric power** by using a **wider range** of **renewable resources**.
2) This is needed to cope with any future rise in energy consumption, as **almost all potential HEP sites** have been **exploited**.
3) **€2.5 billion** was invested in **developing renewable energy** and **energy efficiency** in **2006**. One of the main projects is to **triple wind power capacity**.
4) Research into **solar power** aims to **increase the percentage** of the **Sun's energy** that can be converted **into electricity** from 17% to 50%.
5) The state also provides **funding** for companies to **research and develop biofuels** to use for transport instead of oil, e.g. producing biodiesel from salmon waste.
6) As a **wealthy nation** (unlike Chad), Norway is able to **invest in research** in order to develop a **sustainable energy supply**.

1) Norway is **energy-rich** so doesn't have to worry about **energy security** in the short term.
2) It can concentrate on developing a **long-term sustainable energy supply**.
3) **Some aspects are already sustainable**, e.g. using hydropower for electricity generation, but **others aren't**, e.g. relying on oil for transport.
4) Policies such as **investing in energy efficiency** and **renewables**, and putting **high taxes on oil**, **promote sustainability**.
5) The **political stability** and **wealth** of the country allow it to pursue **energy sustainability**.

Practice Questions

Q1 What are Norway's main energy resources?

Q2 Why is Norway particularly suited to using hydroelectric power?

Exam Question

Q1 Describe how Norway's energy supply is becoming more sustainable. [15 marks]

My energy resources are running a bit low after all that...

So that's energy done. Learn these two pages and you'll be all set for the exam. As long as you can still remember the other pages that is... You might want to look back over them to check... well OK, you might not want to but you should do it anyway.

Global Patterns of Health, Disease and Death

This section is for AQA (Health option).
This section's all about global health issues. Where you live in the world affects your health in many different ways.

Health is Better in Wealthier Countries

1) **Health** is defined as your **physical**, **mental** and **social well-being**, and the **absence of disease**.
2) Health **varies** between different parts of the world.
3) Health is **difficult** to **measure**, which makes it pretty difficult to **compare** the health of people in two places. There are things you **can measure** that **indicate health** though (they're called health indicators... imaginative).
4) An example of a health indicator is **healthy life expectancy** (**HLE**) — this is the **number** of **years** a newborn child can **expect** to **live** in **full health** without major disease. The **global pattern** of HLE is shown on the map below:

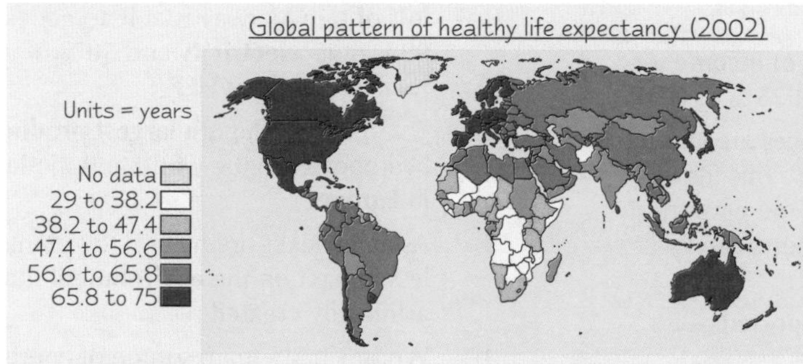

- The map shows **HLE** is **highest** in **wealthier countries** such as the **UK**, **USA** and **Australia**.
- **HLE** is **lowest** in **poorer countries** such as those in **sub-Saharan Africa**.

Sub-Saharan Africa includes all the countries south of the Sahara Desert.

5) How **healthy** a country is **depends** on how much **disease** there is in the country, and what **types** of **diseases** there are.

Global Morbidity Patterns are Different Depending on the Type of Disease

1) **Morbidity** means **illness**.
2) Morbidity **indicators** include:
   - **prevalence** — the **total** number of **cases** in a **population** at a **particular time**.
   - **incidence** — the number of **new cases** in a **population** during a **particular time period**.
3) You can use these indicators to **compare global patterns of illness**.
4) **Global patterns** of morbidity **differ** depending on the **type** of **disease** you're looking at:
   - **Infectious diseases** (e.g. malaria, HIV/AIDS) — these are often **more common** in **poorer countries**.
   - **Non-communicable diseases** (e.g. cancer, heart disease) — these are often **more common** in **wealthier countries**.

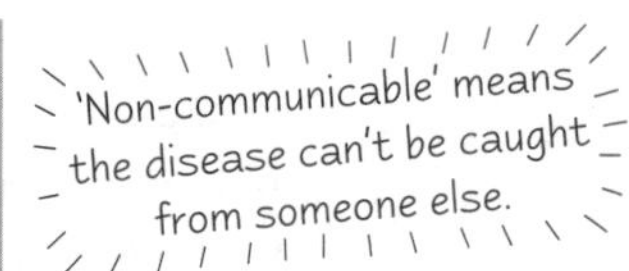

'Non-communicable' means the disease can't be caught from someone else.

1 Morbidity pattern of infectious diseases

- The map shows the **global morbidity pattern** of the **infectious** disease **tuberculosis (TB)**.
- There's **high TB morbidity** in **poorer** countries, e.g. countries in **sub-Saharan Africa**.
- There's **low TB morbidity** in **wealthier** countries, e.g. the **UK**, **USA** and **Australia**.

Global morbidity pattern of tuberculosis (TB) (2005)

Units = new cases per 100 000 of the population

No data
0 to 24
25 to 49
50 to 99
100 to 299
>300

The **reasons** for **high infectious disease morbidity** in **poorer** countries include:

1) **Malnutrition** (due to **poor food availability** and **periodic famines**) — **reduces** the body's **ability** to **fight** disease.
2) **Lack** of **clean water** and **sanitation** — **increases** the **spread** of **infectious** diseases.
3) **Overcrowded** conditions in **urban** areas — **increases** the **spread** of **infectious** diseases.
4) **Poor access** to **health care** — people **can't** access drugs to **treat** and **prevent** infectious diseases.
5) **Limited health education** — people **aren't well-informed** about how they can **avoid** infectious diseases.
6) **Disease vectors** (organisms that spread disease) — these are often **more common** in poorer countries, e.g. the **mosquitoes** that spread **malaria** are more common in **tropical** regions of **Africa**.

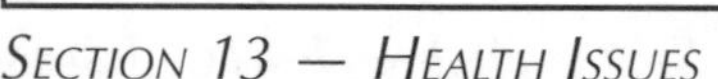

Global Patterns of Health, Disease and Death

2 Morbidity pattern of non-communicable diseases

- The map shows the **global morbidity pattern** of the **non-communicable** disease **breast cancer.**
- There's **high breast cancer morbidity** in **wealthier** countries, e.g. the **UK, USA** and **Australia.**
- There's **low breast cancer morbidity** in **poorer** countries, e.g. countries in **Africa** and **Asia.**

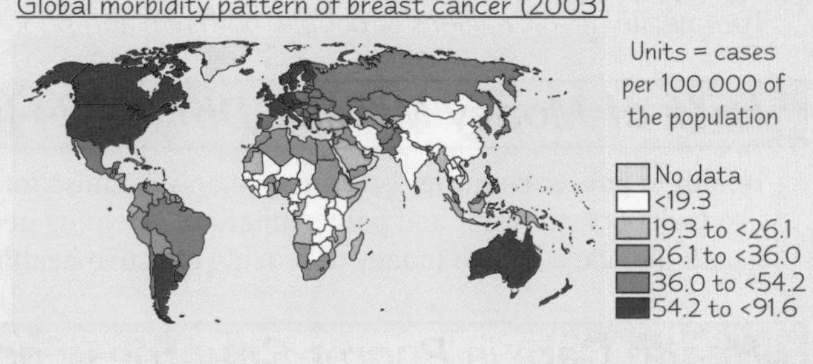

The **reasons** for **high non-communicable disease morbidity** in **wealthier** countries include:

1) **Higher proportion** of **older people** (due to higher life expectancy) — if there are more old people **more** people are **likely** to suffer from **diseases** associated with **old age**, e.g. **cancer** and **heart disease.**
2) **Unhealthy lifestyle** — the **risk** of getting **some diseases** (e.g. cancer, heart disease) **increases** if you're **overweight** or **obese**, eat **unhealthy food** and don't do enough **exercise**. These **factors** are **more common** in **wealthier** countries.

Mortality Patterns Depend on *Morbidity* and the *Ability* to *Treat Morbidity*

1) **Mortality** means **death**. In general, **high morbidity** causes **high mortality**.
2) The **mortality rate** is how many people **die** in a **population** over a **period of time**. You use mortality rates to **compare global patterns of death**.

- The table on the right shows that **wealthier** areas, such as **Northern America** and **Australia**, have a **high mortality** rate for **cancer** (**caused** by a **high incidence** of the disease). But only a **low percentage** of **cases** result in **death.**
- The **mortality rate** from **cancer** is **lower** in **poorer** areas, such as **Middle** and **Eastern Africa** (**caused** by a **low incidence** of the disease), but the **percentage** of cases **resulting in death** is **much higher.**

Global incidence and mortality rates from all forms of cancer (2002)

Area of the world	Incidence rate (cases per 100 000)	Mortality rate (deaths per 100 000)	% of cases resulting in death
Middle Africa	125	105	83
Eastern Africa	152	123	81
Northern Africa	87	70	80
Southern Africa	174	122	70
Central America	144	89	62
Northern America	331	125	38
Northern Europe	252	132	52
Southern Europe	237	122	51
Western Europe	267	131	49
Australia/ New Zealand	299	120	40

The **risk** of **dying** from a disease is **much higher** in **poorer countries** because of:

1) **Malnutrition** — **reduces** the body's **ability** to **fight** disease.
2) **Poor access to health care** — people **can't access** the drugs they need to **treat** the disease.

Health and *Disease* are *World Issues*

1) **Infectious diseases** can **spread** to **other countries** and can even **spread** around the **world** (e.g. **HIV/AIDS** now **affects** people in **all countries**).
2) This means **countries** need to **work together** to help **improve global health** and **prevent diseases spreading**.
3) **Organisations** like the **WHO** (**World Health Organisation**) **work** with **most governments** and in **most countries** to help **eradicate** and **prevent disease**. For example, they run a **programme** of **vaccinations** (**paid** for by **wealthy** countries) to **eradicate polio** (an **infectious disease** mainly found in **poorer countries**).

Practice Questions

Q1 Define health.

Q2 Give an example of how you can measure health.

Q3 What is morbidity?

Exam Question

Q1 Measles is an infectious disease spread by close contact.
Use the map to outline the global pattern of measles morbidity. [10 marks]

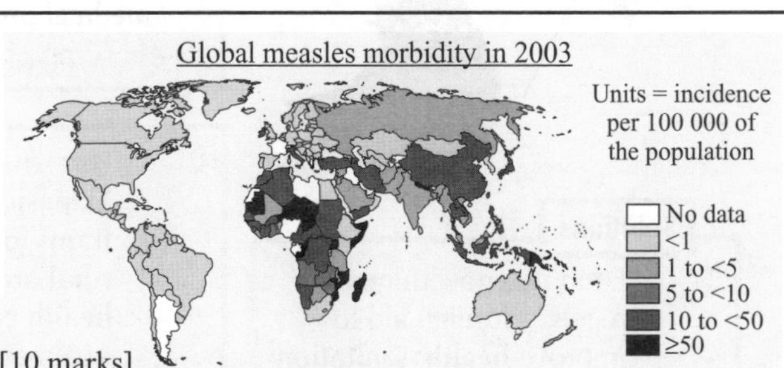

Disease — it's morbid stuff...

This isn't the cheeriest of sections, I know, but that doesn't mean you can get away with not learning it. Sorry. It doesn't help when they make morbidity and mortality such similar words but with different meanings — that's just asking for trouble. So just remember — morbidity means illness and mortality means death. So what are you waiting for, get on and learn it...

Health Care Approaches

These pages are for AQA (Health option).
Poor health affects millions of people, both rich and poor. There are lots of ideas for how to improve health, but no easy fix...

Lack of Money Makes it Difficult to Improve Health in Poorer Countries

Health in **poorer countries** isn't great, mainly because **infectious diseases** are **common** and **spread easily** (because of issues like **lack** of **clean water** and **poor sanitation**). Helping people become healthier isn't easy — the **key barriers** to improving health include a **lack of money** to provide **effective health care** and **difficulties** in getting health care to **remote populations**.

Health Care in Poorer Countries Focuses on Treating Disease

1) In **poorer** countries the **national income** is **low**, so **spending** on **health** tends to be **low** too.
2) A **large proportion** of the **money** that's available for health care is often spent on **treating** large numbers of patients with **diseases**. This leaves **little money** available for **preventative care** (like **vaccinations**) and **health education**.
3) **Preventing disease** is often a **more effective** way to **improve health** than just treating disease.
4) Some poorer countries **rely heavily** on **foreign aid** to help with **health care**, e.g. grants and loans, donated medicines and medical equipment, and volunteer doctors and nurses.
5) **Foreign aid** can help poorer countries **improve health care services** in the short-term, but **longer-term solutions** are needed so countries can become **self-reliant**.

Local Health Care Training Can Improve Health in Remote Populations

1) A **key health care issue** in poorer countries is the **lack** of **medical services** in **remote rural populations**.
2) One solution is to **train local people** in **basic health care** and **employ** them to provide basic health care **services** to their **local communities**. Services include **first aid**, **treating common diseases**, providing **medicines** and **vaccinations**, **pregnancy support** and **midwifery**, and **health education**.
3) There are **advantages** and **disadvantages** to training local basic health care workers:

Advantages

1) It's a relatively **inexpensive** way of **improving health care** and **health education** in **rural** areas.
2) It **creates jobs** for **local** people.
3) It **increases** the **self-reliance** of communities.
4) Local basic health care workers are **unlikely** to **leave** (professionals, e.g. doctors, often migrate to wealthier countries where pay is better).

Disadvantage

Basic health care workers **can't replace** fully trained **medical professionals**. So **long-term solutions** must improve access to **proper medical facilities** and **fully trained staff**.

Case Study: Local Health Care Workers in Ethiopia

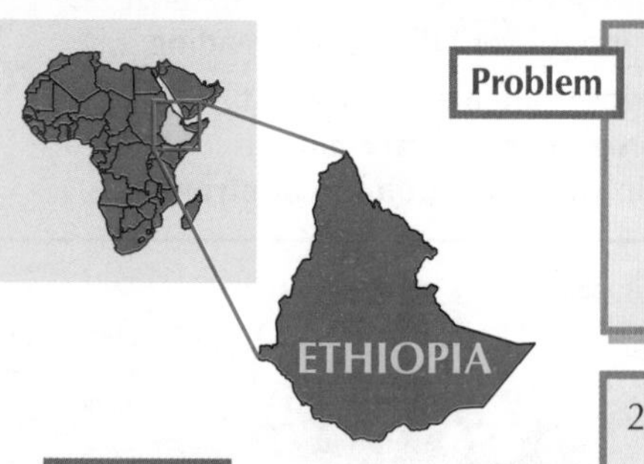

Problem

Ethiopia, in Eastern Africa, is one of the world's **poorest** countries. There's widespread **poor health**, e.g. **life expectancy** is only **52 years** and **infant mortality** is around **8%**. People have **poor nutrition**, **poor sanitation** and **unclean water**. **Infectious diseases** are very common. There's a **shortage** of **medical professionals** and **health facilities**, especially in **remote rural** areas — in some places there are only **three doctors** per **100 000 people**.

Solutions

1) Ethiopia's government receives **foreign aid** to improve **health**, **sanitation** and access to **clean water**. Some of the money's spent on **preventative health care** such as **vaccinations** and **contraceptives**.
2) Foreign aid funds the **Health Extension Programme**, which **trains local health care workers** in **rural** areas. Workers deliver **basic health care** (vaccinations, malaria treatments and maternity care) and **health education** (teaching about family planning, prevention of HIV/AIDS, hygiene and nutrition). But **more** health workers are **still needed** by many communities.
3) **Money** is being used to **prevent disease**. E.g. since 2005, millions of **insecticide-treated bed nets** have been given out — a **cost-effective** way of **preventing** the spread of **malaria** by **mosquitoes**. In **one year**, the number of new **malaria** cases **fell** by **20%**.

Health Care Approaches

Ignoring Advice Makes it Difficult to Improve Health in Wealthier Countries

1) **Health** in **wealthier countries** isn't that good either, partly because of **ageing populations**. This is when there's a **higher proportion** of **older people** in the population — often due to a **high life expectancy** and **low birth rate**.
2) **More people** suffer from **age-related illnesses**, such as cancer and heart disease. This can put a **big strain** on **health services**.
3) **Lifestyle choices** also affect health. Choosing to **eat healthily**, **exercise**, **not smoke** and **reduce alcohol** consumption can **improve** your **health**.
4) The **key barrier** to improving health in **wealthier** countries is people **ignoring advice** on **lifestyle changes** that would **reduce** their chance of **developing disease**.

Stella tried to cut it down to just a few drinks a day...

Health Care in Wealthier Countries Includes Preventing Disease

In **wealthier** countries a great deal of **money** is spent on **preventative health care**, such as:

1) Providing **vaccinations against diseases** (e.g. measles, mumps, meningitis).
2) **Health awareness campaigns** to **promote good lifestyle choices** (e.g. eating healthily and taking regular exercise).
3) **Providing support services** to help people **improve** their **health** (e.g. services to help people stop smoking).
4) **Early diagnosis** (e.g. cancer screening, antenatal screening and screening for heart conditions).

Case Study: Preventing Cervical Cancer in England

Problem

Nearly **3000 women** are diagnosed with **cervical cancer** each year in **England**, which can cause **death** if left **untreated**. **99%** of all **cervical cancers** are **caused** by a virus called **HPV** (human papillomavirus).

Solutions

1) Some forms of cervical cancer are **preventable** by **stopping infection** with **HPV**. An **HPV vaccine** is now offered to **all girls** aged **12-13** in **England**.

2) **Cervical screening** (a **smear test**) is offered to **all women over 25** in **England**. **Unusual cells** (signs of cancer) can be **detected early**, allowing **treatment** to **prevent cancer**. **Death rates** from cervical cancer have **decreased** by nearly **70% since screening** began.

Practice Questions

Q1 What are the main barriers to improving health in poorer countries?

Q2 What are the advantages of training local people in basic health care in rural areas of poorer countries?

Q3 Why does an ageing population contribute to a country's poor health?

Q4 Give four examples of preventative health care that wealthier countries spend money on.

Exam Question

Q1 The graph shows global differences in public health spending per person.

a) Describe the pattern of public health spending shown by the graph. [2 marks]

b) The amount of money available for public health services can affect the health care approach countries use. With reference to one or more schemes, describe the contrasting health care approaches used in wealthy and poor countries. [10 marks]

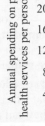

Annual spending on public health services per person (US$)
2000
1600
1200
800
400
0
Central Africa
South-eastern Africa
Northern Africa
Southern Asia
Asia Pacific
Middle East
Eastern Asia
South America
Eastern Europe
North America
Western Europe
Japan

Prevention is the best cure — or so my mum says...

It's not easy to improve the health of populations, in poor or rich countries — you can't just throw money at people. Well, you can, but that'll only help in the short-term. Long-term solutions need to tackle ways of preventing diseases. It's vital that people are educated — this helps people to help themselves. Whether they'll listen or not is another matter...

The Geography of Disease

These pages are for AQA (Health option). *Different diseases affect different countries — but they all have a big impact...*

Diseases *Affect* ***Health, Economic Development*** *and* ***Lifestyle***

The **cost** of a **disease** to any country includes the following:

HEALTH	**Increased poor health** in the population and in some cases **permanent disability** and **death**.
ECONOMIC DEVELOPMENT	**Slow economic development** due to **increasing death rates** (so **fewer taxes** go to the government), **decreasing productivity** (due to **days lost** from **work**) and **increasing health care costs**.
LIFESTYLE	**Increased poverty** (due to **days lost** from **work** and **health care costs**), **impaired learning** (due to **days lost** at **school**) and a **downward spiral** as the poorest families are **trapped in poverty**.

Malaria *is* ***Common*** *in* ***Tropical Regions*** *such as* ***Sub-Saharan Africa***

1) Malaria is an **infectious disease** caused by **parasites**, which are transmitted by **mosquitoes**.
2) Malaria can be **cured** with **anti-malarial drugs**, but **without treatment** it can quickly become **life-threatening**.
3) Malaria can be **prevented** by using **bed nets** and **insecticides** (which kill the mosquitoes that carry the disease).

Distribution of malaria CASES

Most **cases** of **malaria** are found in **tropical** areas, e.g. **sub-Saharan Africa**. In **2006** there were nearly **250 million global cases** of malaria and **86%** occurred in the **poorest** countries in **Africa**. **Reasons** include:

- **Climate** — **mosquitoes** that carry **malaria** can only **survive** in **warm countries** like those in **Africa**.
- **Limited health education** — people **aren't informed** about how to **avoid malaria** (e.g. by using **bed nets**).
- **Poor health care** — people with malaria are **less likely** to be **treated**. This means there are **more infected people** and so **more sources** of the **parasite** for mosquitoes to pick up and transmit.

Distribution of malaria DEATHS

In **2006**, **91%** of **global deaths** from **malaria** were in **sub-Saharan Africa**. **Reasons** include:

- **High number** of **cases**.
- **Poor health care** — **anti-malarial drugs aren't affordable** or **available**, especially to people living in **remote rural populations**.
- **Poor health** and **nutrition** — **reduces** the body's **ability** to **fight infections**.

HIV/AIDS *is* ***Very Common*** *Across* ***Africa*** *but* ***Quite Common Elsewhere***

1) **HIV** (Human Immunodeficiency Virus) is a virus that **destroys** the **immune system**. It eventually causes **AIDS** (Acquired Immunodeficiency Syndrome), which causes **death**.
2) HIV is transmitted by **sexual contact**, **sharing needles**, **blood transfusions** and **contaminated medical equipment**.
3) There's **no cure** for AIDS but you can **slow** the **development** of **HIV to AIDS** by using **antiviral drugs**. HIV can be **prevented** by practising **safe sex**, **screening blood donors** and by using **sterile medical equipment**.

Distribution of HIV/AIDS CASES

66% of the **population** (and **90%** of **children**) **living with HIV/AIDS** are in **sub-Saharan Africa**. **Reasons** include:

- **Society** — people are more **reluctant** to get **tested** for **HIV/AIDS**.
- **Gender inequality** — in some African countries men are **socially dominant**, which makes **women** less likely to insist on **condom** use, and so they're **more vulnerable** to **HIV/AIDS**.
- **Limited health** and **sex education** — people **aren't aware** of what HIV is and **aren't informed** of how they can **avoid it** (e.g. by using **condoms** and **sterile medical equipment**).
- **Limited health care** — people with HIV/AIDS are **less likely** to be **diagnosed**, so they're more likely to **pass on** the disease.

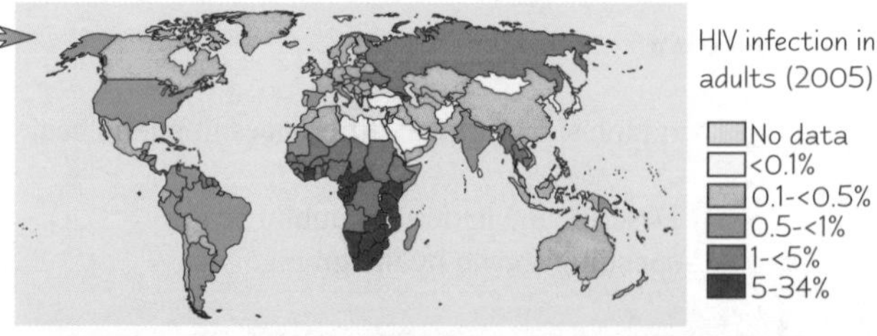

Distribution of HIV/AIDS DEATHS

Over **70%** of **global deaths** from **HIV/AIDS** occur in **sub-Saharan Africa**. **Reasons** include:

- **High number** of **cases**.
- **Poor health care** — **antiviral drugs** that prolong life **aren't affordable** or **available**.
- **Poor health**, **nutrition** and **hygiene** — **increase** the **risk** of other **infections** that can be **fatal** because HIV **destroys** the **immune system**.

The Geography of Disease

Coronary Heart Disease is Becoming More Common in Poorer Countries

1) **Coronary heart disease** (**CHD**) is a disease where the heart doesn't get enough blood. It can lead to a **heart attack**.
2) **CHD** has **no cure** but it can be **controlled** with **treatment** (e.g. **aspirin**, or **surgery** such as a heart bypass operation). **Early diagnosis** and access to **health care** can **increase life expectancy**.
3) The **risk** of developing CHD can be **reduced** by **lifestyle changes** such as **eating healthily**, **exercising** and **not smoking**.

Distribution of CHD CASES

CHD is a **non-communicable disease** — it's **more common** in **wealthier** countries, e.g. the **UK** and the **USA**. **Reasons** include:

- **Ageing populations** — your **risk** of developing CHD **increases** as you get **older**.
- **Lifestyle factors** — an **unhealthy lifestyle** and being **obese** or **overweight increases** your **risk** of developing CHD.

Cases of CHD are **increasing** in **poor** and **newly-industrialised countries** though (e.g. countries in **sub-Saharan Africa** and **India**), as their **wealth increases**. **Reasons** include:

- **Increasing life expectancy** — **more people** suffer from **CHD** because of **ageing populations**.
- **Social**, **economic** and **cultural changes** — people are adopting **Western diets** and **lifestyles**, e.g. smoking.

Distribution of CHD DEATHS

CHD is one of the **world's biggest killers**. It caused **14%** of **global deaths** in **1997**. Over **80%** of deaths occur in **poor** and **newly-industrialised** areas, e.g. **sub-Saharan Africa** and **India**. **Reasons** include:

- **Poor health care** — **treatments** (e.g. **surgery**) **aren't affordable** or **available**.
- **Limited health education** — people **aren't aware** of the **effects** of **lifestyle changes** (e.g. **smoking** and **eating fatty foods**).

Death rates are **falling** in **wealthier** countries though, because of **improvements** in **diagnosing** people **at risk** of CHD, developing **effective treatments**, and **awareness campaigns** to **prevent** the disease.

Cancer is Becoming More Common in Poorer Countries

CHD and cancer are non-communicable diseases, see p. 190.

1) **Cancer** is the **uncontrollable growth** and **spread** of **abnormal cells** in the body.
2) If **detected early** enough, many cancers can be **cured** or **controlled** with **treatment** (e.g. surgery). Many cancers are **detected early** through **awareness** of **symptoms** and **regular screening**, e.g. detecting breast cancer lumps.
3) The **risk** of getting cancer can be **reduced** with **lifestyle changes**, such as **eating healthily**, **exercising more** and **not smoking**. Some forms of **cervical cancer** can be **prevented** by having a **vaccination**.

Distribution of cancer CASES

Cancer is another **non-communicable disease** — it's **more common** in **wealthier** countries, e.g. the **UK** and **USA**. The **most common** types are **prostate**, **breast** and **colon cancer**. **Reasons** include:

- **Ageing populations**.
- **Lifestyle factors**.

Cancer is becoming **increasingly common** in **poor** and **newly-industrialised** countries — especially **liver**, **stomach** and **cervical cancer**. **Reasons** include:

- **Increasing life expectancy**.
- **Social**, **economic** and **cultural changes** (adoption of a more **Western lifestyle**).

Distribution of cancer DEATHS

Cancer is the **world's second biggest killer**, causing **13%** of **deaths** in **2007**. **75%** of those **deaths** were in **poor** and **newly-industrialised** countries. **Reasons** include:

- **Poor health care**.
- **Limited health education**.

Death rates are **falling** in **wealthier** countries though, because of **improvements** in **diagnosis**, **treatment** and **awareness**.

Practice Questions

Q1 Describe the impact of disease on economic development.

Q2 What measures can help prevent the spread of HIV/AIDS?

Q3 Describe the global distribution of coronary heart disease.

Exam Question

Q1 Describe and explain the reasons for the global distribution of malaria and discuss its impact. [10 marks]

Diseases affect the poor and wealthy — but death rates are very uneven...

Irritatingly, any one of these diseases could come up in your exam, so I'm afraid you have to learn them all. But hey — at least some of the points are similar for the examples of poor and wealthy diseases...

Health and Globalisation

These pages are for AQA (Health option). *The distribution of disease is affected by some companies, which sounds a bit weird, but it's true (Scout's honour). A lot of these companies now operate at a global level (globalisation) so they have an impact on global health — in both good and bad ways...*

Trans-National Corporations can Improve Health or Add to Health Problems

Trans-National corporations (TNCs) are companies that operate in **more than one country**. Some TNCs are **very large**, with **huge budgets** and **powerful political influence**. TNCs affect global health by their **actions**:

1) How they **treat employees** — the **wages** they **pay**, their **safety standards** and the **health care** they provide.

   Example — **Namdeb diamond corporation** runs an **HIV/AIDS awareness programme** in **Namibia** and provides its **HIV-positive employees** with **drug treatment**.

2) How they **market products** — such as **tobacco**, **fatty foods** and **breast milk substitutes**.

   Example — There are **concerns** that aiming **fast-food advertising** at **children** may **contribute** to long-term **unhealthy eating** choices and **obesity**.

3) How they **sell products** (such as **tobacco**, **medical drugs** and **medical supplies**) and **how much they charge** for them.

   Example — Many **African** countries have to **rely** on the **generosity** of **overseas governments** and **pharmaceutical companies** to **subsidise drugs** because they **can't afford them**.

4) Which **products** they choose to **research** and **develop** — such as **healthy foods** and **medicines**.

   Example — **Kraft Foods** are **developing** a **new food** that **kills intestinal worms**. It's aimed at **rural Africa**, **Asia** and **South America**, where **intestinal worms** are a **big health problem**.

Pharmaceutical Companies Affect Global Health

Pharmaceutical companies **research**, **develop**, **produce** and **distribute drugs** to treat disease.
They affect **world health** because they can choose **which drugs** to develop and what **prices** to charge.

Research and Production

1) There's **more money** in **wealthier countries** so pharmaceutical companies often choose to **research and produce** drugs for diseases that **mainly** affect wealthier countries (e.g. drugs for impotency). This leads to **improved health** in **wealthier countries.**
2) Some pharmaceutical companies use the **profits** they make in wealthier countries to **subsidise research** into diseases that affect **poorer countries** (e.g. malaria vaccines). This leads to **improved health** in **poorer countries**.

Distribution and Sales

1) Drugs cost **a lot of money** to research and develop, which companies get back from the **sale** of their drugs.
2) Pharmaceutical companies have **exclusive rights** for **20 years** to produce new drugs they've developed. This means they can set **any price** for them because you can't get them **anywhere else**.
3) This affects **global health** because some **poorer countries** may not be able to **afford** the drugs they need.
4) Some pharmaceutical companies, often through **deals** with wealthier countries, provide **free or cheaper drugs** for poorer countries (e.g. anti-HIV drugs).

Case Study: GlaxoSmithKline (GSK)

GSK is one of the **world's largest pharmaceutical companies**.
It **produces** many different **drugs** and **health products**.

Research and Production

1) GSK produces almost **four billion** packs of **medicines** and health care products **each year**, including **one-quarter** of the **world's vaccines**.
2) It produces products for **wealthy countries** (e.g. Pravastatin-RL™, a drug for CHD), and for **poorer countries** (e.g. polio vaccines).

Distribution and Sales

1) GSK makes a **large profit** from drug sales but also **donates** some drugs to poorer countries for **free**. For example, GSK's donated **750 million albendazole tablets** to treat over **130 million people** with **elephantiasis** (an infectious inflammatory disease).
2) GSK also **invests** a large amount of its profit in **community programmes** to help people in need — **3.8%** of their pre-tax **profits (£282 million)** in 2007.

Health and Globalisation

Tobacco Companies Also *Affect Global Health*

1) About a **third** of the **world's population over** the **age** of **15 smokes**. Although **wealthier countries** are starting to **smoke less**, it's becoming a **huge problem** elsewhere — **80%** of **smokers** live in **poorer countries**.
2) Almost **four million** people **die each year** from **tobacco-related illnesses**, such as **lung cancer** and **heart disease**. **Death rates** are **rising** because most **tobacco-related illnesses** take years or decades to develop.
3) Because tobacco-related illnesses take a long time to develop, they're **traditionally** a health problem associated with **wealthier countries** (because people **live long enough** for the disease to develop).
4) As poorer countries develop and **life expectancy increases**, tobacco-related illnesses are becoming **more common**.
5) In **2003**, the **World Health Organisation** (**WHO**) developed a **treaty** called the **'Framework Convention on Tobacco Control'**. The treaty **protects public health** by **restricting tobacco advertising**, **regulating** the **contents** of **tobacco products**, making sure they're **packaged** and **labelled correctly** and **regulating** who they're **sold to**.
6) It's hoped these measures will help to **reduce** the number of global **smokers**, **reducing** the number of **tobacco-related illnesses** worldwide.
7) There are **concerns** that some **tobacco companies** are **targeting** countries that **haven't signed** the **WHO treaty**, so have **fewer restrictions**. Companies are accused of **aggressive marketing** to **target vulnerable populations** (e.g. young people), and **exploiting** people's **lack of knowledge** about tobacco's **health effects**.
8) This could result in **increased tobacco-related illnesses** in these countries.

Some people thought tobacco restrictions had gone too far this time.

*Case Study: Philip Morris International (**PMI**)*

PMI is the **world's largest tobacco company** and **owns** the **world's top selling brand**.

Research and Production

1) PMI **sells** a lot of **tobacco products**. In **2005** it **sold 805 billion cigarettes** worldwide.
2) But PMI does **research** and **develop** some potentially **less harmful tobacco products**, e.g. **cigarettes** that might **reduce** the **exposure** of the **smoker** to **toxic chemical compounds**. These measures could help to **reduce** the number of **tobacco-related illnesses** worldwide.

Distribution and Sales

1) PMI does stick to the **'Framework Convention on Tobacco Control'** in the **countries** that **have signed** it. But it uses a different range of **advertising** and **marketing strategies** in countries that haven't signed up. E.g. PMI **offers** adult **smokers free samples** of **cigarettes** where it's **legal** to do so.
2) PMI does have a **'responsible marketing policy'**. It's **agreed not** to **market products** to **children** and to put **health warnings** on all **marketing materials** and all **packaging**.

Practice Questions

Q1 Briefly describe how research carried out by pharmaceutical companies can affect global health.

Q2 Briefly describe how the distribution and sale of drugs by pharmaceutical companies can affect global health.

Q3 Give one possible reason why the number of tobacco-related illnesses is rising.

Exam Question

Q1 With reference to one or more specific examples, explain how transnational corporations can affect global health. [10 marks]

TNC — aren't they a girl band...

Some of the largest TNCs are wealthier than some of the world's poorest countries — seems a little unfair, doesn't it. People have divided opinions about how much these companies should be doing to improve world health. But don't worry, you don't have to come up with the answer to that problem — you just have to get learning these wonderful pages.

The Geography of Health in the UK

These pages are for AQA (Health option).
Health isn't just different between countries, it's different within countries too. Take the UK for example...

Health is Better in Southern England than in Northern England and Scotland

There are **big differences** in **health** across the **UK**. **Life expectancy** from birth (a measure of health) for **males** born between 2004-2006 is shown on the map.

1) The **general health trend** for the UK is a **North-South divide** — people living in the **South** of England are **healthier** than people living in the **North** of England and in **Scotland**.
2) The **highest life expectancy** at birth for **males** (1991-2001) was in **North Dorset**, South-west England (**79 years**) and the **lowest** was in **Glasgow** (**69 years**).
3) The **trend** of **morbidity** (illness) also **varies** — it has a **similar pattern** to **life expectancy**. E.g. **lung cancer** is **more common** in women living in **Scotland** (about **50% higher** than the rest of the UK) and **less common** in women living in **South-west England** (about **40% lower** than the rest of the UK).

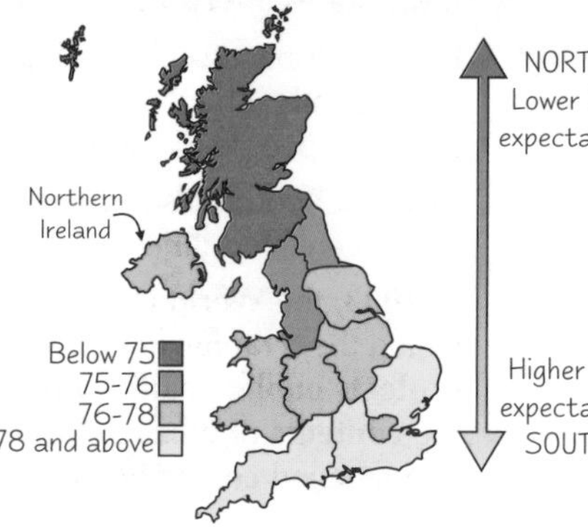

Income Affects Health Patterns in the UK...

There's a **strong link between** how much **money** you earn and how **healthy** you are. In general, **wealthier people** tend to be **healthier** because they have **better access** to **exercise facilities** and **health care**, and are **more educated** about **health issues**. The **pattern** of **household income** in the **UK** broadly **matches** the **pattern** of **life expectancy** (above).

For example, average **household income** (2003/04 to 2005/06) was **highest** in **South-east England** (**£91** a week **higher** than the UK average) and **lowest** in **North-east England** (**£141** a week **lower** than the UK average).

...and so Do Age Structure, Occupation Type, Education and Environment

1 Age structure

1) **Older people** are **more likely** to suffer from **age-related diseases**, e.g. **cancer** and **heart disease**.
2) **All regions** of the **UK** have an **ageing population**, due to **low birth rates** and **increasing life expectancy**.
3) But, **some areas** have a **higher proportion** of old people than others because **more retired people** choose to live there, e.g. **rural** and **coastal areas** like **Devon**.

2 Occupation type

1) If you do a **manual job** (e.g. a **labourer** or a **cleaner**) then you're up to **three times more likely** to suffer from **poor health** than if you do a **non-manual job** (e.g. a **doctor** or an **accountant**). Reasons for this include a **higher risk** of **accidents** and **exposure** to **hazardous substances**, e.g. asbestos.
2) **More people** do **manual jobs** in the **North** of **England**, which may contribute to the **higher levels** of **poor health**.
3) People doing **non-manual jobs** are **more likely** to suffer from **stress** and **mental health problems**. For example, **London** has the **highest proportion** of **people** in **non-manual jobs** and the **highest level** of **self-reported stress**.

3 Education

1) The **better educated** you are, the **more likely** you are to **choose** a **healthier lifestyle** — such as **eating healthy foods**, **exercising regularly** and **not smoking**.
2) This could be because **poor education** means **poor knowledge** of how to stay healthy.
3) In 2003, **18.8%** of the working-age population in **North-east England** had **no educational qualifications**. Only **10.7%** of the working-age population in **South-west England** had **no educational qualifications**. This might contribute to the **difference** in **health** between the two areas.

Some of these factors are linked together, e.g. people with a poor education are more likely to do manual jobs.

4 Environment and pollution

1) If you live in a **polluted area**, like a **big city** or near a **major road**, then you're **more likely** to suffer from **poor health**.
2) For example, **London** has a particularly **high mortality** rate from **respiratory diseases**, thought to be **caused** by the **poor air quality** in the city.
3) In contrast, **Devon** and **Cornwall** in **South-west England** are **countryside areas** with much **less pollution**. This may contribute to the **better health** there.

The Geography of Health in the UK

Gender Influences Health Too

Women tend to **live longer** than men but they're **twice as likely** to have **higher morbidity** from **chronic illnesses**, such as **arthritis**, and are **three times more likely** to suffer from **migraines**. **Women** are also **less likely** to take part in **sports** than men (**18.5%** compared with **23.7%**). Some **leisure facilities** have introduced **'ladies only'** sessions to **encourage participation**.

Health Care Provision is Affected by Ageing Populations

An **ageing population** requires **more money** to be **allocated** to **certain health care services**, for example:

1) **Specialised wards** — to **care** for the **growing population** of **elderly people** who have **ill health**.
2) **Increased screening** for **age-related diseases** (e.g. cancer and heart disease).
3) **More residential care homes** and **carers**.
4) **More mobile health care services** — to **cope** with the **increasing immobilised elderly population**, especially those in **rural areas** without family support.

More older people in a population means **more people** are **retired** and **fewer people** are **working** — this can result in a **declining tax base** to **pay** for **health** and **social services**.

Case Study: Health in South-west England

The **South-west** of **England** has the oldest population structure in the UK — in **2001**, **21%** of the **South-west's** population was pension age or over (60+ for women and 65+ for men). This compares to **19%** in **England** and **14%** in **London**. This will **increase** as **more people** are reaching **retirement age** and are choosing to **live** in **rural** and **coastal** areas.

An **ageing population** affects the **general health** of the area and the provision of **health care**:

1) **Higher rates** of diseases associated with **age** — in the South-west in **2003**, the rate of **breast cancer** was **7% above** UK average, and the rate of **prostate cancer** was **14% above** the UK average.
2) More **carers** and **health workers** are needed — in **2001**, **11%** of the working population of the South-west worked in the **social and health sectors**, compared to **10%** in **London**.
3) More **care homes** are required — **14%** of care homes in England are located in the **South-west** (only 10% are located in London).

1% extra might not seem like a lot but it's over 22 000 people.

Pumping money into **health care services** might **not** be the **best way** to **improve health** in the South-west:

1) Although the **South-west** has the **oldest population structure**, it's still the **healthiest region** in the UK — which **suggests** that **age isn't** the **most important factor** in **poor health**. There's **evidence** in the **South-west** that **low income** is **strongly linked** to **poor health**.
2) **Inland Revenue** figures show that **older people** have **lower personal incomes** than average, so it could be their **low income**, rather than age, that's **mostly affecting** their **health**. So the **most effective way** of **improving health** in the region could be to **focus** on **reducing** the number of **people** living on a **low income**.
3) For example, the **government** provides people **over 60** years old with a **heating allowance** — grants of up to **£4000** to **insulate homes** and make **heating improvements**. This is especially important in the **South-west** because this area has the **highest proportion** of **energy-inefficient homes** in England. The **heating allowance improves health** in the **South-west** because it helps **reduce illness** and **speeds recovery** in the **elderly population**.

Practice Questions

Q1 Describe the general health trend for the UK.

Q2 Why are wealthier people more likely to live healthier lives?

Q3 Name two factors that affect health in the UK.

Exam Question

Q1 Describe how an ageing population in the UK is likely to affect the provision of health care services. [6 marks]

Repeat after me — wealthier means healthier...

So, your health depends on many things but it seems like income's the major factor. Of course, they're all linked — it's hard to afford gym membership and a house by the coast on a low income. Still, there's just no excuse for deep-fried Mars Bars...

Exam Structure

This section is for AQA and Edexcel.
And now onto the unpleasant topic of exams (sorry, I had to mention them sooner or later). It's a pretty good idea to know what's in store for you so there are no nasty surprises on the day.

For all the exams you have roughly 1 minute per mark — so if a question's worth 10 marks you should spend about 10 minutes answering it.

There are Two Edexcel Exam Papers

UNIT 1 EXAM – GLOBAL CHALLENGES

1) It's **1 hr 30 mins** long and there are **90 marks** up for grabs (worth 60% of your AS grade).
2) It tests your knowledge of two topics — **World at Risk** and **Going Global**.
3) You get a fancy **resource booklet** with this paper (with things like **photos**, **maps**, **graphs** and **data** in).
4) There are **two sections** in the paper — **A** and **B**:

SECTION A
- You have to **answer ALL the questions.**
- The questions are worth up to **4 marks each,** so there are **no 'essay' answer questions.**
- There'll be questions where you have to use your **understanding** to **interpret** the **resources**, and questions that **test your knowledge** of the topics.

SECTION B
- You have to **answer ONE question** (which is in **two parts**) from a choice of four.
- **Part (a)** is worth 10 marks — this'll be based on **interpretation** of a resource from the **booklet.**
- **Part (b)** is worth 15 marks — this'll be an **'essay' question**, sometimes needing **case study** material (see page 202).

UNIT 2 EXAM – GEOGRAPHICAL INVESTIGATIONS

1) It's **1 hr 15 mins** long and there are **70 marks** in total (worth 40% of your AS grade).
2) You also get a **resource booklet** with this paper.
3) It tests four topics, but you only have to answer questions on **TWO** of them:

Either Extreme Weather ***OR*** Crowded Coasts
AND
Either Unequal Spaces ***OR*** Rebranding Places

4) For each topic there's **one question**, split into three parts:
   - **Part (a)** is worth 10 marks — this'll be based on **interpretation** of a **resource** from the booklet.
   - **Part (b)** is worth 10 marks — this'll be an **'essay' question**, usually a '**case study** question' (see page 202 for how to answer case study questions).
   - **Part (c)** is worth 15 marks — this'll be an **'essay' question** where you have to write about **'fieldwork and research'** (see page 203 for how to answer these questions).

Exams — who needs them, don't you know who my father is?

There are Two AQA Exam Papers

UNIT 1 EXAM – PHYSICAL AND HUMAN GEOGRAPHY

1) It's **2 hrs** long and there are **120 marks** to be had (worth 70% of your AS grade).
2) It tests **all** the topics you've studied.
3) There are **two sections** — **A** and **B**.
4) Both sections have the **same structure**:

- You have to **answer the FIRST question** and **ONE other** (on the **optional topic** that you've studied) in each section.
- For each question there are a couple of **short-answer parts** — some test your **knowledge** of the topic and some test your **understanding** by getting you to **interpret** a **photo, diagram, map** etc.
- The **last part** of each question is an **'essay' question,** which often needs **case study** material (see p. 202).

UNIT 2 EXAM – GEOGRAPHICAL SKILLS

1) It's **1 hr** long and there are **50 marks** in total (worth 30% of your AS grade).
2) This paper tests your **investigative**, **map-reading**, **graph-reading**, **statistical** and **fieldwork skills** (see pages 207-212 to brush up on these skills).
3) The questions will be based on stuff you've learnt **throughout** the **year** (i.e. on any topic).

Answering Questions

No matter how much you revise you aren't going to do well in your exams if you don't answer the questions properly. This can be trickier than it sounds, but fear not, I've included a whole page on it, because I'm nice like that...

1) Make Sure You Read the Question Properly

It's dead easy to **misread** the question and spend 10 minutes writing about the **wrong thing**. **Five** simple tips can help you avoid this:

There are loads of hints about how to answer the questions in this book in the Answers section at the back.

1) Figure out if it's a **case study question** — if the question wording includes 'using **named examples**' or 'with reference to **one named area**' you **need** to include a case study.
2) **Underline** the **command words** in the question (the ones that tell you **what to do**):

Answers to questions with 'explain' in them often include the word '**because**' (or '**due to**').

E.g. for the question 'Explain how vegetation affects a river's lag time', your answer would include '...more vegetation decreases lag time because it increases interception...'.

'Assess', 'Evaluate' and 'Discuss' all mean pretty much the **same thing**. They're all about **weighing something up**, e.g. the **success** of a coastal management scheme, or the **role** of people in causing desertification in the Sahel.

Command word	Means write about...
Describe	what it's **like**
Explain	**why** it's like that (i.e. give reasons)
Compare	the **similarities AND differences**
Contrast	the **differences**
Distinguish	the **differences**
Assess	the **advantages** and **disadvantages OR** the **arguments for** and **against**
Evaluate	
Discuss	
Examine	**describe AND explain**
Outline	**describe AND explain**
Define	the **meaning** of the word

If a question asks you to describe a **pattern** (e.g. from a map or graph), make sure you identify the **general pattern**, then refer to any **anomalies** (things that **don't** fit the general pattern).

E.g. for the question 'Describe the global distribution of volcanoes', you first need to say that they're mostly on plate margins, *then* mention that a few aren't (e.g. Kilauea in Hawaii).

When writing about differences, '**whereas**' is a good word to use in your answers, e.g. 'Employment in north-east England in 2007 was 6.1% whereas it was 4.1% in the south-west'.

'Examine' and 'Outline' are pretty similar. The main difference is that you do **more explaining** for '**Examine**' and **more describing** for '**Outline**'.

3) **Underline** the **key words** (the ones that tell you **what it's about**), e.g. rivers, population, social impacts etc.
4) For **essay** questions, **re-read the question** a couple of times **whilst you're answering it**, just to make sure you're still **sticking** to what the question is asking you to do.
5) For **all** questions, **re-read** the question and your answer **when you've finished**, just to check that your answer really does address **all parts** of the question being asked. A **common mistake** is to **miss a bit out** — like when questions say 'use data from the graph in your answer' or 'use evidence from the map'.

2) Figure Out Your Structure Before You Start

For any **longer answers**, you need to think carefully about how to **structure** your answer. Jot down the **order** you're going to cover things in under the question. **Label** your **plan** and **answer** clearly so the examiner knows which is which.

Q1 Describe the physical and human factors that can affect river discharge.

PLAN

1. Intro — define 'discharge' and say it's affected by human and physical factors
2. Physical — drainage basin characteristics, weather, rock and soil type, vegetation.
3. Human — impermeable surfaces, drainage systems.

ANSWER

River discharge is the volume of water...

3) Include Relevant Geographical Terms

Use the **proper geography words** for things, e.g. say 'tributary' rather than 'little river', and 'morbidity' instead of 'illness'.

Don't Forget all the Usual Rules

1) Your answer should be **legible** (you won't get many marks if the examiner can't read it), use **correct grammar**, and **everything** should be **spelt correctly** (double-check jazzy geography words).
2) **Use diagrams** where they're appropriate — drawing a diagram can be way **quicker** than describing the same thing in words.
3) If you're **running out of time** at the end of the exam, **don't panic** — just write what you can as **bullet points**. You'll still get some marks for doing this.

Answering Case Study Questions

Geography examiners are even keener on case study questions than they are on tweed jackets with fetching elbow patches...

*Don't Forget the **Three Tips** When Answering **Case Study Questions***

1) For **every question** you need to do the following three things:

   ① **Read** the **question properly.**
   ② **Figure out** your **structure before** you **start.**
   ③ **Include** relevant **geographical terms.**

2) But for case study questions you also **need to**:

   Include **PLENTY** of **RELEVANT DETAILS**

3) This includes things like **place names**, **dates**, **statistics**, **names** of **organisations** or **companies**.
4) Don't forget that they need to be **relevant** though — it's no good including the exact number of people killed in a flood when the question is about the causes of a flood.
5) For many case study questions, a great way to show your specific knowledge is to learn an **annotated map** and re-draw it in the exam (e.g. the California disaster hotspot map on page 72) — but take care to only include labels relevant to the specific question being asked.

Jeremy's case study revealed very few relevant details... black, handle, smells a bit funny...

*Here's an **Example Answer** to a Case Study Question*

'**With reference to one named area**' means you **have** to include a **case study**.

Don't think 'Ah, this is about the bit of coast I've studied' and then write everything you know about a particular coastline. The key words are '**causes**' and '**coastal erosion**' and the command words are '**describe**' and '**explain**', so you need to write about the causes of erosion along a specific coastline (but not about the impacts of erosion).

Q1 With reference to one named area describe and explain the causes of coastal erosion. [10 marks]

PLAN

1. Introduce Holderness
2. Describe the physical causes of erosion — rock type, narrow beaches, powerful waves
3. Describe the human causes of erosion — sea defences

Whenever you write about **causes** it's a really good idea to split them up into **physical** and **human**.

ANSWER

Holderness is a 61 km long stretch of coastline in East Yorkshire. It's eroding at an average rate of 1.8 m/year, and in some places, e.g. at Great Cowden, the rate of erosion is over 10 m/year.

There are many physical causes of the high rate of erosion. There is a long fetch (from the Arctic Ocean), which means that waves that hit the coastline have a lot of energy and so a lot of erosive power. The coastline also faces the dominant wind and wave direction (from the north-east). This also increases the energy of the waves (and so increases their erosive power). Another important physical factor is that the coastline is made from till, which is an easily eroded rock type. As well as being susceptible to corrasion it is prone to slumping when wet. The presence of Flamborough Head also increases erosion along holderness. The longshore drift runs from north to south along the coastline, so Flamborough Head traps sediment from the north. This means that the beach material eroded along Holderness is not replenished. Flamborough head is also made from chalk, which does not produce beach material when eroded (the chalk dissolves rather than forms sand). This means that the beaches along Holderness are quite narrow. Beaches slow the waves, reducing their erosive power. Narrower beaches protect the coast from erosion less than wider beaches.

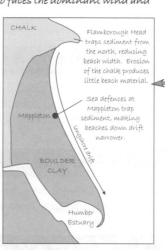

CHALK
Flamborough Head traps sediment from the north, reducing beach width. Erosion of the chalk produces little beach material.
Sea defences at Mappleton trap sediment, making beaches down drift narrower.
Mappleton
Longshore drift
BOULDER CLAY
Humber Estuary

Humans are contributing to the high rate of erosion. This is mainly through the building of sea defences, e.g. at Mappleton. Sea defences trap sediment and starve down-drift beaches of sediment. The thinner beaches don't protect the cliffs as well as wider beaches do.

Include **relevant details**, e.g. if the coast is made from an easily eroded rock type, say exactly **what rock type** it is.

Use relevant **geographical terms**, e.g. **corrasion** and **slumping**.

You can't always include an **annotated map** in case study answers, but for this question including one **helps you** illustrate how **Flamborough Head** and **sea defences** at **Mappleton** increase erosion at Holderness.

Answering Fieldwork & Research Questions

*If you're doing **Edexcel** then you'll have to answer 'Fieldwork and Research' questions in the Unit 2 exam. Unlucky.*

You Need to **Write About What You Did**

1) The questions are really easy to spot — you only get them in the **Unit 2 exam paper** and they'll include the phrase '**fieldwork and research**'.
2) When answering fieldwork and research questions you need to write about **your own** fieldwork and research.
3) You also need to do the following:

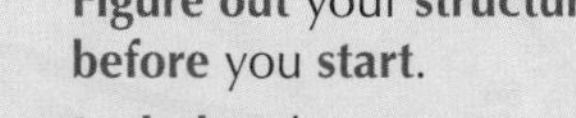

① **Read** the **question properly**.
② **Figure out** your **structure before** you **start**.
③ **Include** relevant **geographical terms**.
④ **Include** plenty of **relevant details**.

This time relevant details are things like **where** you carried out your fieldwork, what **websites** you used to research a place, what the exact **results** were, what **method** you used to investigate something etc.

- If the question asks you to **describe a programme** of fieldwork and research, you need to talk about the **methodology** for your **fieldwork** (what you did) and talk about your **research sources**.
- If you're asked to **describe the results** of your fieldwork and research, don't forget to briefly say **what you did** first.
- If you're asked to use your results to **judge the success** of something, say whether your results showed **if it worked** (and if there were any problems).

Here's an **Example Answer** to a Fieldwork and Research Question

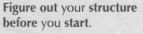

Q1 Describe the results of your fieldwork and research into the success of a rural rebranding scheme. [15 marks]

PLAN:
1. Introduce the Eden Project
2. Describe what fieldwork I did and what the results were
3. Describe what research I did and what the results were
4. Conclude whether it was a success or not

ANSWER:
I investigated the success of the Eden Project, near St Austell in Cornwall. The Eden Project is a tourist attraction that opened in 2001.

I went to St Austell, a town 5 kilometres from the Eden Project, to conduct a questionnaire-based survey asking businesses and people in the street about the impacts of the project. 75% of businesses said that trade had increased since the Eden Project opened. One business owner reported a 100% increase in profits since 2001. 25% of businesses said that trade had remained unchanged or had decreased. These results could be slightly biased though, as the majority of the businesses I surveyed were shops and cafés on the high street and so are more likely to be affected by an increase in tourist numbers. Ideally I would have surveyed a wider range of business types. Of people in the street surveyed, 22% said that they had come to the area specifically to go to the Eden Project. 51% of people questioned said that traffic congestion had become more of a problem since the project opened.

The research I did mainly focused on using the internet to search for positive and negative impacts of the project. Cornwall County Council's website (www.cornwall.gov.uk) states that the Eden Project attracts more than 1 million visitors to the area every year and has contributed more than £100 million per year to the Cornish economy. The Eden Project website (www.edenproject.com) states that an economic impact study estimated that the project had added £800 million to the regional economy in the last 5 years. It also states that 85% of the approximately 500 staff are from the local area. The Eden Project Business Survey conducted in 2003 found that the number of customers had increased for 38% of local businesses questioned. This is much lower than what I found in my fieldwork, but this could be because the number of tourists between 2003 and now has increased. An article in The Independent in 2002 mentioned the traffic congestion problems. The business survey conducted in 2003 stated that 5% of businesses thought traffic had worsened, though this was down from 13% in a 2001 survey.

I think my fieldwork and research shows that the Eden Project has been successful because it has had a huge positive economic impact on the surrounding area. Jobs have been created and trade has increased for most businesses since it opened. Although there have been traffic problems since it opened the Eden Project are trying to minimise these, according to their website, by reducing admission prices for those arriving by bus, bicycle or on foot.

When you have to cover fieldwork and research it makes sense to split them up in your answer.

Include relevant details — don't just say that trade increased for most businesses, give the specific result (e.g. 75%).

If there was something you could have done better then say so.

If there's any reason why your results might be biased then mention it.

Name the websites that you used to research the place.

If there are any inconsistencies between your fieldwork and research suggest reasons why.

Answering Resource Interpretation Questions

Whichever exam board you're doing, you're going to get some questions where you have to interpret a resource. The following pages show you the kind of thing that might crop up. Knock yourself out...

You Might Get a Question Based on an **OS Map**...

Q1 Below is a map showing Cockermouth. Describe what the social and economic impacts of flooding in Cockermouth might be. [10 marks]

See page 210 for how to read OS® maps and give grid references.

PLAN

1. Describe the possible social impacts — hospital, houses, roads
2. Describe the possible economic impacts — brewery, roads, campsite, farms

The question only mentions social and economic impacts, so you shouldn't write about any possible environmental impacts. This makes your structure pretty simple.

ANSWER

Possible social impacts of a flood in Cockermouth include loss of life, inconvenience and disruption to people's lives. The hospital at grid reference 125 321 is very close to the river so could be flooded. The lives of patients could be at risk if it floods.

When you're talking about somewhere specific on the map always give the grid reference.

There are lots of homes close to the river which would be affected if the river flooded (e.g. grid reference 1231). This could put lives at risk. It could also lead to the damage or loss of household goods and personal possessions. This is also an economic impact as they cost money to repair or replace.

Some roads run very close to the river at some points (e.g. the A5086 at grid reference 116 318). If these flood it would disrupt local traffic, which could cause congestion. It may also prevent people from reaching businesses, which would decrease trade.

Include relevant details, e.g. if there's a road that might flood, say what road number it is.

The brewery at grid reference 125 317 is also close to the river so could flood. This would have economic consequences, as production could be stopped, reducing revenue. Equipment could be damaged and have to be replaced, which would also be expensive.

The campsite at grid reference 129 304 could be flooded. As well as disrupting holidays this would cause economic problems. The campsite owners would lose income whilst the ground was unusable for camping, and any facilities damaged by flooding would need repairing or replacing.

There is farmland near to the river, e.g. Green Bank Farm land (grid reference 125 297). If this farmland was flooded it could damage crops or kill livestock. This would be expensive for the farmer to replace.

Answering Resource Interpretation Questions

...or a Photo

The best thing to do first is write a list of the landforms you can see (just so you don't miss any out when writing your answer).

The command words in the question are 'describe' and 'explain' so you need to say what each landform is like and give reasons for its formation.

You need to scour the photo to make sure that you've got everything — it'd be really easy to miss the ribbon lake at the top of this photo if you hadn't looked properly.

Include diagrams where they help illustrate your answer.

Q1 Describe and explain the landforms shown in the photo on the right. [8 marks]

PLAN

Describe and then explain how each landform is formed — arête, corrie, tarn, ribbon lake.

ANSWER

There are four main glacial landforms present in the photo.

There is an arête in the centre-left of the photograph. An arête is a steep-sided ridge. It's formed when two glaciers flow in parallel valleys. The glaciers erode the sides of the valleys, which sharpens the mountain ridge between.

There is a corrie on the right of the photo. A corrie is a bowl-shaped hollow. Glaciers form when snow accumulates in a hollow and turns to ice. Basal sliding, along with abrasion and plucking, deepens the hollow into a corrie. When there is enough ice the glacier starts to move downhill. Frost shattering and plucking steepen the back wall of the corrie.

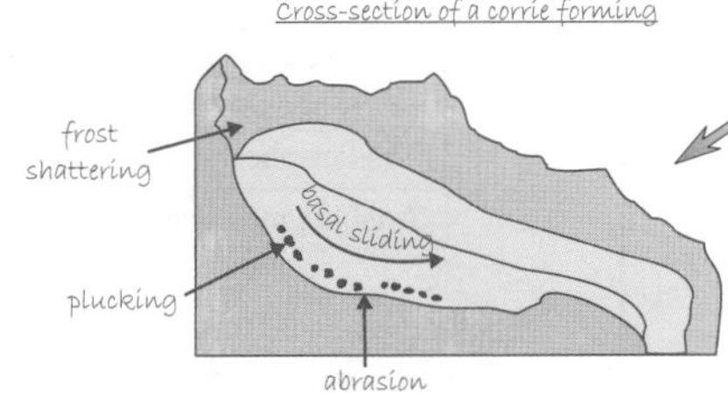

There is also a tarn. Tarns are lakes that form in corries after glaciers have retreated.

There is a ribbon lake at the top of the photo. Ribbon lakes are long, thin lakes that form after a glacier retreats. They form in dips caused by the erosion of bands of less resistant rocks, or behind dams of debris left by the glacier.

...or a Graph

The command word is 'examine' so you need to describe the trends on the graph and give reasons for them.

As well as describing general trends, describe specific details, e.g. hydro-meteorological disasters have increased, but you also need to say that they've increased very rapidly in the last 10 years.

Use evidence from the graph to back up your points (to get accurate figures from the graph it often helps to draw working lines on with a ruler).

Q1 Examine the graph of global disaster frequency on the right. [10 marks]

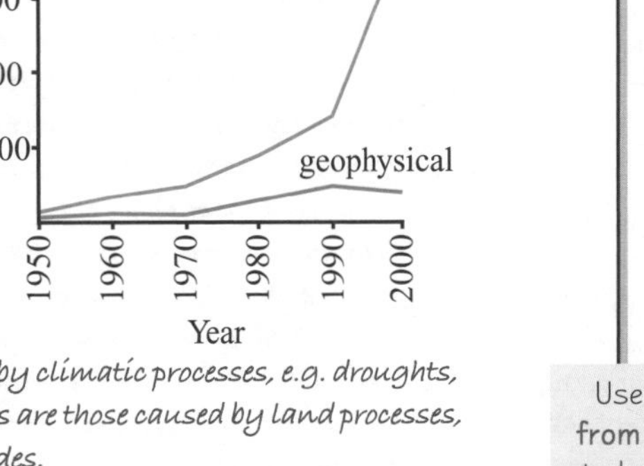

PLAN

1. Define hydro-meteorological and geophysical disasters.
2. Describe the trend shown for geophysical disasters, then describe the trend for hydro-meteorological disasters.
3. Explain the reasons for the trends.

ANSWER

Hydro-meteorological disasters are those caused by climatic processes, e.g. droughts, floods or tropical cyclones. Geophysical disasters are those caused by land processes, e.g. volcanic eruptions, earthquakes and landslides.

The frequency of geophysical disasters has increased in the last 50 years, e.g. there were 10 disasters in 1950, rising to about 40 in 2000. The frequency of hydro-meteorological disasters has also increased over the last 50 years, and has increased very rapidly in the last 10 years (from approximately 150 in 1990 to 390 in 2000).

The frequency of geophysical hazards has remained roughly the same for the last 50 years. The reason for the increase in geophysical disasters could be the increasing vulnerability of populations in hazard prone areas. A hazard is more likely to cause a disaster if the people it affects are more vulnerable.

There are many reasons for the increase in hydro-meteorological disasters. The most likely reason is the increase in the frequency of hydro-meteorological hazards, which may be due to the effects of global warming. El Niño events make hydro-meteorological hazards more difficult to predict and so they are more likely to result in a disaster. Human factors such as rapid population growth, urbanisation and increasing world poverty may also have contributed to the increase by increasing the vulnerability of people affected. Also, the exploitation of resources (e.g. deforestation) can increase the risk of some hydro-meteorological hazards, e.g. flooding and landslides.

However, if the data shown in the graph is based on media information the trend could just be caused by increased media coverage of disasters over the last 50 years.

Answering Resource Interpretation Questions

...or Some **Data**

Q1 Outline how well the information in the table shows the inequalities between Bradford and Harrogate. [10 marks]

This question is asking about how well the **information** in the table shows inequality, **not** about the causes and effects of these inequalities.

Measure	Bradford	Harrogate
Total population (2001)	467 665	151 336
Average detached property selling price (Aug 2001)	£112 723	£191 024
% unemployed (2001)	4.4	1.8
% people of working age claiming a key benefit (Aug 2001)	17	8
% people with 'not good' general health (2001)	10.2	7.21
Police recorded offences of theft from a motor vehicle (Apr 01 - Mar 02)	9961	698
% 15 year old pupils achieving 5 or more A* - C GCSE grades from schools within the area	37.3	68.6
Total number of students aged 16-17 (2001)	10 256	3041
Area of green space (km^2) (Jan 2005)	0.27	1.25

PLAN
1. Define inequality and describe the three types of inequalities.
2. Describe and explain data that shows an inequality.
3. Describe and explain data that doesn't show an inequality.

The command word is '**outline**' so you need to **describe** the information in the table **and explain** how the information does or doesn't show an inequality.

ANSWER

Inequalities are differences in wealth, social opportunity and environmental quality between different areas. There are three main types of inequality — economic, social and environmental. Economic inequalities include differences between income or assets. Social inequalities include differences between types of employment, as well as education or crime levels. Environmental inequalities include differences between pollution, quality of housing or quality of surroundings.

Always **quote data** from the table to back up your points.

The data in the table shows economic inequalities between Bradford and Harrogate. For example, the percentage of people unemployed is higher in Bradford than in Harrogate (4.4% compared to 1.8%). The average selling price of a detached property is higher in Harrogate (£191 024) than Bradford (£112 723). The percentage of people claiming key benefits is lower in Harrogate, at 8%, than in Bradford, where it's 17%. This information tells you that Harrogate is a wealthier area than Bradford.

You can't directly compare the number of thefts from a motor vehicle because the total populations are different. You need to work out thefts per 10 000 of the population.

Try to **manipulate data** from the table where appropriate, e.g. instead of giving the percentage of 15 year olds getting A* to C for each place, give the difference between them.

The table shows social inequalities between the two areas. For example, in Harrogate there were 46 reported thefts from a motor vehicle per 10 000 residents (Apr 01 to Mar 02), compared to 213 per 10 000 residents for Bradford. Bradford also has a higher percentage of people with 'not good' general health (10.2% compared to 7.21%). In addition, the percentage of 15 year olds achieving 5 A* to C grades is over 30% higher in Harrogate than it is in Bradford. Together, this data tells us that there is more social opportunity in Harrogate than in Bradford.

The area of green space is higher in Harrogate, where there's 1.25 km^2, compared to Bradford, where there's only 0.27 km^2. This is an environmental inequality.

However, not all the data in the table shows inequality. The data on total population tells you that Bradford has a larger population, but it doesn't show any inequality. This is because it doesn't tell you anything about the population's wealth or social opportunity, or the area's environmental quality. The table also shows that there are 7000 more students aged 16-17 in Bradford than Harrogate, but both areas have a similar proportion of students (2% of the total population). So, this data doesn't show any inequalities either, because it doesn't tell you anything about the student's education or lifestyle.

The data's been manipulated to show there's **no difference** in the percentage of students.

Investigative Skills

Whether you consider yourself a modern-day Poirot or not, you need to know this basic stuff about investigating things through fieldwork and research.

You Need to Have an **Aim** and a **Hypothesis**

1) When you're doing fieldwork and research you won't get very far without an **aim**, and a **hypothesis** to **test**.
2) An aim is **what you want to find out**, e.g. 'To see if coastal defences at Holderness affect the rate of erosion of the coastline'.
3) A hypothesis is a **specific testable statement**, e.g. 'Coastal defences at Holderness increase the rate of erosion downdrift of the defences'.
4) Both your aim and hypothesis should be **'developed'** — this just means that they have to be **really specific**. E.g. the above aim is better than 'To see if coastal defences affect erosion', and the hypothesis above is better than 'Coastal defences do affect erosion'.

Herman's hypothesis that large brown bears could drive German police cars was very specific (and seemed to be correct).

You Need to **Select** Your **Sites Carefully**

1) When you're investigating an urban area, river or coast you **can't study** the **whole thing**, so you have to **select sites** to investigate instead.
2) Selecting sites can be **tricky** though — you need places that are **easy to get to** (e.g. places with **footpath access**) and **not too far** from a **parking place** (if you've got **heavy equipment** to carry you don't want to be walking for miles). But you also need sites that are a **good representation** of all the things you want to study, e.g. if you're studying how **channel characteristics** change along the **course** of a **river** it's no good selecting three sites at the **top** of the river (sites near the **source only**) — this would be a **biased sample**. You need to select sites at **different stages** along the course of the river, **from source to mouth**.
3) **Systematic sampling** is often used to select sites in geography fieldwork — this involves selecting sites in a **regular**, **structured way**, e.g. **every 2 km** along a coastline, or **every third shop** on the high street. Doing it this way means you should be able to **cover** the **whole area** in an unbiased way.
4) You can also use **random sampling** — e.g. using a **random number table** to find the distance of a site from the source of a river. As long as you're using a big enough sample this should **remove** any **bias**.

You Need to **Collect Data**

1) You'll **collect data** when you're doing your **fieldwork** and when doing your **research**.
2) There are two types of data — **primary** and **secondary**:
    - **Primary** data is data you **collect yourself** (i.e. the data you get from your **fieldwork**).
    - **Secondary** data is data **someone else** has **collected** (i.e. the data you get from your **research**).
3) You might have to **describe** how you collected your data **in detail** in the **exam**. This includes mentioning things like what type of **equipment** you used (e.g. a velocity meter), **how you did it** (e.g. you conducted a questionnaire containing 10 questions) or **what source** it came from (e.g. 2001 census data from www.statistics.gov.uk).
4) Also, point out any **limitations** of the **data**, e.g. whether it could be **biased** due to the collection method.

You Need to Know About **Risk Assessment**

1) When you're out and about doing your **fieldwork** you need to be **pretty careful**.
2) You need to **identify** any **risks** there might be and **take action** to reduce the risks.
3) Risks basically include any way you could **get hurt**.
4) Here are a few examples:

Area	Risk	Action
City	Being run over	Cross roads using pedestrian crossings where possible.
	Abuse (verbal and physical)	Be polite.
		If you're asking people questions make sure you introduce what you're doing and give them an opportunity to refuse to answer.
River	Drowning	Don't go into deep water (e.g. past knee height) or water that's fast flowing.
		Don't tread on slippy rocks (e.g. ones with moss on them).
Coast	Rock falls from cliffs	Where possible, keep away from cliff faces.
	Drowning	See above. Also, make sure you're aware of when the tide's coming in.

Graph and Map Skills

As sure as death and taxes, there'll be graphs and maps in your exam. So make sure you know all the different types...

There are Loads of Different Types of Graphs and Maps

1) There are some types of graphs and maps that you'll have come across lots of times before. These include **line graphs**, **bar charts**, **pie charts**, **scatter graphs**, **atlas maps** and **sketch maps**.
2) Some graphs and maps are trickier than others, so the next three pages are full of tips to help you interpret the tougher ones.
3) When you're **interpreting** graphs and maps you need to remember to **read** the **scale** or **key really carefully**.
4) If you have to read from a graph **draw working lines on** to help you get an accurate figure.

Triangular Graphs Show Percentages Split into Three Categories

1) To read a triangular graph start by **finding the point** you want on the graph.
2) **Follow** the **line** that goes **down** from the **point** to the **lowest end** of the **scale** and record the percentage.
3) Then **turn the graph around** so that the next axis is at **the bottom**, **follow** the **line** down to the lower end of the scale and record that percentage.
4) Do the same for the **third axis**.
5) The three readings should **add up** to **100%**.
6) The graph on the right shows the age distribution of three populations. There are **three age groups** so a triangular graph can be used. **Each point** represents **one population**.

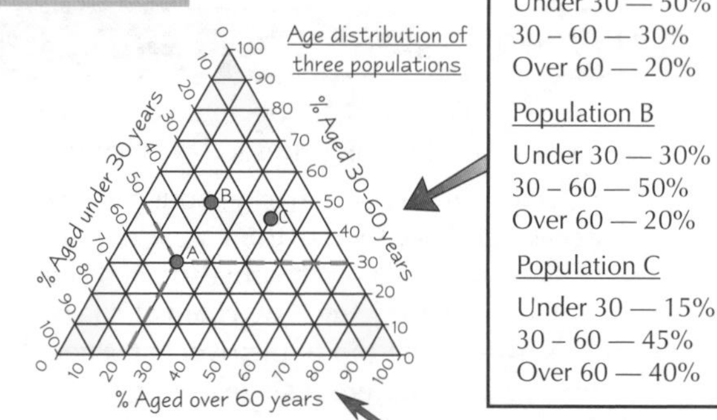

On this scale the lowest end is on the **left**, so to find the percentage you follow the line down and towards the left of the scale.

Dispersion Diagrams Show the Frequency of Data

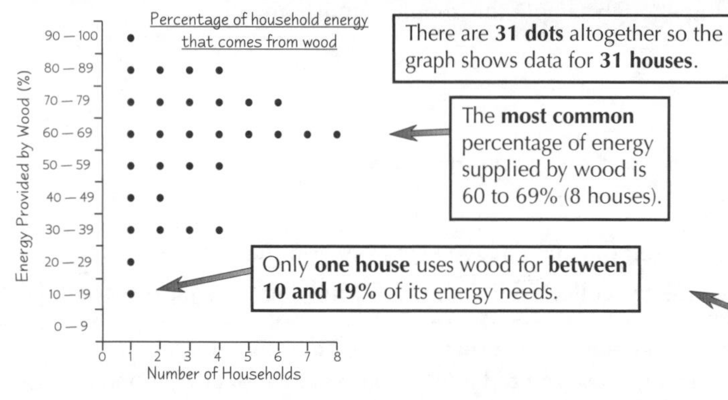

1) Dispersion diagrams are a bit like a cross between a **tally chart** and a **bar chart**.
2) The **range** of **data that's measured** goes on one axis. **Frequency** goes on the other axis.
3) **Each dot** represents **one piece of information** — the **more dots** there are in a particular category, the **more frequently** that event has happened.
4) The dispersion diagram on the left shows the **percentage** of **household energy** that comes from **wood** for **houses** in a **particular village**.

Logarithmic Scales are Used When the Data Range is Large

1) The **intervals** on logarithmic scales are **not fixed amounts** (e.g. they don't go up by 5 every time).
2) Instead, the **intervals** get **increasingly larger** at the top end of the scale (e.g. 10, 20, 40, 80).
3) This lets you fit a **very wide range** of **data** onto one **axis** without having to draw an enormous graph.
4) The graph on the right uses a **logarithmic scale** on the **vertical axis** to show how the world's population changed between 1950 and 2000.

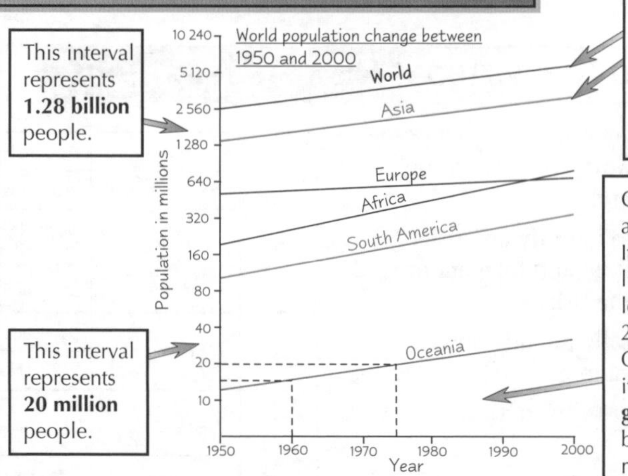

Be careful, it looks like the world's population isn't much bigger than Asia's but that's only because there are **big jumps** at this end of the scale.

Graphs with log scales are **really tricky** to **read**. It's OK if your working line hits a label on the log axis (e.g. there were 20 million people in Oceania in 1975), but if it doesn't it's easiest to **give a range** (e.g. it was between 10 and 20 million in 1960).

Graph and Map Skills

Choropleth Maps Show Information Using Colours and Patterns

1) Choropleth maps show how something **varies** between **different areas** using **colours** or **patterns.**
2) The maps in exams often use **cross-hatched lines** and **dots.**
3) They're straightforward to read but it's **easy to make mistakes** with them as the patterns can be very similar.
4) If you're asked to talk about all the parts of the map with a **certain type of hatching**, look at the map carefully and put a **big tick** on each part with that hatching, to make them all **stand out.**

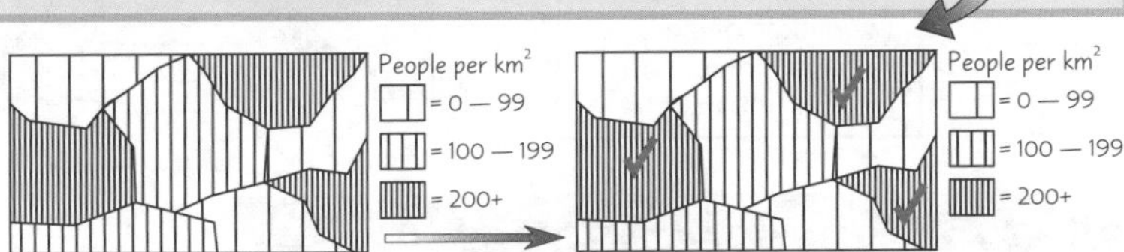

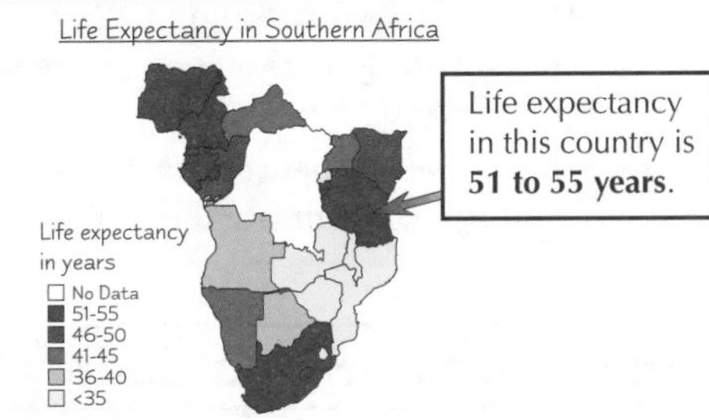

Dot Maps Show Distribution and Quantity Using Identical Symbols...

1) Dot maps use **identical dots** to show how something is **distributed** across an **area.**
2) Use the **key** to find out what **quantity** each dot represents.

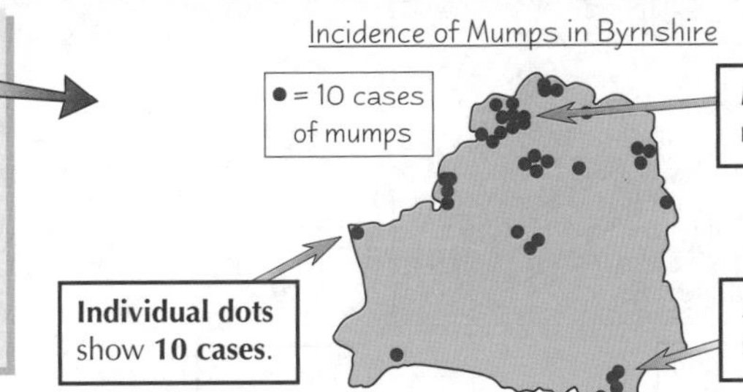

...Proportional Symbol Maps Use Symbols of Different Sizes

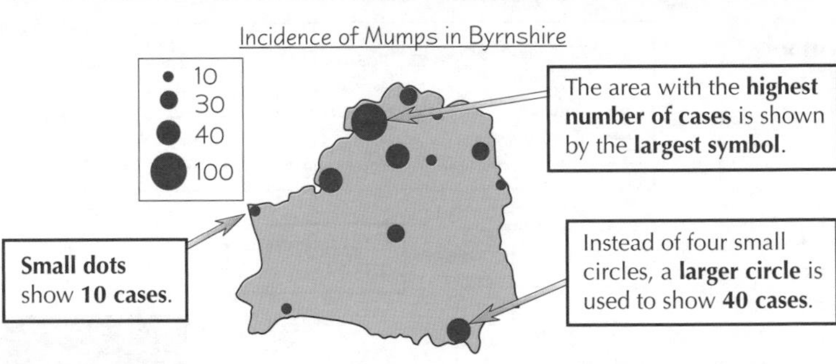

1) **Proportional symbol maps** use symbols of **different sizes** to represent **different quantities.**
2) A **key** shows the quantity each symbol represents. The **bigger** the **symbol**, the larger the **amount.**
3) The symbols might be **circles, squares, semi-circles** or **bars**, but they're always read the **same way.**

Flow Line Maps Show Movement

1) Flow line maps have **arrows** on, showing how things **move** (or are moved) from **one place to another.**
2) The map on the right shows the movement of people **to the UK from** the **USA**, the **rest of the Americas** and the **Middle East.** It also shows the movement of people **from** the **UK** to those areas.
3) It's also a **proportional symbol map** as the size of the arrows show **how many** people are moving.

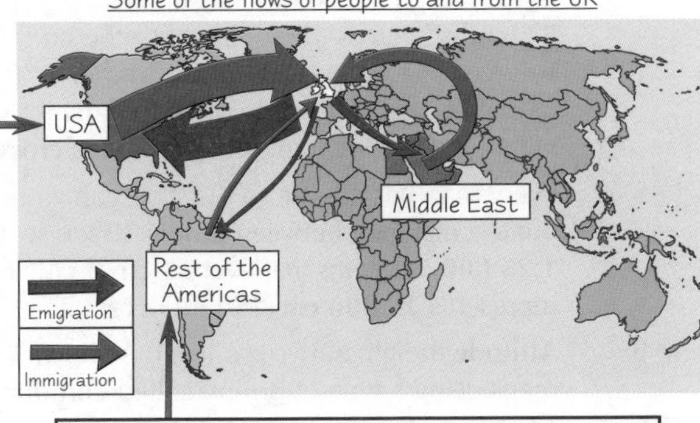

Graph and Map Skills

Isoline Maps Show Where Conditions are the Same

1) **Isolines** are lines on a map **linking** up all the **places** where something's the **same**, e.g. on **weather maps** isolines show places that are the **same air pressure**.
2) If the place you're being asked about lies **on** an isoline you can just **read** the value off the line.
3) If the place is **between** isolines you have to **estimate** the value.

Map of low pressure system

Helsinki and Leece both lie **on** this line so both have a pressure of **996 mb**.

Madrid lies **between** the lines for **988** and **992**. It's pretty much in the middle of the lines, so has a pressure of roughly **990 mb**.

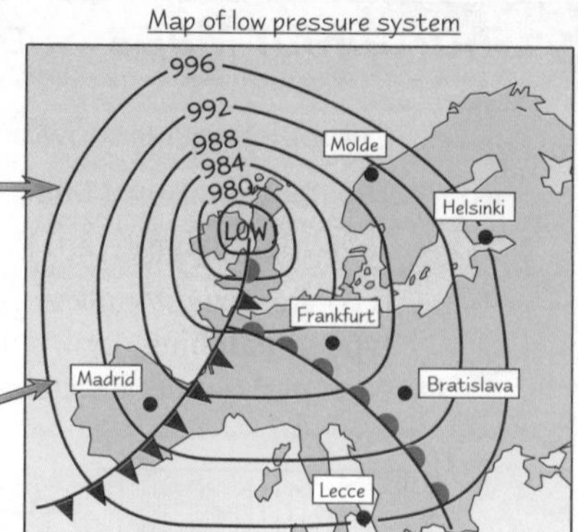

Town Centre Plans Show Detailed Information of Urban Areas

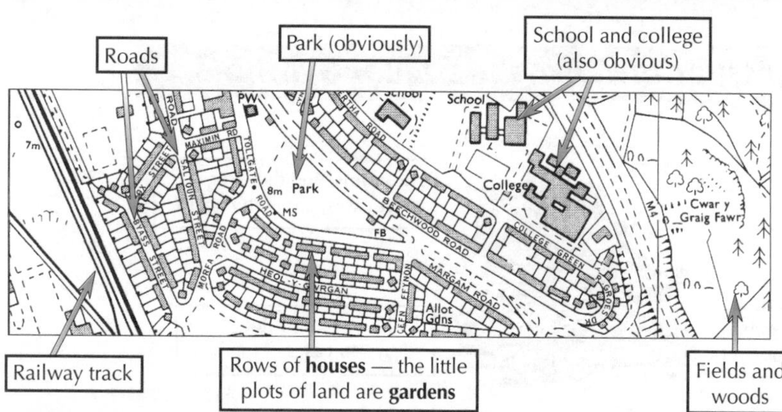

1) When you get a plan, start by looking at the **types of buildings** and what's **around** them.
2) **Small buildings** are probably **houses** or **shops**. **Bigger buildings** are probably **factories** or **schools**.
3) Work out what kind of **area** it is — lots of **car parks** and **shops** mean it's a **Central Business District** (CBD), **houses with gardens** mean a **residential area**.
4) The plan to the left shows a **residential area**.

Ordnance Survey Maps Show Detailed Information of All Areas

1) Ordnance Survey® (OS®) maps use lots of **symbols**. It's a good idea to **learn** the most common ones.
2) You can find places on OS maps using **grid references**.
3) **Four-figure grid references** direct you to a 1 km × 1 km **square** on the map, e.g. for **1534** go **across** to the number **15** (the **eastings** value) and then **up** to the number **34** (the **northings** value). This grid reference refers to the **square above** and to the **right** of the point 1534.
4) **Six-figure grid references** are more precise and can direct you to a more **exact spot** (a 100 m × 100 m square). E.g. for 155341 the eastings value is 155, so go across to 15 again and then a further **5 "tenths"** across the square. For the northings value of 341 go up to 34 and a further **1 "tenth"** of that square. The spot you're looking for is where the easting and northing values **cross**.
5) Every map has a **scale** so that you can work out the **distance between points**. If the scale is **1:25 000**, it means that every **1 cm** on the map represents **25 000 cm** (250 m) in real life.
6) **Altitude** (height above sea level) is shown on OS maps using a type of isoline called **contour lines**. The **closer together** the contour lines are, the **steeper the gradient** is.

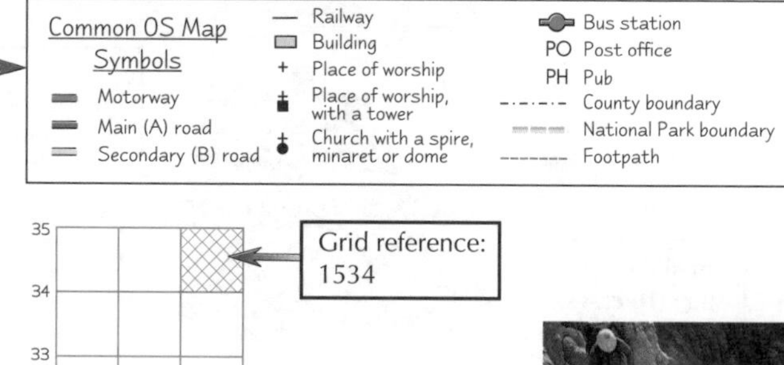

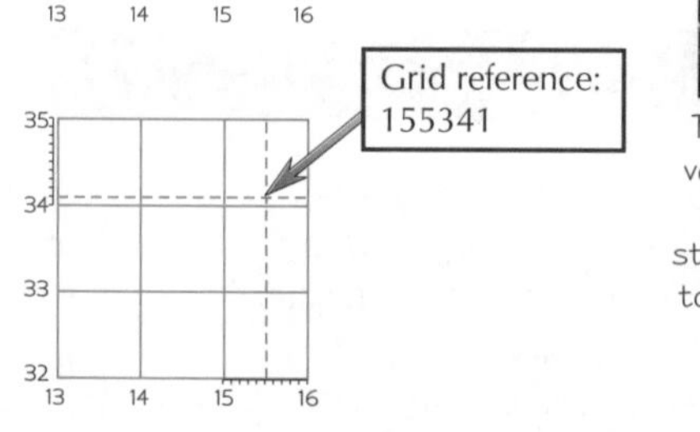

The contour lines did look very close together on the map, but nothing would stop Chaz and Dave getting to the Public House at grid reference 613 574.

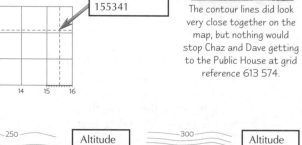

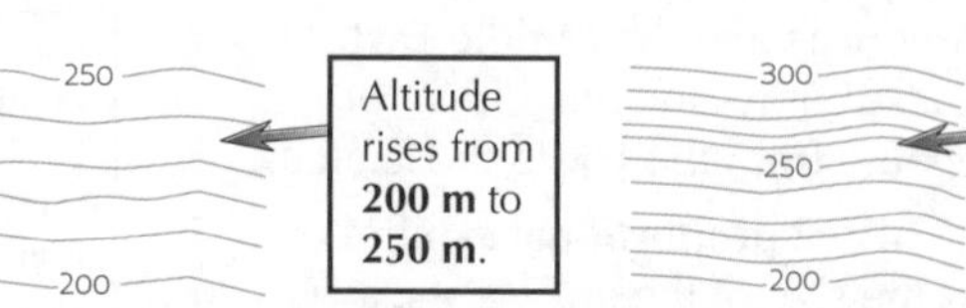

The contour lines on the right are closer together and show a **steeper slope** (there's a **greater increase in height** over the **same distance**).

Statistical Skills

As if knowing about loads of weird graphs and maps wasn't enough, you also need to be pretty familiar with statistics. These next two pages cover the ones you need to know.

There are Different Ways of Finding the Average Value of a Set of Data

1) The **mean**, **median** and **mode** are different ways of finding the **average** value of a set of data.
2) You find the **mean** by **adding up** all the numbers in a set of data, then **dividing** by the number of **sample points**, **n**.

Take a look at the data in this table:

Location	1	2	3	4	5	6	7	8	9	10	11
Temperature in °C	3	7	4	3	7	9	9	5	5	7	6

n = 11, so the mean temperature is: $\frac{3+7+4+3+7+9+9+5+5+7+6}{11}$ = **5.9 °C**.

3) The **median** is the **middle value** in an ordered set of data. So you need to **sort the numbers into order**, then work out which one is in the middle. So for the data above the median is **6 °C**.

3 3 4 5 5 (6) 7 7 7 9 9

If there are an even number of sample points the median is the mean of the middle two numbers.

4) The **mode** is the **most common value** in a set of data. So for the data above the mode is **7 °C**.

3 3 4 5 5 6 (7 7 7) 9 9

Sometimes there isn't a mode, and sometimes there's more than one.

The Interquartile Range is a Measure of Dispersion...

1) The **interquartile range** (**IQR**) is the range of values covered by the **middle 50%** of a set of data.
2) To find the interquartile range you first need to find the median of the values **to the left** of the median. This is called the **lower quartile** (**LQ**). Next find the median of the values **to the right** of the median. This is the **upper quartile** (**UQ**). Then you just **subtract** the **UQ from the LQ** to give you the **IQR**.
3) So, for the data above, the **LQ** is **4** and the **UQ** is **7**, and the interquartile range is UQ – LQ = 7 – 4 = **3 °C**.

LQ Median UQ
3 3 (4) 5 5 (6) 7 7 (7) 9 9
IQR

4) The interquartile range tells you about the **spread** of data **around** the **median**. If it's a **big** number, it shows that the numbers are pretty **spread out**. And yep, you've guessed it — a **small** number means that a lot of the data is pretty **close** to the **median**.

...and so is Standard Deviation

1) The **standard deviation** is a bit trickier to calculate than the IQR, but it's often a **more reliable** measure of dispersion (spread). The symbol for it is σ.

The formula is $\sigma = \sqrt{\frac{\sum(x-\bar{x})^2}{n}}$

Σ just means 'sum of', and $\bar{x}$ is just a way of writing 'mean'.

2) To calculate it, it's easiest to **work out** the **individual bits** in the formula **first**, e.g. the mean. It's a good idea to **draw** a **table** to help you. Below is a simple example for the set: 5, 9, 10, 11, 14.

- For these numbers, the **mean** is (5 + 9 + 10 + 11 + 14) ÷ 5 = **9.8**. This is shown in the 2nd column in the table.
- For each number, **calculate** $x - \bar{x}$ (3rd column in the table).
- Then **square** each of those values (4th column) — remember that the square of a **negative number** is always **positive**.
- Then **add up** all the squared numbers you've just worked out — this will give you $\sum(x-\bar{x})^2$.
- Now just **divide** your total by **n**, then take the **square root**.
- In this example, n = 5, so $\sigma = \sqrt{\frac{42.8}{5}}$ = **2.93** (2 d.p.)

x	$\bar{x}$	$x-\bar{x}$	$(x-\bar{x})^2$
5	9.8	−4.8	23.04
9	9.8	−0.8	0.64
10	9.8	0.2	0.04
11	9.8	1.2	1.44
14	9.8	4.2	17.64
		Σ	42.8

Standard deviation can be represented by σ or **s**.

3) If the standard deviation is **large**, the numbers in the set of data are **spread out** around the **mean**. If it's **small**, the numbers are **bunched** closely around the mean.

Statistical Skills

Make Sure You Know How to Find Spearman's Rank Correlation Coefficient

The Spearman's Rank correlation coefficient is a handy way to find out whether two sets of numbers are **correlated** (there's a **relationship** between them). The example below uses the test to see if **river discharge** (m^3/s) and **rainfall** (mm) are correlated.

1) The bad news is that it's a bit of a pain to calculate. The first step is to give a **rank** to each number in both sets of data. The **highest** number is given rank **1**, the second highest is given rank 2... you get the idea.
2) Then you **calculate 'd'**, the **difference** between the ranks for each item, e.g. if the ranks for River F are 4 and 6, the difference is –2.
3) Next you **square 'd'** and **add up** the **d^2 values**.
4) Finally you need to work out the **Spearman's Rank Correlation Coefficient** (known as r_s).

The formula is: $r_s = 1 - \frac{6\sum d^2}{n^3 - n}$

River	Discharge	Discharge rank	Rainfall	Rainfall rank	d	d^2
A	14	5	28	5	0	0
B	19	4	27	6	2	4
C	9	9	15	8	–1	1
D	6	11	9	11	0	0
E	21	3	35	3	0	0
F	13	6	30	4	–2	4
G	22	2	36	2	0	0
H	35	1	38	1	0	0
I	5	12	6	12	0	0
J	7	10	14	9	–1	1
K	11	8	10	10	2	4
L	12	7	20	7	0	0
					$\sum d^2$	14

5) So for the example above, $\sum d^2 = 14$ and n = 12. So $r_s = 1 - \frac{6 \times 14}{12^3 - 12} = 1 - \frac{84}{1716} = 1 - 0.05 = \mathbf{0.95}$.
6) The number you get is always **between –1** and **+1**.
7) A **positive number** means the variables are **positively correlated** — as one variable **increases** so does the **other**. The **closer** the number is to 1 the **stronger** the correlation.
8) A **negative number** means that the two sets of variables are **negatively correlated** — as one variable **increases** the other **decreases**. The **closer** the number is to –1 the **stronger** the correlation.
9) If the coefficient is **0**, or near 0, there probably isn't much of a relationship between the figures.
10) The value of r_s in the example above was **0.95**, which is **close to 1**, so there's a **strong positive correlation** between the **data** for river discharge and rainfall.

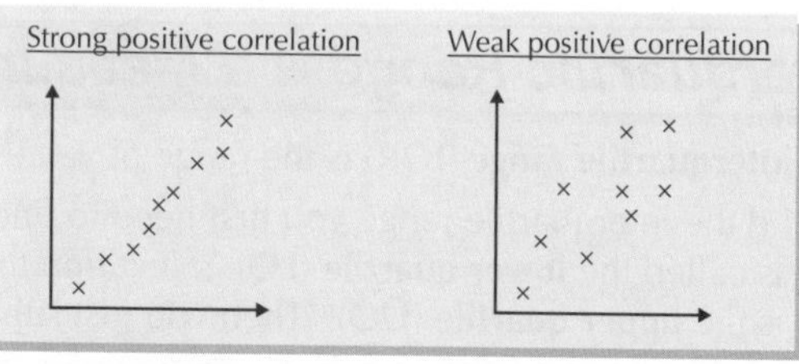

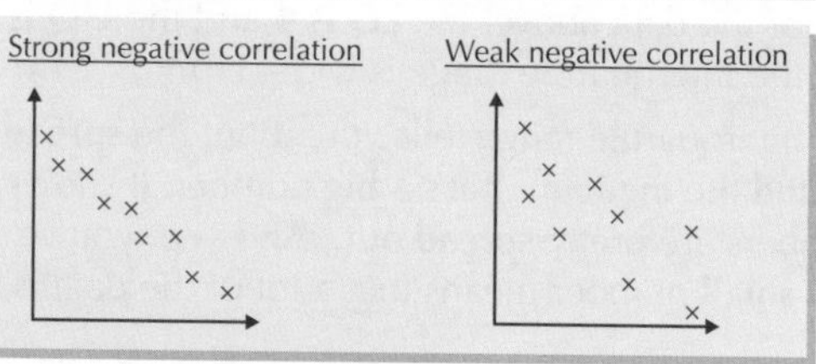

You Have To Check the Correlation Is Significant Though

1) A **Spearman's Rank correlation coefficient** might tell you that **two sets of numbers** are **correlated.** But you need to check whether this is evidence for a **genuine link** between the two quantities you're looking at. (You sometimes get correlations between sets of data **by chance**, even if there's no underlying relationship. For example, there **is** a correlation between river discharge and rainfall **for the data shown above**, but this might have been a fluke and there might be **no real relationship** between the two things.)

2) You can check whether it's evidence for a genuine link by looking at the **probability** that a correlation would happen by chance. If there's a 5% (or higher) probability that a correlation is because of chance then it's **not significant** evidence for a link. If there's a **0.1% or less** chance, then it's **very significant** evidence for a link. (This is what's meant by the **significance level** of a statistical test — it's a kind of 'cut-off' probability.)

3) To test whether the value of r_s is evidence for a relationship between discharge and rainfall, you'll need a **graph** like the one on the right. You'll also need to know the **degrees of freedom** (this is just n – 2, so in the example above degrees of freedom = 12 – 2 = **10**). Since r_s = **0.95**, you can use the graph to find that this correlation has a **less than 0.1%** probability of being due to chance. This means you have **very significant** evidence for a **relationship** between river discharge and rainfall.

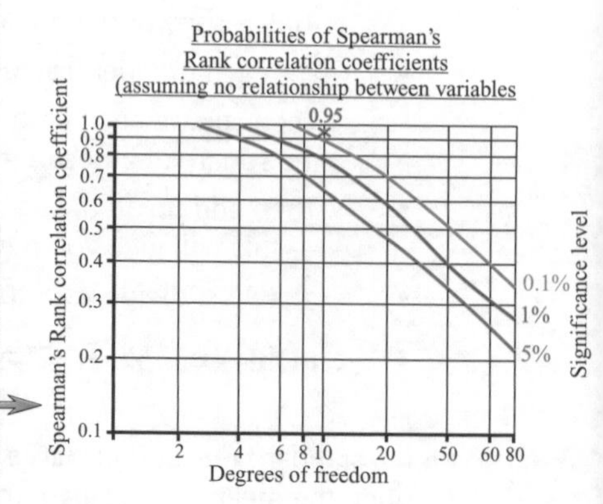

Answers

Section 1 — Rivers and Flooding

Page 3 — The Hydrological Cycle

1 *Maximum of 4 marks available.*
In wet seasons, precipitation exceeds evapotranspiration, creating a water surplus — ground stores fill with water as there's more surface runoff and higher discharge, so river levels rise ***[1 mark]****. In drier seasons, precipitation is lower than evapotranspiration — ground stores are depleted as some water is used by plants and humans and some flows into the river channel, but isn't replaced by precipitation* ***[1 mark]****. At the end of a dry season, there's a deficit (shortage) of water in the ground* ***[1 mark]****. This has to be paid back in the next wet season (ground store recharge)* ***[1 mark]****.*

Page 5 — River Discharge

1a) *Maximum of 2 marks available.*
Lag time = 12 hours ***[1 mark]****.*
Peak discharge = 35 cumecs ***[1 mark]****.*
b) *Maximum of 4 marks available.*
Vegetation intercepts precipitation and slows its movement to the river channel, increasing lag time ***[1 mark]****. So deforestation will reduce interception, resulting in a decreased lag time* ***[1 mark]****. The more vegetation there is in a basin, the more water is lost through transpiration and evaporation directly from the vegetation before it reaches the river channel, reducing peak discharge* ***[1 mark]****. So deforestation will reduce transpiration and evaporation, causing an increase in peak discharge* ***[1 mark]****.*

Page 7 — River Processes

1 *Maximum of 5 marks available.*
Erosion by hydraulic action happens as the pressure of the water breaks rock particles away from the bed and banks ***[1 mark]****. Abrasion (corrasion) occurs when eroded pieces of rock in the water scrape and rub against the bed and banks, removing material* ***[1 mark]****. Attrition is when eroded rocks smash into each other and break into smaller fragments* ***[1 mark]****.*
Erosion by cavitation occurs as air bubbles in turbulent stretches of water implode causing shockwaves that break pieces of rock off the banks and bed ***[1 mark]****. Corrosion erosion (solution) is the dissolving of rock by chemical processes* ***[1 mark]****.*

2 *Maximum of 6 marks available. This question is level marked.*
HINTS:
- *Start off by defining what the critical erosion velocity curve shows, e.g. 'The critical erosion velocity curve shows the minimum velocity needed to pick up and transport particles of different sizes'.*
- *Then you need to describe how it's different for different particle sizes, e.g. 'It's lowest for sand (particles between 0.1 mm and 1 mm), but it's higher for particles that are both larger (e.g. gravel, pebbles and boulders) and smaller (e.g. clay and silt)'.*
- *Finally explain why clay and silt require a faster velocity to be picked up and transported than sand (they tend to stick together more, so it takes more energy (velocity) to erode them), and do the same for larger particles (they require more velocity as they're heavier).*

Page 9 — The Long Profile and Channel Characteristics

1 *Maximum of 3 marks available*
A river's hydraulic radius is a measure of how efficient the river is ***[1 mark]****. It's calculated by dividing the river's cross-section area* ***[1 mark]*** *by the length of its wetted perimeter (the total length of the banks and bed that are in contact with the water)* ***[1 mark]****.*

2 *Maximum of 6 marks available. This question is level marked.*
HINTS:
- *It's fairly easy to structure your answer to this question. You can either talk about each stage of the river in turn and describe how the processes change. Or you can talk about each process in turn and describe how it changes as you go down the river.*
- *The questions says 'outline' so you need to describe what's happening and explain why, e.g. 'In the lower stage of a river, there's less erosion because turbulence is lower and sediment particle size is reduced (reducing erosion due to abrasion)'.*

Page 11 — River Landforms

1 *Maximum of 4 marks available*
Levees are natural, raised embankments formed when a river overflows its banks ***[1 mark]****. During a flood, material is deposited across the whole flood plain as the river loses velocity and energy due to increased friction* ***[1 mark]****. The heaviest material (e.g. sand and gravel) is dropped first, closest to the river channel* ***[1 mark]****. Over time, this material builds up on the river bank, creating a levee* ***[1 mark]****.*

Page 13 — Causes and Impacts of Flooding

1 *Maximum of 6 marks available. This question is level marked.*
HINTS:
- *The question asks you to 'outline' — this means describe the physical characteristics and explain why they would increase the risk of flooding.*
- *Focus on one characteristic at a time and give a full explanation, e.g. 'Drainage basins with impermeable ground (such as clay soils) don't allow infiltration of surface water. This increases surface runoff, which increases river discharge and increases the risk of flooding'.*
- *Cover a range of physical characteristics in detail, e.g. sparse vegetation, high drainage density, circular basin, steep slopes, etc.*

2 *Maximum of 5 marks available.*
Urban areas have large areas of impermeable tarmac and concrete ***[1 mark]****, so when it rains, surface runoff is very rapid* ***[1 mark]****. Urban areas also have gutters and drains, which quickly take runoff to the rivers* ***[1 mark]****. Both of these reduce lag time* ***[1 mark]****, which increases discharge and so increases the risk of flooding* ***[1 mark]****.*

Page 15 — Causes and Impacts of Flooding — Case Studies

1 *Maximum of 10 marks available. This question is level marked.*
HINTS:
- *Focus your answer on the impacts of flooding — write about the effect flooding has on society, the economy and the environment.*
- *The question asks you to use two named examples, so use two case studies you've learnt (e.g. the South Asia flood and the Carlisle flood).*
- *'Compare' means you should describe the impacts that are similar in poor and wealthy countries, and those that are different. For example, 'When South Asia was flooded in 2007 over 2000 people died, but only three people died in the Carlisle floods of 2005. The death toll in South Asia was high for many reasons, e.g. because many people living there rely on agriculture, so were reluctant to evacuate and leave their land and livestock unattended. Also, many children couldn't swim so they drowned in the floods'.*

Page 17 — Flood Management Strategies

1 *Maximum of 8 marks available. This question is level marked.*
HINTS:
- *This is a sneaky one — to answer the question you need to know that most soft engineering defences don't use man-made structures.*
- *Explain how flooding can be reduced using soft engineering defences, and explain how each defence works. For example, 'Flooding can be reduced by restoring the river to its natural state, e.g. by removing man-made levees. This allows the river to flood naturally. The water spreads out over the flood plain, which reduces river discharge and so decreases flooding downstream'.*
- *You don't need to include weather forecasts and flood warnings, as these don't actually reduce flooding (they only reduce the impacts of flooding).*

Answers

Page 19 — Flood Management Strategies — Case Studies

1 Maximum of 10 marks available. This question is level marked.
HINTS:
- The question asks you to refer to 'named examples', so you need to write about at least two case studies (e.g. the different approaches used on the Yangtze River and in Abingdon).
- Start off by describing what type of defences have been implemented in each place, e.g. 'Hard engineering defences, such as dams and levees, have been used along the Yangtze river in China'.
- Next write about the success of the schemes — say whether they have reduced flooding and describe any problems they have caused. For example, 'The Three Gorges Dam on the Yangtze River is thought to have successfully reduced major flooding from once every 10 years to once every 100 years. However, it has had many negative impacts, e.g. people have had to relocate as the reservoir behind the dam builds up. It's thought that between 1.3 and 2 million people will have been forced to relocate by the time the reservoir is full'.
- Don't forget to stuff your answer full of specific details about the case studies, e.g. 'There are 3600 km of levees along the middle and lower parts of the Yangtze'.

Section 2 — Coastal Environments

Page 21 — Introduction to Coastal Environments

1 Maximum of 4 marks available.
2 marks available for characteristics of constructive waves, from any of the following points: Constructive waves are flat and gentle **[1 mark]**. They have a low frequency **[1 mark]** of about 6-8 waves per minute **[1 mark]**. Their swash is greater than their backwash **[1 mark]** which carries material up the beach and deposits it **[1 mark]**.
2 marks available for characteristics of destructive waves, from any of the following points: Destructive waves are tall and steep **[1 mark]**. They have a high frequency **[1 mark]** of about 10-14 waves per minute **[1 mark]**. Their backwash is greater than their swash **[1 mark]** and removes beach material **[1 mark]**.

2 Maximum of 6 marks available. This question is level marked.
HINTS:
- 'Outline' means describe and explain, so first you need to list the erosion processes that affect cliffs — these include abrasion/corrasion, hydraulic action, quarrying and corrosion/solution.
- Don't write about attrition — it's not a type of erosion that affects cliffs (it's the erosion of rocks in the water by smashing together).
- Then for each type of erosion you need to explain how it erodes cliffs, e.g. 'Hydraulic action is where air in cracks in cliffs is compressed by waves. The pressure exerted by the compressed air breaks bits of rock off the cliff'.
- For top marks you also need to explain how sub-aerial weathering makes cliffs more vulnerable to erosion, e.g. 'Freeze-thaw weathering weakens cliffs and so makes them more vulnerable to erosion'.

Page 23 — Coastal Landforms

1 Maximum of 5 marks available.
Weathering and wave erosion forms a notch in a cliff **[1 mark]** at the high water mark **[1 mark]**. This eventually develops into a cave **[1 mark]**. Rock above the cave is unsupported and so collapses **[1 mark]**. As this process is repeated the cliff retreats, leaving behind a flat wave-cut platform **[1 mark]**.

2 Maximum of 6 marks available. This question is level marked.
HINTS:
- Spits are formed by longshore drift — to get top level marks you'll need to describe the process.
- Describe where spits are likely to form, e.g. 'Spits tend to form where the coast suddenly changes direction, such as across a river mouth'.
- Explain what a recurved end is, and how it's formed.
- Make sure you include what happens behind the spit, e.g. 'The area behind the spit is sheltered from the sea and often forms salt marshes'.
- Include a diagram (or a series of diagrams, like on page 23) to illustrate the formation.

Page 25 — Coastal Erosion — Case Study

1 Maximum of 10 marks available. This question is level marked.
See page 202 for a full worked answer to this question.

Page 27 — Sea Level Changes

1 Maximum of 8 marks available. This question is level marked.
HINTS:
- The question asks for possible impacts, so you need to write about what the impacts might be in the future.
- Make sure you include all the main impacts — more frequent and more severe flooding, submergence of low-lying islands and changes in the coastline.
- For each impact describe what could happen and give an example to back up your point if possible, e.g. 'Low-lying coastal islands may be submerged if sea level rises, e.g. if it rises 0.5 m, most of the Maldives would be submerged'.
- Don't forget to include that the main impacts have further impacts, e.g. decrease in tourism, damage to infrastructure etc.

2 Maximum of 8 marks available. This question is level marked.
HINTS:
- The question asks about coastal submergence, so you need to explain how it happens, e.g. 'Coastal submergence happens when the sea level rises relative to the land'.
- Then you need to explain how the rise in sea level may occur, and the difference between eustatic and isostatic change.
- The question also asks for a range of landforms, so make sure you talk about more than one (e.g. cover rias, fjords and Dalmatian coastlines).
- For each landform, describe how it's formed and its main features, e.g. 'Rias are drowned river valleys. They are wide and deep at the mouth, becoming narrower and shallower further inland'.

Page 29 — Coastal Flooding

1 Maximum of 10 marks available. This question is level marked.
HINTS:
- The question says a named coastal area. It might sound obvious, but remember to write about a case study, not just the general causes and effects of flooding.
- Talk about both the physical and human causes of the flooding, e.g. 'Coastal areas in south-east Asia were flooded by a tsunami that was caused by a submarine earthquake measuring about 9.0 on the Richter scale off the coast of Indonesia. However, human activity, such as destruction of mangrove forests in Thailand to make way for fish farms, and coral mining in the Indian Ocean, meant that a lot of the coasts' natural protection was missing. This made the effects of flooding worse'.
- Make sure you know whether each effect is social, economic or environmental because you might not always get asked for all three.
- Include plenty of facts and figures and make plenty of place-specific statements to show that you really know the case study, e.g. 'A quarter of hotels in southern Thailand were forced to close for at least 6 months because of damage from the flooding'.

Page 31 — Coastal Management

1 Maximum of 6 marks available. This question is level marked.
HINTS:
- First you need to describe what hard engineering defences and soft engineering defences are and give a couple of examples. E.g. 'Hard engineering defences are built structures, e.g. revetments, groynes and sea walls'.
- Then go on to explain why soft engineering defences are more sustainable, e.g. 'Soft engineering defences usually require much less time and money to maintain than hard engineering defences. They also create habitats like dunes and marshland, e.g. coastal realignment leads to the formation of marshland. Hard engineering defences often disrupt natural processes'.
- Finish up with a conclusion, e.g. 'Soft engineering schemes have a lower environmental impact and a lower economic cost than hard engineering schemes, so are more sustainable'.

Page 33 — Coastal Management — Case Studies

1 Maximum of 15 marks available. This question is level marked.
HINTS:
- The command word in this question is evaluate, so you need to talk about the costs and benefits of your chosen scheme.
- The question doesn't specify whether you need to write about a hard or soft engineering scheme, so the choice is yours. Make sure you pick one that you know loads about, so you can get plenty of detail in your answer.

Answers

- *Whatever scheme you choose, the benefits are likely to be things like saving land, housing, transport routes, and industry, and preserving natural habitats. The costs will include things like the price of setting up and maintaining the defences, the appearance of the defences and the possible effects on adjacent areas of the coast.*
- *Examiners love 'specific and detailed reference' to the case study, so it's always good to have some numbers to back up your points, e.g. '£2 million was spent on two rock groynes and 500 m of revetment at Mappleton in 1991'.*
- *But don't just scribble down all facts — you need to explain why these measures were used and the effect that they've had, e.g. 'They were built to protect the village and the B1242 road. The scheme has successfully protected these areas, but the groynes have starved down-drift beaches of sediment, which has caused increased erosion of the cliffs south of Mappleton'.*

Page 35 — Coastal Population Growth

1 *Maximum of 10 marks available. This question is level marked.*
HINTS:
- *You need to write about two locations and they need to be contrasting (i.e. very different). So you could cover either the development of a wealthy and poor location, or the development of an industrial port and a tourist resort.*
- *The question is asking you to explain (i.e. give reasons) why the population of the two locations has grown rapidly, so you need to write about the causes of the growth, e.g. 'Tourism grew in Brighton in the 18th century as people believed that bathing in seawater was good for their health. Brighton's population grew as people migrated to the area attracted by the jobs tourism provided'.*
- *Make sure you include plenty of relevant facts about the two locations, e.g. 'Following the discovery of oil in the region, the population of Dubai City quadrupled between 1968 and 1975, as foreign workers flooded into the city to work in construction and oil production'.*

Page 37 — Coastal Development and Conflict

1 *Maximum of 10 marks available. This question is level marked.*
HINTS:
- *This question is asking you to examine so you need to describe the impact of the development, and explain why this leads to conflict, e.g. 'Road building and construction of tourist amenities can destroy ecologically important land, such as sand dunes. This creates conflict between tourists, who demand improved infrastructure, and conservationists, who want to preserve these valuable coastal areas'.*
- *You're only asked to examine the environmental impact, so don't start talking about conflict between tourists and locals because of traffic congestion. Stick to things that affect the environment.*
- *There are four main activities linked with development that have an impact on coastal environments: tourism, overfishing, aquaculture and industrialisation. Structure your answer so you describe the impact of each of these in turn. You can even find links between some of them, e.g. 'Demand from tourists for fresh, local fish can lead to overfishing'.*

Page 39 — Coastal Development and Conflict

1 *Maximum of 10 marks available. This question is level marked.*
HINTS:
- *This is similar to the question on page 37, but this time you need to focus on specific case study details, not just the theory.*
- *Again, there'll be a few main activities having an impact on the environment which you can use to structure your answer. Be careful though because they might not be exactly the same for your chosen areas as they are in the general case, e.g. for Dubai, it's 'oil production', not just 'industrialisation'.*
- *It might be tempting to write a whole load of stuff about conflict, but the question doesn't actually ask for it. You won't get top marks for answering what you THINK the question is asking you. You're only asked about how development has threatened the coastal environment.*
- *As ever with questions like this, you need to get in lots and lots of place-specific details to back up your points. It's no good just saying 'more tourists in Dubai are damaging the coast' — you need to give details, e.g. 'The number of tourists visiting Dubai is forecast to increase from about 7 million in 2007 to 14 million by 2015. This increased tourism will lead to more sewage, litter and erosion of the coastline'.*

2 *Maximum of 15 marks available. This question is level marked.*
HINTS:
- *Structure your answer to explain your fieldwork plans, how you carried out those plans and how you used research sources.*
- *Make sure you say what you aimed to find out with your fieldwork and research, e.g. 'To assess the impact of tourism on the area and the potential conflict, I looked for articles in the local newspaper that described tourist development, and I interviewed different stakeholders'.*
- *Include details of where you studied, where you looked for information and what fieldwork you carried out.*

Section 3 — Cold Environments

Page 41 — Distribution of Cold Environments

1 *Maximum of 15 marks available. This question is level marked.*
HINTS:
- *The question only mentions glacial and periglacial environments, so don't write about alpine or polar environments.*
- *Start by defining each environment, e.g. 'Glacial environments are areas of land covered by ice (either glaciers or ice sheets)'.*
- *Then describe where each environment is found (i.e. its distribution). Don't forget to include examples. E.g. 'Glacial environments are found at high latitudes, e.g. the Antarctic Ice Sheet is above 60°, and at high altitudes, e.g. there are glaciers in the Himalayan mountains (the highest mountain range in the world)'.*
- *Then explain why they're found there. E.g. 'Glaciers and ice sheets only form where it's really cold. High latitude areas are really cold because they receive little solar radiation. The Sun's energy hits the Earth at more of an angle at high latitudes, so it's spread out over a larger area'.*
- *For extra marks explain why glacial environments aren't found on low altitude land in the middle of continents.*

Page 43 — Glaciers

1 *Maximum of 3 marks available.*
A glacial budget is the balance between accumulation (the input of snow and ice into a glacier) and ablation (the output of water from a glacier) over a year ***[1 mark]***. If the glacial budget is positive, accumulation is exceeding ablation, and the glacier is advancing ***[1 mark]***. If the glacial budget is negative, ablation is exceeding accumulation, and the glacier is retreating ***[1 mark]***.

2 *Maximum of 5 marks available.*
In warm-based glaciers, the base temperature is warmer than the melting point of ice, so melting occurs. The meltwater acts as a lubricant, making it easier for the glacier to move downhill ***[1 mark]***. Ice at the surface also melts if the temperature reaches 0 °C. Meltwater moves down through the glacier and lubricates it even more ***[1 mark]***. In cold-based glaciers the base is cold, so there's very little melting at the bottom of the glacier. The ice is frozen to the valley floor ***[1 mark]***. So warm-based glaciers move faster than cold-based glaciers ***[1 mark]***, which means they erode the landscape more ***[1 mark]***.

Page 45 — Glacial Processes

1 *Maximum of 4 marks available.*
At the head of a glacier the valley is steep, so there's a strong gravitational force pulling the ice downwards ***[1 mark]***. This makes the ice move quickly ***[1 mark]***. The tension created causes the ice to crack into layers, which slip downwards over each other ***[1 mark]***. This is called extensional flow ***[1 mark]***.

2 *Maximum of 4 marks available.*
Glaciers pick up debris by plucking ***[1 mark]*** and abrasion ***[1 mark]***. Plucking is when ice thaws and then refreezes around rocks. When the glacier moves forward, it plucks the rocks from the valley floor or wall ***[1 mark]***. Abrasion is when debris carried by the glacier scrapes material off the valley walls and floor ***[1 mark]***.

Page 47 — Glacial Landforms

1 *Maximum of 8 marks available. This question is level marked.*
See page 205 for a full worked answer to this question.

2 *Maximum of 3 marks available.*
Lateral moraine is deposited where the sides of the glacier were ***[1 mark]***. Medial moraine is deposited in the centre of the valley where two glaciers converge ***[1 mark]***. Terminal moraine is deposited as semicircular hillocks at the end of the glacier ***[1 mark]***.

Answers

Page 49 — Fluvioglacial Processes and Landforms

1 *Maximum of 2 marks available.*
Kame terraces are piles of sorted deposits that run along the valley walls ***[1 mark]****. They're deposited by meltwater streams that run between the glacier and the valley sides* ***[1 mark]****.*

2 *Maximum of 4 marks available.*
Delta kames are formed when meltwater streams flow into a proglacial lake ***[1 mark]****. When they flow into a proglacial lake, they slow down and deposit the sediment they're carrying on the ice* ***[1 mark]****. These deposits are known as deltas* ***[1 mark]****. After the ice has melted the deltas are deposited on the valley floor, forming delta kames* ***[1 mark]****.*

Page 51 — Periglacial Processes and Landforms

1 *Maximum of 6 marks available. This question is level marked.*
HINTS:
- *Start by explaining what's meant by patterned ground.*
- *State the two ways that patterned ground is formed — by frost heave and frost contraction.*
- *Explain how each process causes stones to form patterns on the surface of the ground, e.g. 'Frost contraction occurs when temperatures drop very low in winter — the ground contracts, causing polygon shaped cracks to form in the permafrost. The cracks get filled in with stones forming polygon patterns on the surface'.*

Page 53 — Issues in Cold Environments

1 *Maximum of 6 marks available. This question is level marked.*
HINTS:
- *The main types of development in cold environments are mining, fishing, oil extraction, tourism and hydroelectric power production.*
- *For each type of development, describe how it can damage the environment and give an example. E.g. 'Oil spilt when it's being transported can lead to the death of birds and marine life. For example, when the Exxon Valdez tanker crashed off the coast of Alaska over 40 million litres of oil were spilt, which killed over 250 000 birds and fish'.*
- *Include that cold environments have fragile ecosystems, which means that they struggle to recover from damage.*

2 *Maximum of 6 marks available. This question is level marked.*
HINTS:
- *Start by describing the traditional way of life of native tribes, i.e. what their lifestyle was like before development of tundra areas.*
- *Then say what development has taken place, e.g. whaling, sealing and fishing by newcomers.*
- *Finally, explain how this development has affected the native tribes, e.g. by bringing diseases and depleting their resources.*
- *Include any relevant facts you can remember, e.g. 'When newcomers arrived in Canada in the late 19th century and early 20th century, they brought diseases like tuberculosis, which killed 90% of the Inuvialuit tribe'.*

Page 55 — Issues in Cold Environments — Case Study

1 *Maximum of 15 marks available. This question is level marked.*
HINTS:
- *Start off by describing what resources are found in the Antarctic and what type of development they attract.*
- *Then explain how the Antarctic is being protected by the Antarctic Treaty — i.e. it bans some development and controls other activities.*
- *Describe which activities are banned (mining, oil extraction and whaling) and explain why they're banned — the possible environmental impact of mining and oil extraction could be huge, and the whale population has decreased due to whaling. Don't forget to include the names of the protocols that ban them.*
- *Then say which activities are allowed but controlled (tourism, scientific research, fishing). Explain how they're controlled and how the measures reduce their environmental impact and make them more sustainable.*
- *Finish off by talking about any issues, e.g. illegal fishing.*

Section 4 — Hot Desert Environments

Page 57 — Desert and Desert Margin Characteristics

1a) *Maximum of 6 marks available. This part is level marked.*
HINTS:
- *Start by describing what the rainfall is like — say which months have no rainfall, which months do, and which month has the highest rainfall, e.g. 'Riyadh receives no rainfall from June to September. It typically rains from October until May, with most rain falling in April (average 29 mm)'.*
- *You get higher marks if you manipulate the data, so count up the total rainfall for the year and say if Riyadh has an arid or semi-arid climate, e.g. 'The total rainfall in Riyadh is about 100 mm per year, which is less than 250 mm per year, so it has an arid climate and is classed as a desert'.*
- *Next describe the temperature throughout the year.*
- *Remember to quote data from the graph to back up your points.*

b) *Maximum of 5 marks available. This part is level marked.*
HINTS:
- *First, say that if it's 25° north of the equator it's located in an area of circulating air known as a Hadley cell.*
- *Then you need to explain how the circulating air leads to low precipitation, e.g. 'As air rises at the equator, the moisture that it holds condenses and falls as rain. The dry air descends over Riyadh, creating an area of high pressure. Winds blow outwards from this area, meaning no moisture can be brought in, so there's very little precipitation'.*

c) *Maximum of 4 marks available.*
The total amount of vegetation in Riyadh will be low ***[1 mark]*** *because the lack of water makes it difficult for plants to grow* ***[1 mark]****. Any vegetation present will be specialised to collect, store and conserve water* ***[1 mark]****. Vegetation is likely to include shrubs, grasses and cacti* ***[1 mark]****.*

Page 59 — Processes in Hot Desert Environments

1 *Maximum of 8 marks available. This question is level marked.*
HINTS:
- *To get full marks you need to describe all four types of mechanical weathering that occur in hot desert environments — thermal fracture, frost shattering, wetting and drying, and salt weathering.*
- *Write a brief paragraph about each type of weathering, e.g. 'Thermal fracture is caused by the large daily temperature variations in hot desert environments. Rocks expand during the day (when it's hot) and contract at night (when it's cold). Sometimes outer layers of rock flake off because they warm up and cool down more quickly than the inner layers (exfoliation). Individual grains can also fall off because different minerals within the rock expand and contract at different rates (granular disintegration)'.*
- *Include diagrams to help you explain the processes involved.*

2a) *Maximum of 3 marks available.*
Exogenous rivers have a source outside the desert margin and they flow throughout the year despite evaporation reducing their volume ***[1 mark]****. Endoreic rivers terminate inland in the form of an inland sea or delta* ***[1 mark]****. Ephemeral rivers flow intermittently or seasonally after rainstorms* ***[1 mark]****.*

b) *Maximum of 6 marks available. This part is level marked.*
HINTS:
- *Start your answer by describing what flash floods and sheet floods are.*
- *Then describe how both types of flood transport material. Make sure you point out that flash floods have more energy and so can carry larger pieces of rock.*
- *Be specific in your answer — don't just say, 'Flash floods carry large pieces of rock', instead say, 'Flash floods carry large pieces of desert rock by traction'.*
- *The question asks about erosion — so make sure your answer includes how both types of floods erode the desert surface by abrasion and attrition.*

Page 61 — Landforms in Hot Desert Environments

1 *Maximum of 7 marks available. This question is level marked.*
HINTS:
- *You need to describe and explain the formation of both yardangs and zeugen to get full marks. Make sure you don't get them confused.*
- *First explain what yardangs are and how they're formed, e.g. 'Yardangs are narrow, streamlined ridges. Strong winds (blowing in one direction) carry sand in suspension, which erodes rocks by abrasion. Softer rock is eroded faster than harder rock, so ridges of hard rock are created'.*
- *Then do the same for zeugen.*

Answers

- You could include diagrams of each to help explain how they're formed. For example, draw one like this for yardangs:

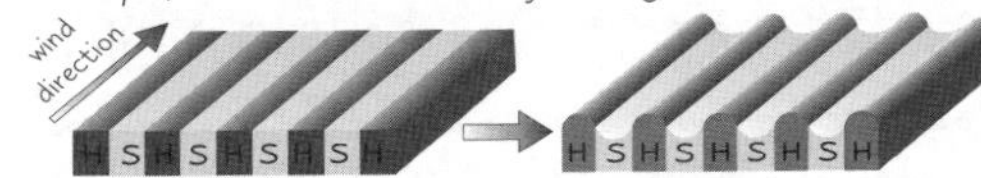

2a) Maximum of 3 marks available.
Landform A is a sand dune/barchan/crescent-shaped sand dune **[1 mark]**. Landform B is an alluvial fan **[1 mark]**. Landform C is a wadi **[1 mark]**.

b) Maximum of 4 marks available.
A mesa is an isolated, flat-topped, steep-sided landform found only in arid places **[1 mark]**. It's a type of inselberg **[1 mark]** made of hard rock that's more resistant to erosion than the surrounding rock **[1 mark]**. It's formed when the surrounding softer rock is eroded away by wind or water, leaving the harder rock mesa standing out **[1 mark]**.

c) Maximum of 4 marks available.
Feature E could be a salt lake or a salt pan **[1 mark]**. Salt lakes form when desert rivers are endoreic/terminate inland **[1 mark]**. The water can't leave the lake and evaporation is high, resulting in a lake with a high salt content **[1 mark]**. Some salt lakes are ephemeral — evaporation is so high that they dry up at certain times of the year, leaving the salt behind to form salt pans **[1 mark]**.

Page 63 — Desertification

1 Maximum of 10 marks available. This question is level marked.
HINTS:
- Split your answer into two — first cover the physical causes, then the human causes.
- For each cause, explain how it leads to desertification, e.g. 'Climate change is causing an increase in temperature in some areas. This increases the rate of evapotranspiration, which dries soils out and lowers surface water levels. Vegetation dies due to lack of water and so there are fewer roots to hold the soil together. This leads to an increase in soil erosion'.
- Make sure you explicitly say how each one leads to either soil erosion or the land being less fertile (e.g. because the salt content has increased).
- Don't forget that there are a number of ways that irrigation leads to desertification.
- As a final point, include how an increase in population can increase overgrazing, overcultivation and deforestation.

Page 65 — Desertification Case Study — The Sahel

1 Maximum of 15 marks available. This question is level marked.
HINTS:
- This question asks you to evaluate the strategies, so you need to say if they worked, if they caused any problems and if they had any extra benefits, e.g. 'Jatropha curcas is being grown around crops in Mali to protect them from wind erosion. The strategy has reduced erosion in the area and has also reduced rural poverty, as oil from the plant can be sold'.
- Include whether each strategy is sustainable or not.
- As always with case study questions include plenty of relevant details, e.g. 'Yields of some crops increased 40% in Burkina Faso as a result of contour bunding'.

Page 67 — Desertification Case Study — Southern Spain

1 Maximum of 15 marks available. This question is level marked.
HINTS:
- The question asks you to compare strategies, so you need to write about the similarities and differences between the strategies used to tackle desertification in Spain and the Sahel.
- Start off by describing the similarities in the strategies used in the Sahel and Spain, e.g. 'Both the Sahel and Spain are implementing strategies to increase the level of vegetation, as loss of vegetation is a major cause of desertification in both areas'.
- Then explain the differences in the strategies used, e.g. 'In Spain lots of money is being spent on transferring water from one place to another, whilst in the Sahel the focus is on working with what little water they have, by conserving rainwater (using contour bunding) and growing plants that are suited to drought conditions'.

Section 5 — World at Risk

Page 69 — Global Hazards

1 Maximum of 15 marks available. This question is level marked.
HINTS:
- You need to structure your answer into clearly separate parts, e.g. write a short introduction, then divide the main answer into two main sections talking about the number of deaths, and then the economic losses. At the end write a short conclusion.
- In your introduction define what 'disaster' means, e.g. 'A disaster occurs when a hazard (something that's a potential threat to human life or property) actually seriously affects humans'.
- In each of the two sections (number of deaths and economic losses), start by describing in detail how they are changing, e.g. 'On a global scale, the number of deaths caused by disasters has been decreasing, but the trend has recently levelled off'. The question's worth 15 marks so make sure you give plenty of detail.
- Then you should explain why this is happening, e.g. 'Deaths are decreasing because of improvements in risk management strategies. But the trend is levelling off because there are an increasing number of vulnerable people, meaning more people are affected by disasters, and so more are likely to be killed'.

Page 71 — Hazard Distribution

1 Maximum of 3 marks available.
Earthquakes occur because tectonic plates don't move in a uniform way **[1 mark]**. Some parts move faster than others, which causes pressure to build up **[1 mark]**. When the pressure becomes too much the plates crack or jerk past each other, causing an earthquake **[1 mark]**.

2 Maximum of 10 marks available. This question is level marked.
HINTS:
- Make sure you have a clear structure — write an introduction, then describe where they occur, followed by a section explaining why volcanoes occur there.
- In the introduction, define 'volcano', e.g. 'A volcano is a point where magma has risen from below the Earth's surface and been ejected above ground'.
- Next describe the global distribution of volcanoes, e.g. 'Volcanoes can be found all along the mid-Atlantic ridge. They are also found around the edges of the Pacific Ocean, particularly around Japan and Indonesia, and along the west coast of America. They're also found in the centre of the Pacific Ocean in Hawaii'.
- Now explain why volcanoes happen at each of the locations you've described. Make sure you use appropriate language, e.g. 'The mid-Atlantic ridge is a constructive boundary. Here the mantle is under pressure from the overlying plates, and when they move apart pressure is released and the mantle melts, forming magma. This is less dense than the plates so it rises and can erupt to form a volcano'.

Page 73 — Disaster Hotspot Case Study — California

1 Maximum of 15 marks available. This question is level marked.
HINTS:
- Start by introducing the key terms in the question — define the term 'disaster hotspot', e.g. 'A disaster hotspot is a vulnerable place at risk from two or more hazards'.
- Next describe and explain each of the hazards that threaten California, e.g. 'California is at risk from earthquakes because the San Andreas fault runs the length of the state. This forms part of a conservative plate boundary — where two plates are moving past each other. Earthquakes occur here because pressure builds up as the plates move past each other. Eventually the plates crack or jerk past each other, releasing energy as an earthquake'.
- Include specific examples for each hazard, e.g. 'Two or three large earthquakes occur every year, and there have been disastrous earthquakes before, e.g. the San Francisco earthquake (1906), which destroyed much of the city'.
- Include a section explaining why the population is vulnerable e.g. 'California is a wealthy state, but some people are very poor, so they have a lower capacity to cope when affected by a disaster'.

Answers

Page 75 — Disaster Hotspot Case Study — The Philippines

1a) Maximum of 4 marks available.

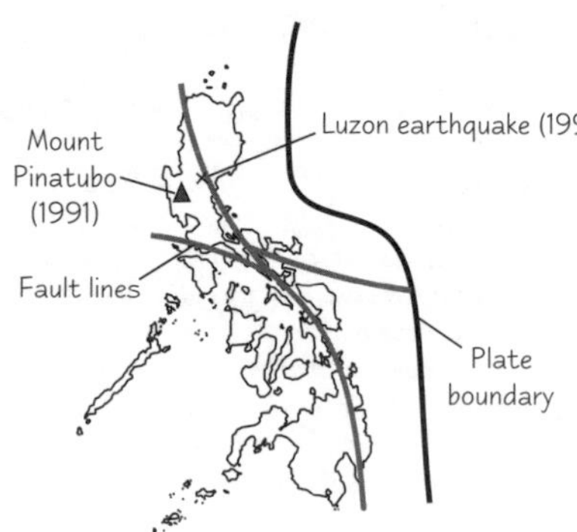

1 mark for each of the following: a volcano disaster, an earthquake disaster, and the approximate positions of the plate boundary and fault lines.

b) Maximum of 15 marks available. This question is level marked.
HINTS:
- 'Compare' and 'contrast' means you need to talk about the similarities and the differences between the two disaster hotspots.
- You can structure this in different ways, but make sure you compare the two places — don't just write about them separately, e.g. 'Both California and the Philippines are at risk from volcanoes, earthquakes, landslides, tsunamis and droughts, but the Philippines is also at risk from typhoons'.
- Define the term 'disaster hotspot' e.g. 'A disaster hotspot is a vulnerable place at risk from two or more hazards'.
- Write a paragraph for each hazard. Make sure you include which place is vulnerable to each hazard — California, the Philippines or both.
- Write a paragraph about the populations of both places, e.g. 'Both the Philippines and California have many settlements built in hazardous areas, e.g. the Aeta tribe in the Philippines live on the slopes of Mount Pinatubo, a volcano, and over 70% of California's population live within 30 miles of a fault line. However, the population of California is more wealthy and there's a better infrastructure to cope with hazards, so it's likely that fewer lives would be lost in a disaster in California than in the Philippines'.

Page 77 — Evidence for Climate Change

1 Maximum of 10 marks available. This question is level marked.
HINTS:
- To get full marks you need to outline (describe and explain) a number of sources of evidence for long-term climate change, e.g. ice cores, pollen analysis and indicators of sea-level change.
- Structure the answer to have an introduction, then separate sections outlining each of the sources of evidence and finish with a conclusion.
- In your introduction, define the key terms of the question such as 'climate change' and 'long-term', e.g. 'Climate change is any significant change in the weather of a region over a period of at least several decades'.
- For each source of evidence describe it and then explain how it's used to determine past climate, e.g. 'Scientists can drill deep into ice sheets (huge masses of ice) to extract cores of ice. When the ice was formed, gases were trapped inside it. Scientists can analyse these gases to tell what the temperature was when the ice formed'.

Page 79 — Causes of Climate Change

1 Maximum of 15 marks available. This question is level marked.
HINTS:
- Start by stating that humans are causing global warming, e.g. 'There's a scientific consensus that the rise in average global temperature, especially over the last century (called global warming) is being caused by human activity'.
- Then split the rest of the answer into two parts covering the two main human activities that cause climate change — enhanced greenhouse gas emissions and destruction of natural CO_2 sinks.
- Describe and explain how each activity contributes to global warming, e.g. 'Human activity, e.g. burning fossil fuels, means more greenhouse gases are released into the atmosphere. More greenhouse gases increase the greenhouse effect, which warms the planet more'.
- Where possible quote facts, e.g. 'In the last 150 years atmospheric levels of CO_2 have increased from 280 ppm (parts per million) to 380 ppm. This is thought to be mostly due to human activity'.

Page 81 — Impacts of Climate Change

1 Maximum of 15 marks available. This question is level marked.
HINTS:
- Start by describing global warming and some of its impacts, e.g. 'Global warming is the rise in average global temperature over the last century. Impacts include... '.
- Then you need to explain that people are trying to predict what changes will occur, using the example in the question, e.g. 'The Intergovernmental Panel on Climate Change (IPCC) has developed a number of different emissions scenarios. They range from predictions where emissions won't increase any more, to scenarios where they increase a lot'.
- Then write a paragraph on each of the reasons why these predictions are difficult to make, e.g. 'Scientists don't know how much of the emissions will be absorbed by natural CO_2 sinks like oceans and plants'.
- To get full marks you should explain at least four reasons why predictions are difficult to make.

Page 83 — Climate Change — Case Studies

1 Maximum of 10 marks available. This question is level marked.
HINTS:
- The question is asking about the specific impacts in a named area — this means using a case study, e.g. the Arctic or Africa.
- Write an introduction defining what global warming is, then name the place you're going to talk about and describe where it is, e.g. 'Global warming is having significant impacts on the Arctic — the area around the North Pole'.
- Then split your answer into two sections — ecological impacts and environmental impacts. Remember to quote facts when you're describing the impacts, e.g. 'Increasing temperatures are causing the area of sea ice (frozen sea water) in the Arctic to shrink at an increasing rate — some scientists think there won't be any in the summer by 2030. Polar bears need sea ice to hunt for food, so loss of sea ice may mean they become an endangered species'.

Page 85 — Coping with Climate Change

1 Maximum of 15 marks available. This question is level marked.
HINTS:
- It would be a good idea to explain why global agreements are complex before you go into your named example. It'll have more impact this way.
- Write an introduction explaining that climate change is a global hazard, there are lots of strategies to cope with it (at many levels), and global agreements involve lots of different groups (key players).
- Briefly explain who all the key players are and how they influence agreements on how to cope with climate change. You can then go on to say that agreements are difficult because there are different views and levels of influence between and within all the groups.
- Write a detailed section on a named example, e.g. Kyoto Protocol.
- It's important you quote as many relevant facts as you can, e.g. 'The Kyoto protocol is an international agreement between more than 170 countries to cut greenhouse gas emissions'.

Page 87 — Global Hazards — The Future

1 Maximum of 10 marks available. This question is level marked.
HINTS:
- You'll need to use material from p. 86 for this answer.
- Don't forget to structure your answer. First link global warming to famine and water shortages, e.g. 'Changes in temperature and precipitation brought about by global warming can result in drier conditions in some areas, leading to water shortages, and a decreased ability to grow food'.
- Then write a section linking water shortages to conflict, e.g. 'Conflict can occur where there isn't enough of a resource for different groups, e.g. increasing water shortages due to global warming could lead to conflict over the diminishing water resource'.
- Use examples, e.g. 'The Nile river's two main tributaries flow through Sudan and Ethiopia. These join together and the river then flows through Egypt. If Ethiopia and Sudan need to use more water from the tributaries because of global warming, Egypt's supply will be reduced, and conflict may occur'.

Answers

Section 6 — Extreme Weather

Page 89 — Extreme Weather Events

1 Maximum of 10 marks available. This question is level marked.
HINTS:
- Start off by stating what tropical cyclones are.
- Then describe the conditions needed for tropical cyclones to form, e.g. 'Tropical cyclones form over warm water (26.5 °C or higher at the surface)'.
- Next, explain where tropical cyclones are found, linking the distribution to the conditions needed for cyclones to form. E.g. 'Tropical cyclones are found in the tropics because the sea water temperature in this region is high enough for cyclones to form. They're not found below 5° latitude because the Coriolis effect isn't strong enough to make the winds spin'.
- If you can, add in a relevant example, e.g. if you're writing about distribution mention that Hurricane Katrina developed in the south-eastern Bahamas in August 2005.

Page 91 — Extreme Weather Events

1 Maximum of 10 marks available. This question is level marked.
HINTS:
- Start off by stating what an anticyclone is and the extreme weather conditions that it can cause, i.e. droughts and heatwaves.
- Then describe how anticyclones can lead to drought conditions. E.g. 'Anticyclones are areas of high pressure caused by sinking air. No air can rise, which means there's no condensation and no precipitation. If the anticyclone remains stationary for a long period of time (because it's cut off from a jet stream) it can cause drought conditions'.
- Next describe how anticyclones can lead to heatwaves. E.g. 'Anticyclones that remain stationary for a long period of time (blocking anticyclones) can lead to reduced cloud cover and higher temperatures as more solar radiation is absorbed by the land. If the blocking anticyclone lasts for a long time it can cause a heatwave'.

Page 93 — Extreme Weather — Fieldwork and Research

1 Maximum of 15 marks available. This question is level marked.
HINTS:
- This question asks you to describe and explain how you would investigate the link between weather conditions and a depression, so it's not enough to say what you did, you've got to explain why as well.
- Describe what fieldwork you did. E.g. 'I made a weather diary and recorded how pressure, wind speed, precipitation and temperature changed over time. This allowed me to see the correlation between extremely low pressure (depressions) and wind speeds and rainfall'.
- Include details of exactly how you carried out your fieldwork, giving reasons for your choices. E.g. 'I took readings from the same place each day (to make sure that nothing else affected the readings) and I did this for ten days. This period of time was long enough to allow me to see any patterns that emerged'.
- Then describe what research you did to further investigate the links and why you did this. E.g. 'I used the internet to look up reliable sources of data (e.g. from the Met Office) to see if this secondary data agreed with the primary data that I collected from my weather diary'.

Page 95 — The Impact of Extreme Weather

1 Maximum of 10 marks available. This question is level marked.
HINTS:
- The question asks you to explain the factors that influence the impact of extreme weather events — it's not asking you to explain the impacts themselves.
- Start with an introduction saying what the three key factors are — severity of the event, economic development of the area affected and vulnerability of the people affected.
- Then explain each of the three factors in detail, e.g. 'The bigger and more intense a weather event is the more severe it is. The greater the severity of the event the bigger the impact will be'.
- The best way to show how the impact of an event can differ due to each factor is to compare two separate, specific weather events. E.g. compare the impact of two tornadoes that differ in severity or compare the impact of two hurricanes that hit economically different areas.
- When using examples include relevant details, e.g. don't just say one tornado was more severe than another, state what category each tornado was.

Page 97 — The Impact of Extreme Weather

1 Maximum of 10 marks available. This question is level marked.
HINTS:
- This question asks you for one or more named examples, which means you'll need to use at least one case study — e.g. you could use the Murray-Darling Basin drought in Australia, or the Carlisle flood.
- First, you need to describe the social, environmental and economic impacts of your chosen weather event. E.g. 'One of the environmental impacts of the Murray-Darling Basin drought is that there's less vegetation and more soil erosion in the area, as well as increased wildfires and dust storms'.
- Use specific data in your descriptions. For example, instead of saying 'Unemployment has increased', say 'Unemployment has increased to 7% above the national average for Australia'.
- Then, you need to explain the impacts of the weather event. So you need to talk about how the severity of the weather event, the economic development of the area and the vulnerability of the population influenced the impact of the drought. E.g. 'Australia is a more economically developed country, so it's able to lessen some of the impacts of the drought. For example, 1500 small businesses have received income support from the government to help them survive'.

Page 99 — Increasing Risk from Extreme Weather

1 Maximum of 10 marks available. This question is level marked.
HINTS:
- Start with an introduction explaining that there are two main factors that have contributed to the increased risk of flooding occurring — climate change and poor land management (population growth increases the risk from floods).
- Then write about each of the factors in separate paragraphs. Make sure you explain how each factor is believed to cause an increased risk of flooding. E.g. 'Many scientists believe global warming has contributed to the increased frequency and severity of flooding in the UK. This is because higher temperatures (due to global warming) result in changes in global air circulation and ocean currents, which means some places in the UK will receive more rainfall due to more storms. Greater rainfall increases the risk of flooding'.

Page 101 — Increasing Flood Risk — Fieldwork and Research

1 Maximum of 15 marks available. This question is level marked.
HINTS:
- This question asks you to describe and explain how you have investigated physical factors that affect flooding, so it's not enough to say what you did — you've got to explain why you did it as well.
- Start your answer by writing the name and location of the river you studied.
- Then describe the fieldwork you carried out to explore the link between physical factors (e.g. precipitation, surface runoff, infiltration rates) and flooding. E.g. 'I measured the amount of rainfall in the area by using a rain gauge. I left the rain gauge in the same place beside the river and measured the amount of rainfall it had collected, at the same time each day for seven days'.
- Then describe the research you carried out into the link between physical factors and flooding. This could include rainfall data you looked up on the Met Office website or reports from the National Water Archive.
- Remember to only include fieldwork and research into physical factors, as the question requires — not human factors.
- Try to use lots of geographical terms in your answer, e.g. precipitation, discharge, hydrograph, infiltration, flood return intervals. But be careful, make sure you know exactly what they mean before you use them.

Answers

Page 103 — Managing Extreme Weather

1 Maximum of 10 marks available. This question is level marked.
HINTS:
- *The question says 'outline' so it's asking you to describe and explain.*
- *Make sure you describe a range of ways in which new and more powerful technology has improved the management of extreme weather events, e.g. more accurate weather forecasts, drought-resistant crops, hurricane-proof and flood-proof buildings.*
- *Give appropriate examples to back up your answer. E.g. 'The Met Office uses supercomputers, which are more powerful and have faster processing speeds than previous models. This means scientists can run more complex weather models, making the forecasts more accurate. Forecasting accuracy rose from 79% in 1980 to 86% in 1996, because of computer upgrades'.*
- *Remember to explain how each of these things has improved the management of an extreme weather event. E.g. 'More accurate weather forecasts mean that earlier warnings can be given. This gives people more time to protect their houses or evacuate, which reduces damage and loss of life'.*

Page 105 — Drought and Water Management

1 Maximum of 10 marks available. This question is level marked.
HINTS:
- *The question asks you to refer to at least two named examples, so you should use at least two case studies you've learnt about, e.g. drought management in Australia and south-east England.*
- *Describe a range of drought management strategies used in each of your examples and include as much detail as you can. E.g. 'Perth, in Australia, has a desalination plant that supplies the city with 17% of its water by filtering, treating and desalinating seawater and mixing it with the public water supply'.*
- *The question asks you to 'discuss the sustainability', so for each strategy you describe you need to say if it's sustainable and why. E.g. 'Perth's desalination plant is powered by renewable energy (from wind farms) and permanently reduces water use, so it is sustainable'.*

Section 7 — Globalisation

Page 107 — Introduction to Globalisation

1 Maximum of 15 marks available. This question is level marked.
HINTS:
- *First write a short introduction, then divide the answer into four sections explaining why TNCs, new markets, improved communications and international organisations have accelerated globalisation.*
- *In your introduction give a short definition of what globalisation is, e.g. 'Globalisation is the process of all the world's systems and cultures becoming more integrated'.*
- *In each of the four sections you need to describe what the factor is and explain how it's accelerating globalisation. For example, 'Improved communications are improvements to transport mechanisms, e.g. aeroplanes or high-speed rail, as well as to information exchanges, e.g. the internet and e-mail. Individuals and businesses have easier access to places that are further away (and to more products brought from far away) and they can communicate instantly with any part of the world. The world seems smaller as distance becomes less important'.*

Page 109 — Global Groupings

1 Maximum of 4 marks available.
LDCs are countries defined by very low incomes, poor health, low education and economic instability ***[1 mark]***. LDCs have economies based on agriculture ***[1 mark]***. In comparison, NICs aren't fully developed countries, but they're more wealthy than LDCs and their economies are growing quickly ***[1 mark]***. NICs have economies that have recently moved from agriculture to manufacturing and exporting ***[1 mark]***.

2 Maximum of 2 marks available.
Being in a trade bloc means it's easier to trade for all the different goods and services a country needs, because trade is less restricted. So countries can specialise in producing the things they're good at making and trade for the things they're not good at making ***[1 mark]***. Member countries of the trade bloc benefit from comparative advantage because production increases for each country as they're concentrating on what they do best ***[1 mark]***.

Page 111 — Trans-National Corporations

1 Maximum of 4 marks available.
Mergers ***[1 mark]***, acquisitions ***[1 mark]***, sub-contracting ***[1 mark]*** and Foreign Direct Investment (FDI) ***[1 mark]***.

2 Maximum of 10 marks available. This question is level marked.
HINTS:
- *You need to make sure you write your answer about one named example.*
- *Structure your answer by writing a short introduction, then write two sections on how the TNC has grown, and how the labour force is divided.*
- *Use the introduction to define TNCs and name the example you're using, e.g. 'TNCs are large companies that produce, sell or are located in two or more countries. The largest retail TNC is Wal-Mart'.*
- *In the first section introduce your example and describe how it has grown, e.g. 'Wal-Mart is a chain of department stores started by Sam Walton in Arkansas, USA. It first grew by opening new stores across Arkansas, then across the USA. It has grown more recently across the globe by buying retail companies in other countries, e.g. ASDA in the UK and Seiyu in Japan. Wal-Mart is currently trying to expand into NICs, e.g. in India it's working with a company called Bharti Enterprises'.*
- *In the second section talk about the spatial division of labour, e.g. 'Wal-Mart sub-contracts the production of a lot of its goods to NICs like China and Malaysia. Some Wal-Mart production has been moved back to more developed countries because they were criticised for exploiting cheap labour in poorer countries, e.g. George clothing have switched a lot of their production to the UK'.*

Page 113 — Global Winners and Losers

1 Maximum of 4 marks available.
Switched-on countries are countries that are well connected to global networks ***[1 mark]***. Trade, money, people and information easily flow between them — they're global hubs ***[1 mark]***. People in switched-on countries are significant consumers and producers of goods and services ***[1 mark]***. Energy usage and the ecological footprint are large because of the high levels of production and consumption ***[1 mark]***.

Page 115 — Consequences of Globalisation

1 Maximum of 15 marks available. This question is level marked.
HINTS:
- *For this answer you should start with a short introduction. The main part of your answer could then be divided into three sections where you evaluate strategies at different levels: governments, businesses and individuals.*
- *Remember, evaluate means talk about both the advantages and disadvantages of something.*
- *The introduction should briefly cover what the problems caused by globalisation are, e.g. 'Increased global trade means people have access to more products at low prices, so they can afford to be more wasteful. Lots of waste ends up as landfill'.*
- *Then you should write three sections evaluating the strategies to solve the problems, e.g. 'Businesses can use more recycled materials to make their products, e.g. recycling old drinks cans to make new ones. This reduces the amount of waste going into landfill sites, but could increase carbon emissions and oil pollution if the recycled material is shipped long distances'.*

Section 8 — Population

Page 117 — Population Change Basics and the DTM

1 Maximum of 10 marks available. This question is level marked.
HINTS:
- *Write an introduction briefly explaining what the DTM is, e.g. 'The Demographic Transition Model (DTM) shows how the population of a country changes over time through five stages. The model shows birth rate, death rate and total population'.*

Answers

- *The question asks you to refer to the DTM, so you can use this to structure your answer — start by explaining what stage of the DTM the country was in in 1600. E.g. 'In 1600 the birth rate and death rate were very high (38 and 37 respectively) and the population was low (2 million). The country was in Stage 1 of the DTM. Birth rate was high because there was no birth control or family planning, and education was poor. Also, infant mortality was high, so people had more children to replace those who'd died. The death rate was high because of poor health care, sanitation and diet, which led to disease and starvation'.*
- *Next, describe how the data changes and relate the changes to the stages of the DTM, e.g. 'Between 1600 and 1800, the death rate decreased (from 37 to 18 per 1000 per year) and the population had more than tripled, from 2 million to 7 million. The birth rate had dropped very slightly from 38 to 35 per 1000 per year. The country had reached Stage 2 of the DTM'. Don't forget to give reasons for the changes.*
- *Make sure you use data from the table in your answer.*

Page 119 — Applying the DTM

1 Maximum of 15 marks available. This question is level marked.
HINTS:
- *Start with an introduction briefly explaining the DTM.*
- *The question asks you to discuss the uses and limitations, so you need to talk about the advantages and disadvantages.*
- *Write a section on what the DTM can be used for and why it's useful (the advantages), e.g. 'The DTM can be used to forecast how a population may change, which can help governments decide on policies such as one-child limits or immigration laws'.*
- *Then explain each limitation of the DTM (the disadvantages), e.g. 'The original data used to create the DTM was from more developed, richer countries (e.g. European countries, Japan and the USA). This means it might not be a valid model worldwide — what happened in these countries might not be the same as what's happening in others, e.g. countries in Asia or Africa'.*

Page 121 — Population Structure and Migration

1 Maximum of 4 marks available.
Push factors are the things that make people want to move out of the place they're in **[1 mark]**. *They're negative factors about the place they're leaving, e.g. lack of jobs or poor living conditions and services, fear of political persecution* **[1 mark]**. *Pull factors attract people to a new place* **[1 mark]**. *They're positive factors about the place they're moving to, e.g. better jobs and more job opportunities, better living conditions and services* **[1 mark]**.

Page 123 — Changes in the UK Population Since 1900

1 Maximum of 10 marks available. This question is level marked.
HINTS:
- *Write an introduction explaining what is meant by 'internal factors', e.g. 'Populations can change in lots of ways, e.g. changes in the average family size. These changes can be caused by internal factors — things that are happening within the country or area'.*
- *For each factor state what it changed, then explain how it caused the change, e.g. 'Life expectancy in the UK has changed since the introduction of the NHS in 1948. Free health care for everyone has led to increased life expectancy — from around 50 in 1900 to 77 for men and 81 for women today'.*

Page 125 — Impacts and Management of Population Change

1 Maximum of 15 marks available. This question is level marked.
HINTS:
- *First, briefly explain what an ageing population is, e.g. 'An ageing population is a population where the proportion of older people (over 65) is increasing'.*
- *Then write a section describing and explaining each social effect. E.g. 'An ageing population means there's increased pressure on public services such as hospitals and hospices. More people are needed to care for the elderly, so more carers and nurses will need training'.*
- *Next write about the economic effects, e.g. 'There could be increased taxes for the working population. Pensions and services are paid for by taxes, so if there's a greater proportion of older people claiming pensions and support, there'll be higher taxes for the working population'.*

Page 127 — Managing Populations — Case studies

1 Maximum of 10 marks available. This question is level marked.
HINTS:
- *Remember, evaluate means you need to talk about whether the strategies have been successful or not.*
- *Introduce the named example, and say briefly how the population has been changing, e.g. 'Uganda has a youthful population — in 2007, 50% of the population were under 15 and only 3% were over 65. The youthful population is increasing because the birth rate is high — 48 babies are born for every 1000 people each year'.*
- *Next talk about any strategies that have been used to manage the population change, e.g. 'The use of contraceptives and family planning has been encouraged in Uganda to try to slow the increase in the youthful population, e.g. the government has brought in free contraceptives like condoms'.*
- *Finally, assess the strategy, e.g. 'Family planning clinics aren't widespread, so many people don't have easy access to birth control. This may explain why the strategy has been unsuccessful — since 1991 the birth rate has increased'.*

Page 129 — Migration into Europe

1 Maximum of 10 marks available. This question is level marked.
HINTS:
- *In the introduction say that the consequences of migration can be in Europe (the destination), and in the countries that migrants are leaving (the source). Introduce the main headings the consequences can fall under — demographic, economic, social, cultural, political and environmental.*
- *Then write a paragraph for each of the headings, discussing the consequences for both the source and destination countries, e.g. 'Migration into Europe results in demographic changes (e.g. changes in population structure and characteristics). Most migrants are of working and reproductive age, so the population structure of European destination countries will have an increased proportion of people of these ages. The population structure of source countries will have a reduced proportion of people of these ages'.*

Page 131 — Intra-EU Migration

1 Maximum of 10 marks available. This question is level marked.
HINTS:
- *Start by defining intra-EU migration and introducing the named example you'll be using, e.g. 'Intra-EU migration is migration between two countries within the European Union. Many people have migrated to the UK from Poland since it joined the EU in 2004'.*
- *Next write a section on the reasons for this migration. Divide the reasons into push and pull factors and write a paragraph on each, e.g. 'Push factors show why people left Poland. For example, unemployment was high in Poland (around 19% in 2004) so people left Poland to find work in the UK — they were economic migrants'.*
- *Then write two sections on the consequences — one for each country in your example, e.g. 'Poland's population has shrunk because so many people have migrated to other countries, e.g. it fell 0.3% between 2003 and 2007'.*

Page 133 — Rural-Urban Migration

1 Maximum of 10 marks available. This question is level marked.
HINTS:
- *First of all define rural-urban migration, and introduce the named example, e.g. 'Rural-urban migration is the movement of people from areas with low population density (rural) to areas with high population density (urban). Massive rural-urban migration has been going on in China, where 300 million people are now thought to live in cities'.*
- *Then write a section describing the push factors, e.g. 'One of the push factors from rural areas in China is poverty. In 2004, 26.1 million people were living in absolute poverty in rural areas (too poor to afford enough food or clothing). So people are migrating to urban areas to escape poverty'.*
- *Finish by writing a section describing the pull factors, e.g. 'One of the pull factors to urban areas in China is higher wages. Average income is three times higher in urban areas than rural areas and the difference is getting bigger. So people migrate to increase their income and escape poverty'.*

Answers

Page 135 — Megacities

1 Maximum of 10 marks available. This question is level marked.
HINTS:
- Define megacity and introduce the two that you're going to talk about, e.g. 'Megacities are metropolitan areas with a population of over 10 million people. London is a megacity in the south-east of the UK with a population of around 13 million, and Mumbai is a megacity on the west coast of India with a population of more than 20 million people'.
- The question is asking you to compare, so you need to talk about the similarities and differences.
- Write a paragraph comparing the two cities for each of the following things — the urban cycle, economy and housing patterns.
E.g. 'The population of Greater London is increasing. It's grown by 1 million since 1981. This is partly because there's a large number of international migrants, e.g. in 2006 there was a net gain of almost 70 000 international migrants. The population of Greater Mumbai is also growing, but much more rapidly. It's grown by more than 6 million since 1971. Unlike London, it's because so many people are moving into Mumbai from the rest of India, rather than from international migration'.

Page 137 — Urban Sustainability

1 Maximum of 10 marks available. This question is level marked.
HINTS:
- You should write a good definition of sustainable development in your introduction, e.g. 'Sustainable development means growth in a way that lets the people living now have the things they need, but without reducing the ability of people in the future to get what they need. It means developing in a way that doesn't irreversibly damage the environment or use up resources faster than they can be replaced'.
- Next you should write a few sections describing the things an urban area could do to become more sustainable, and explaining how these things help. E.g. 'An urban area could become more sustainable by building more carbon-neutral homes. These are houses that generate as much energy as they use by having things like solar panels to produce energy. Carbon-neutral homes increase the amount of housing without increasing the ecological footprint of the area, so the environment isn't damaged as much for future generations'.

Page 139 — Urban and Rural Characteristics

1 Maximum of 6 marks available. This question is level marked.
HINTS:
- Cover one characteristic at a time and for each one explain how population change and migration can affect it, e.g. 'As young, wealthy professionals move to redeveloped urban areas, they increase the wealth of those areas. This can improve inner city areas, but can also mean that the younger original residents can't afford to live in these areas any more'.
- Remember that the question says 'explain', so you need to say why population change and migration can affect the character of urban areas, e.g. 'Younger people could migrate into urban areas to look for work, which would affect the population structure of the area. This could also affect the provision of services, as younger people (of reproductive age) require more schools and childcare services'.
- The question only asks you about the character of urban areas, so don't start talking about how rural areas are affected.

Page 141 — Urban and Rural Characteristics — Case Study

1 Maximum of 15 marks available. This question is level marked.
HINTS:
- Start by naming your region and the two areas you've chosen, and describe and compare their characteristics. E.g. 'The wards of Fishwick (inner city area) and Lea (rural/urban fringe) can be found in Preston, a city in the North-west of England. Fishwick has lots of high-density, 19th century housing, whereas Lea has large detached and semi-detached houses with gardens and driveways'.
- Then for each of the different characteristics, describe and explain any effects they have on the social welfare of the residents in your chosen areas, e.g. '74% of people in Lea (rural/urban fringe) described their general health in the 12 months leading up to the 2001 census as 'good'. This was only 64% for Fishwick. This may be because a higher percentage of people in Fishwick live in houses that are likely to be cold and damp due to a lack of central heating — 17.5% of houses in Fishwick have no central heating, compared to 5.6% in Lea'.
- Include data from the table on p. 140 in your answer, and don't forget to use appropriate terms such as suburban area, occupancy rate, professional sector.

Section 9 — Unequal Spaces

Page 143 — Introduction to Inequalities

1 Maximum of 10 marks available. This question is level marked.
See page 206 for a full worked answer.

Page 145 — Causes and Effects of Urban Inequalities

1 Maximum of 10 marks available. This question is level marked.
HINTS:
- Look at each row of data in the table and think about whether it shows any inequality — economic, social or environmental.
E.g. the third row shows economic inequality because 62% of parents in two-parent families received income-related benefits, compared to 89% of lone parents. Write down the type of inequality next to each row of data.
- Next, note down any causes and effects you can think of next to each inequality. Try to find links between the inequalities too.
- Structure your answer — for each type of inequality, write down the data that supports it from the table, then discuss the possible causes and effects of that inequality. E.g. 'Only 56% of lone parents were in employment compared to 81% of parents from two-parent families, which is a social inequality. This could've been caused by a lack of child-care facilities in the area, which meant lone parents had to stay at home to look after their children rather than work. It could also be due to a lack of education — if the lone parent couldn't get a good enough job to pay for child-care facilities. An effect of this inequality is that lone parents have lower incomes, so fewer can afford to rent or live in detached housing (only 8% of lone-parent families lived in detached housing, compared to 28% of two-parent families)'. Repeat this with all three inequalities — economic, social and environmental.
- Write a short summary at the end that explains how causes and effects can be linked, which may lead to a cycle of decline, e.g. 'A lower percentage of lone parents are employed, so they're more likely to have lower incomes and receive income-related benefits. This means they're less likely to be able to afford to go back into education and less likely to get a better paid job, which could pay for child-care facilities. In turn, this worsens the economic and social inequalities between lone parents and two-parent families, causing a cycle of decline'.

Page 147 — Strategies to Reduce Urban Inequalities

1 Maximum of 10 marks available. This question is level marked.
HINTS:
- First, think of two schemes that could have been introduced into a city to tackle city centre traffic, e.g. a park-and-ride scheme, congestion charging, public transport passes (e.g. Oyster card in London).
- Then for each scheme, state what it is and describe how it would decrease city centre traffic. Try to include the key players involved and the scale on which it would be carried out. E.g. 'A park-and-ride scheme could have been introduced into City X, which allows people to park their cars outside the centre and travel in by public transport. They're carried out on a local scale by the local authority'.
- Next you need to evaluate the success of each scheme. Look at the table and decide what pieces of data show that there's been an effect on city centre traffic. You need to look for data that shows a decrease in the number of cars in the city, a decrease in air pollution or an increase in public transport.
- Include the data in your answer and explain how it shows that the schemes have/haven't been successful. E.g. 'In 1995, there were 753 124 vehicles passing through the city centre on average each month, which decreased to 215 376 vehicles by 2005. So there was less traffic in the city centre after the schemes were introduced, suggesting they've been successful'.

Answers

Page 149 — Urban Inequalities — Case Study

1 Maximum of 10 marks available. This question is level marked.
HINTS:
- 'One named example' means a case study in an urban area, e.g. Cardiff.
- First, plan your answer. Jot down the main inequalities in that area, then write a cause and effect next to each inequality. There may be multiple causes and effects of each inequality.
- Begin your answer by describing the inequalities of your chosen urban area, e.g. 'There's economic inequality between the north and south of Cardiff, with the less wealthy generally living in the south'.
- Next, discuss the key causes of the inequalities, e.g. 'The decline of industry in the 20th century (e.g. coal exports stopped in 1964), caused high unemployment in Cardiff, especially in the south of the city where workers from the docklands lived. This led to lower incomes and economic inequality between the north and south of Cardiff'.
- Then describe the effects of the inequalities and explain how they resulted from the inequality. To gain higher marks, describe how inequalities are linked. E.g. 'Lower wages (economic inequality) in the south of Cardiff have led to poorer health, because people have less money for food, prescriptions etc. People with poor health and a lack of money for smart clothes are less likely to gain employment, which leads to further economic inequality in the south of Cardiff'.
- Make sure you learn the details of your case studies so you can quote data where possible, e.g. 'Lower wages in the south of Cardiff mean that fewer people are able to buy their own homes. For example, the 2001 census shows that only 12.5% of residents in Butetown (south Cardiff) owned their own house, compared to 20.9% in Cathays (north Cardiff)'.

Page 151 — Causes and Effects of Rural Inequalities

1 Maximum of 10 marks available. This question is level marked.
HINTS:
- First, define polarisation, which is when the inequalities between two groups of people become extreme, e.g. the rich are very rich and the poor are very poor.
- Then describe the causes and effects of inequalities in rural areas. Explain how an inequality leads to polarisation. Repeat this for two or three different inequalities. E.g. 'A lack of access to affordable housing in rural areas has caused social inequality between wealthy people who can afford to buy a house and local people on lower incomes who can't. Wealthy people have also bought second homes in rural areas, driving up property prices. In turn, they become wealthier as property prices increase, but people on lower incomes are less able to get on the property ladder. This increases polarisation between the rich and poor in rural areas'.
- Include how inequalities are interlinked and that they can lead to a cycle of decline, which can cause polarisation as inequalities become worse.

Page 153 — Strategies to Reduce Rural Inequalities

1 Maximum of 10 marks available. This question is level marked.
HINTS:
- Describe specific examples of strategies from each of the four groups on p. 152 — introducing appropriate technologies, community schemes, transport and services schemes, and employment schemes.
- The question asks you to 'describe' the strategies, so make sure you include as many details as you can about each one, e.g. the name of the strategy, where the strategies are carried out and how they operate. E.g. 'The Village Enterprise Fund in East Africa gives people skills to set up and run their own businesses, e.g. small farms, bicycle repair workshops and tailors'. It provides local people with business training, financial grants and mentoring'.
- Make sure you address the question and say what inequality each strategy is trying to reduce and how it does this. E.g. 'The Village Enterprise Fund aims to reduce social inequality in rural areas by giving people new skills, and to reduce economic inequality by helping people to set up their own businesses in rural areas'.

Page 155 — Rural Inequalities — Case Study

1 Maximum of 10 marks available. This question is level marked.
HINTS:
- First, think of a case study you know that covers inequalities in a rural area, e.g. Llangynidr and Llanelly Hill in the Brecon Beacons National Park.
- Then, jot down the main inequalities of the area and a few causes and effects of the inequalities. Look for any ways in which the inequalities are linked.
- Structure your answer — begin by describing the inequalities of your chosen rural area and their causes. E.g. 'There's economic inequality between places situated in the centre of the Brecon Beacons National Park, such as Llangynidr, and those on the outskirts of the park, like Llanelly Hill. The more wealthy areas are in the centre of the park. These inequalities are partially caused by the decline of coal and iron industries to the south of the National Park, which caused high unemployment in areas like Llanelly Hill. This led to lower family incomes and economic inequality'.
- Describe the effects of the inequalities and explain how they resulted from the inequality. To gain higher marks, describe how inequalities are linked — the effect of one inequality may be the cause of another inequality, leading to a cycle of decline. E.g. 'High unemployment in Llanelly Hill means people have lower average family incomes. This means residents of Llanelly Hill are less likely to be able to get on the property ladder, because they don't have enough money to buy their own house. There's a lack of affordable housing in the area, so this causes polarisation between residents of the National Park who can afford their own house and those who can't'.
- Use data to support your points where possible, e.g. '13.3% of people in Llanelly Hill have 'not good' health, compared to 8.9% in Llangynidr'.

Section 10 — Rebranding Places

Page 157 — Introduction to Rebranding Places

1 Maximum of 10 marks available. This question is level marked.
HINTS:
- To get full marks you need to give reasons why urban, rural and coastal areas might require rebranding.
- Write a paragraph for each kind of area, covering why it might go into decline and need rebranding. For example, 'Rural areas can go into decline because of the decline of agriculture and its effect on the economy. The lack of job opportunities leads to the out-migration of young people, resulting in an ageing population. Services such as shops, schools and post offices close as people move away to find work, leading to a spiral of decline as economic problems and social isolation become worse'.
- Quote facts and mini case studies where possible, e.g. 'An example of an urban area that was in need of rebranding is Bilbao in Northern Spain. It was a successful industrial port until the decline of industry in the 1970s and 1980s. This led to high unemployment and many social problems'.

Page 159 — Urban Rebranding Strategies

1 Maximum of 10 marks available. This question is level marked.
HINTS:
- You need to include a range of urban rebranding strategies — so cover regeneration (changing the built environment), re-imaging and using sport as a catalyst.
- The question says 'with reference to named examples' so you need to include relevant mini case studies for each strategy.
- Make sure you explain how the rebranding strategy has led to regeneration. For example, 'Urban rebranding can involve marketing a place with a new image. Some coastal towns have been re-imaged, e.g. Eastbourne Borough Council used the slogan 'Change Your View' to try and change Eastbourne's reputation as a tourist and retirement destination for older people. The campaign has promoted attractions like extreme sports and theme parks, to try and attract younger visitors. It's helped bring new tourists to the area, which in turn brings in more money and investment, helping to regenerate the area'.
- Quote facts and relevant data where possible, e.g. 'The development of the Emirates Stadium, Arsenal FC's £430 million new ground in North London, has provided 2500 new homes and 2600 new jobs for the area'.

Page 161 — Urban Rebranding — Case Study

1 Maximum of 10 marks available. This question is level marked.
HINTS:
- You need to write about one case study for this question. You can use any case study you know well, e.g. New Islington.
- The question says 'evaluate' so you need to comment on how successful the scheme has been.

Answers

- *Start by describing why the area needed to be rebranded (don't forget to include relevant facts). For example, 'New Islington is a replacement for the Cardroom estate, which had experienced a spiral of decline. By the mid 1990s the area had social problems like high unemployment and crime, and 50% of the houses were empty'.*
- *Then describe the details of the scheme, e.g. 'New Islington is a flagship development. New facilities in the development include 1700 new homes, a primary school and a community football pitch. The estimated cost is £250 million'.*
- *Next, discuss the strengths and weaknesses of the development. For example, 'One of New Islington's strengths is that the development has improved the area's infrastructure by improving public transport, e.g. New Islington has a new tram stop. This makes the area more attractive to new residents, and should stop it from becoming isolated'. You could also include points on how the development is environmentally friendly and has involved local people in the planning. A weakness of New Islington could be that experts have criticised it for not having much social housing. You could also mention that some residents are unhappy with the development, e.g. 'Some residents have complained that the new social housing has been built far away from the public spaces and other amenities in the development. This has led them to feel less important than new residents'.*

Page 163 — Rural Rebranding Strategies

1 *Maximum of 10 marks available. This question is level marked.*
HINTS:
- *To get full marks you need to discuss a range of named examples. Structure your answer to cover named examples of regeneration, re-imaging and integrated projects. Write a paragraph for each.*
- *You can use any relevant case studies you know, but make sure you cover how the place has been rebranded. For example, 'Rural regeneration can involve introducing new technology to a rural area. In the remote Highlands and Islands area in Scotland, a £70 million project was set up to connect communities to high-speed broadband. It meant that the Highlands and Islands Enterprise (HIE) could then market the area as a good place to base small businesses, encouraging new residents who could work from home and bringing extra income to the area'.*
- *Quote facts and relevant data where possible, e.g. 'The children's TV programme Balamory was filmed in the village of Tobermory on the Isle of Mull. The village has had up to 160 000 extra visitors every year since the show launched in 2003, and the tourist economy has been boosted by around £5 million a year'.*

Page 165 — Rural Rebranding — Case Studies

1 *Maximum of 10 marks available. This question is level marked.*
HINTS:
- *'Compare' means talk about the similarities and differences. So you need to write about how the effects of at least two rural rebranding schemes are similar or different.*
- *You can use any rural rebranding case studies that you know about, e.g. the Eden Project and the Jurassic Coast. Include the positive effects and negative effects of the different schemes. This could include things like the creation of jobs, the amount of traffic, and how residents feel about the rebranding.*
- *Write a paragraph for each comparative point you make. For example, 'The Eden Project has had a positive economic impact on the surrounding area, e.g. it's led to a £75 million facelift project for St Austell town centre. The Jurassic Coast rebranding has also had a positive impact on the local economy, e.g. West Bay's new £16 million Jurassic Pier has doubled visitor numbers to the area since 2004'.*
- *Make sure you compare any negative effects too. For example, 'The Eden Project has created serious traffic problems in the area. This makes it less environmentally sustainable, as well as irritating visitors and local residents. On the other hand, the Jurassic Coast area doesn't have as big a problem with traffic and pollution because tourists aren't just attracted to one location'.*
- *Quote facts and relevant data where possible, e.g. 'The Eden Project has had a positive impact on the surrounding area — it's influence has helped local businesses make around an extra £150 million every year'.*

Page 167 — Evaluating Rebranding Strategies

1 *Maximum of 15 marks available. This question is level marked.*
See page 203 for a full worked exam answer.

Section 11 — Food Supply Issues

Page 169 — Global Food Distribution

1 *Maximum of 5 marks available.*
*Intensive farming produces as much as possible from the land **[1 mark]**. It has a high input of capital or labour relative to land area **[1 mark]**. Extensive farming has a low input of capital and labour relative to land area **[1 mark]**. Extensive farming produces less food from the land than intensive farming **[1 mark]**, but has less environmental impact and offers better animal welfare **[1 mark]**.*

2 *Maximum of 8 marks available. This question is level marked.*
HINTS:
- *Start by describing the role of TNCs in the global food industry, e.g. in production, processing and distribution.*
- *To get full marks you need to discuss at least three advantages and three disadvantages of the involvement of TNCs.*
- *Give specific examples where possible, e.g. 'Cargill™ employs local people to trade and distribute their produce in Pakistan, which benefits the local economy'.*
- *Discuss points from different angles, e.g. 'Although some local people benefit from the job opportunities that TNCs provide, local companies that can't compete with the TNCs often go bankrupt, and this causes unemployment in the area'.*
- *Link points together, e.g. '...and this causes unemployment in the area. Another effect of smaller companies going bankrupt is delocalisation of food supplies'.*

Page 171 — Changes in Demand

1 *Maximum of 4 marks available.*
*The demand for high value food exports from developing countries has increased **[1 mark]**. The demand for seasonal products all year round has also increased **[1 mark]**. 1 mark for each reason up to a maximum of two marks. Reasons include: rising incomes **[1 mark]**, an increasing culture of high consumption **[1 mark]**, increased demand for exotic products in developed countries **[1 mark]**.*

2 *Maximum of 8 marks available. This question is level marked.*
HINTS:
- *To get full marks you need to describe a range of environmental issues relating to the globalisation of the food industry (e.g. deforestation, damaging effects of intensive farming, transporting food / food miles).*
- *Write a paragraph for each environmental issue, covering the negative environmental impacts. For example, 'Transporting food releases carbon dioxide into the atmosphere. Carbon dioxide is a greenhouse gas, which contributes to climate change'.*

Page 173 — Increasing Food Production

1 *Maximum of 6 marks available. This question is level marked.*
HINTS:
- *To get full marks you need to describe what the technologies and methods are and give their disadvantages, e.g. 'Mechanisation brought in by the green revolution involves the use of expensive machines. Farms that can't afford these machines could go bankrupt, leading to unemployment and food shortages'.*

Page 175 — Controlling Food Production and Supply

1 *Maximum of 15 marks available. This question is level marked.*
HINTS:
- *This question is about EU market policies so don't write about non-market policies.*
- *EU market policies include: subsidies, tariffs, intervention (including pricing) and quotas.*
- *To get full marks you need to cover at least three EU market policies.*
- *For each policy you need to describe what it is, then explain how it controls the level and nature of agricultural production, e.g. 'Subsidies are payments made to farmers. They can control production by encouraging farmers to produce particular products'.*
- *Quote facts and give real-life examples where possible, e.g. 'In 2006 EU farmers were paid €1 billion to produce dairy products' and 'Tariffs of 18-28% are applied to imported beef products'.*

Answers

Page 177 — Managing Food Supply — Case Studies

1 Maximum of 10 marks available. This question is level marked.
HINTS:
- *First describe the strategies used to manage food supplies in Bangladesh.*
- *Strategies include: investment in green revolution technologies, investment in improving infrastructure, diversification, free market policies and food aid.*
- *Then discuss the sustainability of each strategy you describe, e.g. 'Investment in green revolution technologies is not sustainable because of the high cost and the environmental impact (falling water tables and soil salinisation due to irrigation, water pollution from agrochemicals, and soil degradation due to overcultivation)'.*
- *Quote facts and give real-life examples where possible, e.g. 'Between 1974 and 2000 the use of high yielding rice seeds, increased irrigation and increased use of agrochemicals increased rice production from 11.7 to 23.1 million tonnes'.*

2 Maximum of 15 marks available. This question is level marked.
HINTS:
- *To 'compare' the management of food supplies in the two countries you need to look at the similarities and differences between them.*
- *Start by describing and explaining the aim of food supply management in Bangladesh and China, e.g. 'Food supply management in Bangladesh aims to provide enough food for the population, as there isn't enough at the moment. Chinese management is focused on producing enough food within the country to be self-sufficient, as it has a history of food shortages'.*
- *Next, describe and explain the similarities in the management of food supply in China and Bangladesh, e.g. 'Both China and Bangladesh have invested in transportation infrastructure to improve the transport of produce around the country'.*
- *Then describe and explain the differences between the two countries, e.g. 'Bangladesh has removed subsidies, eliminated quotas and reduced import tariffs to encourage food imports as this increases the amount of food available to feed the population. In contrast, China limits imports in order to protect the market for local produce, encourage production and improve food security'.*
- *Discuss the sustainability of the contrasting strategies, e.g. 'Self-sufficiency may not be a realistic and sustainable strategy in China as the limited amount of arable land available is being reduced as the country becomes increasingly urbanised. Free market policies in Bangladesh may not be sustainable because they increase susceptibility to rising food prices, and maintain reliance on food imports – more sustainable solutions may involve improving local production and reducing imports'.*

Section 12 — Energy Issues

Page 179 — Energy Resources

1 Maximum of 6 marks available. This question is level marked.
HINTS:
- *Start off by describing what renewable and non-renewable resources are.*
- *Include examples of renewable and non-renewable resources.*
- *Explain why it can be difficult to classify resources as renewable or non-renewable (because some resources are only renewable if carefully managed).*

2 Maximum of 6 marks available. This question is level marked.
HINTS:
- *Start off by explaining what the term 'energy mix' means.*
- *Then describe the energy mix of a particular country, e.g. 'In 2008 the UK got 33% of its energy from petroleum (oil), 40% from natural gas, 17% from coal, 8% from nuclear and 2% from other sources'.*
- *Finally describe how the amount an energy source contributes has changed and give reasons for the change, e.g. 'The use of coal has fallen 40% since 1990. This is due to the closure of coal mines in the UK and a move to less polluting oil and gas'.*

Page 181 — Global Energy Distribution

1 Maximum of 15 marks available. This question is level marked.
HINTS:
- *Start off by explaining why the amount of energy that a country produces could increase or decrease.*
- *Then explain why the amount of energy a country consumes could change.*
- *Go on to energy trading next. Explain what energy trading is and why it's needed.*
- *Describe how the amount of energy that a country needs to import (or is able to export) could change and how this would affect trade, e.g. 'After Brazil discovered new supplies of oil it was able to become energy self-sufficient and no longer needed to import energy'.*
- *Explain why some countries might decide to change their energy supplier, e.g. to reduce their dependence on a particular country or to receive imports from a more stable and therefore more reliable region.*

Page 183 — Impacts of Energy Production

1 Maximum of 10 marks available. This question is level marked.
HINTS:
- *Start off by describing why a replacement for fossil fuels needs to be found, i.e. fossil fuel use is environmentally damaging and they will run out.*
- *Describe the advantages and disadvantages of nuclear power in relation to fossil fuels, e.g. 'Accidents at nuclear power plants can cause more serious environmental damage than accidents at fossil fuel plants, as radioactive material can be released into the environment. However, if accidents are avoided fossil fuels cause the more serious environmental problems as burning them leads to global warming and climate change, whereas the environmental impacts of nuclear energy are much smaller'.*
- *Using your arguments for and against nuclear power, come to a conclusion on whether it's a suitable replacement for fossil fuels. It doesn't matter whether you think that nuclear power is a good replacement for fossil fuels or not, as long as you can give reasons for your choice.*

Page 187 — Sustainable Energy

1 Maximum of 4 marks available.
Biomass is material that is or was recently living **[1 mark]**. It can be burnt directly to release energy **[1 mark]**. Biomass can also be used to produce biofuels like ethanol **[1 mark]**, which are burnt to release energy **[1 mark]**.

2 Maximum of 6 marks available. This question is level marked.
HINTS:
- *'Compare' means talk about the similarities and differences.*
- *Start off by describing the similarities between wave energy and tidal energy, e.g. they both rely on seas/oceans, they both involve the use of turbines to convert the energy into electricity.*
- *Then describe the differences between them, e.g. 'Although both wave and wind energy use turbines to generate electricity, tidal energy is a reliable and constant source of energy (as tides are regular events), but wave energy isn't. If there's no wind no waves are produced and that means electricity can't be generated. This is a big disadvantage of wave energy'.*

3 Maximum of 8 marks available. This question is level marked.
HINTS:
- *Start off by explaining why energy use isn't sustainable (i.e. the energy that we use comes from unsustainable sources), but that there are things that can be done to make energy use more sustainable.*
- *Then explain that energy use can be made more sustainable by conserving as much energy as possible.*
- *Describe the different strategies that conserve energy in the home, e.g. insulation, energy-efficient boilers, features that absorb the Sun's energy.*

4 Maximum of 10 marks available. This question is level marked.
HINTS:
- *Start by explaining why transport isn't sustainable at the moment, e.g. using oil for transport depletes non-renewable resources and releases greenhouse gases.*
- *Explain that energy conservation can make transport more sustainable and describe strategies that can conserve energy, e.g. park-and-ride schemes and congestion charging.*
- *Then explain how technologies that run off sustainable energy sources can improve sustainability of transport. Describe at least two and explain why they improve sustainability of transport, e.g. 'Hybrid fuel vehicles use more than one source of fuel. If a vehicle runs on an ethanol and petrol mix then less fossil fuels are used and less greenhouse gases are emitted, making the vehicle more sustainable than those that just run on petrol'.*
- *Technologies include hydrogen fuel cell vehicles, hybrid fuel vehicles and vehicles that run off other renewable energies, e.g. wave power.*

Answers

Page 188 — Managing Energy — Case Studies

1 Maximum of 15 marks available. This question is level marked.
HINTS:
- Start by describing Chad's energy resources and its energy mix.
- Explain which aspects of Chad's energy supply aren't sustainable, e.g. 'Currently, oil is used to generate electricity. This is unsustainable as oil will run out one day and its use contributes to global warming. If Chad is to generate electricity in a more sustainable manner, a different energy source must be used'.
- Describe aspects of Chad's current energy supply that are sustainable or have the potential to be sustainable, e.g. '90% of Chad's energy is supplied by biomass. This has the potential to be a renewable resource, but at the moment it's overexploited, making it unsustainable'.
- Then explain how supplies could be made sustainable, e.g. 'If the Household Energy Project was successfully implemented over a larger area, more of the country's biomass resources would be better managed, becoming renewable and therefore sustainable'.
- Include details of any aspects of Chad's energy supply that are a barrier to sustainability, e.g. 'The revenue from Chad's oil exports could be invested in projects to improve the sustainability of energy supplies, e.g. the Household Energy Project. This doesn't happen though, due to the high level of corruption in Chad, which is a serious barrier to sustainability'.

Page 189 — Managing Energy — Case Studies

1 Maximum of 15 marks available. This question is level marked.
HINTS:
- Start by describing Norway's current energy supply and briefly explain which aspects of it are sustainable, e.g. '50% of Norway's energy is supplied by HEP which is a renewable source of energy and (once established) is sustainable'.
- Then explain which aspects of Norway's energy supply are unsustainable and what methods are being used to improve their sustainability, e.g. 'Norway relies on oil for transport, which as a non-renewable resource is unsustainable. Biofuels are being developed to replace oil. This will make energy supply for transport more sustainable as long as the sources of materials used to produce the biofuels are managed properly'.
- Other methods that Norway is pursuing to improve sustainability include development of wind power and development of solar power.

Section 13 — Health Issues

Page 191 — Global Patterns of Health, Disease and Death

1 Maximum of 10 marks available. This question is level marked.
HINTS:
- Take your time to study any maps or graphs you get — look carefully at the title, key and units.
- The map shows the global pattern of measles morbidity (measles cases) — don't get this confused with measles mortality (deaths due to measles).
- The question asks you to 'outline' the pattern — in other words, you should 'describe and explain' it.
- When describing the pattern, say what the map shows and quote relevant data for the most and least affected countries. E.g. 'The countries most affected by measles are mostly in Africa — some countries had over 50 cases per 100 000 of the population in 2003. Measles morbidity is low in North America, South America and Australia, which had less than 1 case per 100 000 of the population in 2003'.
- Give reasons why the pattern is like this, e.g. 'The countries mostly affected by measles are those in poorer areas of the world. There's limited health education in Africa so many people aren't informed about how they can avoid infectious diseases, like measles. Also, overcrowded conditions in urban areas of poorer countries means that measles is more likely to spread to other people'.
- Remember, the general trend is that poorer countries have higher mortality and morbidity than wealthier countries — but always point out any exceptions to the rule. E.g. 'The map shows that measles also affects wealthier countries like Italy'.

Page 193 — Health Care Approaches

1a) Maximum of 2 marks available.
Public health spending is high in Western Europe, North America and Japan **[1 mark]** and particularly low in Africa, Asia and South America **[1 mark]**.

b) Maximum of 10 marks available. This question is level marked.
HINTS:
- To get full marks, you need to describe the differences in health care approaches used in poor and wealthy countries — and refer to at least one scheme (case study).
- Start with the main difference — e.g. 'Poor countries have less money, which is mainly spent on treating diseases, whereas wealthier countries have more money to spend on treatments, prevention and awareness of diseases'.
- Give examples of the main approaches to health care used in poor and wealthy countries, and describe at least one specific scheme you've studied. E.g. 'Many people live in remote rural areas in sub-Saharan Africa, so have limited access to health care and medical services. One inexpensive health care approach is to train local people as basic health care workers. For example, the Health Extension Programme in Ethiopia trains people who live in remote rural areas as local health care workers. Workers can then deliver basic health care and education to people in their local communities'.
- Use statistics where relevant, e.g. 'Insecticide-treated bed nets helped the number of malaria cases to fall by 20% in just one year'.
- The question doesn't ask you to discuss or evaluate, so don't go on about advantages or disadvantages.

Page 195 — The Geography of Disease

1 Maximum of 10 marks available. This question is level marked.
HINTS:
- Start off by describing the global distribution of malaria — the main countries affected by malaria (with a statistic) and those least affected.
- Give reasons for the uneven distribution of malaria cases and explain each reason, e.g. 'Mosquitoes that carry malaria can only survive in tropical climates, such as those found in sub-Saharan Africa'.
- 'Discuss its impact' means you should explain a range of effects that malaria has on a country's health, economic development and lifestyle. E.g. 'Malaria has a big impact on a country's economic development because of the number of people dying, decreasing productivity due to days lost from work, and increasing health care costs'.

Page 197 — Health and Globalisation

1 Maximum of 10 marks available. This question is level marked.
HINTS:
- Start off by describing what is meant by a Trans-National Corporation (TNC).
- Explain how TNCs can improve global health and how they can add to global health problems. E.g. 'Pharmaceutical companies can improve health in wealthier countries by choosing to research and produce drugs for diseases that mainly affect wealthier countries, such as drugs for impotency. However, this can add to health problems in poorer countries because money isn't being spent on life-saving drugs for diseases such as malaria and HIV/AIDS'.
- To get full marks, you need to give a range of examples of how specific TNCs (like GSK or PMI) affect global health. E.g. 'The pharmaceutical company GSK helps to improve global health by investing a large amount of their profit (e.g. £282 million in 2007) in community programmes to help people in need'.
- You can take a mixture of examples from different case studies if you want, as long as each example backs up whatever point you're making and doesn't just repeat points you've already made.

Page 199 — The Geography of Health in the UK

1 Maximum of 6 marks available. This question is level marked.
HINTS:
- Start off by describing what's meant by the term 'ageing population'.
- To describe how ageing populations will affect the provision of health care services, you need to cover examples of services needed by the elderly. For example, 'An ageing population has different health needs, such as the need for more mobile health care services to cope with the increasing immobilised elderly population. This is a particularly important way of providing health care to elderly people in rural areas who don't have family support'.

Acknowledgements

Page 26 — Graph adapted from Climate Change 2001: The Scientific Basis. Contribution of Working Group I to the Third Assessment Report of the Intergovernmental Panel on Climate Change. Figure 5. Cambridge University Press.

Page 29 — All three photos © iStockphoto.com

Page 36 — Seaside resort land use model reproduced by permission of HarperCollins Publishers Ltd © Prosser, Bishop & Raw, 2000.

Page 41 — Antarctic diagram reproduced from 'Fundamentals of the Physical Environment' by Peter Smithson, Ken Addison and Ken Atkinson, Third edition June 2002, Chapter 24, Polar Environments, Fig. 24.2. © 2007, Routledge, member of the Taylor & Francis Group.

Page 57 — Data used to construct the Riyadh climate graph from: http://www.climate-charts.com/Locations/s/SD40438.php © Climate-Charts.com

Page 62 and 66 — World map of desertification risk and vulnerability to desertification map of Spain reproduced from U.S. Department of Agriculture: National Resources Conservation Service, Soil Survey Division, World Soil Resource, Washington, D.C.

Page 69 and 205 — Graph reproduced with kind permission from EM-DAT: The OFDA/CRED International Disaster Database: www.emdat.net, Universite catholiqué de Louvain, Brussels, Belgium.

Page 76 — Short-term climate change graph adapted from Crown Copyright data supplied by the Met Office.

Page 76 — Medium-term climate change graph reproduced with thanks to the NOAA for the graphic and to the Alley (2000) paper for the underlying data.

Page 76 — Last 1000 years of climate change graph reproduced with kind permission from Climate Change 2001: The Scientific Basis, Contribution of Working Group I to the Third Assessment Report of the Intergovernmental Panel on Climate Change, SPM Figure 1. Cambridge University Press.

Page 81 — Graph of emissions scenarios modified and based on Special Report of Working Group III of the Intergovernmental Panel on Climate Change on Emissions Scenarios (IPCC 2000).

Page 81 — Data used to compile table of sea level rise modified and based on Climate Change 2007: The Physical Scientific Basis. Working Group I Contribution to the Fourth Assessment Report of the Intergovernmental Panel on Climate Change. Cambridge University Press.

Page 83 — Map reproduced with kind permission from the World Resources Institute, http://www.wri.org.

Page 90 — Map of drought risk © UCL Global Drought Monitor.

Page 98 — Natural disasters graph reproduced from Centre for Research on the Epidemiology of Disasters (CRED), Emmanuelle Bournay, Environment and Poverty Times #3: Disaster issue, 2005, United Nations Environment Programme.

Page 122 and 126 — Data used to construct the UK population pyramids reproduced with kind permission from National Statistics online. Reproduced under the terms of the Click-Use license.

Page 127 — Data used to construct the population pyramid for Uganda, source: U.S. Census Bureau.

Page 132 — World population graph reproduced with kind permission from Jean-Paul Rodrigue (underlying data from the United Nations).

Page 140 — Data used to compile the table on Preston, source: National Statistics website: www.statistics.gov.uk. Crown copyright material is reproduced with the permission of the Controller Office of Public Sector Information (OPSI).

Page 143 and 206 — Data used to compile the table comparing Bradford and Harrogate, source: National Statistics website: www.statistics.gov.uk. Crown copyright material is reproduced with the permission of the Controller Office of Public Sector Information (OPSI). Reproduced under the terms of the Click-Use license.

Page 145 — Data used to compile the table comparing lone parents to two parent families Copyright © 2001 One Parent Families Scotland.

Page 148 — Data used to compile the table comparing Cathays and Butetown is taken from the following sources: National Statistics website: www.statistics.gov.uk, © Cardiff Community Safety Partnership 2001 & Crown copyright material is reproduced with the permission of the Controller Office of Public Sector Information (OPSI).

Page 154 — Data used to compile the table comparing Llangynidr and Llanelly Hill source: National Statistics website: www.statistics.gov.uk. Crown copyright material is reproduced with the permission of the Controller Office of Public Sector Information (OPSI). Reproduced under the terms of the Click-Use license.

Page 157 — With thanks to Science Photo Library for permission to reproduce the Guggenheim museum photo.

Page 158 — Photo of Burj-al-Arab hotel © iStockphoto.com

Page 164 — Photo of the Eden Project © iStockphoto.com

Page 168 — Barley production map reproduced with kind permission from the Food and Agriculture Organization of the United Nations, http://oregonstate.edu/instruct/css/330/five/BarleyOverview.htm with data from FAOSTAT, http://faostat.fao.org/default.aspx.

Page 168 — Calorie map reproduced with kind permission from the World Resources Institute, http://www.wri.org.

Page 179 — UK energy mix pie chart © Crown copyright reproduced under the terms of the Click-Use license.

Page 179 — France's energy mix pie chart reproduced with kind permission from Obeservatoire de l'énergie.

Page 180 — Global Energy Production map & Global Energy Consumption map "From www.worldtravelatlas.co.uk copyright © Columbus Travel Media Ltd 2009."

Page 190 — Healthy Life Expectancy map reproduced from UNEP/DEWA/GRID-Europe, GEO Data Portal, Healthy Life Expectancy (HALE), 2002, United Nations Environment Programme.

Page 190 — TB map © WHO, 2008. All rights reserved. World Health Organisation, http://www.who.int/ith/maps/tuberculosis_2008.jpg

Page 191 — Breast cancer map reproduced with thanks to WHO © International Agency for Research on Cancer, March 2003. Data from Stewart B. W. and Kleihues P. (Eds): World Cancer Report. IARCPress. Lyon 2003. http://www.who.int/bookorders/anglais/detart1.jsp?sesslan=1&codlan=1&codcol=76&codcch=16#

Page 191 — Cancer table, Cancer Research UK: http://info.cancerresearchuk.org/cancerstats/geographic/world. November 2008.

Page 191 — Global measles map reproduced with thanks to WHO, from the WHO/IVB database, 2004 © WHO 2004. All rights reserved. http://www.who.int/vaccines-surveillance/graphics/NY_graphics/glob_inc_measles_map.jpg

Page 193 — Graph © Copyright 2006 SASI Group (University of Sheffield) and Mark Newman (University of Michigan), www.worldmapper.org

Page 194 — HIV map © WHO, 2008. All rights reserved. World Health Organisation, http://www.who.int/ith/maps/HIV_infection2005_en.gif

Page 198 — Data used to construct the UK life expectancy map reproduced with kind permission from National Statistics website: www.statistics.gov.uk. Crown copyright material is reproduced with the permission of the Controller Office of Public Sector Information (OPSI). Reproduced under the terms of the Click-Use license.

Page 204 and 210 — Mapping data reproduced by permission of Ordnance Survey® on behalf of HMSO © Crown copyright (2008). All rights reserved. Ordnance Survey® Licence No. 100034841.

Page 208 — World populations graph, data from *World Population Prospects: 2008 Population Database* © United Nations, 2009. Reproduced with permission.

Page 209 — Movement map source: International Passenger Survey, Office for National Statistics © Crown copyright reproduced under the terms of the Click-Use License.

Every effort has been made to locate copyright holders and obtain permission to reproduce sources. For those sources where it has been difficult to trace the originator of the work, we would be grateful for information. If any copyright holder would like us to make an amendment to the acknowledgements, please notify us and we will gladly up date the book at the next reprint. Thank you.

Index

Index

Index